Women of the Mountain South

OHIO UNIVERSITY PRESS

Series in Race, Ethnicity, and Gender in Appalachia

Series editors: Marie Tedesco and Chris Green

Memphis Tennessee Garrison: The Remarkable Story of a Black Appalachian Woman, edited by Ancella R. Bickley and Lynda Ann Ewen

The Tangled Roots of Feminism, Environmentalism, and Appalachian Literature, by Elizabeth S. D. Engelhardt

Red, White, Black, and Blue: A Dual Memoir of Race and Class in Appalachia, by William R. Drennen Jr. and Kojo (William T.) Jones Jr., edited by Dolores M. Johnson

Beyond Hill and Hollow: Original Readings in Appalachian Women's Studies, edited by Elizabeth S. D. Engelhardt

Loving Mountains, Loving Men, by Jeff Mann

Power in the Blood: A Family Narrative, by Linda Tate

Out of the Mountains: Appalachian Stories, by Meredith Sue Willis

Negotiating a Perilous Empowerment: Appalachian Women's Literacies, by Erica Abrams Locklear

Standing Our Ground: Women, Environmental Justice, and the Fight to End Mountaintop Removal, by Joyce M. Barry

Shake Terribly the Earth: Stories from an Appalachian Family, by Sarah Beth Childers

Thinking Outside the Girl Box: Teaming Up with Resilient Youth in Appalachia, by Linda Spatig and Layne Amerikaner

Once I Too Had Wings: The Journals of Emma Bell Miles, 1908–1918, edited by Steven Cox

Women of the Mountain South: Identity, Work, and Activism, edited by Connie Park Rice and Marie Tedesco

Women of the Mountain South

of the

Mountain South

IDENTITY,
WORK,
AND
ACTIVISM

Edited by
Connie Park Rice
and Marie Tedesco

OHIO UNIVERSITY PRESS   ATHENS

Ohio University Press, Athens, Ohio 45701
ohioswallow.com
© 2015 by Ohio University Press
All rights reserved

To obtain permission to quote, reprint, or otherwise reproduce or distribute material from Ohio University Press publications, please contact our rights and permissions department at (740) 593-1154 or (740) 593-4536 (fax).

Cover images: (*front*) Children of neighboring white and black miners, southern West Virginia, 1932. *James T. Laing, photographer; (back)* Coal Miner's Widow, Gilbert, West Virginia, 1970s. *Jeanne Rasmussen Photographer, Jeanne Rasmussen Collection, Archives of Appalachia, East Tennessee State University, Johnson City, Tennessee.*

Printed in the United States of America
Ohio University Press books are printed on acid-free paper ∞ ™

25 24 23 22 21 20 19 18 17 16 15   5 4 3 2 1

Library of Congress Cataloging-in-Publication Data

Women of the Mountain South : identity, work, and activism / edited by Connie Park Rice and Marie Tedesco.
    pages cm. — (Race, ethnicity and gender in Appalachia)
 Summary: "Scholars of southern Appalachia have tended to focus their research on men, particularly white men. While there have been a few important studies of Appalachian women, no one book has offered a broad overview across time and place. With this collection, editors Connie Park Rice and Marie Tedesco redress this imbalance, telling the stories of these women and calling attention to the varied demographics of those who call the mountains home. The essays that make up *Women of the Mountain South* contradict and debunk entrenched stereotypes of Appalachian women as poor and white, and they bring to life women too often neglected in the history of the region. Each focuses on a particular individual or a particular group, but taken as a whole, they illustrate the diversity of women who live in the region and the richness of their life experiences. The Mountain South has been home to Cherokee, African American, Latina, and white women, both rich and poor. Civil rights and gay rights advocates, environmental and labor activists, prostitutes, and coal miners—all have worked, played, and loved in the place called the Mountain South and added to the fullness of its history and culture. The collection is supplemented with key documents that make the volume ideal for the classroom. Contributors: H. Adam Ackley, Katherine Lane Antolini, Joyce M. Barry, Deborah L. Blackwell, Carletta A. Bush, Wilma A. Dunaway, Barbara J. Howe, John C. Inscoe, Lois Lucas, Penny Messinger, Louis C. Martin, Evelyn Ashley Sorrell, Connie Park Rice, Marie Tedesco, Karen W. Tice, and Jan Voogd"— Provided by publisher.
 Includes bibliographical references and index.
 ISBN 978-0-8214-2150-5 (hardback) — ISBN 978-0-8214-2151-2 (pb) — ISBN 978-0-8214-4522-8 (pdf)
 1. Women—Appalachian Region—Social conditions. 2. Women—Political activity—Appalachian Region. I. Rice, Connie Park. II. Tedesco, Marie.
 HQ1438.A127W66 2015
 305.40974—dc23

2015001218

For Opal Kemp, Twila Price,

and all the women of the Mountain South

Contents

Acknowledgments		xi

Introduction: A Tapestry of Voices
Women's History in the Mountain South
CONNIE PARK RICE 1

PART ONE: IDENTITY AND WOMEN OF THE MOUNTAIN SOUTH

One — Women in Cherokee Society
Status, Race, and Power from the Colonial Period to Removal
MARIE TEDESCO 23

Two — Mothers' Day v. Mother's Day
The Jarvis Women and the Meaning of Motherhood
KATHARINE LANE ANTOLINI 45

Three — Female Stereotypes and the Creation of Appalachia,
1870–1940
DEBORAH L. BLACKWELL 74

Four — Women on a Mission
Southern Appalachia's "Benevolent Workers" on Film
JOHN C. INSCOE 95

Five — Embodying Appalachia
Progress, Pride, and Beauty Pageantry, 1930s to the Present
KAREN W. TICE 117

Documents

Moravian *Lebenslauf* (Memoir or Life's Journey) 141

Petition for Divorce 144

Women of the Mountains
Rev. Edgar Tufts 147

Rebel in the Mosque: Going Where I Know I Belong
Asra Q. Nomani 153

An Undocumented Mexican Mother of a High
School Dropout in East Tennessee
Maria Alejandra Lopez   158

Questions for Discussion   170

PART TWO: WOMEN AND WORK IN APPALACHIA

Six   Challenging the Myth of Separate Spheres
            Women's Work in the Antebellum Mountain South
            WILMA A. DUNAWAY   173

Seven   Cyprians and Courtesans, Murder and Mayhem
            Prostitution in Wheeling during the Civil War
            BARBARA J. HOWE   195

Eight   Professionalizing "Mountain Work" in Appalachia
            Women in the Conference of Southern Mountain Workers
            PENNY MESSINGER   217

Nine   "'Two fer' the Money"?
            African American Women in the Appalachian Coalfields
            CARLETTA A. BUSH   244

Ten   Flopping Tin and Punching Metal
            *A Survey of Women Steelworkers in West Virginia,
            1890–1970*
            LOUIS C. MARTIN   270

Documents

The Indenture of Mary Hollens   295
The Testimony of Mrs. Maggie Waters   297
A Working Woman Speaks   306
The Pikeville Methodist Hospital Strike   312
Poetry from the *Coal Mining Women's Support Team News*   315

Questions for Discussion   323

PART THREE: WOMEN AND ACTIVISM IN THE MOUNTAIN SOUTH

Eleven   In the Footsteps of Mother Jones, Mothers of the Miners
            Florence Reece, Molly Jackson, and Sarah Ogan Gunning
            H. ADAM ACKLEY   327

Twelve	"She Now Cries Out"	
	Linda Neville and the Limitations of Venereal Disease Control Policies in Kentucky	
	EVELYN ASHLEY SORRELL	350
Thirteen	Garrison, Drewry, Meadows, and Bateman	
	Race, Class, and Activism in the Mountain State	
	LOIS LUCAS	372
Fourteen	*Ethel New v. Atlantic Greyhound*	
	Fighting for Social Justice in Appalachia	
	JAN VOOGD	402
Fifteen	"Remembering the Past, Working for the Future"	
	West Virginia Women Fight for Environmental Heritage and Economic Justice in the Age of Mountaintop Removal Coal Mining	
	JOYCE M. BARRY	418

Documents

The Petition of Margaret Lee · 443

The Fight for Suffrage · 446

Abortion in the Mountain South · 452

Helen Louise Gibson Compton: Founder and Proprietor
of The Shamrock
Carol Burch-Brown · 459

At the Intersection of Cancer Survivorship, Gender, Family, and
Place in Southern Central Appalachia: A Case Study
Kelly A. Dorgan, Kathryn L. Duvall, and Sadie P. Hutson · 466

Questions for Discussion · 474

Epilogue: Reflections on the Concept of Place in the Study
of Women in the Mountain South
A Roundtable Discussion with the Authors · 475

Contributors · 493

Index · 499

Photographs follow pages 166, 319, and 470

Acknowledgments

First and foremost, we thank all the contributors for their excellent essays and endless patience during the creation of this book. Likewise, we thank Gillian Berchowitz, Ohio University Press director, for her insights and her faith in the project. We extend special thanks to Isaac Emrick for the maps he created for this project; to Lisa Mixon, granddaughter of Bessie Edens, for permission to use Bessie Edens's Southern Summer School writings; to Tom Laing, son of James T. Laing, for the use of his father's photograph for the cover of this book; and to Lou Martin and Kate Black for their insightful suggestions. Last but not least, we thank Kenneth Fones-Wolf for suggesting we embark on this endeavor.

A number of persons provided invaluable assistance to us during the course of the project; without them, we could not have completed the book. Thanks very much to L. Nicole Crabbe at the Archives of the Moravian Church in America, Southern Province, Winston-Salem, North Carolina; Michael Ridderbusch and Catherine Rakowski at West Virginia and Regional History Center; Sharyn J. Mitchell and Lori Myers-Steele in Special Collections and Archives at Hutchins Library, Berea College; Amy Collins and Laura Smith at the Archives of Appalachia at East Tennessee State University; Steve Cotham and Sally Polhemus at the Calvin M. McClung Historical Collection at the Knoxville Public Library; Jim Baggett and Catherine Oseas at the Birmingham Public Library; Sara Abdonishani, Ruth Bryan, and Jason Flahardy from Special Collections at the University of Kentucky; the staff at the Alabama Department of Archives and History; Kay Peterson at the Archives Center of the National Museum of American History; Kelly Wooten at Duke University; and the staff at the Martin P. Catherwood Library at Cornell University.

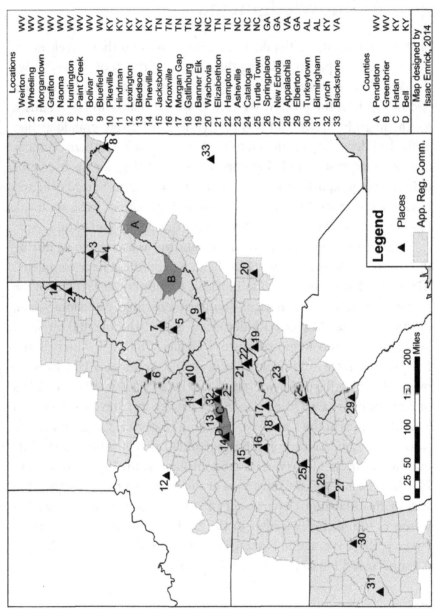

Selected sites in *Women of the Mountain South*

INTRODUCTION

A Tapestry of Voices

Women's History in the Mountain South

CONNIE PARK RICE

> As a river is born deep inside the earth in springs
> that gather into streams and join to become a river,
> so people's lives gather into families and communities
> and become part of the river of history.
>
> —Wilma Dykeman, *The Tall Woman*

Thoughts of the Mountain South, those mountain counties south of the Mason-Dixon Line and the flow of the Ohio River, evoke numerous images of a region and a mountain people often disassociated with northern Appalachia. Yet the images themselves are contradictory, depicting the Mountain South as an isolated yet resource-rich region, and its people as isolated, illiterate, poverty ridden, and coal dependent, or as a culturally rich region with picturesque mountains and inhabitants who value strong family and community ties, humor, and beautiful music. It is all of those things and more. This collection of essays examines the history of the Mountain South and, occasionally, its social, economic, and political ties to its neighboring states in the North and West through the eyes of mountain women.

Why use the term "Mountain South"? Recent scholarship in regional studies focuses on considering regions as social constructions that change with time; therefore, to be in the forefront of discourse in regional studies, it is important to recognize that the term "Appalachia" is a social construction, and a recent one at that. Not only have the boundaries of Appalachia changed over time, but the name of the area within those boundaries has changed. Formerly referred to as the "southern mountains," "southern backcountry," "Mountain South," or "southern uplands," the region is now called "Appalachia." William Goodell Frost defined it as "Appalachian America." Perhaps the *idea* of Appalachia first appeared in Will Wallace Harney's travelogue, "A Strange Land and a Peculiar People," printed in *Lippincott's Magazine* in 1873. Local color writers of the late nineteenth and early twentieth centuries continued the creation of Appalachia as a distinct region inhabited by unique people who possessed certain definable traits, both positive and negative. While "mountain people" were staunch individualists determined to live their lives free from outside interference, they also were tied to large kin networks. Respect for kin and dedication to caring for kin are qualities associated with residents of the region, yet the patriarchal structure of families often meant that women had few choices in life, except to bear and raise large families. Women were caring mothers, yet also lascivious in their sexual habits. Men were caring fathers, yet also domineering over their "womenfolk." Mountaineers possessed common sense but were ignorant in regard to "book learning." These Appalachian stereotypes and images, as well as many others, still hold power, even though they represent essentialist views of the region's inhabitants. In 1990 anthropologist Allen W. Batteau stated that "Appalachia is a frame of reference, not a fact."[1] Indeed, the region is, and has been, characterized by racial, ethnic, and socioeconomic class diversity. It is this diversity that this volume explores: there is no "Appalachian woman," but there are many Appalachian women.

As a result, the history of women in the Mountain South is as rich and varied as its people and its regions. Although many women suffered the limitations imposed on them by those who accepted a patriarchal construction of gender, many refused to be constrained and directed their own life experiences, which varied and changed according to the social, economic, and political conditions of time and place. Their experiences differ because the women were, and are, diverse. They are women of all races, ethnicities, ages, classes (social and economic), religions, and sexual orientations; and they all have a history.

For teachers of Appalachian history courses who seek to include the history of women in the Mountain South, the diversity of women's experiences makes it difficult to present a singular portrait of women throughout the region. Often, instructors make selections from a variety of good essays or settle on one particular book that examines the role of women, particularly when additional books are required to cover other topics. In the last four decades, scholars have produced, and continue to produce, many fine studies on women in Appalachia, but few provide a broad overview of women across time and place. This book begins to fill that void. Intended as an introduction to the history of women in the Mountain South, *Women of the Mountain South: Identity, Work, and Activism* focuses on three dominant themes over two hundred years of history in various geographic locales. A few essays in this book provide synopses of scholarship essential to the understanding of women in the Mountain South; others provide new insights into the experiences of Appalachian women. The attempt to cover specific topics, eras, and places revealed the scope and limitations of current studies on women's history in the region. The scarcity of primary documents written by mountain women themselves limits understanding of their thoughts and experiences during the frontier and colonial eras.[2] The legendary exploits of women such as Mad Anne Bailey, Elizabeth Zane, Rebecca Boone, and others often overshadow historical analysis of women on the Appalachian frontier; and while the exploits of men are well documented, very little is known about their wives—for example, John Sevier and his wife, Catherine S. Sevier. Surprisingly, in a region vital to, and still (in numerous ways) obsessed with the Civil War, only a few historians have investigated the wartime roles of mountain women. Unsurprisingly, the industrial era from 1880 to 1920, the focus of numerous studies in Appalachian history, continues to produce the highest number of studies on women in the region. The role of women in the establishment and organization of religious groups demands more investigation. In recent years, several scholars have addressed the role of women in Catholic organizations, but no one has examined the role of religion in mountain women's daily lives.[3] Analysis of women's

Introduction: A Tapestry of Voices   3

sexuality and gender identity is also limited. For the most part, studies on gay, lesbian, bisexual, and transgendered life in the region have focused on men.[4] The arrival of minority women in Appalachia, particularly the growing number of Hispanic/Latina and Muslim women, and the maintenance and blending of cultures resulting from the encounter need to be explored. Without a doubt, there is still a lot left for historians to investigate.

A historiography of women in the Mountain South makes it clear that for the most part women remained on the periphery, marginalized by the actions and experiences of the men in their lives. In contrast to the historical narratives written by and about women at the national level, historical works on mountain women written in the antebellum era are almost nonexistent.[5] Sidney Saylor Farr's *Appalachian Women: An Annotated Bibliography* lists only one, Rufus Anderson's publication of *Memoir of Catherine Brown, A Christian Indian of the Cherokee Nation,* published in 1825.[6] Between 1850 and 1960, however, the number of books and articles published on mountain women steadily grew. The majority were autobiographies and biographies of well-known or prominent mountain women, from Nancy Ward to Rachel Jackson to early female pioneers in education, medicine, music, or religion; narratives of women captured by Native Americans such as Mary Draper Ingles and Jemima Boone; memoirs and stories of Appalachian mothers, grandmothers, and "aunts", stories relating the experiences of being a preacher or miner's wife; or tales of a mountain girl who made good against all odds. By far, the women who made it into those history books were white. One of the earliest exceptions to this is African American Anna D. McBain's short essay, "What It Means to Be a Teacher," printed in *Berea Quarterly* in 1901.[7]

Local color writers of the late nineteenth and early twentieth centuries had an impact on historical work, as many historians tried to place women within the context of the images of Appalachian women created by those writers. Mostly in works of fiction, the writers created lasting stereotypes, portraying the mountain woman either as a young, beautiful, innocent, white girl at the height of her sexuality or as a woman haggard and worn from the domestic duties and childbearing forced on her by a patriarchal society. Yet a third image depicted the woman who managed to survive a life of toil and hardships as strong and enduring, a woman (often embodied as a "granny woman") of great wisdom, power, and influence who sustained traditional mountain culture. Historical works tended to promote the latter image (in biographies of mothers and grandmothers) or to document either those who worked to overcome problems in the region (benevolent workers) or those who overcame the problems themselves to become successful.[8]

In the 1960s, the War on Poverty (1964) and the creation of the Appalachian Regional Commission (1965) drew the nation's attention to the region and to the plight of families suffering from high rates of poverty, unemployment, and a lack of health care. The emphasis on women and children led people both inside and outside Appalachia to reexamine the lives of women in the region. The civil rights and women's movements of the 1960s and 1970s also encouraged women to reevaluate their lives and roles within the family and within their communities. The women's movement, along with the movement of "history from the bottom up" that gave rise to the social history movement and the acceptance of women into graduate programs in history departments throughout the region, sparked a new interest in the history of women in Appalachia. Aided by the creation of women's and Appalachian studies programs in colleges and universities throughout the region and the establishment of the Appalachian Studies Association in 1977 (which encouraged discourse and activism among community women and women in academia), the history of women in the Mountain South began to flourish. Much of the credit goes to Helen Lewis, who recognized the discrimination that women academics faced and played an active role in the development of Appalachian studies.[9]

By the late 1970s, although historians and other scholars still wrote essays on coal miners' wives, the majority of works on women in the coalfields concentrated on the women who went down in mines themselves. Publications on women written by the staff members of the Coal Employment Project (1977–2000), *Appalachian Heritage, Mountain Life and Work, Southern Exposure,* and the Council on Appalachian Women's (CAW) *Magazine of Appalachian Women* (MAW) and *Appalachian Women* focused on women's work, health, art (particularly in the fields of music and literature), education, religion, and history (memoirs and

Introduction: A Tapestry of Voices   5

interviews with "grannies" continued). These early feminist writers focused almost exclusively on women and the recovery and documentation of women's roles in history.

Yet many of these works continued to set forth an essentialist perspective of "Appalachian" women that accepted the social and historical construction of a universal female identity in the region. Many feminist scholars, and the feminist movement overall, continued to champion the late nineteenth- and early twentieth-century idea that there was such a thing as an "essential nature of woman." The maternalist care ethics approach of the late twentieth century holds to this essentialist view. Even Sidney Saylor Farr, in the introduction to the first significant compilation of works on Appalachian women in 1981, wrote that "mountain women are warped or shaped by their environment, the mores of their culture, the restrictions of their religious beliefs, and the traditions handed down from mothers and grandmothers" and that they "are very insular." She concluded that based on the compiled works, mountain women "do have some special powers and special hardships."[10]

During the 1980s, a growing historiography on women in the Mountain South emerged from the research and writing of scholars from all disciplines. David Whisnant's *All That Is Native and Fine: The Politics of Culture in an American Region* (1983) un-romanticized Appalachian culture and laid the foundation for future studies with his examination of Progressive Era reformers— missionaries, nurses, and teachers—the so-called fotched-on women from outside Appalachia whose biased but "well-meaning" efforts to preserve or modernize mountain culture threatened the culture itself. Challenging and rejecting the romanticized and stereotyped interpretations of women in the Mountain South, scholars began to use postmodern feminist theories to challenge the universalist and essentialist writings on Appalachians and Appalachia.[11] Scholars used gender analysis, how societies construct and teach masculinity and femininity, to examine the impact of gender on individual and institutional structures of power and its social, economic, and political impact on women. Jacquelyn Dowd Hall's "Disorderly Women: Gender and Labor Militancy in the Appalachian South" (1986), a complex study of striking female textile workers in Elizabethton, Tennessee, and Sally Ward Maggard's "Class and Gender: New Theoretical Priorities

6 CONNIE PARK RICE

in Appalachian Studies" (1986) introduced feminist approaches to Appalachian studies.[12] Since then, feminist theory has played a prominent role in the study of mountain women.

In their essay "Appalachian Studies, Resistance, and Postmodernism" in *Fighting Back in Appalachia: Traditions of Resistance and Change* (1993), Alan Banks, Dwight Billings, and Karen Tice maintain that the field of feminist studies promotes the use of a "deconstructive strategy" to disassemble the myths and stereotypes of Appalachian women and to examine the diversity and plurality of women's experiences in the Mountain South. The resulting conclusion is that women in the Mountain South have multiple identities that do not stem from geography or culture but from political dynamics and social change.[13] Maggard's feminist criticism of Appalachian historiography continued with the essay "Will the Real Daisy Mae Please Stand Up? A Methodological Essay on Gender Analysis in Appalachian Research" (1994), followed by essays on gender and education (1995) and gender, class, and labor (1998, 1999).[14] While many of the feminist studies on Appalachian women came from women's studies scholars, others used the same methodology in their works. Geographer Ann Oberhauser applied gender to her analysis of women, work, and geography (1995), and historian Sandra Barney examined the role of gender in the construction of Appalachian "otherness" (1996, 1999). Two seminal works on women in the region come from historian Theda Perdue, who examined the cultural persistence of Cherokee women in *Cherokee Women: Gender and Cultural Change, 1700–1835,* and sociologist Wilma A. Dunaway, who examined the impact of race and class on women's work in the Mountain South in both *The African American Family in Slavery and Emancipation* and *Women, Work, and Family in the Antebellum Mountain South.*[15]

In 1999 Patricia Beaver edited a collection of essays for a special issue of the *National Women's Studies Association Journal* titled "Appalachia and the South: Place, Gender, and Pedagogy."[16] Among those essays, perhaps the most used are Beaver's "Women in Appalachia and the South: Gender, Race, Region, and Agency" and Barbara Ellen Smith's "'Beyond the Mountains': The Paradox of Women's Place in Appalachian History." That same year, Smith published an edited volume, *Neither Separate nor Equal: Women, Race, and Class in the South,*

Introduction: A Tapestry of Voices　7

containing seven essays that examine the political economy of women in Appalachia.[17] In "'Beyond the Mountains,'" Smith argues that anyone writing the history of women in Appalachia should consider the "implicitly gendered constructions of Appalachia," in which men play the dominant role, and challenges writers to look at the ways in which women have made and shaped history and contested traditional constructions, thereby creating a new feminist historiography that "challenges conventional conceptions of the region, its history, and who has created both."[18]

Sandra Barney's groundbreaking work, *Authorized to Heal: Gender, Class, and the Transformation of Medicine in Appalachia, 1880–1920* (2000), followed by Melanie Beals Goans's *Mary Breckinridge: The Frontier Nursing Service and Rural Health in Appalachia* (2008), addresses the politics of gender and class that occurred during the transformation of health care in the mountains.[19] Both works reveal the historical role of women in the professionalization of health care in Appalachia and the appropriation of that history by men.

Mary K. Anglin's "Toward a Workable Past: Dangerous Memories and Feminist Perspectives" (2000) and Elizabeth S. D. Engelhardt's essay "Creating Appalachian Women's Studies: Dancing Away from Granny and Elly May" (2005) both argue the benefits of a feminist approach.[20] Engelhardt argues that feminism and Appalachian studies have much to offer each other. Feminism, according to Engelhardt, "can help Appalachian studies get beyond the questioning of stereotypes" to investigate the historical, cultural, and material causes of stereotypes" and to make and analyze connections between individuals and institutions, while Appalachian "tools of class analysis could help feminism move on to resolving its class struggles."[21] Engelhardt's work has resulted in two books on women and feminism in the Mountain South, *The Tangled Roots of Feminism, Environmentalism, and Appalachian Literature* (2003) and *Beyond Hill and Hollow: Original Readings in Appalachian Women's Studies* (2005).

The goal of feminist history, defined as historical work infused with concern about the past and present oppression of women, is to reread the work of female writers and artists to demonstrate the significance of women's voices and choices in the past. A feminist approach to studies of mountain women encouraged an even more inclusive analysis of race, ethnicity, gender, age, place, and sexuality in Appalachian studies, a field dominated by the study of the class struggles of men.

Lately, Appalachian studies scholars have sought to place women's history in a global perspective. Scholars such as Barbara Ellen Smith, Stephen L. Fisher, Elizabeth S. D. Engelhardt, and Mary K. Anglin are at the forefront of this movement in Appalachia, challenging regional scholars to look beyond the Appalachian region and old concepts of Appalachian exceptionalism to examine the common concerns of women throughout the world, particularly those living in mountain regions.[22] How do mountain women around the world contest economic injustice, established power structures, and environmental degradation? What can Appalachian activists teach them? And what can they teach us?[23]

In 2010 *Appalachian Journal* printed a special issue titled "Women in Appalachia." The issue contains the work of some of the most prolific historians of women in the Mountain South, including Barbara J. Howe, Deborah L. Blackwell, and Penny Messinger, all of whom also contributed to this collection of essays. Other recent works include Erica Abrams Locklear's *Negotiating a Perilous Empowerment: Appalachian Women's Literacies* (2011); Helen M. Lewis, Patricia D. Beaver, and Judith Jennings's *Helen Matthews Lewis: Living Social Justice in Appalachia* (2012); and Joyce M. Barry's *Standing Our Ground: Women, Environmental Justice, and the Fight to End Mountaintop Removal* (2012).[24] Researchers of all disciplines increasingly document the complexity and diversity of women and place.

So what does the concept of place mean for the historical analysis of women living in the region? And what does it mean for the future of Appalachian studies? Is Appalachia a distinct place or not? "Place," or a sense of place, can suggest a sense of belonging—and, thereby, exclusiveness and a separation from those who do *not* belong. "Place" can be prescriptive, if it creates parameters whereby only certain ideas or qualities and characteristics of people linked to place are acceptable (a form of essentialism). And, in Appalachian studies, focus on place often leads to analysis from the perspective of the outworn binary of "outsider/insider." Admittedly, "place" is central to Appalachian studies in

Introduction: A Tapestry of Voices　9

many respects. Events unfold "in place" and are linked from local place to the larger "region." Place also is evocative, especially of emotional attachment (and often found in literary works); but emotional assertions of "place" cannot substitute for the historical analysis of people, poverty, events, or power relations in a local place, or in their linkage to region and nation.

Although students, scholars, and activists who study the region still have a lot to learn, the essays in this book provide different perspectives of the diversity of mountain women and their experiences throughout the region. Focusing on the three dominate themes of mountain women's history, identity, work, and activism, the essays illustrate the ways in which women have shaped, and have been shaped by, the social, economic, and political history of Appalachia.

Part 1 of *Women in the Mountain South* explores identity, that is, how women interpreted and perceived their lives in social, economic, and political terms, as well as how others perceived them, and how those perceptions changed over time and place. While essentialist writings depicted a universal "Appalachian" identity, recent scholarship recognizes the plurality and complexity of Appalachian identity. Phillip Obermiller and Michael E. Maloney in "The Uses and Misuses of Appalachian Culture" argue against the indiscriminate use of culture based on generalized and stereotypical cultural traits and claim that no single "mountain culture" applies to twenty-five million people in thirteen states. They argue that while there may be numerous local cultures based on "belief and behavior sets tied to specific places," it may be better to substitute the concept of culture for that of Appalachian identity.[25]

The social constructions of race, ethnicity, and gender, social and political institutions, the perceptions of benevolent workers, local color writers, scholars, the media, and mountain women themselves have shaped and altered the images and identities of Appalachian women. In the first essay on identity, "Women in Cherokee Society: Status, Race, and Power from the Colonial Period to Removal," Marie Tedesco examines the place of native, white, African, African American, and mixed raced women in evolving Cherokee society. The power to determine Cherokee identity, based on clan affiliation through a Cherokee mother, belonged to Cherokee women. Cultural borrowing and diffusion led to

10 CONNIE PARK RICE

major changes in the Cherokee nation and weakened its matrilineal base of society. Yet the persistence of Cherokee identity, and its link to race and to white concepts of race gender, continually marginalized black Cherokee women and created a race prejudice that still exists today.

In "Mothers' Day v. Mother's Day: The Jarvis Women and the Meaning of Motherhood," Katharine Lane Antolini illustrates the fact that motherhood has many meanings, depending on class, race, place (urban or rural), and, particularly, time. As gender ideals shifted, the *mothers'* day that Ann Reeves Jarvis created in the 1850s had a far different meaning than the one her daughter, Anna Jarvis, conceived at the turn of the twentieth century. While Ann Reeves Jarvis's "mothers' day" emerged from rural efforts for health reform and the war-torn counties of a divided state during the Civil War, it was "Mother's Day," a day to honor an individual's parent, that became a national holiday. In the process, the identity of "mothers' day," rooted in service by and for mothers and communities in need, was altered. Yet while the region maintains its claim on the idealized version of "mothers' day," Ann Reeves Jarvis's original definition of motherhood created a lasting maternal model for social organizing.

The gendered nature of stereotypes and the centrality of those gendered and feminized images to the concept of Appalachia are the focus of Deborah L. Blackwell's essay "Female Stereotypes and the Creation of Appalachia, 1870–1940." Blackwell investigates the role of women (from both inside and outside Appalachia) and institutions in the creation and perpetuation of the stereotypes. While mountain women sometimes used the images as a means of social, economic, or political agency, benevolent workers used them to obtain charitable aid and industry used them to excuse their exploitation of the land and its people.

In "Women on a Mission: Southern Appalachia's 'Benevolent Workers' on Film," John C. Inscoe analyzes the media's portrayal of female benevolent workers in the films *I'd Climb the Highest Mountain*, *Christy*, and *Songcatcher*. Over time, Hollywood presented an increasingly feminist portrayal of the workers. More important, the movies illustrate how people inside and outside Appalachia have perceived each other across cultural boundaries, thereby highlighting the issue of "cultural otherness."

Introduction: A Tapestry of Voices 11

In the last essay on identity in part 1, Karen W. Tice reveals the ways women's bodies and images are sites of representation, assimilation, belonging, and racial and cultural identity in the Mountain South in "Embodying Appalachia: Progress, Pride, and Beauty Pageantry, 1930s to the Present." Tice examines the gendered, racialized, and class-based nature of beauty pageants and the personal and political agendas behind them. She demonstrates that the pageants promoted a sense of place, promoted and protected white femininity, and in the case of black pageants, reinforced class and color hierarchies. At the same time, contestants represented the commercial and political interests of the region, particularly those of railroads, oil, coal, and gas.

Primary documents included in the section enhance understanding of women and identity in the Mountain South. In the "Moravian *Lebenslauf* (Memoir or Life's Journey)," Moravians, Cherokee, and blacks, although united in their love of God, maintain racial distinctions. "Petition for Divorce" reveals how marriage and divorce had the ability to shape a woman's social, political, and economic identity in the early nineteenth century. Edgar Tuft's perception of mountain women illustrates the making of female stereotypes and "identity" and how they became a basis for reform efforts in the Mountain South in the document "Women of the Mountains." "Rebel in the Mosque: Going Where I Know I Belong" and "An Undocumented Mexican Mother of a High School Dropout in East Tennessee" reveal the difficulties of recent immigrants, Muslim and Hispanic, to socially and economically integrate into local communities while maintaining their ethnic and cultural identity. In combination, the essays and documents in this section reframe what it means to be "Appalachian." Although the population in the Mountain South has been culturally and genetically blended throughout its history, racism persists in the mountains, and the region continues to maintain an image of cultural whiteness.

The nature and diversity of women's work is the topic of part 2. Based on race, ethnicity, and class, variations in the labor experiences of women in the Mountain South existed both inside and outside the domestic environment of home. Women's work consisted of both paid and unpaid labor, public and domestic work, and what anthropologist

Carol Stack refers to as "kin work," the responsibility of caring for the sick, the elderly, and the young.[26]

The first essay in this section, Wilma A. Dunaway's "Challenging the Myth of Separate Spheres: Women's Work in the Antebellum Mountain South," argues that the concept of separate spheres cannot be applied to Appalachia. Instead, gender lines blurred, with mountain women performing tasks that outside the mountains were seen as "unsuitable" for women. Regardless of the legal and cultural standards that kept many women from working outside of the home, women's labor contributed to the family economy and survival. Dunaway maintains that women's work came in many forms and was shaped by race, class, and gender, all of which had economic value regardless of being paid or unpaid work.

"Cyprians and Courtesans, Murder and Mayhem: Prostitution in Wheeling during the Civil War," written by Barbara J. Howe, does much to dispel the stereotypical images of Appalachian women. Her study reveals a hierarchal profession based on class, race, and ethnicity. Contrary to the dominant image of Appalachians as rural folk, female prostitutes were predominantly urbanites. Lacking both power and agency, many of these women entered prostitution as a consequence of economic distress, alcoholism, abuse, or homelessness.

In contrast, Penny Messinger examines the central role of middle-class white women from outside the region in the movements to reform Appalachia in "Professionalizing 'Mountain Work' in Appalachia: Women in the Conference of Southern Mountain Workers." Through the Conference of Southern Mountain Workers, these reformers asserted their authority to define both the region and its needs and created and institutionalized their vision of Appalachia as a recognizable geographic and social region. The female leadership of the CSMW carried out a rural and feminized Progressive agenda in the mountains that contributed to the development of social work as a profession.

In ""Two fer" the Money'? African American Women in the Appalachian Coalfields," Carletta A. Bush examines the gendered and racialized myth surrounding black women's employment in the coal industry in the 1970s. The "two fer" myth alleged that black women had an employment advantage over men and white women because the coal industry could, under affirmative action guidelines, claim the

Introduction: A Tapestry of Voices 13

employment of two minorities by hiring one black woman and that, subsequently, the successful entrance of these minorities into the work force would lead them to take jobs from white men. Those few who were hired faced discrimination that limited their advancement and made them among the first to be fired when the coal industry began to decline. In the end, the myth served to preserve white male privilege in the mining industry, while dividing women miners and eliminating the power they could gain through unity.

The sex typing of jobs and sexism among union workers in the steel industry is the focus of Louis C. Martin's "Flopping Tin and Punching Metal: A Survey of Women Steelworkers in West Virginia, 1890–1970." Martin shows that despite numerous changes in the steel industry over decades, a gendered division of labor in the steel industry remained in place, making the women's experiences "surprisingly consistent" over the next eighty years. Working conditions for women did not improve until legal challenges against discrimination occurred in the 1970s.

The documents in part 2 highlight the impact of class and gender on women's work. "The Indenture of Mary Hollens" reveals how women without means were often forced to survive in the late eighteenth and early nineteenth centuries. "The Testimony of Mrs. Maggie Waters" illustrates the lack of jobs available for women living in the coal mining regions of Appalachia, forcing women to take in boarders or do laundry to supplement the family income. The Summer School for Women Workers in Industry held in Arden, North Carolina, in 1930, attempted to educate women on labor economics, union activism, and public health. In "A Working Woman Speaks," Bessie Edens of Hampton, Tennessee, describes the conditions women faced in the artificial silk (rayon) industry, efforts to organize, and need for married women to work. Efforts of mountain women to obtain decent wages and better working conditions are also the focus of "The Pikeville Methodist Hospital Strike" and "Poetry from the *Coal Mining Women's Support Team News*." The documents reveal women's impetus for participating in the workforce, their continual attempts to improve working conditions, and the methods they employed to achieve their goals.

The dominant role of women activists in Appalachia is the topic of part 3. Community activism on all levels has shaped the construction and reconstruction of Appalachian identity and continues to do so today. Like the other topics in this book, gender, race, and class have influenced the focus and methods of activism in the region. Women's petitions for freedom, for divorce, and for recognition of their legal right to inherit, antislavery petitions, and more helped mountain women to make strides toward obtaining their own rights and, in the process, transform their political identity. Efforts to organize churches, schools, and communities and to protect their families and communities through sanitation and health reforms created good communities in which to live. Mountain women have fought for better social and economic conditions and for justice. They have fought for protection and survival of their husbands, families, and neighbors in coal communities throughout Appalachia. They have fought for the preservation of the environment and the land. And they have fought for and against each other. Geography, moral values, cultural traditions, religious beliefs, political ideology, race, ethnicity, and class often have divided mountain women on issues such as abolition, politics, suffrage, abortion, and gay rights. Regardless of their stance on issues, mountain women have found a variety of ways to express their opinions, make changes, or promote their causes.

H. Adam Ackley's "In the Footsteps of Mother Jones, Mothers of the Miners: Florence Reece, Molly Jackson, and Sarah Ogun Gunning" analyzes the maternal model of Appalachian community organizing based on the lives of some of Appalachia's best-known and best-loved women activists. All of these women expanded the traditional Appalachian definitions of maternal authority and women's work and brought national attention to the poor working conditions found in the timber and coal mining regions of the Mountain South.

Motherhood and sexuality are the focus of Evelyn Ashley Sorrell's essay "'She Now Cries Out': Linda Neville and the Limitations of Venereal Disease Control Policies in Kentucky." Sorrell found that when Progressive Era reformers attempted to eliminate blindness in infants due to veneral disease, specifically gonorrhea and syphilis, mountain women were deemed responsible for spreading the disease. The solution, therefore, was to control women's, rather than men's, sexuality.

"Garrison, Drewry, Meadows, and Bateman: Race, Class, and Activism in the Mountain State" examines the lives of four middle-class

Introduction: A Tapestry of Voices 15

black women who fight to ease conditions in the black community and initiate social and political change in the fields of politics, social work, education, and health care. Author Lois Lucas demonstrates how, working both inside and outside the confinements of race and gender, these women drew on their education and the skills they learned in the black clubwomen's associations and fraternal auxiliaries to provide racial uplift in the age of Jim Crow. Jan Voogd also looks at race in Appalachia and discusses one of the earliest examples of the civil rights movement's legal challenges to segregation in transportation in *"Ethel New v. Atlantic Greyhound:* Fighting for Social Justice in Appalachia." Three months pregnant and tired from standing up for 80 miles of a 350-mile bus trip in western Virginia, Ethel New defied institutionalized segregation, regional mores, and cultural expectations when she refused to move from a seat on a segregated bus. In doing so, she not only defined herself but found the means and power to challenge segregation in a court of law.

In the last essay in this section, "'Remembering the Past, Working for the Future': West Virginia Women Fight for Environmental Heritage and Economic Justice in the Age of Mountaintop Removal Coal Mining," Joyce M. Barry analyzes the role of West Virginia women in the fight against mountaintop removal coal mining. Barry argues that despite the historic link between women's activism and male resistance in the coalfields of West Virginia, women have created their own path in the fight against mountaintop removal. In this fight, women operate outside the coal industry and against the interests of male labor in an effort to protect their families, their communities, and the environment.

The essays and documents in part 3 document the maternal nature of women's activism in the Mountain South. Using their maternal role as protectors of their families, their communities, the environment, and the land, women fought both for and against numerous causes. In "The Petition of Margaret Lee," Lee fights to obtain freedom for both herself and her children. Women extended their maternal duties to address issues such as temperance or suffrage, as seen in the documents included in "The Fight for Suffrage." Women's bodies and sexuality, and the control of both, have always been, and continue to be, contentious issues as seen in the documents included in both "Abortion in the Mountain South" and "Helen Louise Gibson Compton: Founder and Proprietor of The Shamrock." Limited access to health care in rural areas of the Mountain South and rising cancer rates in the region have increased the importance of family in health care issues as seen in "At the Intersection of Cancer Survivorship, Gender, Family, and Place in Southern Central Appalachia: A Case Study." Health concerns also play a vital role in activists' continuing interest in the environment.

The essays and documents in part 3 reflect issues that were, or continue to be, controversial throughout the region. For the most part, the examples of activism in this section of the book illustrate only one side of the issues discussed. Women of the Mountain South fought, and continue to fight, on both sides of the issues. In this regard, place has little impact, for women in the same "places" of the Mountain South often chose, and continue to choose, opposing sides. Women were antisuffragists as well as suffragists; union and anti-union; civil rights workers and racists. Issues such as abortion, gay marriage, and immigration continue to divide women in the region, just as these issues divide women throughout America. Perhaps nothing has divided women of the Mountain South more than the issue of mountaintop removal—perhaps because it strikes at the heart of "Appalachian" maternalism. Mountaintop removal forces mountain women to choose between jobs and environment; between feeding and clothing families today and their health tomorrow; between preserving the past and the desire for a better future.

In the epilogue, contributors to this volume discuss the concept of place as it applies to the Mountain South and to their work. Diverse and pluralistic, the *real* Appalachia consists of many places, where people of different social classes, religions, races, ethnicity, and sexual orientation live while maintaining a variety of traditions and interests. Yet there remains an elusive and intangible element to the place or "places" of the Mountain South that continues to make the region "distinct," one that appeals to the heart of all of those who call it home.

NOTES

1. Allen W. Batteau, *The Invention of Appalachia* (Tucson: University of Arizona Press, 1990), 199–200.

2. Major exceptions include works on Cherokee women, particularly Theda Perdue's *Cherokee Women: Gender and Cultural Change, 1700–1835* (Lincoln:

Introduction: A Tapestry of Voices 17

University of Nebraska Press, 1998); Tiya Miles's *Ties That Bind: The Story of an Afro-Cherokee Family in Slavery and Freedom* (Berkeley: University of California Press, 2006); and Wilma A. Dunaway's pioneering *Women, Work, and Family in the Antebellum Mountain South* (Cambridge: Cambridge University Press, 2008). These are works that illustrate the existence of, even if difficult to find, primary documents on women in the Mountain South.

3. See Helen M. Lewis and Monica Apple, *Mountain Sisters: From Convent to Community in Appalachia* (Lexington: University of Kentucky Press, 2004); Barbara J. Howe, "Pioneers on a Mission for God: The Order of Visitation of the Blessed Virgin Mary in Wheeling, 1848–1860," *West Virginia History: A Journal of Regional History*, n.s., 4, no. 1 (Spring 2010): 59–92; and Barbara J. Howe, "Expansion Despite 'National Difficulties': The Order of the Blessed Virgin Mary in Wheeling, 1861–1870," *West Virginia History: A Journal of Regional History*, n.s., 5, no. 2 (Fall 2011): 59–101; also see Carolyn Knight, Sarah Poteete, Amy Sparrow, and Jessica C. Wrye, interviewers, "From the Ground Up: The Community-Building of Marie Cirillo," *Appalachian Journal* 30, no. 1 (Fall 2002): 30–56.

4. See Kate Black and Marc A. Rhorer, "Out in the Mountains: Exploring Lesbian and Gay Lives," *Journal of the Appalachian Studies Association* 1, no. 1 (Fall 1995): 18–28; and Jeff Mann, *Loving Mountains, Loving Men* (Athens: Ohio University Press, 2005).

5. There are numerous historical accounts of women's history outside of the region from women: Mary Rowlandson's autobiography of her capture by Native Americans in 1676; Boston native Sarah Kemble Knight's and Elizabeth House Trist's travel narratives; Elizabeth Ashbridge's story of her rise from an indentured servant to a Quaker preacher; Phoebe Palmer's *The Way of Holiness* (1843); and Margaret Fuller's history *Women in the Nineteenth Century* (1845). There is an even bigger gap in the historical narrative of black women in Appalachia compared to black women's narratives on the national level. Nationally, Jarena Lee's *Life and Religious Experience of Jarena Lee* appeared in 1836; publication of Zilpha Elaw's *Memoirs of the Life, Religious Experience, and Ministerial Travels and Labors of Mrs. Zilpha Elaw, An American Female of Color* occurred in 1845; and Julia A. J. Foote's *A Brand Plucked from the Fire* followed in 1879.

6. Sidney Saylor Farr, *Appalachian Women: An Annotated Bibliography* (Lexington: University Press of Kentucky, 1981), 34.

7. Anna D. McBain, "What It Means to Be a Teacher," *Berea Quarterly* (May 1901): 19–21, listed in Farr, *Appalachian Women*, 15.

8. See for example, Col. John H. Dillard's "The Story of Rowena Roberts," *Mountain Life and Work* 4, no. 1 (April 1928): 19–20, 31. Success usually meant getting an education and moving out of the mountains.

9. Jessica Wilkerson, Jessica Cline, and David P. Cline, "Mountain Feminist: Helen Matthews Lewis, Appalachian Studies, and the Long Women's Movement," *Southern Cultures* 17, no. 3 (Fall 2011): 48–65.

10. Farr, *Appalachian Women*, 4.

11. Alan Banks, Dwight Billings, and Karen Tice, "Appalachian Studies, Resistance, and Postmodernism," in *Fighting Back in Appalachia: Traditions of*

Resistance and Change, ed. Stephen L. Fisher (Philadelphia: Temple University Press, 1993), 292.

12. See Jacquelyn Dowd Hall's "Disorderly Women: Gender and Labor Militancy in the Appalachian South," *Journal of American History* 73, no. 2 (September 1986): 354–82; Sally Ward Maggard's "Class and Gender: New Theoretical Priorities in Appalachian Studies," in *The Impact of Institutions in Appalachia: Proceedings of the Eighth Annual Appalachian Studies Conference,* ed. Jim Lloyd and Anne G. Campbell (Boone, NC: Appalachian Consortium Press, 1986), 100–113; and Banks, Billings, and Tice, "Appalachian Studies, Resistance, and Postmodernism," 283–302.

13. Banks, Billings, and Tice, "Appalachian Studies, Resistance, and Postmodernism," 292.

14. Sally Ward Maggard, "Will the Real Daisy Mae Please Stand Up? A Methodological Essay on Gender Analysis in Appalachian Research," *Appalachian Journal* 21, no. 2 (Winter 1994): 136–50; Sally Ward Maggard, "Gender and Schooling in Appalachia: Lessons for an Era of Economic Restructuring," *Journal of the Appalachian Studies Association* 7 (1995): 140–51; Sally Ward Maggard, "'We're Fighting Millionaires!': The Clash of Gender and Class in Appalachian Women's Union Organizing," in *No Middle Ground: Women and Radical Protest,* ed. Kathleen Blee (New York: New York University Press, 1998), 289–306; Sally Ward Maggard, "Gender, Race, and Place: Confounding Labor Activism in Central Appalachia," in *Neither Separate nor Equal: Women, Race, and Class in the South,* ed. Barbara Ellen Smith (Philadelphia: Temple University Press, 1999), 185–206; and Barbara Ellen Smith, "Walk-Ons in the Third Act: The Role of Women in Appalachian Historiography," *Journal of Appalachian Studies* 4, no. 1 (Spring 1998): 5–28

15. See Ann Oberhauser, "Towards a Gendered Regional Geography: Women and Work in Rural Appalachia," *Growth and Change* 26, no. 2 (Spring 1995): 217–44; Sandra Lee Barney, "Bringing Modern Medicine to the Mountains: Scientific Medicine and the Transformation of Health Care in Southern West Virginia, 1880-1910," West Virginia History 55 (1996): 110–26, and "Maternalism and the Promotion of Scientific Medicine during the Industrial Transformation of Appalachia, 1880–1930," *NWSA Journal: A Publication of the National Women's Studies Association* 11 (Fall 1999): 68–92; Perdue, *Cherokee Women*; and Wilma A. Dunaway, *The African American Family in Slavery and Emancipation* (Cambridge: Cambridge University Press, 2003) and *Women, Work, and Family in the Antebellum Mountain South* (Cambridge: Cambridge University Press, 2008). Also see Thomas Hatley, "Cherokee Women Hold Their Ground," in *Appalachian Frontiers: Settlement, Society, and Development in the Preindustrial Era,* ed. Robert D. Mitchell (Lexington: University Press of Kentucky, 1991), 37–51; Tiya Miles, "The Narrative of Nancy, A Cherokee Woman," *Frontiers: A Journal of Women's Studies* 29, nos. 2 and 3 (2008): 59–80; and Tiya Miles, "'Circular Reasoning': Recentering Cherokee Women in the Antiremoval Campaigns," *American Quarterly* 61, no. 2 (June 2009): 221–43.

16. Patricia Beaver, ed., "Appalachia and the South: Place, Gender, and Pedagogy," *NWSA Journal: A Publication of the National Women's Studies Association* 11, no. 3 (Fall 1999).

Introduction: A Tapestry of Voices 19

17. See Barbara Ellen Smith's "'Beyond the Mountains': The Paradox of Women's Place in Appalachian History," *National Women's Studies Association Journal* 11, no. 3 (Fall 1999): 1–17; Smith, *Neither Separate nor Equal*.

18. Smith, "'Beyond the Mountains.'"

19. See Sandra Barney, *Authorized to Heal: Gender, Class, and the Transformation of Medicine in Appalachia, 1880–1920* (Chapel Hill: University of North Carolina Press, 2000); and Melanie Beals Goans, *Mary Breckinridge: The Frontier Nursing Service and Rural Healthcare in Appalachia* (Chapel Hill: University of North Carolina Press, 2008).

20. See Mary K. Anglin, "Toward a Workable Past: Dangerous Memories and Feminist Perspectives," *Journal of Appalachian Studies* 6, nos. 1 and 2 (Spring, Fall 2000): 71–99; and Elizabeth S. D. Engelhardt, "Creating Appalachian Women's Studies: Dancing Away from Granny and Elly May," in *Beyond Hill and Hollow: Original Readings in Appalachian Women's Studies,* ed. Elizabeth S. D. Engelhardt (Athens: Ohio University Press, 2005).

21. Engelhardt, "Creating Appalachian Women's Studies," 11.

22. See Stephen L. Fisher and Barbara Ellen Smith, eds., *Transforming Places: Lessons from Appalachia* (Urbana: University of Illinois Press, 2012); Engelhardt, "Creating Appalachian Women's Studies," 7–8; and Mary K. Anglin, "Moving Forward: Gender and Globalization in/of Appalachian Studies," *Appalachian Journal* 37, nos. 3–4 (Spring/Summer 2010): 286–94.

23. Fisher and Smith, *Transforming Places,* 325.

24. See Bruce E. Stewart, "An Appalachian Odyssey: An Interview with Patricia Beaver," *Appalachian Studies Journal* 37, nos. 3–4 (Spring/Summer) 2010: 164–82; Erica Abrams Locklear, *Negotiating a Perilous Empowerment: Appalachian Women's Literacies* (Athens: Ohio University Press, 2011); Helen M. Lewis, Patricia D. Beaver, and Judith Jennings, *Helen Matthews Lewis: Living Social Justice in Appalachia* (Lexington: University Press of Kentucky, 2012); and Joyce M. Barry, *Standing Our Ground: Women, Environmental Justice, and the Fight to End Mountaintop Removal* (Athens: Ohio University Press, 2012).

25. Phillip J. Obermiller and Michael E. Maloney, "The Uses and Misuses of Appalachian Culture," Urban Appalachian Council Working Paper No. 20, May 2011. Available at http://uacvoice.org/pdf/workingpaper20.pdf (accessed June 1, 2012), 11. This study focuses on concepts of culture and identity in relation to urban Appalachians.

26. Stewart, "Appalachian Odyssey," 177. Patricia Beaver attributes the concept of "kin work" to anthropologist Carol Stack.

PART ONE

Identity and Women of the Mountain South

She knows the weight not only of her own years;
she has dwelt since childhood in the shadow of
centuries gone.

—Emma Bell Miles, *The Spirit of the Mountains*

CHAPTER ONE

Women in Cherokee Society

*Status, Race, and Power from the
Colonial Period to Removal*

MARIE TEDESCO

Until the mid-twentieth century, historians by and large had treated the history of Southern and Central Appalachia as the history of whites and their triumphant conquest of the region. Native Americans, the Cherokee in particular, figured in the development of the region primarily in relation to Northern European and British white males enforcing their political, religious, and economic systems and values on natives—even though historical and ethnographical evidence demonstrates that in the frontier areas of Southern and Central Appalachia, for example, cultural borrowing and diffusion between whites and Native Americans were commonplace.[1] Cherokee women figured only marginally in historical accounts of the region, even though some early chroniclers, notably traders Alexander Longe and James Adair, Lieutenant Colonel Henry Timberlake, traveler William Bartram, and Moravian missionary Martin Schneider, commented—sometimes astutely—on the social and economic roles of Cherokee women in their societies.[2] But too often western cultural values that privileged patriarchy in social organization, Christianity in religion, and gender division of labor that in theory kept women in the home, prevented contemporary observers from "seeing" and understanding native cultures different from those of the West.

Considering that history as a discipline emerged in the West as a product of mid- to late nineteenth-century positivism that privileged Western white "civilized" cultures and the white males considered responsible for social, economic, and political "progress," it is not surprising that historians—and anthropologists and sociologists as well—long investigated native cultures only as they compared unfavorably to western cultures or as they contained "remnants" of barbarism left behind by white westerners.[3] Interestingly, from the positivist perspective, "refined" treatment of women in Western civilization was a hallmark of civilization; maltreatment of women, as well as the allegedly low status they held in native cultures, marked the "savage" state of indigenous peoples. The contradiction inherent in nineteenth and early twentieth-century approaches to the position of women in Western and native cultures can be seen in the concurrent marginalization and idealization of women. Native women in many tribes, including the Cherokee, occupied social, religious, economic, and political roles unfamiliar to many contemporary observers and later scholars. While even early white travelers often commented on the role of Cherokee women in Cherokee life, until recently the twentieth-century historian ignored the role of women in native cultures.

A few pioneer historians of Native Americans, notably Angie Debo, Carolyn Thomas Foreman, and Henry T. Malone, published works as early as the 1940s and 1950s, prior to the social history boom of the 1960s and 1970s that saw historians increasingly pay attention to previously marginalized groups, among them Native Americans, African Americans, and southern and eastern European ethnic groups. As the concept of "history from the bottom up" gained adherents among historians, nonelites, many of whom left few written documents, entered the historical record.[4] The aforementioned historians relied to a great extent on memoirs and ethnological studies (e.g., by James Mooney and John R. Swanton) to write their histories, which largely focused on men and included women only to an insignificant degree. In more recent years, however, a number of historians have written important histories that investigate the roles of women in Cherokee society. My intent is not to tread over the same ground covered by these historians but, rather, to focus, if even briefly, on the "place" of native, white, African, African American, and "mixed-race" women in an evolving Cherokee society that subsequent to white contact departed from Cherokee traditions and adopted many features of white Western Christian society.

In traditional Cherokee society, Cherokee women occupied the center: to be Cherokee meant to have a Cherokee mother and, hence, Cherokee clan affiliation.[5] As Cherokee men were drawn into the European and English orbit economically, politically, and socially, they adopted Western patriarchal values and standards of behavior. Even though women held on to traditional roles in, for example, agriculture and making baskets for market, while resisting the federal government's "civilization" program, adoption of Western, patriarchal values and behavioral standards upset the gender balance of traditional Cherokee society by privileging men over women and shifting men to the center and pushing women to the periphery.[6]

How did nonnative women fare in traditional Cherokee society? In accordance with traditional Cherokee customs and traditions, non-Cherokee native women at times were integrated into Cherokee clans and white women who married Cherokee men became accepted members of society, although not clan members. Most women of African descent, however, first entered Cherokee society in the degraded status of slaves in a racial system of slavery. Yet some free women of African descent entered Cherokee society as wives or sexual partners of Cherokee men. Female descendants of Cherokee-black relationships became marginalized members of Cherokee society.[7]

The few white women who lived among the Cherokee did so primarily as wives of Cherokee men, wives of white missionaries, or as missionaries themselves.[8] Notable among white women who entered Cherokee lands and interacted with the Cherokee, especially the women, were the wives of Moravian missionaries, who in actuality often performed the duties of missionaries.[9] Even though prior to an 1825 change in marriage laws white wives could not produce Cherokee children, the wives of Cherokee men and their children often became part of a Cherokee elite—something that could not happen with women of African descent and their children.[10]

Women in Cherokee Society 25

NATIVE WOMEN IN TRADITIONAL CHEROKEE SOCIETY

Traditional Cherokee society originally derived from Iroquoian structures and ways of life, because the Cherokee were, according to leading recent scholars, once part of the northern Iroquoian tribes until probably the thirteenth century or so. How and why the Cherokee came to occupy the Southern Appalachian region is unknown. What is known is that the Cherokee speak a language historical linguists termed "southern Iroquoian," as distinguished from "northern Iroquoian." The language split occurred roughly 3,000 to 3,500 years ago; when the Cherokee migrated to the Southern Appalachian region is debatable, as is whether or not they first migrated to what later became northern Georgia and northern Alabama, and then east and north to what later became eastern Tennessee and western North Carolina.[11] By the early sixteenth century the Cherokee had a presence in East Tennessee and western North Carolina and, subsequently, during the eighteenth and early nineteenth centuries, they expanded into North Georgia and northern Alabama. The Cherokee occupied such towns on the Little Tennessee River as Chilhowee, Chota, Tellicoa, Echota, and Tanasi; New Echota and Tanasqui in North Georgia; Catatoga and Turtle Town in western North Carolina; and Turkeytown in northern Alabama.[12]

Like the Iroquois of the North, the Cherokee of the South were matrilinial in regard to social and familial organization, as well as identity; that is, each Cherokee traced descent through her/his mother's side of the family. The essence of being Cherokee meant to have a Cherokee mother and to be affiliated with the clan of the mother.[13] For children, all that counted was kinship to the mother's side of the family; those on the father's side were not kin, even though these persons were treated with respect. Clan membership demanded that one married outside of one's own clan; the married couple lived in the wife's house, which included multiple generations. The husband's relocating to the wife's town weakened the man's connection to his clan but at the same time helped to strengthen ties among towns.[14] Economically, in terms of trade, strong ties aided towns; in times of war or famine, cooperation among towns could make the difference in towns surviving or succumbing.

But more than anything else, the matrilineal system signified the power and respect that Cherokee women held on many levels in

Cherokee society. The power of the clan resided in its linkage to blood and identity. The power of identity, *of being* Cherokee, went back to women. As Tiya Miles claims, women were the center of the clan structure; they "possessed clan and passed it on to their children through bloodlines."[15] Without a Cherokee mother, one was not a Cherokee and thus stood outside Cherokee laws and behavioral prescriptions. It was possible for a person to be adopted into a clan, but only with the permission of the woman who headed the clan. Circumstances that encouraged adoption included wars that depleted the native population, mercy shown those captured in acts of revenge or those orphaned by deaths of parents, or freeing of those enslaved. Clans rarely adopted slaves, African or native, because to be a slave meant to reside outside the boundaries of freedom defined by clan membership.[16]

Cherokee marriage embodied the principles of the matrilineal and matrifocal structures and reflected the power and importance of the clan structure, which not only governed social relations of persons but also served as the source of judicial power and law.[17] One could not, upon penalty of death, marry within one's own clan; to do so was incestuous and taboo. Intraclan marriage would weaken the clan and its alliances and strengths and, hence, the power of the matrilineage.[18] English trader and sometime political agent for the colony of South Carolina Alexander Longe observed in the early 1700s that men could not marry women in their own clan because, as a Cherokee priest said to Longe, they considered them "'proper sisters.'"[19] While the bonds between spouses often were strong, the kinship bonds of the clan were stronger. Longe, writing from the perspective of a member of a patriarchal society, stated that for Cherokee husbands "their wives is nothing akin to them."[20]

On what basis, then, did Cherokee men and women marry, and were the "bonds of marriage," as whites called them, strong and lasting? And did it matter to the Cherokee and to the structure of Cherokee society that the marriage bonds be lasting ones? Often a Cherokee woman married for affection, but more often she married to please parents. To understand the latter, it is necessary to understand that the bonds between Cherokee parents and children were quite strong, to the point where some Western observers thought that Cherokee parents "spoiled" their children. Yet Cherokee children greatly respected their parents and desired to please them, perhaps even to the point of marrying someone not of their own choice.[21] While a number of Cherokee marriages lasted many years, it is true that many lasted only a short time, perhaps a few months. Separation or what westerners call "divorce," was easy, and the choice to separate could be made by either the man or woman. For a number of the white traders, travelers, and political officials who observed and wrote on the Cherokee, "easy" divorce, often initiated by women, indicated lax morals, lack of "civilization," and absence of strong religious beliefs.[22]

The power of the clan can be seen in the matrifocal nature of Cherokee marriage and living arrangements. As Frenchman Louis-Philippe noted in his 1797 diary of travels in America, "Among the Cherokees . . . the family is reckoned around women rather than men as in our society. They claim that only motherhood is sure."[23] Once a couple agreed to live together, the man moved to the residence of the woman. That residence consisted of an extended kin family headed by an elder woman and housing members of the wife's clan. Within the marriage, husband and wife each had their prescribed yet complementary roles, all within the overarching Cherokee belief in balance and harmony.[24] Duties of one spouse were as important as those of the other. The couple had, and raised, children; the mother taught the daughter to be a Cherokee woman by passing on to her knowledge of farming, trading, making clothes, and preparing meals. The mother's uncle(s) passed on to the son knowledge of hunting, being a warrior, and farming. Both parents told their children legends and stories that conveyed behavioral standards and penalties for violating such standards.[25]

Because the Cherokee community did not view marriage bonds as necessarily lasting for life, divorce was easy, with either partner being able to dissolve the relationship. But when the bonds were dissolved, the husband left the dwelling and went back to the house of his mother or sister. If it happened that the man did not want to dissolve the marriage but the woman did, more often than not the wishes of the woman prevailed, perhaps even to the point of her driving the man from the house.[26]

Because it was not imperative that marriage bonds endure for a lifetime, what westerners call adultery usually did not excite the passions of spouses and did not violate legal and religious prescriptions. In fact, the Cherokee had no laws against adultery. Adair considered that the absence of laws against adultery not only revealed the "savage" and uncivilized nature of Cherokee culture but also revealed the untoward power held by women.[27] Raymond Fogelson agrees that absence of adultery laws "suggests that women possessed unusual authority and power in eighteenth-century Cherokee society."[28] Theda Perdue emphasizes that women controlled their own sexuality, something foreign to eighteenth- and nineteenth-century white Christian society. Perdue also relates that straying wives usually did not elicit much response, but straying husbands did, because their actions created communal disharmony. But any conflicts resulting from clashes between straying men, their wives, and mistresses were confined to the families concerned.[29]

Control of sexuality, at least as it related to a Cherokee woman's engaging in sexual relations with a Cherokee man, was concomitant with the power of the woman. A woman could engage in sexual relations prior to marriage with no shame attached to such activity. She also could engage in extramarital sexual liaisons, and, within reason, a husband and family accepted these extramarital engagements. Promiscuity, however, was not accepted and was not rampant among Cherokee women.[30]

Sexual liaisons between Cherokee women and white men, however, often involved securing the permission of the woman's family and, perhaps, of the village chief. As Perdue explains, just as chiefs controlled foreigners' access to trade with a village or to where foreigners lived in the village, so they controlled or, at the least, played a significant role in permitting sexual access of foreigners to Cherokee women. Allowing, perhaps encouraging, relations between women and white traders both allowed incorporation of the foreigner to the village in a seamless manner and forged a friendly relationship with traders who had goods desired by the Cherokee. Because the rewards of maintaining friendly relations with white traders were manifold, often women from prominent clan families became the partners of white traders (e.g., Nancy Ward, who married trader Bryan Ward, was the niece of Chief Attakullakulla;

Women in Cherokee Society 29

their daughter Betsy then married Joseph Martin, North Carolina agent to the Cherokee).[31]

Polygyny, perhaps seemingly out of place in a culture that ascribed sexual power to women, was not unheard of, but its practice varied from place to place within Cherokee regions and towns and depended on such circumstances as depletion of male population through warfare. Cherokee men practiced two types of polygyny: mother-daughter polygyny and sororal polygyny. These marriage forms may have benefited women in different ways. Sororal polygyny contributed to the development of a strong female-bonded household within the matrilineal structure, while the marriage of related women to the same man reduced competition for household and agricultural resources.[32] White observers, such as James Adair (who referred to the "corrupt Cheerake" man who marries mother and daughter) and Louis-Philippe, found such practices repugnant, as did Christian missionaries to the Cherokee.[33] Except for the Moravians, who allowed Cherokee male converts to Christianity to keep their wives, other Christian missionaries required the husband with multiple wives to retain only the first wife. Missionaries, who brought to the Cherokee both patriarchal practices and a Christian ethic that emphasized a different type of morality linked to marriage and fidelity, played a prominent role in the 1824 Cherokee Council's decision to outlaw polygamy, as well as other practices found repugnant to whites (e.g., the Cherokee ball game that featured nude ballplayers).[34]

One should note, however, that while it is important to understand Cherokee polygyny within the context of Cherokee cultural values, it also is important to avoid valorizing it and denying its possible negative impact on Cherokee and other women. As Tiya Miles explains in *Ties That Bind*, a polygynous society condoned multiple sexual relationships and thus in a household that included a black female slave and a Cherokee or white wife, the Cherokee master may have felt "entitled" to make sexual advances toward the female slave and the slave may have been acculturated to expecting those advances.[35] The added dimension of race complicates sexual relations here, to be sure, but that dimension should not obscure polygyny's possible negative impact on Cherokee or white women who did not want to succumb to the sexual advances and become part of a polygynous household.

Until the destruction wrought by eighteenth-century wars with whites that destroyed many Cherokee towns, the town was the center of political and judicial life. Each town had a town council in which both men and women were active. But the bulwark of the town and the town council, in essence, was kinship—the clan system. Within each town were several households that belonged to each matrilineal clan. Members knew one another; they knew what others needed; they knew who had been wronged. Destruction of towns destroyed social, political, judicial, and religious units. Families dispersed, many to live in nuclear units, as did whites. The political function of the town council came to be replaced by the Cherokee National Council, established in 1794.[36] Women's voices, heard often in town councils, initially were heard at national council meetings. For example, women addressed the national council on the vital issue of land cessions in the late 1790s and early nineteenth century, as well as the removal crises of 1817. But the influence accorded women by the decentralized town system eroded as Cherokee men adopted a centralized system that they thought would enable them to counter white authority and power better than the decentralized town system. By 1827, then, when the Cherokee National Council drew up the constitution, no women's voices were heard, even though in previous years the Cherokee considered land cessions to be women's concern, because women tended the land and owned the dwellings in which families lived and raised children.[37] By 1830, certainly, as Miles notes, women were disempowered politically.[38] In traditional Cherokee society, war women, those younger women who had performed admirably in conflict, and beloved women—older, usually postmenopausal elder women held in high esteem—who may have been war women in their earlier days, were respected and listened to by all.[39] By 1830, however, Cherokee society had evolved to emphasize the role of men exclusively in war and politics, so that war women and beloved women no longer held a place.

Sexual division of labor reflected Cherokee beliefs in balance: men and women each carried out certain tasks at certain times, although they also helped one another in their work. For instance, in spring men and women cleared fields and planted crops, especially in the large fields that were, in essence, communal fields. In summer women

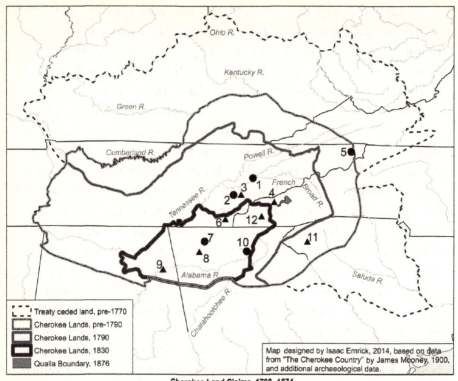

Cherokee Land Claims, 1700–1874
Selected places: 1. Knoxville, **2.** Fort Loudon, **3.** Little Tallassee, **4.** Kituhwa, **5.** Watauga Settlement, **6.** Hiwassee, **7.** Springplace Mission, **8.** New Echota, **9.** Turkeytown, **10.** Dahlonega, **11.** Keowee, **12.** Cowee

tended to the crops in the large fields and in the smaller gardens that were family gardens and were owned through the generations by the woman's family; in fall and winter men hunted, at times accompanied by women who gathered nuts and firewood. Most often in winter, however, women stayed in their warm homes, while the men hunted in the cold.[40] In the nut-gathering months from September through December, women gathered hickory nuts and chestnuts from forest trees, as well as from trees that grew within or close to villages. The nuts, cooked into breads, combined with corn grits, and pounded into fine particles and combined with water to make milks, comprised an essential part of the Cherokee diet by providing fat and protein.[41]

Inside the house was the domain of the woman, who performed domestic tasks of cooking, cleaning, making clothing, and teaching their female children how to be Cherokee women by imparting knowledge about foods and food preparation, making clothes, tilling fields and tending to plants, and making plants into medicinal cures.[42] A Cherokee mother also transmitted knowledge concerning the nature of womanhood—and manhood—to her female children. Especially important was the legend of Selu, the first woman, the Corn Mother who was murdered by her sons, and Kana'ti, the first man and hunter.[43]

The above summarizes women's activities in traditional Cherokee society; by 1800 or so, the Cherokee had long been in contact with whites, so that traditional activities had evolved and changed. Women dominated traditionally subsistence agricultural activities. But as agriculture came to be valued for surpluses of corn, grain, and livestock that could be traded out of Cherokee territory, men assumed more important roles, especially in raising and trading cattle. Commodities valued for export suited production on large farms using large numbers of workers, a situation amenable to the use of slave labor and favoring those Cherokee plantation owners who held large numbers of slaves.[44]

The shift to the market economy in corn, grains, and livestock did not mean that Cherokee women abandoned their traditional roles of trading baskets, food products, and household goods. They maintained these and other agriculture practices, such as raising cotton, and some even became entrepreneurs (e.g., war woman and beloved woman Nancy Ward operated an inn and ferry; a woman named Oo-dah-less owned wagons that hauled goods throughout Cherokee Nation).[45] But elite women who ran plantations often were what whites and Cherokee later referred to as "mixed bloods," part Cherokee and part white, or white women married to Cherokee men who had white ancestry.[46]

RACIAL IDENTITY AND THE CHANGING STATUS OF WOMEN IN CHEROKEE SOCIETY

In traditional Cherokee society, slavery was a common institution, dependent on war and the capture of prisoners of war. On rare occasions, a clan matriarch might accept a prisoner of war destined to become a slave as a replacement for a lost clan member. In such an instance, the person would be accorded clan membership and would therefore become Cherokee. Traditional Cherokee slavery was not racial, then.[47] But not long after contact with whites—perhaps as early as the Juan Pardo expedition in 1540—Cherokee encountered enslaved Africans

Women in Cherokee Society 33

who accompanied white explorers. For a long period of time, Cherokee would have seen Africans only in positions of subservience to whites and in a condition of "not freedom," so they quickly came to correlate "black" with "not free." As the Cherokee became enmeshed in the international European trading system in which they traded raw materials, predominantly deerskins, to the English and Spanish for manufactured goods, they also began to trade both Indian and black slaves to whites and to capture Africans to be enslaved to Cherokee masters.[48] As they did so, the Cherokee started on a path that led to their accepting the racial basis of slavery and the weakening of the matrilineal basis of Cherokee society by denying to the offspring of a union between a Cherokee woman and black man the right to be Cherokee. Black and Cherokee came to be mutually exclusive categories.[49]

The Cherokee National Council in 1824 and 1825 passed two laws on intermarriage that signaled a shift away from the traditional understanding of being Cherokee, and of Cherokee marriage, to western patriarchal definitions of marriage and racialized slavery. On November 11, 1824, the council passed a law prohibiting intermarriage between Negro slaves and Indians or whites; the punishment for violating the law was fifty-nine stripes for Indian or white men who married black female slaves and twenty-five lashes for Indian or white women who married black male slaves. Further, the slave owner who allowed intermarriage was to be fined fifty dollars.[50] It is critical to understand, as Fay Yarbrough explains, that the law specified Negroes as slaves and thus revealed that Cherokee lawmakers in the early 1820s had accepted equating black with "not free."[51] Moreover, because the law specified Negroes as slaves, it also implied that Negroes could not be citizens (by definition, free persons) and could not enjoy the rights and privileges of citizenship.[52] The following November the council passed a law that acknowledged the offspring of Cherokee men and white women as Cherokee, with all the rights and privileges of being Cherokee, just as if the mother was Cherokee.[53]

Yet, even though the council's actions signaled a weakening of traditional matrilineal society, it was not yet ready to abandon matrilineal practices completely. The 1827 constitution granted limited citizenship to offspring of Cherokee women and free black men. But as will be discussed later, the 1839 constitution prohibited intermarriage between any free female or male citizens and any person of color.[54]

Prior to forced removal of the Cherokee in the East to Indian Territory in 1837–38, a few prominent Cherokee men, among them John Ridge and Elias Boudinot, married white women they had met at the Foreign Mission School in Cornwall, Connecticut.[55] While it had been common enough for white traders and soldiers to marry Cherokee women or take Cherokee women as mistresses, it had been less common in preremoval times for white women to marry Cherokee men. For one thing, except for missionary women or the wives of male missionaries, few white women ventured into Cherokee lands. The exceptions were some missionary women or wives of missionaries, who interacted with one another and with Cherokee women, most often at the mission stations, for reasons of commerce (trade of goods), religion (conversion to Christianity), or education (of women and/or their children). In most instances interaction occurred through Cherokee women going to the missions; the exception may have been with Anna Rosina Gambold, the wife of a Moravian missionary to Springplace in North Georgia. A botanist, Gambold gathered plants and seeds from both Cherokee lands and her own substantial garden. Anna Smith claims that the sheer size of Gambold's collection of dried plants and seeds (12,000 to 14,000 dried plant specimens and 100 packets of seeds sent to the Reverend Henry Steinhauer in 1818) suggests that despite her inability to speak the Cherokee language, she communicated with Cherokee women in her botanical efforts.[56] Moravian women and Cherokee women, in many respects, led parallel lives within their respective cultures, a similarity that encouraged mutual respect.[57]

But interaction between the two did not mean intermarriage between white women and Cherokee men. What encouraged the marriages of white women to Cherokee men were the circumstances of acculturation that led Cherokee men to venture beyond the boundaries of Cherokee lands to become involved with whites, for example, in politics or in obtaining Western-style education. Both Elias Boudinot and John Ridge met their white spouses at the Foreign Mission School in Cornwall, Connecticut. After their marriages, which were scandals in the North, the couples returned to Cherokee territory to live the lives

Women in Cherokee Society 35

of acculturated, not traditional, Cherokee.[58] Although the marriages were scandalous in white society, they were less so in Cherokee society, even though the presence of white wives raised the question, at least among the acculturated Cherokee, of the status of the couples' children. For traditional Cherokee, there was no question that the children of white mothers were not Cherokee. But acculturated Cherokee men who had come to accept patrilineal and patriarchal structures wanted to see their children accepted as Cherokee and as heirs to their property. The changes in marriage laws reflect the influence of Cherokee acculturated elites who had veered from traditional matrilineal structures and customs. Thus, in 1825 the Cherokee National Council passed a new marriage law that gave to the children of white women and Cherokee men the status of Cherokee, just as if they had been born of Cherokee mothers. These children also became citizens of Cherokee Nation.[59]

But while the national council accorded limited citizenship to descendants of Cherokee women and free black men, it did not follow the pattern of the 1825 law by deeming as Cherokee the offspring of the unions of Cherokee men and free black women. Why was this so? More than likely, the Cherokee National Council, which contained a number of men with white ancestry, sought to place on one side Indian and white, and on the other black, to fit the racial binary of the United States.[60] Refusal to legitimize the union of Cherokee men with either free black women or black enslaved women denied offspring Cherokee citizenship, yet did not prohibit Cherokee men from having sexual relations with black women. Because the council's decrees said nothing about Cherokee slave masters having sexual relations with their slave "property," masters could engage in such relationships without fear of recrimination.[61]

By the time of removal in 1837–38, the Cherokee, in particular through the actions of the National Council, had attempted, and failed, to demonstrate to whites that Cherokee and whites could coexist. Continuing interaction among Cherokee, whites, and blacks had altered traditional Cherokee society, so that its matrilineal structure had been weakened—though not destroyed—and the role of native Cherokee women in many respects diminished. The elites of Cherokee nation had adopted white attitudes toward patriarchy and patrilineal structures, as well as toward race. All blacks had become marginalized in Cherokee Nation, but perhaps black women in particular, as they came to represent not only the servitude of blacks, but also of women, in patriarchal society.

From removal to the beginning of the Civil War in 1861, through its promulgation of laws, Cherokee Nation, as of September 1839 one united nation with the seat of government located at Tahlequah, Indian Territory, continued to restrict the marriage and sexual choices of women, especially native women, and to restrict the activities of all blacks, free or enslaved. In 1839, for example, the National Council passed two laws that revealed its racial bias. "An Act to Prevent Amalgamation with Colored Persons" prohibited free (i.e., Cherokee or white) males or females from marrying "any slave or person of color not entitled to the rights of citizenship under the laws of this Nation."[62] Since persons of color were not citizens, neither Cherokee nor whites living in Cherokee nation could marry a person of color. For Cherokee women, that meant that the children of an illegal union with a black person, slave or free, could not produce a Cherokee citizen. For a Cherokee slave master, sexual relations with a slave woman were not necessarily illicit, but marriage with a black woman, slave or free, was illegal and the children of any such union would be "not Cherokee."

Also in 1839, the Cherokee National Council passed "An Act for the Punishment of Criminal Offenses." Included was the crime of rape: "Any person charged with the offense of having committed a rape on any female, he shall be punished with one hundred lashes on the bare back; and upon the conviction of any negro [sic.] for the aforesaid offense against any free female, not of negro [sic.] blood, he shall suffer death by hanging."[63] As in the South, then, the rape of a woman by a black male was considered more heinous than the same crime committed by a white or Cherokee male. Cherokee males, like their white counterparts in the South, demonstrated fear of the black man as noted by punishment meted out for committing the crime of rape and thus taking "possession" of the free, not-black women of Cherokee nation. The meaning of the statute is manifold. Were black males of such a degraded state that correction of behavior could only fail and, thus, death was the only suitable punishment? Was the sexual behavior of black men especially to be feared? What about women of African descent? Did they matter not at all? Raping them was not a crime.[64]

Women in Cherokee Society 37

BEYOND 1839

The National Council proceeded to pass a number of other laws that restricted the behavior of persons of African descent. For example, in 1840 the council passed a law prohibiting "any free negro [sic.] or mulatto, not of Cherokee blood," from owning property.[65] Another law passed in 1841 forbade anyone from teaching any "free negro [sic.] or negroes [sic.] not of Cherokee blood, or any slave belonging to . . . citizens of the Nation, to read or write."[66] While the language of these laws allows latitude to those who have Cherokee blood, nonetheless, it is clear that the council was moving toward the southern system of slave codes that restricted behavior of persons of color. It is also clear that the Cherokee National Council, if not all Cherokee citizens, had adopted the racial attitudes of white society, overall, and of racial legal statutes common to the South. Moreover, Cherokee identity and being, once easily determined by the matrilineal structure that dictated that the child of a Cherokee mother was Cherokee, now had been blurred both by weakening of matrilineality and adoption of racialist thought and laws by elite Cherokee and the National Council.

Questions of identity, of who is Cherokee and who is not Cherokee, continued to haunt Cherokee Nation, especially, but not only, Cherokee Nation West (i.e., the nation established by the Treaties of 1817 and 1819 with the U.S. government, and the nation settled by Trail of Tears survivors). Identity came to be linked to race and to gender, and to the continued efforts of the federal government to force the Cherokee, and other tribes living on reservations, to forsake Indian identity and tribal ties by accepting the land allotments created by the 1887 Dawes Severalty Act.[67]

The Cherokee as an identifiable people have survived, perhaps even prospered. Both Theda Perdue and Carolyn Ross Johnston attribute to Cherokee women a remarkable persistence of identity that has survived slavery in Cherokee Nation and the attempts of the US government to alienate the Cherokee and other tribes from their tribal heritage. All this is true, but while women have persisted, so have the nagging questions of race, race prejudice, and identity in Cherokee Nation. The status of descendants of slaves held by Cherokee masters and their right to vote in national Cherokee elections, for example, remains controversial.[68] While the strength of being Cherokee, as tied to "being woman,"

38 MARIE TEDESCO

has persisted through story and through the work of Cherokee women who have become chiefs (e.g., Joyce Dugan and Wilma Mankiller) the strength of a racialism that marginalizes the black Cherokee unfortunately also has persisted in Cherokee Nation.

NOTES

1. As discussed by Terry C. Jordan and Matti Kaups, *The American Backwoods Frontier: An Ethnic and Ecological Interpretation* (Baltimore: Johns Hopkins University Press, 1989).

2. See *Adair's History of the American Indians,* ed. Samuel Cole Williams (Johnson City, TN: Watauga Press, 1930). Theda Perdue notes that as observant as he was, Adair did not understand that Cherokee society was matrilineal, that is, that the Cherokee traced descent through the mother. Therefore, to be Cherokee meant one had to have a Cherokee mother; blood relatives were only those traced through the mother's lineage, while those from the father's lineage were not considered blood relatives at all. Perdue also notes that Adair had both a Cherokee wife and a Chickasaw wife. See Theda Perdue, *Cherokee Women: Gender and Culture Change, 1700–1835* (Lincoln: University of Nebraska Press, 1998), 4 and 198n11.

3. For a brief definition of positivism, consult "Positivism," *Dictionary of Social Science,* ed. Craig Calhoun (London: Oxford University Press, 2002), Oxford Reference Online, http://www.oxfordreference.com.ezproxy.etsu.edu. For an older but more in-depth explanation of positivism, see Nicola Abbagnano, "Positivism," trans. Nino Languilli, in *The Encyclopedia of Philosophy* (New York: Macmillan and Free Press, 1967), 414–19.

4. See Angie Debo, *The Road to Disappearance: A History of the Creek Indians* (Norman: University of Oklahoma Press, 1941); Carolyn Thomas Foreman, *Indian Women Chiefs* (Muskogee, OK: Star, 1954); and Henry T. Malone, *Cherokees of the Old South: A People in Transition* (Athens: University of Georgia Press, 1956). The Leftist historian Jesse Lemisch coined the term "history from the bottom up" in his 1968 essay "The American Revolution as Seen from the Bottom Up," in *Towards a New Past: Essays in American History,* ed. Barton J. Bernstein (New York: Pantheon, 1968), 3–46. Among the twelve essays in the collection, not one investigated the lives of women or women as important historical actors. Eleven of the twelve authors were men.

5. Perdue, *Cherokee Women,* 41–42; Tiya Miles, *Ties That Bind: The Story of An Afro-Cherokee Family in Slavery and Freedom* (Berkeley: University of California Press, 2005), 50; and Circe Sturm, *Blood Politics: Race, Culture, and Identity in the Cherokee Nation of Oklahoma* (Berkeley: University of California Press, 2002), 30–32.

6. Thomas Hatley, "Cherokee Women Farmers Hold Their Ground," in *Appalachian Frontiers: Settlement, Society, and Development in the Preindustrial Era,* ed. Robert D. Mitchell (Lexington: University of Kentucky Press, 1991), 37–51; Hill, *Weaving New Worlds: Southeastern Cherokee Women and Their Basketry* (Chapel Hill: University of North Carolina Press, 1997), esp. the introduction (xv–xxii) and prologue , 1–34; and Perdue, *Cherokee Women,* 3–11.

Women in Cherokee Society 39

7. On black women in Cherokee society, see Miles, *Ties That Bind;* Wilma Dunaway, *Slavery in the American Mountain South* (Cambridge: Cambridge University Press, 203), 15–17, 201–5; and Wilma Dunaway, *The African-American Family in Slavery and Emancipation* (London: Cambridge University Press, 2003) under pertinent topics on women in the slave family. Patrick Minges's book *Black Indian Slave Narratives* (Winston-Salem, NC: John F. Blair, 2004) contains selected Works Progress Administration (WPA) narratives on African Americans who were enslaved by Cherokee and other native tribes. The WPA narratives, now on-line (http://memory.loc.gov/ammem/snhtml), contain other first-person accounts of black women and men enslaved by the Cherokee and other tribes.

8. Missionary women include, especially, the Moravian sisters, all of whom can be considered missionaries, as well as the wives of the designated "official" male missionaries whom the Moravians sent to Springplace in northern Georgia, the Moravian mission established in 1801. For instance, Anna Rosina Gambold, the wife of missionary John Gambold, was as influential as he in bringing the gospel to the Cherokees. Wives and daughters of designated missions of Protestant churches (Methodists excepted) taught school and ran mission stations. On the Moravians, see Anna Smith, "A Community of Women: Cherokees and Moravians in the Early Nineteenth Century," paper presented to the 2002 conference German Moravians in the Atlantic World, Winston-Salem, NC, http://www.wfu.edu/history/events /moravians (published as "Unlikely Sisters: Cherokee and Moravian Women in the Early Nineteenth Century," in *Pious Pursuits: German Moravians in the Atlantic World,* ed. Michelle Gillespie and Robert Beachy [New York: Berghahn Books, 2007], 191–206); and William G. McLoughlin, "The Cherokees and the Moravians," chap. 2 in William G. McLoughlin, *Cherokees and Missionaries, 1789–1839* (New Haven: Yale University Press, 1984), 35–53.

9. The Moravian Church traces its heritage to the late fourteenth and early fifteenth centuries and to Jan Hus, a religious leader in Bohemia whom the Catholic Church considered a heretic and who was, as a consequence, burned at the stake in 1417. (Rowena McClinton, "Introduction," in Anna Rosina Gambold, *The Moravian Springplace Mission to the Cherokees,* ed. Rowena McClinton (Lincoln: University of Nebraska Press, 2010), 25. For a brief history of the Moravian Church, see the entry "Moravian Brethren," in *Oxford Dictionary of Christian Churches,* http://www.oxfordref.com (accessed through East Tennessee State University proxy server).

10. Faye Yarbrough, "Legislating Women's Sexuality: Cherokee Marriage Laws in the Nineteenth Century," *Journal of Social History* 38, no. 2 (Winter 2004): 389–90. Intermarried elite families include those of James Vann, John Ross, Narcissa Owen, Elias Boudinot, John Ridge, and the Bushyheads; the last mentioned were descendants of John Stuart, British commissioner of Indian affairs south of the River Ohio.

11. Raymond D. Fogelson, "Cherokee in the East," in *Handbook of North American Indians,* ed. William C. Sturtevant, vol. 14, *Southeast,* ed. Raymond D. Fogelson (Washington, DC: Smithsonian Institution, 2004), 337; and James Mooney, *Myths of the Cherokee* in *James Mooney's History, Myths, and Sacred Formulas of the Cherokees* (Fairview, NC: Historical Images, 1992), 16.

12. Fogelson, "Cherokee in the East," 338; and Gerald F. Schroedl, "Overhill Cherokees," in *Tennessee Encyclopedia of History and Culture,* ed. Carroll Van West et al. (Nashville: Tennessee Historical Society and Rutledge Press, 1998), 713.

13. By the end of eighteenth and the beginning of the nineteenth century, there were seven clans, but more than likely there were a larger number before that time, when conflict with Europeans and exposure to European diseases, especially smallpox, had caused a population decline and, more than likely, a weakening and shrinkage of membership in some clans. Mooney reported that there were fourteen clans originally, while Fogelson relates that nineteenth-century anthropologist Lewis Henry Morgan claimed the Cherokee "anciently" had ten clans. See Mooney, *Myths of the Cherokee,* 212–13; and Fogelson, "Cherokee in the East," 346.

14. Fogelson, "Cherokee in the East," 346; Miles, *Ties That Bind,* 50.

15. Miles, *Ties That Bind,* 50.

16. Ibid., 51; Perdue, *Cherokee Women,* 98; and Theda Perdue, *Slavery and the Evolution of Cherokee Society, 1540–1866* (Knoxville: University of Tennessee Press, 1979), 8–9, 12. But see Tiya Miles's account of Molly, a black slave purchased by a white trader and given to the clan of the Cherokee wife he murdered, in *Ties That Bind,* 56–57.

17. John Phillip Reid, *A Law of Blood: the Primitive Law of the Cherokee Nation* (New York: New York University Press, 1970), esp. 37–41; and Fay Yarbrough, "Legislating Women's Sexuality," 386–88.

18. Sarah Hill, *Weaving New Worlds: Southeastern Cherokee Women and Their Basketry* (Chapel Hill: University of North Carolina Press, 1997), 30.

19. Alexander Longe, "A Small Postscript on the Ways and Manners of the Indians Called Cherokees," ed. David H. Corkran, *Southern Indian Studies,* XXI (October 1969): 32, pdf available at http://rla.unc.edu/Publications/NCArch.html; and Perdue, *Cherokee Women,* 44.

20. Perdue, *Cherokee Women,* 44.

21. Perdue, *Cherokee Women,* 43–44. Perdue's comments are based on the nineteenth-century observations of John Howard Payne, an actor, magazine editor, and diplomat who visited Georgia in 1835 and there met Chief John Ross, who gave him original materials on Cherokee customs, religious rites, and relations with the US government. Payne used these materials to write a series of articles favorable to the Cherokee in his magazine, as well as an unpublished history on Cherokee Nation. His papers (fifteen volumes total) are contained in the Edward E. Ayer Collection in the Newberry Library, Chicago. For a brief description of the paper, consult http://www.newberry.org/catalogs-and-guides. Perdue also consulted an 1829 diary entry of a Moravian missionary to the Cherokee.

22. Carolyn Ross Johnston, *Cherokee Women in Crisis: Trail of Tears, Civil War, and Allotment, 1838–1907* (Tuscaloosa: University of Alabama Press, 2003), 14–15; Perdue, *Cherokee Women,* 44–45; and Hill, *Weaving New Worlds,* 31.

23. Louis-Philippe, *Diary of My Travels in America,* trans. Stephen Becker (New York: Delacorte Press, 1977), 76–77.

24. As Michelle Daniel notes, in the Cherokee world view maintaining social harmony was so valued that it took precedence over individual desires and needs.

Women in Cherokee Society 41

She also relates that British traveler William Fyffe observed in 1761 that the Cherokee rarely quarreled among themselves. He attributed lack of quarreling to fear of "barbarous revenges," but it is the case that valuing harmony was responsible for lack of disputations. See Michelle Daniel, "From Blood Feud to Jury System: The Metamorphosis of Cherokee Law from 1750 to 1840," *American Indian Quarterly* 11, no. 2 (Spring 1987): 99.

25. Johnston, *Cherokee Women in Crisis*, 23–25; Perdue, *Cherokee Women*, 42–43; and Hill, *Weaving New Worlds*, 31–34.

26. Johnston, *Cherokee Women in Crisis*, 14; and Perdue, *Cherokee Women*, 44. As Perdue notes, Mooney's collection of stories contains two, "The Owl Gets Married" and "The Huhu Gets Married," that feature women driving their husbands from the home. See Mooney, *James Mooney's History*, 291–93.

27. Adair, *Adair's History*, 145–46.

28. "On the 'Petticoat Government' of the Eighteenth-Century Cherokee," in *Personality and the Cultural Construction of Society: Papers in Honor of Melford E. Spiro*, ed. David K. Jordan and March J. Swartz (Tuscaloosa: University of Alabama Press, 1990), 165.

29. Perdue, *Cherokee Women*, 56–57. Perdue notes (p. 56) John Howard Payne's observation that priests had several methods for changing the wandering ways of a wife. So while most husbands of straying wives accepted their actions, some did not and sought to change their ways.

30. Ibid.

31. Theda Perdue, "Race and Culture: Writing the Ethnohistory of the Early South," *Ethnohistory* 51, no. 4 (Fall 2004), 704.

32. Perdue, *Cherokee Women*, 174–75; and Hill, *Weaving New Worlds*, 96.

33. Adair, *Adair's History*, 177; and Louis-Philippe, *Diary of My Travels*, 72–73.

34. William McLoughlin, "Fractured Myths: The Cherokees' Use of Christianity," in *The Cherokees and Christianity, 1794–1870: Essays on Acculturation and Cultural Persistence*, ed. Walter H. Conser Jr. (Athens: University of Georgia Press, 1994), 178; and McLoughlin, *Cherokees and Missionaries, 1789–1839* (New Haven: Yale University Press, 1984), 217.

35. Miles, *Ties That Bind*, 45.

36. In *Blood Politics*, 40–43, Sturm discusses the process by which towns came to relinquish autonomy to a more centralized political system beginning in the early eighteenth century.

37. Perdue, *Cherokee Women*, 106–7; Tiya Miles, "'Circular Reasoning': Recentering Cherokee Women in the Antiremoval Campaigns," *American Quarterly* 61, no. 2 (June 2009): 223–24; and Gambold, *The Moravian Springplace Mission to the Cherokees*, "Voices in Cherokee Councils," 68–72.

38. Miles, "'Circular Reasoning': Recentering Cherokee Women," 225.

39. On war women and beloved women, see ibid., and Perdue, *Cherokee Women*, 39.

40. Perdue, *Cherokee Women*, 19–20, 70–73 and Johnston, *Cherokee Women in Crisis*, 11–12.

41. Hill, *Weaving New Worlds*, 9–10. Hill notes that William Bartram, on his 1775 trip that went through Cherokee lands, observed the nut trees growing close to and in Cherokee villages. Although it is not known whether or not women were responsible for the trees being planted there, it is logical to presume that since women were responsible for gathering nuts and making foods from them, they had something to do with the planting of the trees. See Mark Van Doren, *Travels of William Bartram* (1791; repr. New York: Dover Publications, 1955), 38.

42. Hill, *Weaving New Worlds*, 34; and Johnston, *Cherokee Women in Crisis*, 23. It was the mother's brothers or other male relatives on the mother's side, not fathers—who were not considered kin, because they were not of the same clan as the mother and children—who taught boys how to be hunters and warriors.

43. Johnston, *Cherokee Women in Crisis*, 24. For the story of Selu and Kaná ti, see Mooney, *Myths of the Cherokee*, 242–49.

44. Wilma Dunaway, "Rethinking Cherokee Acculturation: Agrarian Capitalism and Women's Resistance to the Cult of Domesticity, 1800–1838," *American Indian Culture and Research Journal* 22, no. 1 (1997), 157, 159, 161. On the development of plantation slavery in Cherokee territory, see Theda Purdue, "The Development of Plantation Slavery," chap. 4 in Perdue, *Slavery and the Evolution of Cherokee Society*, 50–69.

45. Dunaway, "Rethinking Cherokee Acculturation," 163, 166.

46. Among slaveholders, James Vann was a "mixed-blood" who had multiple (exact number unknown) wives, some of whom had white ancestry and three of whom were sisters; John Ross had Scots ancestry; his first wife, Quatie Brown Ross, who died on the Trail of Tears, had white ancestry, and his second wife was a white woman from Philadelphia. On Ross's wives, see Tiya Miles, *The House on Diamond Hill: A Cherokee Plantation Story* (Chapel Hill: University of North Carolina Press, 2010), 53–55; and on Vann, see William McLoughlin, "James Vann: Intemperate Patriot," in *The Cherokee Ghost Dance: Essays on the Southeastern Indians, 1789–1861* (Macon, GA: Mercer University Press, 1984), 46. John Ridge was an acculturated Cherokee who married Sarah Northrup, a white woman he met at the Foreign Mission School in Cornwall, Connecticut. Writer Narcissa Owen's father was Thomas Chisholm, a slaveholder and last chief of the Arkansas Old Settlers who had removed to Arkansas lands in 1807, and son of John Chisholm and a Cherokee woman with Scots ancestry. On Ridge, see Theresa Strouth Gaul, "Introduction," in *To Marry an Indian: The Marriage of Harriet Gold and Elias Boudinot in Letters, 1823–1839*, ed. Theresa Strouth Gaul (Chapel Hill: University of North Carolina Press, 2005), 8. On Owen, see Karen L. Kilcup, "Introduction," in *A Cherokee Woman's America: Memoirs of Narcissa Owen, 1831–1907*, ed. Karen L. Kilcup (Gainesville: University Press of Florida, 2005), 1, 17.

47. Perdue, *Slavery and the Evolution of Cherokee Society*, 4–6, 8–9, 11–12.

48. Ibid., 36–49, passim; and Sturm, *Blood Politics*, 48–51.

49. Perdue, *Slavery and the Evolution of Cherokee Society*, passim, 36–49; and Fay Yarbrough, "Legislating Women's Sexuality, 389.

50. A. H. Murchison, "Intermarried-Whites in the Cherokee Nation Between the Years 1865 and 1887," *Chronicles of Oklahoma* 6, no. 3 (September 1928): 1, http://

digital.library.okstate.edu (accessed October 17, 2011); and Yarbrough, "Legislating Women's Sexuality," 388–89.

51. "Legislating Women's Sexuality," 389.

52. Ibid., 391.

53. Murchison, "Intermarried-Whites in the Cherokee Nation," 1.

54. Yarbrough, "Legislating Women's Sexuality," 389–90.

55. Johnston, *Cherokee Women in Crisis*, 43–46; and Gaul, "Introduction," 3–7.

56. Daniel McKinley, "Ann Rosina (Kliest) Gambold (1765–1821), Moravian Missionary to the Cherokee, with Special Reference to Her Botanical Interest," *Transactions of the Moravian Historical Society* 28 (1994): 62–63, 65, 83.

57. Anna Smith, "A Community of Women: Cherokees and Moravians in the Early Nineteenth Century," http://www.wfu.edu/history/events/moravians/papers/smith.doc (accessed May 20, 2011), 3–6, 8; and William McLoughlin, *Cherokees and Missionaries, 1789–1839* (New Haven: Yale University Press, 1984), 248–49.

58. For reactions in Connecticut to the engagement and marriage of Boudinot and Gold, see Johnston, *Cherokee Women in Crisis*, 43–45; and Gaul, "Introduction," 1–3, 10–14.

59. Yarbrough, "Legislating Women's Sexuality," 388–89.

60. Ibid., 401.

61. Ibid., 394.

62. *The Constitution and Laws of the Cherokee Nation Passed at Tah-le-quah, Cherokee Nation, 1839* (1840; facsimile, Wilmington, DE: Scholarly Resources, 1975), 18.

63. Ibid., 17.

64. See Yarbrough's discussion, "Legislating Women's Sexuality," 391.

65. *Constitution and Laws of the Cherokee Nation*, 41.

66. Ibid., 53.

67. For information on the Dawes Severalty (General Allotment) Act, as well as the 1906 Burke Act on allotment, see *Encyclopedia of American History, 7th ed.*, ed. Richard B. Morris and Jeffrey B. Morris (New York: HarperCollins, 1996), 625–26. Carolyn Johnston discusses the allotment crisis in *Cherokee Women in Crisis*, 129–44; and Circe Sturm discusses the Dawes Act in *Blood Politics*, 78–81.

68. See, for example, Justin Juozapavicius, "Cherokees Told to Take Back Slaves' Descendents," *Atlanta Journal-Constitution*, September 13, 2011, http://www.ajc.com/news/nation-world/ cherokees-told-to-take-1179886.html.

CHAPTER TWO

Mothers' Day v. Mother's Day

The Jarvis Women and the Meaning of Motherhood

KATHARINE LANE ANTOLINI

In 2008 Mother's Day celebrated its centennial. Over four hundred people commemorated the anniversary at the former church in Grafton, West Virginia, that hosted the first official Mother's Day service on May 10, 1908.[1] In a lovely sanctuary adorned with arrangements of white carnations, families listened to messages of praise for all mothers, sang hymns accompanied by a century-old pipe organ, and enjoyed the serenading of a local children's choir. Many across the country joined in similar holiday services, of course, but what made the Grafton celebration unique was its tribute to the native founders of Mother's Day, Ann Reeves Jarvis and her daughter, Anna Jarvis. Few people outside West Virginia recognize their names. Yet on every second Sunday in May, we mail the cards, buy the flowers, place the long-distance phone calls, and make the brunch reservations to honor our mothers because of these two women and their aspirations to establish an annual day of maternal tribute.

According to legend, a young Anna first heard the special plea for a mother's day during a "Mothers of the Bible" lesson taught by her mother, the superintendent of Andrews Methodist Church's Primary Sunday School Department. She listened as Mrs. Jarvis closed the morning class with a simple prayer that allegedly "burned" forever within the daughter's heart and soul. "I hope and pray that someone,

45

sometime, will found a memorial mothers day commemorating her for the matchless service she renders to humanity in every field of life," her mother wistfully told her students. "She is entitled to it."[2] When Mrs. Jarvis died in May 1905, Anna repeated her mother's prayer at her burial and promised, "by the Grace of God," to fulfill her mother's greatest wish. "I went directly from the grave to my room and began to plan for Mother's Day," she later claimed.[3]

Anna's plan began with an aggressive letter-writing campaign to any local or national figure she believed could advance her self-proclaimed Mother's Day Movement. In appeals to influential figures such as commercial giant John Wanamaker, former president Theodore Roosevelt, and *Ladies Home Journal* editor Edward Bok, she described the pressing need to take one day out of our busy, selfish lives to remember the "mother of quiet grace, who through her self-denials, devotion, and patience" gave her children a better chance in life.[4] Within three years Anna had fulfilled her graveside promise and successfully organized the first official Mother's Day services in the United States, the first a morning program, hosted by her mother's home church in West Virginia, and then a second, much grander, afternoon observance at the Wanamaker Store Auditorium in Philadelphia with approximately 15,000 people in attendance.[5]

Anna renewed her letter-writing campaign every spring to remind politicians, church groups, and national fraternal organizations to reserve the second Sunday in May in honor of Mother's Day. The enormity of this task led her to incorporate the Mother's Day International Association, headquartered out of her Philadelphia home and primarily financed by Anna for over thirty years. The organization served as a driving force behind the day's recognition and perpetuation throughout the early twentieth century. That fact that Mother's Day was observed in every state in the country, including the territories of Hawaii and Puerto Rico, at least three years before its official sanctioning as a national holiday stands as a testament to Anna's leadership and the early success of her movement. Finally, in 1914, six years after Congress first dismissed the idea of a maternal memorial day with jokes of an impending "mother-in-law day," Anna sat proudly in the gallery to witness Congress's formal designation of Mother's Day. She also graciously accepted the pen President Woodrow Wilson used to sign the first presidential Mother's Day proclamation. It called only for the display of the American flag on all governmental buildings and individual homes as a public expression of love and reverence for American mothers.[6]

Today Mother's Day remains a widely observed holiday. Over 80 percent of Americans reportedly celebrated the day in its centennial year. Most bought gifts, obviously, as opposed to displaying the American flag in maternal tribute; subsequently, Mother's Day has become the second highest gift-giving day behind Christmas and a multibillion-dollar industry for retailers.[7] Yet neither Anna Jarvis's life-long dedication to the day's observance or its enormous commercial appeal can completely explain the holiday's success. Mother's Day owes its longevity to its cultural gift for reinvention, not its floral and greeting cards sales, because to observe Mother's Day is to join the discourse over the true meaning of motherhood. At the core of every Mother's Day celebration is an image of a mother deemed worthy of memorializing. The day would be meaningless without a model of motherhood, or criteria of "good mothering," to serve as a measurement of praise. Thus the holiday provides the perfect platform for the cultural debate over the intrinsic value of motherhood and the appropriate boundaries of women's maternal influences. Since the nineteenth century, various social, commercial, and political movements have appropriated this ritual act of honoring mothers in order to redefine and harness the symbolic power of motherhood in American society.[8]

The holiday's susceptibility to conflicting maternal imagery began with the Jarvis women and their personal interpretations of that legendary Sunday school prayer. Both envisioned a day commemorating women for their "matchless service" as mothers, but they did not venerate the same maternal roles. For Ann Reeves Jarvis, a woman's maternal influence transcended the traditional domestic sphere to directly serve "humanity." She imagined a celebration of motherhood that included civic leadership and service; mothers united in public works to empower themselves and help to empower others. "Mothers must have faith in God, faith in the church, faith in their country, faith in their community, faith in their family," Mrs. Jarvis believed. All of which rested first on mothers' "large faith in themselves."[9] Thus to honor

Mothers' Day v. Mother's Day   47

motherhood was to affirm the full potential of the maternal role within both the home and community. Anna, however, shared neither her mother's perspective on motherhood nor the maternal experience that bore it. As a spinster living with a bachelor brother and a dependent sister, Anna celebrated motherhood through the eyes of a daughter. The unheralded work of mothers who sacrificed quietly and unobtrusively for their families everyday was worthy enough of praise from her perspective; she often referred to Mother's Day as a great "home day" to stress the celebration's domestic location. Instead of a day reserved exclusively for mothers in celebration of their maternal influence, as envisioned by Mrs. Jarvis, Anna designed a day reserved for "sons and daughters to honor themselves by showing gratitude to the [mother] who watched over them with tender care in childhood days."[10]

The Jarvis women embody the contrast between a Mothers' Day (possessive plural) signifying the collective power of mothers and the impressive breadth of their maternal role and a Mother's Day (possessive singular) honoring a sentimental image of motherhood as defined by those most dependent on a mother's care—her children. The first design offers mothers an active role in their own tribute, while the other reduces them to a more passive figure of praise. After her mother's death, Anna championed the domestic portrayal of motherhood as the foundation of the Mother's Day observance and its only legitimate representation. "We celebrate Mother's Day as sons and daughters and not as mothers," Anna emphasized. "Therefore, perhaps, it is right that a mother's daughter should be its leader."[11] As a consequence of her daughter's leadership, the history and significance of the original Mothers' Day was lost to the deliberate distortion of Mrs. Jarvis's maternal legacy and Anna's crusade against its modern representation.

THE MOTHERS' DAY LEGACY LOST

The scholarly accounts of Anna's life typically remark on her "ambiguous" relationship with her mother. In the absence of primary historical evidence, the Grafton lore describing a mother-daughter relationship fraught with personal conflicts has, unfortunately, earned unfair significance over the years.[12] Yet Anna never publicly spoke of a mother-daughter relationship based on anything but absolute love and mutual esteem. Mother's

Day, after all, was meant to serve as a testimony of a child's love for her mother and the home she governed. As evidence of her love, Anna based the celebratory design of Mother's Day on personal tributes to Mrs. Jarvis. She chose the second Sunday in May to mark the anniversary of her mother's death and selected her mother's favorite flower, the white carnation, as the day's official emblem. Her request for children to visit or write letters home on Mother's Day reflected her own bouts with homesickness, after finally leaving home at the age of twenty-seven, and the significance she placed on her correspondence with her mother while separated.[13] But at the heart of the Mother's Day observance was Anna's modest portrait of Mrs. Jarvis as the quintessential symbol of nineteenth-century motherhood—a woman who found true fulfillment only in motherhood and carved her identity from her selfless dedication and service to her family, friends, and faith. Based on that maternal portrait, Anna saw no better memorial to motherhood than a day that promised a mother that which was her greatest joy—"the loved ones she lived for."[14]

As Anna memorialized her mother, however, she minimized the complexity of Mrs. Jarvis's maternal identity. Details of Ann Reeves Jarvis's life and work that fell outside her daughter's idealized perspective of motherhood were conveniently excluded from the historical account of Mother's Day—especially Mrs. Jarvis's advocacy of a proactive Mothers' Day. Although Anna swore that Mother's Day was more than just "maudlin sentiment," she rarely portrayed the power of motherhood beyond the traditional boundaries and she never directly acknowledged the aspects of Mrs. Jarvis's life that celebrated a public dynamic of motherhood. In its place, she used her Mother's Day International Association to cultivate a sentimental persona of her mother for public consumption, one that she used to endorse and defend a Mother's Day celebration rooted in idyllic domesticity. Thus, the first step in reclaiming the lost Mothers' Day legacy is to reveal the history obscured by Mrs. Jarvis's deceptive maternal facade—one crafted by her daughter upon lies of omission. Fortunately, Anna's stories of her mother are not the only records of Mrs. Jarvis's life. In combination with more "objective" sources, it is possible to see beyond a daughter's one-dimensional maternal image and obtain a richer understanding of Ann Reeves Jarvis, the woman and community leader.[15]

Mothers' Day v. Mother's Day 49

Anna was the tenth of thirteen children born to Granville and Ann Reeves Jarvis, one of only four Jarvis children to live to adulthood. By the time of Anna's birth in May of 1864, Mrs. Jarvis had already buried seven children, ranging in ages from three months to six years. In a cruel twist of fate, she lost one of those children, her oldest daughter, Annie Elizabeth, on the same December day in 1856 that she gave birth to daughter Columbia. Annie died one hour before her baby sister's birth, according to family lore, and the timing at first convinced Mrs. Jarvis that God gave her Columbia to replace the daughter He took from her. Tragically, Columbia succumbed to measles in 1862, along with her older sister Clara, young brother Ralph, and baby sister Marry.[16]

Mrs. Jarvis was not the only mother in Taylor County, (West) Virginia, to lose children to the measles, typhoid, and diphtheria epidemics that swept through the community. The entire region experienced appalling infant and child mortality rates, fueled mainly by the poor sanitary conditions that allowed sickness to thrive, especially through the contamination of local water supplies. The national public health movement of the mid-nineteenth century initially conceptualized the link between infant mortality and deficient sanitary precautions as primarily an urban dilemma. Thus reform measures were centered in major cities throughout the Northeast and Midwest, leaving rural communities, especially those in the Mountain South, isolated from the larger movement's demands for a large-scale civic response to the obvious health risks. The limited availability of professional physicians in the mountains exacerbated issues of public health even further, increasing a community's vulnerability to the spread of communicable diseases.[17]

In 1858 Mrs. Jarvis organized Mothers' Day Work Clubs to combat the devastating health crisis that threatened every area family. To inspire collective action, she appealed to a mother's responsibility to safeguard her family, as it was a duty all mothers could share. As exemplified by the organization's name, Mrs. Jarvis aspired to unite women in the intertwining, and mutually beneficial, work of familial and community service.[18] Historian Norman Kendall, a former Sunday school classmate of Anna's, described Mrs. Jarvis as the most magnetic personality he had ever known, explaining her ability to motivate the mothers around her to join her clubs and embrace for themselves a larger civic role.

"In her organized 'Mothers Work,' she always sought to secure goodwill community cooperation in order to obtain the best things for a modern progressive neighborhood," he remembered.[19]

The club members first gathered in local churches to listen to area physicians lecture on the health concerns facing each community and learn of their recommendations on how best to address them. Mrs. Jarvis relied heavily on the advice of her brother, Dr. James Reeves, who was already known for his work with typhoid fever epidemics in northwestern Virginia.[20] As a professionally trained physician, he was instrumental in helping individual clubs design and implement health programs tailored to address the immediate needs of their respective neighborhoods. All the clubs eventually sponsored households requiring assistance in improving their overall health conditions. Through regular visits, club members educated families on the importance of proper sanitation, reinforced the necessity of boiling drinking water, and inspected all milk fed to children for contamination. They worked to ensure that families received proper medical care by providing medicine and even employing women to help care for homes where mothers before had silently suffered alone from tuberculosis. When necessary, they quarantined households to prevent a county-wide epidemic.[21] The lack of established medical professionals in the region allowed the Mothers' Day Work Clubs a vital degree of autonomy in implementing their community programs. Although they sought medical advice in their initial planning, the clubs were not under the control of area physicians and, consequently, did not face the same obstacles experienced by regional women's clubs in the twentieth century. Nineteenth-century physicians were more likely to view the assistance of area women's clubs as a necessity in safeguarding community health instead of a bothersome interference or direct threat to their authority.[22]

When Virginia joined the Confederacy in the spring of 1861, the state's western counties became the first front of the Civil War. Both sides recognized the strategic importance of the village of Grafton as the transportation hub where the Baltimore and Ohio and Northwestern railroads intersected. Securing western Virginia ensured not only the control of the vital Baltimore and Ohio line but access to potentially vulnerable transportation routes in Pennsylvania and Maryland.[23]

Mothers' Day v. Mother's Day   51

Living four miles south of Grafton at the time, the Jarvis family quickly found themselves caught in the middle of the Union and Confederate forces battling for regional control. Though over forty western counties of Virginia voted to reject the Southern state's ordinance of secession, communities were far from unanimous in their support for the Union, ultimately resulting in a civil war within the larger Civil War. Mrs. Jarvis thus struggled to command the attention of the area women now consumed by the war around them and their conflicting loyalties. She first attempted to lead by example. In May of 1861, she alone offered a prayer over the body of Thornsbury Bailey Brown, the first Union soldier directly killed by enemy fire in the war, when others refused to publicly express their condolences out of fear of retribution by Confederate loyalists.[24]

In the midst of such social and political chaos, Mrs. Jarvis managed to hold her Mothers' Day Work Clubs together, convincing the various branches to remain neutral and united in their work in the face of the wavering allegiances of each town. Her efforts to rise above the turmoil made her a local hero. The escalating hostilities and growing presence of military encampments in the region increased the threat of disease. In a war where soldiers were more likely to die of disease than in battle, any service provided by the Mothers' Day Work Clubs would have been invaluable to the surrounding communities.[25] According to legend, Union colonel George R. Latham of the Grafton Guards approached Mrs. Jarvis, hoping to enlist the essential services of her clubs. He needed the group's help to stop the typhoid and measles epidemics already spreading through the camps of both armies. Soldiers were dying faster than they could be buried, he stressed. Mrs. Jarvis agreed to help with the stipulation that all soldiers would receive the women's assistance regardless of the color of their uniforms. "We are composed of both the Blue and the Gray," she cautioned the Colonel. Unfortunately, the legend fails to detail the clubs' assistance in combating the epidemics. The account boasts only of the collective "gratitude and highest recommendations" offered from the many soldiers they tended. Lost to history is the full story of the war from the women's perspective. The same epidemics that took the lives of soldiers, for example, took the lives of five Jarvis children.[26]

Yet the celebrated work of the women to heal the wounds of the Civil War did not end with the war itself. Feelings of distrust and bitterness ran deep among the veterans returning home to Taylor County to live beside those they once considered the enemy. Although West Virginia furnished more soldiers to the Union fight than the Confederate cause, rebel guerilla bands had roved and raided the mountains during the war. Many cities and towns changed hands several times, leaving civilians with rival sympathies vulnerable to economic retribution and physical violence; every county recorded atrocities inflicted upon civilians by both Union and Confederate troops. In the immediate aftermath of the war, communities in neighboring counties threatened and attempted to forcibly expel Southern sympathizers and returning Confederate soldiers.[27] It was apparent that the passage of time was doing little to ease underlying hostilities and communities worried about the potential violent consequences.

In 1868 the Mothers' Day Work Clubs agreed to meet yet another challenge. Mrs. Jarvis rallied the women to bring their families and all the area soldiers to a meeting at the Pruntytown Courthouse, the current county seat, in order to begin the public healing process. She warned them to refer to the meeting simply as a "mothers' friendship day," in hopes that the respect men had for their mothers, if not each other, would bring them to the courthouse steps. An immense crowd of veterans gathered on the designated day, many of them allegedly armed. Wary town officials pleaded with Mrs. Jarvis to cancel her plans, but she refused, declaring defiantly that she was no coward. Shrewdly, she had directed the women to separate the men upon arrival, as a means to disarm their collective animosity and deter any violence. She knew that the day's success depended on the men's ability to stand as individuals, not as soldiers, so they could perhaps view each other as they once did before the war.[28]

Despite their initial suspicions, the men remained to listen to Mrs. Jarvis. She stood before them, flanked by two teenage girls dressed in blue and gray, and clearly explained the gathering's message of forgiveness and unity. Eventually more women dressed alternatively in blue and gray came forward to link hands with Mrs. Jarvis, and they led the crowd in choruses of "Dixie" and "The Star Spangled Banner." Mrs. Jarvis appealed to the men to offer their neighbors a hand in reconciliation as they sang their last song, "Auld Lang Syne," in a final gesture of peace and absolution. Witness recalled veterans weeping and shaking hands by the first chorus.[29] "It was a truly wonderful sight to see the boys in blue and the boys in gray meet, shake hands and say, 'God bless you, neighbor; let us be friends again.'"[30] Mrs. Jarvis and her Mothers' Day Work Clubs received full credit for the successful reunion. This "remarkable event," according to a local minister, was clear proof of "what a good woman can do."[31]

The Mothers' Day Work Clubs positively exemplified the collective social power of women and the potential scope of their maternal role and influences. Their motto, "Mothers Work—for Better Mothers, Better Homes, Better Children, Better Men and Women," reflected their heightened self-awareness and maternal confidence.[32] They recognized the magnitude of the "matchless service they rendered," not just for their families, but "to humanity in every field of life," as poignantly captured by Mrs. Jarvis in her original Mothers' Day prayer.

Anna was four years old when the mothers of Taylor County reunited their community from the courthouse steps. She was the only daughter of the three born during the war years to survive past infancy. Although too young to witness directly the events that made her mother a respected public figure, she most certainly heard the stories while growing up. She was twelve years old when she first overheard her mother's wish for a maternal memorial day and, by then, should have known the famed events in her mother's life that inspired her Mothers' Day model. Her childhood friend Howard Kendall obviously knew the stories and eagerly recorded them in his published history of Mother's Day. But what Anna failed to grasp as a girl, she also failed to understand as a woman of forty-one, the age she was when her mother died and she first embarked on her Mother's Day movement. Anna never discussed her mother's legendary roles in the Mothers' Day Work Clubs or the Mothers' Friendship Day in any of her surviving private or public documents. It is a glaring absence when compared to the reminiscences of those who knew Mrs. Jarvis and readily recorded the stories of her inspiring acts of community leadership.[33]

Nonetheless, from Anna's perspective it is an understandable absence. Stories of maternal activism did not serve her promotion of

Mother's Day and the sentimental model of motherhood it was designed to memorialize. Anna restricted Mrs. Jarvis's maternal persona to the prescribed boundaries of a Victorian feminine ideal because it best suited her designs of a familial celebration. No other era imbued the home and motherhood with more sentiment than the nineteenth century and its defense of gendered spheres of influence. Child-rearing literature, directed for the first time primarily at mothers, valorized the sanctity of the home and the redemptive power of maternal love over the corruptive individualism and materialism of the outside world.[34] A mother's love was "eternal," "unquenchable," and "irrepressible."[35] It was not just the physical care she provided that bonded her children to her, but her role as the affectionate moral educator entrusted to instill the emotional fortitude needed for her children to one day prosper as adults in a changing society. Authors of maternal advice assured every woman that to preside over a loving and pious home with such skill that her family would "rise up and call her blessed" was "nobler than to rule an empire." And if she succeeded in her wise and gentle rearing of her children, then her influence upon them would endure long after they left the nurturing protection of the home.[36]

The recurring themes of duty, love, faith, and sacrifice that composed the nineteenth century's maternal ideal provided the framework for Anna's account of her mother's life. Buried among Anna's surviving papers is an unfinished biography, entitled "Recollections of Ann M. Jarvis 1833–1905." After their father's death in 1902, Anna and her brother Claude repeatedly begged their mother to join them in Philadelphia so they could be reunited once more as a family. Mrs. Jarvis finally agreed to move from Grafton two years later, when her declining health prevented her from remaining on her own. Surrounded by her children, she died of heart failure the following May.[37] In the wake of Mrs. Jarvis's death, Anna began the account of her mother's life and final illness in response to the many condolences sent to the family over their loss.[38] For unknown reasons, Anna never completed the biography, and it remained among her personal documents for over forty years. Clearly evident within this manuscript's several drafts and hand-scribbled rewrites is the sentimental maternal model that later served as the foundation of the Mother's Day celebration. It is, in essence, the original

Mothers' Day v. Mother's Day 55

draft of Mrs. Jarvis's maternal persona and the first step in dismantling her Mothers' Day legacy.

Anna admitted that she was not an objective biographer of her mother's life. "It is a daughter who writes [this]," she confessed, "a daughter who loved her more than any one else, and who feels she represented the highest type of motherhood."[39] Anna exposed her skewed perspective throughout the entire narrative by refusing to portray Mrs. Jarvis's as anything other than that embodiment of the "highest type of motherhood." Even in the description of her mother as a child, Anna identified her as a "little mother" who helped to raise her younger siblings:

> The discipline that came with these responsibilities, that made duty
> her every-day religion, that made her life one of loving sacrifice
> and self-denial to all around her, and deprived her of so many of
> the pleasures that came to each and all of the other members of her
> family, [molded] her life throughout its course. She joyfully pushed
> aside self-gratification, and gave comfort to those around her.[40]

Anna repeated this imagery continually throughout the manuscript. Her mother was a "mother to all," "a living sacrifice," a woman who "filled her place in the household with remarkable tenacity of purpose" and whose "immeasurable" maternal love was surpassed only by the Christian faith that sustained her through the tragic loss of nine children. Ultimately, Anna believed it was lives like her mother's that made the "earth wholesome."[41]

The Ann Reeves Jarvis of historical record is barely recognizable beneath the mawkish prose. Without explanation, Anna chose to exclude her mother's famous public roles in the Mothers' Day Work Clubs and Mothers' Friendship Day and relegate her activism to the proper feminine confines of only home and church. Mrs. Jarvis's life reads as if it literally ended at the front door of the Jarvis home or on the steps of the Andrews Methodist Church. Anna praised her mother's refined and discriminating tastes, her love of reading, and her "faculty of absorbing it in a way that she could apply it."[42] Yet she failed to expound upon her mother's public invitations to lecture on subjects ranging from classical literature to children's health issues, often before substantial crowds.[43] She described her mother's pride in preventing the Civil War from dividing her church into Northern and Southern denominations, but not of the gratification she must have felt after reuniting an entire community through her Mothers' Friendship Day.[44] And Anna ignored her mother's direct involvement in the governing of church business, beginning with the church's construction, to highlight only her twenty-five years of dedication as a Sunday school teacher.[45] Anna effectively minimized her mother's active roles in the various aspects of her life by either disregarding evidence of her assertive leadership or by reducing them to passive acts of sacrifice and service to others.

Only once in the narrative does Anna hint at Mrs. Jarvis's ambivalent feelings about her life of familial and maternal sacrifices. At the age of seventy-two, Mrs. Jarvis shared with her daughter one of her biggest disappointments as they passed the Girls Normal School of Philadelphia one day. "How I wish I could go to college," she told her daughter that day. "I would make such good use of my opportunities." Anna recorded her reaction to the ostensible regret and sincerity that mingled within her mother's words:

> If this mother of [13] children, whose ambitions had been restrained by the ties of motherhood, homemaking, years of frail health, and finally the financial losses of my father, had led a selfish life and devoted herself as faithfully to her own pleasures and ambitions as she did to those of others her achievements would [un]doubtedly have brought her unusual honors, and made her a woman of prominence in her undertakings.

It is a startling revelation on Anna's part, considering her selective exclusion of the very acts that earned her mother unusual honors during her life and made her a woman of prominence within her local community. (Or that Anna never seemed to recognize the irony within her own life. As an independent single woman, she found an outlet for her own ambitions by personally rejecting the maternal role she strove to commemorate with her Mother's Day Movement.) Just as quickly as Anna acknowledged her mother's regret over opportunities lost, however, she dismissed them as irrelevant. "But after all, was she not a masterpiece as a Mother and gentlewoman[?] We who love her best as life's most precious gift to us, think so."[46]

Mothers' Day v. Mother's Day   57

The simultaneous glorification of home and motherhood inherent in the sentimental maternal image clearly defines the social boundaries of a woman's maternal influence. The power of a mother's love dwells in her capacity for self-denial and willingness to sacrifice in service to her family. The grandiose notions of women's undeniable maternal destinies or the indestructibility of a mother's love does not inevitably translate into real power outside the domestic sphere. According to historian Jan Lewis, the sentimental doctrine of motherhood was not designed to provide women a new sense of empowerment:

> It grew out of an ideology whose objective was to vanquish power with love, to replace selfishness with affection and virtue. Thus, the doctrine of maternal influence was bound to take away with the same hand that which it gave. Mothers could be powerful only if they renounced power, loved only if they renounced love, immortal only if they were willing to die.[47]

When Anna draped Mother's Day and her mother's memory in the same maudlin sentiment, she too lavished praise on motherhood while simultaneously restricting the full potential of a woman's maternal role.

Publicly Anna always gave her mother credit for the original inspiration for Mother's Day, referencing that infamous Sunday school prayer, but never did she discuss her mother in ways that contradicted the image first cultivated in her unfinished biography. Anna's deception is difficult to detect by those unfamiliar with the original history of Ann Reeves Jarvis or her Mothers' Day vision. Since no one challenged Anna's exclusion of her mother's activist legacy, she was not forced to deny it directly on record. A closer examination of her Mother's Day International Association's letterhead, however, reveals provocative evidence of the false persona Anna created of Mrs. Jarvis. For over thirty years, Anna purposely confused her name with her mother's, referring to her in all public documents as Mrs. Anna M. Jarvis. When questioned about the frequent confusions with their names, Anna swore she was named for her mother and they both shared the same middle initial. But to distinguish between them, she often dropped the "M." from her full name in public records, as she felt it properly belonged to her mother—"its original owner thru baptism."[48]

Mrs. Jarvis's middle initial was, indeed, an "M" (though there is still confusion over whether it stood for Maria or Marie), but her birth name definitely was not Anna—as her daughter clearly knew. According to birth records and the family bible, Anna did not have a legal middle name and was most likely named for the older sister who died in 1854. Still, the true motivation behind Anna's deliberate distortion of their names is open to speculation. Jarvis family biographer and Mother's Day historian Howard Wolfe viewed the act as Anna's *selfless* attempt to make her mother famous posthumously. Due to the difficulty in carrying forth a movement in someone else's name, Anna claimed the identical name as her mother in order to share the credit for founding Mother's Day.[49] That certainly is a noble and even reasonable justification for Anna's actions. Yet Wolfe's defense of Anna is perhaps too generous when one considers the full scope of her career as Mother's Day advocate and self-proclaimed defender. If it was Anna's honest attempt to equally share the spotlight as Mother's Day founder (something she adamantly refused to do with anyone else), why not reveal her mother's full history and alternative maternal commemoration? Why not embrace those who celebrated motherhood in the same spirit originally intended by her mother? On the contrary, Anna repackaged Ann Reeves Jarvis's legacy, name and all, and even condemned all attempts to use the possessive plural spelling of Mother's Day. "You may always key the impostor thru this false spelling," she warned.[50]

THE MOTHERS' DAY LEGACY REBORN

When Anna incorporated her Mother's Day International Association, she trademarked a white carnation emblem, the words "Mother's Day," and the phrase, "Second Sunday in May," all of which appeared on the association's official letterhead. She frequently included disclaimers in memos, letters, and formal press releases stating that Mother's Day was neither a holiday nor common property void of copyright restrictions.[51] Mother's Day was her sole intellectual and legal property; therefore she felt justified in challenging anyone who she believed violated her copyrighted ownership. Her public protests of commercial industries, especially the floral, candy, and greeting card business, made for great media press during her lifetime and long after her death. But Anna faced a

Mothers' Day v. Mother's Day 59

variety of adversaries in her crusade against the commercialization of Mother's Day. Her lengthy list of what she dubbed "anti-mother propagandists" also included the charities that used Mother's Day in their promotional campaigns. Anna expressed her dismay with the maternal charities she often referred to as the "expectant mother rackets" in a 1931 Mother's Day speech:

> They say a million dollars' worth of flowers are sold for this day. I never thought it would mean that. . . . But even stranger than commercialization by tradesman is that the public has allowed professional welfare workers to exploit its sentiment for motherhood in [a] manner of which I never dreamed. I am more than amazed; I am dismayed. I deplore particularly that committees of prominent men and women have commercialized this day in the name of needy mothers. . . . I wanted to focus attention all over the country at once on the unrecognized service that mothers do.[52]

What made the maternal charities particularly threatening to Anna was their attack on the sentimental model of motherhood and its veneration of a woman's inherent maternal nature. Anna's celebration of motherhood held sacred the physical and emotional work of mothers within the home. It never questioned a mother's intrinsic abilities or doubted her worth to her family. In contrast, the modern model of motherhood emerging in the early twentieth century called upon the growing fields of pediatrics, psychology, and child development to assist women in raising their children. Being a good mother required more than natural instincts and unconditional love; it required adequate training and steadfast medical supervision. The proponents of the new "scientific" model of motherhood, named for its advocating of modern scientific principles in child rearing, also created a "New Mother's Day" to help spread its message—to Anna's chagrin.[53] The New Mother's Day message offered a model of public assistance for motherhood reminiscent of Mrs. Jarvis's original service-oriented Mothers' Day. They even used (although not consistently) the possessive plural spelling that identified them as "imposters" from Anna's perspective.

Topping the list of "expectant mother rackets" were two New York City organizations, the Maternity Center Association (MCA) and the

Golden Rule Foundation, which designed programs to address the city's raising maternal and infant mortality rates throughout the early twentieth century. Beginning in 1917, the MCA operated clinics and coordinated citywide health agencies to educate expectant mothers on the necessity of prenatal and postnatal care and improve the quality of all available medical services. The Golden Rule Foundation, incorporated in 1929, raised funds to assist private charities and welfare agencies that provided services to impoverished women and children.[54] Both groups unapologetically used Mother's Day in their educational and fundraising campaigns throughout the 1930s, dismissing Anna's charges of copyright infringement and threats of legal repercussions.

The MCA, for example, used the slogan "Let's Make Mother's Day Mean a Better Chance for Mothers Everywhere" in its first Mother's Day campaign in 1931. They hoped to re-channel the "vacuous sentimentality" surrounding the holiday into a national movement to save the lives of American mothers. A promotional cartoon featuring Uncle Sam rocking a recently orphaned baby expressed the organization's hope to rally a country to meet a serious health problem. With both hands on the cradle, Uncle Sam looks solemnly at a sign exposing the United States' shameful maternal death rate, the highest in the civilized world. "Uncle Sam is troubled—sixteen thousand mothers every year fail to answer roll call on Mother's Day," grimly notes the caption. "They lost their lives performing woman's greatest duty, maternity."[55] The Golden Rule Foundation entitled their annual Mother's Day campaigns "Observing Mothers Day the Golden Rule Way" and asked Americans to honor mothers with charitable gifts instead of trivial tokens of affection. In this time of economic crisis, millions of needy mothers prayed for flour, not flowers, and required clothes instead of confections, urged the Foundation. "How better can we honor Mothers on Mothers Day than by doing in her name for other mothers and dependent children . . . what she would do so graciously, aboundingly and lovingly, if it were within her power?"[56]

Congress aided the new Mother's Day campaigns by introducing into the original 1914 Mother's Day Flag Resolution a call to contribute to charitable agencies in honor of motherhood. Anna tried to stall the resolution when it was first proposed in 1933 by writing over fifty

Mothers' Day v. Mother's Day 61

personal letters and telegrams, including direct appeals to President Franklin Roosevelt to exclude the charity promotion in his Mother's Day proclamation. She never reconciled her anger over the intrusion of charities on Mother's Day, as evidenced by her annual written protests, despite the obvious need generated by the Great Depression. In Anna's forceful opinion, the reduction of Mother's Day to a "beggar's day" sanctioned the economic exploitation of the day's venerable meaning and subsequently demeaned motherhood.[57] "Mother's Day celebration is not for charity, but for gratitude to the living, and reverent memories for the deceased," she pleaded with President Roosevelt. "'Charity' with its sting is not associated with Mother's Day. We use the word 'gratitude,' as your Excellency would in a gift to the Mother of your heart and the Nation."[58]

Anna's efforts to protect Mother's Day from the taint of charitable solicitations, especially the Golden Rule Foundation and the Maternity Center Association, pitted her against the elite women of New York society who dominated the organizations' various committees and boards. That included members of President Roosevelt's family and administration. Both Roosevelt's wife and mother served as honorary chairwomen of the Golden Rule Foundation's Mother's Day committee. Eleanor Roosevelt became a tireless spokeswoman for the campaign's message of maternal assistance, and her mother-in-law, Sara Delano Roosevelt, presented the committee's first national Mother of the Year Award in 1935.[59] Both women publicized the Mother's Day campaigns of the MCA as well, along with Secretary of Labor Francis Perkins. Perkins served as the organization's executive secretary in the 1920s and sponsored their work through the Labor Department's Women and Children's Bureau throughout the 1930s.[60]

Although Anna tempered her criticism of the maternal charities when appealing directly to President Roosevelt, she aggressively accused both the First Lady and Secretary Perkins of the illegal and unethical use of Mother's Day. In 1935 she charged Eleanor Roosevelt with "grand larceny of human reputation and achievement" for her misrepresentation and encroachment upon the work of the Mother's Day International Association. Later that same year, she compared Francis Perkins's sanctioning of the MCA's Mother's Day operations to

Mussolini's seizing of property in Africa. Anna also demanded Perkins's resignation for perceived attempts to divert federal funds to aide her private maternity concerns.[61]

It was more than just the flagrant disregard of her legal copyright that fueled Anna's resentment of maternal charities and health organizations. It was the clash of fundamental maternal models. These groups challenged the sentimental foundation of Anna's Mother's Day celebration with their sponsorships of community activism and their endorsement of the tenets of scientific motherhood. They offered a modern representation of Ann Reeves Jarvis's Mothers' Day legacy. Both the nineteenth-century Mothers' Day Work Clubs and the twentieth-century MCA, for instance, sought medical and community solutions to combat appalling maternal and infant mortality rates. Both trusted the guidance of medical authorities and touted education as the best tool in empowering mothers to guard their own health and ensure the survival of their children. And just as Mrs. Jarvis's club members went door to door to advise local families on how to improve sanitary conditions, MCA nurses and social workers combed New York City blocks and climbed tenement steps to offer their assistance and provide direct medical care.[62]

In addition, married women (and presumably mothers) served in the majority of MCA administrative offices and dominated the membership of every governing board, with the exception of the medical board and finance committee.[63] Anna despairingly referred to the women as the "committee of prominent ladies" and often portrayed them as frivolous women with enough personal wealth to save all the needy mothers in New York City themselves. In a letter to her cousin, she ridiculed their promotion of a Mother's Day luncheon at the Warldorf-Astoria in the early years of the Depression; she imagined the socialites all dressed in their elegant clothes and jewels discussing the plight of "poor mothers," oblivious to the apparent hypocrisy. She especially enjoyed agitating the committeewomen by sending telegrams to their husbands informing them of their wives' blatant infringement of Mother's Day.[64] Even President Roosevelt received telegrams addressing his wife's sordid charity work.[65]

Regardless of Anna's opinion, the prominent women who lent their social notoriety, economic connections, political clout, or organizing

Mothers' Day v. Mother's Day 63

talents to the work of the MCA contributed to an extensive health movement in the name of motherhood and in the original spirit of Mothers' Day. Under its female leadership, the MCA Mother's Day campaigns reached a national audience. Its publicity efforts in the first 1931 campaign, for example, included advertisements and articles in thousands of national periodicals, including promotions for special radio talks sent to every daily newspaper in the United States. The national news network CBS broadcast speeches presented at the first annual MCA Mother's Day luncheon in New York City—the luncheons later ridiculed by Anna—over forty-five of its radio stations. Despite their national profile and leadership, however, the MCA stressed local community activism from the very beginning and reached out especially to various women's clubs. A women's club, for instance, financed and directed the MCA's first prenatal clinic in 1917.[66] Each spring, the organization offered free "promotional kits" for any groups wishing to lead their own holiday campaigns. The kits provided complete outlines for town meetings, church sermons, radio talks, political proclamations, newspaper articles, and advertisements, all designed to empower a group's effort to secure better maternity care in their individual communities. The MCA received hundreds of requests for the promotional kits during each of its Mother's Day campaigns throughout the 1930s.[67] The MCA's "committees of prominent ladies" may never have worked directly with impoverished New York City mothers as licensed nurses and social workers, but their successful organizing, fund raising, and publicity efforts nonetheless represented "maternal service to humanity" as once exemplified by the community leadership of Mrs. Jarvis and her Mothers' Day Work Clubs.

What served as honorable examples of maternal tribute for the Golden Rule Foundation and the MCA smacked only of pity and disdain to Anna. Her sentimental model of motherhood sought to praise the strength of the maternal influence within the home and not exploit its weakness for public sympathy. "Let us have one day of the year when even the 'poor mother' may feel exalted and not have the word 'poor' rubbed into her thru the brutal word 'charity.'"[68] Anna's criticism of the MCA exposed the potential danger the advocating of scientific motherhood posed to the sanctity of the home and a woman's maternal autonomy. In the introduction to *The Story of the New Mother's Day,*

MCA president Mary Kresch warned readers that despite the advances in medical science women continue to die needlessly in childbirth. "At least half of these women are a sacrifice to ignorance, carelessness or incompetence. Do not take my word for this, I am only expressing the conservative opinion of leaders of medical thought," she assured them.[69] MCA literature consistently emphasized how mothers needed to be *taught* precisely why they required medical care and instruction, as it was such a strange concept for them to view pregnancy, childbirth, and child rearing as anything but natural biological events or extensions of the female role. It was the MCA's duty, nonetheless, to overcome women's initial resistance to their offers of scientific advice and explain to them all they did not know about being good mothers and properly raising their children, which apparently was a great deal based on the extensive list of lessons designed for their Mothers' Clubs Talks.[70]

Although proponents of scientific motherhood hoped to raise the status of mothers to the heights of skilled professionals, analogous to the professionalism of the public sphere, contemporary critics and middle-class mothers feared the toll that adherence to evolving medical theories and child care experts took on women's maternal confidence and identity.[71] Modern historians have echoed the same criticisms, documenting the undermining of women's maternal autonomy and the eroding trust in traditional female networks as real consequences of a mother's adherence to the tenets of scientific model.[72] For there was one significant difference between the members of Ann Jarvis's Mothers' Day Work Clubs in the nineteenth century and the modern public health nurses and social workers of the MCA. Both carried a similar message about the importance of education and science in improving maternal and infant health, but Jarvis's club members spoke *as mothers,* no doubt tempering their advice with their own maternal experiences. Public health nurses, in comparison, were single women. Their authority to dispense child care advice to mothers rested on their professional training, not maternal experiences. Many mothers, however, particularly working-class and poor mothers, valued maternal experience over "book learning" and often rejected the unsolicited advice of public health nurses. The rejection only strengthened the belief of public health professionals that working-class and poor mothers were ill equipped to properly

Mothers' Day v. Mother's Day 65

raise their children—viewing their disinterest in scientific child-care methods as a sign of their ignorance, not as evidence of their maternal confidence.[73] Karen Tice documented the same situation between early twentieth-century female settlement workers and mothers living in rural Appalachia. Although educated on the latest child-care practices, the settlement workers' status as single women weakened their legitimate authority to correct the traditional child-care methods of regional mothers. As one mother astutely noted, "These here quare women has got a sight of booklarning, and if they was to spend their opinions on books, I'd listen to 'em. But what does a passel of old maids, that hain't got a baby to their names, know about babies?"[74]

While the sentimental maternal model glorified women as natural caretakers of the home, the competing scientific model demanded deference to child care experts and the intrusion of public agencies to protect children from the rampant maternal ignorance, carelessness, and incompetence cautioned by the MCA President. Ironically, then, the MCA's Mother's Day campaigns may have honored motherhood through rallying community activism in its name, but it also potentially hindered the collective confidence of mothers by encouraging their dependency on (typically) male medical authority. Anna's criticism of the maternal charities hinted at the contradiction of their Mother's Day message. Hidden beneath her inane rants over unauthorized fund-raising sales of white carnations, was an honest fear of weighing a mother's worth against a calculated technical standard. For Anna, Mother's Day entitled even the poorest and uneducated mother to unconditional commemoration; she did not deserve to be pitied for her apparent misfortunes, reminded of her maternal failures, or made a source of public social debate.

In 1931 a *New York Times* reporter asked Eleanor Roosevelt and fellow Golden Rule Foundation chairwoman Mrs. John Finley to comment on Miss Anna Jarvis's accusations of infringement and threats of legal action against their Mother's Day campaign. Mrs. Roosevelt appeared sincerely puzzled by the Mother's Day founder's reaction to their organization's charitable efforts. "I think she misunderstands us," she explained. "She wanted Mothers' Day [spelling in original] observed. We want it observed, are working for its observation and are really aiding her." To which Mrs. Finley added, "We are helping her to a better observance of the thing she loves. In so far as she is working for a better observance of the day we are working with her."[75]

It was more than just a simple misunderstanding to Anna. She considered the 1930s charitable campaigns as a direct assault on her Mother's Day work. And in all fairness, Anna's fervent defense of Mother's Day was not wholly unjustifiable—despite the frequent ridicule her eccentric behavior elicited from her contemporaries. When the Golden Rule Foundation called for a "better observance" of Mother's Day and the Maternity Center Association wrote a 'new Mother's Day story,' they effectively insinuated that Anna's sentimental model, and especially her national leadership as official founder, had become obsolete and meaningless in the modern era.

Inevitably, Anna's greatest success was, sadly, the source of her greatest heartache. She triumphantly led a national and international movement to establish a maternal memorial day and secured her place in history as Mother's Day's official founder. But her thirty-year battle to restrict the holiday's observance to her rigid "sentimental specifications" drained her emotionally, physically, and financially. She lived the final years of her life partially deaf, blind, and destitute in a mental hospital in Pennsylvania, allegedly coming to regret her role in the day's creation.[76] Yet in the end, Anna's failure to suppress irrevocably Mrs. Jarvis's Mothers' Day legacy, despite her best efforts, serves to highlight further the intrinsic source of the holiday's cultural longevity. Mother's Day's symbolic celebration of the maternal role provides all of us who observe it the power to ponder the true meaning of motherhood in modern society and construct for ourselves a maternal ideal worth memorializing.

NOTES

1. Andrews Methodist Church, the site of the first Mother's Day service, is now the International Mother's Day Shrine and Museum, dedicated to preserving the history of Mother's Day and the Jarvis family. It is open to the public between April and October and hosts a Mother's Day service every May. For more information, visit the official website: www.mothersdayshrine.com. The Anna Jarvis Birthplace Museum in Webster, West Virginia, (about four miles south of Grafton), also celebrates the history of the Jarvis family and their role in the founding of Mother's Day. The museum is open to the public for tours by appointment. For more information visit the official website: www.annajarvishouse.com.

Mothers' Day v. Mother's Day   67

2. Barbara Robinson, "Mother's Day: What a Good Woman (or Two) Can Do," *Mature Years* (Spring 1993): 15; Howard Wolfe, *Behold Thy Mother: Mother's Day and the Mother's Day Church* (Kingsport, TN: Kingsport Press, 1962), 190–91, 267.

3. Robinson, "Mother's Day," 15.

4. "White Carnation" (1984), 153–58, Howard Wolfe Collection, International Mother's Day Shrine and Museum, Grafton, WV. "The White Carnation" is an unpublished collection of transcribed documents of Anna Jarvis and the Mother's Day International Association. The letters Anna sent to John Wanamaker (February 26, 1908), Theodore Roosevelt (March 6, 1908), and Edward Bok (February 5, 1908) shared similar wording and quotes.

5. Wolfe, *Behold Thy Mother*, 192–95.

6. *New York Times*, "Against A Mother's Day," May 10, 1908; US Congress, Senate, Senator Burkett of Nebraska speaking for a Mother's Day Resolution, 60th Cong., 1st sess., Cong. Rec. 42 (May 9, 1908): 5971–74. According to the Mother's Day International Association, parts of Canada, Mexico, South America, China, and Japan were also celebrating Mother's Day by 1911. Mother's Day International Association, *The Mother's Day Movement: International Honor Day for Everybody and Every Land* [1912] 3, Mother's Day Archives, International Mother's Day Shrine and Museum; Wolfe, *Behold Thy Mother*, 190–99, 205; "White Carnation," p.175–76. House Joint Resolution 263 designating Mother's Day passed on May 8, 1914. President Woodrow Wilson issued his presidential proclamation on May 9, 1914.

7. The National Retail Federation estimates that consumers spent just over $15 billion on Mother's Day gifts in 2008. Flowers, greeting cards, and special dinners ranked as the top three gift categories. National Retail Federation, "Consumers Will Still Spend For Mother's Day, Just Not As Much, According to NRF Survey," April 22, 2008, www.nrf.com.

8. Ann Reeves Jarvis and Anna Jarvis were not the only ones to promote the idea of a maternal memorial day in American history. In 1872, for example, Julia Ward Howe designated June 2 as Mother's Peace Day. The day was observed primarily by peace organizations until the early twentieth century. Other lesser-known individuals and groups have also identified themselves as the real founders of Mother's Day, claiming they advanced the idea of a Mother's Day before Anna Jarvis; see Katharine Antolini, "Memorializing Motherhood: Anna Jarvis and the Struggle for Control of Mother's Day" (PhD diss., West Virginia University, 2009), 20–65.

9. Norman F. Kendall, *Mothers Day: A History of Its Founding and Its Founder* (Grafton, WV: D. Grant Smith, 1937), 32.

10. Eleanor McNulty, "Miss Anna Jarvis Recounts the Founding of Mother's Day to Eleanor McNulty," *Children: The Magazine for Parents* 11, no. 5 (May 1927): 30; Mother's Day International Association, *Mother's Day Movement*, 3; "White Carnation," 9–13, 172.

11. "Mother's Day International Association address," n.d., Mother's Day Archives.

12. James P. Johnson, "How Mother Got Her Day," *American Heritage* 30, no. 3 (April/May 1979): 16–19; Kathleen W. Jones, "Mother's Day: The Creation, Promotion and Meaning of a New Holiday in the Progressive Era," *Texas Studies in Literature and Language* 22, no. 2 (Summer 1980): 176–77. Both authors describe

Mrs. Jarvis as a controlling figure who purposely restrained her daughter's ambitions to fit the boundaries of proper womanhood. They describe the motivations behind Anna's Mother's Day Movement as either a daughter aggressively seeking an outlet for ambitions once denied to her or as a form of "pathological mourning" in order to reconcile her grief with the resentment she felt toward her mother while she was alive.

13. Anna first moved to live with her Uncle James Reeves in Chattanooga, Tennessee. By 1892 she was living in Philadelphia with her brother Claude. "White Carnation," 177–80; Johnson, "How Mother Got Her Day," 16–19; Leigh Eric Schmidt, *Consumer Rites: The Buying and Selling of American Holidays* (Princeton: Princeton University Press, 1995), 244–55.

14. "White Carnation," 53.

15. Most historical accounts of Ann Reeves Jarvis are based on memorial tributes and the retelling of legends. They offer a skewed account of their own through their uncritical celebration of Mrs. Jarvis. However, the secondary historical accounts of Mrs. Jarvis's life include the aspects of her community service and leadership excluded from her daughter's history of Mother's Day.

16. Anna Jarvis, "Recollections of Ann M. Jarvis," 1905 (?), Draft A, Anna Jarvis Papers, West Virginia Regional History Collection, West Virginia University, Morgantown, WV. The unpublished, unpaginated manuscript consists of two rough drafts of an account of Ann Reeves Jarvis's life and death. The drafts are identified as Draft A and Draft B; James P. Johnson, "Death, Grief, and Motherhood: The Woman Who Inspired Mother's Day," *West Virginia History* 39 (1978): 189. Popular histories of Mother's Day and the current written accounts of the Jarvis family identify only eleven or twelve Jarvis children. However, the various sources disagree on the identity of the children, and names that appear on some lists do not appear on others—including the personal account of Anna Jarvis. Howard Wolfe's genealogical account of the Jarvis family is the main source identified by most histories. He identifies twelve Jarvis children (see *Behold Thy Mother*, 261). I base my history on the work of Olive Dadisman, the curator of the Anna Jarvis Birthplace Museum. She has uncovered, to date, the records for thirteen children born to Granville and Ann Jarvis. The names and dates do not fully correspond with Wolfe. He refers to Annie Elizabeth Jarvis as Anna A. Jarvis, and Dadisman did not find the birth records of a Wesley Jarvis included on Wolfe's list. Children discovered by Dadisman but not included in Wolfe's account: Alonzo Eskridge Jarvis (September 28, 1851–April 4, 1853), Margaret Jarvis (April–July 1863), and Ellen Jarvis (stillborn 1868). The exact cause of death for all the children is presently unknown.

17. Richard A. Meckel, *Save the Babies: American Public Health Reform and the Prevention of Infant Mortality, 1850–1929* (Ann Arbor: University of Michigan Press, 1990), 11–39; Sandra Lee Barney, *Authorized to Heal: Gender, Class, and the Transformation of Medicine in Appalachia, 1880–1930* (Chapel Hill: University of North Carolina Press, 2000), 41–70, 100–4.

18. The original spelling of Mothers' Day Work Club is unclear. "Mothers" appears in its plural form, possessive plural, and possessive singular forms

Mothers' Day v. Mother's Day 69

throughout various publications. I use the possessive plural form, as I believe it best reflects the intention for collective action.

19. Kendall, *Mothers Day*, 11, 3.

20. Doctors practicing medicine in Appalachia in the early nineteenth century varied in their levels of education. Dr. James Reeves began his medical training under two different preceptors and attended lectures at Hampden Sydney College, in Richmond, Virginia. He graduated from the University of Pennsylvania in 1860. He went on to have a successful career in public health, eventually establishing the American Public Health Association and both the West Virginian State Medical Society and the State Board of Health. L. D. Wilson, MD, "James Edmund Reeves, M.D.," *Transactions of the Medical Society of West Virginia* (1896): 1–9; Wolfe, *Behold Thy Mother*, 250–51; for a discussion of early nineteenth-century physicians practicing in Appalachia, see Barney, *Authorized to Heal*, 41–70.

21. Robinson, "Mother's Day," 13–14; Howard Wolfe, "The Second Sunday" (1983), Howard Wolfe Collection, 21–22; Wolfe, *Behold Thy Mother*, 182–83.

22. Barney, *Authorized to Heal*, 41–70, 122–51.

23. W. Hunter Lesser, *Rebels at the Gate: Lee and McClellan on the Front Line of a Nation Divided* (Naperville, IL: Sourcebooks, 2004), 31–38; Clayton R. Newell, *Lee vs. McClellan: The First Campaign* (Washington, DC: Regnery Publishing, 1996), 87–107; John W. Shaffer, *Clash of Loyalties: A Border County in the Civil War* (Morgantown: West Virginia University Press, 2003), 49–128.

24. Kendall, *Mothers Day*, 10; Wolfe, "Second Sunday," 24–25; The following sources detail the death of Thornsbury Bailey Brown but do not include the story of Mrs. Jarvis: Lesser, *Rebels at the Gate*, 53–54; Shaffer, *Class of Loyalties*, 70–71; Stanley A. Tenney, "Taylor County in the Civil War," in *A History of Taylor County West Virginia*, ed. Taylor County Historical and Genealogical Society (Grafton, WV: Taylor County Historical and Genealogical Society, 1986), 62.

25. John Duffy, *The Sanitarians: A History of American Public Health* (Urbana: University of Illinois Press, 1990), 110; Drew Gilpin Faust, *This Republic of Suffering: Death and the American Civil War* (New York: Vintage Books, 2008), 137–70; Lesser, 159–72.

26. Robinson, "Mother's Day," 13–14; Wolfe, "Second Sunday," 21–22; Wolfe, *Behold Thy Mother*, 182–83; For a detailed account of Colonel George R. Latham and military campaigns in western Virginia, see Frank S. Reader, *History of the Fifth West Virginia Cavalry, formerly the Second Virginia Infantry, and of Battery G, First West Virginia Light Artillery* (New Brighton, PA: Daily News, 1890).

27. Shaffer, *Class of Loyalties*, 4, 84–129, 154, 163.

28. Robinson, "Mother's Day," 14; Wolfe, *Behold Thy Mother*,185–86.

29. Wolfe, "Second Sunday," p. 22–26; Wolfe, *Behold Thy Mother*, 185–86.

30. Kendall, *Mothers Day*, 4; J Edgar Williams, *The White Carnation and Mother's Day* (Detroit: Northwestern Printing Company, 1950), 44.

31. Wolfe, *Behold Thy Mother*, 186.

32. Kendall, *Mothers Day*, 8.

33. Ibid., 11–13. Kendall's Mother's Day history offers the best evidence of Ann Reeves Jarvis maternal activism. He records the memories of those who admired her community leadership.

34. Julia Grant, *Raising Baby by the Book: The Education of American Mothers* (New Haven: Yale University Press, 1998), 15–24; Christina Hardyment, *Dream Babies* (Oxford: Oxford University Press, 1984), 33–86; Sharon Hays, *The Cultural Contradictions of Motherhood* (New Haven: Yale University Press, 1996), 29–35; Jan Lewis, "Mother's Love: The Construction of an Emotion in Nineteenth Century America," in *Mothers and Motherhood: Readings in American History,* ed. Rima Apple and Janet Goldmen (Columbus: Ohio State University Press, 1997), 52–71. For an exclusive discussion on the changing view of fatherhood in relationship to the elevation of motherhood in the nineteenth century and/or the declining role of fathers in the direct rearing of children, see Stephan M. Frank, *Life with Father: Parenthood and Masculinity in the Nineteenth-Century American North* (Baltimore: John Hopkins University Press, 1998), 23–54; John Gillis, *A World of Their Own Making: Myth, Ritual, and the Quest for Family Values* (Cambridge, MA: Harvard University Press, 1996), 179–200; Ralph LaRossa, *The Modernization of Fatherhood: A Social and Political History* (Chicago: University of Chicago Press, 1997), 21–40.

35. Lewis, "Mother's Love," 58.

36. Quoted in Hays, *Cultural Contradictions,* 30; For more discussion of nineteenth-century maternal ideals, see also Mary P. Ryan, *The Empire of the Mother: American Writing about Domesticity, 1839–1860* (New York: Harrington Park Press, 1985), 45–70; Maxine L. Margolis, *Mothers and Such: Views of American Women and Why They Changed* (Berkeley: University of California Press, 1985) 11–61.

37. Johnson, "Death, Grief, and Motherhood," 192; Claude Jarvis to Mrs. Ann Reeves Jarvis, June 3, 1903, Anna Jarvis Papers.

38. Jarvis, "Recollections," Draft B.

39. Ibid. The full quote includes "the highest type of motherhood and womanhood." In my opinion, however, Anna does not actually distinguish between the two feminine roles in the account of her mother's life. Since length constraints for this essay prevent a complete discussion of the manuscript's content, I feel the inclusion of "womanhood" in the quote would be misleading.

40. Jarvis, "Recollections," Draft A.

41. The quotes, and/or the sentiment behind them, are scattered throughout both drafts.

42. Jarvis, "Recollections," Draft A.

43. Kendall, *Mothers Day,* 11–12; Wolfe, "Second Sunday," 34.

44. Jarvis, "Recollections," Draft A; Kendall, *Mothers Day,* 9.

45. Wolfe, "Second Sunday," 30.

46. Jarvis, "Recollections," Draft A.

47. Lewis, "Mother's Love," 59–60.

48. Wolfe, "Second Sunday," 40.

49. Ibid., 35–36, 84.

50. "White Carnation," 247.

51. Johnson, "How Mother Got Her Day," 19; Wolfe, *Behold Thy Mother,* 208; "White Carnation," 180.

52. "Mothers Honor Unknown Soldier: Miss Jarvis, Founder of Mother's Day, Protests Ways in Which It Is Exploited," *New York Times,* May 11, 1931.

Mothers' Day v. Mother's Day   71

53. *The Story of the New Mother's Day* (New York: Maternity Center Association, 1935).

54. Golden Rule Foundation, *Observing Mothers Day the Golden Rule Way,* May 14, 1933. Copy located in the Franklin D. Roosevelt Library, Hyde Park, NY. The following sources provide an overview and discussion of MCA services since the early twentieth century: Laura E. Ettinger, *Nurse-Midwifery: The Birth of a New American Profession* (Columbus: Ohio State University Press, 2006); *Maternity Center Association, 1918–1943* (New York: Maternity Center Association, 1943); *Maternity Center Association Log, 1915–1975* (New York: Maternity Center Association) 1975; Sara Twerdow, "The Maternity Center Association as a Vehicle for the Education for Motherhood" (MS thesis, New York School of Social Work, 1947). The organization still exists in New York City. However, it changed its name to Childbirth Connection in 2005.

55. "The Mother's Day Campaign: An Account of the Publicity Used by the Maternity Center Association," *American Journal of Nursing* 31, no. 7 (July 1931): 839; *Gazette Virginian,* "Facing Facts on Mother's Day," Halifax County, VA, May 7, 1931; *Ackley World Journal* "Facing Facts on Mother's Day," Ackley, IA, May 7, 1931.

56. Golden Rule Foundation, *Observing Mothers Day,* 1.

57. US Congress, Senate, Observance of Mother's Day, 73rd Cong., 1st sess., S. Res. 16, Cong. Rec., 77, no. 1 (March 1933): 125; "White Carnation," 59; Anna Jarvis to Franklin Roosevelt, April 18, April 29, May 3, 1933; February 6, April 24, April 27, 1934; March 7, March 21, April 4, April 22, 1935; April 15, 1936; March 18, April 8, April 18, 1938, Franklin D. Roosevelt Library.

58. Anna Jarvis to Franklin Roosevelt, April 15, 1936, Franklin D. Roosevelt Library.

59. "Mother's Day Fund Planned for Needy," *New York Times,* March 3, 1931; "Georgian Named Typical Mother," *New York Times,* April 5, 1935; "'Typical Mother' Broadcasts Plea," *New York Times,* May 13, 1935; Mary Krech, Maternity Center Association President, to Miss Marguerite Le Hand, President Roosevelt's personal secretary, April 15, 1935, Franklin D. Roosevelt Library; Charles V. Vickrey to Franklin Roosevelt, March 31, 1942, Franklin D. Roosevelt Library. The Golden Rule Foundation's Mother's Day Committee became American Mother, Incorporated, in 1950. It has awarded a Mother of the Year every year since 1935. Today the organization considers itself the official sponsor of Mother's Day; www.americanmothers.org (accessed 2014).

60. "Maternity Center to Give Luncheon," *New York Times,* May 7, 1933; Ettinger, *Nurse-Midwifery,* 76; *Campaign Suggestions for Mother's Day, May 12, 1935* (New York: Maternity Center Association, 1935), B 3–6.

61. Anna Jarvis to Eleanor Roosevelt, May 14, 1935, Anna Jarvis Papers; "White Carnation," 75.

62. *Maternity Center Association, 1918–1943,* 1–38; *Maternity Center Association Log, 1915–1975,* 1–20; Twerdow, "Maternity Center Association," 9–13.

63. Mary Krech to Miss Marguerite Le Hand, April 15, 1935, Franklin D. Roosevelt Library; *Maternity Center Association, 1918–1943,* 82–84.

64. "Charity Charlatans," n.d., Anna Jarvis Papers; "White Carnation," 59, 171.

65. Anna Jarvis to Franklin Roosevelt, May 15, 1933, March 6, 1935, Franklin D. Roosevelt Library.

66. *Maternity Center Association Log, 1915–1975*, 6; "Club Women Support Maternity Aid Drive," *New York Times*, May 9, 1931.

67. "Mother's Day Campaign," 839–40; *Story of the New Mother's Day*, 6–15. For an example of a surviving copy of a MCA Mother's Day campaign informational kit, see *Campaign Suggestions for Mother's Day, May 12, 1935*.

68. Anna Jarvis to Franklin Roosevelt, April 27, 1934, Franklin D. Roosevelt Library.

69. *Story of the New Mother's Day*, 2; *Campaign Suggestions for Mother's Day, May 12, 1935*.

70. *Story of the New Mother's Day*, 5; *Maternity Center Association, 1918–1943*, 5–9; *Routines for Maternity Nursing and Briefs for Mothers' Club Talks* (New York: Maternity Center Association, 1935), 49–83. These pages outline the lessons for the association's series, Mothers' Club Talks.

71. Rima Apple, "'Training' the Baby: Mothers' Responses to Advice Literature in the First Half of the Twentieth Century," in *When Science Encounters the Child: Education, Parenting, and Child Welfare in 20th-Century America*, ed. Barbara Beatty, Emily D. Cahan, and Julia Grant (New York: Teachers College Press, 2006), 195–211; Grant, *Raising Baby by the Book*, 137–60.

72. For a detailed discussion of the tenets of "scientific" motherhood, see Hays 19–50, 44; Hardyment, *Dream Babies*, 89–222; Margolis, *Mothers and Such*, 11–107; Rima Apple, Perfect Motherhood: Science and Childrearing in America (New Brunswick, NJ: Rutgers University Press, 2006), 34–55; Rima Apple, "Constructing Mothers; Scientific Motherhood in the Nineteenth and Twentieth Centuries," in Apple and Goldman, *Mothers and Motherhood*, 90–110; Barbara Ehrenreich and Deirdre English, *For Her Own Good; Two Centuries of the Experts' Advice to Women* (New York: Anchor Books, 2005), 215–30; Daniel Beekman, *The Mechanical Baby: A Popular History of the Theory and Practice of Child Raising* (Westport, CT: Lawrence Hill, 1977), 109–205.

73. Grant, *Raising Baby by the Book*, 84–85.

74. Karen Tice, "School-Work and Mother-Work: The Interplay of Maternalism and Cultural Politics in the Educational Narratives of Kentucky Settlement Workers, 1910–1930," *Journal of Appalachian Studies* 4, no. 2 (Fall 1998): 211.

75. "Asks Aid For Needy on Mothers' Day," *New York Times*, March 11, 1931.

76. Wolfe, *Behold Thy Mother*, 208; Oscar Schisgall, "The Bitter Author of Mother's Day: The Strange Story of Anna Jarvis, Who Was Convinced That Her Great Success Was Also Her Defeat," *Reader's Digest* 76, no. 457 (May 1960): 64–66.

CHAPTER THREE

Female Stereotypes and the Creation of Appalachia, 1870–1940

DEBORAH L. BLACKWELL

In 1939 intrepid cartoon dancer Betty Boop starred in a short entitled *Musical Mountaineers.* The plot centered on Betty's car running out of gas in the (unnamed) mountains and her encounter with the locals. From the initial scene, which starts with the outline of a moonshine jug, through the conclusion, when "Zonk Peters" and his family fill up her car with "corn drippin's," the stereotypical imagery of backwards hillbillies dominates the cartoon. Betty complains in a frustrated huff about being stranded "a thousand miles from nowhere." Her first observation about the Peters' dilapidated cabin is that "it looks like the people who moved out don't live here any more." After being confronted by the entire gun-toting Peters clan, Betty's girlish exclamations of fear turn to delight when the family begins demonstrating their "natural" musical talents. The female characters display some of the stereotypical "mountain woman" qualities; Ma is first seen plowing the garden, while the menfolk lie around; she and her daughter brandish rifles and sport corncob pipes; and they make beautiful music from primitive instruments while giving Betty a taste of mountain dancing.[1] Thus, in the span of a six-minute cartoon, virtually every familiar stereotype about mountain men and women served as shorthand for hilarity.

These stereotypes, which were in fact very familiar to Americans nationwide by the time *Musical Mountaineers* debuted in 1939, were not creations of that decade. Depictions of Appalachian mountain residents by outsiders were widely publicized in the latter part of the nineteenth century, as the region was opened up to the exploitation of its mineral and human resources. Many scholars have noted that these publicly traded images served a variety of functions, from excusing exploitation, to validating claims to charitable aid, to selling novels. Less often examined, however, is the issue of the gendered nature of these stereotypes and what the images of Appalachian women, in particular, can reveal about the complex nature of gender dynamics in the late nineteenth and early twentieth centuries. This essay considers a number of different sources to characterize the production of stereotypes about Appalachian women and then discusses the lingering effects of such images on the region. Focusing primarily on the time period between 1870 and 1940, the essay emphasizes the importance of gender and ideas about femininity to the idea of Appalachia. The question of gender is often a more subtle or overlooked subtext in fiction, fund-raising literature, newspaper accounts, and film, and the essay analyzes selected examples of each category in order to further explore that subtext. Even as J. W. Williamson notes that the stereotypical notion of the hillbilly "is, most frequently, male,"[2] the question of gender analysis becomes critical when examining the stereotypical lives of women in the mountains and what those stereotypes may tell us about their reality.

As the field of Appalachian studies has grown over the last three decades, historians and other scholars have often devoted attention to the causes and consequences of these stereotypes of mountain residents. Henry Shapiro's *Appalachia on Our Mind: The Southern Mountains and Mountaineers in the American Consciousness* was among the first works to consider the creation of Appalachian stereotypes by religious and secular reformers and local-color novelists in the late nineteenth and early twentieth centuries. Allen Batteau, in *The Invention of Appalachia*, discussed how fiction writers in particular used "Appalachia . . . [as] a representation of the chaos and disorder on the periphery of commercial and industrial expansion."[3] Portrayals of the so-called hillbillies as both depraved and noble have persisted throughout the twentieth century, even as mountain music has gone national and as film and television have provided new outlets for these stereotypes. According to J. W. Williamson in his book *Hillbillyland: What the Movies Did to the Mountains and What the Mountains Did to the Movies,* the hillbilly character often serves as "[a part of] the conflicted urban memory of necessary frontier rudeness that produces the rural fool who up-ends our complacent assumptions about ourselves."[4] As a marker of class identity, argues Williamson, the notion of the hillbilly provides positive possibilities for politicians and Nashville recording artists and at the same time diminishes and mocks those rural poor who do not have the ability to pick up and discard the term at will. Indeed, historian Anthony Harkins identifies this dual, class-based nature of the hillbilly concept as the key source of the stereotype's popularity and persistence, allowing audiences both to identify with a romanticized past and to embrace the promise of modern life. As a case study in white male "otherness," then, the hillbilly embodies all the good and bad qualities of a mythic Anglo-Saxon past.[5]

Less frequently examined, however, have been the stereotypes generated concerning Appalachian women, as well as the role of women in creating and perpetuating these stereotypes. Scholars such as Barbara Ellen Smith have noted this omission and have suggested avenues for productive inquiry. Smith points out that the traditional focus on poverty and class conflict "have led us to a unilateral, exclusionary construction of inequality, whereby all forms of oppression tend to reduce to the single relationship of social class."[6] Ignoring gender as "a site of power, contestation, and history-making," she suggests, leaves scholars with an incomplete understanding of the lives of Appalachian women. The pervasive source problem, however, may necessitate analyzing other types of historical materials in order to create a viable history of Appalachian women. Smith argues that "the history of women in Appalachia will not be discovered exclusively, perhaps even primarily, in the official documents of institutions, even those that they founded and shaped." Rather, she asserts, "the historical agency of Appalachian women, especially working-class women, is to be found as much in jokes, 'old wives' tales,' and fugitive actions as in the public events and records of conventional history."[7] Such an invitation to broaden the historiography of Appalachian women suggests that further examination of stereotypes may yield useful analysis.

Elizabeth Engelhardt also finds potential usefulness in the examination of stereotypes of Appalachian women. Engelhardt posits that feminism's focus on the relationships between "the personal and the political" or rather "individual and institutional structures of power" provides an avenue for the study of Appalachian women's history and questions of image and stereotype in Appalachian studies more generally.[8] Engelhardt, who opens her essay with a discussion of a 2002 University of Virginia–West Virginia University football halftime show, believes that the examination of "Granny" and "Elly May" stereotypes could yield "theorizing that might illuminate the intentions of and privilege acquired by the viewer of Appalachians who is employing those stereotypes."[9]

Opposing stereotypes such as the "Granny" and "Elly May" constructions have not, of course, been confined to one particular group of women. In her landmark 1985 work *Ar'n't I a Woman? Female Slaves in the Plantation South,* Deborah Gray White begins by tackling the two major stereotypes of female slaves as a way of trying to move her readers past the reliance on those very images as well as toward a greater understanding of the production of historical evidence. "Mammy" and "Jezebel" are not just pervasive tropes, according to White but are also important ways of justifying slavery based on the affection between masters and slaves (Mammy) as well as slaves' supposedly inherently debased nature (Jezebel).[10] White's work suggests that the study of Appalachian stereotypes would benefit similarly from a greater focus on the creation and use of female images in a variety of frameworks. Engelhardt warns that a similar Appalachian studies reliance on "Granny" and "Elly May" to sum up women's experiences has stunted the field's growth.[11] And yet, White's explanation of how dominant groups create and utilize stereotypes as a means to further marginalize oppressed groups holds particular resonance for a consideration of the stereotypes of Appalachian women that pervaded the fiction, news reports, fund-raising literature, and speeches that appeared in the late nineteenth and early twentieth centuries.

Also missing from many previous studies is consideration of the role played by the creators of those images, many of whom were themselves female and who appear to have been acutely aware of the delicate balancing act that they had to maintain. As the definitions of "true

Female Stereotypes and the Creation of Appalachia

womanhood" and femininity were being challenged in the United States by female reformers and suffragettes, stereotypes of Appalachian women provided outlets for cultural anxiety and means for justifying industrialization and benevolence work among a supposedly backward population. As Anthony Harkins notes in his book *Hillbilly: A Cultural History of An American Icon,* one of the sources of the more positive stereotypes of Appalachian culture stemmed from the widespread belief that the region supported clearly defined and unchanging gender roles, in contrast with the beginnings of a more public presence for many northern, urban women as the twentieth century began.[12] Historians of women benevolence workers long have acknowledged that their subjects often prescribed one vision of femininity to their clients while transgressively practicing another in their own lives.[13] Depending on the audience, those competing femininities —and occasionally masculinities as well—may tell us as much or more about the producers of the images as they do about the lived experiences of mountain residents.

The notion that a group of people proves their inferiority through gender roles has a very long history in the United States. Captain John Smith described the Powhatan Indians of Virginia as one such group, noting that "the men bestow their times in fishing, hunting, wars, and such manlike exercises, scorning to be seen in any woman like exercise, which is the cause that the women be very painful and the men often idle. The women and children do the rest of the work."[14] For Smith, concerned with encouraging settlement in early colonial Jamestown, such an explanation made the Powhatans appear to be an easy conquest. William Byrd II's early eighteenth-century depictions of rural North Carolinians includes the observation that "the Men, for their Parts, just like the Indians, impose all the Work upon the poor Women."[15] Deborah Gray White notes in *Ar'n't I a Woman?* that whites justified treating African Americans so poorly because of the "fact" that black women were suited to field work by their cultural heritage and their physical strength.[16] Black women's supposed "inferiority" to white upper-class women thus set African Americans, as a whole, apart from whites.

Stereotyping Appalachia was also not new to the late nineteenth and early twentieth centuries. As noted by Katherine Ledford, explorers as far back as the early colonial settlements thought of the mountains as a place apart from the rest of the world. Ledford finds that colonial and antebellum travelers' accounts, in particular, reflect both images of degeneracy and of yeoman virtue, often within the same narrative. John Lederer, a German national commissioned by Virginia governor William Berkeley to explore the western mountainous regions of the colony in 1669 and 1670, viewed the landscape as overwhelmingly dangerous and threatening in his published accounts. Ledford suggests that "Lederer's characterization of the mountains as a harsh, cruel environment represents colonial anxieties about growing hostilities among frontiersmen and coastal elites over land-ownership and settlement patterns."[17] Lederer wrote comparatively little about the people living in the mountains, however. By the time William Byrd III launched his explorations of the same region in the 1720s and 1730s, the land appeared much more valuable for its natural resources. That change was accompanied, however, by an increasingly negative view of mountain residents, who seemed to the wealthy Byrd to be lazy, unkempt, and thus unfit stewards of the natural beauty in which they lived.[18] Antebellum commentators such as Frederick Law Olmstead also found residents of "backcountry" America to be rough, crude, and ignorant, albeit in Olmstead's case not necessarily as a sign of an entirely different race of people.[19] During and after the Civil War, novelists and missionaries alike often cited the Unionist sympathies of the mountains as a part of their appeal to target audiences in the Northern states.[20] Even so, in the early industrializing period that followed the Civil War, many of the images produced about the region served in much the same way as did stereotypes of African American slaves; images of stupidity, laziness, and violent behavior helped justify economic exploitation as the Appalachians became essential to the nation's coal and timber production.[21] Appalachia as a setting of simultaneous beauty and danger thus intermingled with national anxieties about economics and class status.

Local color fiction writers, more concerned with entertainment and profiting from stories that included a sense of "cultural hierarchy,"[22] often set their stories in the most isolated and rural parts of the mountains and used "Appalachia . . . [as] a representation of the chaos and disorder on the periphery of commercial and industrial expansion," according to Allen Batteau.[23] The feuds, the poverty, and the ignorance of the native mountaineers in their stories fostered the belief in the supposed "otherness" of the mountain residents. That "otherness" extended to stereotypes of white Appalachian women in much of late nineteenth- and early twentieth-century fiction and nonfiction. Anthony Harkins identifies several female tropes in the work of the local colorists: "the beautiful but ignorant mountain lass; the overworked and crudely attired drudge who struggles to care for her oversized family; or . . . the bonneted, toothless crone who lives out her remaining years smoking a corncob pipe awash in a haze of melancholia."[24] One of the most successful of the local color writers was Kentuckian John Fox Jr., whose many novels and short stories about southwestern Virginia and eastern Kentucky reflect many of the literary stereotypes of the day. Though he was most famous for *The Trail of the Lonesome Pine* (1908), which focused on the romance between a mountain woman and an outsider man, Fox began playing with that theme much earlier. In 1892 Fox wrote the novella *A Mountain Europa*, originally serialized in *The Century* magazine and published in book form in 1899. *A Mountain Europa*'s perspective on mountain women in general, and the heroine in particular, provides a remarkably illustrative example of Appalachian gender stereotyping.

As *A Mountain Europa* begins, Clayton, the university student turned coal mine operator, catches his first glimpse of the enchanting Easter as she is following a "curious" and rather unladylike custom by riding a bull up the mountain (though it is worth noting that she is riding sideways, rather than straddling the bull). Her gruff and dismissive demeanor astonishes Clayton, who had become accustomed to worndown and meek mountain women. He later consults with Uncle Tommy Brooks to find out more about her, to which Uncle Tommy responds:

> She's a cur'us as I ever seed. . . . [T]he gal does the work. She ploughs with that bull, and does the plantin' herself. She kin chop wood like a man. An' as for shootin,' well, when huntin's good 'n' thar's shootin'-matches round-about, she don't have to buy much meat. . . . She air a cur'us critter . . . shy as a deer till she air stirred up, and then she air a caution; mighty gentle sometimes, and ag'in stubborn as a mule.[25]

Plenty of men have tried to tame the fair Easter, warns Uncle Tommy, but she will have nothing to do with them. The novella focuses on

Clayton's growing fascination with Easter, and their love story develops as he begins teaching her more of the ways of the "settlemints," expanding her mind and fancying himself a Pygmalion-like figure to her Galatea. To Clayton, Easter is an exotic creature whose violation of middle-class gender norms attracts him at first, but it is her transformation into a "lady" that seals his commitment to her. He sees her as a creature apart from those women of the mountains who were "haggard and careworn at thirty."[26] The tragic end of their love story comes when Easter's drunken fugitive father accidentally shoots her instead of Clayton. Such a tragic ending to the story leaves open the question of whether or not Easter could have completed her transformation in Clayton's urban world. Even so, Fox clearly underscores the notion that, however beautiful the natural setting of the mountains may be, the qualities of "true womanhood" were endangered by life in the mountains, with its "backwards" civilization populated with violent feudists and backwards moonshiners.[27]

The wave of industrialization that swept through the mountains in the late nineteenth century was accompanied by a wave of missionaries and secular benevolence workers who were instrumental in adding to the popular image of mountain women and men. William Goodell Frost, for many years the president of Kentucky's Berea College and self-proclaimed "discoverer" of the Appalachian residents he dubbed "our contemporary ancestors," was one of many educators who traded in images of an Appalachia unchanged from the era of the American Revolution.[28] In an attempt to emphasize the charitable worthiness of their organizations and the mountain people, Frost and others chose to ignore the signs of change in the region and to romanticize the persistent poverty.

One of the authors most responsible for popular culture's representations of Appalachia's residents was Lucy Furman, who penned both fiction and nonfiction about her experiences working at the Hindman Settlement School in Eastern Kentucky. Furman, who initially came to Hindman for a short visit with her school friend Katherine Pettit, stayed for several years and spent most of the rest of her career devoted to the school's success. She wrote a series of fund-raising letters for the school that focused primarily on the "mothering" efforts of the settlement

Female Stereotypes and the Creation of Appalachia 81

workers. Emphasizing a maternal sense of responsibility both described the way that the teachers thought of themselves and was also a tactic likely to bear fruit with the women and men who donated money to the school. By not challenging the still-alive "separate spheres" notion of "woman's place," and yet following the national reform rhetoric that justified women's public roles as "civic housekeeping," Furman joined female benevolence workers, such as Jane Addams and Julia Lathrop, around the country in utilizing the rhetoric of maternalism.[29]

Even so, elements of Furman's maternalist writing demonstrate specifics particular to the Appalachian context. At least in the early years of Hindman Settlement School, and with the apparent blessing of school leaders, Furman utilized some of the more "colorful" aspects of mountain life in her writing, while still trying to be sensitive to the feelings of mountain residents. In many of the school's fund-raising letters, Furman advised her readers at the end of her letter to "please do not let this get into print."[30] In a letter describing the "Home Life of the Little Boys" that contained that particular request, Furman tells her readers that "there are only one or two of our little boys who have not been drunk at some time" and points out that "it is interesting to hear the boys brag about the shootings and killings their fathers and brothers have been in." She closed with the observation that the boys "are capable, warm-hearted, loving and responsible to a remarkable degree, and it is a privilege to be able to teach them their first prayer and to show them day by day a better way to live."[31] Calling, as this imagery does, on both the most persistent negative stereotypes of mountain males as drunken and violent, it is not surprising that Furman and the Hindman directors did not want to risk offending their clients by reinforcing those images to outsiders. Lucy Furman thus was trying to have it both ways: play into the uglier prejudices of her audience while attempting to protect the residents from national broadcasts of their troubles. In doing so, the possibility of bringing a maternalist "woman's touch" to these children's lives is held out to potential donors as a worthy cause for their philanthropy. In doing so, Furman implicitly criticizes the mothers of these mountain children; as Karen Tice notes, Furman and other "reformers considered the fate of mountain children precarious because of class-based maternal incompetence and insufficient resources: mountain mothers typically relied upon tradition and neighbors for child rearing advice instead of "expert" knowledge."[32]

Furman's nonfiction fund-raising articles led her to begin writing short stories and novels about her Hindman experiences. Her 1913 book, *Mothering on Perilous,* continued the themes of her earlier work in terms of Appalachian gender. The main character, a fictionalized version of herself, works as a housemother for a group of twelve young boys at a mountain settlement school. In addition to the descriptions of daily life that make up much of the book, Furman very clearly addresses the issue of herself as a mother figure and the mothers that the boys left behind them to come to school. Schools like Hindman were specifically organized to promote the maternal connection between teachers and students, and "the educational work of settlement schools was regularly equated with mothering."[33] In one chapter entitled "About Mothers," Furman's character encourages the little boys to talk about their mothers as a way of bonding with them, especially with the children whose mothers had died. The stereotypes of impoverished, long-suffering, abundantly fertile, and often ill mountain women are fully present in *Mothering on Perilous,* but the sentimental nature of the boys' attachment to their mothers and the frequently noted desire of mothers that their children receive an education provide an additional dimension to the stereotype.[34] Such a seeming contradiction in imagery was, in fact, not unusual; Karen Tice notes that the settlement women's dependence on the good opinion of mountain parents led to a delicate balancing act on the part of school leaders.[35] At the same time, however, settlement school leaders were keenly aware of the need to appeal to the hearts and wallets of wealthy benefactors from outside the region. That Furman intended *Mothering on Perilous* as an appeal to the long-established prejudices of potential donors seems likely, and in fact was successful in drawing the single largest donation the school ever received.[36]

Lucy Furman's short story *Sight to the Blind* is an even more pointed depiction of women in Appalachia, both the natives and the "quare women" who established the settlement schools. The story centers on an old woman known as "Aunt Dalmanutha," whose blindness was perceived by local preachers as punishment for blaspheming God at the funeral of her only daughter. When the nurse from the local settlement

Female Stereotypes and the Creation of Appalachia 83

school suggests that in fact she has cataracts and that surgery could restore her sight, Aunt Dalmanutha is skeptical at first but finally agrees to go to Lexington for treatment. She returned to the mountains with both her sight and her teeth intact, praising God and those around her. After recounting the story of her rebirth from a bitter and backward old woman to one with hope, health, and love in her heart, Aunt Dalmanutha proclaimed herself to be "a ree-surrected woman . . . I know I am free, restored, and saved; I know my Redeemer liveth."[37] Even though Aunt Dalmanutha's illnesses left her, her use of highly emotional religious expressions to relate her joy continues to set her apart from the settlement women, whose superior scientific knowledge was the key to saving Aunt Dalmanutha's sight. These sharp contrasts in the characterizations of both mountain women and settlement women further notions of the usefulness of gender to understanding the development and promulgation of the stereotypical mountain white.

Many benevolence workers were, in fact, acutely aware of the need to balance carefully the noble with the savage in their portrayals and of the need to protect the feelings of their clients. From their earliest arrival in the region, the missionaries and reformers often worried about the images they created in their writing. Ethel DeLong Zande,[38] the co-director of Pine Mountain Settlement School, wrote to one supporter that "we people who are connected with schools for the improvement and development of the mountain people necessarily can present only certain aspects of the things that we know. Whatever we write is for the purpose of presenting the most worthwhile things about the mountain people."[39] "Worthwhile," of course, could be translated to mean those things that were most attractive about the mountain residents to those individuals most likely to donate money. Historian David Whisnant offered a sharp critique of such attitudes in 1983's *All That Is Native and Fine*, charging that such overly careful creation of Appalachian imagery reflected an unwillingness to challenge the forces of economic destruction gathering around mountain residents. Thus they "promised a solution [to the region's problems] that entailed no social cost and confirmed rather than challenged the status quo."[40] Indeed, settlement workers wrote their articles and letters for an audience that did not want the gender or class status quo to be questioned. If that meant trading

84   DEBORAH L. BLACKWELL

in less-than-flattering stereotypes, then that was a calculated risk these women took.

Controlling the distribution of stereotypes required a variety of different techniques. Katherine Pettit, for one, took matters into her own hands and refused all press coverage of her fund-raising speeches, seemingly for fear of being quoted or misquoted in ways that would damage her ability to work effectively in eastern Kentucky. This makes her frustrating to the historian trying to trace her motivations, but the absence tells us a great deal about how delicate an issue publicity could be. Sometimes, though, publicity was meant to get into print: Ethel De-Long wrote two articles for her *Smith College Alumnae Quarterly*, the first in 1912 and the second in 1914. "Many people," she lamented, "do not distinguish between [the mountain] stock and the 'poor whites,' of whom are the clay-eaters and snuff-dippers."[41] As a result, "they have been judged by externals alone, and, proud with the sense of their own capacity, are often deeply hurt by the phrase 'poor whites,' and by an attitude of well-meant pity."[42] In distinguishing mountain residents from the proverbial "poor white trash," DeLong evinced concern both for the dignity of her clients and for an appeal based on their ability to reform, given the proper tools and guidance.

Another author associated with the Hindman Settlement School, one with a different agenda, provides interesting contrasts in his descriptions of mountain women and settlement leaders. Author William Aspinwall Bradley visited the Hindman Settlement School in eastern Kentucky for six months in 1913 and subsequently published a poetry collection entitled *Old Christmas* in 1917. Many of his poems dealt with the women who ran the settlement school. Bradley particularly focused on sexual themes, in keeping with the stereotype of mountain women as promiscuous. Several of the poems made reference to the settlement school workers with whom he had made his home, including the "Mountain Angel" to whom the volume was dedicated.[43] Unfortunately, those references were often imaginative in a way that seriously upset many of those at Hindman and continued the trend of portraying mountain women as uncivilized and sexualized. The most inflammatory stereotypes appeared in the poem entitled "The Strange Woman," about a settlement school worker who married a mountain

Female Stereotypes and the Creation of Appalachia   85

man after being seduced by him. As the poem began, however, her love had turned to hatred, and she lay in wait to shoot her husband as he returned from visiting his mistress. The poem's opening stanza summed up the general tone and direction of the rest of the verses:

> What spell was on me when I wed
> This brutal boy who seeks my bed
> Only when drunk. His kiss—his *sight*—
> I loathe. I shall kill him to-night,
> If he comes back as last he came,
> With bloodshot eyes, with face aflame,
> Making foul jest of my hot shame,
> To force what once I freely gave
> Ere I became his cabin slave.[44]

In a seeming reversal of the theme of Fox's *A Mountain Europa*, the "strange woman" had been corrupted by her experiences in the mountains, resulting in her descent into savagery and the abandonment of her former "true woman" self. This belief in the destructive nature of the Appalachian setting on "womanly" qualities was consistent with the identification of mountains as a setting on the periphery of "civilization."[45] This insider/outsider binary is common in many stereotypical depictions of life in the mountains. In Bradley's case, the outsider woman was brought down by the insider man, while in Fox's story, the outsider man elevates the insider woman, only to lose her to the depravity of her insider father. Both stress the transformative effects of love on women; their desire to fall in love transcends their regional origins. Even so, in both cases the mountains ultimately function as corrupters of women. Interestingly, though, authors like Lucy Furman—and Bradley himself, as discussed below—stress the idea that women benevolence workers who came to the mountains were the ones who could really transform men through their maternal attributes. All of these works, however, depend on notions of Appalachian white women as a class apart from urban middle-class white women.

The images that Bradley's poetry evoked was clearly not the romanticized mountain region of the sentimentalists, nor was it intended to uplift anyone's ideals; this was salacious entertainment. At least one of the settlement women drew distinctions between Bradley's poetry and the writing of benevolence workers, who felt the need to monitor carefully their public statements. In December 1918, Ethel DeLong Zande wrote a letter explaining her position on *Old Christmas* to Marshall Allaben, the Presbyterian Church (USA) home missions board representative to the mountains. She began by observing that for mountain residents "sex is the tremendous interest necessarily where there is no travel or education or outlook through books." She argues, however, that "of course we people who write circulars to secure funds for our schools must always emphasize the qualities of the mountain people which we consider make them a peculiarly interesting problem. But it doesn't surprise me at all that a disinterested observer who sojourns for six months in the hills should deal with questions of sex almost primarily."[46] Zande went on to comment further on the value of such a book to posterity. "It seems to me highly desirable however that somebody should come along who writes of things we [settlement workers] necessarily could not write of but which we know to be perfectly true. Surely in fifty years when these conditions have changed utterly it will be worthwhile to have stories dealing with the motives of the people in the region."[47] This is a fascinating attitude coming from one who wrote multiple appeals for Pine Mountain Settlement School; in some respects, it addresses the idea that what attracted attention to the mountains was the widely held belief that the region was "uncivilized."

Old Christmas was not the only evidence that Bradley took inspiration from his time at Hindman Settlement School. In 1918 *Scribner's* published his article "The Women on Troublesome." Once again, his focus was again on the settlement women, but with the intent of publicizing the extent of their work rather than capitalizing on sexualized fiction. He described the region as racked by feuds and violence; he quotes one mountain woman as saying, "This air the hell o' Kaintucky!"[48] The Appalachian women in Bradley's article were not the aggressive, sexualized creatures of his poetry; rather, they are the needy downtrodden looking for outsiders to bring them the education they so desperately want. According to Bradley, when Katherine Pettit first traveled in the mountains, before she had any notion of starting a settlement school, she was confronted by a mountain mother who was not satisfied

Female Stereotypes and the Creation of Appalachia 87

with the meager attention paid to her desire to learn to bake biscuits. The mountain resident's parting words to Pettit, as related by Bradley, sounded a call to womanly duties: "Well, we allowed that you uns as knowed how had come to show us uns as don't, but you hain't."[49] The founding mythology of Hindman always put a respected local man named "Uncle" Solomon Everidge at the center of the community's desire for education from the "quare women," but in Bradley's version, the outspoken need of women to protect their children from a life of feuding also played into Pettit's agenda.[50] These were people "cut off from all contact with the currents of modern progress," rendering them tragically ignorant and lacking in moral training.[51] Bradley really poured on the imagery for *Scribner's* middle-class audience, in an argument that challenged the social Darwinism of that age:

> These scions of a superb stock were victims of circumstances rather than of their own undisciplined passions, which were the result, not the cause, of their economic condition. They never, even at their worst moments, lost a sense of the destiny which had been denied them, of the heritage which here in what had once been the wilderness, their fathers had somehow forfeited. . . . And it was upon these [people] that "the women" counted to aid them in their struggle to rescue this flotsam and jetsam of a submerged race.[52]

The women who mattered in the scenario envisioned by Bradley were the settlement women; other than a few reactions to their presence, mountain women are rarely in the forefront of Bradley's description. The implication of their social invisibility is hard to escape in his work; for him, decades of fear and hopelessness have kept mountain women from achieving much of anything for themselves or their children.

Mythmaking about Appalachian residents in general and women in particular brought these paradoxical stereotypes together: that they were overworked and lazy; religious and violent; overly masculine and overly feminine. These binaries suggest that stereotypical Appalachian women, as (mis)understood by outsiders, functioned as outliers in the development of the twentieth century's "New Woman." Certainly these stereotypes persisted well past the initial burst of enthusiasm for the region into the 1920s and especially the 1930s, when the combination of national poverty and nostalgia for a supposedly simpler past once again refocused attention on the Southern Appalachians.

Many silent films continued the narratives established by earlier local color writers and settlement teachers: white Appalachian women were strong but vulnerable; overworked yet exuberantly joyous; poor but dignified. A silent movie from the 1920s about a female character called Harum-Scarum provides a remarkable parallel to Fox's *A Mountain Europa*; Harum-Scarum is intrigued by the dapper young industrial agent who comes to survey the mountains, and she eventually sneaks away from a dance to listen to his plans for the land and to accept his wedding ring.[53] Such oversimplification of the development of the Appalachian region was so familiar to the general public by the 1920s that no real story development—or sound—was required to get the moviemaker's point across. At the same time, however, fictional Appalachian women had access to greater options in terms of narrative tolerance of differences, albeit in impermanent ways. Williamson's history of movie stereotypes considers the "hillbilly gals," as he calls them, to be "mock males," where part of their "otherness" stems from their lack of adaptation to middle-class America's gender norms.[54] He cites several examples of silent films where title characters "were allowed symbolic moments of equal power through violence," either by forcing men to marry them, punishing men for attempting to attack them, or shooting men for causing trouble of some sort.[55] Though the Appalachian women in these silent movies do not experience "anything approaching permanent equality," they do have transgressive moments of freedom, much as their male compatriots did.

Interestingly, there are some examples in this period where Appalachian white women seem to have used elements of these stereotypes to their advantage. Williamson refers to this as "playing dumb but showing smart," in reference to politicians who sought a connection with their constituents.[56] Newspaper accounts of the 1929 trials of striking women textile workers in Elizabethton, Tennessee, provide one example of this phenomenon. Jacquelyn Dowd Hall's discussion of these "disorderly women" includes stories of two women who were on trial for having created disturbances during the textile strike. Trixie Perry appeared in court wearing a dress made of red, white, and blue bunting to answer charges of mocking the National Guard's efforts to control the

Female Stereotypes and the Creation of Appalachia   89

strikers. When confronted with the accusation that she had threatened a soldier, she responded that she did so only to get him to get his gun out of her face. Another woman who called herself Texas Bill made the most of appropriating gender stereotypes to her purposes. Normally clad in men's clothes and freely utilizing profanity, she was referred to by the defense attorney as the "Wild Man from Borneo." She appeared in court, however, in an elegant coat and picture hat and assumed a very ladylike dignity while on the stand.[57] The actions of both Trixie Perry and Texas Bill demonstrate that manipulating stereotypes of mountain women could have benefits for the women who were able to play with "outsider" America's ideas about gender. These were not the pitiful elderly grandmothers or the ignorant, oversexed nymphs of much of Appalachian stereotyping, and the degree to which they managed that delicate balance of "playing dumb but showing smart" indicates the potential for greater historical agency on the part of Appalachian white women than has traditionally been acknowledged.

In reference to the 1939 Betty Boop cartoon *Musical Mountaineers* cited at the outset of this article, it is clear that images of Appalachian women were so clearly a part of the national mythology that they required no explanation and, indeed, served as a shorthand indicator of mountain "backwardness." Betty herself was in the process of undergoing changes: the advent of the Hayes Code in Hollywood dictated that her skirts become longer and her legendary flirtatiousness be toned down.[58] One of the most intriguing images in the cartoon is at the beginning, when Ma is plowing the fields while the men sleep away the day. Appalachian women, as the cartoon indicates, fall into that same tradition; carrying a heavy burden of family sustenance by being the main sources of farm labor reverses the assumption of mainstream American culture of the man as principle breadwinner.

The gendered messages of *Musical Mountaineers* continue in the spontaneous song performed at the end of the cartoon. The chorus of the song repeats the phrase "who cares, who cares," as indicative of the laziness of mountain residents. The verse about the mother figure is especially interesting: "She chews all day in them thar hills, she don't care nothin' 'bout fuss and frills."[59] Reminiscent of Ethel DeLong Zande's lament about the characterization of mountain people as "snuff dippers," this line simultaneously claims a mainstream male privilege of tobacco consumption while at the same time further separating mountain women from their "flatlander" sisters by denying interest in pretty—presumably manufactured—finery. Read another way, though, the line could also be a subtle critique of mainstream femininity's obsession with "fuss and frills." For 1930s America, suffering in the Great Depression, the happiness evidenced by the Peters clan in their broken-down home and with their simple possessions played on dominant cultural longings for a mythical preindustrial—and presumably happier—past. These "Musical Mountaineers" thus served the audience both as individuals to look down upon and as a glimpse at a past that supposedly once existed.

Just as female stereotypes evolved nationally in the late nineteenth and early twentieth centuries, so too did the potential for more multidimensional appraisals of white Appalachian women. Yet the question of how these stereotypes informed and constrained real women remains a more difficult one to answer. Throughout the twentieth century, a re-energizing of the simultaneous nostalgia for and condemnation of Appalachia seems to have come in waves, especially during the Depression of the 1930s and the Great Society of the 1960s. With these came renewed depictions of naturally talented craftspeople, impoverished illiterates, and violent drunkards. And yet more sympathetic portrayals emerged as well, informed in part by the increasing number of Appalachian natives—men and women—who produced social science literature, journalism, and mass media. Deconstructing earlier depictions of Appalachian women and the stereotypes created and reified by these depictions allows us the possibility of greater understanding of the overall history of the region and the artifacts left for historians to analyze.

NOTES

1. *Musical Mountaineers,* dir. Dave Fleischer (Paramount Pictures, 1939). Available online at http://www.youtube.com/watch?v=hEEXylFBfKk (accessed November 30, 2008).

2. J. W. Williamson, *Hillbillyland: What the Movies Did to the Mountains and What the Mountains Did to the Movies* (Chapel Hill: University of North Carolina Press, 1995), ix.

3. Allen Batteau, *The Invention of Appalachia* (Tucson: University of Arizona Press, 1990), 72.

4. Williamson, *Hillbillyland,* 16.

5. Anthony Harkins, *Hillbilly: A Cultural History of an American Icon* (New York: Oxford University Press, 2004), 6–7.

6. Barbara Ellen Smith, "Walk-Ons in the Third Act: The Role of Women in Appalachian Historiography," *Journal of Appalachian Studies* 4, no. 1 (Spring 1998): 6.

7. Barbara Ellen Smith, "'Beyond the Mountains': The Paradox of Women's Place in Appalachian History," *National Women's Studies Association Journal* 11, no. 3 (Fall 1999): 8–9.

8. Elizabeth S. D. Engelhardt, "Creating Appalachian Women's Studies: Dancing Away from Granny and Elly May," in *Beyond Hill and Hollow: Original Readings in Appalachian Women's Studies*, ed. Elizabeth S. D. Engelhardt (Athens: Ohio University Press, 2005), 7.

9. Engelhardt, "Creating Appalachian Women's Studies," 8. The halftime show took place in 2002 during a West Virginia University–University of Virginia bowl game and included a very "Elly May" type of character. See Engelhardt, 1–2.

10. Deborah Gray White, *Ar'n't I a Woman? Female Slaves in the Plantation South* (New York: W. W. Norton, 1985, 1999), chap. 1.

11. Engelhardt, "Creating Appalachian Women's Studies," 3.

12. Anthony Harkins, *Hillbilly: A Cultural History of an American Icon* (New York: Oxford University Press, 2003), 6.

13. See, for example, Robyn Muncy, *Creating a Female Dominion in American Reform, 1890–1935* (New York: Oxford University Press, 1991), and Karen W. Tice, *Tales of Wayward Girls and Immoral Women: Case Records and the Professionalization of Social Work* (Urbana: University of Illinois Press, 1998).

14. Captain John Smith, "Of the Natural Inhabitants of Virginia," from *Captain John Smith of Willoughby by Alford, Lincolnshire; President of Virginia and Admiral of New England. Works: 1608–1631*, ed. Edward Arber, The English Scholar's Library, no. 16 (Birmingham, 1884), excerpted in *Readings from Settlement to Reconstruction*, vol. 1 of *America Firsthand*, ed. Robert Marcus, John Giggle, and David Burner, 7th ed. (New York: Bedford/St. Martin's Press, 2004), 22.

15. William Byrd II, *The History of the Dividing Line*, cited in Katherine Ledford, "A Landscape and a People Set Apart: Narratives of Exploration and Travel in Early Appalachia," in *Back Talk from Appalachia: Confronting Stereotypes*, ed. Dwight B. Billings, Gurney Norman, and Katherine Ledford (Lexington: University Press of Kentucky, 1999), 59.

16. White, *Ar'n't I a Woman?*, chap. 1.

17. Ledford, "A Landscape and a People," 54.

18. Ibid., 59.

19. Harkins, *Hillbilly*, 24–25.

20. Kenneth W. Noe, "'Deadened Color and Colder Horror': Rebecca Harding Davis and the Myth of Unionist Appalachia," in *Back Talk from Appalachia*, 67–84. Noe focuses on Davis, whose fiction took a more nuanced approach to the region and thus was unlike many of her contemporaries.

21. Henry D. Shapiro, *Appalachia on Our Mind: The Southern Mountains and Mountaineers in the American Consciousness, 1870–1920* (Chapel Hill: University

of North Carolina Press, 1978), and Batteau, *The Invention of Appalachia,* are two of the most important works in defining this imagery and its connection to the rapid economic shifts of the period. The classic overview of Appalachian industrialization in the late nineteenth and early twentieth centuries is Ronald D. Eller, *Miners, Millhands, and Mountaineers: Industrialization of the Appalachian South, 1880–1930* (Knoxville: University of Tennessee Press, 1982).

22. Harkins, *Hillbilly,* 29.

23. Batteau, *The Invention of Appalachia,* 72.

24. Harkins, *Hillbilly,* 32–33.

25. John Fox Jr., *A Mountain Europa* (1899), chap. 2, http://www.fullbooks.com/A-Mountain-Europa.html (accessed February 23, 2009).

26. Ibid.

27. Harkins, *Hillbilly,* 39.

28. Shapiro, *Appalachia on Our Mind,* 115.

29. A discussion of both Jane Addams's and Julia Lathrop's use of maternalist strategies may be found in Robyn Muncy, *Creating a Female Dominion in American Reform* (New York: Oxford University Press, 1991), chaps. 1 and 2. Addams was the cofounder and director of Hull House in Chicago and a key figure in the settlement house movement; Lathrop directed the federal Children's Bureau as the first woman to head a federal government bureaucracy. The phrase "civic housekeeping" comes from a speech given by Addams to the National American Woman Suffrage Association Convention in February 1906 entitled "The Modern City and the Municipal Franchise for Women" (excerpted in *Major Problems in American History,* vol. 2: *Since 1865,* ed. Elizabeth Cobbs-Hoffman and Jon Gjerde, 2nd ed. (New York: Houghton Mifflin, 2001), 125–26).

30. See, for example, Lucy Furman, "Home Life of the Little Boys," December 1908, box 1, folder 2, Hindman Settlement School Papers, Berea College Archives.

31. Ibid.

32. Karen W. Tice, "School-Work and Mother-Work: The Interplay of Maternalism and Cultural Politics in the Educational Narratives of Kentucky Settlement Workers, 1910–1930," *Journal of Appalachian Studies* 4, no. 2 (Fall 1998): 196.

33. Tice, "School-Work and Mother-Work," 208.

34. Lucy Furman, *Mothering on Perilous* (New York: Macmillan, 1913), 92–99, available on Google Books, http://books.google.com/books/about/Mothering _on_Perilous.html?id=qSE1AAAAMAAJ (accessed November 30, 2008).

35. Tice, "School-Work and Mother-Work," 209.

36. Jess Stoddart, *Challenge and Change in Appalachia: The Story of Hindman Settlement School* (Lexington: University of Kentucky Press, 2002), 66.

37. Lucy Furman, *Sight to the Blind* (New York: Macmillan , 1914), 71, available on Google Books, http://books.google.com/books/about/Sight_To_The_Blind .html?id=Qd3obkiM5aYC (accessed November 30, 2008).

38. Ethel DeLong married Luigi Zande, a fellow worker at Pine Mountain Settlement School, in 1918. I have chosen to refer to her alternately by her maiden or married name depending on the date of the reference.

Female Stereotypes and the Creation of Appalachia 93

39. Ethel DeLong Zande to Marshall Allaben, December 2, 1918, reel 44, Pine Mountain Settlement School Microfilm Collection, Berea College Archives, Berea, KY (hereafter PMSS microfilm collection).

40. David E. Whisnant, *All That Is Native and Fine: The Politics of Culture in an American Region* (Chapel Hill: University of North Carolina Press, 1983), 85.

41. Ethel DeLong, "Doings on Troublesome," *Smith Alumnae Quarterly* (November 1912), 18.

42. Ethel DeLong, "The Appeal of the Kentucky Mountains," *Smith Alumnae Quarterly* (April 1914), 165.

43. William Aspinwall Bradley, *Old Christmas* (Boston: Houghton Mifflin, 1917). The information concerning his visit is located in the preface of this same book. It is clear from other sources that the "mountain angel" was settlement nurse Harriet Butler (see Ethel DeLong to Harriet Butler, February 7, 1918, reel 46, PMSS microfilm collection).

44. Bradley, *Old Christmas*, 24. For the time this poem was written, it was pretty racy, dealing, as it did, explicitly with sexual desire.

45. Williamson, *Hillbillyland*, 17–19.

46. Ethel DeLong Zande to Marshall Allaben, December 2, 1918, reel 44, PMSS microfilm collection.

47. Ibid.

48. William Aspinwall Bradley, "The Women on Troublesome," repr. from *Scribner's* (March 1918), 1, reel 11, Hindman Settlement School Microfilm Collection, Berea College Archives.

49. Ibid., 2.

50. Ibid., 3–4. Whisnant, *All That Is Native and Fine*, discusses the "Uncle Sol" imagery and the notion of the "quare women" in chapter 1.

51. Bradley, "The Women on Troublesome," 6.

52. Ibid., 9.

53. "Harum-Scarum Steals From the Dance to Meet her New Lover of the Valleys," n.d. (ca. 1920s), shown in *Strangers and Kin*, dir. Herb E. Smith (Appalshop, 1984). This documentary traces many of the stereotypes discussed herein and addresses the problematic nature of these ideas along similar lines to White's *Ar'n't I a Woman?*

54. Williamson, *Hillbillyland*, ix, chap. 8.

55. Ibid., 233.

56. Ibid., 9–10.

57. Jacquelyn Dowd Hall, "Disorderly Women: Gender and Labor Militancy in the Appalachian South," *Journal of American History* 73, no. 2 (September 1986), 327–74.

58. Sean Chadwell, "Technological Determinism and the Poisoned Apple: The Case of *Snow White and the Seven Dwarfs*," *Reconstruction: Studies in Contemporary Culture* 8, no. 2 (2008), http://reconstruction.eserver.org/issues/082/chadwell.shtml (accessed November 30, 2008), is one of the most recent articles to reference Betty Boop's transformation from sexualized icon to a more middle-class conceptualization of femininity.

59. *Musical Mountaineers*.

CHAPTER FOUR

Women on a Mission

Southern Appalachia's "Benevolent Workers" on Film

JOHN C. INSCOE

The "discovery" of Appalachia in the late nineteenth and early twentieth centuries has always loomed large in the vast and growing scholarship on the region. As missionaries, educators, social workers, and academics moved into the southern highlands in increasing numbers, the issue of "cultural otherness," or "how people perceive each other across cultural boundaries," as David Whisnant has termed it, became central to how Americans came to see and understand Appalachia at the time and long afterward. More specifically, this era was one in which, to quote Whisnant again, "mostly educated, urban, middle- and upper-class, liberal 'culture workers' perceived, manipulated, and projected the culture of mostly rural, lower-class working people in the southern mountains during the half century after 1890."[1]

The fact that women were front and center among these so-called benevolent workers has been the focus of much of the historical and literary work devoted to Appalachia's "age of discovery."[2] Given the dramatic possibilities inherent in the incursion of these women into southern highland communities, it seems surprising that they have inspired only limited interest in Hollywood. There are, however, three films produced over the course of a half century that have dramatized those encounters by outsiders with Appalachian residents and their culture. Each of the three centers on the experiences of individual women who,

95

for different reasons and under different circumstances, moved into the southern mountains with a mission. One came as a teacher; one as a musicologist collecting mountain ballads; and one as simply the wife of a Methodist minister assigned to a highland circuit. As such, they reflect the three most basic incentives behind these outreach efforts—education, religion, and culture brokering.

Though heavily fictionalized, all three films are based on the experiences of real women. Corra Harris's loosely autobiographical account of her own experience with her husband's first pastorate in the North Georgia mountains in the 1880s, *The Circuit Rider's Wife* (1910), inspired the film *I'd Climb the Highest Mountain* in 1951. Catherine Marshall, the wife of the celebrated preacher Peter Marshall, produced a best-selling novel, *Christy* (1967), based on her mother's first year as a teacher at a mission school in Tennessee's Great Smoky Mountains in 1910. It was made into a television movie in 1994, which served as the pilot for a short-lived series on CBS. Finally, *Songcatcher* (2000) is an independently produced film loosely based on the experiences of Olive Dame Campbell and her academic quest to capture the ballads and other music of North Carolina's Blue Ridge Mountains, set in 1907.

In one way or another, all three films confront that central issue of that age of Appalachian discovery: the cross-cultural interactions between mountain residents and those who moved into their midst with specific agendas for working with them or for them. How these particular women engaged the Georgia, Tennessee, and Carolina highlanders they encountered in their missions and how those highlanders responded to them serve as a promising means of gauging Hollywood's shifting treatment of Appalachia and its people. Equally significant are the depictions of the female protagonists themselves. The rapport each established with the mountain people they served proved transformative to one degree or another, and each left the region with a very different sense of themselves and their capabilities.

I'D CLIMB THE HIGHEST MOUNTAIN

Corra Harris was a prolific Georgia writer, whose "highly publicized experience in backwoods Protestantism," as one biographer termed it, began as a serial in *The Saturday Evening Post* in 1908, and was pulled together and published as a novel in 1910.[3] While loosely based on her first year of marriage to Lundy Harris in 1887 and his itinerant ministry in Hart County in northeastern Georgia (adjacent to her home county of Elbert), *The Circuit Rider's Wife* was as far from that reality of some twenty-three years earlier as the film version made forty years later was from the novel. In actuality, Corra White was only seventeen years old when she married Harris, her senior by over a decade, and moved only twenty-two miles from her hometown of Elberton to begin that ministry at three churches as assigned by the Methodists' North Georgia Conference. They served but a single, troubled year in that assignment before Lundy was offered a teaching position at Emory College in Atlanta, much to the relief of both husband and wife.[4]

Harris's novel extended both the time frame and the geographical base. She had William and Mary Thompson, their fictional counterparts, appointed to several circuits, including one or two in mountainous areas. Given that Lundy was dying after years of alcoholism and mental instability as Corra was writing it—he committed suicide later in 1910, after the book's publication—Harris's tone is far darker than anything suggested in the screen adaptation. More episodic and rambling than plot driven, her book focused on how hard those years were for the couple, both ill equipped for the arduous life of a circuit-riding ministry, and conveyed real bitterness at the Methodist establishment that provided them—and other itinerant pastors—with so little support and forced them to endure such financial hardship.[5]

Atlanta native Lamar Trotti, one of Hollywood's most prolific screenwriters from the late 1930s through the early 1950s, had long been familiar with Harris's work and had attempted as early as 1945 to get underway a film project based on *The Circuit Rider's Wife*. (Harris herself had tried to sell her books to film producers in the 1910s and '20s but had abandoned such efforts well before her death in 1935.[6]) Trotti's adaptation, which ultimately went before the cameras in 1950, made significant revisions to Harris's novel. He minimized its angry tone, transferred William's spiritual doubts onto Mary, and made them far more fleeting incidents than the serious and sustained struggles with which he grappled in the novel. Trotti also shifted the story's time frame from the early 1880s, at the beginning of the Harris's marriage, to 1910, the year it ended

Women on a Mission 97

so tragically—though of course Lundy's suicide was never referred to, or even hinted at, in his screenplay, as it had been in the novel.

Equally as important a decision was to set the story entirely in the mountains, and within a single congregation and community, decisions that in turn forced a change in title—from *The Circuit Rider's Wife* (since the circuit riding was scuttled) to *I'd Climb the Highest Mountain*. Nearly all of the film was made on location in Habersham and White counties in North Georgia, using quaint locales from chapels and railroad stations to farmhouses, ponds, streams, red clay roads, and vast cornfields in and around Helen, Demorest, Clarkesville, and Tallulah Falls. All of the extras were played by local residents, as were several minor character roles. Trotti assured them that "the picture would poke no *Tobacco Road* fun at them" and joked that "we'll hang the first Yankee actor who tries to fake a southern accent." That commitment to accuracy and the respect shown to the local community paid off in immense good will throughout the state and an enthusiastic reception for the film when it premiered in Georgia a year later.[7]

While the mountain setting, photographed in vivid Technicolor, quickly became—and remains—one of the film's chief assets, the local people to whom the Thompsons minister are anything but backwoods hillbillies. Trotti, who served as producer as well as screenwriter, hired Hollywood veteran Henry King to direct the film, and he too saw this as far more a story of rural America than of Appalachia, a term never mentioned in the film. "It was a film about people who had never been seen in motion pictures," King later recalled in explaining its appeal to him. "I thought it was a story worth telling, a story of America, real Americana."[8] Surprisingly, the spiritual dimension of their story was fully preserved on screen, with much discussion of faith, belief, and spirit, and quite a few scenes set in church.[9]

It was, as were most Hollywood productions of that era, a star-driven vehicle. When the original female lead, Jeanne Crain, had to drop out due to a pregnancy, an even bigger star, Susan Hayward, stepped into the role. (Her husband, William, was played by a mere B actor, William Lundigan, whose casting was said to have irritated Hayward.) Though "wife" came out of the film's title, it remained very much the film's central theme, opening on the day of Mary's wedding to William and covering their first three years of married life, as they bond with each other while dealing with the various challenges and occasional crises of the mountain community they serve. In the opening lines of a voice-over narration by Hayward, she articulates these dual themes: "It was like stepping through a doorway into a new world; a world I'd never seen before, a world I never knew existed." She continued: "My family and friends had warned me. I was a city girl, they'd said; I had no idea what it would be like living in the hills among strangers who knew nothing of the things I'd been brought up with." Then comes the kicker: "But they'd overlooked the one thing that made all the difference in the world—the fact that I love William and that nothing, no power on earth, was going to keep me from his side." Unlike the two other films to be discussed here, Mary Thompson sees herself first as a wife first and a mission worker (or even minister's partner) second, which makes the film as much a story of newlyweds adjusting to each other as it is of outsiders adjusting to mountain society. In short, Mary came to the mountains with no agenda, no sense of mission or service; she was there merely because that was where her new husband was assigned.

From the church services to various social activities—pot-luck suppers, shopping at the general store, a church picnic with baseball game, sack race, and a sing-along—there's little in the film that suggests anything distinctively Appalachian, which in effect means that Mary is simply a city girl having to adjust to rural life. Local speech patterns contain no hint of mountain dialects, nor is the music in the film distinctively regional—songs range from "In the Good Old Summertime" to mainstream hymns like "When the Saints Go Marching In" and "How Firm a Foundation." We see nary a farmer, tenant, moonshiner, or feuding family here. Nearly all of the highlanders with whom the Thompsons interact are professionals or businessmen—a doctor, a merchant who also serves as the church's influential lay leader, and a snobbish woman of wealth who summers at a nearby lake and rides in a chauffeur-driven Model T.

Like the novel, the film consists of loosely woven incidents, some humorous and others more serious. The Thompsons encourage a courtship between a dapper young rogue and the daughter of the merchant who disapproves of this ne'r-do-well but good-hearted suitor. (He threatens to separate the couple by sending his daughter off to Wesleyan College

Women on a Mission 99

in Macon, an option not open to many mountaineers.) When an unspecified "epidemic" breaks out, both William and Mary pitch in and help the local doctor by turning their church into a hospital. While the epidemic seems to subside once William prays hard enough, such relief comes only after Mary has had to watch several of their new congregants die, which leads to her first crisis of faith. She declares to Lundy: "I'm going home. I'm not fitted for this sort of life; I had no business coming here in the first place. It's ugly and awful and a lie." William forces her to stay, reminding her, "You wanted to come here; you accepted this life of your own free will." Quickly sobered and duly penitent, Mary states in a voice-over: "In spite of my weakness, I survived my first crisis. In a way, I'd grown up. I'd become, in fact, my husband's wife."

Further tragedy strikes shortly thereafter. When they take the children of a resistant atheist to the church picnic, a first sign of progress in winning over his godless family, the oldest son accidentally drowns. That, along with Mary's loss of a premature baby, her first, throws her into a deep depression, which she describes in a voice-over: "Of the months that follow, I had little recollection, for I was like one dead myself." And then she reveals the source of her greatest remorse. "In the selfishness of my grief," she proclaims, "I'd begun to commit the greatest sin a woman can commit against her husband: I ceased to care how I looked—I let myself go." As laughable as that statement sounds to us now (and as hard as it was to imagine Susan Hayward ever looking bad—only a plain gray dress suggests she has lost her looks), she is rudely awakened to the problem only when a Mrs. Billywith, who summers on a lake nearby, shows up at church one Sunday in all her finery, and immediately sets her sights on William, insisting that he counsel her on certain Old Testament passages that she can't quite understand. Sensing more feminine wiles than theological concerns, Mary tells her off in one of the film's best-written scenes, and one of the few moments in which we see real spunk—and humor—in Hayward's character. Once the sputtering temptress makes her exit, Mary heads for the general store, buys some flowery pink cloth, and makes a dress that indicates her grief is over, her good looks restored, and her husband all her own. (It is noteworthy that it took an affluent outsider, rather than a local mountain woman, to pose any threat, however remote, to Preacher Thompson's fidelity.)

Mary mounts a campaign to provide Christmas gifts to the needier children "in the hills" and rallies all of the women in the community to help. In depositing toys on the porch of the atheist household, the obstinate father seems to appreciate the joy they bring the children (even if it's his wife who points out to him how happy they are), thus leading to a curious sort of religious conversion brought on by Santa Claus. There's a certain irony in Trotti's inclusion of this scene, given Harris's reference in *The Circuit Rider's Wife* to the fact that the Thompsons themselves were actually the recipients of—and dependent on—such Christmas generosity to supplement the meager income during their year on the circuit.

The film concludes with the Thompsons' departure from the mountains after three years to take up a new appointment in Atlanta. The full community gathers to bid them farewell, and the camera pans over those particular residents whose lives they most seem to have impacted—the once star-crossed lovers who William ultimately married and the merchant whose approval the Thompsons coaxed out of him; the father who told them he'd at least take a more open mind when it came to his children's religious education; and a brief moment that Mary and William spend at the grave of their dead baby. There she tells him that she's learned to love it there and "come to understand that I was jealous of your God, your work, and you." She concludes by embracing him and quoting Ruth: "They people shall be my people; thy God my God; and whither thou goest, I shall go." After assuring his congregation that "part of our hearts remain here in the red clay of your hills," they drive off on the same red clay road by which they'd first arrived in the film's opening, with the swelling strains of a full choir singing "The Lord's Prayer," and the camera rises to pan a white cloud-covered sky.

CHRISTY

In December 1909, Leonora Whitaker, nineteen years old and thus two years older than Corra Harris when she began her mountain mission work, left her family in Asheville, North Carolina, and took a six-hour train trip just across the state line into Tennessee, where she got off at Del Rio, a few miles east of Newport on the French Broad River. Arriving just after a major snowstorm, it was another day before she found someone, the local postman, to escort her on foot seven more miles over the mountain to a remote cove called Morgan Gap, where she was to take on the sole teaching position at the newly established Ebenezer Mission School. That incident, as related by Leonora to her daughter, Catherine Marshall, makes up the opening pages of the latter's novel, *Christy,* and the opening scene of its television dramatization in 1994.[10]

In a prologue to her novel, Marshall explained that the impetus for the novel was a 1958 visit with her mother to Del Rio and Ebenezer, where the latter reminisced about the two pivotal years she spent there a half century earlier. By the time she left at the end of 1911, she was Mrs. John Wood, having married Catherine's father, a young minister serving the same community. According to Marshall, Leonora stated that "the story aches to be told, Catherine . . . but I'm not the one to put it on paper. You know, sometimes the dreams of the parents must be fulfilled in the children." Marshall took the hint and realized that, while the story could only be told through her mother's eyes, it would have to be adapted into fictional form. Extensive interviews with her mother provided the basis for what ultimately became her "imagined story" of Leonora Whitaker (renamed Christy Huddleston) and her first year at Ebenezer (renamed Cutter Gap); the result was a nearly five hundred–page novel, published as *Christy* in 1967.[11] It spent ten months on the *New York Times* best-seller list and joined her biography of her late husband, *A Man Called Peter* (1951), the renowned evangelist and chaplain of the US Senate, as the most successful of her multiple books.[12]

Like Leonora, Christy was part of an affluent Presbyterian family in Asheville. In nearby Montreat, where they spent a month every summer, Leonora heard Dr. Edward O. Guerrant speak about the newest of more than fifty mission schools he had established for poor mountain children in Kentucky and Tennessee since 1897.[13] Again, like her real-life counterpart, Christy volunteered her services as a teacher on the spot, and within a year, despite parental reservations, she arrived at Ebenezer, a mere nineteen years old, with a year and a half of college education from Flora McDonald College in eastern North Carolina.

Given the book's popularity, it is hard to understand why it took so long to adapt it to film. MGM studios purchased the film rights to it from Marshall in the late 1960s but let it languish until its option expired in 1986. At that point, producer Ken Wales bought the rights and approached CBS about turning it into a TV series, selling it as a wholesome family drama that could replicate the appeal of earlier series such as *The Waltons, Little House on the Prairie,* and *Dr. Quinn, Medicine Woman.* The network gave Wales the go-ahead to develop a twenty-episode series, which he did over the next few years. By 1993 CBS was ready to move into production and selected Townsend, Tennessee, on the edge of the Great Smoky Mountain National Park, as the site where it would be filmed. (Del Rio was considered too remote to bring a film crew there.)[14]

The series aired in 1994 and 1995, with the two-hour pilot debuting on Easter Sunday to huge ratings for CBS. Although the network chose not to extend the series beyond its original run, it was soon picked up by the Family Network, which aired it all again over the next few months. The series was much lauded by evangelical Christian organizations like the Christian Television and Film Commission and the National Religious Broadcasters, and it quickly acquired a cult following that led to multiple websites, online fan clubs, and rebroadcasts of the series on Christian networks, along with newly produced special holiday movies. In 2001 a new miniseries, called *Christy: Return to Cutter Gap*, was produced on the PAX network, at least in part the result of an aggressive online campaign by fans of the original series who wanted to see more. Since 1997 an annual gathering of fans, known as Christyfest, has been held in either Del Rio or Townsend.[15]

The pilot, which will be the focus here, opens with the train ride and grueling hike over to Cutter Gap by Christy (played by eighteen-year-old Kellie Martin), where she is quickly thrust into the drama of highland life. Her postman-escort warns her "to either warn your neighbors of your presence or take a chance of being greeted with the barrel of a rifle," an ominous introduction to the world she is about to enter. While visiting the first family along the postman's route, a man with a serious head wound, Tom Allen, is brought to their door, followed shortly by an imposing doctor on horseback, McNeill, with a Scottish brogue, who insists on operating immediately. As the distraught wife of the then comatose man arrives and debates with the doctor whether or not surgery is necessary, certain themes of mountain life are introduced—from superstitions (Mrs. Allen swings an ax into the floor to cut her husband's pain) and religious fatalism ("it's in God's hands") to distrust of outsiders

Women on a Mission 103

and their modern ways—all of which Christy will find herself combating in other circumstances over the coming months. There's also the first reference to a family feud in the community—with one onlooker suggesting that the patient may not have been the victim of a mere accident, given the Allens' long-standing antipathy toward the Taylors.

Christy is quickly taken under the wing of Alice Henderson, a middle-aged Quaker missionary from Pennsylvania, who is in charge of the Cutter Gap school and serves as the young teacher's mentor and sounding board. Although there seems to be no mention of a historical counterpart to Miss Alice, as she's called (Leonora Wood never mentions any such female supervisor or mentor in her factual account of her years at Ebenezer), she represents a mainstay of the mission school movement in the southern highlands at the time—the many strong, take-charge women who headed up several of the Guerrant schools and others in Kentucky, North Carolina, and elsewhere in the highlands in the early twentieth century.[16] Miss Alice is one of the novel's most compelling characters, and as embodied by Tyne Daly (who won an Emmy for the role), is fully as commanding a presence in the film. Yet her function is a rather enigmatic one, in that she seems to float above the actual operation of the school, offering little tangible relief in the classroom, despite how overburdened and in need of help Christy seems to be.

An equally pivotal character is the young minister, David Grantland, modeled on Marshall's father, John Wood. While physically attractive, as Christy notes early on, he remains a rather aloof and humorless with almost everyone in the community, except Christy, to whom he's obviously attracted. Grantland (played by Randall Batinkoff) seems to relish his role as her mentor and guide into this strange new culture, but far more than his more nuanced characterization in Marshall's book, he appears in the film to have little sympathy for the highlanders he is ministering to. His judgmental and rigid approach to reforming their ways and saving their souls wins him few friends (certainly far fewer than does Christy's far more sympathetic and empathetic approach to the same constituency), and makes him a far less appealing character in the pilot, though he softens up some in certain episodes that follow.

It is Christy's role as teacher and her trial-and-error approach to the challenges of relating to her mountain pupils that forms the core of the pilot's plot, as it does of Marshall's novel. Christy faces a large class of eager pupils in a still partially built, single-room schoolhouse, who range in age from five to grown boys her own age. Here she appears both naive and inept, as she attempts to bring order to the class, while distracted by the smell—and sound—of hogs rooting under the floorboards and a pet raccoon one young student keeps in his desk. The children are too cute by half, with one, full of self-assurance, proclaiming, "Teacher, I've come to see you and swap howdies," and others making equally disarming comments reflecting the quaintness of mountain speech but also the other-worldliness of this society for Christy and for the viewer.

In this scene and others early in the film, Christy comes off as far more innocent and inexperienced than does the Mary Thompson character in *I'd Climb the Highest Mountain.* In part this is because Susan Hayward was in her mid-thirties and Kellie Martin was only eighteen when they made their respective films, and because Hayward, one of big screen's more forceful personalities, could only go so far in acting demure and innocent. One of the strengths of *Christy* on film along with later episodes in the series is the dramatic arc that traces her growing self-confidence and maturity as she continues to wear down local opposition to both the school and to the outsiders seeking to change their mountain ways. Almost all of this resistance comes from adult males, and it is clear throughout that this is a far more patriarchal than matriarchal society.

While some of the mountain women seem willing to stand up for their children's welfare, the film never flinches from the reality that wives and daughters were often intimidated and even abused by husbands and fathers, and that they were cowed by men in general, a truth that Christy finds as troubling as the dire poverty she sees wherever she looks. Both are problems she feels powerless to address in any meaningful way. She visits the home of one of her youngest students, named Mountie, who seems to be mute, to ask the parents about her problem and what can be done about it. Only Mountie's mother is at home, and she seems not only fatalistic about her daughter's speech defect ("I reckon if the Lord wants Mountie to talk, she will"), but also deferential to her husband on the matter of seeking some sort of treatment or counseling ("My man wouldn't like it—he don't believe in fussing over no girls").

Women on a Mission 105

Moonshine soon comes into play, as bottles of liquor are discovered hidden under the school, and the rather self-righteous young Reverend Grantland and Christie herself stand bound and determined to turn over to authorities Birds-eye Taylor, the head of that clan and "the most likely culprit . . . a notorious moonshiner who had nothing but contempt for our mission," according to Christie's voice-over. This sets off what is by Hollywood standards a rather enlightened debate on the subject, as Dr. MacNeill lectures the young preacher and teacher on their high-minded moralism and offers a spirited defense of why corn liquor is in effect their only "cash crop" and, as such, an economic necessity for the people of the cove. "These people *still* scratch out a bare living," he tells them, and selling liquor is their only source of money in this cash-poor economy. Grantland insists that "it's still the Devil's work" and is the cause of many quarrels and killings, but MacNeill insists, "I'm warning you, they don't see it that way." It's hard to think of another film that addresses those issues so fully and robustly and in much the same terms that mission workers would have faced them around the turn of the century. Marshall's novel is the source of scenes such as this, but it's to the credit of the screenwriter, Patricia Green, that so much of this ambivalence is preserved in the teleplay.[17]

Like *I'd Climb the Highest Mountain*, Christy's story as dramatized for television did not shy away from a strong spiritual context. On several occasions she (like Mary Thompson) experiences moments of self-doubt and crises of faith the first time after her visit to Mountie's home, where she first witnessed the extreme poverty and the mother's reluctance to buck her callous husband and seek help for her daughter. She is discouraged enough to declare to Miss Alice that she doesn't belong there and should return home. Alice (in Tyne Daly's finest moment in the film) lectures her on the inner light that's so central to Quaker faith and service and tells Christy that "that light will only come when you open your eyes to the pain and grief around you." She challenges Christy, now fully exposed to the harsh realities of mountain life, to decide: "Were you meant to come here and serve and work or were you only running away from home?" Christy later prays about her motives and tells God that yes, she may first have come for fun and adventure, "but I think you had something different in mind. You can use me in this cove. Well, God, here I am." (It's no wonder that the Christian media has embraced the film and the series as ardently as they have for so long.)

To the film's credit, as with the book, the problems endemic to this highland society and the attitudes of those perpetuating them are never solved by Christy or her coworkers, and there are few, if any, individual conversions or repentances that allow for a feel-good conclusion to either the film or the series that followed. What little impact these benevolent workers have is modest, and achieved only incrementally, while the major issues of poverty, moonshine, and feuding remain as daunting as ever by film's end.

The climax comes when the Taylors set fire to the school, leading Christy to decide that she's made no headway on that front. Miss Alice urges her to forgive them, if they are indeed the culprits. Christy finds it harder to forgive herself, and she concludes to herself that the "fire is a sign that I've done more harm than good here." She decides to leave, to slip away without notice to anyone, but in stopping by the school for one final look, she is overwhelmed by memories of the children. When Mountie arrives, quite conveniently, and speaks her first word, Christy of course changes her mind. The film ends with all the children gathered around her, as Mountie recites the alphabet to her beaming teacher and Miss Alice arrives at the front steps, witnesses the warm scene inside, and proclaims: "Christy Huddleston, I think thee will do."

SONGCATCHER

Six years after *Christy* had its television debut, a feature film, *Songcatcher*, appeared in theaters. Certainly the most ambitious and sophisticated screen treatment of "culture brokers" in Southern Appalachia, this independently produced film, written and directed by Maggie Greenwald, suggested more complex dynamics in play in terms of how outsiders interacted with insiders and the impact of that interaction on both. Filmed almost entirely in Madison County, North Carolina, just north of Asheville, Greenwald's story is loosely based on Olive Dame Campbell's experience in discovering and collecting Old English ballads in the North Carolina mountains, a venture that began with her first trip through the region with her husband, John C. Campbell, in 1907.[18]

Greenwald stated in an interview that her initial interest in the subject was the origins of country music and the much earlier mountain ballads and folk music from which it evolved. She and her husband,

Women on a Mission 107

David Manse, a musician and her collaborator on the film, put the music front and center and went to great pains to recruit local and regional performers as consultants in both selecting songs and accurately performing them.[19] Greenwald was also intrigued that it was primarily women, as teachers and missionaries moving into the southern mountains, who first discovered and initiated efforts at collecting and preserving that music. "They soon came to the realization," she said, "that these were not backward, ignorant people, but people with an incredible culture, rooted in the music." Thus, along with their agenda of recreating the music and the culture it reflected, Greenwald was equally intent on using a largely feminist framework through which to relate its discovery and preservation. (It is telling that of the story's eight principal characters, six of them are female.)[20]

Greenwald candidly acknowledges that Olive Dame Campbell served as the basis for Lily Penlaric, though reviews and commentary by several Appalachian scholars suggests that traces of a variety of other historic figures are also evident in the character, from writers and teachers to academics and musicologists.[21] She sets the film in 1907 because that was the year of Campbell's first venture into the southern highlands, and the year in which she first heard a mountain version of the British ballad "Barbara Allen," a song that until then she knew only as an English ballad, sung to her by a student at the Hindeman Settlement School in Kentucky.

Olive Dame Campbell was not a professor or a musicologist as Lily Penlaric is; nor was she single. She was a Massachusetts native who moved south with her new husband (his second marriage), educator and minister John C. Campbell, in 1907, as he undertook an extensive study of Appalachian society and culture by traveling through the region from Kentucky and Virginia through Tennessee, North Carolina, and Georgia. After discovering this regional version of English, Scottish, and Scots-Irish ballads and folk songs, Olive began collecting and documenting this music, meticulously copying words and transcribing the tunes on a piano. Her cinematic counterpart writes in a letter to a colleague: "What a remarkable discovery this is. The songs are virtually intact, according to the oldest known versions, with wonderfully idiosyncratic local changes in a lyric or phrase here and there." From 1907 to 1915 Campbell collected over seventy ballads. In the latter year, she met the eminent British authority on folk songs and dance, Cecil Sharp, in Boston, shared her findings with him, and in 1917 they published jointly a selection of those songs (thirty-nine) in a seminal volume entitled *English Folk Songs from the Southern Appalachians*.[22]

Greenwald uses much of this scenario in the film she wrote and includes a character named Cyrus Whittle, based on Sharp, who is referred to early in the film as a potential academic rival but appears as a character only in the movie's final scene. Penlaric (Janet McTeer) is lured to the North Carolina mountains after being denied full professorship at an unnamed New England college, not by a husband, but by her younger sister. Elna Penlaric is one of two teachers who run the Clover Settlement School, which seems to be for girls, though we never see any students or classes in session. A teenage girl, Deladis (Emmy Rossum), lives with the two and sings "Barbara Allen" to their northern guest on her first night there. As was the case with Campbell, this performance sets Lily onto the realization that the Appalachians are a repository of early British folk music, and she's quick to begin an intense effort at collecting and recording as many such songs as she can. *Songcatcher* benefits from a much more tightly woven plot than do either of the earlier films discussed, as Lily confronts, befriends, and alienates a number of local residents, who react in a variety of ways to her "meddlin,'" especially her attempts to exploit or capitalize on their culture. She is stiff, uptight, and uncomfortable upon her arrival in the Blue Ridge, and somewhat condescending, even dismissive, toward the first residents she encounters. It is only with her discovery of their rich musical heritage that her attitude begins to change as she comes to appreciate and to advocate for them (especially women) and their way of life.

The issues of "cultural brokering" are explored far more astutely here than in either of the other two films. This is especially evident in a pivotal exchange between Lily and a skeptical Tom Bledsoe (Aidan Quinn) that suggests the stakes at play. His granny Viney Butler (wonderfully played by Pat Carroll) has been won over by Lily and agreed to let her record her singing. Lily insists that she can use their music to win public sentiment and to show the world that mountain people are not all "dirty, ignorant savages." Tom responds that "the only way to preserve our way of life is to keep your way of life away from us." She challenges an unscrupulous

Women on a Mission 109

agent of a coal mining company trying to buy up local farmland. (This is of course one of Greenwald's most egregious factual flaws, given that there is no coal in the North Carolina mountains.) The agent, Earl Giddens, who's from the area, suggests the self-awareness of at least some highlanders in terms of how they're perceived by outsiders. When Viney Butler threatens to shoot him if he doesn't get out of her yard, he tells her: "Viney, that kind of talk gives city folk a terrible impression of us hillbillies." He tells her how much better off she'd be by spending her latter years in a town, where, he says, "you might even learn to read and write," to which she replies: "I was born on this mountain and I'm going to die on it . . . and so are you." Then, "Get goin', Giddens!," she yells as she cocks her rifle, and he scurries off.

One of *Songcatcher*'s more remarkable scenes comes midway through, when the coal company's owner and his refined and vastly overdressed society wife attend a tea party given by the two schoolteachers. In something of a tour de force, Greenwald uses them and the presence of a Baptist preacher who's also one of the guests to address, if only fleetingly, a variety of issues regarding the role of educators and "culture brokers" in the region. Just three lines of dialogue in this extended scene suggest the range of attitudes and approaches to the education of mountain people by outsiders. The wife of the coal owner states, with utter naiveté: "I endorse the English idea; we must educate by example. If we teach these ruffians to serve tea properly, they will want refinement and will seek it out." Elna stifles her disdain at such a premise and says simply: "I believe we must ask the mountain people what they want and what they need," to which the mine owner himself retorts: "Educating these savages is a waste of money. If you want to help these children, you should get them out of their hovels and put them to work." Given the mere lip service these issues receive, it's easy to write off such scenes as attempts to cram far too much into what's already a very issue-oriented narrative. On the other hand, no other film before (or since) has made any effort even to acknowledge these conflicting ideas, much less dramatize them even in the deft but fleeting way Greenwald does here.

The film moves too rapidly through a series of rather unlikely climaxes, as the teachers—who are lesbian lovers—are spied in an affectionate embrace by a young man, Deladis's beau. He is repulsed, and he recruits a handful of his cronies to burn down their house and the school, which destroys Lily's discs of the songs she'd worked so hard to record. Even more implausibly, a woman storms into the local church during a Sunday service and guns down her lover, a man who Lily had persuaded to return to his wife and many children. This too comes across as gratuitous, as if any Appalachian-based story must include at least one such murderous vendetta.

The movie's conclusion also fails to ring true. With much of her work destroyed, Lily declines her sister's proposition that she stay and help her rebuild the school. Instead, having fallen in love with Tom Bledsoe, the two of them, along with Deladis, decide to move to an unnamed big city and make a new start recording and marketing mountain music, another anachronism, given that there was no viable recording industry for another decade at least. As they move down a steep mountain road toward their new life, they just happen to run into, of all people, Cyrus Whittle (based on Cecil Sharp), who is coming up the mountain to seek her out. After a brief exchange, she passes along all of her surviving notations and passes the torch, so to speak, to him. He promises that any publication that comes out of his work will appear under both of their names. As the threesome continues down the road, the final credits roll over a third version of "Barbara Allen," this one a contemporary, upbeat rendition sung by Emmylou Harris.

For all of its historical inaccuracies, overstuffed plot points, many of which are left unresolved at film's end, and the issues it embraces, often with only fleeting lip service, *Songcatcher* is nevertheless (in my opinion) the most serious and sophisticated treatment of Appalachia ever captured in a feature film. To her considerable credit, Maggie Greenwald is unusually attuned to the many implications of the region's discovery by the outside world and realizes that there were no easy answers in terms of the problems that such exposure brought, nor easy judgments as to the good or ill done by those with even the best of intentions in terms of what they thought they were doing for the highlanders in whose midst they put themselves.

THESE FILMS' three protagonists came to the mountains under different circumstances. It is curious that two of the three did not travel

Women on a Mission 111

far from home to the mountain missions they served—Corra Harris/ Mary Thompson moves only a few counties away in Georgia; Leonora Whitaker/ Christy Huddleston merely crosses the state line from highland North Carolina to highland Tennessee—and yet their respective films depict them as being exposed to a society and culture as foreign to them as it was to New Englander Lily Penlaric. However exaggerated this clash of cultures may seem as laid out in both fiction and film, those interactions and negotiations made across cultural boundaries provide much of the thematic thrust and dramatic conflict so crucial to both genres. Yet this too has a basis in fact; like Harris and Whitaker, many of the region's benevolent workers—Mary Martin Sloop, Martha Berry, May Stone, and Katherine Pettit, for example—all came into the highlands from other parts of their own states and approached the people and problems they found there in much the same way as those who traveled much farther to do so.

Each of the three leads is meant to be a sympathetic character, though in the case of Penlaric, she is decidedly less so at the beginning and becomes appealing only as her attitude and behavior improves over the course of the story. The basis for that improvement is quite simply her growing appreciation for the highland people and their culture. Lily asks her sister upon arrival if she really feels safe among "these savages" and then is interested only in their music; when her sister asks her what she thinks of their school, she has nothing to say. Only gradually does she come to appreciate them as individuals and their culture as a whole, and by the film's end, she treats them with genuine affection and respect. So to a lesser degree do Mary Thompson and Christy Huddleston, though they seem to enter the region with fewer preconceived ideas or animosity toward mountain people, so that the dramatic arcs in their stories have more to do with their overcoming their own insecurities and self-doubts, as we watch them maturing, growing, and ultimately emerging as giving, self-assured women.

It is their good will, affection, respect, and advocacy for their congregants, students, or research subjects that makes these women so appealing and ultimately admirable characters for us as viewers, which in turn suggests that the filmmakers expect us to see mountain people in the same light, which we do. In *I'd Climb the Highest Mountain*, they are good-hearted country people more reflective of wholesome Americana than of Appalachia, given that anything suggesting regional otherness has been carefully removed. *Christy* seriously portrays the problems that plague the region, while still giving most of the mountain characters some sense of dignity and certainly sympathy (in part by keeping children front and center). *Songcatcher* does much the same but adds to that a sense of savvy self-awareness and pride on the part of highlanders who refuse to let themselves become mere pawns for those coming in to "uplift" them. (Not coincidentally, it is almost exclusively mountain men who Hollywood scriptwriters see in real need of reform, and each film provides one or two menacing figures—a feuder, a moonshiner, or even a two-timing husband or beau—to make the point.)

Finally, it is easy to trace an increasingly feminist approach in these films in their treatment of both the benevolent workers and the mountain residents they come to serve. It is not surprising that in a 1951 film based on a 1910 novel, the film's protagonist is first and foremost a helpmate to her husband, and that pleasing him becomes as much a goal as serving the Appalachian Georgians he's brought her with him to do. Local women are very much in evidence throughout, but not one of them emerges as a formidable force or memorable character in the film.

In our 1994 film, drawing largely on the emerging feminist sensibilities of the late 1960s novel on which it is based, Christy is not only single, she's a mere nineteen years old. She has a strong sense of purpose—if less so of self—and is mentored by a very wise, independent, and forceful woman who can handle a rifle as well as any man who challenges her. Among the Tennesseans to whom they reach out are several key female characters who are far from liberated in terms of the deference they give—and occasional abuse they suffer—in this decidedly patriarchal and chauvinistic society. Although Christy is courted by two eligible young men in the book and the film, she is still single when the film, and even the series, ends, although her real-life counterpart left as a bride.

Finally, our one film created by a woman and unveiled at the turn of the twenty-first century presents us with three willful, independent career women, two of them in a lesbian relationship, the third almost defiantly single as she struggles in the still very masculine world of academic research. They interact with a range of mountain women and

Women on a Mission 113

girls, coming to the defense of those oppressed or wronged, and cheering on those with minds and wills of their own, from an elderly granny to their own adolescent protégée. For the most part, these women are portrayed as willful and self-assured enough to stand up to the men misbehaving around them. In perhaps the scene that most strains credibility, a spurned lover shoots the man who'd deserted her. (It suggests, one supposes, that mountain women could also have violent tempers, and that mountain men could be redeemed—the man shot had just returned to his wife and children—though in this case, at a high cost.)

The last word should go to Cratis Williams, who in his seminal 1961 dissertation, "The Southern Mountaineer in Fact and Fiction," became one of the first scholars to write on the clash between southern mountaineers and these "benevolent workers." "'Missionaries' dedicated their efforts to the salvation of [the mountaineer's] soul," Williams wrote, "and to changing his social behavior patterns and his standard of living to preconceived patterns and standards that were often unlike anything that had ever been on land or sea but that helped to 'lift' him from the stagnation of the eighteenth century into the standardization of the twentieth."[23]

While that was indeed the intent of many of those mission workers, in these films that description could only be applied to *Christy*. There is very little going on in either *I'd Climb the Highest Mountain* or *Songcatcher* that suggests Hollywood had succumbed to that particular formula in its depiction of the mountain people with whom either Mary Thompson or Lily Penlaric find themselves interacting. If the first minimizes the cultural differences of north Georgians, thus suggesting there's little need for "uplift," the latter embraces and even romanticizes that mountain culture as one to be valued and preserved. In both, indeed in all three, Appalachians are, for the most part, treated with dignity and respect, though it is the women—both outsiders and insiders—who come off far better than their male counterparts.

NOTES

1. David E. Whisnant, *All That Is Native and Fine: The Politics of Culture in an American Region* (Chapel Hill: University of North Carolina Press, 1983), xiii.

2. The term "benevolent worker" seems to stem from Henry D. Shapiro, *Appalachia on Our Mind: The Southern Mountains and Mountaineers in the Southern Consciousness, 1870–1920* (Chapel Hill: University of North Carolina Press, 1978),

see esp. chaps. 2 and 6. The scholarship on these women, both as individuals and as a group, has been extensive since. For a recent sample, see several articles in a special issue of *Appalachian Journal* (37, nos. 3 and 4 [Spring-Summer 2010]), which focuses on women in and of Appalachia.

3. John M. Talmadge, *Corra Harris, Lady of Purpose* (Athens: University of Georgia Press, 1968), 10.

4. Biographies of Harris include Talmadge's *Corra Harris* and Catherine Oglesby, *Corra Harris and the Divided Mind of the New South* (Gainesville: University of Florida Press, 2008); and several essays, most notably Donald Mathews, "Corra Harris: The Storyteller as Folk Preacher," in *Georgia Women*, vol. 1: *Their Life and Times*, ed. Ann Short Chirhart and Betty Wood (Athens: University of Georgia Press, 2009), 341–69.

5. Oglesby, *Corra Harris and Divided Mind*, 29–31, 115–16; Talmadge, *Corra Harris*, 10–11, 46–47.

6. Talmadge, *Corra Harris*, 143. On Trotti, see Kay Beck, "Lamar Trotti," in *The New Georgia Encyclopedia*, www.georgiaencyclopedia.org, last accessed June 4, 2011.

7. Talmadge, *Corra Harris*, 14–15.

8. Frank Thompson, ed., *Henry King, Director: From Silents to 'Scope* (Los Angeles: Directors Guild of America Publication, 1995), 157. The book is a compilation of interviews with King, who directed over a hundred films between 1919 and 1962.

9. Ibid., 158.

10. Marshall's nonfiction account of her mother's experience appears in Catherine Marshall, *Dearest Mother, Dearest Friend: Godly Inspiration from the Journals and Letters of Catherine Marshall* (Nashville: J. Countryman, 2002), 15–16.

11. Catherine Marshall, *Christy* (New York: McGraw Hill, 1967), "Prologue," 1–7; quotes from pp. 5–6, 7. Oddly, Marshall uses the fictional names for places and people used in the novel in this otherwise factual prologue.

12. Catherine Marshall, *A Man Called Peter: The Story of Peter Marshall* (New York: McGraw-Hill, 1951). She ultimately wrote more than twenty works of fiction and nonfiction. *A Man Called Peter* was made into a film in 1955, starring Jean Peters as Catherine and Richard Todd as Peter.

13. Marshall, *Dearest Mother, Dearest Friend*, 15–16. On Guerrant and his schools, see Mark Huddle, "Home Missions Revisited: Edward O. Guerrant and the 'Discovery' of Appalachia," an introduction to a recent edition of Guerrant's *The Galax Gatherers: The Gospel among the Highlanders* (Knoxville: University of Tennessee Press, 2005), xi–xl; and J. Gray McAllister and Grace Owings Guerrant, *Edward O. Guerrant: Apostle to the Southern Highlanders* (Richmond: Richmond Press, 1950).

On a personal note, my maternal grandmother also heard Guerrant speak in Montreat several years after Leonora Whitaker did and was likewise inspired to become a teacher at two of his schools in Kentucky. For a description of her experience, see John C. Inscoe, "Memories of a Presbyterian Mission Worker in the Kentucky Mountains, 1918–1921: An Interview with Rubie Ray Cunningham," *Appalachian Journal* 15, no. 2 (Winter 1988): 144–60.

Women on a Mission 115

14. There are multiple websites devoted to both the book and the various TV versions of *Christy*, on which some of the following information is drawn. See also the entry on "Christy" in Rudy Abramson and Jean Haskell, eds., *Encyclopedia of Appalachia* (Knoxville: University of Tennessee Press, 2006), 1699–1700; and "The Filming of Christy," in Susan Sawyer, *It Happened in Tennessee* (Guilford, CT: Globe Pequot Press, 2002), 100–3.

15. This film is also known as *Christy: The Movie*. See "Resurrecting Christy," *Christian Teens Weekly* (April 2001), reproduced on the most comprehensive of several websites devoted to "Christy" in all of its various manifestations: www.tvshow_christytripod.com; last accessed May 11, 2011. See also www.christyfest.org; last accessed May 11, 2011.

16. These include women like Katherine Pettit, May Stone, Ethel DeLong Zande, Cora Wilson Stewart, all of whom founded or supervised schools in Kentucky; Mary Sloop and Lucy Morgan in North Carolina; and Martha Berry in Georgia.

17. While Green is given sole credit for writing the pilot, it is interesting to note that three of the four writers of the subsequent series were also women—Green, Dawn Prestwich, and Nicole Yorkin—who together were part of the writing team of such TV dramas as *L.A. Law, Chicago Hope, Pickett Fences,* and *Judging Amy.*

18. Elizabeth McCutchen Williams, ed., *Appalachian Travels: The Diary of Olive Dame Campbell* (Lexington: University Press of Kentucky, 2012), offers a vivid account of her first venture into the region.

19. Interviews and running commentary on the film by Maggie Greenwald and David Manse appear on the DVD of *Songcatcher* (Lionsgate, 2003). Both also noted that they used the original notations by Campbell and Cecil Sharp in their arrangements of the fourteen ballads performed in the film.

20. They are Lili Penlaric, two settlement house teachers—her sister Elna Penlaric and Harriet Tolliver—and three mountain women or girls—Viney Butler, Deladis Slocum, and Alice Kincaid. The only comparable male parts are those of Tom Bledsoe and Fate Honeycutt.

21. They include writer Emma Bell Miles, anthropologist Ellen Churchill Semple, teachers Katherine Pettit and Lucy Morgan, musicologist Dorothy Scarborough—the first to record this music, with a dictaphone, in 1930—and Maude Karples, Sharp's assistant. See review of *Songcatcher* by Betty Smith, *Appalachian Journal* 30, nos. 2 and 3 (Winter/Spring 2003): 248–53; and Arthur Krim, "Appalachian Songcatcher: Olive Dame Campbell and the Scotch-Irish Ballad," *Journal of Cultural Geography* 24, no. 1 (Fall/Winter 2006): 91–112.

22. It is surprising that no one has produced a full biography of either John or Olive Dame Campbell, despite the fact that their extensive papers are held by the Southern Historical Collection at UNC-Chapel Hill. Among the best treatments of her are Krim, "Appalachian Songcatcher"; Whisnant, *All That Is Native and Fine,* chap. 2; and Williams, *Appalachian Travels.* Greenwald quote from her commentary on the DVD of the film.

23. Cratis D. Williams, *The Southern Mountaineer in Fact and Fiction,* CD-ROM of *Appalachian Journal* edition (2011), 144.

CHAPTER FIVE

Embodying Appalachia

Progress, Pride, and Beauty Pageantry, 1930s to the Present

KAREN W. TICE

The westernized beauty-contest prototype of individuated competition has proven to be malleable, molded to fit an array of historical, regional, and cultural contexts. It has been modified continuously in response to shifting idealizations of gendered, racialized, and class-based beauty and respectability to promote a variety of agendas, including touting community solidarity and modernity, promoting tourism and trade, union recruitment, showcasing civic and cultural pride, and providing opportunities for assimilation, upward mobility, and self-advancement. Attaching abstract values to women's bodies, behaviors, and aspirations through beauty pageantry has been a popular strategy for many rural and ethnic communities, including Appalachia, in the United States and internationally, to showcase community norms, gendered distinction, cultural citizenship, and regional identities.[1]

Beauty pageants are about beauty, bodies, and idealized femininity, but also about political issues central to contestants, sponsors, and audiences. Beauty pageants represent a multitude of personal and political agendas and subject positions. Vast differences and contradictions in meaning and aesthetics exist within and among beauty pageants, their contestants, and sponsors. Robert Lavenda concludes that community queen pageants are "ideologically hybrid rather than totalizing and unified, susceptible of several different possible interpretations for outsiders, for organizers, and especially for participants."[2] Business and social elites of Appalachian communities, for example, have used beauty pageants and queen festivals to contain labor unrest and social divisions, to promote tourism and commerce, to market commodities such as coal, to showcase embodied excellence, and to herald their membership in cultural and global economies.

Not all pageants, however, are commercialized promotions of place, products, and hegemonic femininity. Some are designed to subvert gendered and racialized norms. The Ivanhoe Jubilee Festival in Appalachian Virginia, for example, is part of a grassroots community revitalization effort. One of its most popular events is a men's beauty pageant in which men cross-dress as women and compete for the title of Miss Jubilee. Women also cross-dress as men in a "hunk show."[3] Ivanhoe community activist S. Maxine Walker sees these performances as consciousness-raising events since

> so many of the men here have this attitude about the "little woman" and this little attitude about how they should be "made-up little dolls," and all the men go around. See, in Ivanhoe, it's kind of OK for a man to go out on a woman. But God help a woman who fools around. Or has an affair! So I think in a men's beauty pageant, it's a way for us to look at the "painted doll" attitude and it is kind of like to make a joke about it, but it's a political joke. And it's a change for the women to really see the way men feel about them, but it's also a way for the women to get back at men.[4]

Mary Ann Hinsdale, Helen M. Lewis, and Waller conclude that while male beauty pageants may not be the way to solve gendered problems in the region, they nonetheless provide a "mirror to see the distortions of everyday life."[5] Thus, beauty pageants are rich cultural sites for exploring the contradictory oscillations of race, class, region, gender, sexuality, commerce, community values, group affiliation, belonging, representation, and rerepresentation, as well as the display of normative and, even occasionally, transgressive selves and oppositional projects.

COAL, COMMERCIALIZATION, CULTURE, AND CAREERISM

Beauty pageants are most often designed to showcase hegemonic ideals of beauty, hyperfemininity, middle-class comportment, and aspiration. But sometimes they also serve as sites of struggle over representation, assimilation, exclusion, belonging, and racial and cultural identity.[6] Pageants have been justified by some contestants and promoters as vehicles for countering the simplistic stock images of Appalachian women and the region that are deeply embedded in popular culture and the national imaginary. Tales of a strange land and odd people lacerated by fierce feuds and lawlessness, lacking basic middle-class proprieties and civilized gendered relations have constituted the core of travel, fictional, and academic writing about Appalachia and mountain women in the late nineteenth and early twentieth centuries.[7] Exotic stock caricatures such as toothless, wizened grandmothers, feral and fertile young woman with large broods of barefoot children, and homespun, long-suffering, "stand by your man" women were part of this cultural imaginary. While many of these controlling images have persisted throughout the twentieth century, others have been reformulated and modernized. Popular images of Appalachian women as men-seeking, vacuous beauties (such as the buxom blonde Daisy Mae in Al Capp's long-standing (1934–77) cartoon strip *Li'l Abner;* Elly May Clampett and her gun-toting, pipe-smoking Granny on *The Beverly Hillbillies;* and Daisy Duke of the *Dukes of Hazzard)* coexist with images of mountain women as labor radicals and as activist daughters of coal miners *(Harlan County, U.S.A.* and *A Coal Miner's Daughter).* Network documentaries on Appalachia have often recycled historical images of the unfit Appalachian mother prevalent in the literature of the early twentieth century of settlement schools.[8] *20/20*'s 2009 special "A Hidden America: Children of the Mountains," for example, featured numerous poverty-stricken mountain mothers who have succumbed to drugs and their children to Mountain Dew.

Dolly Parton provides an alternative image of Appalachian womanhood that embodies the complexities and ambiguities that run throughout pageantry as well as celebrity. Buxom and blond, enterprising and glamorous, she has successfully managed to emphasize her sexuality, femininity, voluptuous body, and big hair, but also her Appalachian

Embodying Appalachia 119

roots, wholesome Christian values, and business savvy. Pamela Wilson has labeled Parton's bifurcated image—sexualized icon and wholesome role model—as a "mountain of contradictions."[9] In 2008 Parton finished her world tour to promote the release of her CD, *Backwoods Barbie*. Lines from her title song, "Backwoods Barbie," evoke the contradictions of beauty, wholesomeness, performance, and authenticity not only in her professional career but in the amateur world of beauty pageantry as well: "I am just a backwoods Barbie, too much makeup, too much hair. Don't be fooled by thinking the goods are not all there."

Such contradictions also characterize the ambitions and contortions of Appalachian beauty queens as they navigate the crosscurrents of glamour, tradition, modesty, community values, commercialization, careerism, and normative femininity in mountain pageants. Promoters and contestants alike often justify pageant participation as a strategy to subvert both essentialized notions of Appalachian women and attributions of regional backwardness and cultural deficiencies. Much as Christine Yano observed in her study of Japanese beauty contests, some Appalachian beauty pageants can be understood as spectacles of "emplacement," a process of "situating oneself within the larger mainstream community," yet trumpeting "particularities and a strong sense of 'place.'"[10] Contestants in mountain pageants often justify their participation as a way to celebrate regional heritage, cultural pride, local history, and familial roots.

Malana Piatt said that she participated in the 2003 Pennsylvania Bituminous Coal Queen competition because "it is our area—it is our heritage. If you are from this area you would understand what a powerful meaning it has."[11] Over the years, many contestants in this festival have had family members who worked as miners and justified their participation in the coal festival as honoring this labor history. Jessica Levo, a daughter of a coal miner, hoped that she would win the title of Bituminous Coal Queen so she could visit the underground mine where her father had worked. Amy Snodgrass, the 2007 winner of the Miss West Virginia Coal Festival in Madison, West Virginia, and granddaughter of a coal miner, said that "this pageant was about representing him. The coal festival is about everyone coming out to celebrate coal mining."[12] Pageant supporters in both states testify to the importance of coal for community cohesion. At the Pennsylvania Bituminous Coal Festival, elementary school age boys appear on the pageant stage wearing miner's helmets and lights, and testimonials are given by industry spokespersons about the glory of coal. Many former queens are invited back to the coal festivals to reunite with their mountain roots, and one who had moved to Philadelphia boasted that she was one of the few people in the city who knew the difference between kinds of coal.[13]

In addition to celebrating local history and heritage, coal contestants justify their pageant participation by trumpeting the self-advancement, personal empowerment, public recognition, celebrity, and career opportunities they receive through pageant experiences. They point to professional contacts, educational scholarships, and upward mobility, as well as the opportunities to enhance public speaking skills, self-confidence, and poise through beauty pageantry. West Virginia's coal queen Snodgrass, for example, asserted that "pageants are not a negative thing. I think there's a lot of positive that can come out of them. I've met new people, made new friends, improved my interview skills, and improved my self-confidence."[14]

During her reign, Ronni Kramer, the 2005 Pennsylvania Bituminous Coal Queen, dined at the home of the president of the Pennsylvania Coal Association, officiated at several parades, attended a coal miner banquet, spoke to the Pennsylvania legislature, and toured an underground coal mine—a ceremonial gesture that characterizes many beauty pageants in Appalachia. She planned to use her $1,500 pageant scholarship to attend West Virginia Junior College and major in executive office technology. Kaitlyn McCall Pieri, the 2006 Pennsylvania Bituminous Coal Queen, said simply that her year-long reign as coal queen had been "a transformation for me, just as a lump of coal transforms into a beautiful diamond."[15] Pageant sponsor William Groves, past president of the King Coal Association and longtime master of ceremonies at the festival, boasted that because of their confidence-building pageant experiences as coal queens, many winners are now successful attorneys, business managers, entertainers, and schoolteachers, and some have done well at other state beauty pageants.[16]

After leaving the runway, many Appalachian ex-beauty queens have continued to fashion careers out of their beauty pageant experiences.

Embodying Appalachia 121

Leigh Patton, for example, was a veteran of the pageant circuit in her home state of West Virginia. She had competed in numerous pageants, including the Miss West Virginia Scholarship pageant, Miss West Virginia USA pageant, Mrs. West Virginia pageant, and the Mrs. West Virginia United States pageant. Today, she works as state director of the West Virginia International Pageant.[17] Other Appalachian beauty contestants have forged careers as beauty pageant consultants, lifestyle and image coaches, and inspirational and motivational speakers. Some sell pageant regalia, including apparel, tiaras, and other pageant necessities.

A significant number of mountain beauty pageants have been designed by business councils and Chambers of Commerce to enhance their cultural status and commercial power by conjoining notions of commerce, community, and a heritage wedded to commodities such as coal. Throughout the twentieth century, numerous coal companies in Appalachia have made ample use of women's bodies to enhance their marketing campaigns. In 1952, for example, members of the King Coal Association and the Carmichaels, Pennsylvania, Chamber of Commerce attended the West Virginia Coal Festival and Beauty Pageant in Bluefield, West Virginia. In the following year, in the midst of massive layoffs at the mines due to mechanization, they established their own coal festival that featured a beauty contest for high school girls in order to "focus attention on this area as the hub of the soft coal region and hopefully spur the lagging industry."[18] They also touted the pageant as being good for community spirit, a "celebration of living culture, a way of life that is both part of our shared history and part of our daily lives."[19]

Fifty years later, this pageant was the subject of a celebratory documentary, *The Bituminous Coal Queens of Pennsylvania,* produced by Patricia Heaton (actress on the TV series *Everybody Loves Raymond*) and David Hunt in 2003. The documentary depicts the careers and homecoming of many former coal queens, including the narrator (Hollywood actress Sarah Rush), the labors of the twenty high school women contestants and numerous community volunteers as they prepared for the 2003 contest, and the virtues of coal. Director Hunt asserted that the film is about "these people and their community. . . . What struck me from day one was the sense of community and home and what it really means. It is a can-do kind of spirit. . . . It really became a homage to small town America."[20] In actuality, the documentary portrays an amalgam of contradictory agendas by pageant supporters, including legitimation of the coal industry, the loss of mining jobs due to mechanization, the promise of mobility and visibility for high school women, homecoming, civic pride, and heritage.

In addition to coal beauty pageants in Pennsylvania and West Virginia, Kentucky civic and business leaders have sponsored coal beauty queens as a long-standing strategy to promote and beautify its coal industry by associating it with feminine beauty, charm, and community unity. The Miss Hazard Coal Carnival, a forerunner of the ongoing Black Gold Festival, was established in Hazard, Kentucky, in 1937. Today, the Black Gold Festival features age-graded beauty competitions for babies up to women in their twenties. Black Gold contestants compete for a modeling scholarship each year in state finals held in Lexington. Other prizes are given for the most beautiful, best hair, best eyes, best dress, and most photogenic. An annual coal festival held in Wellston, Ohio, is sponsored by local banks, coal companies, county officials, and the local chapter of the Republican Party. It features numerous beauty pageants for girls and women of all ages. Its promotion of coal is quite explicit: the 2008 festival theme emphasized the glamour of coal by trumpeting: "Hollywood Light Shines Bright with Coal."[21]

The link between commodities and beauty contests has a long history in both the Mountain South and Deep South. In 1939, for example, the National Cotton Council of America established its Maid of Cotton festival. Promising celebrity, international travel, sophistication, and upward mobility, contestants were told that the winner would "be dressed in clothes fit for a princess . . . honored by famous people at banquets and balls in elegant places . . . lunch with movie stars . . . chat with ambassadors . . . pose for magazine covers . . . and smile for television cameras." They were told that the winner had the challenge of "creating a fresh interest in cotton" and that "every word and gesture [of the Maid of Cotton] counts in winning friends for the nation's leading textile fiber." In addition to being "photogenic" and possessing "a good figure," contestants were expected to be paragons of "culture and refinement." A promising contestant was one who "came from a home where other members of her family are a welcome asset" and "possessed

Embodying Appalachia 123

enough education to assure a disciplined mind—one that can absorb and master basic facts regarding the cotton industry."[22]

Nationally, by the 1930s beauty pageants were increasingly sponsored by a wide spectrum of civic, business, and political organizations. For example, in 1932 the Federal Office of Education recommended beauty pageants in public high schools as a way to create "greater interest in personal care among girls of the school and for giving the girls profitable training to take the place of strenuous exercises during hot days."[23] In 1936 the Democratic National Convention held a national beauty pageant. This popularity of beauty pageants among the middle class opened up new career opportunities for woman as pageant promoters in their local communities. In 1934, for example, Ida Rose Greer of Marion, Virginia, was hired by the Southwestern Virginia Chamber of Commerce, a regional organization serving nine Appalachian counties in Virginia, Tennessee, and West Virginia and the cities of Radford, Bluefield, and Bristol, to coordinate a local dogwood princess pageant in each of counties that would culminate in a region-wide beauty pageant in Bristol, Tennessee. Her responsibilities included publicizing the pageants, securing local sponsors, and serving as master of ceremonies for the ten pageants.[24]

Since then, hundreds of community and industry festivals in Appalachia have marketed mountain food, mammals and reptiles (including pigs, possum, and rattlesnakes), and seasonal celebrations of spring, May Day, and the fall harvest. Currently there are more than seven hundred community and commodity festivals in Kentucky alone each year; many include beauty queen contests. The West Virginia Association of Fairs and Festivals, established in 1932, offers a state-wide beauty pageant in which over seventy-five festival queens compete each year. Its contestants represent numerous commercial interests, including West Virginia Oil and Gas, the Cowen Railroad Festival, the Calhoun Wood Festival, the West Virginia Poultry Festival, and the West Virginia Timber and Wood Products Show.[25] Regional food products such as pawpaws, spoon bread, corn bread, black walnuts, apple butter, fried chicken, and barbecued ribs are also showcased in festivals that crown beauty queens.[26]

Other pageant models besides those that link regional commodities and feminine beauty also shape Appalachian pageantry. Foremost is the Miss America pageant, which helps to cement the relationship between beauty pageants, nation/region, and higher education. Today the southern states host more local preliminaries to national pageants such as Miss America than any other region. West Virginia, Tennessee, Virginia, and Kentucky each hold numerous local and state preliminaries for the Miss America pageant, as well as Miss USA and Miss Teen USA. This proliferation of beauty contests, along with civic and commodity competitions, has earned the South the nickname of the "pageant belt."[27]

PAGEANT PRECURSORS

The genealogy of mountain beauty pageants can be traced to nineteenth-century beauty contests. Always subject to symbolic usage and public scrutiny, women's bodies long have been utilized to advance a variety of political, civic, and commercial projects across the globe. As beauteous figureheads, queens have adorned floats and tableaux, and they have presided over a jumble of working-class and upper-class rituals, pageants, and festivals.[28] The calibrations of class and racialized femininity in beauty competitions have differed over time and place. Some pageants have evoked mythic representations of Greek, Elizabethan, and medieval traditions, others portrayed civic pride and enterprise. Less genteel roots, however, are in the circuses, carnivals, dime museums, and seaside resorts. In 1854 entrepreneur P. T. Barnum held one of the first American beauty pageants in which contestants paraded in the flesh before a panel of judges. Moral outrage over the live display of women's bodies pushed Barnum to offer an alternative, the photographic beauty contest, which by the 1920s had become a regular feature in many white- and black-owned newspapers and magazines, including even the decorous *Ladies' Home Journal*, which had previously denounced beauty pageants as crass commercialism. Today there are numerous online photographic beauty contests, including the West Virginia Heavenly Angels for young girls.[29]

The expansion of visual technologies, commodity consumption, urbanization, and spectacularization in the 1920s ushered in a multitude of new occasions, sites, and ways for women's bodies and behaviors to be displayed and evaluated in the glare of the public eye. A myriad of cultural tensions and moral panics accompanied this enlargement of

Embodying Appalachia 125

women's public presence. Serving as an antidote to the destabilizing specter of suffragettes, flappers, "new women," and immigrants, national beauty pageants were established in the 1920s to preserve traditional idealizations of feminine appearance, propriety, virtue, and place.[30] The first Miss America national beauty pageant, the Super Bowl of beauty pageants, was held in Atlantic City in 1921, a year after women received the vote. Kimberly Hamlin has argued that the popularity of Miss America was due in part to fears that the Nineteenth Amendment, along with women's increased mobility and presence in public life, were undermining conventional understandings of white femininity and gendered boundaries. The first Miss Americas winners were "small, passive, non-threatening women with little or no interest in remaining in the public eye."[31] Contestants were expected to uphold traditional feminine virtues and attend church, as well as abstain from makeup, alcohol, and tobacco. Pageants rules banned married and divorced women and woman who had been pregnant from participating in the contest, and they also stipulated that contestants must "be of good character and possess poise, personality, intelligence, charm, and beauty of face and figure."[32] In 1945 pageants judges were told to evaluate contestants' "beauty of the face, voice, manner of speaking, wholesomeness, disposition, general culture, special talents, health, and care of the body."[33]

Despite their promotion of gendered conventionality, bathing beauty contests such as Miss America ignited an inferno of opposition from both churches and women's organizations, condemning beauty contests as the crass commercial exploitation of women. In 1927, Bishop William Hafey fumed that beauty pageants were simply the "exploitation of feminine charm by money-mad men."[34] To help cushion Miss America from condemnation as the tawdry flesh-peddling exploitation of women, the beauty pageant underwent many makeovers. Lenore Slaughter, director of Miss America for over thirty-five years, made numerous attempts to minimize the pageant's prurient roots as merely a bathing beauty leg show by successfully aligning the pageant with civic organizations such as the Junior Chamber of Commerce, the National Association of Colleges and Universities, the US military, and a variety of corporations. In order to navigate the contradictions inherent in promoting conflicting gender ideologies of modesty and sensuality, flesh and virtue, and decency and titillation, the Miss America pageant attempted to link its beauty contest with athleticism, wholesomeness, and domesticity in the 1920s; higher education, scholarships, and Junior Chambers of Commerce in the 1940s; and, more recently, careerism, evangelicalism, and postfeminist empowerment to subvert opposition to the public display and appraisal of women's flesh.[35]

Despite numerous local particularities among beauty queen pageants, the Miss America pageant institutionalized many pageant orthodoxies, including the scholarship narrative as well as evening gown, talent, question and answer, and community service competitions that unify various beauty competitions, including those that signify and embody Appalachia. More than simply providing the template for mountain pageants, however, the Miss America pageant organization had early business ties to Appalachian Kentucky. Entrepreneur Henry H. Wheeler, the owner of the Ashland, Kentucky–based Sandy Valley Grocery chain that included fifteen regional grocery stores as well as a milling and coffee operation, played a pivotal role in the use of beauty queens to market local businesses, in this case his grocery company, in Appalachian communities. Wheeler was one of the five original business sponsors of the Miss America scholarship that also included Catalina swimsuits and Harvel watches. He understood his investment in beauty queens as both a commercial opportunity and a strategy to promote and protect white femininity. He observed that "the future which faces American womanhood is filled with opportunities on the one hand and fraught with dangers on the other. Certainly the training and incentive which this scholarship provides will go far in enabling the recipient to meet the challenge of that future successfully and constructively."[36]

Throughout the late 1930s and early 1940s, Wheeler brought Miss America pageant winners to advertise his grocery operations in Kentucky, Ohio, and West Virginia, beginning with Bette Cooper, Miss America 1937. However, soon after Bess Myerson, the first Jewish Miss America, came to Kentucky in 1945 to promote the grocery chain, the official relationship between Miss America and the Sandy Valley Grocery Company became strained. Myerson was taken on a tour of the Sandy Valley grocery stores, its head offices, and its cooking school. Later, after a visit to Wheeler's private train, Myerson said that Wheeler

Embodying Appalachia 127

put his head on her lap without her permission. Myerson said that she felt "unnerved," adding "I felt that I had handled this small incident without finesse, that I would never be invited to work again for this sponsor. I was right. Sandy Valley never used me again. And whatever explanations they gave encouraged the Pageant to believe I had been unacceptable in their locality because I was Jewish."[37] Afterward, Lenore Slaughter, the director of Miss America, characterized the Sandy Valley Grocery Company as a small provincial firm not suitable to their national ambitions for pageant sponsorship, and Wheeler ceased underwriting scholarships in 1946.

Despite this debacle, the Miss America pageant and others like it took root throughout the Appalachian region, often serving to stimulate tourism and trade. For example, Huntington, West Virginia, became the pageant capital of Appalachia in the 1960s through the efforts of Miss USA 1961 Joanne Odum, a native. Odum persuaded the Miss World pageant franchise based in London, England, to bring the national competition to her home city in both 1962 and 1963. (The Miss USA–World pageant had previously been held only in seaside resorts or cities such as New York City.) Governor W. W. Barron described the pageant as "a first class promotion that brought West Virginia a great deal of national attention and publicity."[38] Larry Glick of the Tourism and Vacation Bureau said that hosting the national pageant was "the greatest thing that ever happened to Huntington."[39] The city also hosted the Miss United States pageant in 1964. Pageant activities reflected a broad spectrum of promotional agendas and included a visit to a coal mine, dinner at the governor's mansion, dedications of a new tourist information center and the opening of a new Democratic Party headquarters, visits to local clubs and churches, and numerous star-studded entertainments by such celebrity guests as actor Michael Landon (Little Joe on *Bonanza*) and actress Donna Douglas (Elly Mae on *The Beverly Hillbillies*).[40]

Only white women were allowed to participate in these pageant systems. Until 1950 Miss America contestants had to complete a form detailing their racial heritage and ancestry. Pageant rules stipulated that "only members of the white race" could participate.[41] African American women, however, had participated in the contest as slaves in the pageant's Oceanic Majesty's Court, and Native America women were selected as princesses but none were allowed to compete. Native American, Puerto Rican, and Asian American women began to compete in the national pageant for the first time in the 1940s. However, it was not until 1970 that African American women began to compete in Miss America, and none won until 1984. These contestants, however, closely approximated and reinscribed white standards for beauty, body type, attire, hairstyles, and expression.[42]

As beauty pageantry gained popularity among middle-class white women, middle-class African Americans—in part due to their exclusion from white-only pageants—created their own contests to showcase black beauty. Fusing desires for middle-class distinction, racial advancement, and commercial interests, black newspapers, black colleges, cosmetic and hair companies, black social and fraternal organizations, and groups such as the NAACP became sponsors of black beauty pageants. Since the 1920s, middle-class African Americans have created a variety of spaces to display racial pride and gendered excellence.[43] Noliwe Rooks notes that African American migration, urbanization, and consumerism helped to shape the mission of many elite African American women who urged migrant and working-class black women to adopt "redemptive skills . . . to signal an embrace of dominant cultural understandings of womanhood and gentility."[44]

The first national black beauty pageant, the Golden Brown National Beauty Contest, was held in 1925. Like many white pageants, commercial interests were behind this pageant. It was sponsored by the white-owned Golden Brown Chemical Company, which sold cosmetics to black women. Widely promoted by black newspapers, approximately 1,400 women entered the contest. Black colleges also introduced queen pageants throughout the 1920s.[45]

Just as white beauty pageants differed from each other, so did black pageants. Although often designed to counter white representations of black women's presumed immorality and inferiority, black beauty contests sometimes reinforced intraracial hierarchies of class and color. Maxine Craig argues that black contests varied according to whether or not they were "explicitly framed as displays of racial pride, whether or not they incorporated images of Africa or Europe, whether or not they promoted explicitly middle-class images of women, and whether or not they challenged or reinforced the African American pigmentocracy."[46]

Embodying Appalachia 129

Craig argues that the links among racial dignity, class, self-presentation, grooming, and manners were institutionalized by the National Association of Colored Women when club members were urged to be an "ocular demonstration of the swift advancement of the race," an impulse that spread to black colleges.[47] As a result of the contractions of class and color within black pageants, Craig observes that black beauty pageants have been "symbols of both defiance and conventionality."[48] Today many historically black colleges in Appalachia, including Bluefield State University and West Virginia State University, continue to hold campus queen pageants for black women. Predominantly white colleges throughout the southern mountains, such as Berea College, also hold separate pageants for their African American women students. In some cases, black women who have participated in historically white contests have defined their participation as civil rights actions.

KENTUCKY MOUNTAIN LAUREL FESTIVAL

Pineville is a small town in the heart of what once was the feuding country in southeastern Kentucky. Public-spirited citizens started the festival in 1931, partly to counteract the false impression strangers had of that section and partly to give their local pride a boast.[49] The Kentucky Mountain Laurel Festival is "needed to show the rest of Kentucky that everything here [is] not moonshine and chewing tobacco."[50]

Combining the commodity beauty nexus with the Miss America prototype and supported by ideologies of middle-class enterprise, civic pride, and self and community advancement, pageant rituals of idealized femininity in Appalachian mountain communities have been significant sites for consolidating meanings of place, tradition, local enterprise and industry, gendered value and virtue, social hierarchies, and perpetuation of long-standing patterns of racialized and class inclusion and exclusion. Despite narrow models of embodied excellence and visual meritocracy, hundreds of pageant supporters and contestants applaud the opportunities for mobility, empowerment, and entrepreneurship that they believe beauty pageantry provides as well as the promise of promoting their communities with positive imagery.

One of the oldest continuing community beauty pageants in the southern mountains is the Kentucky Mountain Laurel Festival (KMLF), established in 1931 in Pineville, Kentucky, by local elites and state officials as a way to reinvigorate the local economy, promote tourism, counter long-standing popular images of mountain people as uncultured and uncivilized, and refine the area's reputation when national attention was riveted on the protracted coal strikes in Bell and neighboring Harlan County and the violent suppression of union and communist party organizing efforts. One of the KMLF's principal organizers, Bell County attorney Walter Smith, played a key role in suppressing union activity in the area. Smith banned public meetings, turned away trucks bringing food to striking miners at the county line, and is said to have encouraged mob violence and the intimidation of writers such as Theodore Dreiser and John Dos Passos who were there to bring national attention to the miners' plight.[51] Smith was a key part of establishing the KMLF festival, and he served as its first president in 1931 as well as in 1937 and 1938. In addition, he led the festival parade for many years, riding a white horse and wearing a white Stetson hat.

Annie Walker Burns of Harlan County also played a pivotal part in establishing the KMLF. An avid genealogist, she published a book, *Dr. Thomas D. Walker: First White Man of Any Distinction to Explore Kentucky.* While working in the governor's office, she convinced Governor Flem B. Sampson to honor Walker. Sampson noted that "since beauty pageants were becoming the norm nationwide," he thought it appropriate to invite the Commonwealth's colleges and universities to send a representative to compete in the KMLF.[52] Dr. H. L. Donovan, president of Eastern State Teachers College and later president of the University of Kentucky, served as president of KMLF for six years and helped to legitimate the relationship between Kentucky universities and this eastern Kentucky pageant. According to James O. Roan, a longtime member of the festival board, the KMLF was conceived to honor Walker and the blooming of mountain laurel as well as to show the world that the people of southeastern Kentucky had "culture" and pride by showcasing wholesome and attractive Kentucky college women and high school girls.[53] In 1938 the *Louisville Courier Journal* reported that at least eight thousand people attended the KMLF, including trainloads of businessmen from Louisville and Lexington as well as the Louisville Board of Trade.[54]

The 2008 KMLF queen, Kimberly Horne, observed that the festival is still "about pride and tradition."[55] The KMLF, however, imported a variety of traditions, including those of British royalty and the Plantation South. Since 1933, for example, the pageant festival has mimicked British royalty traditions by staging a coronation ceremony, parading forty-eight young girls in long pink frocks, two jesters wearing silver bells over purple tights, ten couriers, and sixteen ladies-in-waiting before the queen, who is clad in a white bell-shaped ball gown and long white gloves. Curtsies are a highly ritualized part of the competition. As Amy Redmon, a contestant in 2008, concluded, "It's your old Southern beauty pageant. There are no score sheets, no talent show. It's just for fun."[56]

With a population of just under three thousand people in Pineville, hundreds of KMLF volunteers, primarily women, devote hundreds of hours to promote an image of the town's genteel "culture and classiness" by serving on festival committees responsible for beautifying the city and overseeing festival arrangements. Past governor Bert Combs observed that the festival was "one of the few pageants in the state that is still home grown. There is a lot of work done by volunteers and locals. It has great charm."[57] Such volunteerism was especially evident in 1977, when Pineville experienced a devastating flood that threatened to halt its festival. Community citizens were intent upon upholding community tradition, however, and through the sustained efforts of numerous volunteers, they cleaned the streets and held the festival. They were later commended for doing so in one of President Reagan's State of the Union addresses. One local citizen wrote that "this indomitable community spirit is typically American, and it is what is so well exemplified in Pineville and its festival."[58]

Today the KMLF celebrates coal, religion, women's beauty and poise, and apple pie. Events include mine rescue competitions, gospel singing, antique and low-rider car shows, Elvis impersonations, a softball tournament, concerts, a golf classic, the governor's luncheon, apple pie contests, "Little Miss KMLF" contests for girls from three months to eleven years old, and princess pageants for high school girls, all culminating in the queen's coronation and the grand ball. The KMLF also features a parade where each campus queen rides on the back of a convertible displaying the name of her university or college. Events are planned to allow visitors and contestants to attend Sunday morning worship opportunities at both Protestant and Catholic churches. Area church services are listed in the KMLF program, and to ensure that queen contestants attend, they are explicitly told in their orientation letters that "everyone is expected to attend mass or the community worship."[59] The local newspaper runs endorsements from businesses, including Kentucky Fried Chicken, Pic-Pac Supermarket, Kentucky Farm Bureau Insurance, the health department, funeral homes, a tire company, a drug store, and a trucking company, as well as local doctors, dentists, and attorneys. Still a major tourist event after seventy-five years, the KMLF now attracts as many as twenty thousand visitors annually. Many people in attendance who have moved away from Pineville travel long distances each year to attend and reunite with the local community.

Although the KMLF has mercantile interests, the festival seeks to construct an alternative image for its queens and princesses—not the sexualized commercialized display of women's bodies but a celebration of virginal femininity and middle-class propriety, style, and appearance. Festival sponsors describe the pageant and its contestants as "rich in tradition, grace, and charm."[60] Contestants must each enact a regionalized and whitened version of respectable femininity that is rooted in the mythology of the Old South. According to operating (screening) rules for the KMLF, which are based on the rules for Miss America, all candidates chosen by their schools to represent them at KMLF must be "single, never having been pregnant, married, or divorced" to compete in the KMLF. In the 1990s two campus queens were barred from representing their universities at the KMLF because they were single mothers. (One of them, the first University of Kentucky homecoming queen from UK's community college system, hired an attorney and held a press conference in order fight the ban on mothers.)[61]

There are no swimsuit, talent, or community service competitions in the KMLF. Instead, five undercover judges "observe the candidates' appearance, personality, manners, poise, and cooperativeness at all festival events."[62] Many contestants believe that because of this judging process, the KMLF is "classy" and vastly different from tawdry and demeaning pageants that showcase women in swimsuits. A recent winner, a University of Kentucky cheerleader, described the festival as "unique

Embodying Appalachia 133

and better" than other pageants since the judges get to "know you personally" and you get to interact with members of the local business and professional elites in their homes. The 1997 queen, Brittany Lea Johnson, agreed, adding that there are no "superficial" interviews or swimsuit competitions at KMLF.[63] However, such assertions overlook the overlaps between the KMLF and other beauty pageants such as Miss America in normalizing the importance of body-centered, gendered distinction, and middle-class proprieties and tastes.

Successful contestants must display middle-class competencies and aspirations and espouse values consistent with those of elite sponsors including poise, self-confidence, social savvy, Christianity, family values, and heteronormativity. Although there is no swimsuit competition, the scrutiny of bodies and appearances nonetheless is a major part of the competition. Beverley Skeggs has rightfully noted that "bodies are the physical sites where the relations of class, gender, race, sexuality, and age come together and are embodied and practiced. . . . Class is always coded through bodily dispositions; the body is the most ubiquitous signifier of class."[64]

Contestants are told that "there are many events in which appearance is the feature." A winning style is expensive at the KMLF, since contestants are expected to be properly dressed for all aspects of the competition. They are told that they need to have a casual sundress and suit, sports clothes, a cocktail dress, and a floor-length white ball gown that will allow them the range of motion to curtsy to the governor. At the same time, their male escorts are required to have a white dinner jacket, black trousers, and bow tie. Although the requirements for dress and appearance are made explicit, contestants are expected to have already internalized other markers of middle-class taste and dispositions, including etiquette, makeup, comportment, personal enterprise, moderation, small talk, and table manners as they dine and socialize in the homes of the local elite. Contestants are expected to be genteel, socially savvy, and artful in their class-coded gendered performances.

After seventy-five years, little has changed in the staging and performances of the KMLF, where traditions of white faces, southern ladyhood, purity, charm, and heritage continue to prevail. In 2000 nineteen white university students competed for the crown of laurel buds and blooms and a $3,000 scholarship. In addition to the selection of the KMLF queen and princess, a Miss Congeniality, Miss Photogenic, and Best Escort were chosen. The audience was treated to a lengthy processional of queen contestants clad in long, white bell-shaped gowns and over-the-elbow white gloves. They were accompanied by a "miniature court" consisting of scores of elementary school-age children carrying small bouquets of mountain laurel wrapped in white doilies, the nineteen princess candidates, and the queen's escorts. In 2000 Kentucky governor Paul Patton presided over the coronation ceremony. After a flag-raising ceremony and the National Anthem, the Lord's Prayer, and "My Old Kentucky Home," each campus queen contestant came forward to the edge of a reflecting pool and performed a formal curtsy reminiscent of English court and May Day rituals.[65]

Sarah Hargis, the 2007 KMLF queen representing Center College in Danville, Kentucky, pointed out that contestants not only have to know how to curtsy but also must impress the judges with their "poise" and "substance." Over the course of three days all the girls attend luncheons and dinner parties, mingling with prominent Pineville figures. A panel of secret judges observes each girl's manners, poise, character, and personality. Then, on the final day, the girls dress in white wedding dresses and long white gloves to perform a creative yet elegant curtsy to the governor of Kentucky. After observing the substance of the girls throughout the week, this curtsy becomes the deciding factor of who becomes queen.[66]

Significantly, Hargis's mother is from Honduras, making her the first woman of color to win the KMLF tiara. All previous KMLF queens, however, have been white women with extensive family roots in Kentucky, suggesting the importance of sponsorship and class connections.[67] Board members also tend to come from elite mountain and bluegrass families, including C. V. and Marylou Whitney (heirs to the Vanderbilt fortune), numerous Kentucky governors, district judges, and local business and political elites. Festival sponsors, judges, host families, and contestants are also predominantly white. In recent years, some of the festival organizers have actively sought the participation of black women from Kentucky State University. However, when one of the African American campus queens attempted to breach some of the

Embodying Appalachia 135

class and racial fortifications that have been operative since the KMLF's inception, she found the experience deeply distressing:

> There were only two black families in all of Pineville, and I stayed in the home of elderly white folks . . . I spent time with the black family who was hosting my black escort. I felt comfortable there since I was with black folks. The pageant was all about being a lady. You do not even know what they are judging on. The girl who won had a sister who won a few years prior. I do not know if that factored into her winning. You know you had to curtsy to the governor, you had to wear white including your gloves. The purity thing is what they want with that association. An uncomfortable experience. They are constantly watching you.[68]

Although she did cross the KMLF color line, the "tradition" of showcasing white college women as signifiers of Appalachian culture and excellence remained intact.

APPALACHIAN BEAUTY PAGEANTS such as the KMLF perpetuate longstanding racial, gender, and class legacies and hierarchies. Although pageant supporters tout the numerous purported benefits of pageants, including educational scholarships, career advancement, skill development, cultural capital, community cohesion, local commerce, tourism, and Appalachian cultural heritage, beauty pageants raise deeply troubling questions about body-based gendered distinction; the commercialization of women's bodies to sell products, communities, and Appalachian culture; and belonging and difference in the region. Designed at least in part to counter Bell County's history of coalfield violence and labor suppression, the KMLF, for example, offers a truncated version of heritage and local culture, selecting and revering certain elements of imagined tradition and legacy while suppressing many others. The numerous coal festivals throughout Appalachia also use selection and suppression, as well as women's bodies, to help their marketing crusades clean their product and their image. Despite the efforts to challenge stereotypes, in the main Appalachian beauty pageantry perpetuates restrictive and exclusionary patterns of culture, heritage, memory, belonging, and gendered normativity and exceptionality throughout the region, creating very few winners but many losers.

NOTES

1. See Rupal Oza, "Showcasing India: Gender, Geography, and Globalization," *Signs* 26, no. 4 (Summer 2001): 1067–95; Joan Sangster, "Queen of the Picket Line: Beauty Contests in Post-World War Two Canadian Labor Market," *Labor: Studies of Working-Class History of the Americas* 5, no. 4 (2008): 83–106.

Radhika Parameswaran, "Global Queens, National Celebrities: Tales of Feminine Triumph in Post-Liberalization India," *Critical Studies in Media Communication* 21, no. 4 (December 2004): 346–70; Shanti Kumar, "Globalisation, Nationalism, and Feminism in Indian Culture," *South Asian Journal*, no. 4 (July–September, 2004); William Callahan, "The Ideology of Miss Thailand in National, Consumerist, and Transnational Space," *Alternatives: Global, Local, and Political* 23, no. 1 (January 1998): 1–33.

2. Robert Lavenda, "'It's Not a Beauty Pageant': Hybrid Ideology in the Minnesota Community Queen Pageants," in *Beauty Queens on the Global Stage: Gender, Contests, and Power*, ed. Colleen Ballerino Cohen and Richard Wilk, with Beverly Stoeltje (New York: Routledge, 1996), 31.

3. Mary Ann Hinsdale, Helen M. Lewis, and S. Maxine Waller, *It Comes from the People: Community Development and Local Theology* (Philadelphia: Temple University Press, 1995), 118.

4. Ibid., 117.

5. Ibid., 118.

6. See, for example, "Miss Indian America: Regulatory Gazes and the Politics of Affiliation," *Feminist Studies* 31, no. 1 (Spring 2005): 64–94; Nhi Lieu, "Remembering 'the Nation' through Pageantry: Femininity and the Politics of Vietnamese Womanhood in the *Hoa Hau Ao Dai* Contest," *Frontiers* 21, nos. 1 and 2 (2000): 127–51; Natasha Barnes, "Face of the Nation: Race, Nationalisms and Identities in Jamaican Beauty Pageants," *Massachusetts Review* 35, nos. 3 and 4 (Autumn 1994): 471–92; Judy Tzu-Chun. Wu, "'Loveliest Daughters of Our Ancient Cathay': Representations of Ethnic and Gender Identity in the Miss Chinatown U.S.A Beauty Pageant," in *Beauty and Business: Commerce, Gender, and Culture in Modern America*, ed. Phillip Scranton, (New York: Routledge, 2001), 278–308; and Shane White and Graham White, *Stylin': African American Expressive Culture from its Beginnings to the Zoot Suit* (Ithaca, NY: Cornell University Press, 1998).

7. See, for example, Danny L. Miller, *Wingless Flight: Appalachian Women in Literature* (Bowling Green, OH: Popular Press, 1996); Sally Ward Maggard, "Will the Real Daisy Mae Stand Up: A Methodological Essay on Gender Analysis in Appalachian Research," *Appalachian Journal* 21, no. 2 (Winter 1994): 136–50; Jacqueline Dowd Hall, "Disorderly Women: Gender and Labor Militancy in the Appalachian South," *Journal of American History* 73, no. 2 (1986): 354–82; Karen W. Tice, "School-Work and Mother-Work: The Interplay of Maternalism and Cultural Politics in the Educational Narratives of Kentucky Settlement Workers, 1910–1930," *Journal of Appalachian Studies* 4, no. 2 (Fall 1998): 191–224.

8. Tice, "School-Work and Mother-Work."

9. Pamela Wilson, "Mountains of Contradictions: Gender, Class, and Region in the Star Image of Dolly Parton," *South Atlantic Quarterly* 94, no. 1 (Spring

Embodying Appalachia 137

1995): 109–34; Chris Holmlund, *Impossible Bodies: Femininity and Masculinity at the Movies* (New York: Routledge, 2002); J. W. Williamson, *Hillbillyland: What the Movies Did to the Mountains and What the Mountains Did to the Movies* (Chapel Hill: University of North Carolina Press, 1995).

10. Christine Yano, *Crowning the Nice Girl: Gender, Ethnicity, and Culture in Hawaii's Cherry Blossom Festival* (Honolulu: University of Hawaii Press, 2006).

11. *The Bituminous Coal Queens of Pennsylvania*, dir. David Hunt and Jody Eldred (Four Boys Films, 2004).

12. Danielle Massey, "There Is Royalty Among Us," http://www.marshallparthenon.com/home/index.cfm? (event posted September 11, 2008).

13. *Bituminous Coal Queens*.

14. Massey, "There Is Royalty."

15. "Coal Queen Reflects on Experience," *Observer-Reporter* (Washington, PA), August 18, 2007.

16. Marylynne Pitz, "Movie Documents Bituminous Coal Queens," *Pittsburgh Post-Gazette*, June 11, 2006.

17. www.wvinternationalpageant.com, accessed January 15, 2014.

18. Greene County Pennsylvania, "Historical Facts About the PA Bituminous Coal Show; 1953–2008," http://www.co.greene.pa.us/secured/gc2/history/rec-historyhtm#coal-show accessed 09/15/14.

19. Ibid.

20. Pitz, "Movie Documents."

21. www.wellstoncoalfestival.com, accessed January 15, 2014.

22. Maid of Cotton collection, (no box no.), Auburn University Archives, Auburn, AL.

23. Deborah Wolfe, "Beauty as a Vocation: Women and Beauty Contests in America" (PhD diss., Columbia University, 1994), 97.

24. Collection 465, box 1, folder 9, Appalachian State University Archives Boone, NC.

25. http://www.jennyspageantpage.com/2006wvaff.html.

26. http://www.kentuckypageants.com/About%Us.htm, accessed January 15, 2014.

27. See for example Elizabeth B. Boyd, "Southern Beauty: Performing Femininity in an American Region" (PhD diss., University of Texas at Austin, 2000); Jerrilyn McGregory, "Wiregrass County Pageant Competitions or What's Beauty Got To Do With It," in *"There She Is, Miss America": The Politics of Sex, Beauty, and Race in America's Most Famous Pageant*, ed. Elwood Watson and Darcy Marti (New York: Palgrave Macmillan, 2004), 125–34; Charles Reagan Wilson, *Judgment and Grace in Dixie: Southern Faiths from Faulkner to Elvis* (Athens: University of Georgia Press, 1995).

28. Lois Banner, *American Beauty* (Chicago: University of Chicago Press, 1983).

29. http://www.geocities.com/wvaheavenlyagls/julywinners.html, accessed August 15, 2009.

30. Liz Conor, *The Spectacular Modern Woman: Feminine Visibility in the 1920s* (Bloomington: Indiana University Press, 2004).

31. Kimberly Hamlin, "The First Miss America Pageants, 1921–1927," in Watson and Marti, *"There She Is, Miss America,"* 32.

32. *American Experience,* Primary Sources: 1948 Pageant Contract, http:/www
.pbs.org/wgbh/amexmissamerica/filmore/ps.html, accessed January 15, 2014.

33. Susan Dworkin, *Miss America 1945: Bess Myerson's Own Story* (New York:
Newmarket, 1987), 116.

34. *New York Times,* November 30, 1927.

35. Dworkin, *Miss America 1945;* Sarah Banet-Weiser, *The Most Beautiful Girl
in the World: Beauty Pageants and National Identity* (Berkeley: University of California Press); R. A. Riverol, *Live From Atlantic City: A History of the Miss America Pageant* (Bowling Green, OH: Popular Press, 2002); Candace Savage, *Beauty
Queens: A Playful History* (New York: Abbeville Press, 1998); and Frank Deford,
There She Is: The Life and Times of Miss America (New York: Penguin, 1971).

36. Dworkin, *Miss America 1945,* 96–97.

37. Ibid., 178.

38. Joseph Platania, "Miss USA," *Huntington Quarterly Magazine,* 1999.

39. Ibid.

40. Ibid.

41. Beretta Smith-Shomade, *Shaded Lives: African American Women and Television* (New Brunswick, NJ: Rutgers University Press, 2002); Shirley Jennifer Lim,
A Feeling of Belonging: Asian American Women's Public Culture, 1930–1960 (Philadelphia: Temple University Press, 2006).

42. See Sarah Banet-Weiser, *Most Beautiful Girl in the World,* and G. Reginald
Daniel, *More Than Black: Multiracial Identity and the New Racial Order* (Philadelphia: Temple University Press, 2002) for a discussion of racial containment and
accommodation in the Miss America pageant.

43. Maxine Leeds Craig, *Ain't I a Beauty Queen? Black Women, Beauty, and
the Politics of Race* (New York: Oxford University Press, 2004); Shane White and
Graham White, *Stylin': African American Expressive Culture from Its Beginnings to
the Zoot Suit* (Ithaca, NY: Cornell University Press, 1998).

44. Noliwe Rooks, *Ladies Pages: African American Women's Magazines and the
Cultures That Made Them* (New Brunswick, NJ: Rutgers University Press 2004), 9.

45. Karen W. Tice, "Queens of Academe: Campus Pageantry and Student Life,"
Feminist Studies 31, no. 2 (2005), 250–83.

46. Craig, *Ain't I a Beauty Queen,* 46–47.

47. Ibid., 32.

48. Ibid., 70.

49. William Stucky, "Mountain Laurel Pageant in Old Feuding Country," *New
York Times,* May 9, 1948.

50. "Festival Draws Thousands to Celebrate the Blooming of Mountain Laurel," *Pineville Sun,* May 25, 2000, C2.

51. John Hevener, *Which Side Are You On? The Harlan County Coal Miners,
1931–39* (Urbana: University of Illinois Press, 1978).

52. http://www.kmlf.org, accessed January 14, 2014.

53. "Festival Draws Thousands."

54. Bryan Collier, "6th Laurel Festival Closes with Record Attendance," *Louisville Courier Journal* (1938), University of Kentucky Special Collections, box 199.

Embodying Appalachia 139

55. Brandy Calvert, "Another Festival Wrapped Up," *Middlesboro Daily News*, May 28, 2008.

56. Brian Johns, "Transylvania Student Wins Crown," *Lexington Herald-Leader*, May 28, 1928, B1.

57. Ibid.

58. Unknown author, KMLF organizational records, University of Kentucky Special Collections, May 15, 1986, box 199.

59. Author personal correspondence with Michele Roan, chair of the KMLF Advisory Board, "Letter to Prospective Contestants," February 2000.

60. Kentucky Mountain Laurel Festival, "Celebrate the Millennium," (2000), 1.

61. Thomas Tolliver, "UK Queen Hopes Public Opinion will Change Rules for Pageant," *Lexington Herald-Leader*, May 4, 1991, B1.

62. "Kentucky Mountain Laurel Festival Operating Guidelines," University of Kentucky Special Collections, 1986, box 199.

63. Barbara Ward, "Student Models Small-Town Values," *Lexington Herald-Leader*, June 26, 1997, B1.

64. Beverley Skeggs, "(Dis)Identifications of Class: On Not Being Working Class," in *Pierre Bourdieu 2*, ser. Sage Masters of Social Thought, ed. Derek Robbins (Thousand Oaks, CA: Sage, 2005), 207–44.

65. The author attended the 2000 KMLF, including the coronation, the coronation ball, the governor's breakfast, and receptions, interviewing contestants, escorts, and pageant sponsors.

66. Sarah E. Hargis, "From Queen to Real Life," http://www.centre.edu /mycentrellife0607, accessed January 15, 2014.

67. Beverly Fortune, "Laurel Candidate has 'Royal' Lineage," *Lexington Herald-Leader*, May 19, 2002, J4.

68. Author interview with Kentucky State University queen, March 3, 2005.

Moravian *Lebenslauf* (Memoir or Life's Journey)

The Moravians trace their origins to the fourteenth- and early fifteenth-century teachings of Bohemian reformer Jan Hus, condemned as a heretic and ordered burned at the stake in 1415 by the Council of Constance. In 1457, some Hussites founded a church dedicated to piety and simple living. The church subsequently thrived, but the Thirty Years War (1618–48) in Europe inflicted serious damage on the church, so that few followers remained. In the 1720s, however, a small number of followers, along with other religious dissidents, found refuge on the estate of nobleman Nicholas Ludwig von Zinzendorf of Saxony. The church of Hus experienced a rebirth (as the Brüdergemeine or Renewed Moravian Church) and soon began sending missionaries throughout the world. Some of these missionaries emigrated to the English North American colonies, first to Savannah, Georgia; then to Pennsylvania, where they founded Bethlehem; and then to North Carolina, where they established Bethabara, Bethania, Salem, and Wachovia.

As Pietists, Moravians believed in the real presence of Jesus Christ, from whom the inflow of divine grace allowed followers to achieve a new life. Living a moral and pure life not only demonstrated the presence of Jesus in their lives but also emboldened followers to establish missions (for example, the Springplace Mission to the Cherokee in North Georgia, founded in 1801) to bring others to Jesus. Moravians often kept track of their spiritual lives through the *Lebenslauf* (German for "course of life"). Early in Moravian history, the individual kept her/his Lebenslauf or memoir to detail spiritual struggle and progress. But because increasingly many Moravians were illiterate or barely literate, others, especially the minister, added bits to the memoir, particularly at the time of death or just prior to the reading of the memoir at the follower's death.

In spite of their determination to live moral lives, some Moravians owned black slaves. Their basis for justifying slave ownership resided in European beliefs in the superiority both of the white race over the black in regard to physical and mental qualities and of white civilization over black societies. Zinzendorf even claimed that blacks possessed a permanent character flaw that made it necessary for them to be enslaved before they could be saved. Emancipation meant not emancipation from earthly slavery, but emancipation from sin.

As was the case with other Christian denominations, blacks, both free and enslaved, became members of the Moravian Church. In the Salem region, there resided free and enslaved black Moravians, who kept track of their spiritual lives through the medium of the memoir. Following is the memoir of Rahel, a slave woman. Apparently the minister of the church at Bethania in western North Carolina wrote most of Rahel's memoir and was present at her death. This memoir, part of the diary of the church at Bethania, was written in German and translated in 1989 by Frances Cumnock. The church at Bethania included both black and white congregants until 1844, when a separate black church was established. The white minister was Johann Jacob Ernst.

Entries in the Bethania Diary, 27, 28, and 29 September 1782 Concerning the Life and Homegoing of Rahel, c. 1762–1782

27th ... The Negro woman, Rahel, this evening passed out of time, truly confident

28th in reliance on Jesus' merit. She was buried [on the 28th] on the knoll behind Spoenhauer's field to the north.

29th ... The following is [relevant] to note regarding the circumstances of the life of the Negro woman Rahel. She was born in Virginia and bought by Br. Peter Hauser when she was in about her fifteenth or sixteenth year. According to her statement, she was baptized in her fourth year, through the Presbyterians, at her mother's request. [Her mother] reared her according to her own understanding in true reverence toward God, who rewards good and punishes evil. Her bodily *Constitution* indicated that she had been considerably *ruinirt* [damaged] during her childhood years by hard work and [excessive] cold. During the four years and several months that she spent here, we were not able to perceive any special signs in her of a true change of heart. Nevertheless, when asked whether she knew the Saviour and loved him, with a joyful countenance she answered "Yes." On 7 September she suffered a severe attack of diarrhea. It soon turned into dysentery (*die rothe Ruhr*), against which all remedies were applied to no avail. During her illness she oftentimes was asked whether she would find joy in going out of time. She said: "Oh yes, I will gladly go to the Saviour. I have prayed to him that he might forgive all my sins and have mercy upon me, his poor creature." Shortly before her end, when it was believed that she took no more *Notiz* [notice] of anything, a Sister asked her: "Now, Rahel, will you go now to the Saviour and are you certain of your situation?" She opened her eyes then and with a truly joyful look answered: "Oh yes. He has forgiven me for everything and I am going to him." Immediately thereafter [her life] went out as does a light. She was about nineteen or twenty years old.

Source: Translated from the same document in the Moravian Archives, Winston-Salem, North Carolina, by Frances Cumnock, Archives Translator, December 1989, The Archives of the Moravian Church in America, Southern Province, Winston-Salem, North Carolina.

Petition for Divorce

Based on English common law, marriages in the American colonies united a woman's identity with that of her husband, the legal master of the marriage relationship. Women had no legal identity apart from their husbands: they could not sue or be sued, make contracts, own property, control their own wages, or serve as trustees, estate executors, or legal guardians. Any property and wages a woman brought into the marriage legally belonged to her husband, and she had no means of protecting her financial interests and no security if her husband died. Women also faced the risk of mistreatment by husbands who engaged in adultery and drunkenness, were physically cruel, or abandoned their families. There was power in owning land and labor; married women owned neither.

Following the American Revolution, most southern governments gave the power to grant divorces to their state legislatures. Yet a divorce was almost impossible to obtain in antebellum America, and divorce was strongly condemned in Virginia. The predominant church in Virginia, the Anglican Church, recognized only "bed and board" divorces, legal separations in which the wife received financial support, but neither party could remarry. However, the husband still controlled the property. The Virginia General Assembly granted the state's first actual act of divorce in 1803. In 1827, the Virginia legislature gave Superior Courts of Chancery the power to grant divorces but continued to grant divorces itself until 1850, though only to white Virginians. Most black marriages were not recognized. The state permitted divorce on the grounds of adultery, cruelty, bigamy, and desertion. Surprisingly, in the antebellum era more divorces were granted to women than to men, and most Virginia women retained sole custody of their children without male guardianship. While divorce freed a woman and her property from her husband's control, a woman did not necessarily receive financial support, and both parties were frequently denied the right to remarry, resulting in financial hardship for many women. In addition, society often frowned upon divorced women, particularly if they attempted to remarry. In the following petition, written in 1823, Peggy Cox requests a divorce from her husband on the grounds of cruelty and abandonment. Her husband had already "married" another woman, Elizabeth Hartford, in Ohio in 1818 and the couple had four children. Peggy Cox did not remarry until 1828.

Peggy Cox

To the Honorable the members of the General Assembly of Virginia the petition of Margaret Cox of Greenbrier County respectfully represents.

That in the autumn of year 1816 she your petitioner then Margaret Price, intermarried with a certain Henry Cox of said County with whom your petitioner lived until the fall of 1817. That the early part of her married life, was attended with the utmost peace & cordiality between her & her said husband, which inspired your petitioner with a hope, nay with the anticipation of a long life of uninterrupted peace, constancy & fidelity, which ought ever to attend conjugal life—But your petitioner has not been the wife of the said Henry Cox more than ten or eleven months, when those bright prospects of happiness which she had so warmly cherished in her mind, vanished and were succeeded by the most trying calamities—Not only was your petitioner deprived of the love & affection of a husband, not only was she denied the privileges of a dutiful wife, the protection & support of him, to whom she had a right to look to with confidence, but that husband became her most cruel & wanton enemy—That without the least provocation or inducement on the part of your petitioner by the said Henry Cox regardless of the sacred vow—calous to every generous, & human feeling—cruelly forced your petitioner with her infant in her arms, from her bed and home—and compelled to throw herself and child upon the charity of the world. Your petitioner, at first supposing her said husband activated by momentary passion, endeavored to reconcile him, to the terms of peace but to no purpose, the said Henry Cox was inexorable and threatened your petitioner that if she did not depart his house he would take her life—and that if she ever returned to his bed again, he would secretly conceal a knife in bed with him, and when your petitioner was asleep he would cut her throat— Not only did he make these threats but provided actually to carry them into execution—but the life of your petitioner was saved in consequence of the blow about to be dealt being providentially averted—Thus your petitioner, stript of every means of protection at the house of her husband, for the safety of her life, & that of her infant child, was compelled to seek for shelter in a more hospitable mansion—That your petitioner, was deprived

Petition for Divorce 145

of every means of support for her self & child, and must have suffered for the common necessaries of life, had it not been for the kind interference, of compassionate individuals.

Some short time after your petitioner & her infant had been thus cruelly driven from her bed and home—the said Henry Cox who had some time previously, has had illicit intercourse with a certain Betsey Hartford, of the same neighborhood, eloped with her the said Betsey Hartford to the state of Ohio where he has ever since been living with the said Betsey Harford in the character of man and wife—That he has had by the Said Betsey four children—as will be seen by the affidavits here with exhibited of his own acknowledgements.—

That the said Henry Cox, in January of 1823 came to the county of Greenbrier, and executed to your petitioner, an agreement on his part, never here after to set up any claim to any property, real or personal which she might here after require [acquire]—but your petitioner is advised, that such an agreement is not valid & binding & that the said Henry Cox notwithstanding said agreement can at any time assert his right to any property which, your petitioner may hereafter by her industry & frugality acquire—And that your petitioner is apprehensive & [ ] believes that the said Henry Cox when ever he is informed that your petitioner has obtained property will come forward, assert his right and again deprive your petitioner of the means of subsistence, for herself & child;

That the said Henry Cox also in said agreement in[ ] his willingness that the matrimonial tie may be broken and that they may be hereafter, two people. To this your petitioner most cordially subscribes, and prays that this Honorable body would gratify their wishes, upon this subject.

Your petitioner therefore prays that your honorable "body" would pass a law divorcing your petitioner from the said Henry Cox (as it is his wish and the honest desire of your petitioner)—But should this be not granted then your petitioner prays that your Honorable body would make [ ] & binding his agreement of the 15th of Jan'y 1823 by passing a law securing unto your petitioner, the property she has & may hereafter acquire by her own industry or otherwise, against the claim or demand of the said Henry Cox—and as in duty bound she will ever pray be.

Margaret Cox

Source: Cox, Margaret, Petition for Divorce, Greenbrier County, Virginia, December 3, 1823, Legislative Petition Digital Collection, Library of Virginia, Richmond, Virginia.

Women of the Mountains

REV. EDGAR TUFTS

During the home mission movement (c. 1880–1940), missionaries from "mainline" Protestant churches, the Church of Jesus Christ of Latter-Day Saints, the Catholic Church, the Seventh-Day Adventist Church, and the Salvation Army targeted the Appalachian region in an attempt to intellectually and culturally "modernize" the people who lived there. On the basis of stereotypes and frequently patronizing misconceptions of the region, church officials and leaders assumed mountain folk were intellectually and culturally inferior to the rest of the nation. Adopting educational ideas similar to those of the freedmen's schools for African Americans after the Civil War, the settlement house movement, and the social welfare efforts of urban America in the Progressive Era, churches established schools throughout the region that taught academic subjects, industrial/vocational education, and the religious tenets of their particular denomination. Many churches had been in the region before: Moravians, Congregationalists (Presbyterians), Baptists, and Methodists all established missions among the Cherokee between 1757 and 1820. However, during the home mission movement, the goal of missionaries was to educate white children in the mountain south in academics, religion, and culture.

Seminary student Edgar Tufts organized a Presbyterian church at Banner Elk, North Carolina, in 1895, returned as its pastor in 1897, and founded an all-female high school in 1899. The lack of educational facilities in the area and the distance mountain women had to travel to attend school led Reverend Tufts to build a dormitory that housed fourteen girls and one teacher. He named the boarding school after the teacher, Elizabeth McRae. In 1903, he added benefactor Susanna Lees's name to the school. It was chartered as Lees-McRae Institute in 1907. Tufts also established a boys' school approximately twenty-five miles from Lees-McRae. After the boys' school burned, Lees-McRae became a coeducational facility in 1927. The school became

Lees-McRae College in 1931 and obtained senior college status as a four-year college in 1990.

In this 1899 pamphlet titled "Women of the Mountains," Tufts lists the reasons he felt a school for women in the mountains of North Carolina was necessary.

Women of the Mountains

Rev. Edgar Tufts
Principle Girls Department
Lees-McRae Institute
Banner Elk, N.C.

The Executive Committee of Home Missions
of the Presbyterian Church
in the United States

Perhaps nowhere in our land, not even among the negroes, do the women suffer greater hardships and more deprivations than they do in the mountains. Beginning with the tender years of early childhood, down to old age, theirs is a lot of hard labor, few comforts, few opportunities and often extreme poverty. No wonder that the freshness of youth is early wiped from their brows, and that premature wrinkles cover their care-worn faces.

That there are many exceptions no one is more aware than the writer. But on the other hand, no one who is at all familiar with the conditions can deny the statements that I shall make.

Hardships of Girlhood Days. The mountain woman is born to work. This begins as soon as she is large enough to hold the baby, if there should be one, which is usually the case. Washing dishes, bringing in wood and cleaning up the house are begun not many years after she has learned to walk. Milking the cows, cutting wood and hoeing corn are considered a part of her duties, as much as it is the privilege of her older brothers to loaf around the village store or the blacksmith shop. Many a time have I seen a small girl going to the mill with a peck of corn on her shoulder, or coming from the store with a twenty-five pound sack of flour on her hip, or bending over a washtub doing the work of a grown woman.

The difficulties of attending school are numerous and often insurmountable.

The idea is common among the mountain parents that their girls do not need much education. If they can read and write, that is as much and sometimes more than they themselves can do, and as it sufficed for them it ought to answer for their girls. This spirit is a difficulty that is hard to overcome even with the combined efforts of teacher and pupil.

It is very hard for the girls to be spared from home. They are called upon to help with all kinds of work in the house and outside, as there are practically no servants in the mountains. So when the mother is sick or broken down, which is often the case by the time her children are ready for school, there is nothing to do but keep the girls at home to do the work.

When these circumstances are surmounted, the question of money comes up. A boy could get work at a sawmill or perhaps sell enough of his father's timber to pay his way through. But having the misfortune to be a mountain girl, she cannot do either, amid her parents being not much in favor of her going off to school anyway, her chances will depend in nearly every instance on receiving a scholarship. And even when the scholarship is secured, there comes the difficulty of getting to school. Living, as perhaps she does, forty miles from a railroad, it is no easy matter in the face of indifferent parents to get herself and her trunk to the school.

Then, having reached the school, there comes the difficulty of remaining. In nearly every case her parents tell her that if she gets homesick they will send for her. If she does not, some member of the home is almost sure to be "ailing;" and, of course, the girl must come home at once.

Their Sparse Pleasures. The few pleasures that surround the average mountain girl's life are due in part to the hard work that devolves upon her early in life, in part to her isolated home, and in part to the wrong ideas that her parents entertain about amusements. Two incidents in my own experience will illustrate this: On one occasion at a gathering of some young people, for the purpose of peeling and cutting apples to dry, I introduced some old-fashioned parlor games. It is needless to say that those present enjoyed the games very much. A few days after this, an old man, a member of my church, came to me and in the most solemn manner said: "I hear that you have been leading off the young people into worldly amusements." I explained to him that the games we had played were perfectly harmless and such as had been played a hundred times in Christian homes. But no explanation satisfied him that what I had done was not a gross sin.

On another occasion, while spending the night at a certain home, the children asked their father's permission to go to a candy stew at a neighbor's house. He told them that they might go if I (the preacher) approved of such things. Of course I sided with the children, for which they thanked me very heartily. But I think I won their good will at the expense of their father's confidence, for he has never seemed to have much faith in me since.

Notwithstanding their hardships, there are thousands of gems among them, as pure and as beautiful as any people ever produced. For one thing

Women of the Mountains 149

they are usually strong and healthy. Simple living, outdoor exercise, and plain wholesome food have produced iron constitutions. They are also as bright and as ambitious as any class of girls in any part of our land. More than that, they are as modest and as pure, as a rule, as girls " our most refined homes. All they need in order to produce as fine types of cultivated Christian womanhood as can be found anywhere, is the same opportunities that the girls have in other places.

Hardships of Married Life. Married Life, which is often begun at a very early age, brings no let-up from the hard labors that have been weighing heavily upon her shoulders since early childhood. Indeed, they are now increased, for there will be babies to care for while the work is being done. If company comes, she is expected to wait on the table while the men eat. On "Meetin' Day," if she can go to church at all, she has to take with her the children. If her husband goes, he sits with the men on one side of the church. If during the service the children are obstreperous (and they usually are), she has to take them out until they can be quieted. If there is sickness in the neighborhood she is sure to be present, even though she has to take with her a nursing babe and leave it in an adjoining room while she waits on the sick.

Difficult enough would all this be even if surrounded by every convenience which the water is carried is a hundred yards from the house; that the barn where the milking is done is very open and across the road; that the home is small, dark and full of big cracks; that the stove is small and worn out; that the wood pile is not under a shed; that whether the men work or not they expect their breakfast at daylight; that when sickness comes it is sometimes impossible to get a doctor, it will be seen that her life is a hard one.

On a cold fall day, I once saw a woman fully a mile from her home with an infant on her hip and a bag strapped across her shoulder into which she was gathering galax leaves to sell, while another baby just able to walk was at her side. This is a picture of the hardships of hundred of the women of the mountains.

Beside these terrible burdens, there is the day by day, month by month living without any change. No social gatherings to which she can go, except the monthly meeting at the church, which, by the way, if it meant nothing more than an opportunity for the people to meet together and sing, would be worth the cost. No pictures on the walls, except perhaps the advertisements on the papers that have been pasted over cracks. No music to enliven the home, except the crying of the baby and the fussing of some of the older children. No books, except maybe an old worn-out hymn book or a fine print Bible.

Yet there are some as fine types of womanhood to be found among these people as ever adorned any home. Their kindness of heart and hospitality are without bounds. That they use tobacco and snuff in large quantities goes without saying. But I never heard of one being under the influence of liquor, accused of stealing, or guilty of any kind of gambling, or afraid of hard work. Their Greatest Need. What is most needed for the social, moral and spiritual uplift of these mountain women? Important and helpful as other things are, we say, without hesitation, nothing is equal to a Christian Industrial School, located in their midst, and peculiarly adapted to their special needs. To meet these requirements, and to best accomplish this end, the following things are necessary:

The school should be located in the mountains. Mountain flora do not thrive in the low country, neither do mountain youths. Not only so, but a school can be run very much more cheaply in the mountains than in other places. Another reason is that the mountain girls are painfully timid. They will attend school at home when no power under the sun would induce some of them to go to a distant school.

The school should be permeated with the religion of Jesus Christ. The mountain people are naturally religious; they love the services of the church. No subject is more attractive to them than the Bible. Nothing will do more for them than the pure Gospel. And there is no better way of bringing them under Its influence than through a school that is founded and conducted on the eternal principles of God's Word.

The school should be industrial. This is important especially as there are practically no servants in the mountains, and since there are many resources in the country to make the people comfortable. But alas! too often they are like the people who have shivered over a coal mine, with the black diamonds protruding on all sides, not knowing how to use their resources.

The school in many instances should be run in the summer, with vacation in time in the coldest part of the winter. This for the following reasons: First, it will tend to break down the too frequent custom of putting girls on the farm, and instead teach them the more important duties of housekeeping. Second, it can be conducted much more cheaply and more pleasantly, owing to the saving in fuel and the abundance of country produce at this season. Third, it will put the girls at home during the winter, when the family are together more than at any other season, and when their influence will be worth the most.

The school should have if possible a department under a Christian physician, or a trained nurse, for the instruction of the older girls in matters that pertain to their future welfare and the care of the sick in their own homes.

It follows from some of the reasons given that the school in most instances at least should not be co-educational.

Women of the Mountains 151

* * *

Such a school as described above is the Girls' Department of the Lees-McRae Institute at Banner Elk, N. C., of which Rev. Edgar Tufts is the Principle. It has been in operation for seven years, and has proved the wisdom of every point mentioned. During its brief history it has educated in part over 400 girls, many of whom are today letting their lights shine in the dark corners of the mountains. Its sphere of usefulness ought to be greatly enlarged. It could be doubled with a comparatively small amount of money.

Source: Edgar Tufts, "Women of Appalachia," Digital Library of Appalachia, http://www .dla.acaweb.org/cdm/compoundobject/collection/LeesMcRae/id/80/rec/1.

Rebel in the Mosque
Going Where I Know I Belong

ASRA Q. NOMANI

Asra Nomani moved to the United States from India in 1969. Her father, Zafar Nomani, came to America in the mid-1960s as part of India's "brain drain," a diaspora of Indian immigrants attracted to American universities to study and work. When she was ten years old, the family moved to Morgantown, West Virginia, where Nomani went to high school and then attended West Virginia University. Her mother, an entrepreneur and activist, owned and operated Ain International, an international boutique in Morgantown, for twenty-two years.

As a Muslim in a non-Muslim culture, Asra Nomani often found ways to reconcile the two. However, in October 2003 when she took a stand for the right of Muslim women to walk through the front door of mosques and to pray in the main worship hall at her local mosque, Nomani became an activist for Muslim women's rights. On March 1, 2005, she posted "99 Precepts for Opening Hearts, Minds and Doors in the Muslim World" on the doors of the Morgantown mosque and served as the lead organizer of the woman-led Muslim prayer in New York City on March 18, 2005. In "Rebel in the Mosque: Going Where I Know I Belong," Nomani describes her challenge to the Morgantown mosque and the Muslim community's response. Nomani, a reporter for the *Wall Street Journal* for fifteen years, is the author of *Standing Alone in Mecca: An American Woman's Struggle for the Soul of Islam* and *Tantrika: Traveling the Road of Divine Love.*

MORGANTOWN, W.VA.—On the 11th day of the recent Muslim holy month of Ramadan, in a pre-dawn lit by the moon, my mother, my niece and I walked through the front doors of our local mosque with my father, my nephew and my infant son. My stomach churning, we ascended to a hall to pray together.

Islamic teaching forbids men and women praying directly next to each other in mosques. But most American mosques have gone well beyond that simple prohibition by importing largely from Arab culture a system of separate accommodations that provides women with wholly unequal services for prayer and education. And yet, excluding women ignores the rights the prophet Muhammad gave them in the 7th century and represents "innovations" that emerged after the prophet died. I had been wrestling with these injustices for some time when I finally decided to take a stand.

I had no intention of praying right next to the men, who were seated at the front of the cavernous hall. I just wanted a place in the main prayer space. As my mother, my niece and I sat about 20 feet behind the men, a loud voice broke the quiet. "Sister, please! Please leave!" one of the mosque's elders yelled at me.

"It is better for women upstairs." We women were expected to enter by a rear door and pray in the balcony. If we wanted to participate in any of the activities below us, we were supposed to give a note to one of the children, who would carry it to the men in the often near-empty hall. "I will close the mosque," he thundered. I had no idea at that moment if he would make good on his threat. But I had no doubt that our act of disobedience would soon embroil the mosque, and my family, in controversy. Nevertheless, my mind was made up.

"Thank you, brother," I said firmly. "I'm happy praying here."

In fact, for the first time since the start of Ramadan, I was happy in prayer. In the nearly two months since that day, I have entered the mosque through the front door and prayed in the main hall about 30 times. My battle has been rather solitary; only four women, including my sister-in-law, and three girls have joined me from time to time. And yet I feel victorious.

In a sense, the seeds of my rebellion go back to childhood. I am a 38-year-old Muslim woman born in Bombay and raised in West Virginia. My father and other men started the first mosque here in Morgantown in a room they rented across from the Monongalia County Jail. When we were young, my brother used to join them in prayer. I don't remember ever being invited. What I do recall is celebrating one Muslim holiday trapped in an efficiency apartment with other women, while the men enjoyed a buffet in a spacious lounge elsewhere. As I grew older, I felt increasingly alienated because I didn't feel I could find refuge in my religion as a strong-willed, open-minded woman.

When I became pregnant last year while unmarried, I struggled with the edicts of some Muslims who condemned women to be stoned to death for having babies out of wedlock. I wrote in the Washington Post about such judgments being un-Islamic, and my faith was buoyed by the many Muslims who rallied to my side. To raise my son, Shibli, as a Muslim, I had to find a way to exist peacefully within Islam.

I had tried to accept the status quo through the first days of Ramadan, praying silently upstairs, listening to sermons addressed only to "brothers." After so many years away, I felt I would be like an interloper if I protested. But my sense of subjugation interrupted my prayer each time I touched my forehead to the carpet. I lay in bed each night despising the men who had ordered me to use the mosque's rear entrance. "Your anger reveals a deeper pain," my friend Alan Godlas, a professor of religious studies at the University of Georgia, told me when I described the conflict I felt.

It was true. I had witnessed the marginalization of women in many parts of Muslim society. But my parents had taught me that I wasn't meant to be marginal. Nor did I believe that Islam expected that of me. I began researching that question, and I found scholarly evidence overwhelmingly concludes that mosques that bar women from the main prayer space aren't Islamic. They more aptly reflect the age of ignorance, or Jahiliya, in pre-Islamic Arabia. "Women's present marginalization in the mosque is a betrayal of what Islam had promised women and [what] was realized in the early centuries," says Asma Afsaruddin, a professor of Arabic and Islamic studies at the University of Notre Dame.

And that marginalization seems, if anything, to be worsening. CAIR, the Council on American-Islamic Relations, has concluded, based on a 2000 survey, that "the practice of having women pray behind a curtain or in another room is becoming more widespread" in this country. In 2000, women at 66 percent of the U.S. mosques surveyed prayed behind a curtain or partition or in another room, compared with 52 percent in 1994, according to the survey of leaders of 416 mosques nationwide.

And yet, notes Daisy Khan, executive director of ASMA Society, an American Muslim organization, "The mosque is a place of learning. . . . If men prevent women from learning, how will they answer to God?"

The mosque was not a men's club when the prophet Muhammad built an Islamic ummah, or "community." Nothing in the Koran restricts a woman's access to a mosque, and the prophet told men: "Do not stop the female servants of Allah from attending the mosques of Allah."

The prophet himself prayed with women. And when he heard that some men positioned themselves in the mosque to be closer to an attractive woman, his solution wasn't to ban women but to admonish the men. In Medina, during the prophet's time and for some years thereafter, women prayed in the prophet's mosque without any partition between them and the men. Historians record women's presence in the mosque and participation in

Rebel in the Mosque 155

education, in political and literary debates, in asking questions of the prophet after his sermons, in transmitting religious knowledge and in providing social services. After the prophet's death, his wife Aisha related anecdotes about his life to scribes in the mosque. And Abdullah bin Umar, a leading companion of the Prophet and a son of Omar bin al-Khattab, the second caliph, or leader of Islam, reprimanded his son for trying to prevent women from going to the mosque. "By the third century of Islam, many [women's] rights slowly began to be whittled away as earlier Near Eastern . . . notions of female propriety and seclusion began to take hold," said Afsaruddin.

The Fiqh Council of North America, which issues legal rulings for the Islamic Society of North America (ISNA), supports women's rights in the mosque. "It is perfectly Islamic to hold meetings of men and women inside the masjid," the mosque, says Muzammil H. Siddiqi, a Fiqh Council member. He adds that this is true "whether for prayers or for any other Islamic purpose, without separating them with a curtain, partition or wall."

All too often, however, the mosque in America "is a men's club where women and children aren't welcome," said Ingrid Mattson, an Islamic scholar at the Hartford Seminary and an ISNA vice president.

One of the issues working against American Muslim women—an issue not much discussed outside the Muslim community—is the de facto takeover of many U.S. mosques by conservative and traditionalist Muslims, many from the Arab world. Most of these are immigrants, many of them students, who follow the strict Wahhabi and Salafi schools of Islam, which largely exclude women from public spaces. They stack our mosque library with books printed by the government of Saudi Arabia, where Wahhabi teachings reign. Here in Morgantown, students from Saudi Arabia and Egypt, mostly male and conservative, were virtually nonexistent 10 years ago. More precisely, there were three. Today there are 55, and their wives regularly glide through the local Wal-Mart wearing black abayas, or gowns. (Ironically, the Saudi government says that partitions and separate rooms aren't required in mosques.)

Sadly, the students' presence emboldens (or in some places cows) American mosque leaders, many of whom try to rationalize the discrimination against women through a hadith, a saying of the prophet: "Do not prevent your women from (going to) the mosques, though their houses are best for them." But scholars consider this an allowance, not a restriction. The prophet made the statement after women complained when he said Muslims get 27 times more blessings when praying at the mosque.

Much of this discrimination is also practiced in the name of "protecting" women. If women and men are allowed to mix, the argument goes, the mosque will become a sexually charged place, dangerous for women and distracting to men. In our mosque, only the men are allowed to use a microphone to address the faithful. When I asked why, a mosque leader declared, "A woman's voice is not to be heard in the mosque." What he meant was that a woman's voice—even raised in prayer—is an instrument of sexual provocation to men. Many women accept these rulings; their apathy makes these rules the status quo.

I am heartened that some Muslim men are fighting for women's rights. On that 11th day of Ramadan last month, when I made clear that I would pray in the main hall, my 70-year-old father stood by me as a mosque elder said to him, "There will be no praying until she leaves."

"She is doing nothing wrong," my father insisted. "If you have an issue, talk to her." Four men bounded toward me. "Sister, please! We ask you in the spirit of Ramadan, leave. We cannot pray if you are here." But my answer was: I have prayed like this from Mecca to Jerusalem. It is legal within Islam, I said. I remained firm.

The next day, the mosque's all-male board voted to make the main hall and front door accessible solely by men. My father dissented. Mosque leaders have not prevented me from worshiping in the main hall while the decision receives an internal legal review. "Grin and bear it. It will change one day," one American Muslim leader suggested to me. A woman in my mosque pleaded with me not to talk about any of this publicly. But gentle ways protect gender apartheid in our mosques, and we do no one a service by allowing it to continue, least of all the Muslim community. So I have filed a complaint against my mosque with CAIR, whose mandate is to protect Muslim civil rights.

After one of the final nights of Ramadan, considered a "night of power," my father gave me an early eidie, a gift elders give on Eid, the festival that marks the end of the holy month. He handed me a copy of the key to the mosque's front door, sold the night before at a fundraiser. I traced the key's edge with my thumb and put it on my Statue of Liberty key chain, because it is here in America that Muslims can truly liberate mosques from cultural traditions that belie Islam's teachings.

"Praise be to Allah," my father told me. "Allah has given you the power to make change."

I rattled the keys in front of my son, who reached out for them, and I said to him, "Shibli, we've got the keys to the mosque. We've got the keys to a better world."

Source: Asra Nomani, "Rebel in the Mosque: Going Where I Know I Belong," *Washington Post* (Outlook), December 28, 2003.

An Undocumented Mexican Mother of a High School Dropout in East Tennessee

MARIA ALEJANDRA LOPEZ

The following document is based on a phenomenological study on undocumented Mexican immigrant mothers of high school students who have lived in the United States for at least five years and received social services. Most of these mothers emigrated from rural areas of the central and southern Mexican states of Guanajuato, Michoacan, and Queretaro, among others. According to the participants, socioeconomic conditions forced them to leave their homelands hoping to find a better life in the United States.

Ten undocumented mothers of high school students living in the United States were interviewed from a phenomenological perspective. They were monolingual Spanish speakers (only one mother spoke a native Mexican dialect as a first language and Spanish as a second language), parents of several children, and unskilled laborers with little formal education. This research explored the experiences of these mothers, their beliefs and values, and their relationship with their children's school and the community in general. The study confirmed some known outcomes, but also revealed other findings that are critical to the development of school and social service programs.

These mothers shared their joys and tribulations in the United States. The main issues they faced were (1) financial struggles, (2) lack of communication (with the school and the society in general), (3) isolation, and (4) lack of control. Their lack of documents affected their chances to obtain a good job and to access benefits such as social services. None of the participants spoke English, so communication with the school and the community in general was minimal. They mainly interacted with Spanish-speaking people, family members, and some friends, and they felt intimidated when they attempted to speak in English. They reported isolation in their lives. As a consequence of their lack of English command, they had a limited social network, basically remaining in their homes, or participating in a few social activities with other Hispanic people. Last, they reported that they experienced lack of control in the education of their children as well as the school staff.

To summarize, these mothers reported experiences of both joy and struggle. They maintained a positive attitude, and emphasized the advantages of living in the United States, such as free schools that provided breakfast and lunch for their children, jobs for themselves and their husbands, and a future. In Mexico, to the contrary, they said it was expensive to send their children to school, food was not free at school, and they had to pay for school supplies, which impeded their efforts to send their children to school. Additionally, they said they struggled financially in Mexico. Despite their continued struggles in the United States, participants of this study seemed satisfied to be living there and remained hopeful about their future.

THE IMAGE OF HISPANIC STUDENTS

Interviewer: Tell me about your experience as a mother of a child in high school . . .

Participant: I was very involved in my kid's problems because, actually, Diego started perfectly fine, we demanded [of] him a lot, when he just started high school, our store started getting a lot of time and energy from us, so we neglected our responsibility about demanding [more of] Diego, like grades, and study. So, as the store was growing, I mean, he was given a car to go to school, he did not take the bus, and all our problems started from there, because he was given a cell phone to communicate with us, we spent less time with him, our little child was always with us. So it was *catastrophic,* the beginning of our store, because there was money to get more things, so we neglected his school. Our younger little boy did not go to school at that time, but Diego went to school. So he started driving, he started having money, he started using his cell phone, he had his friends in his car, and he did not go to class. I mean, when he went to class he was a very well

An Undocumented Mexican Mother 159

behaved kid. Everybody liked him, they saw him achieving things and all that, but when he said "I am not going to school today I am going out," he would go out with his friends, he would say, "Hey, I have money, let's go, I take you to that city, let's go to that other city, let's go there . . . ," and he would go out with a bunch of five or six friends.

I: Uh-huh . . .

P: So, the school did not communicate with me, they did not tell me anything about that, or they did, they asked him to tell me and he did not say anything to me, I did not know anything until a year and a half after all those problems started, I did not know anything (pause).

I: Uh-huh, you did not know anything . . .

P: No, and I thought my son was doing fine, I asked him, "How are you doing Diego?" He said "I am doing fine, I have a grade that may be a little low but I will be okay." And we believed him, dad, mom, we all believed him (pause).

I: Uh-huh.

P: But it was so horrible when, I mean, the disappointment when, it was like two years later when I found out (pause).

I: How did you find out?

P: I found out because, some friends told me, I did not find out through the school, because, I believe Diego faked my signature, and when they (the school staff) asked him to go with his mom, he asked some of my friends to go to the school, and he told them (school staff) they (my friends) were his aunts and they signed for me, well (pause).

I: Did the school tell you?

P: No, Diego told me later, he told me that one of my friends went to school for her daughter, and he told my friend, "Look, my mom is working, you know, she is pregnant, she has a lot of problems with the baby, would you mind signing something for me? They are going to tell you something about me, but I am going to be there." She (my friend) told him, "Oh, yes, Diego, of course, tell your mom I said hello ok?" And she signed, and I believe that Diego faked my signature before that, he signed all the documents they sent me, he, he signed, and when he wanted to get permission to skip school, he signed, he would write a letter saying I wanted them to excuse him to miss school.

160 IDENTITY AND WOMEN OF THE MOUNTAIN SOUTH: DOCUMENTS

I: And the school never said anything?

P.: The school is okay with that, I feel that the school does not apply a *mano dura* (firm hand) with Hispanics and with Hispanics' problems, because the Hispanic child is problematic. The Hispanic child in himself is problematic, so they (the teachers) would say "shut up" or "sit down," but they (the kids) would answer in Spanish. Sometimes they do not want to pay attention or they do not care about what they are told. I feel they are happy when they (the kids) are in ELL (English Language Learners) classes with other Hispanic kids. They have a great time there, a lot of fun (pause).

I: You mean the kids or the teachers?

P: No, the kids, students, teachers have no control, they cannot demand more than that to them, because we Hispanics work a lot. Americans understand their language, a phone call from the teacher, or the principal, or anybody. A phone call to a dad and that is perfect, but we do not, we must go with somebody else. Like the school counselor, we have in town, but he is overwhelmed with his job, I think he does not even bother himself to do anything. He would just send a little letter, and the letter was gone before I went to get it, because Diego took it, signed it, and sent it back to school (pause).

I: You said something very interesting before. You said that the Hispanic child is problematic. Say more about that . . .

P: Yes, Hispanic children are, um, I noticed that with Diego, when he first came from Mexico here, he was just nine years old, and I saw how they, I saw the teacher-student relationship. I saw them (teachers) getting very frustrated and giving up (pause).

I: Say more about that. What did you see?

P: They told them, "Do not speak in Spanish; speak in English." They said that in English of course, and the kids said, "I do not speak English." They were sitting on the floor, on their desks. Even though the teachers wanted to punish them, they just gave them after school detention for five minutes, or half an hour. Diego came home sometimes, like half an hour later and I asked him, "Hey, why are you coming late?" and he said, "Oh, I just talked in a class and they gave me a 30 minute after school detention at the principal's office or whatever."

I: He was in after school detention . . . ?

An Undocumented Mexican Mother 161

P: Yes, so, um, a lot of kids had that problem, when Diego went to school, there were a few Hispanics, I believe there were like five or six Hispanic children with him, just a few, so, they did not apply a *mano dura* (firm hand). They said "We cannot handle them" but they (children) were not that bad, they were a little bad, they were very good at math (pause).

COMMUNICATION

I: Let me ask you something. How was the communication between you and the school when all this happened? You said the school did not contact you, I mean, they sent you letters but Diego intercepted them, so how was that, have they ever called you? Did you go to the school? Did you talk with anybody?

P: No, two years after all that happened, the first semester in high school was good. The second semester was okay, neither good or bad, but the second year was bad until the third year. Um, so, when I found out he was doing bad, that was the second year he did not go to school, he did not have any credits. He was supposed to have, like, twenty credit hours and he only had like nine credit hours, the ones he got in his first year. He passed to the next grade, the next grade, and the next grade (pause).

I: So he passed grades even though he did not have enough credits?

P: Yes, I do not understand that . . .

I: The school did not call you, did not say like "Look . . . ma'am" . . . ?

P: (Interrupting). No, this was at the very end, after two years, so, um, we went to a meeting, we talked with a counselor and with a whole bunch of people, a judge, all of them. So then, I did not go to that meeting, my husband and Diego went to that meeting. And they (school staff) told him (husband) was going to have to pay fifty dollars a day, because he missed too many school days . . .

I: Do you remember how many days he missed?

P: No, I do not remember, but if a semester has, let's say, if a semester has a hundred classes, he attended forty classes, and missed sixty classes. So, yes, he crossed the limit, and they said, "This is not Diego's problem, this is Diego's parents' problem."

I: Who said that?

162 IDENTITY AND WOMEN OF THE MOUNTAIN SOUTH: DOCUMENTS

P: Um, the, the people who attended that meeting, I do not know who they were . . .

I: Was that at the school?

P: No, it was not at the school, in another . . .

I: The board of education . . .

P: Yes, there, the board of education . . .

I: I remember that your husband told me there was a meeting at the BOE and somebody told him that he had a problem . . .

P: Yes, so, we told them, "Um, this is the first time I hear this, I did not know anything. How can you do this to me?" They said, "You did not know anything because you do not care about your child, but this happened, we sent you hundreds of letters during all this time, and it has been two years, and you ignored the letters." So, my husband comes home and asks me, "Did you know anything about those letters?" and I said, "I have never seen them, I have never read them. I have never responded to those letters, because I never had them in my hands." So Diego told us, "I signed the letters, I responded to those letters, I took them to the school." So I was ignorant of all that, we are the parents, and we did not know anything. So they said, "If you do not take care of this, if Diego continues to miss school days, or if he takes any of his classmates with him, you either go to jail or you have to pay fifty (50) dollars every time he misses a school day."

THE EFFORT TO STAY IN SCHOOL

P: So, um, when we were going to take him out of school, after all that happened, we talked with a school counselor. My husband and I went to the school to talk with them, they wanted us to say that he was going to leave the school, I mean, like "Diego is not going back to school, he is not going to attend school, anymore, he is going to start a home-school program . . . '

I: They wanted you to say that . . .

P: I think so, but I could not take him out of school because of his age, he was about to be seventeen years old, he had to go to school, so they said, "After the break, he is going to be eighteen years old, so then you can take him out of school."

An Undocumented Mexican Mother 163

I: Uh-huh . . .

P: So we told them, they sent us downstairs, we went to talk with somebody else, because, I, I wanted him to stay in school until he was eighteen. So he said, "Look, he can stay in this school, that is not a problem, but he has to promise he is going to cooperate, and when he is eighteen years old, it does not make any sense for him to stay here." So they said, "Home school is better for him, you have to supervise, him, you have to watch him, you have to demand of him, because he is going to be home studying, working on school projects, and you will know what he is doing, he is not going anywhere. We have no problem if he wants to stay in school, but he has to come to study, not to play, or miss school days."

I: Uh-huh.

P: So they said, "Well, if you want him to stay here that is fine, but home school would be his best option, we are not running him off, but we cannot handle him, and you cannot handle him, so we have to make some drastic decisions, he has court, he has to go to court." So we took him to court, he had several court days. We went to court one day, the judge grumbled to me, that was horrible, she grumbled to him, and said, she said to him, "Look, your mother is Mexican, she is not a US citizen, she is *illegal,* your father is *illegal,* you should not be in this country, and you do not even want to go to school. You know what I can do? I can send you back to your country, with your mom and dad." So Diego told her, "They have a job here" and she said, "What do they have?" He said, "They have their own business." So the judge said, "I can take their business away from them and send you back to your country with nothing in your hands, you want that?"

A MOTHER'S DREAMS

I: It sounds like he wants to work now . . .

P: Um, sometimes he says he is tired and bored of working . . .

I: Well, he can change his mind, he is young . . . Let me ask you this, what are your expectations for him as a mother?

P: Well, like any dreamer mom, I would like him to get married, to have his family and at least to have a technical degree, a career, short but something to be able to defend himself, here. Because, he does not have a social security, if we do not have any documents to be in this country so we are a Don Nadie (Mr. Nobody), right? And without a degree, it is even worse. What helps him a lot is that he speaks English, and he is a very charismatic child, he has, he has a lot of, um, he is very good communicating with people, he has good manners (don de gentes) . . .

I: He is very nice . . .

P: Yes, and people treat him well anywhere. Americans, Hispanics, but I would like for him that, um to grow as a person, so that he could get at least a short career. He is going to be a dad, he has a girlfriend, the girl is pregnant, they became independent, they live together, they pay their bills, I tell him, "Well, that is perfect, but I would like for you to marry her."

I: Tell me about that, I do not know that, I am from Argentina; is it important for you to get married instead of living together? How is it in your culture?

P: In our culture, um, if you get married, you comply with your partner; you can be with that person all the time, but with God's laws, and with civil laws. Yes, you protect your children, if you get divorced, your children will be unprotected, and without a father, without papers. You have your father and mother's last names. In a marriage, otherwise, we are natural children, you are only your mom's child, you have your mom's last name. So, yes, in our culture getting married is something very good, so you have your documents as a couple, and your children are protected. If you are not there, if the father is not there, children have rights to get things from their father, or a good last name, and to be a child within the marriage, but um, he agrees with the American liberalism ideas . . .

I: Say more about that . . .

P: Well, he is like Americans, he says, "No, I do not need a piece of paper. I do not want to get married." And his girlfriend says that, too. She says, "Now we love each other, and if we do not love each other anymore we can part ways" (pause).

I: Do you believe Americans do that . . . ?

P: No, I do not believe that . . .

I: So why did you say that he agrees with the American liberalism ideas . . . some Americans get married . . . they like getting married . . .

An Undocumented Mexican Mother 165

P: Really?

I: I guess . . .

P: But the kids at school, his classmates, they are seventeen, eighteen years old, they have their girlfriends, they make them pregnant and leave. They start dating other people, the girls start dating other men, they do not live together, the babies live with their grandparents. He did not do that when he was in school, but he is doing it now that he left school . . .

I: Uh-huh. I thought you were talking about living together, something I noticed about Hispanics is that they live together but consider that as "being married," they say "my wife" or "my husband," I respect that . . .

P: Yes, yes, in fact, they do that, most Hispanics like "cohabitation" (union libre) . . .

I: They cohabitate sometimes for 20, 30 years . . .

P: Yes, but some people cohabitate and they leave and cohabitate with somebody else and . . .

I: It could be, it could be . . .

P: And they do not care about their kids, and then there is a lot of children with different dads and moms and so, and Americans do that, they are married and they are with other people. We, Hispanics are more conservative, the family is more traditional, my husband's family is all about getting married, my family, too. There is all kind of people from all over the world, and there are people who only like cohabitation, but I do not agree with that . . .

I: You do not agree with that.

P: I do not agree with that, we told Diego, he asked his girlfriend's hand, they have been together for four years . . .

Source: Maria Alejandra Lopez, "Listening to Undocumented Mothers: The Experiences of Undocumented Mexican Mothers of High School Students Living in the U.S. and Receiving Social Services" (PhD diss., University of Tennessee, Knoxville, 2010).

Great-grandmother Eve (1800–1860), with Bible.

Civil War mother and child.

Sarah Seals (1840?–1913), born and held in bondage in Monongalia County, West Virginia. Courtesy of Laura Michaels.

Woman, river baptism, Pocahontas County, West Virginia, 1910. *West Virginia and Regional History Center, WVU Libraries.*

The Higginbotham baby stays at home with a black nurse, while father and mother work in the West Point Cotton Mill, West Point, Clay County, Mississippi. *Library of Congress, National Child Labor Committee Collection, Lewis Wickes Hine, photographer.*

(*left*) Sisters Hilda and Helen McCormick, c. 1924. *Marion County, West Virginia.*

(*below*) Maude Welsh making Indian pottery, Cherokee, North Carolina. *National Park Service, June 1952, Abbe Rowe, photographer. From the Joe Jennings Collection, Archives of Appalachia, East Tennessee State University, Johnson City.*

Part 1: Identity and Women of the Mountain South

Questions for Discussion

1. Discuss the blending of cultures in the Mountain South that Tedesco describes in her essay on the Cherokee and how such blending affected the identity of persons of mixed heritage. Did the Cherokee establish a pattern of cultural sharing that continues today? Where and when? In regard to identity, do you think that persons with Cherokee ancestry, especially partial Cherokee ancestry, experience rejection by mainstream white culture today?

2. Is the Mountain South a distinct and identifiable region? Discuss characteristics of the Mountain South usually applied to the Appalachian region. How have these characteristics evolved over time?

3. In what ways are individual and community identity linked to place?

4. How has "cultural otherness" been used both outside and inside the region to define the region?

5. Analyze the concepts of race, gender, and identity in the Mountain South, from the early nineteenth century to the present. How have these evolved and changed over time?

6. What does identity mean? What attachments do you have to place? Do you identify with a specific place (your home place or an adopted place)?

PART TWO

Women and Work in Appalachia

In Appalachia, as elsewhere, the gainfully employed create their own strategies for resistance and selective compliance with those for whom they labor. Yet others fight for the right to work, while all endeavor to live with dignity amid the contradictions of the changing centuries.

—Mary K. Anglin, *Women, Power, and Dissent in the Hills of Carolina*

CHAPTER SIX

Challenging the Myth of Separate Spheres

Women's Work in the Antebellum Mountain South

WILMA A. DUNAWAY

She looketh well to the ways of her household, and eateth not the bread of idleness.

—Christopher Marshall, Diary[1]

In a period when so many feminist writers are questioning separate spheres assumptions, recent scholarship often reduces women to a racially and economically homogeneous group who are confined in their homes.[2] Not only do such popular culture claims ignore the realities of the lives of poor white, Native American, and enslaved and free black females, but they also ignore the few revisionist works that have emerged about Appalachian women's work and community roles.[3] Conceptually, we need to stop being blinded by oversimplified stereotypes about women being trapped in housebound labors outside the reach of market forces, an idea that is a ghost from the separate spheres legacy.[4] If we search only for unpaid labors that were "manifestations of their private roles as housewives and mothers," we miss the real "dialectics of waged and unwaged labor" that characterize most women's resource accumulation.[5] First, we must move away from the naive notion that all work done by women in households was *without* economic value and was *outside* the market. From a feminist standpoint, we need to be careful about broad use of the phrase "labor force," which refers narrowly to waged occupations, for we cannot judge a woman's income-earning capacity solely by her employment in a waged occupation outside her home. Historically in the United States and worldwide today, women have generated most of their household resources outside waged occupations.[6] Second, we need to employ a "multigridded conceptualization" of women's work, taking into account differences of race, class, ethnicity, marital status, religion, and rural/urban location.[7] Third, we must stop stereotyping Appalachians with an overstated "rural isolation" that neither reflects the capacity of women to market commodities nor gives voice to those females who resided in or near towns.[8]

METHODS OF RESEARCH AND ORGANIZATION OF THE STUDY

I made a concerted effort to locate and include as many women's transcripts as possible, so I drew upon a wide array of archived manuscripts, missionary letters and journals, diaries, letters, the Appalachian Oral History Project (1977), the archival collection of Civil War veteran questionnaires,[9] the *Foxfire* collections,[10] emigrant narratives, and slave narratives. I triangulated hundreds of such primary and archival sources with statistical analysis of samples drawn from public records. With respect to many patterns of women's lives, I am able to "fill in the gaps" caused by the lack of female narratives through analysis of gendered patterns that are evident in a large database of nearly 20,000 antebellum households drawn from Cherokee censuses, frontier county tax lists, and antebellum census manuscripts for 215 counties in nine states. To acquire a rich reservoir of details about women's occupations and livelihoods, I drew four household and farm samples from nineteenth-century census manuscripts for Appalachian counties. In order to reserve as much space as possible for substantive analysis, I have posted at a permanent electronic archive an extensive discussion about research methods and about the primary sources that I have used to end historical silences about Appalachian women.[11]

I will call into question the separate-spheres thesis that Appalachian women's work has traditionally been confined to home and a small area near the dwelling. To varying degrees, depending on their class and racial positions, antebellum Appalachian women engaged in a complex portfolio of agricultural and nonagricultural labors that defied separate spheres norms, including farm labor and income-earning labors within and outside their households. What is striking is the degree to which female labors were so similar across racial boundaries for those women who were poor. Only those females who resided in households wealthy enough to afford slaves or paid servants could avoid back-breaking labor, and less than one-half of Appalachian women were enumerated in census manuscripts as having no occupation other than "homemaker." In the sections that follow, I will examine the diverse labor portfolios of Appalachian women, which included

- economically valuable agricultural labors within the household,
- economically valuable nonagricultural labors within the household,
- income-earning labors within the informal sector, and
- waged labor outside the household.

ECONOMICALLY VALUABLE AGRICULTURAL LABORS WITHIN THE HOUSEHOLD

While a majority of all Appalachian women worked at field labor and outdoor farm tasks to some degree, class and race determined the extent to which a woman worked regularly at heavy manual labor. Even though the cultural ideal may have been that southern ladies did no field work, the vast majority of Appalachian women undertook agricultural labors in order to ensure the survival of their households.[12] More than one-third of white adult females, half of free black females, 95 percent of Cherokee females, and two-thirds of enslaved females worked in agriculture, doing the same backbreaking field work and farm tasks that were stereotyped to be men's work.

Despite pressures from the US civilization program, Cherokee women resisted cultural change in order to maintain their dominance in subsistence food production in their communities and households.[13] When Cherokees were forcibly removed in 1838, missionaries and Indian agents were still complaining that females had not become "civilized" enough to abandon the fields and leave such labor to their men.

Challenging the Myth of Separate Spheres 175

In the later antebellum period, travelers commented on the groups of Cherokee women who were still visibly growing and marketing crops.[14] Similarly, nearly one-half of free black females and two-third of enslaved females worked alongside men at backbreaking field labor. One of every three farm owners in the region held slaves, and these middling and larger farms more often employed black women in their fields than males. Slave girls entered the fields at a younger age than boys because owners thought females were better physically coordinated and exhibited higher crop-picking rates.[15]

Even though an overwhelming majority of white Appalachian households were engaged in farming, only about half of them owned land in 1860.[16] One-fifth of the region's farm owners held fewer than a hundred acres, averaged less than $300 in assets, and were impoverished by national standards. Because most of these farms could not afford to hire hands, women and girls regularly engaged in field labor and outdoor farm tasks. Half the Appalachian Civil War veterans were born into such households, so their family details give rare voice to the mothers and daughters in such circumstances. Without any demeaning criticism, these men indicated that their female kin worked in the fields, tended livestock, milked cows, cultivated garden patches, and assisted with the annual hog slaughtering and meat processing.

While most non-slaveholding middle-class females were able to avoid rigorous farm tasks, 25 percent of these wives combined heavy housework with some outdoor work. Except for the sons of slaveholders, the Civil War veterans almost never employed the phrase "women's work" or any other term that segregated females into a sphere separate from "men's work." In fact, a majority of Appalachian veterans included within the scope of "housework" many outdoor farm tasks that the cult of domesticity reserved for males. About one of every three Appalachian wives resided in a household that owned or hired slaves, and about one-quarter of the large non-slaveholding farm owners hired servants for their wives.[17] These females never engaged in field labor, heavy manual tasks, or waged labor to supplement family income. In comparison to elite wives, women did more housework in middle-class slaveholding households, but they still did far less manual labor than poorer females.

Like their counterparts in other sections of the country, some antebellum Appalachian women acquired their own agricultural land. Fewer than 8 percent of the region's farm owners were females, but nearly one-fifth of the white female heads of household owned their own farms. Three-quarters of them were middle income or better in economic status, and they fared slightly better than their male counterparts. Female farm owners averaged 374 acres, while males averaged only 335 acres; moreover, female owners averaged nearly $2,000 more in total wealth than male owners. In these households, the female owners hired laborers or held slaves, but they still did not fit the idealized image of the "cult of domesticity" because they engaged in farm management that was typically considered men's work.

In sharp contrast, nearly two of every five Appalachian farm operators were tenant farmers or sharecroppers for landlords who were producing cash crops and livestock herds for export.[18] These landless farm laborers lived a precarious existence, and they were constantly on the move in search of employment. Because more than four-fifths of these households failed to produce enough food to meet their household consumption needs, the productive inputs of wives were essential to family survival. Virtually every wife whose tenant or cropper husband worked in close proximity to the home was expected to contribute labor as an assistant to the market-oriented production of her spouse. As part of the process in which labor and resources were transferred within households, the tenant or cropper wife and her children were expected to become "unpaid employees" in the cultivation of the landlord's cash crops.

In addition to females in households that operated farms, another 15 percent of white Appalachian women were identified in census manuscripts as waged farm laborers.[19] These women lived in some of the most desperately poor households in the region, and their families moved repeatedly in search of new employment. Most of these women would have worked in day laborer households in which "wages" often amounted to no more than subsistence. It was common for the females in these poor white households to work the fields alongside white or black males. Poor white women also worked alongside slaves at community work parties, like cornhuskings or log rollings.

We should not just view these women as one-dimensional females we should pity because they were victims of menial toil assigned to

Challenging the Myth of Separate Spheres 177

them by patriarchal husbands and fathers. Most of these women did field labor without any recognition that they were stepping across gender boundaries into "men's work." Primary documents demonstrate far less cultural dominance by the "prevailing southern ideology" of "gracious, fragile, and deferential" wives an daughters than feminists like Elizabeth Fox-Genovese have claimed.[20] Isolation in a separate feminine sphere was a luxury that most Appalachian women were not afforded. Rather, their households operated as inequitable resource pooling units, in which every member was expected to contribute labor and survival resources to ensure the persistence of their families. Perhaps Caney Hall best expressed the idea that white household members knew they had to function together as a survival unit when he said, "People lived hard. Didn't believe we couldn't work. All of them—not just one." Hall's oral history does not include a single comment that indicates any recognition on his part that there should be a separate sphere for females.[21] Second, some women actually preferred outdoor farm work over domestic duties. June Ehle and Julie Price summarized their mothers' philosophies about a "woman's place in life," that sphere being "work at anything to get food for her family."[22] Many enslaved women preferred field work over domestic service. Assignment to the master's household increased the likelihood that females would be sexually exploited by white males. In their productivity levels, some of the enslaved women competed with males.

The third reason that women did field labor was that husbands and fathers became ill or died. In fact, nearly 10 percent of the Civil War veterans described mothers who took charge of farms in such circumstances. The fourth explanation for female field labor derived from the need to free males for nonagricultural work. Enslaved women were assigned to field labor to release males for occupations that would earn their owners greater profits. Similarly, nearly one-fifth of the Civil War veterans described poor or middle-class white mothers who took charge of farm work in order to free their fathers to undertake nonagricultural occupations. The fathers of one of every eight of the veterans left farm management to their wives while they pursued commercial enterprises, professions, or artisan trades that kept them away from home for long periods of time.[23]

ECONOMICALLY VALUABLE NONAGRICULTURAL LABORS WITHIN THE HOUSEHOLD

In addition to their farm labors, females also engaged in several forms of economically valuable nonagricultural labor for their households. During annual slaughtering and meat processing, the entire white family participated, and there was no clear gender-segregation in tasks. On middle-class farms and small plantations, one of the most unladylike roles of wives was their participation in and supervision of the slaughtering and meat processing. On middling to large plantations, however, most of the work was done by slaves, and every enslaved female had a job to do for which there was no gender division. Appalachian women also contributed economically to their households through their outputs of poultry, maple sugar, dairy and orchard products, garden produce, ginseng, and herbs. In 1840 Appalachian women produced 11 percent of the country's poultry, nearly 10 percent of its orchard products, more than 10 percent of home manufactures, and nearly 15 per cent of the ginseng and herbs. Even though they comprised only 5 percent of the country's 1840 population, Appalachian women generated more than 8 per cent of women's household outputs of these items nationally. Per capita, Appalachian farm women accounted for more than five dollars in these outputs while the typical American farm woman brought in only about three dollars to her household through these activities.[24]

However, the most economically-significant of these occupations was home-based textile production. Across all racial and class lines, females had engaged in such production at some level in every historical era before the Civil War. After the Revolutionary War, one of the most hidden market activities was female participation as "disguised industrial proletarians" in textile production.[25] By the late eighteenth century, the Southern Appalachian countryside was exhibiting patterns of labor organization that were typical of protoindustrialization, characterized by the coexistence of agriculture, household-based craft work, and centralized factory production. Also referred to as cottage industries by some writers, these rural handicraft industries occurred in regions where there was a surplus of underemployed rural laborers who had few occupational options, as was indeed the case in antebellum Southern Appalachia.[26] Because household survival could not be ensured

Challenging the Myth of Separate Spheres 179

through agriculture alone, many adults became involved in "the part-time or full-time transition from land-intensive agrarian production to labor-intensive craft production."[27] From the frontier years until the Civil War, Cherokee, white, and black females engaged in home-based textile manufacturing.

There were 2,495 indigenous households when the *Cherokee Phoenix* reported 2,792 plows, 2,428 spinning wheels, and 769 looms.[28] By that account, there were nearly as many spinning wheels as horses. These statistics make it appear that every household had a spinning wheel and that one-third of the families had acquired looms. By 1835 the numbers had grown to 2,484 weavers and 3,129 spinners, seemingly indicating that nearly three-quarters of the 4,328 adult women could spin while more than half could weave.[29]

On Appalachian frontiers, the most significant nonagricultural labor in which white women engaged was household textile manufacturing. After the Revolutionary War, US textile production displaced the heavy imports that had characterized the colonial period, and women accounted for most of that output in their homes.[30] In 1810 only 7.4 percent of US cloth was produced by factory machinery. Nationally, the United States had only 1,776 carding machines and 1,682 fulling mills to process cotton, flax, and/or wool into thread or yarn. Fewer than 2 million pounds of cotton and wool were spun in mills, while households spun more than 26 million pounds. Because the country was heavily dependent upon household textile production, the early national censuses acknowledged the economic value of this type of women's work. In the Appalachian counties of North Carolina, for example, women's spinning was even more extensive. The census enumerated 1.7 wheels for every adult white western North Carolina female, indicating that a majority of households had both the small wheel for flax and the large wheel for wool and cotton. In addition, more than half the households reported flax brakes, indicating a heavy output of linen and linsey-woolsey. Since the census distinguished household looms and the cloth "made in families" from factory textiles and equipment, it is clear that women were weaving 13.4 yards in their homes to every yard of cotton or wool cloth produced by factory equipment. There were cloth mills in only four Appalachian counties, so households wove nearly 7.5

million yards of cloth valued at more than $3.6 million. More than half the white adult females owned looms, and they averaged nearly 207 yards of cloth annually, valued at more than $100. Per capita, Southern Appalachian weavers created 2.6 times more yards of cloth than other US females. Unfortunately, we cannot use those census reports to determine what proportion of that textile production was actually done by slaves within elite or middle-class households.[31]

Though they represented less than 8 percent of the US population, adult Southern Appalachian females produced nearly one-third of the country's cloth in 1810. Not all the fabric traded by women stayed in their resident counties, as is evidenced by distant businesses that advertised in Appalachian newspapers. One Richmond commission merchant was "set up more particularly with a view of doing a Western Country business."[32] In southwestern Virginia and East Tennessee newspapers, he offered to trade all sorts of European imports for good-quality cotton, linen, and woolen cloth. For export to West Indies plantations, an eastern North Carolina commission merchant sought to purchase cloth produced in western North Carolina. Boothe and Dews, an auction and commission house at Knoxville, offered to market on consignment "every description of dry goods," including "cotton yarn" and fabrics that could be exported to the Deep South.[33]

According to Dublin, women continued these frontier patterns of home-based production and accounted for the vast majority of the country's clothing throughout the antebellum period. Early factories "did not so much replace household manufacture as complement it. By mechanizing the slowest, most laborious steps in the production process, the carding and fulling mills actually contributed to increasing production of cloth in the home."[34] In similar fashion, a majority of post-1820 Appalachian textile production occurred in homes, and antebellum historians commented on the economic significance of this form of women's work. While small factories carded wool, most of the spinning and weaving was done in homes. In fact, there were only 43 cents worth of clothing finished in factories or artisan shops to every $2.65 worth of home textile manufactures. For example, the 1840 per capita value of western North Carolina household manufactures was more than twice the per capita value of the outputs of all US households.

Challenging the Myth of Separate Spheres 181

By 1850 the households in this Appalachian subregion were averaging nine times the outputs of other American families. Home textile manufacturing declined in this period only in the Appalachian counties of Maryland, Tennessee, Virginia, and West Virginia, where the greatest number of clothing factories had emerged.[35]

In 1860 only 16 percent of white wives and female heads of household in the United States were identified in census enumerators as seamstresses, spinners, or weavers.[36] However, the vast majority of women described in Appalachian oral histories engaged in these occupations. More than 90 percent of the mothers described by Civil War veterans either produced their own textiles or supervised servants or slaves in the spinning, weaving, and sewing processes. Half of all western North Carolina households owned spinning wheels, and three-quarters held linen and flax equipment.[37] Because of their economic significance, state laws designated spinning and weaving equipment to be the property of wives, therefore exempt from their husbands' debts or estate settlements. Census data and other primary sources indicate that a majority of the women who thought of themselves as skilled textile artisans were poor, nonwaged workers in their own cottage industries. Women's household textiles were marketed to stores, shops, or public town markets; sold or traded to more well-to-do women who wanted to be relieved of the most onerous labor involved in textile production; or produced as part of "putting-out systems" operated by factories, clothing artisan shops, or stores.

Household-based textile protoindustrialization was a multiprocess labor system that required a variety of tasks ranging from menial labor to highly skilled artisanship, but few women were skilled enough to do all the tasks.[38] On the low-skill end of the process, the vast majority of white women carded wool while only two-fifths completed the tedious steps to process flax. While most spun, knitted, sewed, and quilted, only about two-fifths had acquired the complex weaving skills and equipment.[39] Poor women's textile protoindustrialization continued for three reasons. In the region's small towns, there were very few commercial enterprises that produced finished clothing. In the entire vast geographical area, there were only forty artisan shops reported as manufacturers of clothing, gloves, mitten, and hats, and caps, and there were only seventy-two clothing factories located in fewer than one-third of the region's counties.[40] Second, more prosperous women employed textile workers to do most of the manual labor or to supervise their slaves. Third, there was a market for finished goods among more affluent households. Most middle-class women did not undertake the most backbreaking, time-consuming initial steps to process wool, flax, or cotton. Even though they utilized the finished thread, yarn, and cloth to engage in knitting, sewing, and quilting, middle-class farm women were rarely spinners, weavers, or seamstresses. Instead, they hired the wool spun on shares, then they utilized the finished yarn to knit.[41]

Some women participated in the textile putting-out system organized by factories, stores, or artisan shops. Many retail stores advanced raw materials and equipment, paying women one-third in cash and two-thirds in yarn or supplies. In some towns of western Maryland, Blue Ridge Virginia, and West Virginia, artisan shops consigned work to household-based women who were either paid wages or allocated a small share of the output. In heavily industrialized Wheeling, West Virginia, 119 women labored in their homes for milliners, dressmakers, and merchant tailors, who advanced them the wool, cotton, or cloth to card, spin, weave, or sew finished goods. In that town, the vast majority of needleworkers were seamstresses who did contract piecework for eight merchant tailors.[42]

Textile protoindustrialization was a form of superexploitation of women who juggled their time between agriculture, household chores, child rearing, crafts, informal sector marketing, and sometimes waged labor.[43] Many poor women did most of their textile production and quilting in the fall and winter months "because there wasn't enough time while the crops were being tended."[44] Other females worked late into the night, after a day of farm and household work.[45] Even though textile production was essentially "women's work," there was no gender distinction between boys and girls by poor mothers who produced fabric or clothing. Until they were teenagers, boys helped their mothers and sisters with textile tasks.[46]

Textile protoindustrialization was not generally accompanied by sustained increases in the standard of living of the workers or their families.[47] There was a vast economic divide between the small shop owners and the women who worked in cottage industries. In 1860 the

Challenging the Myth of Separate Spheres 183

typical woman who owned a textile shop earned about $632 annually and had accumulated nearly $2,000 in household wealth. In contrast, females who worked in their homes as seamstress, spinner, or weaver averaged about $61 annually, keeping their families well below the national poverty line. Those wives who did textile production in addition to their farm labor averaged only about $49 in cash annually.[48] In addition to these income inequalities, the working conditions posed health risks. According to one physician, there was no occupation that was "more unhealthy or which yield[ed] . . . a higher death return than the several classes of . . . dress makers, milliners, and those engaged in and for the several large tailoring establishments."[49] Many oral histories include comments about the harmful effects on eyes, hands, shoulders, and backs; and much of the hard physical labor would have endangered the health of pregnant women and their fetuses. For example, carding was one of the simplest tasks but was "a wearisome job and hard on the shoulders."[50] Charles Broyles's mother "worked by tallow candle light" in the evenings, while Dorie Cope kept her small flax loom near the only window where she could hope to get some sunlight on overcast days.[51] Due to lack of space, women often completed much of their preparation for weaving and spinning in the cold outdoors.[52]

In addition to these forms of home-based protoindustrialization by Cherokee and white females, slaves on small Appalachian plantations routinely engaged in textile production. The smaller the plantation, the more likely it was to depend almost exclusively on slave production of fabrics, bedding, and clothing.[53] In fact, enslaved Appalachian women were assigned to produce cloth eleven times more frequently than other US slaves.[54] Enslaved females clothed the entire labor force, minimized the cash outlay of their masters for manufactured goods, and supplied their owners with surpluses to sell. Burning pine torches, candles, or rag lamps, women worked late into the nights to produce assigned quotas of textiles. The vast majority of enslaved Appalachian women were assigned daily quotas of spinning that were to be done in the evenings after the day's field work. Except to supervise, very few mistresses participated in textile manufacturing.

By combining their varied skills, slave women completed a manufacturing process that required significant labor input every day, all year round. In the first stage, women spent many hours preparing the raw materials.[55] Wool preparation was a time-consuming process that began (with washing and cleaning. Women used two sets of metal cards, one to separate fibers and one to comb wool into rolls for spinning. After ginning, raw cotton was cleaned of stems, seeds, and debris before it could be carded. In the second stage, women spent many hours spinning the raw fibers into threads or yarns. In the third stage of textile production, threads or yarns were treated to prevent shrinkage, to whiten them, or to add colors. At the top of the hierarchy of artisans were the weavers, who specialized in the fourth and most complex stage of textile production. Before weaving could begin, however, the women spent eight to ten hours filling the loom with threads. The typical daily quota for a weaver was six to seven yards of cloth.

Except on the smallest slaveholdings, only a few women transformed the fabric into the final items of clothing. In the final stage, seamstresses and tailors collected and sized patterns, then cut and sewed garments. Individually at night, women cut scraps from old clothing to piece quilt tops in front of the fireplace. Because there were not enough slaves on many Appalachian plantations to complete all the needed textile specialties, women organized communal work parties. The neighborhood's most reputable artisan supervised the work, assigned tasks, and set quotas for spinning, dyeing, weaving, rug making, or sewing.

INCOME-EARNING LABORS WITHIN THE INFORMAL SECTOR

In addition to these home-based labors, three-quarters of all women earned cash or acquired household resources through informal sector trading. A much higher proportion of antebellum women participated in the informal sector than in any other income-earning activity. All over the world and in every historical era, women have been overrepresented in the informal sector. Because of barriers to their equitable participation in waged occupations and because the wages for domestic service were so low, the informal economy was "thrust upon women as a last resort" in the nineteenth century.[56] In 1860 more than two-fifths of white Appalachian women, two-thirds of free black women, and a majority of Cherokee and enslaved women engaged in nonwaged informal sector outputs in an attempt to earn cash or to trade for household resources.[57]

Challenging the Myth of Separate Spheres 185

After the Revolutionary War, Cherokee women peddled baskets, chickens, pottery, chestnuts, and wild berries to adjacent whites. Women also produced and traded buckeye-wood dough trays, stone pipe bowls, rhododendron hominy ladles, indigo, and oil from butternuts and walnuts. Women gathered, cured, and shipped to Charleston large quantities of ginseng and other herbs for reexport to European cities. During the winter, women sold brown sugar cakes to nearby whites. Cherokee cabins were surrounded by large numbers of fruit trees, from which women marketed fresh and dried produce. Some indigenous women bartered lidded, double-weave cane baskets to white households. Judging from store records, Cherokee women transacted trades of crafts and produce more frequently than white or black females.[58]

A majority of the mothers described by Civil War veterans earned income through informal sector exchanges of their butter, cheese, farm outputs, and home manufactures. Such exchanges were economically significant to households and to communities. In 1840 white Appalachian women exchanged through informal sector activities $1.00 in household outputs to every $1.70 generated through the formal trade in manufactured commodities.[59] Oral histories and other primary sources document all sorts of informal sector marketing by females. For those women without access to urban centers, there was the option of exchanges with peddlers. One-half the wives of farm owners and two-thirds of the women in landless farm households marketed whatever produce or crafted items they could spare. In more than half of the poor farm-owner households, both men and women produced grain and livestock surpluses for exchange; and women in three-fourths of them reported to census enumerators that they had sold market produce. Farm women also generated household cash through their production of butter, cheese, beeswax, orchard products, home manufactures, market produce, poultry, and ginseng. Women's production of surpluses and marketing of these items was so common that census enumerators valued them in monetary terms. For example, the 1850 census for Tazewell County, Virginia, valued at $51,000 women's outputs of maple sugar, beeswax, honey, butter, cheese, wool, flax seeds, and textiles. In fact, white females produced $1.00 in household products for every $3.46 in male-dominated agricultural crops.[60] On average in 1860, the region's white farm women generated nearly $63.00 in items to trade in the informal sector, a level of output that was 1.3 times the national average.

Valued at more than $9 million by census enumerators, women's farm outputs made significant contributions to their local economies. In the Appalachian counties of the Carolinas, women's farm outputs had greater economic value than did manufactured or extractive commodities, and industrial outputs were not far ahead of women's outputs in the Appalachian counties of Alabama, Georgia, and Kentucky. In West Virginia, farms were producing only $1.63 in agricultural commodities to every dollar accumulated by women from informal sector activities. In small farm owner households, women averaged more than $100 worth of commodities, accounting for nearly one-fifth of family income. Even a middle-class farm owner's wife produced more than 2 percent of the total household income. However, wives in tenant or sharecropper households generated as much as three-quarters of the cash income acquired by the households.[61]

Denied access to most forms of visible wage labor or commodity production, free blacks were almost totally dependent upon exchanges in the "underbelly" of the market. Tolls for stall space or for inspections put the town market-house out of their economic reach. As a result, these women engaged in illegal street vending and door-to-door peddling of their wares. Since they were almost never permitted store accounts, they had no means of bartering directly with local merchants. One of every ten free black women (as well as nearly 5 percent of white women) were identified in 1860 census manuscripts as washwomen, while another 12 percent (compared to 1.5 percent of white females) were enumerated as prostitutes. Even though the vast majority of Appalachian slaves engaged in garden cultivation and household production, less than 12 percent of their households ever earned cash or participated in monetary transactions. In most instances, slave women traded their surplus produce, food items, and crafted items to their own masters.[62]

WAGED LABOR OUTSIDE THE HOUSEHOLD

Even though present in smaller numbers, females were also visible in formal waged occupations. In 1820 women and children represented nearly 12 per cent of the region's manufacturing labor force, and they

Challenging the Myth of Separate Spheres 187

were already highly visible in those occupations in which they would be concentrated in the later antebellum period. In fact, they were employed in every nonagricultural economic sector, and the vast majority of them were employed in occupations that have been culturally ascribed by many scholars to be the kinds of "men's work" that were closed to females. By the 1830s, Appalachian women were earning income in nearly every industrial sector. In 1840 slightly more than 14 percent of the manufacturing and industrial labor force was female.[63] Because of their extensive home-based skills, women were employed more frequently in factory textiles production than in any other industrial sector. Females comprised two-thirds of the labor force in textile manufacturing.[64]

Even though males continued to hold most manufacturing positions, women had entered every economic sector by 1860. Almost one-third of the white wives of landless farm operators and nearly one-fifth of the white wives of poor and middle-class farm owners reported wage-paying nonagricultural occupations to census enumerators. Nearly 7 percent of the white women, one-fifth of the free black women, and nearly 15 percent of the enslaved women were employed in town commerce, professional services, domestic service, hotels and inns, travel enterprises, and transportation systems. Black women were much more likely to be employed in industrial jobs than were white females. Nearly one-quarter of all free blacks worked in manufactories, mills, and extractive industries, and more than one of every ten free black women and one of every twenty enslaved females were employed in such industrial jobs.[65] Women had a significant presence in grain milling, leather tanning, and liquor distilling, and a mixed labor force of enslaved and poor white women comprised 79 percent of the laborers who manufactured tobacco. Females represented one-quarter to one-third of the labor force in paper manufacturing and printing. Women supplied most of the labor to manufacture baskets, brooms, carpets, pottery, mattresses, soap, and candles and to process foods sold commercially.[66] Even though the work was dangerous and backbreaking, women were employed in all types of mining and timbering. Free and enslaved females accounted for 15 percent of the workers in extractive industries. Women comprised nearly 2 percent of those employed to smelt copper ore and 6 percent of the salt-manufacturing workers.[67]

In addition to their roles in industry and textile production, 6.4 percent of white females, more than one-fifth of free black women, and nearly 14 percent of enslaved females worked at income-earning activities in towns. About 4 percent of white women owned shops and stores or were professionals and artisans, and another 1 percent identified themselves as commercial laborers. Free black women supplied labor for public works, for retail enterprises, for inns and hotels, and for artisan shops. Even though free blacks were seven times less likely to own land than their white counterparts, a lucky few females owned their own shops, and about 5 percent of them operated boardinghouses or were traders.[68] Enslaved females were nearly twice as likely to be engaged in commercial jobs as white women.[69] Only about 2 percent of white women worked as domestic servants, while nearly 8 percent of free black women and about 7 percent of the region's enslaved women did.[70]

Even though white females were rarely hired to work on railroads, canals, or roads or at mineral spas, a few immigrant women were used for the least skilled jobs. More than 8 percent of slaves and about 6 percent of free blacks, about one-third of them women, were employed by transportation companies.[71] Enslaved women were disproportionately represented among the laborers hired by towns to maintain roads and turnpikes. Southern railroad construction surpassed national averages after 1845, and railroad development had occurred in fifty-three Appalachian counties by 1855.[72] Since railroad construction companies solicited laborers at $150 annually, Appalachian masters contracted one-fifth of their annual slave hires to these transportation companies, one-third of them women.[73]

The Southern Appalachians were dotted with 134 mineral spas, which were annually patronized by 10,000 to 15,000 tourists.[74] All the larger spas owned male and female slaves and advertised to lease slaves during their busy seasons. Male slaves were employed for the most visible occupations, such as valets, waiters, musicians, coachmen, hustlers, and guides, while even larger numbers of women supplied the hidden domestic labor. Appalachian slaveholders hired out surplus female laborers to service baths, clean, wash clothes, and cook.[75] In addition to spa tourism, more than one-third of the Appalachian counties supplied grain sales and inns for itinerant livestock drives. In the 1850s, drovers moved nearly 2.5 million hogs, nearly 600,000 cattle, and almost

Challenging the Myth of Separate Spheres 189

200,000 horses and mules annually through Appalachian counties. At one-day intervals along the network of livestock trails, commercial "livestock stands" provided stables, pens, pastures, and feed for the herds and lodging for the drovers.[76] Black and Cherokee females operated a few of these stands, and females were overrepresented among the laborers at these enterprises. The most visible businesswoman was the inn or hotel operator, but less than 1 percent of white and free black women owned such establishments. Even though few white women owned inns, hotels, restaurants, and mineral spas, black females were overrepresented among the laborers at these establishments as well.[77]

THERE IS NO reliable primary evidence that a majority of Appalachian women accepted the cult of domesticity or desired to be isolated in their homes or families. Elite gender conventions did not constrain the labor decisions of a majority of women who meshed together a diverse portfolio of agricultural and nonagricultural labors. Most women superimposed several types of income-generating labor upon their domestic responsibilities, and they often produced market commodities or rendered services in their homes. In the poor white, Cherokee, free black, and enslaved households that comprised a majority of the population, there was no clear gender division of labor that bifurcated work into "women's production for subsistence" and "male-dominated production for exchange."[78] Even though women were subordinate to men legally, politically, and economically, there were no separate spheres when it came to the female labors that were essential to family survival. On the one hand, households were arenas for both reproductive work and productive income-earning labors. On the other hand, women did not isolate themselves inside their households, nor did they leave the public economic sphere to males. In reality, more than two-fifths of antebellum US white women worked outside their homes, most white and nonwhite females earned income through informal sector activities, and it was not unusual for wives of all classes and racial groups to accumulate cash through home-based occupations. Even though class and race determined the likelihood that a woman would engage in hard manual labor, most females wove together a creative tapestry of labors in order to accumulate a consumption fund adequate to sustain their households.

NOTES

1. William Duance, ed., *Extracts from the Diary of Christopher Marshall Kept in Philadelphia and Lancaster during the American Revolution, 1774–1781* (Albany: Joel Munser, 1887), 158.

2. Rudy Abramson and Jean Haskell, *Encyclopedia of Appalachia* (Knoxville: University of Tennessee Press, 2006), 170.

3. Jacquelyn Dowd Hall, "Disorderly Women: Gender and Labor Militancy in the Appalachian South," *Journal of American History* 73, no. 2 (1986): 354–82; Virginia Seitz, *Women, Development and Communities for Empowerment in Appalachia* (Albany: State University of New York Press, 1995); Mary K. Anglin, *Women, Power and Dissent in the Hills of Carolina* (Urbana: University of Illinois Press, 2002).

4. Julie Matthaei, *An Economic History of Women in America: Women's Work, the Sexual Division of Labor, and the Development of Capitalism* (New York: Schocken Books, 1982); Linda Kerber, "Separate Spheres, Female Worlds, Woman's Place: The Rhetoric of Women's History," *Journal of American History* 75, no. 1 (1988): 9–39.

5. J. L. Collins and Martha Gimenez, eds., *Work without Wages: Domestic Labor and Self-Employment within Capitalism* (Albany: State University of New York Press, 1990), 25–47.

6. Lourdes Beneria, *Gender, Development and Globalization: Economics as if All People Mattered* (London: Routledge, 2003).

7. K. V. Hansen and I. J. Philipson, ed., *Women, Class and the Feminist Imagination: A Socialist-Feminist Reader* (Philadelphia: Temple University Press, 1990), 139–40.

8. Mary K. Anglin, "Toward a Workable Past: Dangerous Memories and Feminist Perspectives," *Journal of Appalachian Studies* 6, nos. 1 and 2 (Spring/Fall 2000): 82.

9. G. W. Dyer and J. T. Moore, eds., *The Tennessee Civil War Veteran Questionnaires* (Easley, SC: Southern Historical Press, 1985).

10. Eliot Wiggington, ed., *Foxfire Book* (Garden City: Anchor Books, 1972); and Eliot Wiggington, ed., *Foxfire 8* (Garden City: Anchor Books, 1983).

11. My companion website is http://scholar.lib.vt.edu/faculty_archives/appalachian_women.

For a map of the regional boundaries that I apply, see Dunaway, *Women, Work and Family in the Antebellum Mountain South* (New York: Cambridge University Press, 2008), 2; Dunaway website. For a brief description of the samples, see Dunaway, *Women, Work and Family*, 11–12. For published primary sources, see Dunaway, *Women, Work and Family*, 271–79.

12. Elizabeth Fox-Genovese, *Within the Plantation Household: Black and White Women of the Old South* (Chapel Hill: University of North Carolina Press, 1988).

13. Daniel Richter, *Facing East from Indian Country: A Native History of Early America* (Cambridge: Harvard University Press, 2001).

14. Dunaway, *Women, Work and Family*, 132–40.

15. Wilma A. Dunaway, *Slavery in the American Mountain South* (New York: Cambridge University Press, 2003), 54–57.

16. Wilma A. Dunaway, *The First American Frontier: Transition to Capitalism in Southern Appalachia, 1700–1860* (Chapel Hill: University of North Carolina Press, 1996). Also see Dunaway website, table 27.

17. See Dunaway website, tables 11, 26.

18. For more information about tenants and sharecroppers, see Dunaway, *First American Frontier,* 91–106.

19. For more information about farm laborers, see Dunaway, *First American Frontier,* 106–108.

20. Fox-Genovese, *Within the Plantation Household,* 109.

21. Caney Hall, interview transcript, Appalachian Oral History Project, Alice Lloyd College Library.

22. June Ehle and Julie Price, interview transcript, Appalachian Oral History Project, Appalachian State University Library.

23. Analysis of Appalachian Civil War veteran questionnaires in Dyer and Moore, *Tennessee Civil War Veteran Questionnaires.*

24. See Dunaway website, tables 55, 61, and 62.

25. Maria Miles, *Patriarchy and Accumulation on a World Scale* (London: Zed Books, 1986), 118.

26. Peter Kriedte, Hans Medick, and Jurgen Schlumbohm, *Industrialization before Industrialization: Rural Industry in the Genesis of Capitalism* (Cambridge: Cambridge University Press, 1981), 117, 219.

27. Hans Medick, "The Proto-Industrial Family Economy: The Structural Function of Household and Family during the Transition from Peasant Society to Industrial Capitalism," *Social History* 1, no. 3 (October 1976): 297.

28. *Cherokee Phoenix,* March 20, 1828.

29. William G. McLoughlin and Walter H. Conser Jr, "The Cherokees in Transition: A Statistical Analysis of the Federal Cherokee Census of 1835," *Journal of American History* 64, no. 3 (December 1977): 695.

30. Stephen Innes, ed., *Work and Labor in Early America* (Chapel Hill: University of North Carolina Press, 1988), 44.

31. Derived from analysis of national and Appalachian county totals in US Census Office (1814: 5–7). Analysis of census enumerator manuscripts for the western North Carolina counties.

32. *Knoxville Gazette,* March 10, 1841.

33. Derived from analysis of US Census Office (1814: 2–7). *Knoxville Gazette,* March 10, 1818, August 15, 1787, January 21, 1840.

34. Thomas Dublin, *Women at Work: The Transformation of Work and Community in Lowell, Massachusetts, 1826–1860* (New York: Columbia University Press, 1979), 4.

35. US Census 1865; Calculated using table 7.1 in Anglin, *Women, Power and Dissent,* 197); See Dunaway website, table 36.

36. Matthaei, *Economic History of Women in America,* 114–19.

37. Margaret Smith and Emily Wilson, North Carolina Women Making History (Chapel Hill: University of North Carolina Press, 1999), 311n11.

38. Franklin Mendels, "Proto-Industrialization: The First Phase of the Industrialization Process," *Journal of Economic History* 32, no. 1 (1972): 249–50.

39. See Dunaway website, table 37.

40. Derived from analysis of Appalachian county data in US Census Office (1865).

41. Sophia Roberts Transcript, Appalachian Oral History Project, Alice Lloyd College. Derived from analysis of a systematic probability sample of 2,795 female heads of household drawn from the 1860 Census of Population manuscripts. For the antebellum national poverty line, see Lee Soltow, *Men and Wealth in the United States, 1850–1870* (New Haven: Yale University Press, 1975).

42. Susanna Delfino and Michele Gillespie, eds., *Neither Lady nor Slave: Working Women of the Old South* (Chapel Hill: University of North Carolina Press, 2002), 145n55.

43. Mendels, *Proto-Industrialization*, 254.

44. Kathy Thompson, ed., *Touching Home: A Collection of History and Folklore from the Copper Basin, Fannin County Area* (Orlando: Daniels Publishers, 1976), 140.

45. Wiggington, *Foxfire Book*, 30.

46. Dyer and Moore, *Tennessee Civil War Veteran Questionnaires*, 202, 212, 871, 877.

47. Mendels, *Proto-Industrialization*, 252.

48. Derived from analysis of a systematic probability sample of 2,795 female heads of household drawn from the 1860 Census of Population manuscripts. For the antebellum national poverty line, see Soltow, *Men and Wealth in the United States*.

49. James Reeves, *The Physical and Medical Topography, Including Vital, Manufacturing, and Other Statistics of the City of Wheeling* (Wheeling, WV: Daily Register Book Job Office, 1870), 26–27.

50. Frances Goodrich, *Mountain Homespun* (New Haven: Yale University Press, 1931), 51.

51. Dyer and Moore, *Tennessee Civil War Veteran Questionnaires*, 27; Florence Bush, *Dorie: Woman of the Mountains* (Knoxville: University of Tennessee Press, 1992), 26.

52. Wiggington, *Foxfire 8*, 101–2.

53. Wilma A. Dunaway, *The African-American Family in Slavery and Emancipation* (New York: Cambridge University Press, 2003), 169.

54. Less than 6 percent of US slave women produced cloth, while more than half of Appalachian slave women were employed at textile production. See Fogel and Engeman, *Without Consent or Contract: The Rise and Fall of American Slavery*, vol. 1: *Markets and Production: Technical Papers* (New York: W. W. Norton, 1992), 139.

55. A few large plantations sent their wool to nearby mills for carding into yarn, but most slaves completed the entire process by hand. See Fogel and Engerman, *Without Consent or Contract*.

56. Michele Hoyman, "Female Participation in the Informal Economy: A Neglected Issue," *Annals of the American Academy of Political and Social Science* 493, no. 1 (1987): 70–76.

Challenging the Myth of Separate Spheres 193

57. Dunaway, *Women, Work and Family,* 132, 187.

58. Ibid., 187–88.

59. Ibid., 189.

60. See Dunaway website, table 38.

61. Dunaway, *Women, Work and Family,* 155.

62. Ibid., 132, 190–91.

63. See Dunaway website, table 35.

64. Dunaway, *First American Frontier,* 148

65. See Dunaway website, table 41.

66. Ibid., table 35.

67. Derived from analysis of Appalachian county data in US Census Office (1865).

68. See Dunaway website, table 41.

69. Ibid., table 23.

70. Dunaway, *Women, Work and Family,* 181.

71. See Dunaway website, tables 24, 41.

72. Dunaway, *First American Frontier,* 215–17, 293.

73. Ibid., 101–2.

74. Ibid., 305–7.

75. Dunaway, *African-American Family in Slavery and Emancipation,* 80–85.

76. Dunaway, *First American Frontier,* 137–39, 237–38.

77. Dunaway, *Women, Work and Family,* 178–86.

78. Matthaei, *Economic History of Women in America,* 114–19.

CHAPTER SEVEN

Cyprians and Courtesans, Murder and Mayhem

Prostitution in Wheeling during the Civil War

BARBARA J. HOWE

The image of an "Appalachian" woman rarely encompasses that of a cyprian, courtesan, *nymph de pave,* or a woman who was "no better than she should be." During the Civil War, however, prostitution "became firmly entrenched" in Wheeling's economy because of the large numbers of transients, including troops, in the city.[1] The prostitutes, who were already a tragic part of the population, gained even more notoriety and visibility, and their stories reveal the seamy underside of urban life in the largest city of the Mountain South at the time. They also challenge any traditional images of Appalachian women.

First, some definitions are in order, for prostitution was a complex business. Jacqueline Baker Barnhart, in her study of San Francisco prostitution, drew on James Murray's *A New English Dictionary* (1888) and *The Unabridged Oxford English Dictionary* for her definitions.[2] By these sources, "prostitute" was the only word used then that referred to "any woman who offered her body for hire or who sold sexual acts for 'base gain.'" "Whore" was a "coarse term of abuse" that could refer to a prostitute, adulteress, or fornicator—any woman "willing to engage in intercourse with men other than her husband." It is not a term found in many Wheeling references. "Harlot," also a "coarse term of abuse," referred to "women who worked in cheap dance halls or entertained in saloons and prostituted as well." "A 'cyprian' could be a prostitute or merely a lewd or licentious woman." Finally, a "strumpet" belonged in the same category as whore and harlot.[3]

At the other end of the social scale for prostitutes, said Barnhart, were the courtesans, who were "only of the highest class," except when Wheeling census keepers were being polite in identifying their occupations. These women were originally women of the court or court mistresses. They were also "often kept by one man at a time, but usually without any pretense of love or permanency," as opposed to a mistress, who was the illicit lover of a married man and who was "a prostitute only if her motives were known to be financial."[4]

Prostitution also depended on madams and bawds. Madams "ran the elite parlor houses and better-class brothels," while bawds presided over cheaper brothels and houses of prostitution, the bawdy houses. Any house of prostitution could be considered to be a brothel, bagnio (originally an Italian bathhouse), or bordello, but the term "parlor house" meant an elite house, while a "crib" was a small, single-room facility often built just to house prostitutes.[5]

The legal framework for regulating Wheeling's prostitution is also important background to the individuals' stories discussed below. William Hening's *The Virginia Justice*, published in 1825 as a guide for the local justices of the peace, had specifically outlawed prostitution. Hening said that lewdness was "properly punished by the ecclesiastical law, yet the offence of keeping a bawdy house" was a matter of temporal law "as a common nuisance, not only in respect of its endangering the public peace, by drawing together dissolute and debauched persons, but also in respect of its apparent tendency to correct the manners of both sexes." In general, common law provided for the punishment of "all open lewdness, grossly scandalous." Punishment could be fines, imprisonment, or "such infamous punishment as to the court, in discretion shall deem proper." A man could be "bound to his good behavior for haunting bawdy houses with women of bad fame, as also keeping bad women in his own house." If a man was indicted for visiting a bawdy house, "it must appear that he knew it to be such a house; and it must be expressly alledged [sic], that it is a bawdy house, and not that it is suspected to do so." A wife who kept a bawdy house could, along with her husband, be "condemned to the pillory," because keeping a bawdy house was "an offence as to the government of the house, in which the wife has a principal share, and also such an offence as may generally be presumed to be managed by the intrigues of her sex." By Hening's interpretations of the laws, it was not illegal to be "a bawd generally."[6]

The 1836 Virginia General Assembly act that incorporated the city of Wheeling gave the city council the authority to pass any ordinances necessary "to secure the inhabitants of said city . . . for the prevention and punishment of lewd, lascivious, indecent or disorderly conduct in the city."[7] The city of Wheeling then had an "ordinance to prevent certain improper practices" as early as January 1842.[8]

The earliest Virginia act specifically related to prostitution was included in the *Report of the Revisors of the Civil Code of Virginia, Made to The General Assembly at December Session 1846.* One of the "offences [*sic*] against chastity, morality and decency" included a reference to prostitution. "Any free person who shall keep a house of ill fame, resorted to for the purpose of prostitution or lewdness," would be punished by "confinement in the jail not more than twelve months and by fine not exceeding two hundred dollars."[9] This did not punish women who were not *keepers* of houses of ill fame, and, of course, it did not punish the men who patronized the prostitutes.

When the city of Wheeling published its codified ordinances in 1855, one prevented "certain improper practices," including "any public lewdness or indecency, whether by word or actions," as well as any public indecent exposure.[10] Unfortunately, there are few details on prosecutions under this act because there are no extant police records other than those in the *Wheeling Intelligencer.*

State and local law to the contrary, though, Wheeling had been a "wide open" city full of transients and prostitutes from its earliest years. European-Americans founded Wheeling in 1769, and David Rose contended that prostitution in the area could be traced back to the camp followers who "provided domestic and sexual service" to the frontier militia that operated in the upper Ohio River valley before the Revolutionary War. By the end of the eighteenth century, Wheeling had earned a reputation for its "lively, if not rowdy, social life" of men ready to pursue their fortunes in the West. Wheeling was a port city, and like others on the route to New

Cyprians and Courtesans, Murder and Mayhem 197

Orleans, gambling, prostitution, drinking, and betting mixed freely. Prostitutes were victims in this carousing life, for Mike Fink and his brother riverboatmen, said Rose, "retained only fleeting ties to women in general," and "their relations to women were violent and misogynistic."[11]

Wheeling's location continued to influence the development of prostitution during the war, as did its economy and political status. Located in the Ohio River valley, it is neither mountainous nor, technically, southern. As the northernmost city in western Virginia, it lies north of the Mason-Dixon Line. The city had 14,083 residents in 1860 and 19,280 in 1870, making it the largest city in what would become West Virginia and the most heavily industrialized city in western Virginia, with glass factories, breweries, iron foundries, cotton and woolen mills, and merchant tailor firms. It was also the most ethnically diverse city in Virginia, with a large population of Germans and Irish but a very small African American population, because free blacks needed legal permission to stay in Virginia, and freedom was nearby in Ohio or Pennsylvania. None of the women discussed in this essay were identified as African-American.[12] Wheeling was the county seat of Ohio County, the capital of the Restored Government of Virginia, and the first capital of West Virginia. The city was removed from the fighting, but its location on the Ohio River, the National Road after 1818, and Baltimore and Ohio Railroad after 1852 made it a major transportation center for troops from the West moving to the front along the railroad.[13]

Some aspects of prostitution did not change during the war, except that military officials helped enforce the law. Proper middle-class Wheeling women, who were mostly native born or, possibly, German immigrants at this time, followed the cult of true womanhood, which emphasized piety, purity, domesticity, and submissiveness for white women.[14] However, the city's prostitutes lived in a totally different world. For example, as middle-class women presided over their nuclear families where servants did the chores and where they might take in boarders, prostitutes created their own "households" where unrelated women and men lived together or where women lived together with their children, sometimes putting those children at risk. Prostitutes also lived in a world of alcohol abuse, crime, and violence that brought them into regular contact with law enforcement officers, although these officers

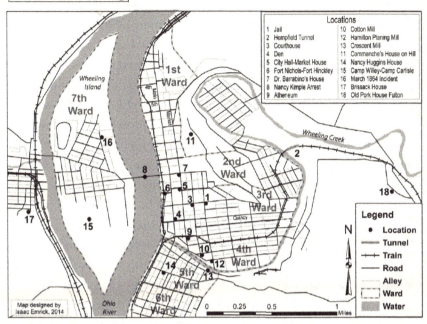

were not always the enemy. And, while proper ladies laced themselves into tight corsets, prostitutes sometimes wore male apparel, although there is no evidence at this time of cross-dressing for sexual purposes.

For example, in 1860, a group of five courtesans who would make news during the war lived in a household with their children in the Fifth Ward. Mary [Ann] McCan [a.k.a. McCann], twenty, Amanda Winesburg [a.k.a. Winesburgh], twenty-one, and Mary McDonald, seventeen, were all born in Virginia, while Linda and Caroline Brady, twenty and nineteen, respectively, were born in Ohio. The other residents were Winesburg's daughter Alice, one, and Louisa and Cora McDonald, three and four, respectively; all were born in Virginia.[15] It is possible that Linda Brady was Melinda Brady, the friend of Mary Ann McCann discussed below. "Courtesan" was being polite, for Winesburg was more often described as "a wretched street walker" and was in and out of trouble with the law from at least 1857 to 1863.[16]

Another prostitution den located in an old barn or stable on Quincy Street between Main and Market streets operated until November 1861. The earliest reference to this in the *Wheeling Intelligencer* came

Cyprians and Courtesans, Murder and Mayhem

in September 1856. The paper had pointed out that it was "generally our plan not to notice the many street quarrels and affairs *du pave* liable to be occurring every hour," but the "shanty environs" were becoming a nuisance to "us poor mortals." The police visited the place, "as usual," and forcibly escorted "a brawling and drunken madam," also described as the "small, abridged Erin, predominantly of the Donnybrook caste, and wholly minus the gentle features of the 'sweet Isle,'" to the mayor's office. He sent her to jail.[17] For years, "rats, bats, prostitutes and rowdies" rendezvoused in the "old castle . . . and all efforts to bar the doors and entrances [had] failed." Citizens asked city council to take the building down, but it "continued to stand as a sad commentary upon the morals of the town" until the owner removed the public nuisance.[18]

Prostitutes were often arrested for alcohol-related offenses. In June 1863, Cinderella Whims "got drunk and proceeded to smash up the crockery and furniture" in the house where she lived with "another woman of like character." When George Santmires [a.k.a. St. Myers?] tried to arrest her, "she set upon him with the fury of an enraged tigress," so the officer had "to raise his hand against her not in the way of kindness." Alderman William Robertson sent her to jail.[19] In 1863 Margaret Bedlar was in "an almost insensible state of intoxication" and covered with bruises when she was found, lying in an alley, about 4:00 a.m. after she was kicked out of the "disreputable house" where she had been living. Born Margaret Baunan, Bedlar had left Wheeling years earlier with a "strolling theatrical company" and had a career of "considerable success" as a "very clever actress" in Philadelphia and Baltimore. It is not clear why her career failed and she ended up back in Wheeling.[20]

Prostitutes also often committed petty crimes, such as robbery and theft, and might initiate attacks. Miss Ritchie, a *nymph de pave,* sought advice from Hannah Smith, a fortune teller who lived in North Wheeling in November 1864.[21] Smith was probably Mrs. Hannah Smith, a widow living on Main Street, but it is not clear if this was the same Miss Ritchie who lived at Fort Nichols, discussed below.[22] When Ritchie could not pay the twenty-five-cent fee, Smith "arose in might wrath and Amazonian strength, and following her into the street, midst cries of terror almost stripped her of clothing, and left her like a dismantled blockade runner in rather a sinking condition."[23]

Murder was the most serious crime that impacted the lives of prostitutes. The case of Mary Ann McCann illustrates how one prostitute interacted with a wide variety of people, including the police, officials of the court, and the military, to get assistance after her infant daughter, Ada May, was killed. The case was not directly related to the war, though, except for the fact that McCann sought help from a military officer. On the morning of Wednesday, May 20, 1863, about 10:00 a.m., Ada May, a two-month-old "small and quite feeble" girl by one definition but "very happy and active . . . for its age," according to her mother, and dressed in a "light frock and bonnet," was found with a "cord drawn tightly around its neck" beneath a pile of boards near Hamilton's planing mill at the foot of Fifth Street in East Wheeling, about a block diagonally southeast of the cotton mill.[24] As Coroner Elijah Day later recalled, the cord was a "worsted cord, such as is usually used in raising window blinds," and it was tied around the baby's neck "so tightly that it caused abrasures in the flesh; the tongue was portruded [sic] and enlarged; the face was much discolored as if the child had died from strangulation."[25]

When he found the baby, Day called a jury to the planing mill, where the group heard testimony from Miss Mary [Ann] McCann, the mother of the "illegitimate" child, the same woman listed as a courtesan in the 1860 census. McCann lived in East Wheeling and said that, on Monday evening, the eighteenth, she had taken her child to spend the night with Mrs. Nesbit, who was not identified as a prostitute and who lived on the second floor of the old abandoned Wheeling Cotton Mill with "a great number" of others. On Tuesday morning, after breakfast, McCann left the mill, leaving her sleeping daughter in Nesbit's care. When she returned, Nesbit refused her entrance and said that a man and woman had come to take the child away, "promising to find it a home." McCann went to get a police officer.[26]

However, instead, she went to the Athenaeum, the auditorium then used as a military prison about two blocks away at John [now Sixteenth] and Market streets, for help and returned with Amanda Winesburg, a well-known prostitute who then lived in East Wheeling, near Mr. Bodley's shop, and who had met McCann on the street, and a soldier, William Gordon of Captain Hamilton's company.[27] Nesbit would not let them come in at first but eventually relented. When they could not find

Cyprians and Courtesans, Murder and Mayhem 201

the child, Nesbit again said the couple had taken the child away. William Long, the child's "reputed father," also went to the cotton mill with McCann, when Nesbit said she would get her baby back in two or three days. Long advised McCann to have Nesbit arrested, so the two went to Alderman J. C. McManaway's, swore out a warrant for Nesbit's arrest, and she went to jail.[28]

Joseph Saulsbury and Henry Jurgens both testified at Nesbit's trial that they had seen a woman whom Saulsbury identified as Nesbit passing by the board pile with a basket on her arm between 9:00 a.m. and 10:00 a.m. on the nineteenth. Neither saw Nesbit place the basket or baby by the pile, but Jurgens saw the woman "stooping down at the place where the child was found."[29] More damaging to Nesbit's story was the fact that Mrs. Margaret Gold [a.k.a. Gould], who lived on the first floor of the cotton mill, and Mary Mills, who lived opposite the cotton mill, both testified that they saw Nesbit leave the house with a basket while McCann was getting a policeman. Gould did not see any couple taking a child. That left Nesbit as the mostly likely murderer, especially since Officer Lancaster testified that he had found a piece of cord identical to that around the baby's neck on the stairway to the cellar at Nesbit's house. The cord was like the green window blind cord that Day had identified and that Gold had given to one of Nesbit's children to keep the peace after they started quarreling over it. Lancaster had had to kick down the door of the cotton mill to arrest Nesbit, who "resisted considerably," so much so that he had to call for help to take her into custody and to the alderman's office.[30]

Thomas Lewis, who also lived at the cotton mill, was arrested and jailed "upon suspicion of having something to do with the late child murder." Lewis and Nesbit were living as a couple but were not married. Nesbit continued to claim her innocence and stuck to her story of the couple taking the child, arguing that "its mother was not fit to keep it, and that he had provided a home for it." Nesbit said she had tried to prevent the man from taking the baby and then added a new twist to the story, claiming that, on Sunday the seventeenth, three nights before the child was found, McCann had attempted to drown the baby in the creek. Long prevented her from doing that.[31] Long also claimed that he had agreed to provide a home for McCann and that she had never threatened to drown herself and Ada May.[32] Lewis was soon cleared of all charges of murder for lack of evidence against him.[33]

Nesbit went on trial in the circuit court in October 1863, after a delay in seating a jury that had not already formed an opinion in the case. Attorney General Aquilla B. Caldwell and Major Flescher appeared for the state of West Virginia, while G. L. Cranmer and J. P. Rogers argued the case for the defense. Most of the defense witnesses testified that Nesbit's "reputation for peaceableness and good order [was] good" but admitted they had had little contact with her in recent years. For the prosecution, Mary Ann McCann and Melinda Brady explained that Lewis "bothered" them two or three times during the night so that the women were unable to sleep; they even threatened to leave if he did not leave them alone. According to Brady, Nesbit wanted Lewis to sleep with Brady because "she had got tired sleeping with him."[34] McCann also claimed that Nesbit had had "a private conversation" with Brady, while Long and McCann were "quarreling" before Nesbit had invited the two women to her house.[35] According to Winesburg, McCann and Long were quarreling because McCann was homeless and would drown herself and Ada May if Long did not provide her with a home. Brady, who had been with McCann along the river bank, confirmed McCann was homeless and desperate when Nesbit came along, offering her "a good supper and bed" at her home.[36]

In addition, Mrs. Wood, who lived in a house facing the cotton mill, testified that she had seen Nesbit's daughter in the door of the mill, holding Ada May, and that Ada May was gone when McCann returned to the house. Bridget Callaghan, who lived downstairs from Nesbit in the cotton mill, also saw Nesbit's daughter with Ada May and Nesbit going down the stairs with a basket, headed toward the planing mill. When she returned, she took the basket upstairs and went to Lewis's place of employment, the Crescent Mill, an ironworks southeast of the cotton mill along Wheeling Creek and just southwest of the planing mill. Mrs. Shaw saw Nesbit coming up the alley near where Shaw lived "with a basket on her arm" and "a little bare footed girl [Lewis's girl] walking by her side." Shaw did not know where Nesbit was going, but she "appeared to be afraid" of Shaw.[37] In spite of what seemed to be overwhelming evidence against Nesbit, the trial ended on October 21 with a verdict of "not guilty."[38]

Cyprians and Courtesans, Murder and Mayhem 203

Although the above cases were only tangentially related to the war, Wheeling's City Council began to look at the potential impact of the war and, perhaps, the upcoming political conventions that would lead to statehood, as early as mid-May 1861. At that time the council considered, but did not pass, an ordinance "for the suppression of houses of prostitution and dispersing those gathered in public places for lewd purposes," just as the first convention of delegates was gathering in Wheeling to establish the Restored Government of Virginia.[39] The detailed amendments the City Council then adopted on May 16 give a sense of the scope of the problem.[40]

> *sec. 1*—if any person shall assemble or be found on any street, alley
> or other public place or in any house, outhouse, stable, shed, fire
> engine, or hose house, board yard, or lot of ground, for the purpose
> of prostitution, lewdness or indecency, or if any prostitute shall be
> found in any such place between sun down or [*sic*] sun up, or if any
> person shall within the limits of the city keep any house or place of
> ill fame or bawdy house or house of resort for prostitutes or keep
> or harbor persons therein for the purpose of prostitution, . . . each
> and every person so offending shall forthwith be arrested by the city
> sergeant or any of his deputies on a warrant issued by the mayor,
> by any alderman of the city, or by any justice of the peace for Ohio
> County or without . . & be subject to trial, fine, or imprisonment
> & labor as is provided . . . provided however that no female shall be
> sent or subjected to the chaing [*sic*] gang or to labor at the public
> works or improvements of the city. . . ."[41]

This ordinance impacted the residents of Fort Nichols, a particularly notorious "household" during the war, and the *Wheeling Intelligencer* frequently used military terminology to describe activities there. Miss Ritchie appeared before Alderman William Robertson in late September 1861 to charge John Nichols "with abusing her. The examination of the case brought a lovely crowd of vagabonds into the office." Nichols and "another old chap by the name of Hinkerton" kept "a sort of den down on Water street which [was] the resort of both male and female vagabonds, and where liquor [was] sold without limit or license." Because the den at the foot of Union Street on the Ohio River was "the

204 BARBARA J. HOWE

constant scene of all kinds of drunken broils," the newspaper argued that it should be "wiped out." In this case, Nichols paid his fine for abusing Ritchie and "returned to his den."[42]

When William Wesley Porter staggered into Fort Nichols in March 1862, "two girls named Brady" refused to admit him. When he could not break in with a battering ram or by throwing bricks at the window, the Bradys "came out of their entrenchments to give him battle." Porter rushed the smaller girl, knocked her down, and then fell down himself. . . . the other woman rushed upon him and beat him most unmercifully over the face and head with a rolling pin." Officer Scroggins arrested Porter, and Alderman Robertson sent him to jail for thirty days.[43] It is not clear if these two Bradys were among those listed in the 1860 census and/or included Melinda [Linda?] Brady.

Still, the attacks continued on Fort Nichols over the course of several weeks, although it seemed "almost impregnable to land attacks," as the attackers were "invariably repulsed with the loss of blood." When John Acheson, "a gentleman of the hard-headed profession" from Pittsburgh, tried "a desperate assault," the occupants "came out of their entrenchments . . . and beat him unmercifully." Acheson tried to get up, but one of the women, "said to be a perfect Amazon," knocked him down with her fist whenever he tried to do so. The police arrested Acheson, and, when he could not pay his five-dollar fine to Alderman Robertson, he went to jail for twenty days.[44]

In early April, the residents of Fort Nichols surrendered unconditionally to the police, and the "formidable establishment [was] now the abode only of bats and owls."[45] However, it soon reopened as Fort Hinckley and was "inhabited by about a dozen of the most abandoned ragamuffins in the city, including remnants of the Hinckleys, Ritchies and Nichols."[46]

Then, in May 1862, the city began to step up the prosecution of "disreputable women," and the number of arrests started to increase.[47] Dr. E. A. Barrabino, who lived at the southwestern corner of Madison and Fourth streets, was one of the first caught in this expanded effort. Barrabino, "an old resident of the city," kept a house "for the resort of prostitutes" until the neighbors complained. When arrested, he paid his ten-dollar fine and costs, promising to appeal his conviction.[48] It is not

Cyprians and Courtesans, Murder and Mayhem 205

clear what type of doctor Barrabino was, but he was not listed as a physician in the 1862 Wheeling business directory.[49]

Later that month, on Friday, May 23, "[i]n accordance with instructions from Mayor [Andrew] Sweeney, the police of the different Wards . . . made a simultaneous descent upon quite a number of houses inhabited by disreputable women, and twenty odd arrests were made." Elizabeth and Sarah Archie, Dora Smith, and Pat Ryan and his wife were arrested at or near the Ryan home. The Ryans paid their fine, but Alderman McCourtney sent the others to jail. Alderman Robertson arrested Linn, Cal, and Louisa Brady and Elizabeth Carr at an infamous hillside house about Fourth Street and sent them to jail.[50] In the First Ward, Officer St. Meyers arrested Mrs. Haymaker, Cinderella Whims, and Miss Manigan; Alderman Miller sent them to jail. When Alex Craig interfered with an officer discharging his duty, the officer "gave Craig a good thrashing." Mayor Sweeney then fined him ten dollars and sent him to jail.[51]

The next night, Mayor Sweeney and Major Swearingen sent "a small detachment of soldiers and policemen" to Nancy Hugens's [Huggins] house on Poverty Point to arrest "several female occupants," including Hugens. Alderman McManaway fined them all ten dollars and costs. Hugens paid her fine, but the others could not afford to do so and were sent to jail for thirty days. Because "the authorities have been making a determined and universal assault upon these houses," the jail was "nearly full of women of bad character."[52] Nancy Huggins [Hugens] continued to be in trouble again in the spring of 1865 when she was arrested, first, for "using abusive language" and then, a few days later, with Susan Frank, for "keeping disorderly houses and creating a disturbance." While Frank was fined at that time, Huggins "successfully vindicated her character," and the charges were dropped.[53]

The "establishment known as Fort Nichols was also overhauled," with John Nichols, George Ritchie, and Mrs. Hinkley arrested and fined during the May 1862 crackdown, but to no avail.[54] The City Council then made further amendments to the ordinance "to prevent certain improper practices" in June 1862.[55] But shortly thereafter there were more problems at Fort Nichols, although the *Wheeling Intelligencer* had "fondly hoped that we should be called upon no more to chronicle the evil doings of this disreputable establishment." On Saturday, June 7, because of "the demoralized condition of the garrison," the residents started fighting among themselves" and were in a fair way to confer a substantial benefit upon society by destroying one another" before the police came. Officers Pender and Scroggins took "Capts. Nichols and Ritchie (who had had some difficulty on the question of authority)" and took them before Alderman George Dulty, who held them in lieu of bail of a hundred dollars "to keep the peace."[56]

But conflict continued. On August 27, 1862, the owner of the Fort Nichols property wanted his rent money. The "disreputable women" drove him out of the house with broomsticks, but Officer Scroggins soon arrested them and sent them to jail.[57] The next month, local residents petitioned Mayor Sweeney to abate "the nuisance," specifically the "disorderly nest of abandoned women." The women were arrested, and Alderman Robertson sent them to jail.[58] In November this house was still "an intolerable nuisance," and residents' complaints were "loud and deep." Allegedly, "a large number of half-grown boys" stayed in the house and spent their time stealing for the "abandoned inmates." As winter approached, the boys were targeting nearby coal bins. Neighbors particularly disliked the fact that, at night, soldiers and citizens came to the area, and not knowing exactly where they were going, "bang[ed] around at the street doors and [tore] down the gates of decent people who [were] so unfortunate as to reside near the disgraceful den." When the police raided the house, everyone except the "proprietress" and one man escaped. Alderman Dulty sent those two to jail.[59]

By mid-October 1863, "quite a number of women of bad repute" lived at Fort Nichols, so "rowdies of different classes" went there often. When the Provost Guard arrived to "quell the disturbance" on Friday, October 9, several members were wounded and one was missing as the guard was repulsed. The guard returned with reinforcements and was able to capture and commit several residents. But there were more disturbances and more arrests two nights later. The *Wheeling Intelligencer* concluded that "the concern ought to be broken up. It is a rendezvous for the worst of characters and should not be tolerated."[60]

Soldiers visited Fort Nichols, but during the winter of 1862–63, soldiers camped on Wheeling Island attracted homeless prostitutes to their

Cyprians and Courtesans, Murder and Mayhem 207

encampment.[61] In March 1864 "a crowd of soldiers assembled around a house of bad reputation at the foot of Fourth street, and proceeded to smash in the windows with bricks and other missiles," firing pistols and alarming the neighborhood. The "gang of abandoned women" in the house fled to safety.[62]

However, if authorities tried to prosecute prostitutes too vigorously, the women sometimes dressed as men and blended into the crowds of strangers in the city.[63] Jennie Powell was one of these women whom Officer Richardson arrested in late July 1864 and sent to jail. She was from Grafton, supposedly married an African American man, and "got him into a difficulty with a lot of soldiers during which he was drowned."[64]

Soldiers sometimes protected the prostitutes:

> Committed—Yesterday morning officer Richardson arrested upon the Suspension bridge a reckless Amazon by the name of Nancy Kimple, who was acting as a bone of contention among a party of soldiers. She was taken before Alderman Robertson and committed to jail. Nancy has lived and encamped with the soldiers for a considerable length of time, and she appears to be firmly bound to some of them in the bonds of iniquity. An attempt was made to arrest her on Saturday but two or three soldiers came to the rescue, drawing revolvers and forcing the officer to release her.[65]

At the end of the war, one prostitute was even found in a barracks, wearing an officer's uniform.[66]

At least one soldier had been a prostitute. The "somewhat famous female soldier," using the alias of "Harry Fitzallen," arrived in Wheeling as a prisoner on the steamer *Bostona, No. 2*, on December 24, 1862, on the suspicion of being a spy for the Confederacy. She had come to Wheeling about 1859 "in the character of a prostitute." It is not clear how long she stayed in Wheeling, but by the time the war broke out she was in Kentucky, where she enlisted "for the love of excitement. She had to quit when her sex was discovered but then enlisted in several different regiments and was arrested several times. By the time she arrived in Wheeling on Christmas Eve, the Glasgow-born woman, whose real name was Marian McKenzie, was about twenty-five years old, "very short and very thick," and "evidently an educated woman, well skilled in the iniquities of the world."[67]

We can only see the police officers' attitudes toward the prostitutes through the eyes of the newspaper reports. Certainly, the police did not ignore the existence of the prostitutes, but, if there was no other crime or violence taking place in the brothels to attract attention, the houses probably operated on a daily basis without fear of interruption. Therefore, when Officer Scroggins was "anxious to break up the dens" in August 1862, it is hard to know if he did so because it was then a high priority to the police or because the public demanded it. Whatever the reason, Scroggins did not have the resources to do this himself, so he resorted to a sting operation that might be familiar to law enforcement officers in the twenty-first century. On Tuesday evening, August 5, 1862, he visited all the houses of ill fame and summoned them to appear in court in a fictitious case. They all arrived promptly at the court, and "when they were all huddled nicely together," Scroggins produced his warrants. This produced "a great excitement among the dissolute tribe, who became so hot as to render strategy no longer available." Officers Pender, Richardson, and St. Meyers provided reinforcements, and those who could not pay their fines went to jail.[68]

It is clear, though, that the relationship between prostitutes and law enforcement officials was not always confrontational, as noted above in the McCann case. For three or four evenings in late January–early February 1863, "abandoned women of the town" asked the aldermen to put them in jail so that they would have a place to sleep. The police were duty bound "to arrest all lewd women found upon the streets after nightfall," and the women usually did not object because they could "scarcely find a more comfortable place to lodge."[69] The next winter, a woman named Archer also asked to be committed to jail because she had nowhere to live. When the alderman could not commit her because she had not committed a crime, she left. Officer Richardson arrested her later that evening for violating a city ordinance, so she ended up in jail, where she wanted to be.[70] While no first name or crime was given in this report, an Elizabeth Archer was arrested frequently for prostitution in 1866.

As other examples of "cooperation" between police and prostitutes, Amanda Winesburg, who was in jail in July 1863, went before Alderman

Cyprians and Courtesans, Murder and Mayhem 209

Dulty as a defense witness to testify that she and Maggie Jones, the jailor's daughter, had heard Miss Maggie Reed, imprisoned for making and flying a Confederate flag in Buckhannon, using "abusive language to the jailor and his wife."[71] When soldiers pursued and annoyed Ann Watson, "a woman of bad character," through the market house in late February 1864, she went to Alderman Robertson's office for protection. Instead of pursuing the soldiers, Robertson took Watson to jail.[72]

Part of the prostitution problem was the fact that Wheeling was a destination for young women "induced" to leave home during the war. Young women who might want to meet a soldier could easily find him. Women driven from their homes by fighting elsewhere in western Virginia could ride the train or travel on the National Road or Ohio River to refuge in Wheeling. A Miss Johnson, "remarkably good looking . . . well and flashily dressed" and a member of a "very respectable family in Pittsburgh," was one such woman who left home in the summer of 1862. By one version of the story, "a young man belonging to the army" brought her to Wheeling. The other version was that she was "no better than she should be" and that she was "a very willing captive." In Wheeling she ended up at the Fifth Ward "disreputable house" of Mrs. Hugans [Huggins/Hugens]. In July, Johnson's cousin came looking for her, and Officers John C. Vail and St. Meyers went to Hugans's house to persuade Johnson to take the train back to Pittsburgh with her cousin. Rumor had it that she was arrested and sent back to Pittsburgh "in consequence of some information which she possessed and which was considered very valuable to others."[73]

Two years later, a Mr. Brissack, an "old gentleman," arrived in Wheeling from Belmont County, just across the Ohio River in Ohio, looking for his daughter, who had "been associating for some days with a lot of disreputable women of the town." Apparently, "a woman of bad character" had left Wheeling to live with the Brissacks, got tired of "country life," and, when she returned to Wheeling, "induced" Brissack's seventeen-year-old daughter to come back with her. A "most incorrigible creature," the daughter only went back with her father when faced with "the most violent threats of arrest and imprisonment."[74]

Wheeling's citizens complained when these homeless "abandoned women" crossed their paths. In April 1864 the city sergeant had so many complaints about these women infesting the city and congregating at the Hempfield Railroad tunnel and near the "old Pork House," both east of the city, where these "respectable people" traveled, that the police were forced to surround the tunnel and capture "a considerable squad of the Cyprians, all of whom were committed to jail."[75] They complained again when, that summer, it was obvious that the morals of the city were deteriorating rapidly, especially in North Wheeling, where "vice, mischief, filth and every abomination . . . abounds in this degraded part of the city." In addition to groups of young men "lounging about . . . and even attacking strangers;—women of doubtful character strolling along with men of worse character than theirs" were common sights. One suggestion to address the persistent crime there was to adopt a law similar to one in Chicago to "rid the city of prostitutes." Another idea was to simply rigidly enforce existing law.[76]

Unfortunately, though, with only one police officer per ward during the war, there was no easy way to stop the crime wave, other than to put prostitutes in jail for awhile.[77] But even that approach was not without problems, for there were so many women in jail in the summer of 1863 for "street walking and other minor offences" that they occupied the entire upper story of the structure. They would "come out of their cells and occupy the hall 'all in a huddle together.' They were all dressed more with regard to coolness and economy that [sic] to neatness or cleanliness." With so many "such characters" in jail year-round, the city incurred "no inconsiderable sum" in keeping them there.[78]

One *nymph de pave*, Ann Pickerson, a "*strange woman* and a stranger to the manners and customs" of Wheeling did not accept her fate without complaint when she was arrested in March 1865 and sent to jail for thirty days because she could not pay her twenty-dollar fine. Indignantly, she informed the alderman that Wheeling was "the residence of a very ungenerous public," unlike Pittsburgh, where "lawyers generally settled such little bills for her." The *Wheeling Intelligencer* proudly editorialized that "Our lawyers don't do such things, Annie. Not muchly they don't."[79]

On a very rare occasion, men were accused of being customers for prostitutes. In September 1863, Officer Santmiers arrested City Councilman Buchanan of the First Ward for "'holding sweet converse'

Cyprians and Courtesans, Murder and Mayhem 211

with a woman of bad repute." Buchanan's excuse was that "he was conversing with the woman for the purpose of eliciting evidence to sustain the [unspecified] charges lately preferred by himself against Santmiers" and that Santmiers arrested him in retribution. Alderman Miller apparently did not believe him and fined him five dollars and costs, per the city ordinance.[80]

Noted Hewetson Ault in his thesis on Wheeling and the Civil War, "at the close of the war the city and its suburbs were infested" with prostitutes.[81] That seems a safe conclusion, given the reports in the *Wheeling Intelligencer*, but, again, there are no extant police records, and circuit court records include no references to the war years.

As the story of prostitution in Wheeling did not begin with the war, nor did it end when hostilities ceased. The first reference to prostitution in the code of the new state of West Virginia came in the 1870 *Code of West Virginia*. This used essentially the same language as the earlier Virginia act, establishing as part of its section on "offenses against morality and decency" that "if a person keep a house of ill fame, he shall be confined in jail not more than one year, and fined not exceeding two hundred dollars."[82]

By that time, there was no house of "*public ill fame*" in Wheeling, but there were "several private brothels or places of assignation for the accommodation of libertines and their paramours." Dr. James E. Reeves, Wheeling's public health officer, estimated the number of prostitutes in 1870 as not exceeding "63 white, and about the same number of colored, persons of well established character." He attributed those figures to "an energetic Member of the Police force."[83]

Reeves estimated the number of prostitutes as not more than seventy-five white prostitutes the next year, "and about the same number of colored, persons of well-established character." He still attributed his figures to "an energetic member of the police force."[84] This was an impossibly high number of African American prostitutes because there were only a total of 390 African Americans in the city in 1870. It was impossible to know the number of "clandestine prostitutes" who, "while they make a trade of their persons, engage in various occupations, and by their singular industry *seem* to be virtuous, if not above suspicion." The last class of prostitutes consisted of "the lowest class of wretched creatures (of which there are but six or eight in Wheeling)—who, besides the vices of their traffic, wallow in the streets and alleys, are drunken, constantly diseased, and spend at least three-fourths of their time in jail." The youngest prostitute Reeves had seen was a girl thirteen and a half years old, "without the least sign of puberty," who was serving a thirty-day prison term and had "severe gonorrhoea."[85] Reeves was most concerned about these prostitutes because he saw them when they went to the city or county prison for medical treatment; there they could be seen "glorying in their brutal estate."[86]

Reeves noted that "despite the sneers of a pharisaical righteousness and prudery, this moral pestilence exists, and is fearfully on the increase all over the land . . . and is, therefore, a subject of terrible importance, [which] presses itself upon the attention of philanthropists and statesmen, regardless of the scowls and scoffs of a mock-modesty that would cover up the ineradicable woes inflicted upon society by this avenging field!"[87] He attributed prostitution to several causes: "a low standard of home education, the desire to shine in fine dress, immoral books, passion, love and desertion, together with idleness."[88] Surely he must have read the police reports in the *Wheeling Intelligencer*, but if he had been able to talk to Mary Ann McCann or the residents of Fort Nichols, he may have understood that the causes of prostitution were more likely economic distress, alcoholism, abuse, and homelessness.

NOTES

1. David Rose, "Prostitution and the Sporting Life: Aspects of Working Class Culture and Sexuality in Nineteenth Century Wheeling," *Upper Ohio Valley Historical Review* 16, no. 2 (Spring/Summer 1987): 49.

2. Jacqueline Baker Barnhart, *The Fair But Frail: Prostitution in San Francisco, 1849–1900* (Reno: University of Nevada Press, 1986), 104.

3. Ibid., ix.

4. Ibid., x. According to the *Oxford English Dictionary*, the earliest use of a sexual connotation for "courtesan" was in 1549. The 1607 reference states that "your whore is for euery rascall, but your Curtizan is for your Courtier" (E. Sharpham in *Fleire Dijb*), online version of OED accessed March 3, 2009.

5. Ibid.

6. William Waller Hening, *The Virginia Justice, Comprising the Office and Authority of a Justice of the Peace, in the Commonwealth of Virginia* (Richmond: Shepherd and Pollard, 1825), 430–31.

Cyprians and Courtesans, Murder and Mayhem 213

7. Wheeling City Council, *Ordinances of the City of Wheeling to which are prefixed the Acts of the Legislature of Virginia, Relating to the City* (Wheeling: Office of the Times and Gazette, 1855), 24–25.

8. City of Wheeling, Minute Record, 1840–1849, January 29, 1842, 119.

9. *Report of the Revisors of the Civil Code of Virginia, Made to The General Assembly at December Session 1846* (Richmond: Samuel Shepherd, 1847), chap. 196, sec. 10, 974.

10. *Ordinances of the City of Wheeling . . . 1855*, 151.

11. Rose, "Prostitution and the Sporting Life," 9, 11.

12. There were ninety-seven free blacks in the 1860 Wheeling census (Francis A. Walker, *Ninth Census*, vol. 1: *The Statistics of the Population of the United States* [Washington, DC: Government Printing Office, 1872], 286). No city-level figures were given for enslaved people in 1860.

13. Walker, *Ninth Census* 1:286. A general history of Wheeling and Ohio County can be found in J. H. Newton, ed., *History of the Pan-Handle; Being Historical Collections of the Counties of Ohio, Brooke, Marshall and Hancock, West Virginia* (Wheeling: J. A. Caldwell, 1879).

14. For a description of the proper roles for white middle-class women at this time, see Barbara Welter, "The Cult of True Womanhood: 1820–1860," *American Quarterly* 18, no. 2, pt. 1 (1966): 151–74.

15. US Census Bureau, Census of Population, Ohio County, Wheeling, 5th Ward, 1860, 1973/2093.

16. *Wheeling Intelligencer*, June 22, 1858.

17. See, for example, ibid., September 13, 1856.

18. Ibid., November 13, 1861.

19. Ibid., June 24, 1863. The spelling of Santmires and St. Myers used in this essay follow those used in the accounts at the time, but no St. Myers can be found in the city directories, and spellings in the *Wheeling Intelligencer* often seem to be phonetic. Therefore, the assumption here is that Santmires and St. Myers are the same person.

20. Ibid., September 19, 1863.

21. Ibid., November 23, 1864.

22. Williams and Co., comp., *Williams' Wheeling Directory. City Guide and Business Mirror, for 1864*, 2nd issue (Wheeling: Williams and Co., 1864), 165. Smith's house was listed on the west side of Main between Adams and Franklin streets.

23. *Wheeling Intelligencer*, November 23, 1864.

24. Ibid., May 21, 1863, June 4, 1863, and October 20, 1863.

25. Ibid., June 4, 1863.

26. Ibid., May 21, 1863, October 20, 1863, and October 21, 1863.

27. Ibid., June 4, 1863, October 20, 1863, and October 21, 1863. There is no case file for this case in the Ohio County Circuit Court records, so it must be reconstructed from the newspaper reports. These reports never gave a first name for Mrs. Nesbit. There are no women with the last name of either Nesbit or Nesbitt listed in the 1860 census or 1864 Wheeling city directory who were identified as widows or who were not living with adult family members.

28. Ibid., May 21, 1863, and October 21, 1863.

29. Ibid., June 4, 1863.

30. Ibid., May 21, 1863, June 4, 1863, October 20, 1863, and October 21, 1863.

31. Ibid., May 22, 1863.

32. Ibid., October 21, 1863.

33. Ibid., May 22, 1863.

34. Ibid., October 21, 1863.

35. Ibid., October 20, 1863.

36. Ibid., October 21, 1863.

37. Ibid., October 21, 1863.

38. Ibid., October 22, 1863.

39. Hewetson Ault, "Wheeling, West Virginia, During the Civil War" (MA thesis, The Ohio State University, 1930), 75 (reference is to *Wheeling Intelligencer*, May 15, 1861).

40. City of Wheeling, Minutes, vol. 6, 1860–67, May 16, 1861, 55.

41. City of Wheeling, Ordinance Book 2, 528.

42. Ibid., September 28, 1861.

43. Ibid., March 11, 1862.

44. Ibid., March 25, 1862.

45. Ibid., April 4, 1862.

46. Ibid., April 9, 1862.

47. Ault, "Wheeling, West Virginia," 75 (reference is to *Wheeling Intelligencer*, May 26, 1862).

48. *Wheeling Intelligencer*, May 7, 1862. Barrabino's address is from Mears and Snavely, comp., *The Wheeling Directory* (Wheeling: Intelligencer Office, 1860), 13; and Williams and Co., *Williams' Wheeling Directory . . . for 1864*, 45.

49. T. Tuther Jr., comp., *The Wheeling Business Directory, for 1862–3* (Wheeling: For the Office of the "Press," 1862), 59.

50. *Wheeling Intelligencer*, May 26, 1862.

51. Ibid., May 26, 1862. Whims was arrested again, along with Rosa Golden, for prostitution in December 1864 (ibid., December 7, 1864).

52. Ibid., May 27, 1862. The newspaper misspelled the alderman's name as Mackmanaway.

53. Ibid., April 15, 1865, April 18, 1865.

54. Ibid., May 26, 1862.

55. City of Wheeling, Minutes, vol. 6, 1860–1867, June 1, 1862, 119.

56. *Wheeling Intelligencer*, June 10, 1862.

57. Ibid., August 28, 1862.

58. Ibid., September 24, 1862.

59. Ibid., November 11, 1862.

60. Ibid., October 13, 1863.

61. Ault, "Wheeling, West Virginia," 75 (reference is to *Wheeling Intelligencer*, February 2, 1863).

62. *Wheeling Intelligencer*, March 10, 1864.

63. Ault, "Wheeling, West Virginia," 75 (reference is to *Wheeling Intelligencer*, April 15, August 1, September 16, 1864).

64. *Wheeling Intelligencer,* August 1, 1864.

65. Ibid., April 5, 1864.

66. Ault, "Wheeling, West Virginia," 75–76.

67. *Wheeling Intelligencer,* December 25, 1862. Further information about Harry Fitzallen, whom the *Wheeling Intelligencer* identified as "Harry Fitsallen," can be found in Larry G. Eggleston, *Women in the Civil War: Extraordinary Stories of Soldiers, Spies, Nurses, Doctors, Crusaders and Others* (Jefferson, NC: McFarland, 2003), 67–68; *Chicago Daily Tribune,* April 18, 1862; and United States Secretary of War, *The War of the Rebellion: A Compilation of the official Records of the Union and Confederate Armies,* ser. 2, vol. 5 (Washington, DC: Government Printing Office, 1899), 121–22. None mention her previous appearance in Wheeling as a prostitute. The *Wheeling Intelligencer* said she identified herself as Miss Fitsallen when she came to Wheeling as a prostitute, but no other sources say she used an alias before she enlisted in the army as a man. The newspaper also said her real name was Marian M'Kinsey, but more authoritative sources use McKenzie.

68. *Wheeling Intelligencer,* August 7, 1862.

69. Ibid., February 2, 1863.

70. Ibid., February 9, 1864.

71. Ibid., July 22, 1863.

72. Ibid., March 2, 1864.

73. Ibid., June 23, 1862.

74. Ibid., July 23, 1864. No first name was given for the daughter, and the Brissacks were not listed in the 1860 census for Belmont County, Ohio.

75. Ibid., April 12, 1864.

76. Ibid., August 20, 1864.

77. Ibid., September 8, 1864.

78. Ibid., July 8, 1863.

79. Ibid., March 15, 1865.

80. Ibid., September 12, 1863.

81. Ault, "Wheeling, West Virginia," 75.

82. *The Code of West Virginia. Comprising Legislation to the Year 1870. With an Appendix Containing Legislation of That Year* (Wheeling: John Frew, Public Printer, 1871), chap. 149, sec. 10, 694.

83. James E. Reeves, *The Physical and Medical Topography, Including Vital, Manufacturing and Other Statistics of the City of Wheeling* (Wheeling: Daily Register Book and Job Office, 1870), 44.

84. James E. Reeves, *The Health and Wealth of the City of Wheeling, Including its Physical and Medical Topography; Also, General Remarks on the Natural Resources of West Virginia* (Baltimore: Sun Book and Job Office, 1871), 138.

85. Ibid., 138; Walker, *Ninth Census,* 1:286.

86. Reeves, *Health and Wealth,* 138.

87. Ibid., 136.

88. Ibid., 138.

CHAPTER EIGHT

Professionalizing "Mountain Work" in Appalachia

Women in the Conference of Southern Mountain Workers

PENNY MESSINGER

Women had a central role within the movements to reform Appalachia during the first half of the twentieth century. Their efforts were sustained and amplified by their participation in the network of reformers who called themselves mountain workers, and whose ranks included missionaries, educators, community workers, health professionals, volunteers, and government employees. This essay examines women's role within the field of mountain work by focusing on the Conference of Southern Mountain Workers, the central organization unifying reformers in the Appalachian South during the middle decades of the twentieth century. The term "mountain workers" appears to express regional identity and working-class status, but the mountain workers were predominantly middle class, as defined by background, education, and occupational status, and few of them were native Appalachians. Instead, their name derived from "mountain mission work," the branch of the Protestant home mission movement focusing on the Mountain South in the years after the Civil War. Created in 1913, the Conference of Southern Mountain Workers (CSMW) was the main organization through which reformers attempted to implement and institutionalize

217

a progressive agenda for Appalachia, and it was unique in its status as a regional organization and for the mix of members and interests represented within.[1] Through the CSMW, mountain workers asserted their authority to define the region and its needs and institutionalized their vision of Appalachia as a geographic and sociological region. The female leaders who directed the program and interests of the Conference during most of the years between 1920 and 1951 were instrumental in establishing professional standards for the field of mountain work. The concerns and agenda of reform that the mountain workers articulated serve to connect them with the themes of national Progressivism, but they also challenge key assumptions about Progressivism, extending the chronological framework of the Progressive Era into the 1950s and shifting its focus from the crowded cities of the East and Midwest to the rural landscape of the Appalachian South. Although this period extends beyond the traditional ending point of Progressivism, World War I, there is a compelling argument for interpreting the organization's history for this period through the framework of Progressivism, especially when one looks at that movement through a gendered lens.

Women were key participants in Progressivism on the national level; centering the narrative upon women changes how scholars view the movement and women's role within it. Focusing on the role of women challenges the periodization of the Progressive Era and the very definition of the movement itself.[2] Earlier scholars have made this point. For example, historian Elisabeth Israels Perry argues that the periodization of the Progressive Era should be expanded to include the Great Depression and New Deal years—when many Progressive reform goals were institutionalized by the federal government—along with World War II. Perry argues that Progressivism ended only in the early 1950s, in part because founders of progressive organizations and publications were no longer capable of continuing their work.[3] Indeed, women's history has shifted our understanding of the agenda and issues of the Progressive Movement, including the delineation between politics and social reform. Most histories of the Progressive movement, Perry writes, have failed to "convey the centrality of women's experiences, ideas, and activities to progressivism."[4] Community work, public welfare, and child saving were the expressions of a political sensibility grounded in women's experiences.[5] These areas, along with public health, education, recreation, and economic development efforts focused upon women, were matters of intense concern and engagement for female reformers. In Appalachia, as nationally, women's experiences and concerns were central to the Progressive reform agenda. Women working in the region's settlements, colleges, medical establishments, and mission centers—that is, mountain workers—presented a female face of Progressivism.[6]

The concerns of the CSMW during its years of female leadership are typical of those pursued by female Progressives elsewhere in the nation. Mountain workers sought professional status for their activities and used tactics and techniques that link them with reformers in other parts of the nation. Female mountain workers came to mountain work through feminized professions including education, nursing, and community work, and often expressed a gender consciousness in speaking as, and for, women. They established training programs at regional colleges and other institutions, set up and ran study tours designed to acclimate mountain workers new to the field, and claimed the right to define the region to outsiders through their quarterly publication, *Mountain Life & Work,* the first journal devoted to the Appalachian region. Olive Dame Campbell and Helen H. Dingman, among other pioneers, were crucial in efforts to define the field of mountain work and to imbue it with professional status, but they did not preserve the field as a female domain. During the 1940s, female founders made way for male successors at institutions throughout the region. This process was replicated within the Conference of Southern Mountain Workers itself during the 1940s, as the organization struggled to redefine its purpose and goals. Women brought professional standards to the field of mountain work, but professionalization restricted the ability of amateurs to enter the field and ended the era of women's leadership in the years after World War II.

PROGRESSIVES IN APPALACHIA

Mountain workers shared much of the vision of social politics held by liberal reformers of the Progressive Era who worked to create the welfare state but who later became uneasy with their creation. The network of female reformers originating in the settlement house movement established key institutions of the early welfare state. Their efforts culminated in the creation of the Children's Bureau and the Women's Bureau, both housed within the Department of Labor. These women utilized the language of self-sacrifice familiar to middle-class Victorian women's culture as they advocated for women and children. However, altruism often competed with a desire for social control, a motivation expressed in Hull House founder Jane Addams's statement, "There's power in me, and will to dominate which I must exercise."[7] These reformers carved out new professions, often turning to government to maintain their initiatives. To some participants within the settlement movement, the growth of the state promised to make private organizations and institutions obsolete.[8] This was not a sign of failure, however, but instead was the goal of many reformers. By initiating endeavors that were then turned over to the state and by expanding the scope of government into new areas, reformers sought to make their efforts permanent. Because women were heavily represented in the ranks of social workers, teachers, and other professionals who staffed these agencies and institutions, women were in effect carving out a new professional space and ensuring that others who followed them would find employment there.[9] In the Appalachian context, the mountain workers' intense focus on education was connected with this strategy. At regional colleges, universities, academies, institutes, and settlement institutions, mountain workers mentored and trained the students from the region who would continue and extend their work. In the case of teaching, nursing, and social work, all of which were heavily feminized occupations within Appalachia as well as within the nation, female reformers who came to the region from other parts of the nation worked to train young mountain-born women who would fill their shoes and continue their efforts both in private and public institutions and organizations.

The story of mountain work intersects in some important ways with the history of Progressivism and liberalism in the three decades after 1920. While the Progressive movement as a whole is defined by its eager advocacy of an expanded role for the state, some reformers were wary of this approach, both because they feared that a government-centered approach could overwhelm their own efforts and because they grew uncomfortable with the centralized authority necessary for the welfare state. These tensions are present in the history of mountain work, just as they are in the history of national reform. Nationally, the enthusiasm for state building is evident in the network of Progressive female reformers that originated within the settlement movement. Maintaining this network within the Children's Bureau during the 1920s, reformers succeeded in implementing many of their long-term objectives during the New Deal.[10] Many female reformers of the Progressive Era utilized maternalist arguments, prioritizing women's responsibilities as mothers and advocating social policies requiring the support of the state. Political scientist Theda Skocpol argues that the maternalist state grew because it had the support of women's clubs, charitable organizations, and other groups that initially drew upon the common bond—exclusion from full citizenship—that united women from different backgrounds. These groups argued for protective legislation, mothers' pensions, and other maternalist policies focused specifically upon women's needs.[11] However, the growth of government was not universally supported by Progressive Era reformers; many private organizations and the professionals who staffed them were uncomfortable with this expanded role for the state. The discomfort with centralized authority increased during the late 1930s,[12] even among the New Deal's liberal architects, who began to rethink their statist ideas. Both the rise of fascism in Europe and the anticommunism of the Cold War era taught American liberals to be cautious about an increased role of the state and facilitated the shift from "reform liberalism" to the "rights-based liberalism" of the post-World War II era.[13]

This bipolar attitude toward centralized authority—and, indeed, public institutions—is evident in the history of the CSMW during these years. Mountain workers who were affiliated with private institutions repeatedly addressed their relationship with public institutions, circling back to the same questions time and again. What was the proper role for private institutions if and when the state provided adequate funding for public schools? Could public institutions address the needs of mountain people as well as private independent schools or religiously affiliated ones did? Mountain workers long had argued that education was a public responsibility, and mission boards often worked together with local governments to supplement teachers' inadequate pay and to

Professionalizing "Mountain Work" in Appalachia 221

recruit and retain trained teachers, taking practical steps to address the inadequate and poorly funded schools that permeated the Appalachian region. Yet many of the mountain workers argued for the distinctiveness of their efforts and depended on the continued existence of private institutions for their livelihoods. The tension between private institutions and expanding public sphere was pervasive within the ongoing conversation about Appalachian reform during mid-century.

THE CSMW AND A FEMALE MISSION

Female missionaries, educators, and other reformers were integral to the network of mountain institutions and organizations from which the CSMW emerged. Most mountain workers, including CSMW founder John C. Campbell, were affiliated with Protestant missionary denominations that had operated in Appalachia since Reconstruction, and their emphasis on social uplift and a sense of religious mission strongly shaped the field of mountain work.[14] The home mission movement's presence was so substantial that Campbell gave honored billing to "the Church Boards of the South and of the North" when describing "the agencies in the field for the betterment of Highland conditions" that were identified in his proposal for initiating study of the Mountain South, and for many years CSMW leaders balanced the representation of missionary groups within the organization's leadership.[15] Campbell was himself a former missionary and educator when he approached the brand-new Russell Sage Foundation with a proposal to study the region and to coordinate reform efforts there.[16] The foundation created a Southern Highland Division to underwrite Campbell's work; it also subsidized the expenses of the CSMW as a means of coordinating and professionalizing the efforts of reformers who were dispersed throughout the region. The yearly conference quickly became a key arena for mountain workers to discuss their activities and plans for agriculture, health care, cultural preservation, and other reforms, foremost among them education. By 1919, when Campbell died, the CSMW was an important regional organization whose members understood their role to be speaking for the region, coordinating the various reform efforts underway within it and acting as an intermediary between Appalachia and the rest of the country.[17]

Although the CSMW operated under female leadership for most of the period between 1919 and 1951, the priorities that female leaders brought to mountain work are little known.[18] In what continues to be the most influential scholarly treatment of the organization, David Whisnant's essay, "Workers in God's Grand Division: The Council of the Southern Mountains," quickly disposes of the fourteen-year tenure of Executive Secretary Helen Hastie Dingman in a couple of sentences, characterizing the period of Dingman's leadership as a time when the "domain of interest and influence [of the CSMW] was reduced to dabbling with the more picturesque aspects of regional folkways (folk songs, folk speech, recreation, and crafts), operating bookmobiles, and distributing used books and clothing."[19] The essay misses the point that such measures grew from the CSMW's central interest in education.

During its years of female leadership, the CSMW took a number of actions that established the organization's primacy in Appalachian reform, while maintaining connections with reformers within the United States and internationally that kept the group in the mainstream of reform efforts of the era. After John C. Campbell's death, his widow Olive Dame Campbell continued to be deeply involved with the CSMW and served as a liaison between the group and the Russell Sage Foundation, which heavily influenced the group's focus and approach throughout the 1920s and 1930s. Campbell's interest in the Scandinavian folk school movement generated ideas about revitalizing rural life and shaped her involvement in the crafts revival among member institutions of the CSMW.[20] Helen Hastie Dingman, who took over Olive Dame Campbell's job as executive secretary of the CSMW in 1928, also maintained connections with national and international reform circles. Dingman was involved in a range of progressive social issues at Berea College, where she taught sociology and trained teachers for careers in rural schools, and she also addressed these issues through the CMSW.[21] During her years as executive secretary (1928–42), Dingman stood at the center of the mountain workers' network. Her career expressed a sense of social mission and activism on behalf of underprivileged people, particularly women and children.[22]

Female leaders of the CSMW relied heavily upon the women who comprised a numerical majority among the mountain workers. Like female Progressive reformers in other parts of the nation, mountain workers

Professionalizing "Mountain Work" in Appalachia 223

improved education and health care, established community centers, marketed crafts, emphasized folk music and culture, promoted recreation, and addressed the needs of women and children. As with female Progressive reformers in other parts of the country, the techniques of female reformers in the southern mountains included cooperation (seeking the *via media*, or "middle way"[23]); speaking from a position of female moral authority (as when missionaries invoked religious motives for their efforts); and publicizing their endeavors with the intent of sharing information and defining an agenda of reform (as they did through *Mountain Life & Work*, the yearly meeting, and regional meetings and study tours).[24]

The era of female leadership also marked an important stage in the professionalization of mountain work, as mountain workers established themselves as experts on the mountain region, coordinated their efforts through their professional organization (the CSMW), and publicized their efforts through *Mountain Life & Work*. Launched in 1925 with funding from Berea College, the publication was initially independent of the CSMW, although it devoted considerable attention to the organization from the start, including one of its quarterly issues dedicated to the yearly conference.[25] Members were urged to support the publication financially, and in 1926 Helen Dingman, who would become executive secretary of the CSMW in 1928, took over as editor. By 1933 Dingman was describing *Mountain Life & Work* as the organization's "official organ."[26] *Mountain Life & Work* filled an important function in the mountain workers' network. The quarterly publication provided a way for mountain workers to maintain contacts beyond the yearly meeting and included brief news articles and literary pieces written by and about CSMW members. It sometimes included items intended for the use of rural teachers. Plans for building playgrounds and other structures appeared in the publication, along with lyrics and music for ballads. Because it also circulated beyond the region among academics and reformers and for many years stood alone as the only publication about the region, the publication created a powerful image of the region as it was understood and experienced by the mountain workers.

The focus of mountain work during the 1920s and 1930s was closely associated with developments in social work. Establishing mountain work as a professional field replicated the process that urban settlement women had followed in establishing social work as a profession. The dialogue among groups, agencies, and individuals who represented private agencies and institutions was a regular feature of the yearly conference meetings, and in their efforts to integrate expertise from disparate fields of knowledge, mountain workers echoed the orientation of social work in the 1920s. Mountain work also followed social work's early focus upon "private agencies and psychiatric treatment of individuals rather than social change," as historian Robyn Muncy notes.[27] The mountain workers' approach was strongly shaped by a continuing affiliation with the Russell Sage Foundation, which was deeply involved in the professionalization of social work in the 1910s and 1920s as part of its initial charge for "the improvement of social and living conditions in the United States of America" and because of Director John M. Glenn's own professional background in social work.[28] The foundation's emphasis on cooperation, association, and voluntary action provided a philosophical foundation for Herbert Hoover's Associational state in the late 1920s. Affiliating itself with CSWM founder John C. Campbell during its first year of operation, the Sage Foundation had expanded its support of Campbell by establishing the Southern Highlands Division (which employed Campbell and his secretary, Edith Canterbury). Although the Southern Highlands Division was ended with Campbell's death, the Sage Foundation continued to provide small subsidies for CSMW activities into the 1940s, and even more important during the 1920s and 1930s, it served as a source of expertise for mountain workers.[29]

While mountain work reflected trends within social work, the organization's focus on such issues as public health nursing, teaching, and "culture work" reflected both the special concerns and the separateness of the women's network in mountain work. This separateness replicated a familiar pattern in women's professionalization. Largely excluded from established professions such as law, medicine, and the ministry, women had created professions of their own. Women entered the professions not by directly competing with men in established fields but, rather, by carving out new areas of expertise that had gone unclaimed by men. Once established, however, these new professions proved attractive to men. The process of professionalization itself limited women's representation even in fields established by women.

Professionalizing "Mountain Work" in Appalachia 225

Gender shaped the actions taken by the CSMW and its members, and the emphasis of the group's program shifted in response to changing leadership. Both men and women participated in the CSMW in the early 1920s, but they often pursued separate interests and tended to cluster separately within the organization. In addition to the consistent themes of mission work, education, and health care, male leaders more strongly emphasized agriculture and industry. When the leaders were female, more attention was directed toward areas and interests of female members, including cultural work, folk arts/handicrafts, and nursing. The "ever-present" elements—including mission work, education, and health care—also had a different focus. For example, female leaders were focused more on the needs of the classroom teacher and her school than upon state-level educational administrations or educational policy. Because concern with education was a central connection among the mountain workers, conference sessions centered around topics such as public and private schools, school funding, adult education, and attendance and retention issues (including truancy and dropout issues), while *Mountain Life & Work* provided instructions and designs for rural schools and playgrounds, as well as music and other materials intended for use by classroom teachers. Female leaders offered sessions and programs to meet the needs of the individual mission worker, often a woman, more often than they addressed the agenda to be pursued by mission executives, who were generally men. This focus reinforced the role of the CSMW as the central professional organization in mountain work.

The segregation of the female mountain workers into specific areas of expertise also reflected the gender hierarchies that existed within mountain work. Both men and women founded and directed educational institutions, but they were staffed primarily by women.[30] Men and women worked as missionaries, but most of the lowly "mission workers" were female. Other occupations reflected similar gender hierarchies: while most physicians were male, most nurses were female. Social workers in Appalachia, as elsewhere in the nation, were overwhelmingly female.[31] While men claimed authority on the problems facing agriculture and on economic development, women took the lead in promoting handicrafts, emphasizing recreation, advocating for children, and dissecting the needs of the rural school.

OLIVE DAME CAMPBELL, HELEN HASTIE DINGMAN, AND FLORENCE GOODELL

Because the executive secretary established the agenda of the yearly conference and accented the issues that he or she considered most important, the central leadership position in the organization allowed for great influence over the organization's focus. Thus, the three women who held the position of executive secretary—Olive Dame Campbell (1919–1928), Helen Hastie Dingman (1928–1942), and Florence Goodell (1950–1951)—kept the concerns of female reformers in the foreground.[32] Even in 1920, during Olive Dame Campbell's first year as executive secretary, the familiar discussions of education and religion were supplemented by a session on public health and another on community work, emphasizing, for the first time, sociological surveys, community organization, extension work, and recreation.[33] In 1922 sessions on education and religion shared equal billing with sessions on agriculture and community activities and agencies (including industry, home economics, health work and rural hospitals, and "community forces").[34] Children's issues, recreation, and handicrafts also received more attention at CSMW meetings during the 1920s and 1930s.

One of the strongest influences from Olive Dame Campbell was her interest in culture, folk arts, and the preservation of rural life. These interests shaped the annual program of the CSMW as well as initiatives among members. In 1922, with a fellowship from the American Scandinavian Foundation, she and Marguerite Butler of the Pine Mountain Settlement School traveled to Denmark and Finland to begin fifteen months of studying Scandinavian folk schools. Campbell was carrying out plans she had made with her husband to study the schools, plans that were interrupted by the onset of World War I. The schools' emphasis on adult education, cultural preservation, and rural revitalization drew their interest.[35] In 1925 Campbell established the John C. Campbell Folk School in Brasstown, North Carolina, to implement her ideas; she would serve as its director until 1947. She was joined by Marguerite Butler, an important leader in her own right. Campbell intended the school as a prototype for a network of institutions that could halt the out-migration of the region's youth and regenerate rural society. The folk school model influenced other regional institutions, including

Professionalizing "Mountain Work" in Appalachia 227

the Opportunity Schools operated by Berea College in the 1920s and 1930s.[36] Campbell also followed the Scandinavian model in spinning off cooperative enterprises from the school, sponsoring several cooperative organizations in Brasstown: a savings and loan association that extended small loans to local farmers, a community (poultry) hatchery, a farmers' association, and the Mountain Valley Creamery Association.[37] Campbell helped to organize other cooperatives in the region. She also publicized their activities by writing articles about the Farmers' Federation of Buncombe County, North Carolina, and about the success of North Carolina's county agents in spreading cooperatives.[38]

Female mountain workers were more interested in cultural topics than in agriculture, however, and their experimentation with cooperative enterprises reached its greatest success in the area of craft production and marketing. The Appalachian craft revival had started in 1890, when the gift of a hand-loomed coverlet sparked the interest of missionary Frances L. Goodrich and led her to nurture a market for coverlets and woven items produced at centers throughout the region.[39] The women who led the effort to commercialize craft production in Appalachia argued that their efforts could give mountain women an income of their own, which was badly needed in many financially strapped mountain families. Gender unity was clearly a motivation: they described themselves as women helping women. During the 1920s, in focused discussions held at the yearly CSMW conference, mountain workers began discussing the creation of a formal, separate organization to produce and market craft items. Marguerite Butler and Olive Dame Campbell attributed this idea to their Scandinavian trip. A cooperative marketing organization, Campbell explained, could ensure 'quality, quantity and a market" and would allow producers to focus on craft production rather than "marketing details."[40]

The cooperative organization that resulted, the Southern Mountain Handicraft Guild, was formally organized in 1930 and renamed as the Southern Highlands Handicraft Guild in 1933. It was created at a meeting of the CSMW by a committee that included Olive Dame Campbell, Helen Dingman, Berea College president Francis Hutchins, Allen H. Eaton of the Russell Sage Foundation, and other mountain workers who were involved in handicrafting as a means of generating income and preserving cultural traditions. The SHHG's first board of directors included Marguerite Butler (John C. Campbell Folk School) as president and May Stone (Hindman Settlement School) as vice president; Clementine Douglas (founder of the Spinning Wheel, the Beaver Lake, North Carolina, hand-weaving center), Lucy Morgan (of Penland, North Carolina), and O. J. Mattil (founder of O. J. Mattil's Woodcrafters and Carvers Shop in Gatlinburg, Tennessee). Helen Dingman served as an ex-officio member and secretary-treasurer of the SHHG. The marketing of handicrafts was sophisticated; mountain workers used the form of a progressive, cooperative organization to advance common goals and (as Campbell put it) to tap "the real market." Although many of those who were involved in the SHHG continued to participate in the CSMW, their efforts in promoting handicrafts in some ways came to overshadow the CSMW itself by the 1940s. They effectively used the image of the handicrafter, who was usually female, to represent the Appalachian region to much of the outside world.[41]

As Olive Dame Campbell came to focus on running the John C. Campbell Folk School, she looked for someone to succeed her as CSMW executive secretary. Helen Dingman was a logical successor; she shared many of Campbell's interests and was a strong leader with progressive social views.[42] Already the editor of *Mountain Life & Work,* she had helped with Campbell's early experiments with adult education and community outreach that preceded the establishment of the John C. Campbell Folk School. Her affiliation with Berea College would also bring needed resources, including office space and clerical assistance, to the organization. Dingman was a native of Spring Valley, New York, and began her early career as a teacher at Dana Hall, a preparatory school for future Wellesley students, but was drawn into mission work after she spent the summer of 1916 in Rocky Fork, Tennessee. In 1917 she began working for the Presbyterian Mission Board in the community of Smith, Kentucky, located in Harlan County. In 1922 she returned to New York in the position of assistant supervisor of fieldwork with the Presbyterian Board of Home Missions, but in 1924 Berea College's new president, William J. Hutchins, persuaded her to take a job at Berea, teaching and supervising student teachers.[43]

Dingman's years as executive secretary overlapped the years of the Great Depression. Financing any program during the Depression was

Professionalizing "Mountain Work" in Appalachia 229

challenging not only because of the overall economic climate but also because the CSMW already operated on a shoestring budget and could manage only a half-time salary for its leader. When the group undertook to expand its program during the mid-1930s, the efforts that were most successful were those that enjoyed support from the female network in mountain work: health work, recreation, and child-centered initiatives. The decision to emphasize recreation rather than to confront directly the economic disaster is puzzling today, but the recreation program succeeded because it had the enthusiastic support of many female mountain workers and was able to attract money from reliable contributors such as the Russell Sage Foundation, the Keith Fund, national sororities, and Smith College.[44] It is also important to keep in mind that the recreation program was developed primarily to serve public and private schools in the region.[45] Even as the fortunes of the CSMW waned in the 1940s, the recreation movement thrived. It almost became an autonomous organization during the early 1950s.

Dingman led efforts to claim professional status for mountain work during the 1930s. The CMSW controlled the agenda of regional reform through hosting study tours, publicizing activities in *Mountain Life & Work* and other publications, and other means. Study tours offered visitors a tour of the region that highlighted the features of member institutions of the CSMW, thus establishing the mountain workers' expertise by recognizing their authority to define the important sites within the region. The study tour was a familiar feature of Progressivism. In his book *Atlantic Crossings,* historian Daniel Rodgers discussed the popularity of study tours in pre–World War I Europe, when "socially concerned Americans could travel to Europe on . . . specially packaged tours." The practice resumed by the 1930s, when a range of European study fellowships, study tours, and the "sociological grand tour" sent Americans in search of potential answers to economic and social problems.[46]

Another effort to establish professional status was the cooperative survey of the Appalachian region, the results of which were published in 1935 by the federal government as *Economic and Social Problems and Conditions of the Southern Appalachians.* In 1929 Dingman had pointed out the need for a comprehensive economic and social survey of conditions in the Appalachian region and to that end convened a committee, chaired by the University of Kentucky's Dr. Thomas Cooper.[47] If mountain work was to be recognized as a professional field, the workers needed information more up-to-date than John C. (and Olive Dame) Campbell's 1921 book, which had drawn upon information from the 1910s and earlier. The 1935 survey was the first comprehensive survey of the region to be undertaken by federal authorities, and perhaps the first official recognition on the part of the federal government that the Southern Appalachians comprised an identifiable social or economic unit. The mountain workers' accomplishment, then, lay in initiating the project, gaining recognition of their region of operation, and in applying the results.

By contrast, the mountain workers' efforts to launch a major new project to train mountain teachers and to provide support to regional schools met with numerous obstacles. The group attracted seed grants from the Earhart Foundation and the General Education Board of the Rockefeller Foundation by the early 1940s, but it lost these funds because it could not hire a full-time executive secretary who was willing to stay in the position. Dingman ran the CSMW as a half-time director, but when she developed cardiac problems in 1937, her illness created a leadership crisis. Several years of restricted activity concluded when Dingman resigned the position of executive secretary at the end of 1941. Over the next decade, the group struggled to find a permanent leader.

The leadership difficulties of the 1940s were partly a result of success. As mountain work became more professionalized, women leaders began to vanish from positions of leadership within the field. Even institutions founded by women, such as the Pine Mountain Settlement School, the John C. Campbell Folk School, and the Hindman Settlement School, chose men to replace their female founders.[48] These transitions also placed men in controlling positions within the CSMW on the Executive Committee, which held the power to appoint new members of the Committee and to select officials of the organization, including the president and the executive secretary. Committee members selected officials from their own ranks and now sought a male leader to carry the group's work into a new era. Despite the strong female presence within the CSMW and the decades of female leadership, the new leaders of the group wanted their new executive secretary to be a man.

Professionalizing "Mountain Work" in Appalachia 231

Initially, the group hired Alva W. Taylor to replace Dingman. Taylor was seventy when he took the job; he agreed to accept the position for two years but stayed for three. The CSMW had no executive secretary during the entire year of 1945 (someone accepted the position but reneged on his agreement before starting). In 1946 the council hired its first full-time director, Glyn Morris, who held the position for one year before resigning. Members of the CSMW's Executive Board were eager for stable leadership but wanted to make sure that they hired the right person. In 1946, they decided that Howard Kester was this person. Kester was a socialist, a southern radical whose social activism in behalf of workers, sharecroppers, and racial integration was partially inspired by Alva W. Taylor.[49] He was also a protégé of Reinhold Niebuhr, perhaps the most influential theologian in mid-twentieth-century America. Kester never became executive secretary of the CSMW, but hiring him became such a high priority that the mountain workers agreed to keep their leadership position vacant for him for more than a year.

The result of this leadership vacuum in the late 1940s was financial disaster, as the mountain workers watched their grants and other forms of outside income melt away. In 1949 financial difficulties forced the CSMW to cut its program, close the office in Berea, and merge operations with those of the Southern Highlands Handicraft Guild, a stronghold of female mountain workers, in Asheville. This female network had provided CSMW's primary source of stability when Florence Goodell arrived in Berea in September 1945. She preceded Glyn Morris by four months and stayed until 1951. She assisted Morris during his year as executive secretary, kept the program operating while the group sought Morris's replacement, and stayed in place through the long wait for Howard Kester. When financial catastrophe struck, Goodell carried out most of the work of the executive secretary. She was voted the title of executive secretary in 1950 and held the post until she resigned in March 1951. Goodell tried to tell other members of the CSMW some hard truths. She suggested dropping "Mountain Workers" from the organization's name because, she argued, it marked the identity of the group as professional "do-gooders" from outside the region. She also argued that mountain people themselves, rather than outside leaders, needed to take control of regional reform, and of the CSMW. Yet there

232 PENNY MESSINGER

seemed to be little support among CSMW officers (including Arthur Bannerman, the CSMW president and spokesman for a larger group of leaders) for her to take over leadership of the group on a permanent basis.[50]

Other female mountain workers, however, seem to have expected that Goodell would carry on the tradition of female leadership within the CSMW on a permanent basis. When she heard of Goodell's resignation, Olive Campbell wrote from Massachusetts, "I am quite shocked to get your word telling of your resigning! I don't know how we are going to get on without you! I feel I ought to be in Gatlinburg—and *do* something; thank goodness Helen is there!"[51] Yet when asked for advice for the group by the new CSMW president, Francis Hutchins, Campbell demurred, saying that she was too far away and no longer in touch with the needs of the region.[52] It's not clear from existing records whether Goodell wanted to continue on as the council's leader, though it does seem that Campbell's decision to disengage from the group reflected a consensus of other female mountain workers, among them Goodell. Responding to Campbell's almost frantic note to her, Goodell wrote that she had always thought of the position as a temporary one, writing as well of her frustrations in trying to meet the needs of the CSMW and the SHHG. Furthermore, she wrote, "I think it's time the Council got a younger, more permanent Executive Secretary. . . . I think she [Helen Dingman] agreed with me, finally, that the Council should make a clean break and plan for the future."[53] With Goodell's resignation in August 1951, the CSMW entered an era in which the network of female mountain workers had gone into eclipse.

Despite some obvious parallels to more recognized and studied urban progressivism, regional scholars who dismiss the mountain workers as ineffectual home missionaries have overlooked their role in shaping Appalachian reform and in pursuing a Progressive agenda into the 1940s. Key themes link the efforts of mountain workers in the Southern Appalachians to their urban counterparts and to the developing profession of social work. A consciousness of the region's educational inadequacies sparked support for community work and outreach efforts that included extension classes and field programs, support for church and independent schools, and recreational opportunities. Mountain workers launched campaigns for improved health care and fought to

Professionalizing "Mountain Work" in Appalachia 233

improve infant and maternal care. They pursued cultural preservation efforts and developed a market for handcrafted products in order to provide mountain women with an income by founding and operating the Southern Highland Handicraft Guild. They drew upon the expertise and funds of the Russell Sage Foundation and other agencies to initiate many of their endeavors, but mountain workers ultimately sought to expand the presence of local and state government in education, health, and other areas. The persistence of mountain workers' efforts to pursue a rural and feminized Progressive agenda into the 1940s calls into question both the traditional understanding of their role in Appalachian reform and the periodization of the Progressive Era.

NOTES

1. In 1944 the Conference of Southern Mountain Workers was renamed Council of Southern Mountain Workers and, in 1954, Council of the Southern Mountains, a name retained by the organization until it disbanded in 1989.

2. See, especially, Elisabeth Israels Perry, "Men Are from the Gilded Age, Women Are from the Progressive Era," *Journal of the Gilded Age and Progressive Era* 1, no. 1 (January 2002), http://historycooperative.press.uiuc.edu/journals/jga/1.1/perry.html, and Robyn Muncy, *Creating a Female Dominion in American Reform, 1890–1935* (New York: Oxford University Press, 1991).

3. Perry, "Men Are from the Gilded Age," paras. 43, 47–48. The question of when the Progressive Movement ended is not a new one. Writing in 1967, Otis Graham Jr. noted that social workers were the staunchest advocates of reform during the 1920s, although he also notes that not all social workers were reformers. Mountain workers closely monitored and followed trends in social work, especially as defined through the Russell Sage Foundation. See Otis Graham Jr., *An Encore for Reform: The Old Progressives and the New Deal* (Oxford: Oxford University Press, 1967), 107–8.

4. Perry, "Men Are from the Gilded Age," para. 16.

5. Ibid., paras. 36–39.

6. Katharine Pettit, May Stone, and other settlement women were involved with the founding of the CMSW. There are two distinct perspectives on their role in the region. David E. Whisnant argues that they were cultural interventionists who facilitated the economic penetration of Appalachia. See David E. Whisnant, "Second-Level Appalachian History: Another Look at Some Fotched-On Women," *Appalachian Journal* 9, nos. 2 and 3 (Winter/Spring 1982): 115–23; and *All That Is Native and Fine: The Politics of Culture in an American Region* (Chapel Hill: University of North Carolina Press, 1983), a work that is highly critical of both Hindman Settlement School (chosen to represent the approach of settlement institutions) and Olive Dame Campbell. See especially chap. 1, "'Hit Sounds Reasonable': Culture and Social Change at Hindman Settlement School,"

and chap. 2, "All That Is Native and Fine: The Cultural Work of Olive Dame Campbell, 1908–1948."

By contrast, scholars such as Nancy Forderhase, James S. Green, P. David Searles, Karen Tice, Sandra Barney, and Jess Stoddard present a more positive view of the settlement women, arguing that these reformers met the very real needs of the mountain people among whom they lived. See Nancy K. Forderhase, "Eve Returns to the Garden: Women Reformers in Appalachian Kentucky in the Early Twentieth Century," *Register of the Kentucky Historical Society* 85, no. 3 (Summer 1987): 237–61; Nancy K. Forderhase, "Settlement School Goes to the People: Pine Mountain School's Community Centers at Big Laurel and Line Fork, 1919–1940," in *The Impact of Institutions in Appalachia: Proceedings of the 8th Annual Appalachian Studies Conference,* ed. Jim Lloyd and Anne G. Campbell (Boone, NC: Appalachian Consortium Press, 1985), 88–99; James S. Greene III, "Progressives in the Kentucky Mountains: The Formative Years of the Pine Mountain Settlement School, 1913–1930" (PhD diss., Ohio State University, 1982); P. David Searles, *A College for Appalachia: Alice Lloyd on Caney Creek* (Lexington: University Press of Kentucky, 1995); Karen Tice, "School-Work and Mother Work: The Interplay of Maternalism and Cultural Politics in the Educational Narratives of Kentucky Settlement Workers, 1910–1930," *Journal of Appalachian Studies* 4, no. 2 (Fall 1998): 191–224; Sandra Barney, "Maternalism and the Promotion of Scientific Medicine During the Industrial Transformation of Appalachia, 1880–1930," *NWSA Journal* 11, no. 3 (Fall 1999): 68–92; Sandra Lee Barney, *Authorized to Heal: Gender, Class, and the Transformation of Medicine in Appalachia, 1880–1930* (Chapel Hill: University of North Carolina Press, 2000); Jess Stoddard, *Challenge and Change in Appalachia: The Story of Hindman Settlement School* (Lexington: University Press of Kentucky, 2002). Stoddard's book includes a detailed historiographical essay (see app. 1, "Social Settlements and Settlement Workers," 225–31) evaluating Whisnant's argument in light of other scholarship about the settlement women. She concludes that his essay about Hindman was simplistic and inaccurate, as was his overall discussion of Appalachian settlement workers.

7. Muncy, *Creating a Female Dominion,* quoting Addams, 3.

8. Political scientist Theda Skocpol disagrees with Muncy's discussion of the creation of the welfare state. She argues that in some instances, such as with the movement on behalf of mothers' pensions during the 1910s and 1920s, professional social workers did *not* turn to the state or support the expansion of the welfare state. Skocpol points out that social workers affiliated with the charity organization movement opposed efforts to create mothers' pensions that would be administered by the state and instead argued that such relief as existed should be administered by private charities and other organizations. Contesting Muncy's conclusions that female reformers affiliated with social settlements built the welfare state, Skocpol argues that in the campaign for mothers' pensions, "the initiative rested almost entirely with the federations of women's voluntary groups, while the social settlement women were only marginally involved (and were certainly not 'directing' anything)." See Theda Skocpol, *Protecting Soldiers and Mothers: The Political Origins of Social Policy in the United States* (Cambridge, MA: Belknap Press of Harvard University Press, 1992), esp. 683n9.

9. This is a central argument in Muncy's *Creating a Female Dominion*. Jess Stoddard describes a similar process of innovation in the history of Hindman Settlement School, which initiated an array of programs as part of its educational mission and turned them over to the local community to operate. In contrast with the many settlement institutions that did not survive into the post–World War II era, Hindman endured by adapting to new circumstances and redefining its mission. See, esp., Stoddard, 142–73. Stoddard's conclusions echo Elisabeth Perry's observations that the decade after World War II was a transitional period that saw the end of many endeavors that began during the Progressive Era.

10. Muncy, *Creating a Female Dominion*. See also Daniel T. Rodgers, *Atlantic Crossings: Social Politics in a Progressive Era* (Cambridge, MA: Belknap Press of Harvard University Press, 2000), for an excellent discussion of the ways that the social policies envisioned by Progressives were realized in the New Deal.

11. The Women's Christian Temperance Union, the General Federation of Women's Clubs, and the National Congress of Mothers were among those large national federated organizations that helped to enact maternalist policies. Skocpol, *Protecting Soldiers and Mothers*, 47–60.

12. According to Otis Graham, many Progressives turned against the New Deal. Despite their role in shaping collective, state-based solutions to social problems, Graham depicts Progressives as individualists who were troubled by their role in facilitating the growth of federal power. Graham, *Encore for Reform*, 71–74.

13. Alan Brinkley, *The End of Reform: New Deal Liberalism in Recession and War* (New York: Random House, 1995), esp. chap. 7.

14. Although the impact of the home mission movement in Appalachia is widely recognized, few scholars have explored its history. In his essay "Home Missions Revisited: Edward O. Guerrant and the 'Discovery' of Appalachia" (Introduction to Edward O. Guerrant, *The Galax Gatherers: The Gospel Among the Highlanders* [Knoxville: University of Tennessee Press, 2005]: xi–xl), Mark Huddle argues that attention to this topic is "long overdue." Recent works about the home mission movement to Appalachia include Mark Banker's "Of Missionaries, Multiculturalism, and the Mainstream Malaise: Insights into the Presbyterian Predicament," *Journal of Presbyterian History* 81, no. 2 (Summer 2003): 77–102, and Chris Allen Green, "The Social Life of Poetry: Pluralism and Appalachia, 1937–1947" (PhD diss., University of Kentucky, 2004).

15. Quotation from "Statement for a Proposed Study Plan of the Southern Highland Section" appended to John C. Campbell to Mrs. John M. Glenn, May 15, 1908, Russell Sage Foundation Archives, Southern Highland Division, box 16, folder 134, Rockefeller Archive Center, Sleepy Hollow, NY (hereafter cited as RSF Archive). John M. Glenn became secretary of the Sage Foundation; his wife, Mary Wilcox Glenn, was also an important figure in the charity organization movement and the early history of social work. From reading the correspondence included in the John C. and Olive Dame Campbell Papers (housed at the University of North Carolina at Chapel Hill) and the records of the Southern Highland Division (in the Russell Sage Foundation Archives), it is clear that reform was a partnership both for the Campbells and the Glenns.

16. The Russell Sage Foundation was established in May 1907 with an initial bequest of $10 million, which was supplemented in 1918 with an additional $5 million gift. See Russell Sage Foundation Finding Aid, RSF Archive. Notably, although John M. Glenn was the chief executive of the Sage Foundation when Campbell suggested his study, he addressed his letter to Mrs. Glenn.

17. My interpretation of the CSMW draws upon my doctoral dissertation: Penny Messinger, "Leading the Field of Mountain Work: The Conference of Southern Mountain Workers, 1912–1950" (PhD diss., Ohio State University, 1998). The most influential treatment of the CSMW remains David E. Whisnant's essay, "Controversy in God's Grand Division: The Council of the Southern Mountains," *Appalachian Journal* 2, no. 1 (Autumn 1974): 7–44, and (in revised form) in David E. Whisnant, *Modernizing the Mountaineer: People, Power, and Planning in Appalachia* (Boone, NC: Appalachian Consortium Press, 1980; repr. 1986). Whisnant's characterization of the CSMW as the central expression of a conservative home mission movement whose locus was at Berea College captures the essence of his critique of the organization. Whisnant presents the CSMW as the first of a sequence of failed twentieth-century reforms aimed at Appalachia whose common element was their inability or unwillingness to confront the reality of economic exploitation by corporate interests. Whisnant situated the organization within a broader context of "a hundred years of exploitative private development in the mountains, and condescending middle-class missionary attitudes and activities that accompanied it" (Whisnant, *Modernizing the Mountaineer,* xv). Although objections to Whisnant's argument about the CSMW were raised by Loyal Jones, Thomas Parrish, and A. H. Perrin, these critiques (published, along with a reply by Whisnant, as Letters to the Editor under the title, "Problems in Revisionism: More Controversy in 'God's Grand Division,'" *Appalachian Journal* 2, no. 3 [Spring 1975]: 171–91), have been less influential than his interpretation. However, some of Whisnant's assertions about Appalachia, most notably his depiction of the Appalachian settlement movement, have been roundly criticized by other scholars (as discussed above).

18. Scholars have written mainly about the eras when men led the CSMW, emphasizing the roles of John C. Campbell (1913–19), Alva W. Taylor (1943–45), and Perley F. Ayer (1951–66). In addition to Whisnant, other scholars who address the history of the CSMW include Allen Batteau, *The Invention of Appalachia* (Tucson: University of Arizona Press, 1990), who closely tracks Whisnant's analysis, and Deborah Vansau McCauley, *Appalachian Mountain Religion: A History* (Urbana: University of Illinois Press, 1995), who emphasizes the group's close affiliation with the home mission movement, which she condemns for its critique of regional religious groups and traditions. Two recent syntheses of Appalachian history include brief discussions of the CSMW. Richard B. Drake, *A History of Appalachia* (Lexington: University Press of Kentucky, 2001) credits the mountain workers for initiating an "Appalachian Conversation" that centered within the Council of the Southern Mountains until 1969–70, when the focus of the organization shifted dramatically (233). John Alexander Williams describes the group's origins and liberal focus in its early decades and its transformation during the 1960s in his

Professionalizing "Mountain Work" in Appalachia 237

Appalachia: A History (Chapel Hill: University of North Carolina Press, 2002), esp. 285 and 361. See also John M. Glenn, "The War on Poverty in Appalachia—A Preliminary Report," *Register of the Kentucky Historical Society* 87, no. 1 (Winter 1989): 40–57.

The extensive emphasis upon John C. and Olive Dame Campbell in regional scholarship is warranted. The book that John C. Campbell began (and Olive Dame Campbell completed after his death), *The Southern Highlander and His Homeland,* is a foundational work about Appalachia. See Henry D. Shapiro, *Appalachia on Our Mind: The Southern Mountains in the American Consciousness, 1870–1920* (Chapel Hill: University of North Carolina Press, 1978), esp. chap. 8. Olive Dame Campbell's cultural work was significant, especially her efforts at ballad preservation and the folk school movement. In addition to Whisnant's treatment of Olive Dame Campbell in *All That Is Native and Fine,* Daniel Rodgers includes a substantial discussion of her involvement in the folk school movement in chapter 8 of his book *Atlantic Crossings.*

19. Whisnant, *Modernizing the Mountaineer,* 11.

20. David Whisnant's extended essay on Olive Dame Campbell in *All That Is Native and Fine* includes an extensive discussion of the Scandinavian folk school movement and its influence on Olive Dame Campbell's efforts, arguing that she was drawn to "the most romantic, nostalgic, and rural" models represented within the Danish movement (136).

21. Helen Dingman's socially progressive causes during her years at Berea included the interracial movement, community work (including the Opportunity School at Berea), contraception, and public health. The professional interests of Dingman's family undoubtedly influenced her: her father and two of her brothers were physicians, and her older sister, Mary A. Dingman, was a major figure in the women's international peace movement in the interwar period and was also involved with the early United Nations.

22. Helen Dingman often mentioned Social Gospel ideals and social justice in her writings; scholars have likewise pointed to Social Gospel influences on the career of her famous sister, Mary Dingman. On Mary Dingman, see *Dictionary of American Biography,* suppl. 7, 1961–65, s.v. "Dingman, Mary Agnes," by Jane A. Benson. On the Social Gospel movement, see Paul A. Carter, *The Decline and Revival of the Social Gospel; Social and Political Liberalism in American Protestant Churches, 1920–1940* (Ithaca, NY: Cornell University Press, 1954). Some historians limit the era of the Social Gospel movement to the 1910s, but Carter argues for its continuation in later decades. Though "Progressive politics had been virtually swept from the stage" by 1920, Carter asserts, "progressive Christianity" persisted (17–18).

23. As Robyn Muncy observes in *Creating a Female Dominion,* the "progressive project" included "a search for the *via media* between nineteenth-century socialism and liberalism," with progressives attempting "to increase equality and 'social cooperation' without sacrificing individual freedom" (45–46).

24. Historians debate the extent to which the Progressive impulse continued after 1920. In his dissertation on Alva W. Taylor (an executive secretary of the

CSMW), Stanley Lincoln Harbison argues that Taylor's Progressive activism continued into the 1950s. See Harbison, "The Social Gospel Career of Alva Wilmot Taylor" (PhD diss., Vanderbilt University, 1975). A similar argument in behalf of the continuity of the reform efforts of Progressive women is presented in J. Stanley Lemons, *The Woman Citizen: Social Feminism in the 1920s* (Urbana: University of Illinois Press, 1973); Muncy, *Creating a Female Dominion;* and Perry, "Men Are from the Gilded Age."

25. Marshall E. Vaughn, the founding editor of *Mountain Life & Work (MLW)*, was the college secretary and director of extension work at Berea College. See Elisabeth S. Peck, *Berea's First 125 Years: 1855–1980* (Lexington: University Press of Kentucky, 1982), 171.

26. Helen H. Dingman, "Our Common Task," *MLW* 9, 2 (July 1933): 1–7; esp. 2.

27. See Muncy, *Creating a Female Dominion,* 83. Muncy also explains that when Sophonisba Breckinridge and Edith Abbot, two key figures in the School of Social Service Administration, advocated social reform, they "were bucking the trend in their determination to dedicate social work to social reform" (83). See also Muncy's discussion of the contrast between the profit-oriented, expertise-hoarding male doctors in public health and the popularizing, non–profit orientation of women in the child welfare movement (esp. 135–49).

28. The quote describing the mission of the foundation is from "Glenn to Manage Sage Foundation: Baltimore Philanthropist Made Active Manager of Charity Plans. To Eradicate Poverty. This, Rather than Relief of Individuals to be the Chief Problem Undertaken," *New York Times*, May 14, 1907. ProQuest Historical Newspapers, *New York Times* (1851–2003), http://0-www.proquest.com.library .daemen.edu (accessed June 25, 2009).

29. During its first four decades, the Sage Foundation was structured into departments that delineated its major interests. These included Charity Organization, Education, Child Hygiene, Recreation, Child Helping, Statistics, Industrial Studies, Surveys and Exhibits, Arts and Social Work, and Delinquency and Penology (Russell Sage Foundation Finding Aid, pp. 1–2, RSF Archive). On the Sage Foundation's role in professionalizing social work, see David C. Hammack, "A Center of Intelligence for the Charity Organization Movement: The Foundation's Early Years," and "A Road Not Taken: The Independent Social Research Institute," in David C. Hammack and Stanton Wheeler, *Social Science in the Making: Essays on the Russell Sage Foundation, 1907–1972* (New York: Russell Sage Foundation, 1994). The Sage Foundation's decision to end its (by then) small subsidy for the CSMW occurred during a major transition within the organization and at a time when it was reconsidering all of its prior programs and focus.

30. Hindman Settlement School, Pine Mountain Settlement School, and the John C. Campbell Folk School are some of the best-known settlement institutions that were founded and directed by women through their early decades. Numerous community centers were started by women, and some of them grew into larger institutions. These included Alice Lloyd College, which originated as a community center founded by Lloyd at Caney Creek, Kentucky, and the Martha Berry Schools. One indicator of female founders is the striking fact that many of the

region's schools were named after the women who founded them. Although teaching became a feminized occupation during the late nineteenth century, the extent of female *leadership* among educational institutions in early twentieth-century Appalachia is notable.

31. On gender hierarchies in the professions, see Dorothy M. Brown, *Setting a Course: American Women in the 1920s* (Boston: Twayne, 1987); and, generally, Jill Conway, "Women Reformers and American Culture, 1870–1930," *Journal of Social History* 5, no. 2 (Winter 1971–72): 164–77. On Appalachian settlements, see Whisnant, *All That Is Native and Fine;* Forderhase, "Settlement School Goes to the People;" and Greene, "Progressives in the Kentucky Mountains."

32. Florence Goodell, who had worked with Helen Dingman in the Presbyterian mission station in Smith, Kentucky, arrived at the CSMW office in 1945 (a year when the position of executive secretary was vacant) to work as office secretary while the organization waited for the group's new executive secretary, former Pine Mountain Settlement School director Glyn Morris, to be discharged from the army. Morris left after one year, creating a vacancy in the leadership position that lasted from 1947 until 1950. Although Goodell was voted the title of executive secretary only in 1950, she had for several years fulfilled many of the responsibilities of the position.

33. Program of the 1920 Conference, box 140, folder 9, Council of the Southern Mountains Records, Southern Appalachian Archives, Berea College, Berea, KY (hereafter CSM Records).

34. Program of the 1922 Conference, box 140, folder 2, CSM Records.

35. John C. Campbell was compiling information about the schools as early as 1909. See Victor Juhler to John C. Campbell, April 30, 1909, box 1, folder 15, Campbell Papers. The Danish term *Folkehöjskole* was sometimes translated as "peasant university, people's college, or high school," in addition to "folk school." Campbell discussed the findings of her study in her book, *The Danish Folk School: Its Influence in the Life of Denmark and the North* (New York: Macmillan, 1928) (translation discussed on vii–viii); the folk school movement is also discussed in Whisnant, *All That Is Native and Fine,* esp. 128–38. Mountain workers' interest in the schools was fostered by the US Commissioner of Education Philander P. Claxton. Claxton would later become a member of the Advisory Committee for the John C. Campbell Folk School.

36. Highlander Folk School, founded by Myles Horton and Don West in Monteagle, Tennessee, in 1932, is another adaptation of the Scandinavian model in the Appalachian region. Highlander became famous for its leadership in unionization efforts and the civil rights movement. The land upon which the school was built was donated to Horton and West in 1935 by Dr. Lillian Johnson, a CSMW member during the 1920s. Johnson had moved to Summerville, Tennessee, in 1915 and initiated a range of community and education programs for adults and children. Historian John M. Glenn wrote that Johnson, who had a PhD from Cornell, had a "distinguished career as an educator and advocate of agricultural cooperatives, temperance, and women's suffrage." On Highlander, see John M. Glenn, *Highlander: No Ordinary School: 1932–1962* (Lexington: University Press of Kentucky, 1988), esp. 17, 35.

37. None of these ventures survived. Their creation and operation was covered extensively in *MLW* during the 1920s and 1930s.

38. Founded in 1922, the federation's business totaled over $680,000 in 1924. See "Farmers' Federation of Buncombe County, N.C.," *MLW* 1, no. 2 (July 1925): 13. On county agents' role in organizing cooperatives, see CSMW program and minutes from 1925 in CSM Records and "My Work in the Mountains by J.M. Feltner," *MLW* 1, no. 2 (July 1925): 11–12.

39. Goodrich was a founder of the CSMW in 1913. See "A Condensed Report of the Southern Mountain Workers Conference," box 140, folder 3, CSM Records. On Goodrich's career, see Henry D. Shapiro, *Appalachia on Our Mind: The Southern Mountains in the American Consciousness, 1870–1920* (Chapel Hill: University of North Carolina Press, 1978), 224–27.

40. Olive Dame Campbell to Francis S. Hutchins, February 23, 1926, box 141, folder 7, CSM Records.

41. See Marguerite Butler, "A Dream Come True," *MLW* 7, no. 3 (October 1931): 1–4; Garry Barker, *The Handcraft Revival in Southern Appalachia, 1930–1990* (Knoxville: University of Tennessee Press, 1991), 5, 13–14; and Allen H. Eaton, *Handicrafts of the Southern Highlands* (New York: Russell Sage Foundation, 1937; repr. New York: Dover Books, 1973). Jane S. Becker's *Selling Tradition: Appalachia and the Construction of an American Folk, 1930–1940* (Chapel Hill: University of North Carolina Press, 1998) follows David Whisnant's interpretation (in *All That Is Native and Fine*) with her attention to the cultural motives in the marketing and sales strategies of the SHHG and other craft producers, emphasizing the ways that these "craft leaders from outside the ranks of local producers used the guild to redefine the meaning of mountain crafts" (8). Philis Alvic, however, reads the evidence differently than Becker, arguing that the Appalachian craft revival was fostered by the largely middle-class advocates of mountain crafts who used culture as a marketing scheme for endeavors focused primarily on helping mountain women generate money for themselves and their families in order to create a viable alternative to outmigration; culture was a secondary, rather than a primary motivation of their efforts. Describing the role of weaving among the range of activities pursued by Appalachian settlements, Alvic writes that "Appalachian settlement schools revived weaving as part of a program of comprehensive reforms that not only addressed problems in education, but also confronted concerns about health care, recreation, and household economy. . . . The mountain workers proposed crafts as a way to supplement the family's income while not substantially altering the rural lifestyle" (Philis Alvic, *Weavers of the Southern Highlands* [Lexington: University Press of Kentucky, 2003], 4–5).

42. In an interview conducted when she was ninety-one, Helen Dingman recounted a deathbed conversation she had had with John C. Campbell in 1919, when he had requested that she stay in Smith, Kentucky, and had told her "I'm looking to you to pull the mountains out for me." See Loyal Jones, "Interview with Helen Dingman," in "Dingman, Helen" folder, Berea College Archives, Record Group 9 (BCA/RG9), Berea College, Berea, KY. Dingman's visit to Campbell is also documented in a 1919 tribute to Campbell by Marshall Allaben, who wrote

that Campbell's "last personal conference, held the afternoon of his death, was with Miss Dingman of Smith, Kentucky." Clipping by Marshall C. Allaben, "John C. Campbell: An Appreciation," *Home Mission Monthly*, November 1919, in box 1, folder pre-1, Campbell Papers.

43. Dingman's correspondence, diary, several typescripts, and other records are held at Berea College. See Helen Dingman Diary, manuscript entitled "My First Trip into the Mountains" and typescript describing the founding of the Smith mission station, in box 1, folders 1, 4, 14, and 18, in Helen Dingman Papers, Southern Appalachian Archive. See also Jones, "Interview with Helen Dingman, February 5, 1976," in "Dingman, Helen" folder, Berea College Archives/Record Group 9.

44. Smith College established the Southern Mountain Workship, which provided funds to send Smith College "girls" (one per year) on a circuit to CSMW member institutions and public schools, teaching recreation. The "workship" program began in 1945 and ran through 1969. In addition to the recreation materials that are part of the Council of the Southern Mountains collection, the workship's history is also detailed in the Southern Mountain Workship Files, Smith College Archives, Northampton, MA.

45. Historian Elisabeth Israels Perry notes that many urban Progressive reformers emphasized healthy recreation, especially as an alternative to dance halls, which they saw as paving a pathway to the brothel. Perry, "Men Are from the Gilded Age."

46. Rodgers, *Atlantic Crossings*, 68–69, 269, 380.

47. Conference minutes from 1929 document the origins of the survey. See box 141, folder 8, CSM Records.

48. Pine Mountain replaced its female leaders with a male leader, Hubert Hadley, in 1930. Olive Dame Campbell resigned as director of the John C. Campbell Folk School in 1946 and was replaced by Dr. Dagnall Folger. At Hindman, the process was delayed but not averted: Elizabeth Watts became the director in 1946 but was replaced by Raymond McLain in 1954. On Hindman and John C. Campbell Folk School, see Whisnant, *All That Is Native and Fine*, 79, 164–65; on Pine Mountain, see Katherine Pettit to William J. Hutchins, June 3, 1930, box 1, folder 1–4, Katherine Pettit Collection, Southern Appalachian Archives.

49. Kester is a central figure in the story of the indigenous Southern radical movement profiled in Anthony P. Dunbar's *Against the Grain: Southern Radicals and Prophets, 1929–1959* (Charlottesville: University Press of Virginia, 1981), which traces the evolution of this movement through the lives of some of its pivotal figures. Robin Kelley also discusses Kester's involvement with the sharecroppers' movement of the 1930s, providing a different perspective than Dunbar on Kester's radicalism. While Dunbar centers his account of the sharecroppers' movement upon the integrated, socialist Southern Tenant Farmers Union (STFU), Kelley's focus is upon the Share Croppers Union (SCU). The members and leaders of the SCU were African American, and many of the leaders were Communists. The STFU and SCU competed for members and exemplified the conflict between socialist and communist groups during the era. See Robin

Kelley, *Hammer and Hoe: Alabama Communists During the Great Depression* (Chapel Hill: University of North Carolina Press, 1990).

50. Although CSMW records from this period are incomplete, it appears that Goodell was not viewed as a permanent executive secretary for the group. Goodell herself emphasized that the arrangements under which she had operated as executive secretary—a quarter-time position with responsibilities divided between the CSMW and the SHHG; the CSMW office located in Asheville while the responsibility for *MLW* and other functions of the groups were still in Berea; and the inadequate financial support for CSMW activities—were frustrating. When she presented the group's Executive Board with a list of suggestions, the reply from the CSMW board president, Arthur M. Bannerman, praised Goodell's ideas but suggested that the group was not willing to move forward under her leadership: "All your ideas under 'Where Is the Council Headed' are very good and something should be done about them. But one additional thought I have very strongly is that the Council ought to have new leadership, for I know full well that for the past year or two I have been a secondrate president and that I should not serve again. ... The Council cannot go forward without some one giving you strong support. If a group is not willing to work vigourously with you, we should face that fact" (A.M.B. [Arthur M. Bannerman] to Dear Miss Goodell, n.d., with correspondence from March 1951, box 2, folder 2, CSM Records).

51. Olive Campbell to Goodie, March 27, 1951, box 2, folder 2, CSM Records.

52. Olive Campbell to Dear President Hutchins, February 16, 1915, box 1, folder 1, CSM Records. The letter is clearly misdated, as Campbell refers to events from 1951 and addresses the letter to President Hutchins, rather than to William Goodell Frost, who would have been Berea College president in 1915.

53. Florence Goodell to Dear Mrs. Campbell, April 9, 1951, box 2, folder 2, CSM Records.

Professionalizing "Mountain Work" in Appalachia 243

CHAPTER NINE

"'Two fer' the Money"?

African American Women in the Appalachian Coalfields

CARLETTA A. BUSH

Coalfield communities welcomed the coal boom sparked by the 1973 oil embargo. The Appalachian region had been losing population to out-migration for two decades, but with new mines opening and existing operations expanding their operations, many migrants saw the boom as a way to return home, and young people saw mining employment as a way to live the American dream. As the wife of a young man with a high school education and limited training, I hoped, as did he, that he would "get in the mines." We were not alone. The demand for these jobs far outstripped the supply, and when women began entering the mines in 1973, the competition for these coveted jobs only increased. I remember hearing prospective miners and other members of the mining community complain bitterly, especially after the first black women were hired. Many people believed that African American women had an unfair advantage, because hiring a black woman was fulfilling "two fer" the price of one under the terms of the 1964 Civil Rights Act.

THE ORIGINS OF THE "TWO FER" MYTH

The 1964 Civil Rights Act was written primarily to end discrimination against African Americans. This act, along with Executive Order 11246 (signed by President Lyndon B. Johnson in 1967), opened the way to underground employment in the nation's mines for women. Since the act's original purpose was to end discrimination against African Americans, many people, both within the coal industry and among the general public, believed that black women would be hired and promoted over their white counterparts. According to Margaret Simms and Julianne Malveaux, the "two fer" myth developed during the early 1970s, after companies began to implement affirmative action guidelines.[1] The myth alleges that black women workers enjoyed an advantage over other groups, because their hiring meant that employers could gain two minorities for the price of one. This was not to be the case for African American women who obtained employment as coal miners during the coal boom of the 1970s and early 1980s. Instead, the majority of the women hired were white women, and later studies would prove that the few black women who obtained employment in the coal industry were in the minority, hired as tokens, mere symbols of affirmative action. As a result, the vast majority of black female miners found themselves on the outside looking in. These women believed that both their race and gender were held against them by their male and female coworkers and supervisors. In the end, the two fer myth served to preserve white male privilege in the mining industry and divided female miners who could have benefited from greater solidarity underground.

A MIGRANT FAMILY GOES HOME

During the mid-1970s, the Gist family was living in Evanston, Illinois, a suburb of Chicago, far from their hometown of Lynch, Kentucky. The daughter and granddaughter of African American coal miners, Cheryl Gist had been born and reared in Lynch, the former coal-company town that U. S. Steel had once touted as the jewel in its crown. Theirs was a two-wage-earner family, but money was still tight. In spite of the conveniences associated with suburban living, Cheryl yearned to see her family once again living in the comfort and security that she associated with small town life.

It was the energy crisis and coal boom that would take the Gist family home to Harlan County. In 1973 leaders of the Organization of the Petroleum Exporting Countries (OPEC) raised the price of oil by 400 percent. As the price of oil soared and gasoline became a scarce

"Two fer' the Money"? 245

commodity, Western nations became increasingly dependent upon nuclear energy and coal, and by the end of the decade coal exports had doubled. The resulting coal boom created new jobs across the coalfields of Appalachia, a surge in in-migration, and growth in the small business sector.[2] The citizens of Harlan County, Kentucky, would share in the boom, and when the "Miners Wanted" sign reappeared at Lynch's U. S. Steel mines, Cheryl's brother-in-law applied for work and was successful. When the news of his good fortune reached Evanston, Illinois, Cheryl's husband decided that the time was right to return to Lynch and seek a job underground. His quest for a mining job was successful as well, and in 1975 the family left Evanston to return to eastern Kentucky. But he would not be the only coal miner in the family. Cheryl, having decided that it was time to go "where she could make some money," followed her husband's footsteps and applied for a job in the mines.[3] By January 1976 Cheryl and her husband were both working the third shift at U. S. Steel's No. 32 Mine. Civil rights legislation passed during the previous decade had created a road home for women such as Cheryl.

WHAT WOMEN WANTED: WELL-PAYING JOBS WITH BENEFITS

By 1970 women comprised nearly 41 percent of the civilian workforce.[4] As inflation crept upward during the ensuing decade, the number of women looking for work rose. Unfortunately, many of these women had limited education and few employment skills.[5] Consequently, most of the occupations open to them paid low wages and failed to provide health benefits. Janice Hedges, in an article in the June 1970 *Monthly Labor Review,* stated that, if women were to find work that fit their abilities, they would have to seek employment outside traditional women's occupations. Fortunately, technology that decreased the physical requirements for many jobs in the skilled trades made them more appealing. As a result, many women turned to the construction industry to obtain employment.[6]

Unfortunately, the economic future for single women who lived in rural, economically underdeveloped regions such as Appalachia was bleak. With its economy undiversified, employment opportunities for unskilled workers were in short supply. The well-paying blue-collar jobs that did exist, such as those available in the extractive industries, were traditionally deemed off limits to women. Nevertheless, the promise of high wages and good benefits made mining jobs especially attractive to the majority of women who needed these jobs the most—single mothers. According to the United Mine Workers of America (UMWA), the majority of the women who applied for jobs underground were single mothers. The union sent out a questionnaire to its female members in 1975. As a result of this survey, the union determined that there were two groups of female miners: divorcées in their mid-thirties with children to support and younger single women "who were generally in mining for the long haul, as a career." Moreover, more than half of the women with children stated that they were the sole breadwinners for their families, and for most of these women, a miner's paycheck meant a way out of poverty.[7]

Women found that obtaining mining jobs, however, was not easy in spite of civil rights legislation. Pressure to refrain from submitting employment applications came from family members, neighbors, and church pulpits. In addition, superstition and legal barriers also kept women out of the mines. Members of mining communities traditionally considered it to be "bad luck" for women to go underground. Because of this, many husbands, fathers, and brothers, most of whom were miners themselves, discouraged the female members of their families from applying for mining jobs. Growing numbers of women, however, were resisting such pressure. Along with young single women, increasing numbers of older married women were finding it necessary to enter the workforce, and they were clamoring for the opportunity to gain entry into traditionally male occupations, regardless of the risk to their health and safety. However, the door to nontraditional occupations such as coal mining would open very slowly and with great resistance from coal operators, male miners, and coal communities.

CIVIL RIGHTS LEGISLATION: THE ROAD TO OPPORTUNITY

President Lyndon B. Johnson signed the Civil Rights Act in 1964. This act, initially constructed to end discrimination against African Americans and considered the cornerstone of Civil Rights legislation, forbids discrimination in hiring and firing, the awarding of benefits and promotions, and working conditions. Three years later, the passage of the

"Two fer' the Money"? 247

Age Discrimination Act would help older women gain employment in the mines. Signed into law in 1967, the Age Discrimination in Employment Act protects individuals, regardless of gender, between the ages of forty and sixty-five.[8] The most important key to entry into the coal industry for women was the amendment of the Civil Rights Act in 1967 with Executive Order 11246. Although the act initially established affirmative action for African Americans, women, and other minorities, it was amended to include sex as a basis of nondiscrimination by federal contractors and subcontractors. In addition, the order established specific goals and timetables for the hiring of women in the construction industry. Employers who hold government contracts valued in excess of $10,000 cannot discriminate on the basis of sex, race, color, religion, or national origin. Furthermore, the law requires employers holding federal contracts in excess of $50,000 to commit themselves to affirmative action programs and the creation of harassment-free workplaces.[9] Although the law requires only that employers make a good faith effort toward compliance, it proved to be a powerful tool for civil rights and women's organizations. The Coal Employment Project used this key to open the door to employment in the coal industry for women.

THE COAL EMPLOYMENT PROJECT

The Coal Employment Project (CEP) was born in 1977 as a one-person project after staff members from Save Our Cumberland Mountains (SOCM) and the East Tennessee Research Corporation, a public interest group from Jacksboro, Tennessee, unsuccessfully asked to tour an underground coal mine. They had submitted names of a group of staffers as required, but while male staff members were granted permission to tour the mine, the one woman on the list was denied access. The coal operator, who was also a criminal court judge, responding to questions concerning the denial, declared that he couldn't "have no woman going underground. The men would walk out; the mine would shut down. Now, if you fellows want to come, that is one thing. But if you insist on bringing her, forget the whole thing."[10]

Shortly afterward the operator's refusal, Neil McBride, the director for the research corporation, called upon attorney Betty Jean Hall, a lawyer from Washington DC who had previously worked as a volunteer

248 CARLETTA A. BUSH

for the corporation, to "do a little research" on affirmative action in the coal industry. Hall agreed. Her research showed that 99.8 percent of all miners were men. Clearly affirmative action was not working in the coal industry. Within days, McBride persuaded Hall to meet him in New York City. He planned to ask various foundations for the funds needed to begin a special project on "women in coal." After the Ms. Foundation for Women agreed to give them $5,000, the pair started the Coal Employment Project to help women find and retain jobs in the coal industry.[11]

Hall moved to Jacksboro during the fall of 1977 to head the CEP and spent the first several months "tracking down" some of the female miners that she had heard about. However, Hall harbored some doubts: first, she wondered if women were physically strong enough to perform all of the jobs required in an underground mining operation, and second, if women were really interested in obtaining employment as miners. As she met with female miners, her first doubt soon vanished. It became clear to her that, while these women realized that there were jobs in the mine that some women could not perform, there were also jobs that some men could not do either. However, there were no jobs in the mines that some women could not do. In addition, she realized that women were interested in obtaining mining jobs when she heard the frequent declaration that they could "bring fifty women here tonight that would love to get these jobs."[12] Publicity on the few women working in the coalfields was fueling women's interest in obtaining mining jobs, and the CEP realized that utilizing the media was one of the keys to both reaching women who were interested in mining employment and attracting support for their cause. The following year, a sexual discrimination suit would provide the CEP with such an opportunity.

SEXUAL DISCRIMINATION AND THE LAW

While not the first lawsuit filed against a major American coal company, the Coal Employment Project filed its most important sex discrimination suit on May 11, 1978, against the 153 coal companies that represented approximately 50 percent of the nation's coal production. The defendants included Peabody Coal, Island Creek Coal, Consolidation Coal, Amax Coal, Eastern Associated Coal, Pittston Coal, Gulf

"Two fer' the Money"? 249

Oil's Pittsburgh Coal, and Midway Coal Mining companies. The CEP filed a complaint with the Office of Federal Contract Compliance, the agency within the US Department of Labor charged with enforcing Executive Order 11246, because many of the companies targeted in the suit supplied coal to the Tennessee Valley Authority (TVA), a major, government-owned electricity producer in the South. Based upon a study that documented the extent of gender discrimination in the industry, the complaint asked the federal government to target the coal industry for special review because of its "blatant" pattern of sex discrimination. In addition, the complaint asked that at least one female entry-level coal miner be hired for every three male entry-level hires until women constituted at least 20 percent of the mining workforce and that job openings be advertised on local radio, in newspapers, and when applicable on television, for at least three days before the openings were filled. Within three weeks of the complaint's filing, the federal government took over responsibility for pursuing the complaint and negotiating a settlement. The Department of Labor announced that it would investigate the complaint, company by company, and target the entire industry for review.[13]

The first major settlement came at the end of 1978, when Consolidation Coal Company (Consol), the nation's second largest coal producer, signed a conciliation agreement. Under the terms of the agreement, Consol agreed to pay seventy-eight women $370,000 in back wages for discriminating against them between 1972 and 1976, because the company had rejected their employment applications even though the women were qualified for employment. In addition, Consol agreed to hire women as miners and to hire one inexperienced woman for every one inexperienced man until female miners comprised 32.8 percent of the workforce.[14]

The first complaints set a precedent and opened up employment by forcing companies to lift the discriminatory ban on women in the mines. Furthermore, most of the negotiated settlements called for the implementation of affirmative action programs. The Kentucky Commission on Human Rights constituted the first known effort to challenge sex discrimination in the coal industry. While the commission did not file its first case on the basis of racial discrimination, racism was definitely part of the problem. The commission's first case was filed on March 18, 1975, on behalf of Melba Strong, an African American woman who had applied for employment as an entry-level miner at a U. S. Steel Company mine in Lynch, Kentucky, in March 1974 and again nine months later. The company refused to hire her both times, instead hiring forty men for entry-level positions during the interim. The commission also filed a case against U. S. Steel on behalf of Joetta Ann Gist on March 19, 1975. Gist first applied for a position as an office clerk in 1971 but was denied the position. She tried once again in 1974, but this time she applied for a mining position. Gist, an African American, alleged that it was "common knowledge" that the company only hired white women for clerical positions and men as miners. She claimed that she was passed over in favor of less qualified men and women for both positions, first because of her race and second because of her gender.[15]

THE CASE OF U. S. STEEL

The Kentucky Commission on Civil Rights investigated the complaints against U. S. Steel separately, and probable cause determinations were made. Since the company refused to negotiate a conciliation agreement, a voluntary written agreement between the parties that would have established a method and timetable to end the company's discriminatory hiring practices,[16] the commission was forced to hold separate hearings in order to consider the evidence and collect testimony. During the hearings, the superintendent of the Lynch District Mines cited "superstition" as the reason behind the company's refusal to hire women as miners, since women were believed to be "bad omens" underground.[17] In a "Brief for Complainants" presented later to commissioners, the women's counsel noted:

> If this was not so serious a matter, such a response would seem humorous. Consider the Respondent, a huge national corporation with thousands of employees, allowing its personnel selection policies to be guided by an old "superstition." Further, so important is this superstition that Respondent indeed knowingly violates state law for three years, federal law for ten years, and its own collective bargaining agreement.[18]

"'Two fer' the Money"? 251

During the hearing, a lawyer for U. S. Steel asked Gist why she thought that the company was guilty of racial discrimination. She asked him, "Who do you see when you look at me?" He replied, "A woman." Gist disagreed. She told him that he saw "a black woman." The attorney quickly dropped this line of questioning.[19] In both Gist's and Strong's cases, the Kentucky Human Rights Commission issued "cease and desist" orders against unlawful discrimination practices. In addition, the commission ordered the company to hire one African American female for every two white employees hired for clerical positions, until 10 percent of the clerical workforce was black. The company was also ordered to hire one female for every three males hired for production and maintenance until 20 percent of these employees were female. This affirmative action plan was to be in effect for five years. In Gist's case, the commission warned the company that it would be fined if any of its employees made any derogatory comments in regard to the plaintiff or other African American female employees.[20]

In spite of the successful outcome of her case, Gist did not work underground. The coal company offered her two choices: she could either work the afternoon shift as an underground miner, or work in one of their warehouses. Since she was then six months pregnant, she decided to work in the warehouse. The company did, however, give her the option of working underground if she ever changed her mind. She chose to remain at the warehouse. In time, Gist worked in the company's warehouses in both Lynch and Cumberland, Kentucky

The steelmaker did not hire another woman to work in their Harlan County warehouses for six years, and when one was hired, it was a white woman. Gist said that the new employee "came in with an attitude" because Gist was black. Consequently, the new worker was not happy to learn that Gist would be responsible for training her. Initially, the tension between the two was palpable, but Gist ignored it, and once the new worker realized that Gist had a very good reputation as a worker and that she was well thought of by her male coworkers, her attitude changed, and the two women developed a positive working relationship.[21]

U. S. Steel was not the only major American corporation targeted by the Kentucky Human Rights Commission. As a result of discrimination cases filed by the commission, Peabody Coal, International Harvester,

Blue Diamond Coal, Island Creek Coal, Gibraltar Coal, and Bow Valley Coal also agreed to hire one woman for every three men hired until their entry-level workforces were 20 percent female.[22]

U. S. Steel Corporation signed a consent decree in 1975 that stated the company's intention to end discriminatory hiring practices, but like many corporations, the company continued to resist hiring women. In 1977 Joan Bondira and Linda Butcher sued the company in Pennsylvania's district court on behalf of hundreds of women who applied for jobs with the steel company but were never hired. Their attorneys, Rosalyn M. Littman and Irving Portnoy, discovered that the applications of these women were never entered into the company's applicant logs, and many were tossed into drawers without being processed. Portnoy contended that this created a "chill effect" where women finally decided not to apply, since they believed that they would never be hired. In fact, Judge Allan Block found that for several months in 1977 the corporation did not hire any women, although it continued to hire men. In addition, the judge determined that a "statistical under hiring" of women existed for a two-year period at U. S. Steel's Gary, West Virginia, mine. After the case was filed, the company began to hire women, but its behavior toward its new hires was not consistent. One witness said that she was called by the company and offered a position the night before the job was to begin and was not put through the usual training procedures. Another witness testified that the job screening and training that she and other women received was more rigorous than that of men who applied for similar positions.[23]

FINALLY: WOMEN GO UNDERGROUND

Bethlehem Steel Corporation was the first major corporation to send women underground when three women went to work at its No. 51 Mine in Ellsworth, Pennsylvania, on August 1, 1974. By November 1978 it had become the largest employer of female miners, with the majority of them working in Kentucky, Pennsylvania, and West Virginia. However, the company's decision to hire women was not of its own choosing but as part of a consent decree the steel companies negotiated to ward off discrimination suits. One of the women was an African American, the first black female to work underground in the state's history: Rosa

"Two fer' the Money"? 253

Pitts, hired in 1977 by Bethlehem Steel for its No. 58 Mine at Mariana, Pennsylvania, under an affirmative action plan. She remembers her first few weeks in the mine, and like her Central Appalachian sisters, she recognizes her importance to the industry: "I'll never forget our first day. The men all lined up on one side of the portal and we could hear them saying under their breaths, 'It's bad luck, women in the mines.' Then one day a few weeks later a shuttle car operator didn't show up for work and the only one who could do the job was a woman. They put her on the shuttle car. We're getting to be indispensable."[24]

THE TWO FER MYTH: DOCUMENTED AND DEBUNKED

According to Kipp Dawson, a former miner from Pennsylvania, African American women were referred to as "twofers." When Dawson was hired, there were no inexperienced men in her training class other than veterans or blacks.[25] As discussed earlier, the two fer myth—that black women workers enjoyed an advantage over other groups, because their hiring meant that employers could gain two minorities for the price of one—developed during the early 1970s, after companies began to implement affirmative action guidelines.[26] Black women have historically been perceived as able to handle racial discrimination better than black men and better prepared to handle sexism than white women. These beliefs fostered the impression that African American women had greater success in finding jobs than the other two groups, elevating them to "superwoman status" in the workforce. Consequently, those who hold such a perception believe that black women take jobs from white men.[27]

An early study conducted on a small group of West Indian women first gave credence to the two fer myth. In 1973 C. F. Epstein studied a small group of highly educated professional women, a high percentage of whom were recent immigrants of West Indian parentage, with experiences and attitudes that were dissimilar to those of other black women in the United States.[28] Epstein's assertion that black women have enjoyed a bonus status in the workforce is not indicative of labor force data. Nonetheless, her work is important, because it describes the unique perceptions made about black women in the workforce. Epstein explained that black women are not perceived to fit stereotypes of white women, black men, or white men. White women are stereotypically portrayed as weak, gentle, modest, soft, mild, tolerant, and tactful, in direct contrast to black women, who have been depicted as strong, independent, striving, and assertive. Janis V. Sanchez-Hucles maintains that the prevalence of these images serve to categorize black women as "others" in American society. As a result, black women are perceived as "strangers" in the workforce and frequently have negative experiences at the workplace.[29]

Whether married or single, with or without children, more black women have historically worked outside the home than have white women. For example, as early as 1890, two out of five black women and girls over the age of ten were employed compared to only one in five white females. In 1984, a year after female participation in the coal workforce peaked, more than half of the female black population in the United States worked, especially those between the ages of twenty-five and forty-four. As did their Appalachian peers, these women worked to ensure their family's survival, since black men have been historically employed in unskilled positions with low pay and few, if any, benefits.[30] Even though affirmative action gave African Americans access to employment in nontraditional jobs such as mining, few black women gained work as underground miners.

By the 1980s, more black women were working than ever before, but most of them worked in low-paid, dead-end jobs without security or benefits. Even with affirmative action programs in place, employment opportunities rarely manifested themselves outside of the service sector. This was especially true in the coal industry. According to Betty Woody, author of *Black Women in the Workplace: Impact of Structural Change in the Economy*, the number of black women working in the coal industry had only increased by 1 percent between 1960 and 1980, while the number of white women coal miners had risen by 14 percent.[31]

The number of black women employed with Cheryl Gist, at Arch Coal's No. 32 Mine in Harlan County, Kentucky, typifies the low number of African American women who gained employment in the mines. Gist, who is now disabled, worked in the mines from 1977 to 1984when she had to quit after suffering a bout of Bell's palsy. According to Gist, there were only a "few" black women employed at the No. 32 Mine.[32] Drenna Thomas worked at two different Arch Coal operations before

"'Two fer' the Money"? 255

she was laid off in 1989. During her fourteen-year tenure underground, she was the only black woman out of seven female miners at Mine No. 33 and one of three black women employed at Mine No. 37. Thomas operated every piece of equipment available at the two mines except the roof-bolting machine.[33]

FIGHTING BACK: THE ASSOCIATION OF WOMEN IN INDUSTRY

Women began to obtain jobs in Alabama coal mines in 1975, but operators tried to limit the number of women who worked in their operations. As a result, officials estimated that of the more than nine thousand miners in the state mines by 1977, only forty were women.[34] To remedy this, women in the Birmingham district formed the Association of Women in Industry (AWI) in the spring of 1978, after they completed coal mining training classes but could not find employment. The organization's goal was to help women find jobs in the district's heavy industries— coal mines, steelworks, and foundries. To help women obtain jobs, the AWI used direct action. For example, activists transported carloads of women to mines to apply for jobs and returned later to check on the status of the applicants. LaMarse Moore met some of these activists outside a mine office where she had applied for a job. She soon joined the organization and accompanied women on the trips to the mines. She said that "we pushed. We fought. We didn't back down. We really fought for it, to get into the mine. . . . We didn't just go and fill out applications to get in the mines. We really fought for it." Obtaining a job in the coal industry was worth fighting for. This was true for women, especially black women. It was "good money," she recalled, "And then you think about the benefits, because I had kids, you know."[35]

Helping women obtain employment in the mines was not AWI's only objective. The organization also strove to help black and white women learn to work together. As Robert Woodrum noted, the AWI faced challenges that were very similar to those faced by union activists when it tried to revive the United Mine Workers of America in Alabama during the 1930s. At a meeting with AWI members in the fall of 1978, national activists discussed the fact that black and white women were unaccustomed to working together. CEP activist Connie White stated that "it seemed that occasionally I could sense some tension between the black and white women—but I think that this was due more to unfamiliarity than to hostility. For black women and white women to show up at the same mine, applying for jobs together, is a really great thing." In spite of the difficulty of crossing the color line, CEP staff estimated that AWI's membership, like the UMWA of their grandfathers, was fairly evenly divided between black and white women. The AWI called for the CEP to call a national conference in 1979 to highlight the challenges that women faced in the mines and to establish unity between women in mining and other heavy industries. AWI members understood that the potential opportunities women had in the mines were part "of a broad movement toward equal rights for all citizens." Racial issues clearly remained central to activists, and they worked to address the "absolute necessity" of building alliances between black and white women working in the mines.[36]

DISCRIMINATION AND HARASSMENT IN THE MINES

By the end of 1980, federal census records indicated that 815 of Alabama's 12,790 coal miners were women, including 108 African American women.[37] Although the number of black women working underground was very small, their gender and race made them highly visible. With the majority of the mining workforce being white and male, it is not surprising that the two fer myth failed to shield African American female miners from discrimination or harassment. Social-psychological studies indicate that African Americans are especially likely to face preconceived stereotypes and high work expectations when there are few or no other black employees in the work setting. This is especially true in situations where a workplace has only one black worker. Black workers who find themselves in these situations are assumed to be incompetent and lazy or find that they are evaluated more harshly than their white coworkers.[38]

Patricia Brown went into the mines in 1980 because she wanted a better life for her children. A widow with three children, in her early thirties, Brown was part of the second group of women hired to work in a large underground mine in Alabama. The men had gotten a "little bit used to women miners," but they still gave Brown and her female coworkers a hard time, cursing the women when they came into the mine. Some white men called Brown a "black bitch," but men of both races

"Two fer' the Money"? 257

made it clear that women did not belong in the mines. The worst times were those spent working on the track when men drew offensive pictures on the walls. Brown believed that they were jealous. Her agitators did not like a woman coming into take a job that a man could come, especially a black woman. Nevertheless, she just worked harder. She was determined that they were not going to "break" her. Talking with white coworkers or going to management or the union was not an option.

> Most of my coworkers were white, and I didn't feel comfortable talking to them. We knew where we stood as black people in the union, and you really didn't feel like you had a voice. Bosses, especially, we would never tell, because you got branded if you go to the company. One of the things you didn't do was go to the company. I didn't want to be branded on top of being a woman and being black.[39]

The UMWA praised its female miners in articles published in the *United Mine Workers Journal* (UMWJ) and other national publications,[40] but female miners gave the union mixed reviews. In Alabama, for example, the union had earned a reputation for not supporting its women members. When Patricia Brown filed a grievance against her employer, Jim Walter Resources, she did so because she believed that the union representative collaborated with the company. Brown said, "In front of them it was one thing, and behind your back it was another thing." Fearing that she would be labeled a troublemaker by both the union and the company, Brown rarely filed grievances with her local union on workplace issues.[41]

Racism continued to be a problem underground. Cheryl Gist stated that she had no trouble with her supervisors as far as job assignment or sexual harassment. According to the UMWA contract, jobs were assigned according to seniority and job classification. However, Gist states that her time underground was fairly brief (seven years), thus giving her very little job seniority.[42] When I asked Gist if she thought that she was treated any differently from her white female coworkers, she said yes, but only at Mine No. 33. She stated that it was a "racial thing." Gist said that while her white female coworker had worked in the mine longer, she believed that the white woman received preferential treatment because of her race.[43] In Alabama many African American women believed that they received more difficult work assignments than either white women or white men and suspected that the Ku Klux Klan had members working as hourly workers and supervisors. Patricia Brown worked with one alleged member of the Klan. Brown stated that he is "friendly toward me. We get along fine on the section. He don't seem to show any prejudice. I told him one day 'I hope you don't sic your boys on me, because half a dozen of them would be killed.' I'd put my .357 on them. I do have a gun. I carry a gun with me all the time." Black women were not the only miners who knew that the Klan was present under-ground. White miner Charlene Griggs told an interviewer that a fellow miner once asked her to join the organization, but she refused. Griggs stated, "The KKK is still around here, but they're quiet. It's no telling how many we've got at the mines. They're not really open about it."[44]

Offers of assistance between miners are also shaped by race and gender. Since the ideal white woman is perceived to be weak, gentle, modest, and dependent upon and subservient to men, white male miners frequently offered them assistance more often than they did black women. In her 1986 study on women coal miners, Kristen Yount found that male miners help their female coworkers because (1) they believed that women are incapable of doing or unwilling to perform the work; (2) they saw themselves as socially trained to help women; or (3) to get the job done. At the same time, while some white female miners resisted any offers of assistance from their male peers, some women willingly accepted it, and others encouraged it. In addition, Yount learned that women who accept offers of assistance do so for two reasons, to "feed" the male ego or because they see men as benevolent coworkers who do not want to see women get hurt. Regardless of either group's motivations, there are negative consequences to accepting excessive offers of assistance. Such women earn reputations as unwilling, unable workers and are not respected by their male co-workers. Consequently, the men increasingly take on these women's work, further reducing opportunities for the women to prove themselves as miners.[45]

DISCRIMINATORY PRACTICES IN TRAINING AND PROMOTION

Coal companies hired women reluctantly during the 1970s, but they balked even more at training and promoting them during the ensuing decade. Galen Martin, executive director of the Kentucky Commission on Human Rights, called this lack of training and promotion a "second generation" problem for female employees. Martin stated that getting women hired was much easier than getting them equal opportunity for promotion, since initial-hire discrimination was "more clear cut" than that involved in denied opportunities for training and advancement; it was difficult to document the number of times women were given opportunities to train on equipment. In addition, Martin stated that it was even harder to determine if men were given more opportunities than women.[46]

Stories abound concerning women who were denied employment, training, and job advancement. From a survey given to its supervisors, the Amax Coal Company realized that it faced a great deal of opposition to hiring women to work in its operations. Company officials discovered that the wives of 90 percent of its foremen did not work outside the home. More important, the majority fervently believed that the coal industry was no place for women. Consequently, with the help of the Fort Wayne Women's Bureau of Industry, the company developed a sensitivity training program. Called "Challenge for Change," the program had two objectives. First of all, company officials hoped that its supervisory personnel would understand why women wanted mining jobs; and second, the officials wanted the supervisors to realize that Amax was committed to hiring and retaining female miners. To that end, in the spring of 1979, Amax unveiled its series of workshops, designed to educate foremen the problems that their female miners encountered in the male-dominated workplace. Held at six different locations over a three-month period, 385 supervisors attended the thirteen workshops.[47]

In spite of the training, problems persisted at Amax operations. Pam Schuble, who worked at Amax's Ayrshire Mine near Chandler, Indiana, shared her plans to file a civil court suit against Amax with fellow female miners at a national conference in 1986. She alleged that while she was qualified to run a drill and had bid on a drill operator job several times, the company refused to promote her. She had been a coal miner for twelve years and had worked as a drill helper for the past six years. Nevertheless, she watched while men with less seniority were trained to operate the drill. Schuble maintained that the company claimed that

260 CARLETTA A. BUSH

women did not know how to run equipment, rendering it pointless to promote them.[48]

Once hired, women often remained delegated to the ranks of general labor for several years and had to fight the company to be trained. Management ignored seniority and passed over women to train men. As one female miner from West Virginia declared: "We build walls, hang curtains, and throw rock dust. You can have seniority and bid for a job, but the foreman won't train you."[49] Johnnie James, a black female miner in Alabama, had a similar experience. Once hired, she believed that her superiors were determined to get rid of her. She also felt that because she was black, she was experiencing worse discrimination than her white peers, since white women hired after James moved off the belt line to other positions while she was still on it after two years. Finally, she filed a grievance in order to receive the training necessary to operate a scoop. According to James, most of the foremen were so used to "doing this stuff, I don't know if they really think twice about it. . . . Anybody in their right mind knows this is discrimination."[50]

Opportunities for training boiled down to favoritism, seniority, and trust. Unfortunately, management trusted men to operate equipment, not women. Given a choice, supervisors usually offered training or a job to the men first. As one female miner noted, "They had a bad habit of keeping the women shoveling the belt [on the job] but sending the men to the section to get started."[51] Thus, women were forced to push the company into letting them operate equipment.

Even when a woman had more seniority than a man, however, she received fewer training opportunities. At a sexual harassment hearing of the Kentucky Commission on Human Rights in 1980, Rita Miller, a miner working in two mines in the White Plains area, described numerous instances of denied opportunities for training with no regard to seniority. Miller told the commission that of the ten women who worked in her mine, none were qualified to operate equipment. In her own case, as she waited to receive the training needed to operate mining machinery, she saw new male hires receive training, in this case on equipment used at the coal's face. Furthermore, these men were placed on a desirable shift, the afternoon second shift, while Miller continued to work on the midnight shift, the same shift she had been assigned

"'Two fer' the Money"? 261

on being hired. Miller also told of a boss who had refused to allow the women in his crew to operate any equipment at all, as well as of a female coworker had labored underground for two years as a rock duster before receiving training to operate machinery.[52]

Unfortunately, female miners could not turn to the union for assistance, and the situation did not improve with the passage of time. When Marat Moore first interviewed Patricia Brown in 1983, she had been one of two black women working at the mine. Moore visited Brown again in 1994 and learned that she had been recently laid off after working underground for fourteen years. When Moore asked her if things had improved with her coworkers as the years passed, Brown said that things were "worse in one way," because the company could "do what they pleased because there are fewer of us. They don't have to answer to anybody concerning minorities and women." And while Brown believed that she "had grown" and realized that there were "outlets" when she had a problem, one thing had remained unchanged, and that was black miners' relationship with the union. Brown stated that "as black people, we still don't have a channel through the union. If issues come up, we don't bother to carry them to the union."[53]

THE END OF THE BOOM AND A NEW BEGINNING

When the coal industry entered into a period of decline that began during the late 1980s, by 1994 Patricia Brown and tens of thousands of other miners found themselves on the unemployment line. Most women were classified as general inside laborers. Since laid-off union miners were hired for available positions at mines listed on their panel papers—papers filed with the union that list training certificates and mines that a laidoff miner is interested in—according to job classification and seniority, female miners had little chance of being called back to the mines. As a result, possessing few training certificates regardless of race, women were the first laid off and the last recalled when hiring began again. Thus, as Betty Jean Hall of the Coal Employment Project observed, "They call back the men as roof bolt helpers and have them [the men] shoveling the belt."[54] That is, even if a company needed general inside laborers, it would call back a man with a particular job classification instead of a woman who should have been recalled and have the man shoveling the belt and performing other tasks usually assigned to general inside laborers.

Life was very difficult for the families of laid-off miners during the 1980s and 1990s. Between 1986 and 1996 the number of mining jobs declined by nearly 60 percent, and the gap widened between the least and most distressed counties in the Appalachian region.[55] As a result, poverty rates rose in the region, especially among black female household heads, many of whom lacked the education, skills, and employment opportunities to obtain a good job. Good paying jobs with benefits would be hard to find in coal-dependent counties, and competition for these jobs would be intense. Gender, and especially race, meant that in most cases these jobs went to white men. For most female miners, especially black women, this meant taking lower-paying jobs with few, if any, benefits.

After declining for more than a decade, employment in the coal industry began to increase in 2001, and by 2009 more than 45,000 miners were working in the nation's coal mines. However, the vast majority of those employed by the end of 2007 were still white and male. Numerical information concerning the number of women currently working underground is virtually nonexistent. However, data from the Mine Safety and Health Administration suggest that approximately 2 percent of the mining workforce is female.[56]

Gender and racial discrimination may indeed be behind this number, at least partially. Yet at the same time, other factors should be considered. Most of the women working during the early 1980s are presently in their late forties to early sixties and have little interest in working at a physically demanding job, especially at their age. While studying female miners in Paonia, Colorado, during the 1990s, Donna Gearhart, a former western coal miner, found that many women understood that they faced "the law of diminishing returns" if they remained in the mines. Although these women realized that they benefited from working in the mines in the short run in terms of wages and benefits, these diminished in the long run as their bodies began to wear from the stress of hard labor. In her dissertation, "Surely a Wench Can Choose Her Own Work," Gearhart argued that some occupations are gender determined because of their unique requirements, and—speaking from her position as a former supervisor in the industry—coal mining, with its exacerbating physical labor, is one of these occupations. She believes that, with their anatomical differences, the law of diminishing returns sets in earlier for female miners than it does for males. Consequently, many women retired or quit to enter other occupations as their bodies suffered from the harsh physical demands. Like Gearhart, many women "looked at the consequences of doing that kind of work, and in most cases made the choice not to do it anymore."[57]

The law of diminishing returns may also apply to family tradition. Historically sons— and later, daughters—followed their fathers, grandfathers, and uncles into the mines. However, after the unemployment line became a more familiar sight than the application line during the closing decades of the twentieth century, many parents and grandparents began urging their children and grandchildren to get a good education in order to avoid working in the mines. The loss of wages and benefits incurred during frequent layoffs are difficult, if not impossible, to make up during times of peak employment, and the effects of mining on miners' health, especially in terms of black lung, are permanent.

Many laid-off miners, both male and female, took advantage of the UMWA/BCOA Training and Education Fund. Established in 1988, this fund provides educational and retraining funds (tuition and fees, books, and stipends) for laid-off miners and their dependents. Between 1996 and 2001, career centers established with this fund and the assistance of the federal and state governments had recruited over 3,300 former miners, trained over 1,800, and placed almost 2,500 in new jobs in five Appalachian states with an average wage of $13.50 an hour.[58] Still in existence, this program—that finances alternative careers for many children of former coal miners—continues to benefit laid-off miners and their dependents.

PRESIDENT LYNDON B. JOHNSON signed the Civil Rights Act in 1964. This act, initially constructed to end discrimination against African Americans and considered the cornerstone of civil rights legislation, forbids discrimination in hiring and firing, the awarding of benefits and promotions, and working conditions. Three years later, the passage of the Age Discrimination Act would help older women gain employment in the mines, but the most important key to entry into the coal industry for women was the amendment of the Civil Rights Act in 1967 with Executive Order 11246. Since the 1964 Civil Rights Act was written primarily to end discrimination against African Americans, many people, both within and without the coal industry, assumed that black women would be hired and promoted over their white counterparts. The two fer myth, developed during the early 1970s, after companies began to implement affirmative action guidelines, alleges that black women workers enjoyed an advantage over other groups because their hiring meant that employers could gain two minorities for the price of one. In addition, since black women have historically been perceived to be able to handle racial discrimination better than black men and were better prepared to handle sexism than white women, hiring black female miners could possibly result in fewer conflicts between male and female miners. Unfortunately for black women, these perceptions clashed with reality.

Demand for mining jobs exceeded the supply during the boom, making competition to "get into the mines" intense. Well-paying jobs with benefits were in short supply in an Appalachian economy that suffered from a lack of diversification. As a result, men and women of all ages saw mining jobs as a way to realize the American dream and obtain financial security for themselves and their families. This was especially important for single mothers, who had long been barred from the trades. Competition for these jobs increased after women, especially black women, began working underground.

Women found that obtaining mining jobs, however, was not easy in spite of civil rights legislation. Cultural traditions and society pressure were barriers to women hoping to work underground. In spite of these pressure, however, growing numbers of women—not only young single women but older married women—who found it necessary to enter the workforce were clamoring for the opportunity to gain entry into traditionally male occupations, regardless of the risk to their health and safety.

Remaining on the job proved to be more difficult. Supervisors resisted training and promoting women. As a result, many women were shoveling the belt line long after men who had been hired at the same time received

"Two fer' the Money"? 265

training to operate mining machinery and work at the mine's face. In addition, women both black and white endured sexual harassment from their supervisors and coworkers. With the UMWA unwilling to support them, many women either quit or sued their employers.

The coal industry entered into a period of decline during the late 1980s, and tens of thousands of miners found themselves on the unemployment line by 1994. Since laid-off union miners were hired for available positions at mines according to seniority and training, female miners had little chance of being called back to the mines. As a result, possessing few training certificates, regardless of race, women were the first to be laid off and the last to be recalled.

In spite of civil rights legislation and the two fer myth, only a small number of black women were hired to work in the mines. Perhaps more important, legislation and the myth failed to shield African American female miners from discrimination or harassment. Since they were highly visible, black women were more likely to face harassment and discrimination and be refused training and promotion than their white peers. Sadly, these conditions, along with the male privilege that exists in the industry, divided women who would have benefited from greater solidarity in the underground.

The minority of black women who obtained employment in the coal industry were hired as tokens and symbols of affirmative action, without advantages. These women found themselves on the outside looking in. As marginalized workers, they were frequently denied the support and camaraderie that they should have enjoyed with their fellow miners, both male and female. For many women, especially black women, "getting in the mines" was a short-lived victory.

NOTES

1. Margaret C. Simms and Julianne M. Malveaux, eds., *Slipping Through the Cracks: The Status of Black Women* (New Brunswick, NJ: Transaction Books, 1986), 7.

2. Ronald D. Eller, *Uneven Ground: Appalachia Since 1954* (Lexington: University Press of Kentucky, 2008), 194.

3. Cheryl Gist, interview with author, Lynch, Kentucky, May 15, 2001.

4. US Department of Labor, Bureau of Labor Statistics, *Women in the Labor Force: A Databook* (2006 ed.), table 2, http://www.bls.gov/cps/wlf-table2-2006.pdf (accessed June 13, 2009).

5. Anne Swardson, "Women Dig into the Coal Industry," *Coal Age* 82 (June 1977): 85.

6. Janice Hedges, "Women at Work: Women Workers and Manpower Demands in the 1970s," *Monthly Labor Review* 93 (June 1970): 19–29.

7. Swardson, "Women Dig Into the Coal Industry," 85. In a study of twenty female miners conducted in 1977 and 1978, Judith A. Hammond and Constance W. Mahoney found that of the twenty women interviewed, fifteen of the women were single mothers, and of the remaining four, two of the women were married to disabled men. These two women also had children. To read more about their study, see Judith A. Hammond and Constance W. Mahoney, "Reward-Cost Balancing Among Women Coal Miners," *Sex Roles* 9, no. 1 (January 1983): 17–29.

8. Robert D. Moran, "Women at Work: Reducing Discrimination; Role of the Equal Pay Act," *Monthly Labor Review* 93 (June 1970): 30.

9. Executive Order No. 11246. 3 C.F.R. 339 (1964–1965 compilation), as amended, Exec. Order No. 11375, 3 C.F.R. 684 (1966–1970 compilation), cited in Thomas A. Barnard and Brenda Clark, "Clementine in the 1980s (EEOC and the Woman Miner)," *West Virginia Law Review* 82 (Summer 1980): 901n8.

10. Sue Thrasher, "Coal Employment Project," *Southern Exposure*, Winter 1981, 48.

11. Betty Jean Hall, "Women Miners Can Dig It, Too," in *Communities in Economic Crisis: Appalachia and the South*, ed. John Gaventa and Barbara Ellen Smith, and Lex Willingham (Philadelphia: Temple University Press, 1990), 53–56.

12. Ibid, 56–57.

13. Thrasher, "Coal Employment Project," 48–50.

14. Linda McMichaels, "Women Coal Miners Can Dig It, Too," *Daily World*, 14 June 1979.

15. Jenny Montgomery, *Women Miners: Complaints of Sex Discrimination Force Coal Industry to End "Male Only" Tradition* (Frankfort: Kentucky Commission on Human Rights, 1986), 3–5; author telephone conversation with Joetta Gist, 22 August 2009. Although Gist states that she was a victim primarily of racial discrimination, her case was filed as a violation of KRS5344 of the Kentucky Civil Rights Act. This provision prohibits sexual discrimination in employment.

16. Office of Adversity and Equal Opportunity at Townsend University, "Affirmative Action—Glossary of Terms," http://www.towson.edu/ODEO/affirmative _action/glossary.asp (accessed October 9, 2014).

17. Montgomery, *Women Miners*, 6–7.

18. Ibid.

19. Joetta Gist, telephone conversation with author.

20. Montgomery, *Women Miners*, 8; Joetta Gist, telephone conversation.

21. Joetta Gist, telephone conversation.

22. "Bias Suits Paying Off for Women Coal Miners," *Louisville Courier Journal*, April–June Clippings, box 85, folder 41, Series IX, CEP Records, Archives of Appalachia, East Tennessee State University, Johnson City, TN.

23. Judith Wollmer, "Victory for Women Underground," *Ms. Magazine*, March 1985, 17.

24. Tim Wheeler, "Women in the Mines," *Daily World*, December 29, 1977, 8.

25. Marat Moore, *Women in the Mines: Stories of Life and Work* (New York: Twayne, 1996), 239.

26. Simms and Malveaux, *Slipping Through the Cracks*, 7.

27. Janis V. Sanchez-Hucles, "Jeopardy Not Bonus Status for African American Women in the Work Force: Why Does the Myth of Advantage Persist?" *American Journal of Community Psychology* 25, no. 5 (1997): 568, 573–74.

28. C. F. Epstein, "Positive Effects of the Multiple Negative: Explaining the Success of Professional Women," *American Journal of Sociology* 78 (1973): 912–35, cited in Sanchez-Hucles, 568.

29. Sanchez-Hucles, "Jeopardy Not Bonus Status," 568–69.

30. Julianne Malveaux, *The Status of Women of Color in the Economy: The Legacy of Being Other* (The National Conference on Women, the Economy, and Public Policy, June 19–20, 1984), 6.

31. Bette Woody, *Black Women in the Workplace: Impact of Structural Change in the Economy* (Westport, CT: Greenwood Press, 1992), 186.

32. Cheryl Gist, interview.

33. Drenna Thomas, interview with author, Lynch, Kentucky, May 15, 2001.

34. Robert H. Woodrum, *"Everybody Was Black Down There": Race and Industrial Change in the Alabama Coal Fields* (Athens: University of Georgia Press, 2007), 206.

35. Ibid., 208.

36. Ibid.

37. Ibid., 210.

38. Diane Hughes and Mark A. Dodge, "African American Women in the Workplace: Relationships Between Job Conditions, Racial Bias at Work, and Perceived Job Quality," *American Journal of Community Psychology* 25, no. 5 (1997): 596.

39. Marat Moore, *Women in the Mines*, 129–32.

40. By 1979 the UMWA realized that they could use women's presence in the mines to paint a more positive image of coal miners. Mike Roberts, a member of District 19, said that "we [the union] need to publicize the fact that women are entering the mines. That will take away some of the feeling that all miners are savages." Bruce H. Joffe, "Today's UMWA Miners: Banking on a New Image, *United Mineworkers Journal* 25, no. 90 (January–February 1979): 23–24.

41. Robert Woodrum, *Everybody Was Black Down There*, 211–12.

42. Cheryl Gist, interview.

43. Cheryl Gist and Drenna Thomas, interviews.

44. Woodrum, *Everybody Was Black Down There*, 211.

45. Kristen R. Yount, "Women and Men Coal Miners: Coping with Gender Integration Underground" (PhD diss., University of Colorado, 1986), 424–26.

46. Montgomery, *Women Miners*, 3.

47. Allanna M. Sullivan, "Women Train for Coal Mining Jobs," *Coal Age* 84 (October 1979): 172–73.

48. "Women Miners Dig Away at Discrimination," *Coal Age* 91 (August 1986): 11.

49. McMichaels, "Women Coal Miners Can Dig It, Too," 2.

50. Molly Martin, ed. *Hard-Hatted Women: Stories of Struggle and Success in the Trades* (Seattle: Seal Press, 1988), 119–21.

51. Constance Mahoney, "Appalachian Women's Perceptions of Their Work Experiences as Underground Coal Miners" (MA thesis, East Tennessee State University, 1978), 33–34.

52. Sexual Harassment Hearings, Kentucky Commission on Human Rights, 10 July 1980. Archive 355, tape 193, CEP Records, Archives of Appalachia, East Tennessee University, Johnson City, TN.

53. Ibid., 136.

54. McMichaels, "Women Coal Miners Can Dig It, Too," 2.

55. Diane K. McLaughlin, Daniel T. Lichter, and Stephen A. Matthews, "Demographic Diversity and Economic Change in Appalachia" (Population Research Institute, Pennsylvania State University, July 31, 1999), http://www.arc.gov/images/reports/demographic/demographics.pdf (accessed July 31, 2010).

56. The Coal Workers' Health Surveillance Program was designed to detect and prevent black lung cases. The National Institute for Occupational Safety and Health (NIOSH) and the Mine Safety and Health Administration (MSHA) are responsible for carrying out this nonmandatory program. According to Anita Wolfe, a public health analyst for the Centers for Disease Control (CDC) and NIOSH, 44,546 miners were eligible for black lung screening between 2005 and 2009. Of the 18,589 miners who took advantage of the program and had lung x-rays taken, 18,266 (98 percent) were men and 322 (2 percent) were women. Anita L. Wolfe, "Re: Employment Info on Women Coal Miners" (July 19, 2010). Personal e-mail (July 14, 2010).

57. Dona G. Gearhart, "'Surely a Wench Can Choose Her Own Work': Women Coal Miners in Paonia, Colorado, 1976–1987" (PhD diss., University of Nevada, Las Vegas, 1996), 218, 222.

58. *The Evolution of Employment, Working Time and Training in the Mining Industry*. Report for Discussion at the Tripartite Meeting on the Evolution of Employment, Working Time and Training in the Mining Industry, Geneva (2002), 52.

CHAPTER TEN

Flopping Tin and Punching Metal

A Survey of Women Steelworkers in West Virginia, 1890–1970

LOUIS C. MARTIN

West Virginian women have worked in the steel industry since the 1890s, when industrialists began constructing tin plate mills in towns and cities across the northern half of the state. Between 1900 and 1970, several forces shaped the experience of these women steelworkers, including the job structure of the American tin plate industry; the relatively static nature of the technology in that segment of production; and the sex typing of steelwork by the companies, unions, and workers. Moreover, steel mills did not offer the Appalachian women of northern West Virginia promising, permanent employment, and their wage work often complemented duties at home as steelworkers' families struggled to achieve a comfortable lifestyle. This encouraged them to continue many of their rural traditions like planting vegetables and raising livestock. Through the decades, major changes within the steel industry restructured work relations significantly but failed to change women's work and bring greater opportunity or better wages. Significant and lasting change did not occur until lawsuits in the 1960s forced companies to allow women to bid on jobs in other departments. Since so little changed before 1970, the historical experience of women in the steel mills of West Virginia remained surprisingly consistent over roughly eight decades.[1]

The history of working women in West Virginia remains largely unwritten. In 1990 historian Mary Beth Pudup noted that the participation of women in the West Virginia economy historically had gone almost completely unexamined. Historians' economic development narratives had focused almost exclusively on market-related activity and portrayed household subsistence as a transitory step to industrial capitalism. As a result, though women continued to perform such subsistence work after the industrial transition, most studies ignored those economic contributions. Finally, few historians had even studied those women who had worked factory jobs in every part of the state in virtually every historical era.[2] After Pudup's groundbreaking essay, several historians took on the challenge of writing the history of working women in West Virginia. First, more historians have acknowledged the contributions of household production to the industrialization of the state.[3] Second, women's wage work has received increased attention as well. Since Pudup's 1990 essay, historians have written about the textile and garment workers in Martinsburg, selectors at the Owens-Illinois Glass Company in Huntington, health care workers in the Service Employees International Union Local 1199, operatives in the Marx Toy factory of Glendale, coal miners, and pottery workers at Homer Laughlin China, to name a few.[4] An examination of women steelworkers in the Mountain State will deepen our understanding of the experiences of working women in the Appalachian economy.

DEFINING WOMEN'S WORK IN THE WEST VIRGINIA STEEL INDUSTRY

Much of the world's capital investment in iron and steel production shifted at the end of the nineteenth century from the United Kingdom and Germany to the United States. One part of this larger industrial restructuring was the migration of tin plate production capacity from Wales to small towns in Pennsylvania, Ohio, Indiana, and West Virginia in the 1890s. The 1890 McKinley Tariff encouraged American investors to build the relatively small mills to roll and coat tin plate, often as an addition to existing mills or an adaptation of old mills. In doing so, industrialists transformed local labor markets by bringing in skilled Welshmen from overseas and hiring men and women from nearby

Flopping Tin and Punching Metal 271

farms and from immigrant enclaves in nearby cities. Companies often located these relatively small mills in rural areas far from the labor strife and high property costs of the cities. West Virginia benefited from this trend, as new tin plate mills were built in Sabraton, Clarksburg, Chester, Weirton, Follansbee, and Wheeling.[5] Of these towns, only Wheeling had a long history of iron and steel production. By the 1870s Wheeling was known nationally as the "Nail City." Highly paid local puddlers produced wrought iron from the city's two hundred puddling furnaces. Skilled heaters and rollers then made the iron into plates that nailers then fed into cutting machines.[6] The puddlers, heaters, and rollers were all men, and their helpers tended to be their sons and nephews. An iron mill, they believed, was no place for women.

Workers created tin plate from steel bars, often purchased from nearby basic steel plants. They heated and rolled the bars into thin sheets, then reheated and rerolled them several times, and sheared them to size.[7] After skilled workers rolled tin plate to the proper gauge, labor crews transported it to the tin house, where it would be dipped in vats of acid, flux, and molten tin and then taken to the assorting room. There, "openers" used knives to pry apart sheets that were partly welded together in stacks, and "assorters" would then inspect and polish the tin-coated sheets. Both openers and assorters, almost all of whom were female, needed to be careful not to slice their hands on the edges of the thin sheets of metal, but the haste of production usually did result in scarred hands and arms.[8]

Tin plate proved to be a useful material for the manufacture of a variety of products, including cans, cigarette and candy tins, ceiling tiles, and all manner of small, thin metal products. As a result, metal fabrication plants sprang up all around the mills, and those plants employed many women as stamp or press operators. Both male and female stamp and press operators performed the monotonous task of placing squares of metal in the machines, cutting or forming the metal, and removing the finished ware from the machine. It is difficult to ascertain exact figures for the fabrication plants, because the US Census Bureau categorized them by product. Anecdotal evidence, however, suggests that these metal shops tended to employ far greater percentages of women than did the tin plate mills. The Phelps Can Company in Weirton, for example, employed 186 men and 185 women.[9] The Marx Toy Company of Glendale employed a workforce that was "largely female."[10]

The movement of capital and labor to the United States was part of an industrial restructuring that changed more than simply the location of the mills. Older technologies and ways of organizing production gave way to new, cheaper methods, and the mills back in Wales suffered from the new tariff and increased competition from American mills. W. C. Cronemeyer, a tin plate executive in the 1890s, observed that American manufacturers made improvements to the production process that reduced the amount of labor and raw materials needed.[11] Often, new mill owners adopted cranes and narrow gauge locomotives that eliminated labor crews.[12] Yet, heating and rolling the sheets still required very skilled and experienced workers who knew their craft well enough to produce very thin-gauge metal, and American manufacturers often recruited skilled crews from Wales. Skilled tin plate workers jealously guarded knowledge of their trade. One son of a Welsh tin plate roller recalled that his people believed that "nobody but a Welshman could make tinplate."[13] As another roller explained, they were "proud of their skill, and the secrets of the trade were passed from father to son as a legacy of great value."[14]

While the rollers and heaters passed their skills on to their sons and nephews, they never passed the secrets of their trade on to their daughters. Women had long been excluded from skilled positions, and the workers who migrated with the tin plate industry attempted to banish women from American mills altogether. Back in Wales, women, employed in a variety of unskilled positions, accounted for as much as 20 to 25 percent of the workforce in the tin plate mills. When Welshmen crossed the Atlantic, they hoped to create an all-male workplace that paid a "family wage" to the male breadwinners, but employers in the fledgling American tin plate industry insisted on employing cheap female labor in certain unskilled positions, primarily in the assorting room. In 1895, Henry William Oliver, president of the Monongahela Tin Plate Company in Pittsburgh, hired a young Welsh woman named Hattie Williams to train other young women. The hiring of Hattie Williams did not signal the beginning of the widespread employment of Welsh women. Instead, employers hired young Eastern European women,

Flopping Tin and Punching Metal 273

especially Poles, whom they believed were stronger and would work for less.[15] It appears that male workers did succeed in excluding women from the dipping works, where heat and fumes made working conditions more trying, and from the rolling mills.

Elizabeth Beardsley Butler observed the openers and assorters at work in Pittsburgh in 1909. Her words capture the exertion required to be an opener. Five to eight sheets, she wrote, would arrive welded together, and the opener had to tear them apart while they were still hot and flexible. Wearing heavy gloves, the women would grab a stack of welded plates and "beat it on the ground" and stick a piece of lead in between the plates to make an opening. Then, she writes: "They forcibly tear apart the plates, holding part of the sheet down with one knee, while tearing the metal with the other. The violence of this work takes all the strength of even the earth-toughened peasant women who have followed their husbands from Poland to the mill country in America." In another room, Butler watched women in a cleaner environment assorting tin plates, an occupation that she described as "less violent." Still, she noted, the repeated lifting and handling of the plates required considerable exertion.[16]

After a massive wave of corporate mergers at the end of the 1890s, many of West Virginia's tin plate mills changed ownership. The United States Steel Corporation, through its subsidiaries, the American Tin Plate Company and the American Sheet Steel Company, owned a rolling mill in Chester, the LaBelle tin plate works in Wheeling, and a mill in Sabraton. Weirton Steel owned rolling mills and dipping works in Weirton and Clarksburg, West Virginia, and Steubenville, Ohio. The Follansbee Brothers Company remained "independent," as did some mills in Wheeling, including the Whitaker Iron Company, which rolled black plate, and the Wheeling Corrugating Company. In 1920 the incorporation of Wheeling Steel brought together the Wheeling Corrugating Company, the Whitaker-Glessner works, and rolling mills and dipping works just across the Ohio River in Martins Ferry and Yorkville, Ohio.[17]

Most of the conditions of employment for women steelworkers in West Virginia were in place by the end of the 1890s and would not change for several decades. The static technology and hiring practices of the mills and fabricating shops provided a surprisingly uniform experience for the women working in the assorting rooms and stamping departments between the early 1900s and the late 1960s. The number of women employed in the tin plate mills remained relatively small, regardless of expansion in the industry generally. In 1914 there were thirty-one tin plate mills in the United States, which employed 4,617 men and only 621 women, who comprised less than 12 percent of the workforce.[18] Even tin plate mills that added basic steel-producing capacity and increased their payrolls many times over typically did not increase the number of female employees, who were still restricted to the assorting room. In the early 1920s Weirton Steel added coke ovens, blast furnaces, and open hearth furnaces and by 1926 had added 7,000 more men to the payroll, but the company still employed only 60 women.[19]

Shift foremen and foreladies made the hiring decisions in most of West Virginia's mills, resulting in uneven employment patterns. A large tin plate mill would typically employ about 500 workers and only about 50 or 60 women. The American Tin Plate Company mill in Chester, West Virginia, employed 450 men but only 9 women.[20] The number of women Weirton Steel employed increased from 108 in 1930 to 293 in 1940 on the eve of World War II.[21] Margaret Heaton grew up in Weirton during the 1930s and fondly remembered the "girls in the tin mill," all wearing their blue uniforms. She also remembered the favoritism and nepotism of the hiring process, noting that "if you was Polish and you knew Anne Kostur, you were guaranteed a job down there."[22] One practice that all the companies shared was the refusal, with few exceptions, to hire African Americans for anything other than basic labor, and African American women were completely excluded from the mill and assorting room jobs.[23]

As a policy, Weirton Steel would not hire married women. Margaret Heaton remembered that "down at the tin mill, if you were married you did not work." She only knew of two married women for whom Weirton Steel made an exception (probably because of nepotism). She said that normally when supervisors discovered that a woman was married, they fired her. This made it difficult for married women in Weirton to find work. Heaton said: "When you got married, you knew that you didn't have a job. That was just understood . . . unless you were a teacher or you were a nurse. You would see some working, but you didn't see too

Flopping Tin and Punching Metal 275

many married women working."[24] Ramona "Boots" Hines, married for ten years, also recalled, "You couldn't work at Weirton Steel if you were married." Some women would "sneak off" to another state to get married, but there was "always somebody to squeal on them." Those who were discovered to be married would be "out of a job."[25] The same does not appear to have been true of Wheeling Steel, at least after unionization in 1937. Many of the women who were active in the union took no efforts to conceal their married status and were openly identified as, for example, Mrs. Betty Lenore and Mrs. Marie Bacue.[26]

Regardless of the variability of hiring practices, the work in the assorting rooms was always the same, and the nature of the work changed surprisingly little for several decades. During the 1930s, the women who worked for Wheeling Steel experienced the job of assorting in much the same way that women had when Hattie Williams started training young women in Pittsburgh in the 1890s. Gizella Dull Brown, daughter of a Hungarian coal miner, worked in Wheeling Steel's assorting room in Yorkville, Ohio, just across the Ohio River from West Virginia. As with many young women, working in the mill was a way for Brown to supplement her parents' income. Flopping tin was difficult, she said, but it did not bother her, since she was young and full of energy. She made new friends at work, kept some "spending money" for herself, and felt a sense of pride in her work. She also had very small scars on her hands, even fifty years later, as reminders of the cuts she suffered. According to Brown, the work was very repetitive: "You turned [the sheets] over, and if you see anything that's bad, you had to take it out and put it in another pile. And then we had to keep the pile straight."[27]

Work in the assorting room in the 1950s and 1960s was just as demanding as it had been twenty years earlier or even sixty years earlier. Boots Hines got a job working in the assorting room in 1959 at Weirton Steel. The job offered her an adequate income to raise her three growing boys, but she remembered that it was not a pleasant place to work: "The first summer I worked in there, I think it was 117 [degrees]. That's where I got this short hair. I had long hair then, and we'd just be soaked. Of course there was no air in the place or anything. It was just like a slave shop."[28] Assorters still inspected the sheets of tin plate individually for flaws and sorted them by hand onto skids based on the nature of the

276 LOUIS C. MARTIN

defect. The *Weirton Steel Employees Bulletin* featured the "Women of the Tin Mill" in 1957, showing pictures of Helen Tonski measuring the height of a stack of tin plate and Catherine Victor holding a "mirror-like" sheet of Weirite (sheet steel with a patented coating). Minnie Pirraglia, being a "safety-minded" employee, wore leather gloves and a heavy apron. The article boasted that the "skill of such veteran Assorters" as Helen Levenson and Merion Knell ensured that Weirton Steel would be synonymous with top quality.[29]

Reminiscent of the experiences of many of the assorters who came before her, Boots Hines said that the edges of the tin plate sheets were "just like a razor blade. You had to be careful." While she never suffered any "real bad" cuts, some of the other women she worked with "had scars all the way up their arms." Each assorter was required to inspect a stack of sheets forty inches high each day, and workers like Boots had to hustle to make their quotas. The foreladies timed the assorters' breaks very strictly, permitting only a fifteen-minute break in the morning and afternoon and a thirty-minute break for lunch. "Not thirty-one min-utes," Hines recalled. "You got thirty minutes." Flopping tin would re-ally "take a toll" on girls who were not used to hard work, but it was the highest-paid work women could find in Weirton. For that reason, there were a lot of women who wanted to work in the assorting room.[30]

Women steelworkers often worked to supplement family income, but their wage labor was just one of several duties they performed to help make ends meet. In 1949 journalist David Dempsey spent a week with steelworkers and found that it was only by "meticulous budget-ing, making many of the children's clothes, keeping a garden, and 'mak-ing out the grocery order with a pruning knife'" that they would have enough left over for an occasional trip to the movies or a ball game.[31] Many of those tasks fell to women. Whether European immigrants or native-born West Virginians, most of these women grew up in rural environments and relied on their rural skills to help their families.

There were plenty of opportunities for women to raise their own food in the mill towns of West Virginia. In the north end of down-town Weirton in the 1920s and 1930s, Margaret Heaton's mother, Julia Illes, a Hungarian immigrant, raised a lot of the family's own food. Illes always planted a big garden. In the spring, she had hot beds with

Flopping Tin and Punching Metal 277

tomato and pepper plants that she sold to neighbors to start their own gardens. The family also had a cow that they grazed on the outskirts of town. They sometimes sold the milk to neighbors and made butter and cottage cheese. Julia also kept chickens in the backyard so the family always had eggs. According to Margaret, since her mother was "on the edge of town there," there were no "rules or regulations" to restrict her agricultural activities.[32]

Other than Wheeling, mill towns in West Virginia often had little other employment for women. For example, Weirton offered few employment opportunities besides the assorters in the tin mill. In 1950 only one in five Weirton women fourteen years and older participated in the labor force. Women could find jobs working as secretaries for some of the professionals in town, as cashiers at local grocery stores, as teachers in public schools, as nurses at the mill, or as domestic workers, but those opportunities were very limited in comparison to the population of working-age women. In Weirton, the leading occupational categories among the 1,683 employed women were clerical (26 percent), factory operatives (19 percent), sales workers (15 percent), service workers (14 percent), professional (including teachers and nurses) (12 percent), and private household workers (7 percent).[33]

Because male steelworkers in Weirton earned a "family wage," the restrictive job market often made little difference to the wives of male steelworkers. Widows and divorcees, however, struggled to make a living. Alma Haning, for example, lived in Weirton, and in 1943, at the age of forty-nine, was forced to confront this unfavorable labor market when her husband died unexpectedly. She got a job as a nurse's aide and complained that she still had to pay, on her meager salary, the same price for goods as people who made "Weirton Steel money." Haning observed that she was not alone, as there were many other women who were struggling. Once married and now "too old or poor to further their education," these women were "forced to take any jobs in hospitals (laundries, dietary, aid) and restaurants, small offices and clerking jobs."[34] This was not an uncommon scenario for women in postwar America. Furthermore, service and retail jobs not only paid low wages but were also often degrading when customers and supervisors treated these women workers with contempt.[35]

278 LOUIS C. MARTIN

Perhaps such restrictive labor markets were what enabled companies to pay women steelworkers low wages. While they were often the best-paying jobs women in the West Virginia mill towns could find, their wages still fell far below what men could earn. The assorters that Elizabeth Beardsley Butler observed in 1909 made less than a dollar a day, which was roughly half of what a male laborer earned.[36] When Boots Hines went to work at Weirton Steel, she recalled that it was a struggle to pay her bills. To make matters worse, women in the assorting room could expect seasonal layoffs as soon as canning season was over, which prevented her from living comfortably. She said that that was "ten years they played with my life," during which she could not buy a house for fear that if she got laid off, while she could probably "feed the boys," she would not "make a big house payment and take care of everything." The boys "were all big eaters," she said.[37]

Poor wages, the monotony of stamping or assorting tin plate, and restricted opportunity made for surprisingly consistent experiences for women steelworkers in West Virginia from the early 1900s through the 1960s. Yet, there were fundamental changes in the steel industry—major technological changes, unionization, and the labor shortage of World War II—that seemingly had the potential to undermine the forces that maintained the status quo.

NEW TECHNOLOGIES, UNIONIZATION, AND WARTIME LABOR SHORTAGES

Technological changes began shortly after the tin plate industry arrived in the United States. As noted above, American manufacturers made several changes during the 1890s, including replacing labor crews with cranes and trains. The most dramatic change to the process came in the 1920s with the perfection of the continuous rolling mill. Such an innovation had eluded technicians for many years because of the thin gauge of metal needed to produce tin plate, but by 1927 they were able to adjust the engines and machine the rolls precisely enough to push a steel slab in one end of a long line of rolls and watch a thin strip of sheet steel emerge at the other. After the adoption of the new process, workers would say that they no longer made tinplate "by the box, they make it by the mile."[38] Rather than producing individual squares of metal,

Flopping Tin and Punching Metal 279

the new process resulted in a massive coil of sheet steel that required new equipment to transport, shear, coat with tin, and ship to customers. Both Weirton Steel and Wheeling Steel constructed continuous rolling mills shortly after the new technology was introduced. The new mills made most of the highly skilled rollers and heaters obsolete.[39] Some crews were kept on for specialty orders, but most were forced to find other employment.

The other important innovation in tin plate production was the development of electrolytic tin plating. During World War II, the government rationed the amount of tin available to manufacturers, forcing them to adopt new technology that used less of it. Electrolytic lines replaced the process of running coils through vats of flux and molten tin. With the new technology, electrolytic plating units used electricity to "bonderize" the tin to the "black plate" (uncoated metal), creating a more uniform and much thinner coating of tin.[40]

The new technologies did not affect the work in the assorting room. The continuous rolling mill fundamentally changed tin plate production and replaced thousands of skilled steelworkers with machine tenders. Yet, enough customers preferred to receive boxes of tin plate rather than coils that steel companies were forced to cut the coils down to size and send them on to the assorting room to be inspected and sorted by quality. And while wartime rationing dictated the adoption of the most modern technology on the tinning lines, there was no incentive to replace the low-wage workers of the assorting room with machines.

As the tin plate industry took root in America during the 1890s, the skilled rollers and heaters were readily admitted in the steelworkers' union, the Amalgamated Association of Iron, Steel, and Tin Workers. The mostly unskilled tin house workers, including the female openers and assorters, were generally excluded. The skilled craftsmen who created the steelworkers' union began with a gendered concept of unionism, since they were partly just codifying unwritten rules of the workplace that often emphasized maintaining a "manly" bearing toward employers and fellow workers.[41] The Amalgamated Association began as a union of skilled, male craftsmen. The 1876 constitution, for example, decreed that the union would "be composed of all iron and steel workers, who are competent workmen and of good character."[42]

280 LOUIS C. MARTIN

Officials revised the Amalgamated constitution in 1877 to make it more inclusive, even explicitly calling upon local lodges to admit assorters.[43] By the 1890s, the clause on membership eligibility simply stated that "all men working in and around" the mills were to be included, "except laborers" who would be admitted at the discretion of the local lodges.[44] When tin house workers approached the leaders of the Amalgamated Association in 1898 to petition for membership, they were advised to form their own union, because they would be better able to protect their interests with a separate organization.[45]

The tin house workers did just that. Of the twenty-one tin plate plants in the United States in 1898, the tinning departments in only six of those plants were unionized. That year, American Federation of Labor President Samuel Gompers issued a call for a convention in Kansas City to create a national organization of the tin house workers. Nine delegates from the six locals met in December, and on January 17, 1899, created the Tin Plate Workers' International Protective Association of America (TPWIPA).[46] According to the constitution, the TPWIPA was comprised of "tin men, risers, tin plate openers, picklers, assorters, boxers, reckoners, tin house shearmen and all men working in tin houses, and all men identified with our craft, except foremen."[47] Many predicted the TPWIPA would fail because their numbers were limited and they had little trade union experience, but by their second convention in May 1900, the union had thirty different lodges.[48] By 1903 the union had negotiated shorter hours for many of the tin house workers as well, and TPWIPA president Charles Lawyer said that while the union's "pathway has not been strewn with flowers, by any means," they had accomplished a great deal in a short amount of time.[49] However, as steel manufacturers drove unionism from the mills during the first decade of the twentieth century, the TPWIPA, too, suffered defeats. A failed 1913 strike in Steubenville, Ohio, against the Weirton Steel Company spelled disaster for the fledgling union, whose few remaining members were absorbed into the Amalgamated Association.[50]

It would not be until the 1930s that the assorters would have another opportunity to unionize. Theresa Ogresovich started "flopping tin" at Wheeling Steel during that time and recalled some of the miserable working conditions assorters faced. Overbearing foreladies, dressed

Flopping Tin and Punching Metal 281

in pink, intimidated and disrespected their subordinates. Assorters, dressed in starched blue uniforms with white collars, often brought bribes and presents to win the foreladies' favoritism. The foreladies never called the women workers by name. They just hissed at them, Ogresovich noted, like "you were a cat." Ogresovich was terrified she would lose her job and actually had nightmares about being fired for making minor mistakes.[51]

Operating the stamping machines and presses of the fabricating plants proved to be far more hazardous than assorting in the mill. Angeline "Sally" Miller experienced the potential horrors of the stamping machines when she started working at Marx Toy Company in 1934. When properly operating, the machines' safety features prevented workers from putting their hands in the path of the press, which came down with tremendous force to cut the metal. She informed her foreman that the press was repeating, meaning that it was unexpectedly going up and down more than once. The foreman instructed her to return to her machine and reassured her that the guard would keep her hands safe. After she started working again, she remembered: "It happened so quickly, I did not feel it. I went to pick up a ware, and I could not pick up a ware." The machine had sheared her fingers off. In shock, she tried to run away, and her coworkers grabbed her and took her to Glen Dale Hospital.[52] It was not the first time they had seen such an accident.

Accidents were among the grievances that inspired many women steelworkers to join unions in the 1930s. The 1933 enactment of the National Industrial Recovery Act (NIRA), which recognized the right of workers to form unions, reinvigorated the Amalgamated Association of Iron, Steel, and Tin Workers. Workers at Weirton Steel were among the first nationwide to test the protections of the new legislation and discovered in the process that the federal government could actually do little to help them. Some ten thousand workers walked out of the company's plants in Weirton, Clarksburg, and Steubenville and formed lodges of the Amalgamated Association. After the company's founder and chairman, Ernest Weir, agreed to elections, workers returned to their jobs but did not find the Amalgamated Association on their ballots. Instead, the company created an employee representation plan and demanded that workers vote for it.

The women of the assorting room did not escape coercion. They were gathered for a party at the Williams Country Club, where they were given cigarettes, beer, and "some hard liquor," according to assorter Katherine Zinaich. Company officials told them if they wanted their "bread and butter every day to vote the right way." Zinaich's bosses then transferred her and another women from the assorting room to the black plate department in an effort to make their work unpleasant. She recalled that management "thought we had too much influence over the other girls."[53] After the rigged election, federal judges refused to enforce the union protections of the NIRA, and Weir continued his vigorous antiunion crusade.

In 1935 Congress enacted the National Labor Relations Act, which created the National Labor Relations Board (NLRB) and was designed to protect unions more effectively than had the NIRA. However, Weirton's steelworkers remained hesitant, having experienced blacklists and unchecked intimidation from the company for three years. Furthermore, Weir's "Hatchet Gang" routinely brutalized organizers from the newly created Steel Workers Organizing Committee (SWOC) of the Congress of Industrial Organizations (CIO).[54] Weirton Steel kept its company union until 1950, when workers opted for an "independent" union that closely resembled the company unions that preceded it.[55]

Other unionization campaigns proved to be far more successful. Workers at Wheeling Steel formed several Amalgamated Association lodges in late 1933 and fought a protracted battle with management. They formed five separate lodges at the Portsmouth, Ohio, plant alone.[56] Workers at the Portsmouth plant agitated for the union for the next three years. In May of 1936 the NLRB ruled that the company had illegally coerced workers into joining an employee representation plan, and in July the workers walked off the job and succeeded in forcing the company to recognize their locals. In August SWOC established an office in Portsmouth and began absorbing the lodges of the Amalgamated Association, whose national officers voted to disband and relinquish all jurisdiction and local lodges to SWOC. With surprising suddenness, Wheeling Steel signed an agreement with SWOC in March 1937 that covered all of its plants.[57] One organizer from Portsmouth told a meeting of steelworkers in Wheeling that they did not appreciate how easily

Flopping Tin and Punching Metal 283

they had gotten their contract compared to the way other members had to "fight for everything they got."[58]

Workers continued to agitate to force the company to abide by its agreement and to negotiate various new local rules, and women played an active role in this ongoing unionization campaign. At an October 1937 meeting of Local 1248 of SWOC, one organizer declared: "We ought to forget our troubles and talk nothing but C.I.O. in our plants." He noted that the "Yorkville girls" had done just that to prevent the company from changing their shifts without their consent.[59] SWOC became the United Steelworkers of America in 1943, and collective bargaining became a permanent fixture in labor relations at Wheeling Steel.

Workers at the Marx Toy Factory and other fabricating plants also unionized. During the course of 1939 and 1940, the toy workers quietly organized among themselves in preparation for a January 1941 union representation election before the National Labor Relations Board. When negotiations with the company broke down in April, Local 149 of the United Paper, Toy, and Novelty Workers' Union, CIO, went on a six-week strike until the company finally agreed to a contract in early May 1941 that offered union recognition, pay increases, a seniority provision, a grievance procedure, and vacation pay for the women who worked there.[60]

Even though women actively participated in the unionization movement of the 1930s and 1940s, gender discrimination in the Mountain State's steel industry persisted. While the United Steelworkers of America managed to improve wages and working conditions for the women at the presses and in the assorting rooms, it did not open up new job opportunities for them. Neither were unions able to protect all workers from accidents on the job. One woman in Wheeling wrote to Franklin and Eleanor Roosevelt in 1944 to tell them that her daughter had lost two fingers to a press at Wheeling Corrugating because, she wrote, the company made "their help work without guards and tongs and bad presses." Her daughter was not alone. Five other young women lost fingers at the plant in one week, she explained. "The girls are some day going to be mothers and do house work. How can they do this without fingers?" CIO officials tried to do everything they could, but "Wheeling Steel runs Wheeling." She hoped that the government could force the company to pay for artificial fingers because "being a mother means dresses to make and button up, and nearly everything means you need your fingers in the home to make good mothers and to rear good citizens."[61]

World War II dramatically changed the basic characteristics of female employment in West Virginia's mills, but these changes proved to be temporary wartime measures. During the war, steel companies hired unprecedented numbers of women to work at many points in the production process that had previously been considered men's work. At first, steel companies transferred male white-collar clerical workers to production jobs and backfilled their positions with women. As the shortage got worse, manufacturers increasingly hired women to be crane operators, operatives at the rolling mills, stampers and metal fabricators, and maintenance workers. Women were also placed in more physically demanding labor jobs but often had to double up on particularly challenging tasks or simply leave some of the heaviest lifting to men. Wheeling Steel promoted Theresa Ogresovich to crane operator, which was less physically challenging than sorting and inspecting tin and paid considerably better wages.[62] Weirton Steel secured defense contracts to produce eight-inch artillery shells for the war effort and employed mostly women in the new shell plant. These workers manufactured the large explosive shells in what had been called "the 23-inch warehouse building."[63] While white women were hired into American steel mills during the war in unprecedented numbers, steel managers typically only placed African American women in the same jobs reserved for African American men: unskilled labor positions in coke ovens, blast furnaces, and sintering plants. Wartime company and government literature often portrayed black women as being tougher or huskier, but after the war they were once again banished from these relatively lucrative mill jobs and relegated to low-paying jobs as domestic servants.[64]

Journalist R. H. Markham watched women at Weirton Steel working in production jobs in 1945. He saw "girls handle 10-ton sticks of red hot steel almost as easily as a powder puff." One "girl without the slightest confusion" sent her "magic crane" to pick up an ingot that had fallen off a conveyor belt "as easily as a cat might put an erring kitten back into the basket." Another woman he observed sat at a lever sending steel ingots into the rolling mills "as easily as an office girl types figures."

Flopping Tin and Punching Metal 285

Markham witnessed a mill mechanized to the point that men became "jinns" and women became "giants," as they shoved steel around like "Jupiter was once reputed to handle lightning bolts."[65] This suggests that mechanization eliminated much of the logic of sex-typing jobs—that is, that the physical nature of steel industry tasks dictated that men perform most of the work. However, historian Jim Rose points out that only the strongest women could meet the physical demands of many labor jobs, such as wielding eighty-pound pneumatic jackhammers.[66] On the surface, the inability to perform demanding labor duties should not have barred women from holding production jobs, but most employees were expected to hire into the company as laborers until they could bid on the more desirable production jobs. Furthermore, negative attitudes about female employment in mills proved to be resilient. *Life* magazine observed that in England and Russia they had always accepted the concept of the "weaker sex" sweating away near blast furnaces or ladles of molten iron, but it was only because of the extraordinary wartime circumstances that American steel companies made this "revolutionary adjustment."[67]

At the war's end, old notions that the steel mill was "no place for a woman" returned. A combination of factors led to the reconstruction of the sexual division of labor, according to historian Ruth Milkman. Some women readily stepped aside for returning veterans. Others were forced out by seniority. And many men and women renewed their commitment to the ideal of female domesticity.[68] USWA Local 1248 in Wheeling spent considerable time debating seniority rules as veterans reentered the workplace. A special provision known as "super seniority" would enable many veterans to "bump" workers with more actual seniority out of jobs. Betty Lenore argued that "service boys are entitled to jobs," but they should not deny the rights of "older people." Ironically, the women in the assorting rooms and on the press lines were not in danger of losing their jobs because of sex typing. One member asked if women "do men's jobs, then why can't the men do the women's jobs?" Another man at the meeting declared, "My wife works. I am going to see that a man gets her job, someone with three or four children." Finally, another man explained the nature of sex typing, observing, "You may have your wife stop working, but some other woman will get the job." Betty Lenore had the last word, explaining, "We know management will not take off women. If I thought that by quitting, some man would benefit, I'd quit. I am conscientious on this question. . . . I have a husband, and it would hurt me more if he is out of work. [But] we cannot tell management to fire the women."[69]

A large number of women were forced out of what the company considered to be men's jobs. Management at Wheeling Steel forced Theresa Ogresovich to return to the assorting room.[70] Gizella Brown voluntarily returned home to raise children. Many other women were forced out of the mills altogether. Management in various industries were the driving force behind the reconstruction of the sexual division of labor after World War II, but the anecdotal evidence from USWA Local 1248 suggests that union officials, returning veterans, and both male and female workers did little to try to permanently redraw the gender lines in West Virginia's steel industry. Unable to return to the life of a housewife for financial reasons, many were instead forced to accept low-wage and low-prestige jobs because of the sexual division of labor.[71]

CIVIL RIGHTS COMES TO STEEL

The enactment of Title VII of the Civil Rights Act of 1964 finally prohibited employment discrimination on the basis of gender and brought women a step closer to economic equality. Many companies felt increasing pressure to change their discriminatory hire and promotion policies as lawsuits mounted. Weirton Steel changed its policy in 1969, according to Boots Hines, so that if a woman could "do a man's job, they could work at it." She jumped at the opportunity and bid on a job in the shipping department, where she worked for the next sixteen years. Many women found that the other jobs in the mill were not as demanding as they had been portrayed. Hines joked that she found out how some men could work so many double shifts: by sitting around for four hours. She said that working in the shipping department was actually less physically demanding than working in the assorting room.[72]

For most women in the steel industry, change did not come until a 1974 court-ordered consent decree instituted one of the largest affirmative action programs in the country. Nine of the largest steel companies were required to hire greater percentages of women and racial minorities into

Flopping Tin and Punching Metal 287

the skilled trades, production, maintenance, and management.[73] With Congress and federal courts on their side, women enjoyed greater access to steel jobs than any time since World War II. The percentage of women in each occupational category in the industry increased steadily after 1975. The proportion of women in sales, clerical, and professional jobs increased by about 20 percent, and their numbers in labor, service, and technical jobs grew by about 10 percent in each category. By 1977 there were 7,413 women working in the steel industry nationwide, comprising 3.4 percent of the total workforce. The number of women at National Steel, Weirton Steel's parent corporation, grew to 636 out of a total of 10,352 employees (about 6 percent), at a time when overall employment in the industry was shrinking. Far fewer women worked at Wheeling Steel's plants (which became Wheeling-Pittsburgh Steel after a merger in 1968) where only 109 women made up 1.2 percent of the total workforce.[74]

The increased presence of women on the shop floor created tensions. Fearful that women would drag down wages or replace family men, many male steelworkers tried to defend the "breadwinner's wage" that they had worked so long to achieve. Steel mills had developed an exclusively male work culture for decades, which actually contributed to the notion that a steel mill was "no place for women." Boots Hines recalled that it was "just one of those things that it just had always been that way, and a lot of the men weren't too happy to have those women come in and work with them."[75] Indeed, many men refused to modify their behavior or stop using offensive language, sometimes shocking their new female coworkers. Hines said that when men used "that word," it actually made her ears tingle.[76] Even relatively banal male culture alienated many women who had little interest in discussing sports, fishing trips, and cars in minute detail.[77] Eventually, most women gained acceptance in the mill. Hines remembered that she learned to stay away from the men who resented women for being in the mill, and her hard work won her the respect of the men on her crew. She even shamed one man into cleaning up his foul language.[78] Other women in the steel industry faced long periods of sexual harassment, continued gender discrimination, and obstinacy in their own union.[79]

Those women who managed to get "men's" jobs in the mill valued the opportunity, but it would be a mistake to glorify that experience.

Boots Hines noted that the shipping department could be just as unpleasant as the assorting room. As a hookup for the crane, she always needed to be alert because the mammoth coils of steel could and occasionally did tip over. Noxious fumes from the coke plant or the sintering plant also made the shipping department an unpleasant work environment. Hines, in fact, disliked working in the mill generally. She said that she hated it the day she started and was "tickled to death" the day she retired, thirty-one years later. After her last day, she threw her steel-toed boots in a trash can. That night she had a terrifying nightmare that she was trapped in a strange part of the mill.[80]

In some ways, West Virginia women had indeed been trapped in a strange part of the mill for nearly eighty years. Restricted to the assorting rooms and the press lines, they were unable to attain promotions to more lucrative and more fulfilling jobs. Monotony and low wages put the jobs of assorting tin sheets and operating presses among the most undesirable jobs in the steel industry in West Virginia. The sex typing of those jobs proved remarkably resilient through several periods of rapid change. Technological changes in the production process eliminated the need for many male laborers as well as many highly skilled male operatives, but companies had little incentive to develop innovations that eliminated cheap female labor. As a result, "women's jobs" in the mill changed little over the decades. World War II labor shortages forced companies to place women in many different jobs throughout the mill, but the war's end also brought an end to the extraordinary breakdown of the gendered division of labor in West Virginia mills. Finally, the unionization of the industry gave workers a voice in their conditions, but that did not enable women to successfully challenge discriminatory hiring policies until the 1960s, because sexism existed within the union as well. Ironically, when women finally broke through the industry's glass ceiling, West Virginia steel producers entered a painful period of layoffs, reductions in force, and bankruptcy that deprived women of the opportunity to achieve the full potential of their careers in steel.

NOTES

1. For previous studies of women steelworkers, see Jim Rose, "'The Problem Every Supervisor Dreads': Women Workers at the U.S. Steel Duquesne Works during World War II," *Labor History* 36, no. 1 (Winter 1995): 24–51; Mary Margaret

Fonow, *Union Women: Forging Feminism in the United Steelworkers of America,* vol. 17 of *Social Movements, Protest, and Contention* (Minneapolis: University of Minnesota Press, 2003); Bill Jones and Ronald L. Lewis, "Gender and Transnationality Among Welsh Tinplate Workers in Pittsburgh: The Hattie Williams Affair, 1895," *Labor History* 48, no. 2 (May 2007): 175–94.

2. Mary Beth Pudup, "Women's Work in the West Virginia Economy," *West Virginia History* 49 (1990): 7–20. For a more general historiographical essay, see Barbara Howe, "The Status of Women's History Research In West Virginia," in *West Virginia History: Critical Essays on the Literature,* ed. John C. Hennen and Ronald L. Lewis (West Virginia Humanities Council, 1993), 149–84.

3. Janet W. Greene, "Strategies for Survival: Women's Work in the Southern West Virginia Coal Camps," *West Virginia History* 49 (1990): 37–54; Paul Salstrom, *Appalachia's Path to Dependency: Rethinking a Region's Economic History, 1730–1940* (Lexington: University Press of Kentucky, 1994); Chad Montrie, "Community in the Midst of Change: Work and Environment for West Virginia Mountaineers," *West Virginia History: A Journal of Regional Studies* 1, no. 1 (Spring 2007). Greene's essay was actually published in the same issue as Pudup's call for increased research in this area.

4. Jerra Jenrette, "'There's No Damn Reason For It—It's Just Our Policy': Labor-Management Conflict in Martinsburg, West Virginia' Textile and Garment Industries" (PhD diss., West Virginia University, 1996); Ginny Young, "Heart of Glass: Women, Work Culture, and Resistance in Huntington, West Virginia's Glass Industry" (MA thesis, Marshall University, 2007); John C. Hennen, "1199 Comes to Appalachia: Beginnings, 1970–1976," in *Class, Culture, and Politics in Modern Appalachia: Essays in Honor of Ronald L. Lewis* (Morgantown: West Virginia University Press, 2009); Kevin Barksdale, "'Beneath the Golden Stairs': Gender, Unionization, and Mobilization in World War II West Virginia," *Ohio Valley History* 4 (Spring 2004); and 45; Carlotta H. Savage, "Women Coal Miners: Another Chapter in Central Appalachia's Struggle Against Hegemony, 1973–1998" (MA thesis, West Virginia University, 1998); Suzanne E. Tallichet, *Daughters of the Mountain: Women Coal Miners in Appalachia* (University Park: Penn State University Press, 2006); Louis C. Martin, "Working for Independence: The Failure of New Deal Politics in a Rural Industrial Place" (PhD diss., West Virginia University, 2008), chap. 5.

5. The structure and geography of the tin plate industry in the 1890s and early 1900s can be gleaned from Louis C. Martin, "Causes and Consequences of the 1909–1910 Steel Strike in the Wheeling District" (MA thesis, West Virginia University, 1999), chap. 3. For a broader discussion of industrial restructuring, see Doreen Massey, *Spatial Divisions of Labor: Social Structures and the Geography of Production* (New York: Routledge, 2nd ed., 1995); Anne E. Mosher, *Capital's Utopia: Vandegrift, Pennsylvania, 1855–1916* (Baltimore: Johns Hopkins University Press, 2004).

6. H. D. Scott, *Iron and Steel in Wheeling* (Toledo, OH: Caslon Company, 1929), 55; Amos J. Loveday Jr., *The Rise and Decline of the American Cut Nail Industry: A Study of the Interrelationships of Technology, Business Organization, and Management Techniques* (Westport, CT: Greenwood Press, 1983).

7. For descriptions of the production process, see Martin, "Causes and Consequences of the 1909–1910 Steel Strike," 5–8; "Manufacture of Tin Plate," *Scientific American* 87 (November 1, 1902), 290; D. E. Dunbar, *The Tin-Plate Industry: A Comparative Study of Its Growth in the United States and in Wales* (Boston: Houghton Mifflin Company, 1915); and William R. Stewart, "Great Industries of the United States: Part IV, Tin and Terne Plate," *The Cosmopolitan* 37 (October 1904): 639–50.

8. For a description of the assorting room see Elizabeth Beardsley Butler, *Women and the Trades: Pittsburgh, 1907–1908,* of the Pittsburgh Survey, ed. Paul Kellogg (New York: Russell Sage Foundation, 1909), 227–28.

9. Peter Boyd, *History of Northern West Virginia Panhandle, Embracing Ohio, Marshall, Brooke, and Hancock Counties* (Topeka: Historical Publishing Company, 1927), 290–91.

10. Barksdale, "Beneath the Golden Stairs," 21.

11. Cronemeyer quoted in William G. Gray, "Tin and Terne Plate," in US Bureau of the Census, *Twelfth Census of the United States of America* (1900), vol. 10, *Manufacturing,* pt. 4 (Washington, DC.: Government Printing Office, 1901), 119.

12. US Congress, Senate, *Report on the Conditions of Employment in the Iron and Steel Industry,* 62d Cong., 1st sess. (Washington, DC: Government Printing Office, 1913), 3:516–22.

13. Bart Richards, interview by Joe Uehlein, February 21, 1974, Pittsburgh, PA, transcript, United Steelworkers of America Archive and Oral History Collection, Historical Collections and Labor Archives (hereafter USA-HCLA), Pennsylvania State University, 6.

14. James J. Davis, *The Iron Puddler: My Life in the Rolling Mills and What Came of It* (Indianapolis: Bobbs-Merrill, 1922), 30–31.

15. Jones and Lewis, "Gender and Transnationality," 175–94.

16. Butler, *Women and the Trades,* 227–28.

17. On the holdings of U. S. Steel, see US Commissioner of Corporations, *Report on the Steel Industry* (Washington, DC: Government Printing Office, 1911–13), 1:1–8. Also see Earl Chapin May, *Principio to Wheeling, 1715–1945: A Pageant of Iron and Steel* (New York: Harper and Brothers, 1945), 200–215, 251–56.

18. US Census Bureau, *Fourteenth Census of the United States,* vol. 10: *Manufacturers* (1919) (Washington, DC: Government Printing Office, 1921), 349.

19. Boyd, *History of Northern West Virginia Panhandle,* 290–91.

20. Ibid.

21. US Census Bureau, *Fifteenth Census of the United States: Population* (1930); *Sixteenth Census of the United States: Population* (1940).

22. Margaret Heaton, interview by author, digital recording, July 28, 2005, Weirton, WV.

23. Based on observations from various oral histories, including author interview with Gizella Brown, tape recording, Summer 2001, Martins Ferry, OH; Margaret Heaton, interview; and histories of the steel industry generally, including Dennis C. Dickerson, *Out of the Crucible: Black Steelworkers in Western Pennsylvania, 1875–1980* (Albany: State University of New York Press, 1986); and Fonow, *Union Women,* 26–33.

Flopping Tin and Punching Metal 291

24. Margaret Heaton, interview.

25. Ramona "Boots" Hines, interview by author, digital recording, March 20, 2007, New Cumberland, WV.

26. Meeting minutes for November 9, 1945 in Minute Book, Amalgamated Association of Iron, Steel, and Tin Workers, Lodge 1248, United Steelworkers of America, District 23 (Wheeling, WV) Records, 1937–1956, box 31 (hereafter Local 1248 Minutes), USA-HCLA.

27. Gizella Brown, interview.

28. Ramona "Boots" Hines, interview.

29. *Weirton Steel Employees Bulletin*, April 1957.

30. Ramona "Boots" Hines, interview.

31. David Dempsey, "Steelworkers: 'Not Today's Wage, Tomorrow's Security,'" *New York Times Magazine*, August 7, 1949, in *American Labor Since the New Deal*, ed. Melvyn Dubofsky (Chicago: Quadrangle Books, 1971), 192–201, quotes on 194 and 196.

32. Margaret Heaton, interview.

33. US Census Bureau, *A Report of the Seventeenth Decennial Census of the United States. Census of Population: 1950*, vol. 2, *Characteristics of the Population*, pt. 48, *West Virginia* (Washington, DC: Government Printing Office, 1952).

34. Alma Haning (Cleveland Ave Weirton) to Arch Moore, May 16, 1957, box GM214a, folder "Questionnaire April 1957—Correspondence." Arch Moore Papers, West Virginia and Regional History Collection, Morgantown, WV.

35. See Fonow, *Union Women*, 80–81, for a description of a female steelworker's experience with the service sector. Also see Ruth Milkman, *Gender at Work: The Dynamics of Job Segregation by Sex During World War II* (Urbana: University of Illinois Press, 1987), 100.

36. Butler, *Women and the Trades*, 227–28.

37. Ramona "Boots" Hines, interview.

38. Bart Richards, interview with Uehlein, USA-HCLA, 4. On the new technology, see *Iron Age*, May 19, 1927, and June 16, 1927.

39. Inez Orler, *Frontiersmen ESOP* (Parsons, WV: McClain Printing Company, 1984), 106; and May, *Principio to Wheeling*, 262–68.

40. *Wall Street Journal*, January 30, 1942, 3; William T. Hogan, *Economic History of the Iron and Steel Industry in the United States* vol. 3: pts. 4 and 5 (Lexington, MA: Lexington Books, 1971), 1121.

41. David Montgomery, *Workers' Control in America: Studies in the History of Work, Technology, and Labor Struggles* (New York: Cambridge University Press, 1979), 11–18. The discussion of a "manly" bearing appears on p. 13.

42. *Constitution, By-Laws, and Rules of Order of the National and Subordinate Lodges of the Amalgamated Association of Iron and Steel Workers of the United States, 1876* (Pittsburgh: National Labor Tribune Print, 1876), 20. The union's constitutions are available on Microfilm Reel 73 of *American Labor Union Constitutions and Proceedings, 1836–1974* (Glen Rock, NJ: Microfilming Corporation of America, 1974).

43. *Constitution, By-Laws, and Rules of Order of the National and Subordinate Lodges of the Amalgamated Association of Iron, Steel and Tin Workers of the*

United States, 1877 (Pittsburgh: Herald Printing Company, 1877), 7. Note that this was during an early attempt to start the tin plate industry in America, and it is not clear whether assorters were primarily male or female at that time.

44. *Constitution and General Laws of the National Amalgamated Association of Iron and Steel Workers of the United States* (n.p., [1892]),7.

45. David Brody, *Steelworkers in America: The Non-Union Era* (Urbana: University of Illinois Press, 1960), 60.

46. Charles E. Lawyer, "History of the Trade Unions: Tin Plate Workers," *American Federationist* 10 (September 1903), 841.

47. *Constitution and General Laws of the Tin Plate Workers' International Protective Association of America* (1901), 3, Microfilm Reel 75 of *American Labor Union Constitutions and Proceedings, 1836–1974* (Glen Rock, NJ: Microfilming Corporation of America, 1974).

48. *Proceedings of the Second Annual Convention of the Tin Plate Workers' Protective Association of America* (1900), 5–7, in ibid.

49. Lawyer, "Tin Plate Workers," 841.

50. Martin, "Causes and Consequences of the 1909–1910 Steel Strike," 84–85.

51. Fonow, *Union Women*, 25, 83–84.

52. Members of the United Toy Workers Union Local 149, interview by George Parkinson, January 7, 1976, transcript, Toy Workers Union Oral History, West Virginia and Regional History Collection, Morgantown, WV; quoted in Barksdale, "Beneath the Golden Stairs," 24.

53. "Threats Charged in Weirton Vote," *New York Times,* October 16, 1934.

54. John Hennen, "E. T. Weir, Employee Representation, and the Dimensions of Social Control: Weirton Steel, 1933–1937," *Labor Studies Journal* 26, no. 3 (Fall 2001): 25–49. Also see Martin, "Working for Independence," 128–150.

55. For the story of the 1950 union representation election, see Elizabeth Fones-Wolf and Ken Fones-Wolf, "Cold War Americanism: Business, Pageantry, and Antiunionism in Weirton, West Virginia," *Business History Review* 77 (Spring 2003), 61–91.

56. See "Roster of Local Union Organizations" in the Portsmouth Central Labor Council's official newspaper, the *Labor Review.* This description came from the Roster in the October 18, 1933 issue.

57. Ibid., May 16, 1936; July 18, 1936; August 22, 1936; and March 12, 1937.

58. February 24, 1939, Local 1248 Minutes, USA-HCLA.

59. October 29, 1937, Local 1248 Minutes, USA-HCLA.

60. Barksdale, "Beneath the Golden Stairs," 25–27.

61. Quoted in *"Slaves of the Depression": Workers' Letters About Life on the Job,* Gerald Markowitz and David Rosner, eds. (Ithaca, NY: Cornell University Press, 1987), 214–15.

62. Fonow, *Union Women,* 83; Rose, "'Problem Every Supervisor Dreads,'" 38–39.

63. Susan Carnahan Lindsey, "Hancock County in World War II" (MA thesis, West Virginia University, 1949), 41–42.

64. Fonow, *Union Women,* 26–33.

Flopping Tin and Punching Metal 293

65. R. H. Markham, "Steelmaking: The 'American Way' Shines Bright Amid Smoke and Toil," *Christian Science Monitor*, May 26, 1945, 11. On sex-typing jobs, see Milkman, *Gender at Work*, 15–20.

66. Rose, "'Problem Every Supervisor Dreads,'" 38–39.

67. Fonow, *Union Women*, 28.

68. Milkman, *Gender at Work*, chap. 7.

69. March 8, 1946, Local 1248 Minutes, USA-HCLA.

70. Fonow, *Union Women*, 83.

71. Milkman, *Gender at Work*, chap. 7; Rose, "'Problem Every Supervisor Dreads,'" 49–50. Milkman argues persuasively that management in the auto and electrical industries were responsible for the return to the prewar sexual division of labor. More research is necessary to determine exactly how the division was reconstructed in West Virginia's mills.

72. Ramona "Boots" Hines, interview.

73. Fonow, *Union Women*, 56–57.

74. Ibid., 58, 71. The increases were calculated between 1975 and 1998 by the US Equal Employment Opportunity Commission.

75. Ramona "Boots" Hines, interview.

76. Ibid.

77. Fonow, *Union Women*, 82.

78. Ramona "Boots" Hines, interview.

79. Fonow, *Union Women*, chap. 4.

80. Ramona "Boots" Hines, interview.

The Indenture of Mary Hollens

During the colonial era, thousands of Europeans signed legal, court-enforced agreements to exchange their labor for passage to America and food, clothing, and lodging during the period of their indenture, usually three to seven years. Few indentured servants arrived in America after the American Revolution. However, indentures continued to occur. Unlike indentured servants from Europe whose bonds were under the control of the courts, most of the indentured persons in Appalachia were American born and bound out through their local, usually county, government. Those who were bound out included indigent adults; illegitimate, orphaned, and mixed-race children; and persons who had no family or whose family could not care for them. Through county poorhouses, persons (predominately women and children) had their labor auctioned off. The majority became house servants or farm laborers. Children's indentures lasted until they reached the age of eighteen or twenty-one. It was also common for poor parents to bind out their children as apprentices, who not only were housed and fed but learned a trade as well. These indentures usually lasted from five to seven years. Although intended to alleviate poverty, indentures often served as means of social and racial control, to both manage those viewed as "public burdens" and reduce the free black population.[1]

The following indenture between Mary Hollen, an underage girl, and her master, John Dunkle, is a good example of apprenticeship indentures in Appalachia. Mary is expected to adhere to moral and social standards and be a "faithful apprentice," and, in return, John Dunkle agrees to provide food, clothing, shelter, education, and pay her a stipend at the end of her service.

This Indenture Witnesseth that John Davis one of the Overseers of the poor for Pendleton County and State of Virginia Doth put and Bind Mary Hollen to John Dunkle the third of Said County and State to Serve him from february one thousand Seven Hundred and Ninety Nine untill she Becomes of Age During all of which term her master faithfully Shall Serve her Secrets keep and all his Lawful Commands Every Whare Gladly Do She Shall Do no Damage to her Said Mastar She Shall not Wast her Mastars Goods nor Lend Unlawfully to Any She Shall not Commit fornication nor Contract Matrimony During the Said term She Shall not play at Cards nor Dice nor Any Other Unlawful Game Wherby her Said mastar may be Damaged With his Own Good or the Goods of Others She Shall not Absent her Self Day nor Night from her Said Mastars Service Unlawfully hant Ail houses taverns nor play houses But in all things Behave herself as a faithful apprentice Ought to Do and the Said mastar Shall procure and provid Sufficient meat Drink Washing Cloathing and Lodging and all Other Necessaries During the said term also her Said Mastar is to Learn her to Read and Right and to Learn her Some aid or art and to Give her twelve Dollars at the End of 2d term and for the true performances of all and Every the said Covanant and Agreement Either of the said parties Bindeth themselves unto the Other formly By these preasents in Witness Whereby we have Set our hands and Seals this Ninth Day of Feb 1801

| | John Davis | (Seal) |

Attst Jesse Morral

his

John   **X**   Dunkle

mark

Source: Indenture of Mary Hollen to John Dunkle, Harry F. Temple Papers, West Virginia and Regional History Collection, West Virginia University, Morgantown, West Virginia.

NOTE

1. See Wilma A. Dunaway, *Women, Work, and Family in the Antebellum Mountain South* (New York: Cambridge University Press, 2008), 251–52.

The Testimony of
Mrs. Maggie Waters

Between April 1912 and July 1913 a violent confrontation took place between striking coal miners and coal operators along Paint Creek and Cabin Creek in Kanawha County, West Virginia. In this prelude to the Matewan Massacre (1920) and the Battle of Blair Mountain (1921), striking miners wanted coal operators to accept and recognize their right to organize, and to bring an end to blacklisting, cribbing (which occurred when coal operators altered coal cars to hold more coal than their specified load but paid miners by the ton for the specified amount when they actually produced more), and compulsory use of the company store. In response, coal operators on Paint Creek and Cabin Creek hired the Baldwin-Felts Detective Agency to break the strike. The agency sent more than three hundred mine guards into the region to aid in the eviction of striking miners and their families from company housing and to ensure the safety of replacement workers (strikebreakers).

Most studies of the West Virginia Mine Wars focus on the striking miners and fail to examine the impact of the strikes on women or the actions women took to protect their homes, husbands, and family. At Paint Creek and Cabin Creek, it was the women who met trains coming into the coal camps in an attempt to educate strikebreakers or "scabs" on the reasons for the strike and to encourage the replacement workers to go home. Occasionally they used funds from the United Mine Workers Union to provide food for strikebreakers' children or to purchase return tickets home. When strikebreakers remained, the women joined picket lines with brooms and buckets to attack both strikebreakers and the mine guards who protected them. When arrested, they often took their babies to jail with them, hoping the annoyance of a crying baby would earn them an early release. Forced evictions from their homes often resulted in beatings, and sometimes rape. When the evicted miners and their families set up tent colonies in nearby Holly Grove, they suffered from hunger, cold, and unsanitary conditions. And when a group of Baldwin-Felts detectives attacked the Holly Grove miners' settlement with machine guns and rifles from an armored train known as the "Bull Moose Special," women took crowbars, pried up the rails, and threw them over the hill.

The violence at Paint Creek and Cabin Creek resulted in a United States Senate investigation into the working conditions of miners in the West Virginia coalfields. Maggie Waters, who ran a boardinghouse owned by Paint Creek Collieries at Banner Hollow, testified to the violence of the Baldwin-Felts detectives and the poverty that resulted from the company store's monopoly.

——

Mrs. Maggie Waters, a witness for the United Mine Workers, being first duly sworn, testified as follows:

Questions by Mr. Houston:—

Q. Where do you live?

A. I am living now at Handley.

Q. Are you married?

A. Yes, Sir.

Q. How much of a family have you?

A. I have six children.

Q. Is your husband dead?

A. No, sir.

Q. Where did you live prior to moving to Handley?

A. At Wacomah, what they call the left hand hollow of Banner.

Q. What is your husband engaged in?

A. At the present time, nothing. He was mine foreman for eight years until June 15th.

Q. At what mine?

A. Banner Mine.

Q. What Company owned that mine?

A. The Paint Creek Collieries Company.

Q. Is your husband one of the strikers?

298 WOMEN AND WORK IN APPALACHIA: DOCUMENTS

A. No, sir; he was discharged, I do not know whether you would call him a striker or not.

Q. How did you come to leave Paint Creek?

A. My husband was fired, and Mr. Green asked us when we intended to leave.

Q. When was that?

A. June 15th.

Q. Con you state the reason for your husband's discharge?

A. Yes, sir. There was three guards went to Frank Russe's house and broke the door open, and with their winchesters opened the house. I went to Mrs. Russe's house and asked her to stay with me until her husband was released. They had him arrested. She wrote a letter to her father. My husband was notified the Monday after that, they had no further use for him. Mr. Green told him it was for taking the miner's wife in. Mr. Green was the Superintendent of the Paint Creek Collieries Company.

Q. Who was this Mr. Russe you spoke of?

A. He was an Italian.

Q. Was he a miner?

A. Yes, he had worked about four years.

Q. Do you know why those guards invaded his home?

A. I do not.

Q. Did they have any child?

A. They had one baby and were expecting another baby soon. The Guards went up and excited his wife so that she went to her washing, and they pointed their guns at her, and she ran to my house as white as a corpse. She was an American woman, the daughter of Mr. Pauley of Blue Creek.

Q. What time of day was this she came to your house?

A. About ten o'clock. She came that morning. I went up for her after we had breakfast, and she was scared because the Guards threw their guns in her face. Her husband was home asleep. She said I will go home. She said she had some washing to do. She was fixing to wash when they went up there and tried to get her to tell something she knew nothing about. They told her she had to tell, and she grabbed her baby and ran to my house. That was about 10 o'clock when she came back.

Q. Was Mr. Russe working at night or during the day?

A. He was not working. He was a striker. I never saw him do anything at all after the strike.

Q. Whose property was he living in?

The Testimony of Mrs. Maggie Waters 299

A. The Paint Creek Collieries Company.

Q. What became of his furniture?

A. His wife sent it to Blue Creek where her father lives, and they threw him out when Frank was in Charleston. They brought his stuff in a wagon with the Guards with the American flag stuck up on the wagon.

Q. Do you know anything about Tony Sevilla and his family?

A. Yes, sir; he was the one they called the Italian. He was there when they killed the Italian.

Q. Who killed the Italian?

A. The Guards.

Q. Who was he?

A. I do not know his name; he was from Boomer. He was shot to pieces. Mrs. Sevilla sent me word to come down. I went to see her Sunday. I staid with her six hours. She dropped on her knees and waved her hands, and made a cross and was mumbling something in her own language I could not understand. When I asked her what was the matter, she was white as a corpse. She said "I am sick". I asked her what caused it, and she said the Guards slapped her on the side of the head and kicked her in the stomach. She expected to be a mother in two months. She was sick from the 9th day of June until the 6th day of August until the child was taken.

Q. Where is she now?

A. She is at Smithers Creek.

Q. What is her name?

A. Sevilla, the wife of Tony Sevilla.

Q. What County is Smithers Creek in?

A. In Fayette County, just across from Montgomery.

Q. When did you see her the last time?

A. I have not seen her since July.

Q. She is the wife of the man who was killed?

A. No, sir; she is the wife of another Italian. Her husband was in Ohio when they were shooting there in her house. They searched her house three times that day.

Q. How many children has this woman, Sevilla.

A. She had one child and was about to have another.

Q. At what hospital was the child born?

A. At the Sheltering Arms Hospital.

Q. Do you know whether that was a natural birth or not?

A. No, sir; it was not a natural birth.

Q. Was the child born dead or alive?

A. It was decade [dead] so the Doctors at the Hospital told me. Doctor Shaffer told her husband to rush his wife to the Hospital. He could do nothing for her.

Q. It was born dead?

A. It was taken by instruments.

Q. Do you know where Mrs. Sevilla is at present?

A. At Smithers Creek.

Q. How did you come to leave?

A. I was burned out.

Q. Whose property were you living in at the time?

A. The Paint Creek Collieries Company.

Q. Do you know how your house caught afire?

A. No, sir; I do not. When I awoke it was falling in. It was between half past three and four that morning. My husband was going with me that day to find something for our children to eat, and the Chief says, "Waters, what are you doing here." And he says "We are hunting something for our children to eat as our house burned down and everything burned up." And he said "Did you see my men." And my husband said "No, I saw nobody." He says "I sent two of my men at 2 o'clock this morning." My husband said "It was funny they did not rescue us."

Q. Did you lose your household effects?

A. Yes.

Q. Were any of your family injured?

A. No, sir.

Q. Are you acquainted with the prices charged by the Company store for groceries and supplies, and the prices charged by independent stores?

A. Yes, sir; I dealt there for eight years, and ran the Company boarding house for the Paint Creek Collieries Company.

Q. State in a general way whether the Companies sell supplies, groceries, etc., cheaper than the independent stores.

A. Higher. When I could buy meat for 13 cents a pound, I paid 25 cents at Wacomah. I told the Clerk that I could get it for that, and he said I could not. I came and bought my meat and showed him the bill. Breakfast bacom [bacon] was 13 cents and 25 to 26 cents at Wacomah; granulated sugar 10 cents a pount [pound], when I could get it anywhere for 6 ½ cents. Flour I paid as much as $8.00 a barrel for and could buy it for $5.25 outside. We were not allowed to buy it off the wagon and deal outside.

Q. Why were you not allowed to deal outside?

The Testimony of Mrs. Maggie Waters 301

A. The Company claimed the County road, and did not let outside wagons in. My son-in-law had worked this road, and the time was turned into the Company. The teamsters said they could not go over it. They said the Company owned this road. I told them the County owned the road, for my son-in-law worked the road and the store turned it into the County, and after that wagons would pass back and forth.

Q. Do you know the names of any of these Guards you have spoken of?

A. No, sir; I never thought enough of one to look him in the face.

Q. Have you ever seen any of them go armed?

A. Yes, and on Sunday too. But to look at one to [?] him, because I do not think enough of him to give him countenance.

Q. Do you know any other acts committed?

A. I saw one throw his gun on a man and search his pockets and empty them out. They made the man stoop over there and pick the things up. They did this and when they got through with him, they marched him down the road and got off the creek and never put his foot back on the Creek again. The man went down over the hill to go to Keeferton or Kinston. Jim Daws saw it too. The man was an Italian and could not speak a word of English.

Q. Is it possible for the average miner working the length of time he usually works during the month and receiving the pay the average miner receives, to save anything from his income?

A. No, sir, not if he deals at the store. It is impossible for him to save anything.

Q. What rent do you pay for that house?

A. $9.00, and there was cracks in it on the outside an inch wide. The chimney was falling down, and I asked Mr. Green to fix it, and he said "let the damn chimney go" On the lower side I could not have a fire in the chimney at all.

Q. How long did you occupy that house?

A. The first time, three years and nine months, and the time I moved back again. It was a jenny lind [Jenny Lind referred to a house built simply. It usually had a foundation of piers made from stone or wood and had no studs in the walls. Boards were nailed to the top and base of the house. As the wood dried, spaces were often left between the boards. Many Jenny Lind houses had battens or 2–3 inch boards nailed over the spaces creating what is commonly known as "board and batten" siding.] and weather boarded on the inside. I had to canvass and paper it myself.

Q. Was it plastered?

A. No, sir; it was ceiled.

Q. What sort of foundation did it have?

A. They were little blocks of wood put under it.

Q. Was it comfortable during the cold winter months?

A. No, sir; you could sit at the fire and burn your face, and freeze your back.

Q. How many rooms?

A. 6 down stairs and four up.

Q. Were you boarding miners?

A. Yes, sir.

Q. What did you charge them for board?

A. $20.00 a month including room. Some months the men did not make enough to pay it.

Q. Did the houses in that neighborhood have running water?

A. No, sir.

Q. Were any places provided where the miners could wash or take a bath?

A. At my house I had a wash house and had to stuff up the holes to keep the men from freezing when they were changing clothes.

Q. Do you know whether the miners were forced to deal at the Company store or not?

A. If they did not deal at the Company store they were kept out of work. They would say to the Mine Boss "that man does not deal with us, do not give him any work." I do not know whether that means to force them or not. I know when men went to board with me, they would say, "please draw my board in the store, or I will not get any work."

Q. Where was the Post Office located at Wacomah?

A. At Mucklow.

Q. Was it at the Company store?

A. They have a Post Office at Mucklow in one corner of the store.

Questions by Mr. Couch:—

Q. Mrs. Waters, describe the occasion when Mr. Frank Russe was arrested. Was that on June 10th?

A. No, sir; the 15th.

Q. Was that the morning the Italians house was shot at?

A. It was the morning the shooting occurred at Wacomah.

Q. The occasion on which the Italian was killed was it not?

A. That same morning Frank Russe was arrested with two or three others and brought to Charleston. It was up the hill, and there was nobody left but me. I live ¼ of a mile away.

The Testimony of Mrs. Maggie Waters 303

Q. The day he was arrested, was the same day the other Italians were arrested?

A. The same day they broke in the house and brought some of the men with guns to Charleston.

Q. Did you see the Guards mistreat Mrs. Russe on that occasion?

A. I was at the house when the Guards were there. She came running to my house and one of the Guards came down the road behind her.

Q. Do you know his name?

A. No, sir.

Q. Do you know about the alleged mistreatment of Mrs. Russe other than what she told you?

A. Her face was white, and I know she was running from the Guards.

Q. Did you see her running from them?

A. I was not there when they were.

Q. You spoke about Mrs. Sevilla. Did you see her mistreated in any way?

A. No, sir; she sent for me afterwards.

Q. Did you know the Guards?

A. No, sir.

Q. You did not see any?

A. No, sir; All I know is that she was sick when I went there, and she dropped on her knees and made a cross over her breast and seemed to be praying. She told me her condition, and I saw enough to prove she was sick.

Q. Did you see any marks or bruises.

A. I saw finger marks on her arm like you had pinched it, and she told me he kicked her in the stomach. She begged him not to kick her as she was going to become a mother. He cursed and told her what he would do.

Q. Do you know his name?

A. No, sir.

Q. Do you know the date?

A. June 15th, the same day the shooting happened. They went through her house when they shot the Italian.

Q. Who owned the house you were living in then?

A. The Paint Creek Collieries Company.

Q. You moved there and then moved away and back again?

A. Yes, sir; twice. The house was burned 9 years ago and the foundation was laid 9 years ago the 4th of last month.

Q. It was built for a boarding house?

A. Yes, sir.

Q. The only one there?

A. Yes, sir; at Banner Hollow. No one kept boarders at Wacomah except a private family would take in one or two.

Q. You went to Mr. Green and told him the chimney was falling in?

A. I showed it to him.

Q. Was your husband ever notified to move out?

A. The Superintendent asked me when we were going to move.

Q. Did they serve a written notice on you?

A. No, sir. He asked me several different times.

Q. Was your husband one of the strikers?

A. He got fired. I suppose he would be one.

Q. Does he belong to the union?

A. No, sir. The Mine Foreman does not belong to the union. They are supposed to give justice between the Operators and the Miners.

Q. Mr. Green said he fired your husband because he took in a Miner's wife?

A. Yes, sir.

Q. Did you hear him tell him that?

A. No, sir, I did not, but my husband told me.

Q. Mrs. Waters, did you ever see or hear any Agent or employee of the Paint Creek Collieries Company stop any person or persons from using the road you have described in front of your house?

A. I never saw it, but other people that lived around there, saw it. All I know is what the [?] told me. They were afraid to come up. Some of those teamsters from East Bank and Pratt.

Q. Did you not say that no miners ever saved anything at all?

A. If you could see the poor wives and children in rags, you would not think they saved money.

Q. I am asking you what you know. Do you wish to be understood as saying no union miner ever saved anything?

A. There may be a few, save a dollar or two, but I do not think they saved enough to amount to anything.

Q. Do you know of any miner being cut out because he failed to deal at the Company store?

A. I do not know anything about the miners affairs. I had the work to look after at the boarding house. I know nothing about their affairs.

Source: "Evidence Taken Before Mining Investigation Commission," West Virginia Mining Investigation Commission Papers, Box 1, Vol. 1, 170–80, West Virginia and Regional History Collection, West Virginia University, Morgantown, West Virginia.

A Working Woman Speaks

Following are two documents written by Bessie Edens of Hampton, Tennessee. Edens worked at American Bemberg, one of two factories manufacturing rayon or artificial silk (as many referred to it in the 1920s) in Elizabethton, Tennessee, a small town in Northeast Tennessee, about ten miles east of Johnson City. The other factory was American Glanzstoff (later North American Rayon); both were owned by the same German corporation. Edens wrote the pieces at the Southern Summer School for Women Workers in Industry, held in Burnsville, North Carolina, in August 1929. Founded in 1927, the school was part of the Affiliated Schools for Workers, which also included three northern schools for women workers. Through 1937, the southern school continued to be held at various locales. It became coeducational in 1938, when it changed its name to the Southern Summer School for Workers, Inc. The school disbanded in 1951. Both the northern and southern schools aimed to educate workers in a wide range of subjects, including labor economics, union activism, public health, and English composition. Although it is not clear how Edens found out about the school, it is likely that union leaders of the Elizabethton local of the United Textile Workers Union of America let her know about it.

My Work in an Artificial Silk Mill

I worked in the Bemberg plant in Elizabethton, Tennessee. It is an artificial silk mill.

The silk is made from cotton waste. They make this waste into a liquid form by using different kinds of chemicals, some very strong acids are used. No one knows the secret of making the silk but a few Germans. The liquid is put into glass funnels about twelve in a row, and these funnels have very small holes in the ends and this liquid runs through the holes and drops into clear water and turns to silk. . . . When the thread is formed in the water it is taken up on a reel that turns slowly . . . and when the reel is full the men lace the skeins with rubber gloves on. If they did not wear the gloves the acids would eat holes in their hands, and if they wear pants with cotton in them, or overalls they are eaten full of holes in a day or so, and the men wear rubber boots or overshoes, because there is water and acids on the floor. The silk is blue looking when it is in the first water. It has to be washed and dried several times before it comes to the textile room where I work. And the wages are very low for the men.

It is dangerous for the men to work in the chemical department. I have known several to lose their eyes by getting something in them in there. And two that I know of lost their lives. And it is very unhealthy for the men in the spinning room. Anyone not used to it can hardly get their breath when they first go in, the ammonia is so strong.

The textile room is in good sanitary condition. We have plenty of air and plenty of light. But the girls have to work so hard. They work ten hours a day and don't make enough to live on.

When the thread first comes into the textile room it is inspected and passed to the winders. The winders wind it on to a bobbin about four or five inches high. Then it comes to the twister where I work. We have long machines with one hundred and sixty spindles on it, a spindle holds one bobbin of thread. We put the thread on every spindle and wrap it on to another bobbin higher up on the machine. One girl operates a machine. A real good operator will keep up every end all the time. But it keeps them very busy all day long. Sometimes the thread is given a harder twist than at other times. We call it a turn. When we give it five turns the machine does not run so fast, a girl can keep that machine up very easily. When we give ten or twelve turns it runs real slowly. Then we have two and one half turns. It runs so fast you can hardly see it. We usually have a real good operator on that and she has to work so hard and fast when it is five-thirty, she can hardly breathe. I have known them to work all day and not take time to go to the wash room, and we only have thirty minutes for lunch.

The girls are all on piece work now. They are supposed to run sixty-five, seventy-five or ninety pounds (according to the turn) for one dollar and eighty cents a day, and so much for extra pounds. Some of the girls run as high as one hundred and twenty-five pounds a day. About the highest any of them made would be fourteen dollars a week, and work like killing snakes for that!

After I had been there a year I was given the job of being a forelady and was paid $16.30 a week. I had to carry passes in my pocket for the girls if they wanted to go to the wash room, and they would have to come and ask me if they could go. Every day they would make new rules and all seemed to be getting harder. If a girl was caught sitting down for one minute she was discharged, and she was not allowed to talk to the girl that worked by her. If I

A Working Woman Speaks 307

happened to help a girl work and the foreman saw me, I would get something like this: "You are not supposed to help any of these girls, you are to see that they do their work and do it well, and if they can't do it we will send them home."

The girls were not satisfied, but were afraid to say anything. I have heard the girls say it was like a jail, but they had to work somewhere. And the men were being treated in the same way. The men stood it as long as they could, and they had a strike a little over a year ago. They did not have a union at that time, and they did not gain anything. Some of them were fired and never allowed to work there again. And the company took some of them back, and the ones that went back formed a secret union. They kept putting more work on them all the time. In January they cut off about half of the girls in our room and I think they cut some of the men off too and told them they would be off for sixty days. They kept the best operators of course, so they doubled their work, and if one said anything about it they were told that they ought to consider themselves lucky because they got to stay and work. And they cut of all the boys that carried bobbins to the girls, so the girls had to do that and it made less wages for them. They did not like it, but all seemed to be afraid to kick about it.

When the Glanzstoff had the first strike the Bemberg girls didn't want to strike because they were afraid and the Glanzstoff girls got less wages than the Bemberg girls. So Bemberg closed down until everything was settled. An agreement had been made that the union people would be treated as well as the non-union. But they did not do what they agreed to do. After the kid-napping [of two union officials by business and civic leaders of Elizabethton] I decided to join the union. I talked to several girls and got them to join. I had been a member one week when the next strike happened. Glanzstoff started it. Several hundred came up to the Bemberg gates. About fifty men and boys climbed the fence and came into the plant. It scared the foreman and Germans stiff. I did not know what it was all about but I had an idea. I saw two boys I knew that belonged to the union, and I asked them what they wanted. They told me to strike. I said alright we will strike. I found five union girls and told them to follow me. We went downstairs and punched our cards and I went on out side. We were out quite awhile and no one followed. I knew there were more union people in there, but they seemed afraid to come out. So we got the boys to open the gate. I never knew how they got it open. Anyway the Glanzstoff people got in, and we five girls led them back into Bemberg. We turned off all machines, blew the whistle and ordered them out. Some of them did not want to go out, but they thought it best.

This plant is owned by several different ones. The Germans are the controlling stock holders. There are several company houses. They are nice little four rooms; or five, six or eight rooms with water, electricity and bathroom in most of them. The rent is not so high now as it was before the strike. A small house that was $34.00 a month is about $22.00 a month now.

Before the strike there was no recreation of any kind. They have ball games now, and an amusement park, where they can go to on Sunday if they wish and I think they have given two big dances since the strike.

Bessie Edens.

Why a Married Woman Should Work

It is nothing new for married women to work. They have always worked. Before the machine age, the women had to spin and weave the cloth for all the garments used by the entire family. After the cloth was woven, they had to cut and make suits, dresses and all the necessary articles. They knit stocking and socks and made all the bed clothing. Women have always worked harder than men and always had to look up to the man and feel that they were weaker and inferior. Nearly all men want us to feel that way.

Now that there are many machines in the world to make all kinds of clothing and every thing we need, what is the married woman expected to do? Her husband does not make enough to support the family if they have a large one. Or sometimes a husband does not want to support them, (there are plenty of men like that), then is a woman supposed to stay in the home and do with out things she really needs because she is married? I say, no. If a married woman has a chance to work and wants to, I say she has a perfect right to do so.

Or sometimes a woman that is married does not have to work, but she has a feeling she would like to earn some money and be independent, would like to know that she could spend her money as she wished, and not feel like her husband has worked for the money and she ought not to spend it so freely. Many women do not like to ask their husbands for money even though they are willing to give to them. I have heard married women say they would much rather do without things than to ask their husbands for the money to get them.

Why should not a married woman work, if a single one does? What would men think if they were told that a married man should not work? And if a married man works, why should not a married woman work if she wants

A Working Woman Speaks 309

to? Is the world made for the unmarried people? If it was like that, how many married people do you think would have the necessary things they would need in life?

If we women would not be so submissive and take every thing for granted, if we would awake and stand up for our rights, this world would be a better place to live in, at least it would be better for the women.

Just suppose that a young girl working in a factory today, and making enough money to buy very nice clothes and go to shows or any where she wishes, and does not have to ask any one for money to pay her way, if she decides to get married and the young man she marries does not make enough money to furnish the home and buy the clothes that he and she have been used to, should the girl just sit down and do without these things because she is a married woman? Or perhaps the husband did make plenty of money, but was selfish with it and wanted to put it all in his business. Is a woman supposed to sit around and be content with the little amount of money he hands out to her?

There are many employers who would rather have married women or old maids to work for them, because they say that the flappers do not have their minds on their work as well as the women with a settled mind. Of course all foremen are not like that, because some of them would rather have the pretty flappers regardless of what kind of work they do. But I say that a married woman has as much right to work as a single one, if she wants to.

Most single girls think that they will work just a year or so and get married and then all will be roses for them. They do not realize that their work has just started in earnest then. If a girl should be so unlucky as to get a husband who liked his whiskey (as a great many of them do) and the husband would like to take his money and spend it all for drinks, and there would not be any money to buy food and perhaps they had children, would it be all right to let the children go without food and clothes? Or would it be better for the poor mother to do washings for different people and earn a dollar a day for the hardest day's work a woman has ever done? And if there was a factory in that place where a woman could get work that would not be so hard as washing, and the pay would be three or four dollars a day or some times more, would it be all right for that woman to say, "Well it ought to be this way, I am married and a married woman has no right to work where she can earn more. That is for the single girls." Well, if the world was like that, I think every girl would show good sense to remain single. Or suppose a woman has been married several years, and had four or five children, and the husband should desert them and leave town with a good looking flapper, and

310 WOMEN AND WORK IN APPALACHIA: DOCUMENTS

the mother and children had no money to buy food or clothes, how would they live if the mother had to wait until she could get a divorce before she could go to a factory to work? Or where, would she ever get any money for a divorce, *poor married woman?*

I know some married women who work because their husbands will not, and never would. The women have to work or starve, and I admire any married woman that is not too lazy to work.

Some girls think that as long as mother takes in washings, keeps ten or twelve boarders or perhaps takes in sewing, she isn't working. But I say that either one of the three is as hard work as women could do. So if they do that at home and don't get any wages for it, why would it not be all right for them to go to a factory and receive pay for what they do?

Bessie Edens.

Source: Bessie Edens wrote these two selections for the 1929 Southern Summer School for Women Workers in Industry's "Scraps of Work and Play" volume, which is archived in the American Labor Education Service Records, 1927–1962, Martin P. Catherwood Library, Cornell University, Ithaca, New York.

The Pikeville Methodist Hospital Strike

On June 10, 1972, more than two hundred support staff (clerks, cooks, nurses' aides, and others) at the Pikeville Methodist Hospital in Pikeville, Kentucky, began a long and violent strike to obtain recognition of their union, the Communication Workers of America (CWA), AFL-CIO. Ninety percent of the striking workers were women—mothers, daughters, wives, and sisters—who had never walked a picket line before. After a nearly a decade of strikes and legislative battles, the strike ended in March 1980 following a court decision in *Methodist Hospital of Kentucky, Inc. v. the National Labor Relations Board* (NLRB).

Grievances began soon after the Pikeville Miner's Hospital (a UMWA hospital) consolidated with the Pikeville Methodist Hospital (Methodist Hospitals of Kentucky), undergoing reorganization that strongly favored the company over the workers. The hospital expanded health care but failed to hire additional staff. Workers faced unreasonable workloads and were often instructed to perform duties they were not trained to do. Coercive management policies due to understaffing resulted in demanding work schedules, unscheduled overtime, and discriminatory suspensions and discharges. Workers had no job security, no promotions, no seniority rights, no retirement benefits, and inadequate medical and unemployment insurance. They averaged $1.75 an hour in wages.[1]

Although the strike ended in October 1974, the hospital refused the union's request to reinstate the employees to their former positions or to accept their applications as new workers. The strike resulted in amendments to the National Labor Relations Act that brought nonprofit health care institutions under the act. The court's decision in 1980 required the hospital to reinstate the strikers to their former positions without prejudice to seniority and required the hospital to reimburse the workers for "earnings lost due to discrimination."[2]

EXCERPT FROM *MOUNTAIN LIFE AND WORK*

The hospital strike in Pikeville, Kentucky, has been to a large extent led by women, the picket line "manned" by women, and the majority of the strikers are women. ML&W—Does the fact that most of you are women have any effect on the picket line?

When there's men around, the people crossing the picket line respect the women.

Any time the women have trouble on the picket line, the men take off. The women'll stand up and fight. They [men] are not even responsible about walking the picket line.

How do you feel about being on the picket line?

I've been called a whore and a bitch since I went out on strike. The night the boy called me a slut made me madder than anything else.

If I know the truth about myself what somebody else calls me doesn't matter.

Would it be better if there were more men on strike?

The women's got more guts than the men.

They've [women] got more determination.

We don't sit and play cards on the picket line like the men do. They have no responsibility about the strike.

Why do the women feel more responsible than the men?

There's more women out on strike.

The women realize what this strike's going to mean to this community and their children. Our women are concerned about what the future generation will have to go through if we don't win this strike.

How has your home life changed since the strike?

I don't have a home life.

I've had so much company since this strike and enjoyed myself.

How will things be different when you go back to work?

I will not respect the scabs. I won't speak to them when I go back in. I'll be writing lots of notes.

You can't have a barrier and work with people; you can't do your best work.

People will say more [about conditions in the hospital], they won't be as afraid.

The Pikeville Methodist Hospital Strike 313

Were you treated any different at the hospital because you were a woman?

No, it was according to who you were and who you knew and how much you were worth.

Do the CWA officials [union officials] treat you differently than if you were men?

I'd say there'd be a difference. Men feel like they know more about things like this than women do. They feel like they can express themselves better.

Do you think the men should have been the leaders?

The majority of what's striking is women. We only have 25 to 30 men on strike. There are 180 women out. The men don't care enough or know enough. I don't know which, to be leaders.

How should the contract be negotiated?

There should be one out of each department sit in on that contract. Housekeeping don't know what the kitchen needs, the kitchen don't know what nurse's aides want, I don't know about the business department. If somebody from each department isn't in on the negotiations, something will be left out.

What if somebody told you that since you were a woman you should stay at home, how would you answer them?

I'd say give our husbands more pay and I'll stay at home. Not really, I enjoy people too much to sit at home. I get in a rut. I'm not a housekeeper, period. If I didn't work, I'd have to find something in the community to do.

When my youngins were small, I'd have enjoyed staying home, but then I couldn't. Now I enjoy getting out, I couldn't stay home.

Source: "WOMEN," *Mountain Life and Work* 48 (November 1972): 3–5.

NOTES

1. Kathy Pellegrino, "Strike Vigil: Pikeville Hospital Picketed," *Kentucky New Era*, April 14, 1973.

2. For a full analysis of the strike, see Sally Ward Maggard, "'We're Fighting Millionaires!' The Clash of Gender and Class in Appalachian Women's Union Organizing," in *No Middle Ground: Women in Radical Protest*, ed. Kathleen Blee (New York: New York University Press, 1998), 289–306.

Poetry from the *Coal Mining Women's Support Team News*

The poems that follow appeared in a publication called *Coal Mining Women's Support Team News,* a newsletter published by regional support groups of Coal Employment Project (CEP) women miners. Support groups existed in East Tennessee, eastern and western Kentucky, Southwest Virginia, western Pennsylvania, and southern Illinois. The parent organization, CEP, was unique among women's organizations in Appalachia, in that it both helped women find employment as miners and advocated on their behalf in regard to such concerns as sexual harassment on the job, safe working conditions, equitable wages, and parental leave.

The Coal Employment Project was born in May 1977, as the Coal Employment Project of the East Tennessee Research Corporation (ETRC). The founding of CEP stemmed directly from an incident in which a mine operator in Campbell County, Tennessee, refused to allow underground a woman who was part of a planned tour sponsored by ETRC and Save Our Cumberland Mountains, both Jacksboro, Tennessee, grassroots organizations. ETRC's director Neil McBride contacted his friend Betty Jean Hall, then working as a lawyer in Washington, D.C., to research the topics of women in mining and federal law on gender discrimination in hiring mining. As a consequence of conducting the research, Hall became interested in the subject of women in mining and agreed to accompany McBride on a trip to New York City to raise funds to start an organization dedicated to researching issues linked to women in mining. Securing a $5,000 grant from the Ms. Foundation allowed the establishment of the Coal Employment Project of ETRC. Hall became CEP's first director.

CEP quickly made an impact. After Hall spent a year conducting research on women in mining and interviewing women miners, CEP filed a gender discrimination in hiring complaint against 153 coal companies. The suit generated a great deal of publicity and resulted in the expansion of CEP and its becoming in July 1978 a separate Tennessee nonprofit organization. CEP moved its office from Jacksboro to Oak Ridge, Tennessee. Soon (in 1979), Hall resigned as director, but stayed on as legal counsel with an office (the Legal Support Office) in Dumfries, Virginia. Over the years, it added field offices in Hazard, Kentucky, and Westernport, Maryland; regional support teams; and a western area coordinator in Denver, Colorado. The national CEP office relocated to Knoxville, Tennessee, in the late 1980s.

CEP worked tirelessly on behalf of women miners, in the face of opposition from both coal companies and the United Mine Workers of America. In the late 1980s, the number of women miners peaked at between three and four thousand, approximately 4 percent of about 98,000 miners total. But the 1990s saw layoffs and reductions in work nationally in coal mines, as demand for coal dropped and as mechanization in underground mining and reliance on surface strip mining led to significant decreases in mining jobs. Women often were victims of the "last hired, first fired" rule. As of 1996, approximately one thousand women worked as miners.

CEP remained active in the 1990s, in both mining and nonmining areas: The slogan of the 1990s captured the essence of the CEP and revealed how the organization had evolved over the years: "Building Women's Solidarity in the Coalfields and Beyond." CEP participated in the Pittston Coal Strike of 1989–90 in Southwest Virginia; it reached out to low-paid women workers in such nonunionized industries as poultry processing; and it became interested in such issues as domestic violence. But hard times in mining, as well as the drying up of CEP's private sources of funding, caused it to close down in 1996.

POETRY FROM THE *CWST NEWS*

Let Us Unite
—a song by Jean Steffey

> Brothers we don't want to take your jobs away,
> Just want a better life with better pay,
> Sisters we don't want your man,
> Just to make the best living we can.
> *
>
> We're willing to go down in a deep dark mine,
> Willing to stand in the picket line,

We'll back the union all the way,
For a better life and a brighter day.
*
We're not saying we can do it all,
Sometimes we'll stumble and we'll fall,
Brothers please lend us a hand,
Divided we fall, united we stand

*(Repeat first verse)

Source: *Coal Mining Women's Support Team News* (hereafter *CWST News*) 1, no. 7 (January–February 1979): 2. Coal Employment Records, Archives of Appalachia, East Tennessee State University, Johnson City, Tennessee (hereafter CER).

Six Good Reasons
By Joyce Dukes

I've got six good reasons for being a woman coal miner.
Their names are Bobby, Jimmy, Johnnie, Beth, Mary and Vickie Sue,
And they are counting on me to pull us through.
Times have been hard, but we are moving toward a better day,
Where women who do equal work can get equal pay.

Lord knows I didn't plan to raise six children all alone,
But somewhere between bottles and diapers and paying the bills,
Nighttime feedings, fever, croop and the chills,
Their father turned and he walked out the door,
Leaving me to try to explain why he won't be coming home anymore.

But we're going to make it, don't you see,
Told that bitchy woman what she could do with her AFDC.
And I went to work in a union mine,
Where the benefits are good and the pay's just fine.

I've got six good reasons for being a woman coal miner,
Their names are Bobby, Jimmy, Johnnie, Beth, Mary and Vickie Sue,
So you see Brother, I need this job just the same as you,
I'm working to support my family—we deserve something too.

Let's stand together and make our union strong,
Let's raise our voices in unified song,

There is room for women and men,
Standing together is the only way to win.

Source: CWST News 3, no. 3 (September–October 1980): 12–13, CER.

A Coalminer's Lament
By Deborah Ralsovich

I work and toll to earn my pay,
Just thankful, I've made another day.

Sometimes I wonder why I'm here—
The sweat, the pain, the constant fear.

I sigh and know why I'm here today,
It's to try and earn an honest day's pay.

The tops a-falling all around,
Clouds of dust rise from the ground.

We sniff and snort that nasty air.
While it fills are lungs without a care.

I know I'll make it one more day—
Cause Fridays always on its way.

The boss is squalling, "Plow that coal"
Tonight we'll set a record goal.

We set our goal then with dismay
A Hershey bar is on its way.

This way of life I'll leave someday,
No jobs to find, I guess I'll stay.

Source: CWST News 3, no. 5 (December 1980): 12, CER.

Way Down in That Deep Dark Hole
By Veronica Marshall

It's a good paying job,
The work is hard,
The air is thick and black.

Your back gets stiff,
And your knees get black,
And that belt keeps moving on,

"Way down in that deep dark hole."

My children say,
"Mama please don't go

"Way down in that deep dark hole."

O children, O children,
Don't you cry.

I have to work somewhere,
Your Daddy's gone three years ago,
And the rent is due,
And I have to feed your hungry ways,

"Way down in that deep dark hole."

Where the fans are blowing
The belts are whining,
And another day starts moving,

"Way down in that deep dark hole."

Source: CWST News 3, no. 7 (February 1981): 6, CER.

Two of the tiny workers, a raveler and a looper, in the Loudon Hosiery Mills, Loudon, Tennessee, 1910. *Library of Congress, National Child Labor Committee, Louis Wickes Hine, photographer.*

The Cherokee Hosiery Mill, Rome, Georgia, 1913. *Library of Congress, National Child Labor Committee, Lewis Wickes Hine, photographer.*

The finishing department at Empire Laundry, Clarksburg, West Virginia, 1914. *West Virginia and Regional History Center, WVU Libraries.*

Conie Mauk, Rebie Farrell, "Moonlight Teachers out after illiterates," Rowan County, Kentucky. *Cora Wilson Stewart Collection, University of Kentucky, Lexington.*

The covering room, Fokker Aircraft Corp. David Anderson, Photographer, 1929. *West Virginia and Regional History Center, WVU Libraries.*

Women sewing at machines in the Goodyear rubber plant in Gadsden, Etowah County, Alabama, during World War II, 1941–45. *US War Department Photo. Alabama Department of Archives and History, Montgomery.*

Betty Jean Hall, cofounder of the Coal Employment Project (1977). The CEP encouraged the hiring of and advocated legally for women miners. Hall served in a number of capacities for CEP, including executive director and legal counsel, 1977–87. Following her CEP career, she practiced public interest law and served as chief administrator and appeals judge for the US Department of Labor Benefits Review Board (1994–2001). *Coal Employment Project Records, Archives of Appalachia, East Tennessee State University, Johnson City.*

Pat Estrada shoveling coal in an underground mine, Harlan County, Kentucky, August 1983. *Photo permission from Marat Moore, photographer. Coal Employment Project Records, Archives of Appalachia, East Tennessee State University, Johnson City.*

Carol Davis Jones: coal miner, Coal Employment Project member, and activist. Jones at present organizes home health care workers in Pennsylvania. *Coal Employment Project Records, Archives of Appalachia, East Tennessee State University, Johnson City.*

Part 2: Women and Work in Appalachia

Questions for Discussion

1. Historically, what has constituted "women's work" in the Mountain South? How have social, economic, and political conditions in the Mountain South shaped the boundaries of women's work in Appalachia?

2. How have race, class, and gender affected women's work in the Mountain South?

3. Who has defined women's work in the Mountain South? And, in what ways has the definition of women's work in the Mountain South shaped their identity?

4. What do these essays and documents tell us about the economic position of women in the Mountain South? Have economic conditions for women in the region improved?

5. Do you think gender integration in underground mines was successful or not? If you were a young woman living in the Mountain South today, would you apply for a job in the mines? Why or why not?

6. What jobs are available to women living in the Mountain South today? Do women have equal opportunities for employment and wages?

PART THREE

Women and Activism in the Mountain South

"Anger and love have kept me going. Love can be a real revolutionary. There is a sense in which you care about people and don't like to see people hurt; you believe in equality."

—Helen Lewis, interview with Libby Falk Jones, *Appalachian Heritage,* Summer 2006

CHAPTER ELEVEN

In the Footsteps of Mother Jones, Mothers of the Miners

Florence Reece, Molly Jackson, and Sarah Ogan Gunning

H. ADAM ACKLEY

Using traditional Appalachian maternal authority in new and unusual ways, mid-twentieth-century Kentuckian labor activists Florence Reece, Molly Jackson, and folksinger Sarah Ogan Gunning drew on the more radical view of mother–labor organizer first pioneered in the region's coal industry and later nationally by Mary Harris "Mother" Jones. By giving leadership not only to a regional labor movement but also to national struggles for socioeconomic justice and civil rights, they directly contradicted the common, domesticated view of Appalachian women as passive and confined primarily to the home.[1] Although Jones hailed from Ireland and lived much of her life in urban Chicago, she worked with striking coal miners in West Virginia from 1897 onward as part of her work with the United Mine Workers of America (UMWA) and soon became associated closely with the West Virginia region.[2] In fact, the West Virginia mining strike of 1913, which the historian Elliott Gorn describes as "one of the longest and bloodiest labor conflicts in American history," marked the height of Jones's fame and influence.[3] Reece and Jackson later drew on Jones's legacy in the central Appalachian region in their own union-organizing efforts on

327

behalf of coal miners. In the late 1950s and early 1960s, Jackson's much younger half sister, Sarah Ogan Gunning, a singer-songwriter of protest songs, also promoted and expanded to a wider national audience their shared legacy of activism for Appalachian miners and their families. Reece and Jackson's labor-organizing influence and success in bringing national attention to regional economic struggles was particularly important to the region and nation after Jones's death in 1930, a year that saw coal company guards shoot so many striking miners on Kentucky's Pine Mountain that Reece remembered its woods covered with their bones throughout the Great Depression.[4]

Like many historians focused on American labor and music, activist Pat Wynne recognizes the importance for the nation of the Central Appalachian labor movement of the Great Depression. It was publicized nationally not only through newspaper accounts but also by recordings and performances of original labor protest songs sung and written by Reece and Jackson, and later remembered in Gunning's songs and interviews. Even though these women were well known to their contemporaries, and still are to scholars for their musical impact on a national audience, Wynne explains how all three are deeply connected specifically to the labor movement of the Central Appalachian region:

> Harlan County, Kentucky, . . . in the 1920s and 1930s, many workers
> and their families found themselves negotiating the transition
> from farming to coal mining. The women were raised as daughters
> of miners and then, at fourteen or fifteen, they married miners.
> Times were desperate and poor. When the unions came to organize
> the miners, Harlan County became a war zone: "Down in Harlan
> County there are no Neutrals there," as Florence Reece sang in
> "Which Side Are You On?"[5]

The editors of the American folk music magazine *Sing Out!* prefaced a 1976 interview with Gunning by highlighting the national importance of these three Appalachian women's protest songs: "Some of the most militant and memorable labor songs in American history were written by strong mountain women fighting for survival in the coal fields of Kentucky."[6] Specifically, as cultural anthropologist Mary Bufwack and music journalist Robert Oermann observe in their comprehensive

328 H. ADAM ACKLEY

survey of women pioneers of American "country" music, *Finding Her Voice: Women in Country Music, 1800–2000*, Reece, Jackson, and Gunning's Harlan County context brought a national spotlight to their labor organizing work and songs. As Bufwack and Oermann explain, "Bloody" Harlan, as home to the state's biggest thirties-era mining strikes, "became the archetype of worker-versus-owner, good-versus-evil" in national depression-era struggles over power and economic justice in general. Nationally, the mining camps of Harlan County thus became a "meeting ground" for political progressives and folk musicians (including Jackson, Reece, and Gunning).[7]

TRADITIONAL APPALACHIAN DOMESTIC MATERNAL AUTHORITY AS CONTEXT

As women's studies scholar Karen Tice recounts, in the century before the Great Depression, many American writers tended to present Appalachian people as "unique in their manner of living and cultural ways," culturally backward and deficient, particularly with regard to the "archaic" rigidity of "an antiquated set of gender norms."[8] Tice notes that writers, educators, and journalists, in and especially outside the Appalachian region, have tended consistently to portray Appalachian women as exerting influence primarily, or even exclusively, within the domestic sphere—particularly in the role of mother or grandmother. This perception of Appalachian women continued to be promoted in recent contemporary popular culture, as journalist Kathy Kahn identifies in her 1970s work on Harlan County.[9] Educators, sociologists, anthropologists, and religious studies scholars such as Sharon Lord, Carolyn Patton-Crowder, Virginia and Clyde McCoy, Diana Gullett Trevino, Patricia Beaver, and Erica Hurwitz agree that in the past, even until very recently, Appalachian women were expected to gain authority within the culture itself through aging, marriage, and child rearing (primarily as mothers), rather than directly through activities in the public sphere.[10] Tice, for example, cites the work of two educators in the region, Ethel deLong and Lucy Furman, during the early decades of the twentieth century, as promoting the idea "that older mountain women and grandmothers possessed special talents and knowledge [that] could easily be enlisted in the educational mission."[11]

In the Footsteps of Mother Jones 329

At the dawn of the twenty-first century, the central Appalachian region still remained distinctive for economic and social factors that continue to limit women's work outside the home, thus reinforcing the domestic maternal role as the only avenue for adult influence for most women of the region. Economists Cynthia Rogers and Kimberly Mencken and sociologist F. Carson Mencken demonstrate that due to the economic dynamics of coal mining introduced in the late nineteenth century, "the Central subregion" of Appalachia (inclusive of West Virginia and southern Ohio) is still one of "the most economically depressed areas in the country" in ways that disproportionately impact women.[12] A regional lack of child care options and far higher rates of disability than elsewhere in the nation limit Central Appalachian women's participation in work outside the home far more than anywhere else in either Appalachia itself or the United States as a whole. Because of the disproportionate absence of social capital in Central Appalachia, particularly in the form of day care and preschools, women of this region tend to be isolated in the home (caring full time for their children and grandchildren, for example) to a significantly higher degree than elsewhere in the United States. According to Rogers, Mencken, and Mencken: "Compared with the rest of the nation and the rest of Appalachia, Central Appalachia has more extractive industries and blue collar occupations, which are [still] not as conducive to female employment (in part because they are less "flexible" and "service" oriented) as are other occupations and industries."[13] These unique regional economic conditions and their gender dynamics were introduced in the late twentieth century and endured through the turn of the millennium, thus affecting Jones, Reece, Jackson, and Gunning as well as the Daughters of Mother Jones working in the region today.

During their years in the region, Reece, Jackson, and Gunning were deeply affected by these unique socioeconomic dynamics, just as Jones had been earlier as a young wife and mother in Tennessee. However, unlike many other Appalachian women of their own time, the tragic losses of their children and husbands, along with the widespread poverty and labor exploitation of their neighbors, drove all four of these particular widows—mothers grieving dead children—out of the home to speak publicly on behalf of other local workers and their families.

Reece, Jackson, and Gunning's outspoken activism and public protest singing were exceptional, challenging the usual limitations placed on women not only in their culture but also, in particular, of their time. Their exceptional behavior, however, seems to draw on a specific earlier model of maternal authority radiating outside the home (when husband and children are dead) outward into public leadership, pioneered in northern Appalachian coal communities by "Mother" Jones. As Meridel LeSueur, who participated in one of Mother Jones's strikes, observed of women's participation in early labor organizing before women won the right to vote, "For a woman to speak publicly was hard to do and not common. Even in my time men got up and left and had meetings in the hall when a woman had the floor."[14] As historian Elliott Gorn demonstrates in his meticulous 2001 biography of Jones, the union ideal to which Jones was originally exposed through her husband, George Jones, a member of the International Iron Molders' Union (IIMU) in Tennessee, was not to "do for" people but to empower them to "do for themselves."[15] After yellow fever caused the death of her husband and children, Jones returned to Chicago, where she had previously spent less than a year as a dressmaker before moving to Memphis. That earlier move to Tennessee for a teaching job had led to her marriage and family life in the region. After her return to Chicago as a widow to resume dressmaking, her life was again thrown into upheaval when her shop was lost to the Great Chicago Fire of 1871. Historian Marie Tedesco explains that within ten years after her husband's death, Jones had become involved in railroad labor strikes and by the 1890s was a key UMWA organizer who "gained fame as an agitator for coal miners, particularly in West Virginia."[16] As a labor organizer from the late nineteenth through the early twentieth century, she helped to organize child mill and mine workers and their families throughout the country, most notably in Appalachia.

Though the labor movement may have been more egalitarian than the dominant culture, possibilities for women to hold union leadership positions were still quite limited. The patriarchal structure and dynamics of the UMWA in particular and the labor movement in general prevented Jones from being able to attend meetings in the early years of her interest in labor and from holding office in spite of the importance of her leadership within the UMWA.[17] At the very least, Appalachian coal miners such as John Brophy, who first met Jones as an organizer in the

In the Footsteps of Mother Jones 331

Pennsylvania coalfields in the 1890s, respected and appreciated her but found her public activism and entry into the mines "an odd kind of work for a woman in those days."[18] At a time when in most places women were not allowed to participate in civic affairs even by voting, Jones acknowledged that some union men "didn't want a woman in the field."[19] She responded to criticisms and questions about a woman's participation in public activism by appealing to a mother's "right" to care publicly for those whom she privately has birthed and nurtured, always struggling alongside them with love. She explicitly evoked the empowering and supportive love of Jesus's mother, Mary, as an example of a self-sacrificial, unconditionally loving, but widely recognized maternal authority.[20]

Thus, although Reece, Jackson, and Gunning's outspokenness built on their traditional authority within their communities as mothers, wives, and elders, by organizing and singing in public venues *beyond* their own homes, churches, and local communities, they used traditional Appalachian maternal authority in new and unusual ways, drawing on the more radical view of mother–labor organizer first pioneered in the region, specifically in the coal industry, by Jones. Reece and Jackson seem to have drawn specifically on the maternal model of Appalachian community organizing pioneered by Jones, while Gunning promoted and expanded on Reece and Jackson's later legacy of Appalachian women's protest songwriting—itself breaking free of its usual domestic context.[21] Gorn argues that Jones intentionally crafted and promoted her public persona as "Mother," building on her maternal authority not only as the mother of her own particular family (the husband and children she had lost tragically) but as a "true mother" representing and leading *all* workers.[22] Jones even "signed all of her letters 'Mother,'" a term by which even American presidents addressed her, Gorn recounts.[23] Unlike Jones, however, Reece, Jackson, and Gunning were born in the Central Appalachian region, maintained ties to the region for much of their lives, and were more than "mothers" to the striking miners. They were also widely recognized beyond the coal industry and region as writers of protest songs that brought the plight of the miners and their families to the attention of a much wider national audience.

These women's role as nationally recognized singer-songwriters of folk ballads whose content and performance style were distinct to

Appalachian women is especially significant. As Bufwack and Oermann so convincingly have demonstrated, there "was a female musical tradition in America long before the advent of entertainment industries. Women's activities as collectors of songs and as singers reflected their central family role as provider[s] and mother[s]" and "bearers of tradition. And because women were so central as teachers and keepers of the culture, a distinct female point of view was passed through the generations."[24] Even though today such scholars as Joe Wilson, John Alexander Williams, and Jane Becker contest the existence of a distinctive Appalachian musical tradition, early to mid-twentieth-century folk music collectors such as Olive Dame Campbell, John and Alan Lomax, and Ralph Peer published and recorded works they argued represented a unique regional folk tradition. Their activities promoting Appalachian folk music as a unique American genre overlapped with the time that Jones, Reece, Jackson, and Gunning were also living and working in the region.[25] Their songs drew on a domestic tradition of women's song in the region, passed down from mothers to daughters each generation, according to Bufwack and Oermann. The women folksingers of the region during the Great Depression era outnumbered men by roughly two to one. Their role as nationally recognized singers reinforced their maternal leadership and union organizing: within Appalachia, just for their singing and songwriting alone, many "were considered community treasures—one culturally distinct way in which their maternal singing had influence beyond their own homes.[26]

Their use of these songs in protest and labor activism was reinforced by the regional folk tradition of women's lament songs. Folklorists and scholars such as Lomax and Campbell observed that Appalachian women's distinct musical tradition included songs of complaint most often sung by Appalachian mothers and grandmothers "as an accompaniment to housework."[27] Though in Chicago and New York, for example, there were women textile workers also striking during this era, it is the Kentuckian mothers Reece, Gunning, and Jackson who most successfully led organized labor by drawing on their particular context, a distinctively Appalachian tradition of musical protest against the hard lot of women and their responsibility to warn others about it through honest and raw motherly singing.

In the Footsteps of Mother Jones 333

MOTHERLY LABOR ORGANIZING IN CENTRAL APPALACHIA VERSUS THE "CULT OF TRUE WOMANHOOD"

Jones paved the way for these later union-organizing Appalachian women as one of the first and "strongest" of the early organizers of Appalachian coal miners. As Gorn argues, her work encouraging women to get involved with labor strikes may be the most important of her many contributions to American labor organizing.[28] In 1897 she included women as she helped organize striking western Pennsylvania coal miners in northern Appalachia, and in 1900 she organized and led as many as 1,500 women in a march on the mining town of Lattimer, West Virginia.[29] Anthropologist Shelley Romalis interprets LeSueur's eyewitness account of Jones's "maternalist politics" as describing a "warrior" who addressed mining company and political authorities "like an angry mother, admonishing them to be human, if they could, to admit the union, to let the workers live."[30]

As Jones and the labor organizers of the Great Depression began their work, the late-nineteenth-century Victorian ideal of motherhood was still promoted to those dominant in American culture (white, socioeconomically privileged), placing a mother at the center of domestic family life in what historians Barbara Welter and Ann Douglas call "the Cult of True Womanhood."[31] According to the ideals of the cult, religious historian Colleen McDannell claims, a mother was to promote "piety, purity, submissiveness, and domesticity," and to function as a spiritual authority within her home.[32] At a time when Americans tended to focus on revival and "religion of the heart," maternal love was so highly valued that, McDannell asserts, "mothers were considered to hold the key to the salvation of their children."[33] Victorian-era mothers exerted maternal influence through love rather than through asserting dominance over those under her care, McDannell explains.[34] Gorn argues that "Mother" Jones intentionally "widened that circle to embrace the whole family of labor."[35] To do so, Gorn further argues, she not only draws in her political speeches and letters on her own experience as a bereaved working-class mother who identifies with and sides with those who are poor and oppressed, but also identifies herself with "Mother Mary," who is both a powerful theological and cultural symbol of maternal authority and of "the cult of womanly renunciation" on a cosmic (rather than purely private) scale.[36] In several of her letters and speeches, Jones unfavorably contrasted Victorian middle- and upper-class "ladies" (which Gorn interprets as her term for the capitalist women she elsewhere derided for living "to please their husbands and show off their wealth") with real "women" made by "God Almighty" alone.[37] In a 1914 speech in New York, Jones exhorted women, "Nevermind if you are not lady-like, you are woman-like. God almighty made the woman and the Rockefeller gang of thieves made the ladies."[38] Just before her death in 1930, one year before the 1931 Harlan County coal mining strike that galvanized Reece and Jackson, Jones repeated this idea to reporters assembled for her hundredth birthday party: "A wonderful power is in the hands of women . . . but they don't know how to use it. Capitalists sidetrack the women into clubs and make ladies of them. Nobody wants a lady, they want women."[39]

Her contemporaries, however, often accused Jones of not fitting the dominant domesticated ideal of motherhood, so, like Reece, Jackson, and Gunning after her, it seems she may have drawn on a working-class definition of motherhood common in Central Appalachian culture, as Lord, Crowder, and Beaver have described, a maternal elder with authority internal to her community (respected by but not opposed to patriarchal authorities).[40] This working-class, Appalachian understanding of maternal authority differs from what Gorn also calls "the cult of womanhood" dominant in other classes and regions, in which mothers were "devoted, nurturing, [and] asexual."[41] Again, Jones's claim to maternal authority as a national and regional labor organizer seems to fit more closely with what Tice, drawing on the writings of deLong and Furman, recounts as an Appalachian understanding of dynamic maternal and grandmotherly authority rather than on the Victorian ideal of women's passivity and submission even within the home.[42] According to Gorn, "Mother Jones' ultimate goal was a living wage for working families, better yet, sufficient pay for men so that women could stay home and children go to school," rather than work in mills or mines.[43] Even in retirement, Jones never ceased her writing and advocacy for labor rights. Thus, as an activist mother whose children and husband were dead, the model of motherhood she exemplified in her own life was certainly not that of "true womanhood" in the passive, romantic

In the Footsteps of Mother Jones 335

Victorian sense. Rather, she lived and promoted economic justice for labor-class families so that mothers with living children or sick husbands would have the opportunity to provide for their needs so that they need no longer suffer malnutrition and neglect and die of easily preventable or treatable illnesses.

While Gorn juxtaposes Jones's maternal image and vows to help protect mothers and children of laboring men with "the implicit threat" of potential violence that could erupt from the masses she organized in rallies and marches, as if maternal authority and violence would be mutually exclusive, Jones herself clearly saw maternal protectiveness and the threat of violence in self-defense as a self-consistent dynamic tension.[44] In her most powerful and best-known organizing work in West Virginia, the force, power, and authority of an elder mother were never-cultural paradoxes, as they may have been for white Victorians. Tice describes regional resistance to most white, educated, upper-class women educators, missionaries, and reformers who came to help from outside the region during and just before the Great Depression, suggesting that socioeconomic class, education, and professional accomplishment were not sufficient for a woman from outside the region to earn credibility and authority.[45] Jones, in contrast, exercised the very kind of maternal authority that working-class Appalachian people of all races seemed to recognize and one to which they responded enthusiastically, which women labor organizers in the region seem to follow even now.

Reece and Jackson renewed Jones's labor organizing efforts in the region in spite of some obstacles that emerged between her time and theirs. The nation's economic downturn during the Great Depression initially eroded both labor organizing in general and women's leadership in the movement in particular.[46] Jackson worked primarily with the Communists' National Miners Union, which Romalis asserts "legitimized wives' support" through woman-organized strike meetings, relief work, and "wildcat strikes," separating women's activities.[47] Reece carried Jones's legacy of pioneering maternal labor organizing more directly, through leadership in the UMWA more generally. And Gunning promoted the labor-organizing legacy of women in Appalachia on a national scale, as Jones had, but mostly indirectly, by continuing to perform Appalachian labor-organizing songs even through the folk music revival of the late 1950s and early 1960s.

Just as Jones had defined Appalachian poverty specifically as a mother's issue, Reece, Jackson, and Gunning did as well—perhaps even more explicitly. Gorn connects Appalachian mothers' reactions to family poverty to the maternal labor-organizing model exemplified in Jones' work: "When insufficient money came into the household, it was women who dealt with making sure there was food on the table, clothes on the children, a roof over their heads," because mothers ran the family household, "the unit of production" for working-class families.[48]

FLORENCE REECE

Florence Reece (1900–1986) often recalled, without further detail, that her father had been killed working a Tennessee coal mine. As an adult, she helped organize local miners with her husband, Sam, who was frequently jailed or hiding from people she described to journalist Kathy Kahn as mining company "gun thugs."[49] As she told Kahn, during one of Sam's flights from the thugs she was desperate to "get word out any way" about the brutal terrorizing of her husband and neighbors "in the aftermath of the violent and failed National Miners Union strike of 1931."[50] Then thirty years old, she composed her first labor anthem, writing the lyrics to her labor organizing anthem "Whose Side Are You On?" on a wall calendar to the tune of an old hymn, "Lay the Lily Low."[51] This song became the anthem for Kentucky's famous Harlan County coal mine strike of 1931. As film reviewer Peter Biskind noted, "There is no bloodier chapter in the history of U.S. labor than the struggle of coal miners, and some of the most violent episodes within this chapter occurred in Harlan County, Kentucky."[52] This site of fierce battles between miners and coal companies culminated on May 4, 1931, and became known by locals as "'bloody Harlan,' particularly after a shootout that left a large number of dead and wounded. Reece's emblematic anthem of the same name "fixed this struggle forever in the folklore of U.S. labor," according to Biskind.[53] Reece explained the striking Harlan workers' motives to Kahn: "All in the world we people wanted was enough to feed and clothe and house our children. . . . The workers offered all they had . . . their hands . . . their prayers."[54]

In the Footsteps of Mother Jones 337

By 1973 Harlan County was once again embroiled in coal miners' strikes, and once again Reece gave leadership to the movement. In spite of Reece's earlier organizing efforts, by this time only 10 percent of workers for Duke Power in Harlan County's Brookside Mine were unionized, and when they voted to join the UMWA as their grandfathers had, a two-year conflict ensued. Barbara Kopple's Academy Award–winning film *Harlan County USA* documents the leadership of wives, mothers, and women workers as fund-raisers, protest and community organizers, and advocates for safety laws, disability and health care, and pension reform in a context where church officials, politicians, and even union leaders were collaborating with coal operators rather than with mine workers. Like their foremothers, who earlier had set labor protest songs to the music of Christian hymns, these women organizers used "revival" language to inspire each other and their men. However, they also carried guns in self-defense after the mine foremen and other company representatives started shooting into their homes and harassing them on the picket lines with clubs and guns, eventually even shooting strikers on the road as they drove past in their trucks. Florence Reece and other elderly women who had lived through the bloody Harlan strikes of the thirties encouraged these younger women both to join the men on the picket line and in union rallies. Addressing the miners directly ten months into the strike, Reece testified, "I am not a coal miner but I am as close as I can be not to be one, my father died and my husband is slowly dying of black lung and we were on strike in bloody Harlan in the thirties, the men got nothing to lose but their chains."[55] She then sang them her song, "Which Side Are You On?" Kopple's film clearly shows that these women's courageous endurance of brutality inspired the men hanging back to come forward onto the picket lines in ever-growing numbers until the strike was finally settled, in 1974, by the intervention of US Secretary of the Treasury William E. Simon, as documented in the film.

MOLLY JACKSON

Like Reece, fellow Kentuckian Molly Jackson (1880–1960), née Mary Magdalene Garland, also focused on "food and children" in her organizing work and protest songs, which folklorist Alan Lomax called "more passionate" and "deeper" than even those of Woody Guthrie.[56] Jackson, the daughter of a Baptist preacher, miner, and union organizer, boasted of joining her outspoken coal-mining father on strikes at age five, just before her mother died of starvation. She was so assertive as a youthful activist that she was first jailed for her family's pro-union activism at age ten.[57] Although originally a midwife, Jackson began writing protest songs after the deaths of one of her very young half-brothers and her second husband from coal mining injuries, and she soon devoted herself fully to union organizing. She was well known in the region for leading wives and children in the singing of her composition "Hungry Ragged Blues," as they entered the mines to convince miners to strike. She later led the miners as they carried signs that said, "Our children must have milk and bread," again connecting her maternal concern for family poverty to labor activism.[58] In a recorded interview, "The Songs and Stories of Aunt Molly Jackson," Jackson explains writing "Hungry Ragged Blues" in desperation after her young niece brought her fifteen thin, barefoot children, in threadbare clothing, who hadn't eaten in days. From walking barefoot in the cold for so long, the skin on the children's feet had split, and their feet were bleeding. Jackson had set up a soup kitchen during a 1931 UMWA coal strike, but it had run out of food six months into the strike. She had not only nothing to feed them, but no clothes or shoes for their return to their homes. This, then, is the song Jackson performed when she testified on behalf of Kentucky coal miners before Theodore Dreiser's National Committee for the Defense of Political Prisoners, in 1931, recounting the desperate situation of coal-mining parents who could not give food to their "children crying for bread" at her soup kitchen for the Bell County coal camp at Glendon Baptist Church. Younger half-sister Sarah Ogan Gunning later told documentary filmmaker Mimi Pickering of this performance that among those more interested in folk music than labor, it was "something new to hear a woman singing labor songs."[59] According to Romalis, this performance "changed, or at least had a significant impact on, the New York left-wing world in the 1930s." As a result, Romalis claims, "Aunt Molly evolved from miner's canary at the beginning of the 1930s to mouthpiece for America's disenfranchised proletariat by the end of the decade."[60]

In the Footsteps of Mother Jones 339

Aunt Molly was also known for guerrilla-style public political aggression not usually considered domestic or maternal, as demonstrated by her shoving the barrel of a pistol into the rectum of a mining company "gun thug" who dared to try to cross a coal miner's picket line set up by local women, who had stripped him naked and held him down.[61] Her involvement in union activities such as these reportedly led to the dissolution of Jackson's third marriage, as foreshadowed in her own account of her husband's employment difficulties, which stemmed from the perception of many in their community, including mining company management, that she was a Communist. As she sang in "I am a Union Woman," "When my husband asked the boss for a job, these are the words he said: 'Bill Jackson, I can't work you, sir; your wife's a Rooshian Red.'"[62] The refrain of the song repeatedly encourages miners to "join the [Communist] NMU."[63] Further contradicting the stereotype promoted by some educators and reformers of Appalachian women's placid natures, Jackson carried two pistols (one for each hand) on the strike lines and promoted and preserved her ideas and legacy through preaching, painting, and writing songs, poetry, and an unpublished autobiography.[64] As Romalis argues, Jackson deliberately "crafted an image" of herself as a "trouble-making, provocative, arrogant, defiant . . . composer-singer of protest songs," a "'ferocious' defender of the downtrodden, indomitable organizer and fundraiser for the miners." She continued to portray herself publicly as a miner's missionary well after leaving the region in 1931 and "to perceive herself as a front-line warrior until her death" thirty years later.[65] To promote the cause of the region's miners, she recorded 150 of her songs for the Library of Congress Archive of Folk Song in 1935 and 1939, touring with traveling folk musicians, and performing in the early New York hootenannies that led to the mid-century folk music revival.[66] Toward the end of her life, she wrote to *Sing Out!* folk song magazine that though she "'never received one cent from anyone out of all the protest songs I have composed,'" she believed her songs taught "'people right from wrong.'"[67]

SARAH OGAN GUNNING

Known for her a cappella songs about watching as her first husband and their babies starved to death during the Great Depression, Sarah

Ogan Gunning (1910–1983) lived in coal mining camps for decades.[68] The daughter of a Kentucky coal miner who died of a mining-related illness, she also lost one of her brothers and a nephew to mining accidents and another brother to black lung. Between 1930 and 1931, local miners, including Gunning's husband, were reduced to two days a week paid labor as a consequence of decreased demand for coal. They saw their choices as either to strike and starve or to work and starve, so Gunning's husband and other family members, including Molly Jackson, chose to strike and joined the communist National Miners Union. In Pickering's 1988 documentary, Gunning observed that during those years, the influence of Molly Jackson and other labor organizers on national and regional politics and economics was at its height, and socialism seemed to be more widely accepted throughout the United States than it is today.[69] However, union efforts made insufficient impact on her family's poverty. By the time Gunning was twenty-eight, her coal miner husband had died of lung disease and malnutrition, and she had lost two of her young children, one to outright starvation and the other to illness, likely brought on by malnutrition.[70]

In her songs and interviews, Gunning repeatedly described her early life as typical for most children of coal miners in depression-era Kentucky. Specifically, her father had periods of intermittent disability due to mining accidents, and as a consequence of the family's financial need, her brothers had to start working in the mines while still children.[71] Gorn describes such "trap boys" (who opened trap doors in the mines for coal carts and mules) as typically working fourteen-hour days, a situation that Mother Jones earlier had publicized and tried to end.[72] In Mimi Pickering's 1988 documentary on her life and work, *Dreadful Memories*, Gunning recounts that, when the children of other mining families died, she would help "lay them out and sit with the mothers until they could put them away. These and other things in my life, is what I composed the songs about."[73] At least once, however, according to her friend Woody Guthrie, she, too, 'had faced guns on the picket line and "sung into the rifle fire of Sheriff Blair's deputies [in Harlan, Kentucky]."[74] Molly Jackson mentioned Gunning's songs during her 1931 work with Dreiser's Appalachian poverty relief campaign in New York, so that the music producers recording Jackson went to Gunning's Kentucky home to record her

In the Footsteps of Mother Jones 341

songs, as well. Appalled by her impoverished living conditions, they took her and her surviving children back to New York with them.[75] Although Gunning was less directly involved with striking Kentucky coal miners than was her more famous half-sibling Molly Jackson, she did publicize the miners' plight nationally through performances at the 1939 New York World's Fair and the initial folk music gatherings of the early 1940s, by singing not only traditional Appalachian women's ballads but also her original compositions about mining camp labor, including "Girl of Constant Sorrow" and "Come All You Coal Miners." She told Pickering that she had written these songs during the Great Depression not only out of her loneliness as a wife and mother after her husband and children's deaths in the Kentucky coal camps but also as a direct result of encouragement by Communist labor organizers.[76] Even before her early public performances in the 1940s, her song "Come All You Coal Miners" had already, in 1937, been recorded for a national audience by Alan Lomax for the Library of Congress, because he considered the tune to be one of the most significant labor organizing anthems of the Appalachian region in the Great Depression.[77]

Unlike Reece's "Whose Side Are You On?," which had focused on the universal theme of social justice, many of Jackson and Gunning's songs focused on the particular plight of women and children in the coal camps. Introducing her autobiographical article, the editors of *Sing Out!* explain that the words to Gunning's "Come All You Coal Miners," for example, "came directly from Sarah Gunning's own tragic experiences in Bell County, Kentucky, and they had one purpose—to organize miners to fight against the inhuman conditions they faced every day of their lives."[78] Romalis argues that although Jackson, in particular, "stood apart and challenged the conservative, mountain culture, constantly testing and stretching the boundaries of appropriate gender behavior, Gunning was less radical, changing an early song called "I Hate the Capitalist System" to "I Hate the Company Bosses," after the demise of the Communist National Miners Union with which Jackson had been involved.[79] Folk music historian Archie Green told Pickering that Gunning's work is important beyond the Appalachian region and her modest level of fame because she synthesized words expressing a Marxist labor protest with traditional Appalachian melodies in a unity of radical labor ideals with women's songs and religious hymns of a traditional culture, citing "Girl of Constant Sorrow" as a specific example.[80] Gunning's works particularly focus on her losses as a widow and bereaved mother but explicitly tie that grief to its context and root causes, family poverty created by unjust economic practices in central Appalachian coal mining camps.

As Romalis recounts, Gunning's mother (Jackson's stepmother) had shared Appalachian women's traditional songs with her, singing spirituals, "old ballads, funny ditties, and children's verses" constantly "while she worked, walked or sat."[81] Gunning later confirmed that her Christian mother "taught us [including brother Jim Garland and half-sister Molly Jackson] most of all the old ballads and spirituals and other songs we know."[82] Although Gunning drew on this legacy of traditional music handed down by her mother, she soon became more famous than Molly Jackson or Jim Garland for her own original songs about the poverty, hunger, and oppression of Appalachian coal miners and their families, inspired by her own and others' experiences in the coal camps.[83] As Gunning recounted toward the end of her life, "I composed a lot of true songs about the coal miners and their families and all the hardships that I had gone through."[84] Her songs promoted union organizing as a response to mountaineers' suffering, just like Reece's and Jackson's. Yet unlike Reece and Jackson, Gunning wrote autobiographically, more for self-expression than for political reasons. She told interviewers that she wrote not just to continue her family's legacy of labor protest nor for fame but because "being able to express my feelings in song has kept me from going nuts. . . . When I get to thinking about the past I get headaches and it makes me feel pretty miserable, but I smile and I try not to make other people miserable."[85] As Romalis notes, "She wanted to record a history of coal-mining people to leave a record for her grandchildren . . . and because she needed the money."[86] She traveled during the very early years of the folk revival just after the Depression, performing not only to support herself and her family but also to raise money for Dustbowl refugees and coal miners.[87] Guthrie wrote that she was a "mother and more than a mother," working not only on behalf of "the children of her own home" but also for other mining families in the region.[88] This, maternal singing and work on behalf of other mothers, then, connects her

In the Footsteps of Mother Jones 343

life and work explicitly to the legacy of Mother Jones, as did the work of Reece and Jackson. Guthrie connected her musical performances of the 1940s back to her involvement with the Appalachian labor struggles of the 1930s. In his view, she was "so full of the Union Spirit that she found time to get out in the wind and rain and the hail of bullets from the deputies' guns, and make up her own songs and sing them to give nerve and backbone to the starving men that slaved in the coal mines."[89] As the editors of *Sing Out!* magazine summarized her legacy:

> The songs she created and sang out of the bitter experiences of her life in the coal mining counties of southeastern Kentucky in the 1920's and 30's reached out to Woody Guthrie, Pete Seeger and many others. Along with the songs of her brother Jim Garland and her half-sister, the late Aunt Molly Jackson, they helped form the basis of the class-conscious folk revival. . . . Her songs are a living reminder of the extremes of poverty that exist continually in this 'richest nation on earth.' They bear witness to the strength of folk traditions [and] of working-class women.[90]

NATIONAL IMPACT AND LEGACY

Indeed, overtly political themes and the struggle for justice dominate Reece, Jackson, and Gunning's songwriting. Bufwack and Oermann describe a distinct tradition of ballads of protest and complaint among Appalachian women that precedes, but includes, Reece, Jackson, and Gunning. However, Reece and Jackson's use of music as a political organizing tool and Gunning's use of music to raise outsiders' awareness of dreadful Appalachian living conditions challenged mountain musical customs, since traditionally women sang their ballads of complaint and protest in the private sphere of the home, to children or to themselves as they performed domestic chores.[91] By singing these songs in the public sphere and using them "to organize coal mining families into the union" and draw national attention to Appalachian suffering, Reece, Jackson, and Gunning all expanded the traditional Appalachian definitions of maternal authority, conventionally practiced in submission to male authority when present, and also of women's work, which Tice demonstrates traditionally focused on "tending the fields" and farms as well as child rearing, housework, and domestic crafts.[92] By drawing on their mountain musical traditions of giving voice to personal maternal grief and protest in resistance to unrelieved suffering of poverty, violence, and injustice in coal-mining communities, these widows whose children were no longer living transgressed domestic limitations to bring these issues to national attention, specifically in their role as mothers.[93]

Through their focus on fighting for socioeconomic justice in the Appalachian mountain region, all of these women carried forward a model of activism pioneered by Jones, bringing national attention to political and economic changes needed to protect families disempowered by the region's coal industry. This maternal leadership model has been carried on in the region more recently in the commitment and leadership women organizers of the 1973 Harlan County, Kentucky, mine strikes and 1990s organizing by women activists of the UMWA and the Daughters of Mother Jones on behalf of mine workers and their families in West Virginia, Virginia, and Kentucky against the Pittston (Pennsylvania) Coal Corporation in 1989–90, in what political scientist Richard Brisbin has called "a strike like no other." As Brisbin explains, the strikers at Pittston countered judicial and corporate accusations of law-breaking violence with language of spiritual resistance as redemptive, very much like the foremothers' protest songs of the Great Depression.[94] Like the Daughters of Mother Jones in the Pittston strike, women community organizers like Maria Gunnoe, Patricia Bragg, and Julia "Judy" Bonds, who fight against mountaintop removal in West Virginia coal mining, are also influenced by the mothering labor activism of Jones, Reece, and Jackson.[95] Bonds, the executive director of Coal River Mountain Watch and a 2003 Goldman Environmental Prize winner, sees little difference between the coal companies' persecution of union organizers in the times of Jones and Jackson and today, except that threats of violence are less public. Instead of "shooting us on the courthouse steps," one of the coal company representatives simply warned at a permit hearing attended by the women labor organizers, "If I were these ladies, I'd be afraid to go home tonight." Bonds responds as any of the maternal labor organizers of the region might have: "You can't scare Appalachian women, and they ought to know that. We've had to fight all our lives."[96] Thus, both through their union activism

In the Footsteps of Mother Jones 345

and voicing of what theologian David Fillingim has called a "hillbilly humanist" maternal commitment to social equality through their labor songs, these women brought mountain values and issues to national attention and again transgressed the traditional perception that Appalachian women's influence was usually assumed to be confined to home, family, and church.

NOTES

1. Kathy Kahn, *Hillbilly Women: Mountain Women Speak of the Struggle and Joy in Southern Appalachia* (Garden City, NY: Doubleday, 1973), xx. Cf. Emma Bell Miles, *The Spirit of the Mountains* (New York: J. Potts, 1905) and Elizabeth S. D. Engelhardt's introduction to *Beyond Hill and Hollow: Original Readings in Appalachian Women's Studies* (Athens: Ohio University Press, 2005) for additional discussion of stereotypes of Appalachian women.

2. Elliott J. Gorn, *Mother Jones: The Most Dangerous Woman in America* (New York: Hill and Wang, 2001), 179.

3. Ibid., 172.

4. Florence Reece, "They Say Them Child Brides Don't Last," in Kahn, *Hillbilly Women*, 6; Pat Wynne, "Teaching Labor History through Song," in *Women's Studies Quarterly: Working-Class Lives and Cultures* 26, nos. 1 and 2 (1998): 187.

5. Wynne, "Teaching Labor History," 187.

6. Sarah Ogan Gunning, "My Name is Sarah Ogan Gunning," *Sing Out!* 25, no. 2 (July–August 1976): 17.

7. Mary A. Bufwack and Robert K. Oermann, *Finding Her Voice: Women in Country Music, 1800–2000* (Nashville: Vanderbilt University Press–Country Music Foundation Press, 2003), 113.

8. Karen W. Tice, "School-Work and Mother-Work: The Interplay of Maternalism and Cultural Politics in the Educational Narratives of Kentucky Settlement Workers, 1910–1930," *Journal of Appalachian Studies* 4, no. 2 (Fall 1998): 191–210.

9. Kahn, *Hillbilly Women*, xxi.

10. Sharon B. Lord and Carolyn Patton-Crowder, *Appalachian Women: A Learning-Teaching Guide* (Newton, MA: Education Development Center, 1979), 65; H. Virginia McCoy, Diana Gullett Trevino, and Clyde McCoy, "Appalachian Women: Between Two Cultures," in *From Mountain to Metropolis: Appalachian Migrants in American Cities*, ed. Kathryn M. Borman and Phillip J. Obermiller (Westport, CT: Bergin and Garvey, 1994), 35–37; Patricia Beaver, "Hillbilly Women, Hillbilly Men: Sex Roles in Rural-Agricultural Appalachia," in Lord and Patton-Crowder, *Appalachian Women*, 65, 70; Erica Hurwitz, "High Lonesome Gospel: Evangelical Christianity in Bluegrass from Bill Monroe to Ron Block" (paper presented at American Academy of Religion Annual Meeting, 1997), 3.

11. Tice, "School-Work and Mother-Work," 207.

12. Cynthia Rogers, Kimberly Mencken, and F. Carson Mencken, "Female Labor Force Participation in Central Appalachia: A Descriptive Analysis," *Journal*

of Appalachian Studies 3, no. 2 (Fall 1997): 189, 191, 198; see also Richard A. Couto, *An American Challenge: A Report on Economic Trends and Social Issues in Appalachia* (Dubuque, IA: Kendall/Hunt, 1994) and Brian Cushing and Cynthia Rogers, "Income and Poverty in Appalachia" (Regional Research Paper 9511. Regional Research Institute, West Virginia University, 1995).

13. Rogers, Mencken and Mencken, "Female Labor Force Participation," 200.

14. Mary Harris Jones, *Autobiography of Mother Jones,* ed. Mary Field Parton. First Person Series 3 (Chicago: Charles H. Kerr, 1990), xi.

15. Gorn, *Mother Jones,* 38.

16. Marie Tedesco, "Mary Harris ('Mother') Jones," in *Biographical Dictionary of American Labor Leaders,* ed. Gary M. Fink (Westport, CT: Greenwood, 1974), 179.

17. Gorn, *Mother Jones,* 46–47.

18. John Brophy, *A Miner's Life* (Madison: University of Wisconsin, 1964), 74.

19. Mary Harris "Mother" Jones to William B. Wilson, November 15, 1901, quoted in Gorn, *Mother Jones,* 93.

20. Gorn, *Mother Jones,* 87–88.

21. Bufwack and Oermann, *Finding Her Voice.*

22. Gorn, *Mother Jones,* 4–5, 7–8.

23. Ibid., 4–5.

24. Bufwack and Oermann, *Finding Her Voice,* x.

25. Joe Wilson, "Country Music in Tennessee: From Hollow to Honkey-Tonk," in *American Musical Traditions,* vol. 3 of *British Isles Music* (New York: Schirmer, 2002), 102; John Alexander Williams, *Appalachia: A History* (Chapel Hill: University of North Carolina Press, 2002), 205, 212–13; Jane S. Becker, *Selling Tradition: Appalachia and the Construction of the American Folk, 1930–1940* (Chapel Hill: University of North Carolina Press, 1998), 60.

26. Bufwack and Oermann, *Finding Her Voice,* 5, 7–8.

27. Ibid., 13.

28. Ibid., 76.

29. Kahn, *Hillbilly Women,* xiii–xiv; Jones, *Autobiography of Mother Jones,* 263.

30. Shelly Romalis, *Pistol Packin' Mama: Aunt Molly Jackson and the Politics of Folksong* (Urbana: University of Illinois Press, 1999), 11; Jones, *Autobiography of Mother Jones,* xii, xi.

31. Barbara Welter, "The Cult of True Womanhood, 1820–1860," in *Dimity Convictions: The American Woman in the Nineteenth Century* (Athens: Ohio University Press, 1985), 21–41; Ann Douglas, *The Feminization of American Culture* (New York: Knopf), 1977.

32. Colleen McDannell, *Material Christianity: Religion and Popular Culture in America* (New Haven: Yale University Press, 1995), 80.

33. Ibid.

34. Ibid., 80, 83.

35. Gorn, *Mother Jones,* 8.

36. Ibid., 31.

37. Ibid., 177.

38. "500 Women Cheer for Mother Jones," *New York Times,* May 23, 1914, 3.

39. "Mother Jones at 100 Years Is Still Fiery; Loudly Denounces 'Capitalists' for Talkie," *New York Times*, May 2, 1930, 25.

40. Tice, "School-Work and Mother-Work," 207.

41. Gorn, *Mother Jones*, 224.

42. Tice, "School-Work and Mother-Work," 207, 210.

43. Gorn, *Mother Jones*, 141.

44. Ibid., 199.

45. Tice, "School-Work and Mother-Work," 191–94.

46. Kahn, *Hillbilly Women*, xv; Jones, *Autobiography of Mother Jones*, xi. Jones's legacy was celebrated in a nationally known song, "The Death of Mother Jones," more popular in central Appalachia from 1930 to 1932 than anywhere else. Gorn asserts that local Appalachian mountain singers kept this song alive so well that even the region's schoolchildren learned the lyrics. Cf. Gorn, *Mother Jones*, 298.

47. Romalis, *Pistol Packin' Mama*, 84.

48. Gorn, *Mother Jones*, 234.

49. Kahn, *Hillbilly Women*, 5–6.

50. Ibid., 9–10.

51. Bufwack and Oermann, *Finding Her Voice*, 116.

52. Peter Biskind, "*Harlan County USA*: The Miners' Struggle." Review of *Harlan County USA. Jump Cut: A Review of Contemporary Media* 14 (1977): 3.

53. Ibid.

54. Kahn, *Hillbilly Women*, 38.

55. *Harlan County USA*, dir. by Barbara Kopple (Cabin Creek Films, 1976). DVD.

56. Romalis, *Pistol Packin' Mama*, 86; Lomax cited in Bufwack and Oermann, *Finding Her Voice*, 115.

57. Bufwack and Oermann, *Finding Her Voice*, 114; Gunning, "My Name," 15.

58. Valentine Ackland, "Aunt Mollie [sic] Jackson—Revolutionary," typescript of interview for *Daily Worker*, n.d., Barnicle-Cadle Papers, 3–4, Schlesinger Library, Radcliffe College, Cambridge, MA; Molly Jackson, "By Aunt Molly Jackson—Monday, Oct. 8, 1945," typescript, n.p., Barnicle-Cadle Papers.

59. *Dreadful Memories: The Life of Sarah Ogan Gunning*, dir. Mimi Pickering. (Appalshop Films, 1988). DVD.

60. Romalis, *Pistol Packin' Mama*, 88, 162.

61. Jim Garland, *Welcome the Traveler Home: Jim Garland's Story of the Kentucky Mountains*, ed. Julia S. Ardery (Lexington: University Press of Kentucky, 1983), 130.

62. Romalis, *Pistol Packin' Mama*, 83; Molly Jackson, "I Am a Union Woman" (Storm King Music), 1966.

63. Ibid.

64. Tice, "School-Work and Mother-Work," 191, 193; Romalis, *Pistol Packin' Mama*, 58, 76–79; Archie Green tape-recorded interview, Sacramento (1957–59), FT 4290, Southern Folklife Collection, Wilson Library, University of North Carolina, Chapel Hill; Molly Jackson, untitled autobiographical notes, typescript, September 5, 1945, Barnicle-Cadle Papers, 8.

65. Romalis, *Pistol Packin' Mama*, 58, 152, 157.

66. Bufwack and Oermann, *Finding Her Voice*, 114.

67. Cited in ibid, 115.

68. *Dreadful Memories.*

69. Ibid.

70. Gunning, "My Name."

71. Romalis, *Pistol Packin' Mama*, 131–32; Gunning, "My Name," 15–16.

72. Gorn, *Mother Jones*, 129.

73. *Dreadful Memories.*

74. Gunning, "My Name," 15.

75. *Dreadful Memories.*

76. Ibid.

77. Bufwack and Oermann, *Finding Her Voice*, 115; Sarah Ogan Gunning, "I am a Girl of Constant Sorrow" (Folk Legacy Records, 1965).

78. Gunning, "My Name," 17.

79. Romalis, *Pistol Packin' Mama*, 59, 128.

80. *Dreadful Memories.*

81. Romalis, *Pistol Packin' Mama*, 129.

82. Gunning, "My Name," 15.

83. Romalis, *Pistol Packin' Mama*, 132–33.

84. Gunning, "My Name," 16.

85. Ibid.

86. Romalis, *Pistol Packin' Mama*, 134, 139, 143; Romalis bases her argument here on Ellen Stekert's tape-recorded interview with Gunning, Detroit (Nov. 6 and Dec. 4, 1964), FT 2788, Southern Folklife Collection.

87. Gunning, "My Name," 16.

88. Woody Guthrie, "Story of Sara Ogan," in *Hard Hitting Songs for Hard-Hit People*. ed. Alan Lomax, Woody Guthrie, and Pete Seeger (New York: Oak Press, 1967), 154.

89. Ibid., 155.

90. Gunning, "My Name," 15.

91. Bufwack and Oermann, *Finding Her Voice*, 14.

92. Tice, "School-Work and Mother-Work," 196, 210.

93. Kahn, *Hillbilly Women*, 3; David Fillingim, "Stand By Your Man and Your Daughters Shall Prophesy: Country Music as Feminist Theology" (paper presented at Popular Culture Association in the South Annual Meeting, 1997), 5.

94. Richard A. Brisbin Jr., *A Strike Like No Other: Law and Resistance during the Pittston Coal Strike of 1989–1990* (Morgantown: West Virginia University Press, 2010), 13.

95. Joyce M. Barry, *Standing Our Ground: Women, Environmental Justice, and the Fight to End Mountaintop Removal*, Ohio University Press Series in Race, Ethnicity, and Gender in Appalachia (Athens: Ohio University Press, 2012).

96. Michelle Nijhuis, "Coal Miner's Slaughter: West Virginia activist Julia Bonds takes on mountaintop-removal mining," *Grist: A Beacon in the Smog* (April 14, 2003), http://www.grist.org/article/slaughter (accessed May 25, 2009).

In the Footsteps of Mother Jones 349

CHAPTER TWELVE

"She Now Cries Out"

Linda Neville and the Limitations of Venereal Disease Control Policies in Kentucky

EVELYN ASHLEY SORRELL

After reading a 1937 newspaper article about Linda Neville's work with the blind, Rory O. Huntsman, the mayor of Scottsville, Kentucky, felt impelled to write to her declaring, "There is no doubt in my mind that if Christ were on Earth today, instead of walking along by the sea of Galilee and picking his disciples from the lowly fishermen, he would walk down the streets of Lexington and say, 'Linda Neville, follow me.'"[1] Neville's success as a savior for the blind and prophet of professionalized medicine solidified her status as a saintly figure among not just her fellow Kentuckians but also nationally within the field of health.

On the surface, Neville seemed a typical Progressive Era reformer, fighting for children born with eye conditions, but a closer look reveals a woman tormented by the cases she saw and struggling to overcome personal and financial limitations that prevented her from saving all the children under her care from a lifetime of darkness. Neville's public health work put children first and pushed mothers to the forefront of blame and to the background of care. Even though Neville single-mindedly sought medical help for the children of poor families in the mountain regions of the state, her work mobilized statewide networks of female reformers and male medical professionals to address the health needs of Kentucky's rural population. In doing so, Neville also unwittingly empowered impoverished mothers to challenge her authority as a reformer, defining for themselves the medical needs of their children and the role professional medicine would have in their lives.[2]

Neville was born in 1873 to John and Mary Neville. Linda's father served as a professor of Greek and Latin at the State Agricultural and Mechanical College and was appointed vice-president of the college in 1899. He retired from his post in 1908 because of bad health.[3] Mary Neville died from cancer when Linda was fourteen years old, and she came of age under the influence of her father, who stressed the value of education and ensured that Linda and her older sister, Mary, went to schools that focused on college preparation.[4] Both Neville sisters received postsecondary educations at Bryn Mawr College. The curriculum at Bryn Mawr deviated from other women's colleges, as its focus was not on the domestic sciences but on courses such as mathematics, Greek, and Latin that prepared women to enter a competitive but restricted job market.[5] In 1895 Linda graduated with a bachelor's degree in Greek and Latin. She returned to Lexington, where she took care of her ailing father and pursued a teaching career. Linda and her sister combined family responsibilities with teaching, which was a common path for women who sought work following graduation.[6]

Beginning in 1899, Neville devoted more time to civic and charitable activities. She first became involved in aiding the poor through her service on the Associated Charities board of directors. Neville visited homes and was "directly acquainted with the poor and their needs." She also worked with the Lexington Civic League and was a member of the Women's Christian Temperance Union. This interest in charity and reform led Neville to discover her life's work as a reformer seeking to care for and alleviate the suffering of the blind. It was a cause close to her heart. Both Neville's father and aunt, Caroline, endured eye ailments that rendered them blind. Through this experience, Neville grew concerned over "helpless sufferers" and soon learned of a contagion sweeping Appalachia and causing a number of adults and children to live a life of darkness.[7]

Neville became involved in identifying and treating trachoma sufferers in the mountains of rural Kentucky.[8] Starting in 1908, Neville worked through the Hindman Settlement School, founded by fellow clubwomen Katherine Pettit and May Stone, to help impoverished children with trachoma while educating parents on how to prevent the infectious eye disease.[9] She collaborated with Dr. J. A. Stuckey, an otolaryngologist, and together they set up trachoma clinics that operated until 1928 when trachoma no longer was an epidemic in eastern Kentucky.[10]

She financed medical costs for impoverished patients through the Mountain Fund, which was established in 1908 after friends and relatives donated money to help the blind in Appalachia. Through Neville's mission to eradicate trachoma, she achieved a respected status among the male-dominated field of medicine and gained experience in legislative lobbying, organizing, and creating charitable societies.[11] Aside from the Mountain Fund, Neville also, in 1910, founded the Kentucky Society for the Prevention of Blindness. Her organizing work was a valuable asset in establishing contact with the professional medical field that Neville became reliant upon in her never-ending campaign to end blindness—a campaign that eventually led her to address the scourge of venereal disease and its role in causing a world of darkness for many "innocent" victims.

Women during the Progressive Era found projects to which they dedicated their lives.[12] It is generally accepted among historians that the Progressive period ended soon after World War I, but Robyn Muncy argued that many women who worked as Progressive reformers continued their initiatives into the 1930s and 1940s.[13] Neville was an example of these continuing reform efforts among female Progressives. Like Neville, many female reformers gained professional power by addressing social problems related to children and mothers, influencing transformations in public health and social work. Much of this work, such as the promotion of scientific motherhood, targeted women with children as recipients of reform.[14] This era of the role of science in the domestic household shaped how Neville viewed the mothers of the children she treated. Women who seemed "uneducated" in the middle-class values of raising healthy children were often met with contempt. In this way, Neville brought a Progressive Era lens to the growing mid-century problem of venereal disease.

Her reform impulses were entrenched and intertwined with her definition of self. Neville wanted the importance of her work with the blind to continue even after trachoma cases had dramatically declined. She reflected on her days battling the disease in a letter to Dr. John McMullen, who was also active in the fight against trachoma through the United States Public Health Service. Needing to find a new cause in which to devote her life, Neville reflected in 1935 about "those old Trachoma Days," writing, "Those mule-back rides, those court-room clinics,—how sad I feel at the realization that all that is so far in the past."[15] But she found a new calling and asserted that "we are in a new stage in Ky. And we use new ways now for meeting our problems. I am getting older, so I must rush to put syphilis on our map just as trachoma was there."[16]

Neville offered varying accounts of how she became aware of the ravages of venereal disease. Ultimately, it was through her work with trachoma patients in the mountains of Kentucky that exposed her to the effects of untreated syphilis and gonorrhea. Neville recalled that when she first started her work with the blind, she was unaware of "social diseases." This ignorance of the presence of venereal infections lasted until 1908, when she came across a family living in a mountain county of Kentucky. Within this family, Neville found blindness in the father and the sixteen-year-old daughter, and in 1913 two younger brothers also suffered loss of eyesight. At first she was baffled by what had caused this familial outbreak in blindness until she brought the family to Lexington to be tested for venereal disease. All members of the family tested positive for syphilis through the Wassermann blood test, which, beginning in 1906, was a popular way to confirm a syphilis diagnosis.[17] The two younger brothers died before treatment began—a tragedy that opened Neville's eyes to the dangers of untreated venereal diseases.[18] The focus on venereal disease represented a second stage in Neville's reform work. Kentucky no longer needed her help in the battle against trachoma, but Neville could not leave the war. Still focused on the prevention of blindness, she discovered a new project in venereal disease and its effects on the eyes of children.

The dangers venereal disease caused to marriage and reproduction had been a concern for doctors nationally since the 1890s. Prince Morrow, a Kentucky native born in Mount Vernon, was among the first doctors to publicize the problem of syphilis and gonorrhea infection as it related to sterility and the inherit dangers it imposed on the continuation of the "white race."[19] In Kentucky the issue remained a silent one, mired in moral decay, until Neville began a new crusade aimed at exposing venereal disease for its dangerous implications for the health of its "innocent victims"—the children.

The tireless reformer blamed the outbreak of venereal disease on soldiers who were intimate with prostitutes while serving in World War I and World War II. She saw no end to the infectious spread in Kentucky, writing, "The presumably large number of gonorrheal women around the aggregations of men/war workers/and soldiers of Kentucky will doubtless mean the birth of many babies whose eyes will be gonorrheal."[20] Neville drew on her Victorian sensibilities relating to sexuality and the suppression of women's sexual feelings.[21] Her views on sexuality placed it in a rigid framework not relevant to the working class.[22] These middle-class and Victorian biases led her to believe that the only victims of venereal disease were the children, and that women were just as responsible for contracting these diseases through relations with their husbands or by engaging in sex outside of marriage. Her Victorian sensibilities related to the proper raising of children through ideas of scientific motherhood and the proper expression of female sexuality shaped the reform work she pursued in Appalachia. Instances of venereal disease in children and their mothers offered an area of public health work where she could fuse her Victorian values with a more modern medical tradition, despite not being trained in the medical field.

Neville used her class, education, and middle-class upbringing to assert her influence in the professional field and set herself apart from lay midwives, whom she criticized as endangering the health of the children they delivered. Although her pursuit of midwife regulations was an extension of the campaign to eradicate blindness, it also represented Neville's self-interested motive for professional status. By the time Neville began addressing venereal disease cases as it related to the ill effects it had on children, the medical process of applying a 1 percent silver nitrate solution in newborns' eyes was firmly in place and backed by state law. The solution was effective in preventing and treating gonorrheal eye infection, but Neville found that many patients she served through the Mountain Fund were not receiving this treatment. One of the earliest cases of venereal disease brought to the fund highlighted this problem. In 1915 a doctor visited the child of an unmarried eastern Kentucky woman, whose stepfather was the father of the child. Neville traveled the distance on horseback, and finding that the baby had a gonorrheal infection, felt that the family was "such poor nurses that it was dangerous to trust them with treatment."[23] The isolation of the mother and child led Neville to a realization on "that cold day in March 1915" that she was "far from the solution of the problem providing prompt and adequate treatment for the gonorrheal babies born in remote and almost inaccessible places, where such babies' families were too poor to provide for them in their homes both doctor and nurse."[24]

Time was not on Neville's side when it came to reaching and treating infants born with gonorrheal infections of the eye. She despaired, thinking about isolated homes in mountain counties with no railroads or highways, and wondered "what would happen if a newborn baby should have gonorrheal pus ooze from under swollen eyelids." But as she asked herself that question, Neville "used to always sadly acknowledge to myself that what would probably happen would be that eyes would become blinded beyond all hope of sight."[25] Neville viewed midwives operating in Appalachia with suspicion because of their lack of knowledge in the value of silver nitrate to prevent blindness. Her support of a more professionalized model of health care influenced her criticism of lay midwives who did not share her faith in medical science.[26] The Frontier Nursing Service, established by Mary Breckinridge in 1925, also addressed the perceived dangers of "granny" midwives and sought to replace them with trained nurse midwives. In 1923 Breckinridge had traveled to eastern Kentucky to perform a comprehensive study of midwife practices in the counties of Leslie, Knott, and Owsley. She interviewed fifty-three midwives and found "a substandard level of care, dangerous practices, and the need for a change."[27]

Breckinridge was critical of "granny" midwives who did not choose their work, but rather felt it had been "thrust upon them." According to their critics, once the mothers gave birth and the babies were dressed, the untrained midwife left, offering very little aftercare.[28] One of the first cases of gonorrheal eye infection Neville experienced was the infant of a single mother who was assisted by a midwife during the delivery. The midwife failed to use preventative drops against gonorrheal infection,

"She Now Cries Out": Linda Neville 355

and Neville did not receive the case until three weeks later, when the damage to the infant's eyes was almost beyond relief.[29] Breckinridge noted midwives' failure to put silver nitrate into the eyes of infants at birth, stating that only ten of the fifty-three midwives investigated used the solution. She also criticized health officers who refused to believe that there were high instances of gonorrheal eye infections emanating from gonorrhea in the mother.[30]

The work of Breckinridge and Neville brought national attention to the health of children born to rural mothers. For example, a 1932 US Senate committee hearing on rural sanitation focused on the poor health of eastern Kentuckians. A number of medical officials and female public health workers testified to what they perceived as the ignorance of both lay midwives and rural mothers in appropriately caring for children at birth. The committee determined that the greatest health challenge facing impoverished areas of the state was the number of children born with gonorrheal eye infections. The committee blamed both mothers and midwives, as rural mothers were perceived as "ignorant of venereal disease" and midwives were "careless" by not using silver nitrate.[31] Thus, initiatives that sought to regulate midwife practices were not entirely separated from mother-blaming rhetoric used by Neville to justify her intervention into the public health field. Midwives and the pregnant women they served were viewed as ignorant because they did not fully embrace the drive to professionalize childbirth and motherhood. This "disorderly" threat to modernization in the rural regions of the state led reformers, shaped in the Progressive Era mold, to turn to state intervention in mandating middle-class ideas of proper child-birthing techniques.

Neville, along with the Kentucky State Medical Association, lobbied the legislature in the 1910s to enact regulations for midwives. In her study on the transformation of rural health in Appalachia, Sandra Lee Barney argued that the regulations, which included supervising the midwife profession, "gradually eliminated alternative practitioners across Appalachia. Ordered by law to obey the principles of scientific medicine, mountain people also were offered attractive inducements to accept their place as patients in the new medical order."[32] The regulation and control of midwife practices that were championed by reformers ushered in a new era of health services in the region. This era was marked by the professionalization of medicine and made physicians the "sole arbiters of medical diagnosis, prevention, and intervention."[33] Neville, who received no medical training, remained active in the medical community through the Mountain Fund and saw her position as caretaker to afflicted children and medical service provider as indispensable. While never diagnosing cases of gonorrhea or syphilis, she oversaw the care given and instructed the nurses who were involved with her "patients."

Statistics regarding the number of venereal disease cases and children born with gonorrheal eye infections or congenital syphilis were underestimated because doctors were not obligated to report incidences of infection until the 1940s, and many rural Kentuckians went untreated because of limited access to medical facilities and care in the rural areas of the state. The social stigma attached to venereal disease also discouraged those infected from seeking professional treatment, instead turning to folk remedies and "quacks" for quick cures.[34] In 1937 Dr. C. M. Moore, assistant collaborating epidemiologist for the City Board of Health in Lexington, reported there were 374 cases of syphilis and 158 cases of gonorrhea known by the board. There also were 11,959 visits made by patients to the venereal disease clinic operated by the health department in Lexington. Moore realized that these statistics did not encompass all possible cases of infection: "The number of gonorrhea cases coming to our attention represents only a small percent of cases occurring among our population. These diseases constitute our major health problem and they are becoming increasingly worse each year."[35] Neville's Mountain Fund statistics indicated she treated fifty-one babies with gonorrheal eye infections between March 1936 and January 1, 1940, and from 1947 to 1958 she received fifty-eight cases of such infection from the Frontier Nursing Service.

Beginning in the 1920s, county health departments extended across the state, which caused health officials to discover more cases of infants and children infected with gonorrhea of the eyes or congenital syphilis. Medical officers, social workers, and county judges often appealed to Neville for financial help in treating these children. Local officials and charity workers viewed Neville as their only hope in obtaining needed

"She Now Cries Out": Linda Neville 357

treatment for the impoverished children suffering from venereal disease. Despite her lack of education in medicine, Neville's public health work afforded her a rare professional status in the medical field, bridging the gap between the "modern" medical field and the bygone days of lay reformers.

She used this status to help the state's most needy children in areas where access to treatment and physicians was limited. Mary Rose McCourt, a charity worker with the Woman's Board of Home Missions in Leslie County expressed her gratitude for Neville's work in rural areas of the state. McCourt asked Neville for assistance in obtaining medical aid for a mother and her nine children, all of whom McCourt suspected of having syphilis. In her letter, McCourt wrote, "We feel so helpless, at times like this, away from our medical advisors, and it is a joy to be able to come to one who is so interested, and who had done so much for our mountain folk."[36]

However, the influx of syphilitic and gonorrheal sufferers seeking help through the Mountain Fund caused a mounting debt. According to Mountain Fund records, four gonorrheal babies cost the entity $1,072.40 for hospitalization and nursing.[37] The debt caused great stress for Neville, who reported that "the GC (gonorrhea) babies have required such long and expensive attention that each June for the past several Junes has found me with a debt that I have had to get paid by getting donations."[38] Neville exploited the children under her care to make an emotional appeal for financial help. By positioning these children as victims of poor parenting, she fomented middle-class interest in her cause.

Her appeals for donations even found their way to the area newspaper, the *Lexington Herald*. The 1937 publication featured a story about five babies who were undergoing treatment for gonorrheal eye infections at Good Samaritan Hospital. Neville and four nurses are prominently pictured above the article, holding the five infected infants. In her appeal for donations, Neville argued that state appropriations were inadequate and invoked the perceived immorality behind gonorrhea and syphilis. She was quoted as saying, "Let us maintain a sympathetic concern for all the babies who are made to suffer pain, and in some cases, permanent blindness because of the sinfulness of people."[39] The perceived immorality of parents influenced Neville to reach beyond treatment and address prevention by pursuing a premarital health bill that prevented couples with venereal disease from marrying. She placed herself on the frontlines of the attack against venereal disease, stating she wished to address the problem as one of health and not morals, but layered within her lobbying rhetoric and casework were moral indictments on the mothers who passed on their afflictions to their children.

Neville's attempts to encourage the involvement of religious institutions in her reform cause were indicative of the influence morality had in her public health work. She appealed to church officials about the need to prevent the spread of venereal disease through the use of emotional language that invoked the suffering of children infected with gonorrhea or syphilis. She offered a retelling of her experiences that dealt with the "many tragedies caused by venereal disease."[40] Neville hoped religious institutions would take a leading role in shaping public opinion toward the acceptance of a proposed premarital health bill. There were difficulties in the way of practical enforcement of the legislation, but "if only the preachers, men of Faith and the preaching of Faith, ought not to deafen the cries of little children, will lead the way Kentucky may cease witnessing the tragedies of blindness."[41] Drawing on her own experience, Neville described herself as "so agonized that she now cries out."[42] She went on to write that "even to unwilling ears she now cries out about the tragedy that is prepared for when by inheritance the tiny baby's blood is tainted with syphilis."[43] Through the retelling of her experiences and the pain she felt for infected children, Neville succeeded in convincing churches to become involved in state control of venereal disease.

Presumptions about the proper role of women in the public sphere, however, limited Neville's success in appealing to churches. The Southern Baptists were a powerful denomination in Kentucky, and Neville "wanted to go before the Baptist group in our state and was told there that, being a woman, I ought not to ask to go on the floor of a Southern Baptist Convention in Kentucky. I did not ask."[44] Neville maneuvered around these limitations by creating a statewide campaign that went beyond churches and legislators. She spoke to community organizations like the Kiwanis and Rotary clubs. Club members, in turn,

"She Now Cries Out": Linda Neville 359

lobbied their churches and legislators for the passage of a premarital health bill. She saw the necessity in recruiting private citizens to take action against venereal disease but put most of her faith behind the power of the churches. Religious officials realized their limitations in controlling the spread of infection, noting that "it is not enough for a church to pass a law that its ministers cannot marry anyone without such a medical certificate, because in that case an afflicted person would go to some magistrate and be married and thus be the cause of misery in the world."[45] Church officials viewed themselves as only one level of protection against the spread of disease and thought legislators and the state held the ultimate power in eradicating the suffering caused by syphilis and gonorrhea. The Episcopalian bishop of Lexington in 1938, Mather Almon Abbott, stated his frank position on the church's role, writing, "I regard the function of the Church to be not primarily legislature, but inspirational. In other words, the Church is not the gun. The Church is the man behind the gun."[46]

Neville was central to obtaining a premarital health bill, which demonstrated the power and authority she held through her work with impoverished children who were infected with venereal disease. In Neville's estimation, the state as well as the church should play a role in preventing a person with venereal disease from getting married and having children. Even though premarital health bills offered medical treatment to couples who sought marriage licenses, the justification behind this legislative public health measure was to preserve the health of children. The focus on children's health placed the actions of mothers under close scrutiny, allowing Neville to serve as an agent of the state in policing the behavior of women who sought help for their children or came to the attention of county charity workers.

Neville, like most reformers, endlessly trumpeted one call to action—the health of babies. This became her motivation for decades and explains why she pursued legislative measures through lobbying rhetoric that placed children at the forefront of care. She too seemed to be ignorant of the underlying issues involving economic conditions, lack of education, and medical access as it related to the spread of venereal disease. Neville was not a trained physician and saw her responsibility lying only with the children she treated and not the mothers of these children, whom she often described as neglectful and ignorant because of their impoverished lifestyles and lack of engagement in scientific motherhood.[47] The fathers of infected children are absent from Neville's case files and from medical literature addressing the infected newborns. Mothers shouldered the blame for becoming infected, becoming pregnant while infected, and giving birth to a child who inherited that infection. It was a "bad" mother who allowed such an event to take place and a blameless father who stood by "helplessly" or was absent throughout the course of infection, conception, pregnancy, and birth.

However, Neville was receptive and less critical of mothers who actively sought her assistance in obtaining medical treatment for their children. For example, Neville immediately contacted a Public Health Service physician working at a trachoma hospital in Pikeville after a mother appealed to her for help in treating her one-year-old daughter. Neville wrote to Dr. Raynor, explaining that Mrs. J. C. Adams needed treatment for her daughter, Johnnie Adams, who was blind and syphilitic. In this particular case, Neville felt she had a *shared* responsibility for the child's health, writing "we want to safeguard the little Johnnie."[48] Unlike the direct intervention of Johnnie Adams's mother, most cases came to Neville's attention through regional charity workers, county judges, and local public health nurses. In these instances, Neville held a less sympathetic view toward the mothers, as she often took the children under her care and only sparingly gave updates on the children's progress. She viewed the women who did not actively seek help for their children's ailment as neglectful and irresponsible mothers because of what she perceived as their selfishness in failing to obtain adequate treatment.

The mothers of the children placed under Neville's care were not passive recipients of this aid. Neville had to build trust with the mothers before they would agree to allow treatment at a hospital. In 1921 Neville took Pauline Meeks, a seven-year-old girl with cataracts and syphilis, under her care. Pauline's mother wrote numerous letters to Neville, pleading for information on her daughter's condition. Mary Meeks, who lived in Webb, West Virginia, which bordered Kentucky, expressed a cautious trust of Neville, writing, "I am so tender hearted so please make haste and get the work done and I am trusting you for you no [*sic*] best and also trusting Pauline in your care you go head [*sic*]

"She Now Cries Out": Linda Neville 361

and do what you think is best and let me hear often as I am so worried."[49] Giving her child over to Neville for medical treatment caused Meeks emotional strain. Her anxiety magnified throughout the course of her daughter's treatment because Neville often left Meeks's letters for updates unanswered. Meeks became more desperate to hear something from Pauline as the months dragged on with only sporadic updates from Neville. Eventually, Meeks decided to write directly to the Children's Free Hospital in Louisville, asking for the return of her child. However, the hospital superintendent, Anna B. Cowles, sought Neville's approval in the matter before sending Pauline back home.[50] Neville granted Mary Meeks's request to be reunited with her daughter after more than a year had passed since Pauline left home.

Though Neville gained status and power as an intermediary between the physicians treating the children and the children's families, mothers were not completely powerless in deciding the length of time for which their children would be under Neville's care. The relationship between Neville and Mary Meeks was built upon a cautious trust and shaped by a common concern for the health of the child. Neville wielded power in the professional field, as hospital officials often submitted their authority to her when deciding if a child should return at the request of the parents, but she was powerless when it came to the wishes of a mother to be reunited with her child. Mothers usurped what authority Neville had by directly writing hospital superintendents and flooding the reformer with letters of concern.

Neville took a sympathetic view of Mary Meeks and her need to be with her child, but in most of her case file notes she expressed sadness toward the children's conditions and borderline disgust concerning the behavior of their mothers. In 1922 Neville had two infants with gonorrheal eye infections under her care. The hospitals were overcrowded, so she had to place both in the same bed. Neville described one of the mothers as "insane" or "feeble-minded" and the other as "what I (and probably the world with me) would call bad."[51] She recalled that the two women did not get along, and it was reported to her that "one of the women tried to smother one of the babies, whether her own or the other woman's baby I do not recall."[52] She expressed disbelief at what she viewed as the mothers' ignorance or uncaring attitudes toward their children, but her overwhelming concern for the children and not the circumstances under which the mothers became impregnated or contracted a venereal disease influenced her harsh judgment.

The middle-class reformer maintained a deep distrust concerning the mothers' abilities to effectively continue treatment once the children were released from her care. In one case she indicated that "the mother's mental condition is such that she could not care for the case properly."[53] She expressed concern over the mother's mental health and abilities but made no mention of the father and his role in caring for the child. She saw herself as a surrogate mother to children suffering from gonorrheal eye infections, even writing to one concerned mother of an infected child that she would "do no good to the baby by visiting it."[54] Her dismay and distrust was often based on the length of time mothers waited before seeking help for their children. Many children that came into Neville's care were emergency cases and had been suffering from gonorrheal eye infections for weeks or living with congenital syphilis for years before receiving treatment.

In a few cases, women Neville criticized openly challenged the reformer's attempts to define them as "bad mothers." Becca McKinney allowed Neville to treat her two daughters, Madgie and Goldie May, for eye trouble related to gonorrhea. Despite being illiterate, McKinney dictated letters to Neville demanding to hear from her children. Offended at Neville's suggestion that Goldie May be put in a feeble-minded institute, McKinney criticized Neville's efforts to cure her daughters. In her response to McKinney's criticisms, Neville wrote: "I am going to write plainly to you. Perhaps you do not know that I have a comfortable home and could sit quitly [sic] in it and enjoy it without ever showing an [sic] concern for your children, whether they become blind or not."[55] Neville expressed anger over what she saw as McKinney's lack of appreciation for her efforts in getting Madgie and Goldie medical treatment. By describing the life of leisure she could enjoy, she criticized the impoverished mother for not showing deference to her authority as a middle-class reformer. McKinney, however, resisted the reformer's power to decide the best course of action for her children. Despite her illiteracy and poverty, the mother of Madgie and Goldie May refused to accept Neville's blame for not doing what was necessary for the health of her children. Eventually, Goldie May and Madgie were returned to Becca McKinney, as she insisted that home was the best place for them, and not in the hands of a middle-class reformer.

Becca McKinney challenged the perception of her as a "bad mother" by criticizing Neville as a "bad reformer." Though in some ways hampered, poor women demonstrated agency through their authority as mothers, just as Neville used her position as a middle-class woman and maternalistic concern to achieve status in the field of public health. Focusing on the "innocent" victims of venereal disease necessitated Neville's need to blame mothers for failing to protect their children from the ravages of gonorrhea and syphilis, but her powers were limited as a reformer who was met with resistance from the mothers whose children she tried to treat.

Rural women's concern for their children contradicted social reformers' rhetoric that perpetuated the stereotype of the neglectful mother. Many, like Becca McKinney, fought for the return of their children, but not all were successful in convincing Neville and the medical officials that the best place for their children was at home. In one of her earlier cases that related to trachoma, but also involved syphilis, Neville oversaw the treatment and rehabilitation of Virginia "Jennie" Owens, who lived in Hazard with her blind mother, Lucinda, before coming to the attention of charity workers in the area. Jennie was ten years old when Mrs. C. O. Chambless, the wife of a railroad contractor, contacted Neville about "a little ragged, dirty, blind girl" who lived in a hut with her "old mother" and begged for food scraps among the railroad workers. The railroad company leveled the hut as an obstruction to its right-of-way, leaving the mother and her daughter homeless.[56]

Chambless experienced difficulty in convincing Lucinda Owens that she and her daughter needed medical treatment for their eyesight and that Neville would help them obtain this form of professionalized intervention. Chambless found Lucinda frantic because someone had "poisoned her mind" into believing that she and Neville were trying to steal her child and put her in a poorhouse. The mother refused to be separated from Jennie and would only agree to treatment if she could go with her daughter.[57] Lucinda's suspicions were substantiated when Chambless secured guardianship of Jennie to "get her away." However,

Owens boarded the train with her daughter, refusing to allow the middle-class women to separate her and Jennie.[58]

This act of resistance allowed not only her daughter but Lucinda to be treated for their eye condition. It challenged the authority of reformers to ferry away children of supposedly "neglectful" mothers. The case of Jennie and Lucinda Owens demonstrated the deep connection between mother and daughter who fought to survive poverty and illness together. Dr. J. A. Stuckey, who treated them both, wrote to Neville about the love they had for one another: "I do not believe that treatment for either of them would have been successful had they been separated. It is as pathetic as it is beautiful to hear them talk to each other in encouraging tones when the painful treatment is being given."[59] However, Jennie stayed in Neville's care after her eyesight was almost entirely restored and Lucinda, still suffering from vision problems, was forced to return home without her daughter. Despite writing to Neville in 1915 asking for information about her daughter, she never saw Jennie again.[60]

After separating Jennie Owens from her mother, Neville shielded her from any information about Lucinda and acted as a surrogate mother until Jennie married and had a child in 1927. The young woman had asked about the whereabouts of her mother when she was a teenager, wanting to know, according to Neville, that Lucinda was not "absolutely wretched."[61] When Jennie discovered that her mother died in 1918, she rebelled against Neville by temporarily running away, leaving a note saying she "would be happier in the mountains."[62] Her return to the mountains after seven years of living in Lexington demonstrated Jennie's connection to her home and family, as well as the power she held to reject Neville's attempt to keep her from past experiences that shaped her life.

Neville expressed deep sadness concerning Jennie's absence, demonstrating her intimate involvement in these cases. She developed a tender attachment to many of the children she helped, which took an emotional toll. Maggie Murphy, an orphan, was one such child Neville agonized over and came to love. Murphy came to Neville's attention in 1920, when a physician in McCreary County asked Neville if she could find a hospital to treat the nine-year-old girl for syphilis. Murphy's father was deceased and her mother, suffering the mental effects of untreated syphilis, had reportedly beheaded her infant son.[63] Neville placed Murphy in the Louisville Free Children's Hospital, but after two years of failed syphilis treatment, the hospital decided to discharge Murphy, leaving Neville distraught as to where to place the child. "Last night I was worrying no little about the future of Maggie Murphy," Neville wrote to the superintendent of the Children's Free Hospital. "I have been thinking so much lately about her and trying to think out the best plans for her."[64]

Murphy was placed with her cousins, who lived in McCreary County, but she soon requested to "return home" to the hospital. Neville also found Murphy's cousins to be "ignorant people" who were unable to give Murphy "proper training."[65] Her harsh views of Murphy's family influenced Neville's dedication to finding a permanent home for Maggie where she could receive the treatment and direction the reformer thought she needed. Neville described Murphy as a "dear, affectionate, good child" who was not mentally bright but who had a "happy, lovely smiling face" and who was "always sweet." She often told Murphy that she loved her. Neville was, indeed, the constant in Maggie's life as she was in and out of hospitals and charitable institutions.[66]

Neville's reform work was unique in that she saw herself as a surrogate mother and a better caregiver than the mothers from whom she took the children. This intimate attachment motivated her unwillingness to allow these children to return to their homes. She thought she could provide them with a better life than the "bad" mothers whom she viewed as neglectful and ignorant of their children's needs. Her middle-class bias and belief in modern medicine influenced how she judged the mothering capabilities of the women who cautiously trusted their children to Neville.

As a lay reformer with respected status in the emerging professionalized field of medicine, Neville pursued venereal disease treatment work through the policing of childbirth practices with the regulations on midwifery and the prevention of marriage among those afflicted with venereal disease through the premarital health law. Both legislative victories were justified as measures promoting children's health. Neville succeeded in appealing for greater state intervention by further propagating and manipulating the stereotype of the ignorant impoverished mother, shifting the focus from women's health to that of their unborn child.

Despite the limitations of Neville's reform work, she created awareness of the health problems impacting the state's poor residents, and rural mothers took advantage of the opportunity to access medical treatment for their children. Even though women were held responsible for their children's health, they used this to demand medical aid from reformers like Neville and other local officials. Neville obtained professional status among medical officials and government authorities, but her power to dictate the lives and actions of the mothers whose children she took under her care was limited. The reformer's criticisms did not limit their power *as mothers*, as they advocated for what they thought was the best course of care for their children. Neville's use of mother-blaming rhetoric to meet fund-raising goals or achieve legislative victories empowered her as a respected public health reformer in the public sphere. But the targets of the "bad mother" discourse were not passive victims of Neville's reform efforts. As subjects of reform, they used Neville's biases to their advantage, gaining free treatment for their children and ultimately having a role in determining to what extent the "prophet" of middle-class values and professionalization of medicine would shape their lives.

NOTES

1. Rory O. Huntsman to Linda Neville, November 1937, Linda Neville Papers, box 73, folder 17, Special Collections, Margaret I. King Library, University of Kentucky, Lexington (hereafter referred to as LNP).

2. In her pioneering article on agency and Appalachian women, Barbara Ellen Smith challenged historians to reenvision women's role in Appalachia and move beyond agency in economic terms. Analyzing the public health movement in the region and women's role in shaping access to medicine is one way in which historians can transcend economic understandings of the development of the region and highlight women's role in shaping Appalachia. See Barbara Ellen Smith, "'Beyond the Mountains': The Paradox of Women's Place in Appalachian History," *National Women's Studies Association Journal* 11, no. 3 (Fall 1999): 1–17. Sandra Lee Barney laid the foundation for exploring women's role in the professionalization of medicine in *Authorized to Heal: Gender, Class, and the Transformation of Medicine in Appalachia, 1880–1930* (Chapel Hill: University of North Carolina Press, 2000). She argued that clubwomen and settlement workers became allies of physicians in bringing professional medicine, which replaced folk remedies and lay midwifery,

to the mountains. Neville was a significant part of this narrative as a proponent of professionalized medicine and a conduit through which mountain women gained access to physicians and hospitals.

3. Judy Gail Cornett, "Angel for the Blind: The Public Triumphs and Private Tragedy of Linda Neville" (PhD diss., University of Kentucky, 1993), 14.

4. Cornett, "Angel for the Blind," 19.

5. Ibid., 20.

6. Joyce Antler, "'After College, What?': New Graduates and the Family Claim," *American Quarterly* 32, no. 4 (Autumn 1980): 419; Cornett, "Angel for the Blind," 26.

7. Cornett, "Angel for the Blind," 31–36.

8. Trachoma is a bacterial infection of the eye that is spread by flies. It has largely been eradicated in the United States.

9. Sandra Lee Barney argued that women's clubs and settlement workers supported one another in their various causes. Drawing on Theda Skocpol, Barney argued that elite and middle-class clubwomen were bound to each other by their ideological ties. Barney, *Authorized to Heal*, 88.

10. Barney, *Authorized to Heal*, 93.

11. For a complete biographical account of Linda Neville's life, see Cornett, "Angel for the Blind."

12. David Whisnant described female reformers in the Appalachian region as "fotched on" women. His work analyzed how reformers used their middle-class biases to shape culture in the region. In what he termed "the politics of culture," Whisnant's work influenced how historians analyze the long-term consequences of middle-class reform in the Appalachian region. See David E. Whisnant, *All That Is Native and Fine: The Politics of Culture in an American Region* (Chapel Hill: University of North Carolina Press, 1983).

13. Robyn Muncy argued that the New Deal represented the culmination of women's reform activities. She used agencies created during the Progressive Era, such as the Children's Bureau and the School of Social Service Administration, to illustrate how they intersected to form a "female dominion" in the male-dominated field of policy making. Muncy focused on the middle-class nature of reform that continued into the 1930s and 1940s. Muncy found that while women sought professional status in the Progressive Era, they discovered men were only willing to accept them as professionals in work that involved women and children. Neville illustrates this argument, as her focus was on children afflicted with eye disorders, which led to a general acceptance by the male-dominated medical community in Kentucky. Robyn Muncy, *Creating a Female Dominion in American Reform, 1890–1935* (New York: Oxford University Press, 1991).

14. Molly Ladd-Taylor and Lauri Umansky, eds., *"Bad" Mothers: The Politics of Blame in Twentieth-Century America* (New York: New York University Press, 1998), 10–11.

15. Linda Neville to John McMullen, February 14, 1935, box 73, folder 5, LNP.

16. Ibid.

17. The blood test was developed by bacteriologist August Von Wassermann in the early twentieth century and was later replaced by the Kahn test, developed by immunologist Reuben Leon Kahn. Allan M. Brandt, *No Magic Bullet: A Social*

History of Venereal Disease in the United States Since 1880 (New York: Oxford University Press, 1985), 147–49.

18. Linda Neville, personal recollection, 1938, box 74, folder 4, LNP.

19. Brandt, *No Magic Bullet*, 14.

20. Linda Neville to Phi Omega Pi, October 19, 1942, box 75, folder 12, LNP.

21. Joan Jacobs Brumberg analyzed sexual maturation in adolescents and cultural changes in the twentieth century. In relation to sexuality, she argued that girls did not talk about sex or their own sexuality before the 1920s. The moral value placed on virginity collapsed as cultural innovations, such as the automobile, created a society where girls became more mobile and less restricted by parental control. A generational divide arose between mothers born in the Victorian Era and their daughters who embraced the Roaring Twenties and a newfound way to express their sexuality, which was forbidden to the generation before them. Neville came of age in the Victorian Era and continued to hold Victorian views about women's sexuality. Joan Jacobs Brumberg, *The Body Project: An Intimate History of American Girls* (New York: Random House, 1997).

22. Kathy Peiss, "'Charity Girls' and City Pleasures: Historical Notes on Working-Class Sexuality, 1880–1920," in *Passion and Power: Sexuality in History*, ed. Kathy Peiss and Christina Simmons (Philadelphia: Temple University Press, 1989). Like the reformers and social workers Kathy Peiss studied, Neville's understanding of sexuality was based on her middle-class upbringing and biases.

23. Linda Neville, "In 1939 Fourteen Babies with Gonorrheal Eye Infection and Two More," January 17, 1940, box 74, folder 11, LNP.

24. Ibid.

25. Ibid.

26. Barney, *Authorized to Heal*, 119–20.

27. Melanie Beals Goan, *Mary Breckinridge: The Frontier Nursing Service and Rural Health in Appalachia* (Chapel Hill: University of North Carolina Press, 2008), 68–69.

28. Ibid., 69.

29. Mountain Fund Case Files, 1911, box 104, folder 17, LNP.

30. Mary Breckinridge, "Midwifery in the Kentucky Mountains: An Investigation by Mary Breckinridge," John C. Campbell and Olive D. Campbell Papers, series 2, Writings, 1895–1965, folder 161, Southern Historical Collection, Louis Round Wilson Special Collections Library, University of North Carolina, Chapel Hill.

31. US Congress, Senate, Senate Committee on Agriculture and Forestry, *Demonstration Work in Rural Sanitation*, 72nd Cong., 1st sess., January 13, 1932.

32. Barney, *Authorized to Heal*, 120.

33. Ibid., 135.

34. Brandt, *No Magic Bullet*, 133.

35. C. M. Moore, "Report on Venereal Disease Cases in Lexington," 1937, box 73, folder 22, LNP.

36. Mary Rose McCourt to Linda Neville, August 21, 1923, box 116, folder 7, LNP.

37. Linda Neville, "In 1939 Fourteen Babies with Gonorrheal Eye Infection and Two More," January 17, 1940, box 74, folder 11, LNP.

38. Linda Neville, "Narrative from Oral or Written Reports," 1941, box 75, folder 1, LNP.

39. *Lexington Herald,* February 21, 1937, copy of article in box 73, folder 12, LNP.

40. Linda Neville, written introduction to church officials, 1937, box 73, folder 11, LNP.

41. Ibid.

42. Ibid.

43. Ibid.

44. Committee on Interstate and Foreign Commerce, *Investigation and Control of Venereal Diseases: Hearing Before the Committee on Interstate and Foreign Commerce,* 75th Cong., 3rd sess., 1938.

45. Deacon Christopher Sparling to Sen. Leer Buckley, February 1, 1938, copy of letter in box 73, folder 20, LNP.

46. Mather Almon Abbott to Linda Neville, September 17, 1938, box 73, folder 3, LNP.

47. Molly Ladd-Taylor and Lauri Umansky argued that mother-blaming was exacerbated during the Progressive Era because of the growth of state power and influx of childbearing experts. Middle-class women promoted a social reform movement historians call *maternalism.* Maternalists used the concept of "good" mothers, or those who had middle-class sensibilities and values, to build a welfare state. Ladd-Taylor and Umansky posited that "good" mother rhetoric caused maternalists to become more critical of mothers who were deemed bad because of their class status or ethnicity. Ladd-Taylor and Umansky, "'*Bad' Mothers,*" 10–12.

48. Linda Neville to Dr. Raynor, February 5, 1922, box 114, folder 3, LNP.

49. Mary Meeks to Linda Neville, September 17, 1921, box 113, folder 14, LNP. Special thanks to Kate Black, retired Appalachian history archivist from the University of Kentucky, and Kathi Kern, associate professor of history, for locating the case files of Pauline Meeks, Madgie and Goldie McKinney, and Jennie Owens. These sources were used in a women's history course taught by Kathi Kern at the University of Kentucky.

50. Anna Cowles to Linda Neville, October 28, 1922, box 133, folder 14, LNP.

51. Linda Neville to A. T. McCormick, June 17, 1922, box 114, folder 32, LNP.

52. Linda Neville, "In 1939 Fourteen Babies with Gonorrheal Eye Infection and Two More," January 17, 1940, box 74, folder 11, LNP.

53. Linda Neville to Dr. A. T. McCormick, June 17, 1922, box 114, folder 32, LNP.

54. Mountain Fund Case Files, 1934, box 122, folder 1, LNP.

55. Linda Neville to Becca McKinney, July 12, 1917, Box 110, folder 27, LNP.

56. Mrs. C. O. Chambless to President of the United Charities, January 7, 1913, box 110, folder 29, LNP.

57. Mrs. C. O. Chambless to Linda Neville, January 23, 1913, box 110, folder 29, LNP.

58. Mrs. C. O. Chambless to Linda Neville, January 26, 1913, box 110, folder 29, LNP.

59. J. A. Stuckey to Linda Neville, January 29, 1913, box 110, folder 29, LNP.

60. Lucinda Owens to Linda Neville, February 15, 1915, box 110, folder 29, LNP.

61. Linda Neville to Dr. Gross, May 4, 1920, box 110, folder 29, LNP.

62. Jennie Owens to Mary Neville, n.d., box 110, folder 20, LNP.

63. Linda Neville to Convent of the Good Shepherd, December 26, 1922, box 114, folder 27, LNP.

64. Linda Neville to Margaret Paddock, July 17, 1922, box 114, folder 27, LNP.

65. Maggie Murphy to Linda Neville, October 30, 1922, box 114, folder 27, LNP; Linda Neville to Convent of the Good Shepherd, December 26, 1922, box 114, folder 27, LNP.

66. Linda Neville to Judge Perkins, March 4, 1923, box 114, folder 27, LNP; Linda Neville to Hattie Perry, March 4, 1923, box 114, folder 27, LNP.

CHAPTER THIRTEEN

Garrison, Drewry, Meadows, and Bateman

Race, Class, and Activism in the Mountain State

LOIS LUCAS

African American men always have enjoyed the franchise in the state of West Virginia and have held political offices in the state since the 1890s. As a result, research on blacks in the Mountain State has focused on the experiences of African American men rather than African American women. In many cases, only scant documentation about the women exists. While the contributions of African American men to the state should not be overlooked, more research on the lives and experiences of African American women needs to be conducted to highlight the contributions and achievements of black women in the state. This chapter focuses on four prominent African American women whose names may be known, but whose experiences and roles in the development of West Virginia are relatively unknown and rarely understood. Insight into the lives of Memphis Tennessee Garrison, Elizabeth Drewry, Lucile Meadows, and Mildred Bateman will provide the foundation needed for a more comprehensive study of black women in the Mountain State.

The experiences and methods of each of these four women were unique. Memphis Garrison was a civil rights advocate. She held a somewhat enigmatic position as an organizer and field secretary for the National Association for the Advancement of Colored People (NAACP).

As a result, Garrison spoke out against discrimination while working as a social worker for a major coal company in southern West Virginia, yet she never addressed the issue of racial discrimination in the mining industry. In 1950 Elizabeth Drewry became the first African American woman to be elected to the West Virginia Legislature. Although she did not shy away from controversy, she tended to support and introduce legislation that favored wage workers, women, and health reform rather than legislation that focused on racial equality. Lucile Meadows was a noted and effective educator who worked to bridge the gap between the races, beginning in the classroom. Despite the political clout she acquired, she chose not to run for election to the legislature at the end of her appointed legislative term. As a medical doctor, Mildred Mitchell Bateman's activist style was markedly different from the others in that she was seemingly less vocal in the public sphere. Nevertheless, her activist style was just as effective in advancing the cause of equality for African Americans in West Virginia. The experiences of all four of these women were shaped by race, class, and the social, economic, and political climate of the Mountain State.

MEMPHIS TENNESSEE GARRISON

Teacher and civil rights activist Memphis Tennessee Garrison (1890–1988) is probably the best known of the four women in this study. Born in Virginia in 1890, Garrison was the daughter of former slaves Wesley Carter and Cassie Thomas Carter, who moved to West Virginia at the turn of the twentieth century. Her father worked as a coal miner, and her mother worked as a housekeeper and nurse for white families, at hotels and boarding houses, and took in laundry. Garrison attended Bluefield State College and later became a teacher and welfare worker for U. S. Steel in the company town of Gary, West Virginia, where her husband, William Melvin Garrison, worked as an electrician and coal company foreman.[1]

Although her father died when she was young, Garrison had the influence and unconditional support of her mother, who lived with her until she died in 1941. "Unlettered, but highly intelligent," deeply religious, and with a gift for organization, Cassie Thomas Carter had a profound impact on Garrison's life. With a supportive husband, no children, and a mother who took care of household chores, Garrison

Garrison, Drewry, Meadows, and Bateman 373

was free to pursue the teaching she loved and the inequalities she found. Active in Republican Party politics and the NAACP, Garrison served as the secretary of the Gary, West Virginia, branch of the NAACP and organized numerous local chapters throughout counties in southern West Virginia. In 1925 Garrison wrote to the NAACP director of branches, Robert W. Bagnall, asking "Why not institute an Annual sale of NAACP Christmas Seals?—Using as a basis for the design the NAACP emblem. We have been selling seals each year for 'Health and Wealth' why not for Justice?" The seals became a significant fundraiser for the organization. In addition to her political activities, Garrison also brought black culture to the southern West Virginia coalfields. With the backing of U. S. Steel, she instituted the Negro Artists Series, which brought well-known black artists into the region. As a teacher, Garrison often worked with special needs children, and her research on children with developmental problems was used at Columbia University. Garrison became the first female president of the West Virginia State Teacher's Association and vice president of the American Teachers Association.[2]

ELIZABETH SIMPSON DREWRY

Born in Motley, Virginia, Elizabeth Simpson Drewry (1893–1979) was the eldest of ten children born to Grant and Katherine Simpson. The family moved to Elkhorn in McDowell County, West Virginia, where Grant Simpson opened a barber shop. By 1910, Elizabeth Drewry was working as a teacher in African American coal camp schools along the Elk River. Educated at Bluefield Colored Institute, Wilberforce, and the University of Cincinnati, Drewry earned a degree from Bluefield in 1933. A member of the Delta Sigma Theta sorority, Drewry became active in black state and national education associations.[3]

Politically active throughout the Jim Crow era, Drewry was a Republican precinct poll worker in 1921, but in 1936 she switched her political affiliation to the Democrat Party. She worked with the American Red Cross, the Northfork Town Council, the McDowell County Public Library, and the NAACP and served as associate chair of the McDowell County Democratic Executive Committee. In 1948 Drewry ran for the West Virginia House of Delegates and lost, but in 1950 she became the first black woman elected to the state legislature. Serving as a delegate from 1951 until 1964,

Drewry introduced legislation in favor of health care reform, teachers, and workers. In her first term she exposed the attempted bribery of legislators by coal operators, and in 1955 she sponsored a bill to allow women to serve on juries in West Virginia. While in the legislature, she chaired the Military Offices and Health committees and served on the Judiciary, Education, Labor and Industry, Counties, Districts, and Municipalities committees. Following a stroke, Drewry retired in 1966.[4]

LUCILE SMALLWOOD MEADOWS

Lucile Smallwood Meadows (1918–1997) was born to Soloman and Lovennia Smallwood in Glen Ferris, West Virginia. Growing up in Glen Ferris, she experienced racial discrimination firsthand. She attended a two-room elementary school for African American children. Although the Smallwoods lived approximately two miles from the nearest high school, Meadows and other black students in the area had to travel twenty-five miles to Montgomery, West Virginia, to attend Simmons High School for blacks because blacks and whites were forbidden to attend school together in the state.

After high school, Meadows went on to attend West Virginia Collegiate Institute, where she earned a Bachelor of Arts degree in education in 1939. She then obtained a position as a teacher in the Fayette County school system, where she taught for over thirty years.

A human rights and civil rights activist, Meadows joined the NAACP as a teenager and worked throughout her life to eradicate social and racial inequalities, particularly in education. Meadows organized the Fayette County Black Caucus in 1976. In 1977 Governor Jay Rockefeller appointed her to the West Virginia Women's Advisory Committee and the West Virginia State Journal Vocational Education Advisory Committee, where she served for eight years. She also served two years on the Governor's Judicial Commission. In 1990 Governor Gaston Caperton appointed Meadows to fill a vacancy in the West Virginia House of Delegates, where she proposed the removal of the obsolete law against black and white children being educated in the same schools from the West Virginia Constitution. During her time in the legislature, Meadows served on the Political Subdivisions, Government Organizations, Constitutional Revision committees, and the West Virginia State Ethics Commission.[5]

Garrison, Drewry, Meadows, and Bateman 375

MILDRED MITCHELL BATEMAN

A trailblazer in the treatment of mental health for over sixty years, Mildred Mitchell Bateman (1922–2012) was the daughter of Presbyterian minister Suder Q. Mitchell and his wife, Ella Lee Mitchell, a nurse. A native of Georgia, Bateman attended Barber-Scotia College in Concord, North Carolina, and Johnson C. Smith University in Charlotte, North Carolina, before earning her MD from the Women's Medical College of Pennsylvania in 1946. After completing her studies, Bateman accepted a position at Lakin State Hospital, a black hospital for the mentally ill in Lakin, West Virginia, for twenty-five dollars a month. She left Lakin to attend the Menninger School of Psychiatry in Topeka, Kansas, and then returned to Lakin, where she served as clinical director before being named as supervisor in 1958. In 1960 she was named supervisor of professional services at the West Virginia Department of Mental Health. In 1962 Governor Wallace "Wally" Barron appointed Bateman director of the West Virginia Department of Health, a position she held for fifteen years. As a result of this appointment, Bateman became the first African American woman to head a West Virginia state agency, and in 1973 she became the first African American woman to serve as vice president of the American Psychiatric Association.[6]

In 1977 President Jimmy Carter appointed Bateman as one of four psychiatrists to serve on the President's Commission on Mental Health. That same year, she became chair of the Psychiatric Department at the Marshall University medical school in Huntington, West Virginia. By 1985 she had become associate clinical director at the school and clinical director in 1996. During that time, Bateman won numerous awards. After receiving awards from the National Medical Association Section on Psychiatry and Neurology, the 1995 E. Y. Williams Distinguished Clinical Scholars Award, the 1996 Wyeth-Ayerst Physician Award for community work, in 1999 Governor Cecil Underwood renamed Huntington State Hospital the Mildred Mitchell Bateman Hospital. Bateman also received a Lifetime Achievement Award from the American Psychiatric Association in 2000 and the 2004 Governor's Award for Civil Rights Contributions.[7]

A GROWING BLACK POPULATION

At the end of World War I, thousands of blacks began their great migration to the North in hopes of escaping the Jim Crow laws of the South.

Many found jobs along the way and never actually moved above the Mason-Dixon Line. West Virginia, with its expanding coal-mining industry, attracted a number of blacks and immigrants who settled in the state's southern coal fields. As a result of the influx of blacks into the region, not only did West Virginia's black population increase significantly, but a distinct black middle class arose and prospered. Out of this group came a number of male African American politicians. Because black males were not denied the franchise in West Virginia, they were able to participate in the political process long before the turn of the century in 1900. Moreover, after women won the right to vote in 1920, within less than fifty years white and black women in West Virginia were running for and holding political offices.[8] Prior to this time, most women in the state had not actively participated in politics. Those who did usually did so within the confines of women's clubs and focused on issues related to women's suffrage, temperance, and various other reform movements.[9]

It is against this backdrop that the lives of Garrison, Drewry, Meadows, and Bateman took shape. Garrison and Drewry were among the first wave of African Americans to migrate to West Virginia with their families during the last decade of the nineteenth century. Both their families left Virginia to seek better employment opportunities in West Virginia. Meadows was the only one of the four women born in the Mountain State. Bateman came to West Virginia at the request of a friend of her parents to assist in the treatment of the mentally ill. Although their reasons for residing in the state varied, they all advocated the importance of personal advancement and racial uplift. As a result, all four women attended college and became members of the middle class in their own right. Three of them—Garrison, Drewry, and Meadows—grew up in southern West Virginia during the boom period of the coal-mining industry.[10]

EXPANSION OF THE BLACK MIDDLE CLASS IN WEST VIRGINIA

As the number of black miners increased, so did the number of black businesses and professional workers. By 1920 the number of blacks in middle-class occupations had increased by 30 percent. In addition to a growing number of professional workers, this group included public

Garrison, Drewry, Meadows, and Bateman 377

schoolteachers, barber and beauty shop owners, hotel and drugstore owners, artisans, and clerical employees. The increasing segregation and discrimination of the Jim Crow era, the continued influx of black migrants into the area, and the expansion of the black working class contributed to the rise of a black middle class.[11] Garrison's and Meadows's parents were not a part of the middle class. However, as schoolteachers, each of them became members of that class. In contrast, Drewry and Bateman's parents were members of the middle class prior to their arrival in the state. Drewry's father was a barber by profession, a skill he brought with him to West Virginia. Bateman's father was a Presbyterian minister and her mother was a nurse.[12]

Historian Carole Marks, in an observation that illustrates the experiences of the Simpson and Bateman families, noted that not all blacks who moved to the North were unskilled laborers, as generally believed. She cites Arna Bontemps and Jack Conroy, authors of *They Seek a City*, who maintain that many migrating blacks had "property and good positions," which they gave up in their efforts to get away from the South.[13]

Fannie Simpson Poole, Drewry's sister, stated in a 1997 interview that the family came looking for work, and they came seeking better opportunities. The Simpson's made up a small but rising middle-class group of blacks in Elkhorn. As Marks notes in her composite about black migrants, the Simpson brothers were not without skills. Not only did Drewry's father and his brothers own their own barber shops, Drewry's father also owned a home in the white section of Elkhorn, the only black family to do so at that time. His barbershop was located in Elkhorn, while his brothers, William and Roscoe, set up their businesses in the neighboring communities of Keystone and Freeman respectively.[14] Grant Simpson's barber shop catered to a black and white clientele. His business was divided into two sections. One side serviced blacks only, while the other side serviced whites. Simpson himself always cut the hair of his white customers, and he was the personal barber of John Lincoln, general manager of the Crozer, Upland, and Page Coal and Coke Companies.[15]

Bateman differs from the other three women in that her parents never moved to West Virginia, she was not born in the state, she did not settle in the southern part of the state, and she was not linked in any way to the mining industry. She came as a medical doctor and settled in Lakin, located in western West Virginia. Her family was already middle class. Bateman's father, Suder Mitchell, was a Presbyterian minister. After graduating from Biddle Memorial Institute in Charlotte, North Carolina, he went on to attend the school's theological seminary and later became the pastor of a local Presbyterian church in the area. When Bateman's mother, Ella, completed her nurse's training at the Lucy Laney School for Nurses in Augusta, Georgia, she became an obstetrics nurse for a white physician.[16]

Members of the black middle class worked hard to disprove the stereotypes attributed to African Americans by white society. Kevin Gaines maintains that "in their desire to counter ... [these] stereotypes, black elites based their authoritative status on ... formulaic racialized conceptions of bourgeois morality." In other words, he points out that they focused on a "vision of racial uplift" based on the idea of self-help. Gaines also states that bourgeois morality was to be evidenced in the home, in the family with the father as the head, in the male's role as protector of the female. He also notes that the same bourgeois morality could be seen in their quest for a college education, and in their focus on respectable behavior for both genders. Moreover, Gaines states that disfranchisement and Jim Crow laws permeated the public sphere to the extent that many African Americans "focused on those private areas perceived to be within their control, namely the domestic realm.[17]

Women were essential in the domestic arena. Their expected role was to bring improvements to the home and family by setting a moral standard of behavior. At the same time, women attempted to create a viable political role for themselves "that would flourish in the nineteenth century."[18] The role of white middle-class women was idealized, as they assumed a "purportedly gentler and more natural role in childrearing."[19] In other words, American middle-class white women, unable to vote or hold political office, constructed a place for themselves based on a woman's place in the home and the idea that a nation could endure if its male citizens were instilled with a sense of public virtue. In her book *Each Mind a Kingdom*, Beryl Satter states that in the years following the Civil War, middle-class women "devoted themselves to uplifting the nation's moral character" by organizing mother's clubs, moral education

Garrison, Drewry, Meadows, and Bateman 379

societies, and social purity leagues, "which were devoted to holding men and women to a single high standard of sexual morality."[20]

Gaines maintains that in the late Victorian Age, respectable sexuality was restricted to reproduction within marriage and marriage "as a sign of monogamous sexual purity conferred status on black men and women." Consequently, many African American reformers adopted the racial views of whites as "home-training" came to serve as the blue print for "social mobility and success."[21] Many white women who attended college were working to bring about social reforms for their own race. College-educated black women, however, were trained to be schoolteachers, nurses, church workers, and domestics. The education black women received at Spelman College in Atlanta, Georgia, for example, was characterized by a strong emphasis on domestic ideology and stressed the importance of students learning to become "good wives and mothers." Spelman focused on developing strong morals, which distinguished it from white women's institutions, where the primary emphasis was on refinement and propriety.[22]

Spelman was not the only African American college to focus on domestic ideology and strong moral character among women. Cynthia Neverdon-Morton reveals that Hampton Institute in Virginia "endorsed the idea that women's influence was a key factor in the progress of Afro-Americans." As a result, the school designed its curriculum for women to train those "who possessed "broader intelligence, higher morality, and proper methods of homemaking."[23] The home and family life were the epitome of middle-class morals and behavior for blacks and whites.[24]

AFRICAN AMERICAN MIDDLE-CLASS VALUES

Yet despite the desire of some African Americans to incorporate the views of whites, it also has been argued that because of their pressing economic needs, most black women could not afford the luxury of remaining at home solely devoted to their marriages and roles as mothers.[25]

Although the general belief of society was that women should work in the domestic sphere to improve the "morality of home and family," African American women had to be both "indoor and outdoor agents" in their efforts to improve their home lives while promoting the social uplift of their race.[26] In other words, black women promoted racial uplift in their homes and in the public sphere. Making the same point, Patricia Hill Collins contends that "African and African American women have long integrated economic self-reliance with mothering." She also notes that although work, "in contrast to the cult of true womanhood," is defined as being incompatible with and in opposition to motherhood, for black women it has been an important and valued dimension of Afrocentric definitions of black motherhood.[27]

In her book *Too Heavy a Load*, Deborah Gray White reveals that Addie Dickerson, a leading clubwoman in Philadelphia and leader in the Northeastern Federation of African American Clubwomen, believed that "women reached their highest function as mothers and directors of the home." She felt, too, that women had to work with other progressives, black and white, to ensure better economic opportunities for black women and to vigorously fight against Jim Crow practices.[28]

The same middle-class values and concerns were evident in Drewry's parents' home. Clearly, Grant Simpson was the head of his household and worked hard to provide for his family. He and his wife, Katherine, instilled in their children the importance of succeeding. Although Katherine Simpson was not a social activist, she was committed to the upkeep of her household and to helping her children maintain a strong sense of achievement, perseverance, integrity, upright behavior, and the necessity of a good education. Mildred Bateman's family also adhered to the same ethos of success. Her parents worked to ensure that all three of their children would be college educated. Although her father did not become the doctor he had hoped to become, the rest of his family worked in the medical profession. Bateman's brother became a general surgeon in Washington, DC, and her sister was a medical technician who married a physician.[29]

Bateman stated that her goals were firmly rooted in her childhood and commented, "I suppose I got the idea of being a doctor from my father. He always hoped to be a physician. He spoke of it often."[30] Her family wanted her to do well, but they encouraged her to take music and become a teacher. She stated, however, that from the time she was six years old, her mind was made up to become a doctor.[31]

Many black parents believed that child-rearing strategies, along with self-discipline and self-assurance, were essential to the success

Garrison, Drewry, Meadows, and Bateman 381

of their daughters in the public and private spheres. Such upbringing partly prepared their daughters "not just for work but for professional positions, activism, and leadership roles."[32] Along with improvements in family life, African Americans saw education as another means of personal and racial uplift. Some black men generally agreed, despite other views on the "the woman question," that black women were entitled to have equal access to education, which most blacks viewed as the major vehicle for racial uplift.[33] Therefore, African American middle-class parents set out to ensure that their children, especially their daughters, would receive the best education they could provide them, the first step toward racial uplift and equality. In her study of eighty African American women who worked in the "feminized professions" between the 1880s and the 1950s, Stephanie Shaw maintains that the parents of these women "intended that these daughters escape the traditional occupational traps most black women had to endure and they expected the daughters to make some difference in the lives of the many people in their communities who did not enjoy the advantages that they did."[34] According to Cynthia Neverdon-Morton, "individual growth and group improvement were inextricably intertwined."[35]

As a single parent, Garrison's mother worked as a laundress and maid to take care of her daughter and provide for her education. She also adhered to the principle that education was essential to personal achievement and racial uplift. While it is not clear whether Meadows's parents were members of the middle-class or not, they also shared the same middle-class values. Early in their daughter's life, they made plans for her to attend college. While the education background of Drewry's parents is not known, it is known that they expected their children to attend college. As college graduates, Bateman's parents expected the same from their children. Higher education was clearly a source of pride for many members of the black middle class.[36]

While blacks sought to improve their lot by refuting the negative stereotypes of their race, black women also attempted to disprove the negative stereotypes of their gender. Middle-class parents did not want their daughters working as domestics, which brought with it the threat of sexual harassment from white men. Work outside the home often meant domestic work in the homes of white people or in hotels. Such work generally exposed black women to "possible dangers . . . [from] . . . the man of the house or delivery boys . . . [who] forced black girls into illicit relationships."[37]

Black parents were well aware that their daughters were especially vulnerable to sexual abuse. Therefore, they attempted to protect them by encouraging them to get an education and not to present themselves in sexual or sensual ways. They also tried to control their daughters' physical appearance by not permitting them to wear makeup until they were almost in their college years. As Fannie Poole reminisced about her family, she confirmed unknowingly what historians have researched extensively to find regarding the way some African American parents reared their daughters: "We usually went to church, played basketball at school, or stayed home. When night time came, we all had to be inside. We were not allowed to wear makeup or date until we were eighteen or nineteen, going off to college."[38] Shaw states that such restrictions were implemented with the hope of warding off sexual abuse and the potential lecherous attentions of young men. The aim of a number of black middle-class parents was to influence other people's, including whites', impression and treatment of their daughters.[39]

Although parents were very aware of the sexual exploitation of black women, they also recognized that their daughters were sensual and sexual beings. Therefore, rather than deny or ignore this fact, as some Victorians did, they acknowledged the possibility that their daughters would consent to a sexual relationship and, therefore, attempted to put safeguards in place to prevent relationships. Shaw explains that some parents, such as Booker T. Washington for example, chose the men who would escort their daughters to social functions while others had parties chaperoned where both males and females were in attendance.[40]

Shaw makes another point that appears to be relative to Elizabeth Drewry's life. She notes that the idea that their daughters could become willing participants in a heterosexual relationship implies that not only white men, but black men, were suspect.[41] While Drewry appears to have been a willing participant in her relationship with William Drewery, it is not known how they met.[42] Although their relationship did lead to marriage, their union was not without controversy. Unlike Garrison, Meadows, and Bateman, who married as adults, by the time she was seventeen Drewry had become a wife and mother.[43] Little is known about

Garrison, Drewry, Meadows, and Bateman 383

William H. Drewery except that he was an educator.[44] For some unexplained reason, he left West Virginia and eventually moved to Chicago.

William Drewery may have left the state as a result of a controversy that arose between him and his wife.[45] Although records reveal an earlier marriage of William H. Drewery to a Della E. Price in Northfork on December 22, 1904, no record has been found of his marriage to Elizabeth Simpson.[46] Whatever the reason for their separation, it may not have been amicable. In a letter she wrote to her daughter, Lucile, Drewry expressed dissatisfaction with her husband. Although she did not explain the cause of her displeasure, her refusal to contact him indicated that they were not living together.[47] If little is known about William Drewery, even less is known about his marriage to Elizabeth. In her discussion of African American clubwomen, Deborah Gray White offers an explanation. She reveals that many leading African American women left few records of their private lives. Most of the collections left are filled with public memorabilia, rather than personal materials. Although White admits that the historian's task is made more difficult when attempting to piece together the private lives of these black women leaders, she argues that they used great strategy by making their cause of racial uplift and their private lives indistinguishable to themselves, their peers, and future generations.[48]

For each of the women in this study, more is known and can be found about their public lives than about their private lives. The wives spoke little about their husbands. Garrison gave some indication that her husband was supportive of her activism. However, he died in 1942, and the majority of her activist work took place after 1945. Meadows's husband appears to have been the most publicly active in his own right. As a member of the Fayetteville City Council, Clinton Meadows shared his wife's interest in community work. Bateman met her husband while the two of them were on the staff at Lakin Hospital. When asked why the African American women of her generation who were public figures spoke or revealed very little about their husbands and their private lives, she explained that it was a protective mechanism. As it was with Garrison and Meadows, she stated that her husband was very supportive of her work, but because he was something of a loner, he did not like the public arena personally.[49]

AFRICAN AMERICAN WOMEN'S ACTIVISM IN WEST VIRGINIA

Whatever their reasons were for remaining silent about their private lives, they were hard workers, and they chose to define themselves in terms of their activist roles and their work outside their homes. These women were strong examples. They put into practice the ideas of self-help and racial uplift. They lived during a time when more women were attending college, taking on jobs outside the home, and participating in the political process as a result of women's suffrage.

Yet blacks often faced exclusion in the various reform movements that swept across the country. Blacks had to contend with racial discrimination in voting, housing, education, busing, and other public facilities. White resistance to the influx of blacks in urban centers, in many cases, turned violent as whites rioted in several cities. Blacks leaving the South were well aware that the North was not Heaven, but they did believe that it was a place where they could freely vote without the fear of being lynched and/or exploited.[50] As a result, the political clout of blacks had grown in the cities, and they were aware that their ballots could make a difference in the blow against racism in the United States. In her study of Ida Wells-Barnett, Patricia Schechter states that educated and urban black women took advantage of the expanded opportunities in civil life that accrued generally to middle-class women during the period.[51]

In West Virginia, south of the Mason-Dixon Line, de facto segregation existed. The only segregation mandated by law was in schools and marriage. As a result, blacks maintained the franchise when states farther south did not. Delegate Harry Capehart, an African American legislator, sponsored the Capehart Anti-Lynching Bill that passed through the state legislature in 1921, establishing a $5,000 fine against any county in which a lynching took place, and the West Virginia Supreme Court upheld the legislation when it fined Greenbrier County for the 1931 lynching deaths of two African American men. They were the last lynchings to occur in the state.[52]

By the 1920s, African Americans had recognized that Booker T. Washington's accommodationist policy for blacks was not sufficient or adequate to bring about racial uplift. As a result of a continuing disillusionment with Washington's views, as well as a number of social, political,

Garrison, Drewry, Meadows, and Bateman 385

and economic circumstances, the decade witnessed the rise of a "New Negro." Gaines maintains that "the success of Bolshevism in Russia, the democratic ideals of World War I, the anti-colonial implications of Woodrow Wilson's Fourteen Points, and the mass migration of blacks to urban areas," all helped to create the conditions "for more militant 'New Negro' intellectuals and leadership."[53] Although black soldiers serving in World War I did little to improve the status of blacks in America, the war did provide the stimulus for the mass migration that fashioned a socially ambitious and increasingly culturally diverse black industrial proletariat.[54]

It was specifically the emergence and expansion of the black coal-mining proletariat that created unusual opportunities for black politicians in West Virginia. Black middle-class leaders created many black Republican clubs, through which they skillfully appealed to the socioeconomic, political, and cultural interests of the growing proletariat electorate. After World War I, many of these leaders established the earliest NAACP branches in West Virginia. As a result, black leaders such as Harry Capehart were able to win civil rights legislation, policy changes, and court decisions favorable to blacks by developing interracial alliances, especially with white Republicans. In addition, increased black migration into southern West Virginia after World War I and the rise of the black working class coincided with the woman's suffrage movement of the 1920s and therefore increased the potential political power of blacks in the state.[55]

Although most women could not vote prior to 1920, it did not diminish the role black women played in black electoral politics.[56] As early as 1916, the McDowell County Colored Republican Organization (MCCRO) recognized the increasing political importance of women and appointed three to its Civic Committee. This committee had the responsibility of investigating the larger social welfare and community issues affecting African Americans.

Following the passage of the women's suffrage amendment in 1920, black women increased their involvement in the political process even more.[57] Even so, middle-class black women's interests had little to do with the Equal Rights Amendment debate that had been played out between the conservative League of Women Voters and the more radical National Woman's Party. Instead, African American women were more interested in issues related to the downtrodden of their own race or people of color throughout the world, rather than in issues limited to middle-class feminists. In her essay titled "Discontented Black Feminists," Rosalyn Terborg-Penn states that although "the economic roles of many white American women were expanding" during the period between 1920 and 1945, the status of African American women remained virtually unchanged. Consequently, "black feminists identified more with the plight of third world people who found themselves in similar situations," working primarily as domestics. Terborg-Penn adds that former black suffragists more likely participated in organizations such as the Women's International League for Peace and Freedom or the International Council of Women of the Darker Races.[58]

Blacks were especially active politically in McDowell County. In 1870, prior to the rise of the coal-mining industry, there were no blacks in McDowell. By 1910 they made up 34.1 percent of the total voting-age male population. The approximately seven thousand whites in the county usually spit their votes between the Republicans and Democrats. However, blacks in the county were solidly Republican and established a number of Colored Republican Clubs throughout the county.[59] As a result, African Americans constituted a formidable political force.

In the southern part of the state, political activism quickly became a very serious matter for African Americans. "I became a Republican when, the first time I voted and they were taking a registration," recalled Memphis Garrison when asked about her interest in politics.[60] She remained a registered Republican for the remainder of her life. Although she explained that she remained a member of the Republican Party because she wanted to and because she felt that by choosing otherwise she was being disloyal to what she had always believed in, Garrison did not always vote Republican.[61]

Garrison never held a state political office, but she was very much involved in the political process. From 1932 until 1940, she served as chair of the Colored Women's Republican Club, working in campaigns both state- and nationwide. Garrison was a keen inside observer of the functions of West Virginia politics. She was well aware that blacks in West Virginia were not helpless, downtrodden people. They were a highly organized and politically skillful constituency.[62]

Garrison, Drewry, Meadows, and Bateman 387

Bateman, like Garrison, did not run for political office but was appointed director of the West Virginia State Mental Health Department in 1962. At the time of her appointment, she was serving as the supervisor of professional services in the department, which had been under the direction of Dr. Charles A. Zeller. When his sudden death left the position vacant, Governor William Barron named Bateman acting director in July of 1962. By December of the same year, he appointed her as permanent director.[63]

Although Bateman met with some prejudices, she always maintained a calm and poised demeanor. Of the four women in this study, she would have been less vocal about a personal injustice. Despite being a woman of a few words, however, she was not afraid to address an issue. Her colleagues described her as a "quiet crusader." Holding her post for more than a decade, Bateman was the first African American woman to head a state department in West Virginia. She increased the number of mental health clinics throughout the state from four to eleven and provided some form of mental health services in all but one county in the state.[64]

Elizabeth Drewry began her political career in 1946, when she ran for the state's House of Delegates. Although she lost her bid for political office in 1946 and again in 1948, she did not give up. Despite the fact that she contested her defeat in 1948, her opponent Harry Pauley was declared the winner. By 1950, however, Drewry had become a lot wiser. Canvassing from door to door and making the right connections, she won her first victory and gained the distinction of becoming the first African American woman elected to the West Virginia Legislature. To her credit, she never lost another election.[65]

When Lucile Meadows ran for the House of Delegates in 1980, she was the first African American woman from Fayette County to do so. Prior to the expansion of the mining industry, Fayette County led the way in sending black representatives to the West Virginia Legislature. The county elected its first black legislator in 1896, Christopher H. Payne.[66] However, Meadows's first bid for office resulted in a defeat. She never ran for office again, but she did remain politically active. She served as president of the Fayette County Democratic Women's Club, as a member of the state Democratic Executive Committee, and as a delegate to four Democratic national conventions. In 1990 Governor

Gaston Caperton named Meadows to fill Representative John Hatcher's vacated seat in the West Virginia House of Delegates when he accepted an appointment as circuit judge.[67]

In their essay on women in southern legislatures between 1946 and 1968, Joanne Hawks and Carolyn Staton reveal that the women of this period were transitional figures who set the stage for female political activists of the 1970s and 1980s. They describe these women as trailblazers for the postwar legislators who followed them. Slowly and steadily they began to occupy seats in the southern legislatures during the 1920s. Hawks and Staton found that "most were short-term legislators; few served more than one or two terms."[68]

What compelled black and white women to step out of the traditional role society defined for them as the keepers and nurturers of their homes and families? The needs of women, children, and persons with mental, physical, and moral handicaps concerned many of these women. In other words, they were progressives who sought to use state government for the improvement of their communities. For the most part, these women were quite accustomed to working in the public sphere as members of women's organizations, as professionals, as businesswomen, or as political party workers. Hawks and Staton contend that through their organizations, these women became familiar with serious issues of social and public concern. They learned how gains could be made through their club work, and "in many cases, their legislative interests mirrored the concerns of the organized groups in which they had worked or held leadership positions."[69]

The issues that concerned a number of white females in politics during the period between 1946 and 1968 included education, health reforms, provisions for child care, aid for the mentally ill and handicapped, care for the aged, and election reform. They believed that legislation was the best means by which to institute needed reforms in society. Although African American women's concerns were the same, the reforms advanced by white women and other progressives did not include blacks, as Jim Crow laws were firmly entrenched, legally and culturally, prior to the late 1960s. Therefore, through their own organizations and professions, black women also addressed issues regarding education, health, children, the disabled, and suffrage.[70] Concomitant

Garrison, Drewry, Meadows, and Bateman 389

with their concerns was their fight against the Jim Crow practices of the South. Consequently, their interest in politics stemmed from their desire to ameliorate the conditions they encountered in the South. Ironically, African Americans in West Virginia were in a position to capitalize on those conditions. As the state of West Virginia created numerous segregated institutions throughout the 1920s, positions of leadership in those institutions provided blacks with political and leadership skills and gave them the ability to control institutions that directly affected the well-being of the black community at large.[71]

In her study of women pioneers in West Virginia politics, Jo Boggess Phillips maintains that the numerous women who served in the state's legislature dared to "break the gender barrier" and entered "the male dominated world of state politics." At a time when the abilities of women were greatly underestimated, women in West Virginia were politically active.[72] One of the first organizations to serve as an outlet for women to address political issues was the woman's club movement. Phillips maintains that women regarded their membership in a woman's club as a means of providing "constructive public service for both their local community and their state." In 1904 the national General Federation of Women's Clubs established a state federation of women's clubs in West Virginia. Phillips states that through their efforts, state clubwomen established libraries, pushed to include home economics as a course in school curricula, set up and operated baby and tuberculosis clinics, purchased milk for schoolchildren, and promoted visual and radio education.[73]

Between 1890 and 1895, the black women's club movement emerged, creating two national associations, the National Federation of Afro-American Women and the National League of Colored Women, which united in 1896 to form the National Association of Colored Women (NACW). Viewing morality and education as the foundation for racial uplift, they established settlement houses, kindergartens, orphanages, and industrial homes for single women. They served as speakers, organizers, fundraisers, and propagandists, using women's reform and community networks to achieve racial advancement and, in the process, tied their organizations firmly into black communities. In the fight against racial oppression, however, black women frequently had to fight against sexism as well. In November of 1896, black women in Wheeling, West Virginia, organized the first women's club in the state associated with the NACW. The Woman's Fortnightly Club of Wheeling, headed by Mamie L. McMechen, had at least ten members.[74] Perhaps the best-known black women's club in the state was the Charleston Woman's Improvement League, founded in 1898. The league purchased a house in 1940 to increase its work in the community and continued to operate until 2006, when the clubhouse was sold.

In 1906, the West Virginia State Federation of Women's Clubs established the chairman of legislation as a new position in their organization, thereby marking the organization's formal involvement in state politics. During the early part of the twentieth century, various women's clubs worked together to pass legislation pertaining to juvenile court law, child labor, the use of municipal taxes for the upkeep of libraries, minimum wage, marriage law, premarital health examinations, a law making parents equal guardians over their children, and the suffrage amendment. At the 1910 West Virginia club convention, the national president, who was in attendance, urged attendees to use their growing influence within the state to stir public opinion to advance social and educational standards in West Virginia.[75]

Cynthia Neverdon-Morton states that "black women were not monolithic in their thoughts and actions." Various factors affected the views they had of themselves. Some had advantages: urban versus rural location, family structure, education, and personal income were four such variables that shaped their social status and self-perceptions. Although differences between urban and rural black women were evident, there was little difference in the means of social uplift between the two groups.[76]

Neither were the women of this study monolithic in their thoughts or actions. They sometimes challenged the status quo, and at other times they worked within the confines of their race and gender. Garrison's forthright determination to fight against discrimination appears to be contradictory to her silence regarding discrimination in coal-company towns. While admittedly a staunch supporter of the NAACP, she also worked as a social worker for U. S. Steel and maintained a special friendship with Colonel Edward O'Toole, the head of the U. S. Steel Coal Company in Gary.[77]

Garrison, Drewry, Meadows, and Bateman

Just as the NAACP "used Garrison as an organizer, propagandist, and fundraiser," she used the NAACP to put forth her agenda of nurturing and instilling racial pride in black children throughout her community, county, and state. It appears also that Garrison may have "used" her friendship with Colonel O'Toole in the same way. Herbert Henderson, a former McDowell County resident and practicing attorney, recalled, "Every black person in McDowell County knew about Memphis Tennessee Garrison. We knew about the things she brought Gary. She had U. S. Steel bring in the Count Basies, bring in the black entertainers, the black intellectuals, the Marion Andersons." Garrison was always able to get monetary contributions from U. S. Steel to help sponsor many of these events.[78]

Drewry worked hard in both rural and urban environments, from her small town in McDowell County to the state capitol in Charleston, gaining a strong political following. *Chicago Defender* reporter Lillian Scott described her as a "self-confident" woman. Scott observed that Drewry was sure in manner, "but not depressingly feminist."[79] Drewry said of herself in a letter to her daughter, Lucile, "I am as hard as tacks. I don't make mistakes and my mind doesn't lead me much wrong."[80]

In 1936, when blacks throughout the country were voting in record numbers for Democratic presidential candidate Franklin D. Roosevelt, Drewry continued to maintain her loyalty to the Republican Party, which she did until the end of World War II. Flexible enough, however, and willing to concede that the Democratic Party was appearing to become more conciliatory, Drewry eventually changed her political affiliation.[81]

Like Garrison, Drewry had close ties with the coal-mining industry. In her first successful campaign, the United Mine Workers backed her. This tie may have had much to do with her silence on discrimination in the mining industry. It appears that both Garrison and Drewry used whatever means or associations they had to advance their causes. For Garrison, the cause of racial uplift focused on educating and encouraging young black children who would grow up to be leaders or great contributors to society. Drewry's cause had more to do with supporting what she often termed the "working man." She was interested in health care reform and providing greater benefits for teachers and laborers. Both women were willing to speak out boldly against injustices, but they also appear to have drawn a line as to what groups they would challenge. Meadows, however, did not appear to have drawn a line when speaking out about racial issues. During her term in the House of Delegates, she introduced a resolution designed to urge President George H. W. Bush to support civil rights initiatives for minorities and women.[82]

Meadows's work and recognition as an educator, along with her civic and political affiliations, brought her into contact with the leading politicians in the state. She worked on Jay Rockefeller's campaign when he ran for governor in 1976 and on the campaign of Governor Gaston Caperton in 1988. She had the ability to deliver a bloc of voting support for the politicians she supported, and they maintained close contact with her. Governor Rockefeller often referred to her as "his friend." They continued to correspond with each other even after he won a seat in the United States Senate. However, despite her political affiliations, she completed her appointed term in the legislature but chose not to run for the office again.

Herald-Advertiser reporter Melinda Hamilton said of Mildred Bateman's appointment as director of the West Virginia State Mental Health Department, "Hers was a new role for black women in the state." Bateman's approach to handling controversy and even personal attacks appears to have been the opposite of Garrison's forthrightness, Drewry's feisty spirit, or the vocal strength of Meadows. Hamilton described her as "a lady with an air of refined dignity."[83] She always displayed the same dignity whether she was working as a doctor or as an administrator.

When compared to the other three, Bateman appeared to have been nonaggressive and a bit too delicate. Perhaps many considered her an unlikely candidate for any political office. Although Dorothy Whitehurst, a coworker of Bateman's for twenty years, described her as "a humble, non-confrontational person," she added, however, that one should not confuse Bateman's style with her being a "wishy-washy or a pushover" type of person. She explained, "I always found her to be focused, goal oriented, and consistent.[84]

Bateman specifically worked hard to change the public's perception of the mentally ill. Rallying to their cause, she argued that they should be treated with dignity and with the view that many could be rehabilitated as useful members of society. Bateman's approach was to be

Garrison, Drewry, Meadows, and Bateman 393

strongly persistent while maintaining her gracious manner. She said of herself, "I think there is always unsureness when I work with a new person, even a new governor, partly because I am black and partly because I am a woman. But as we grow to understand each other, any preconceived ideas about working with me are dispelled." Bateman added that once people got to know her, "they usually tell me I'm one of the toughest people around."[85]

Each of the women in this study had her own activist agenda and style. Each worked within and without the confines of their race and gender, and each adhered to the African American middle-class philosophy of self-help and racial uplift that was so prevalent during the late nineteenth and early twentieth centuries. Although their activist styles varied, they were able to make some valuable contributions to history.

Garrison performed her greatest work through the NAACP. Drewry made history when she became the first African American woman to be elected to the West Virginia state legislature. Meadows's political connections placed her within the inner circle of the state's leading politicians, and they, in turn, recommended or appointed her to key state positions. As a member of the Committee of Constitution Revision in the state legislature, she was able to have arcane language requiring the races to be educated separately removed from the state's constitution.[86] Bateman's pioneering work in mental health eventually landed her a position on President Jimmy Carter's Mental Health Commission.[87]

In her discussion of black middle-class maternal activism, Katrina McDonald puts forth the idea that contemporary black women have revived a form of activism that was "practiced by African American women from the time of slavery to the 1940s." Elaborating further, she contends that although black middle-class women have moved away from the inner cities, it has not necessarily diminished their care or concern for the social degradation and isolation of those in the inner city. In the early twentieth century, black women were trained to take up the responsibility of holding the black community together, while preserving both race and gender.[88]

These activists were convinced that their efforts were necessary for reform and progress. According to Paula Giddings, African American female activists believed that their moral standing "was a steady rock upon which the race could lean."[89] This was the legacy they left to modern African American women. McDonald terms it "normative empathy" or a "synthesis of both personal and social motivation" aimed at bringing about positive change and upward mobility in the black community.[90] Although these are McDonald's words, they reflect the lives of all of the women in this study. They were difference makers in the worlds in which they lived, and their activism in education, medicine, and politics blazed a trail for other African American women to follow in the Mountain State.

BLACK WOMEN AND INEQUALITY IN WEST VIRGINIA

Although blacks enjoyed the franchise early in West Virginia's history, this did not mean that they were free from discrimination. All things were not equal, in that blacks and whites in West Virginia could not marry, they could not attend school together, and they were not permitted in certain places of public accommodation. As a result, blacks had their own establishments, including theaters, restaurants, drugstores, funeral homes, beauty shops, and barbershops, and they had their own doctors and dentists. As did other African Americans in other parts of the United States, they learned to carve out niches for themselves.

While there has been much scholarship on the role and contributions of African Americans to American history, this scholarship has primarily focused on African American men. Only in the last twenty years have the contributions of African American women come to light to a significant degree. However, despite these gains, very little by comparison can be found on the roles of black men or women in Appalachian history. If one were to search archival records, some information could possibly be found on African American men, but seemingly less would be found on African American women in West Virginia.

As a strong advocate of racial equality, Lucile Smallwood Meadows was not only aware of racial prejudices, but gender prejudices as well. In a special document, prepared specifically for her granddaughter, she wrote that "the African American woman has always had to struggle to achieve her goals. Belonging to two groups that have been treated as inferior by American society, Blacks and women were doubly invisible." Meadows told her granddaughter that many African American women

Garrison, Drewry, Meadows, and Bateman 395

were not content to remain invisible, and they struggled to improve their lot as well as that of other African Americans by working to obtain their rightful place in society. But alas, too many records have been discarded, buried, left unread, and generally overlooked. It was important to Meadows to maintain the African American heritage, including the contributions of African American women, and to share it with succeeding generations.

If Meadows was alive today, she would probably acknowledge that new research has begun to fill some gaps, but no doubt she would add that there is still work to do, especially in West Virginia. Indeed, too little is known about the level of activism among women of color in the Appalachian region. Stated bluntly, the documentation of black women's lives was not often considered significant enough to preserve. Today archivists are keenly interested in documenting black women's lives, but for decades this was not the case. Moreover, the racial conditions that existed during the time the women in this essay worked meant that they, with the exception of Lucile Meadows, likely did not give much thought to preserving their own records.

Although limitations exist, the voice of African American women in West Virginia deserves to be heard. Leaving even their limited stories untold because full and extensive documentation is not available is no longer acceptable. While seamless narratives about these women may never be written, pieces of their stories can be told. In the 1960s, some historians cautioned others that African American history was essential for understanding the nation and that a true picture of American history would never be realized without the study of African Americans or other ethnic groups. In the same way, unless even the partial stories of African American women in West Virginia become part of the historical record, we will not have begun to put together a complete picture of West Virginia's past, nor of its women.[91]

NOTES

1. Ancella R. Bickley and Linda Ann Ewen, eds., *Memphis Tennessee Garrison* (Athens: Ohio University Press, 2001), xiv–xxxi; see also M. Lois Lucas, "African American Women's Activism in West Virginia" (PhD diss., University of Kentucky, 2005).

2. Memphis Tennessee Garrison, interview by Bernard Cleveland, December 3, 1975, interview transcript, Marshall University Oral History of Appalachia

Special Collections, James E. Morrow Library, Huntington, WV (herein after referred to as MTGC-OHAMU), 1; Ancella R. Bickley, *History of the West Virginia State Teachers' Association* (Washington, DC: National Education Association, 1979), 67.

3. See Lucas, "African American Women's Activism," and M. Lois Lucas, "Elizabeth Simpson Drewry," *e-WV: West Virginia Encyclopedia,* October 18, 2012, www.wvencylopedica.org/articles/1959.

4. "1st, Only Black Woman Legislator, Mrs. Drewry Dies Monday At 85," *Welch Daily News,* September 25, 1979, 1; "Only Black Woman to Serve State in Legislature Dies," *Charleston Gazette,* September 26, 1979, 4B.

5. Darrell E. Holmes, ed., *West Virginia Blue Book, 1992* (Beckley, WV: BJW Printing, 1992), xxiii–xv; "Committee Listings," in *Acts of the Legislature of West Virginia: Regular and First Extraordinary Sessions, 1992* (Beckley, WV: BJW Printing, 1992), 41.

6. "Mildred Mitchell-Bateman, Mental Health Pioneer, Dies," *Charleston Gazette,* January, 26, 2012; Ancella R Bickley, "Mildred Mitchell-Bateman." *e-WV: The West Virginia Encyclopedia,* October 20, 2010, http://www.wvencyclopedia.org /articles/2003 (accessed March 8, 2014); "Mildred Mitchell Bateman, M.D.," US National Library of Medicine, Bethesda, Md., http://www.nlm.nih.gov/locallegends /Biographies/Mitchell_Bateman_Mildred.html (accessed March 8, 2014).

7. Lifetime Achievement Award presented to Mildred Mitchell Bateman, M.D., F.A.P.A. by the West Virginia District Branch of the American Psychiatric Association, January 2000; "Luncheon Honors Civil Rights Pioneers," *Charleston Gazette,* March 3, 2004, 5A.

8. See Joanne V. Hawks and Carolyn Ellis Staton, "On the Eve of Transition: Women in Southern Legislatures, 1946–1968," in *Women in Politics: Outsiders and Insiders,* ed. Lois Lovelace Duke (Upper Saddle River, NJ: Prentice Hall, 1996), 101.

9. Jo Boggess Phillips, "The Women Pioneers of the West Virginia State Legislature, 1923–1969," *West Virginia Public Affairs Reporter* 14, no. 3 (Summer 1997): 2.

10. See Ronald D. Eller, *Miners, Millhands, and Mountaineers: Industrialization of the Appalachian South, 1880–1930* (Knoxville: University of Tennessee Press, 1982), 138.

11. Joe William Trotter Jr., *Coal, Class, and Color: Blacks in Southern West Virginia, 1915–32* (Urbana: University of Illinois Press, 1990), 145–46.

12. For a listing of the occupations that represented the middle class among African Americans, see Trotter, *Coal, Class, and Color,* 145.

13. Carole Marks, *Farewell, We're Good and Gone: The Great Migration* (Bloomington: Indiana University Press, 1991), 3, 33.

14. Mrs. Fannie S. Poole, interview by author, July 30, 1997, Elizabeth Drewry Collection, Eastern Regional Coal Archives, Craft Memorial Library, Bluefield, WV (hereafter ESDC-ERCA).

15. Fannie Poole, interview; C. Stuart McGehee, "A Busy Time in McDowell History: Looking Back with John J. Lincoln," *Goldenseal* 15, no. 3 (Fall 1989): 56.

16. Dr. Mildred Mitchell Bateman, interview by author, April 11, 2003.

17. Kevin K. Gaines, *Uplifting the Race: Black Leadership, Politics, and Culture in the Twentieth Century* (Chapel Hill: University of North Carolina Press, 1996), 78.

18. E. Anthony Rotundo, *American Manhood: Transformation in Masculinity from the Revolution to the Modern Era* (New York: Basic Books, 1993), 16.

19. Molly Ladd-Taylor, *Motherwork: Women, Child Welfare and the State, 1890–1930* (Urbana: University of Illinois Press, 1944), 4.

20. Beryl Satter, *Each Mind a Kingdom: American Women, Sexual Purity, and the New Thought Movement, 1875–1920* (Berkeley: University of California Press, 1999), 22.

21. Gaines, *Uplifting the Race*, 78; 81.

22. Beverly Guy-Sheftall, *Daughters of Sorrow: Attitudes Toward Black Women, 1880–1920* (Brooklyn, NY: Carlson, 1990), 143.

23. Cynthia Neverdon-Morton, *Afro-American Women of the South and the Advancement of the Race, 1895–1925* (Knoxville: University of Tennessee Press, 1989), 6.

24. Gaines, *Uplifting the Race*, 80.

25. Sharon Harley, "When Your Work Is Not Who You Are: The Development of a Working Class Consciousness among Afro-American Women," in *"We Specialize in the Wholly Impossible": A Reader in Black Women's History*, ed. Darlene Clark Hine, Wilma King, and Linda Reed (Brooklyn, NY: Carlson, 1995), 28. See also Stephanie J. Shaw, *What a Woman Ought to Be and to Do: Black Professional Women Workers during the Jim Crow Era* (Chicago: University of Chicago Press, 1996), 14.

26. Guy-Sheftall, *Daughters of Sorrow*, 156–57.

27. Patricia Hill Collins, *Black Feminist Thought: Knowledge, Consciousness, and the Politics of Empowerment* (New York: Routledge, Chapman, and Hall, 1991), 124.

28. Deborah Gray White, *Too Heavy a Load: Black Women in Defense of Themselves, 1894–1994* (New York: W. W. Norton, 1999), 46–47.

29. Mildred Bateman, interview, April 11, 2003.

30. Melinda Hamilton, "Dr. Mildred Mitchell Bateman, Director of the West Virginia Department of Mental Health," *Herald-Advertiser Sunday Magazine*, April 25, 1971.

31. Ibid.

32. Shaw, *What a Woman Ought to Be and to Do*, 16.

33. Guy-Sheftall, *Daughters of Sorrow*, 162.

34. Shaw, *What a Woman Ought to Be and to Do*, 14. See p. 3 for a list of feminized professions.

35. Michael Fultz, "The Morning Cometh," *Journal of Negro History* 80, no. 3 (Summer 1995): 103.

36. Shaw, *What a Woman Ought to Be and to Do*, 24–25.

37. Sara L. Delany and A. Elizabeth Delany, with Amy Hill Hearth, *Having Our Say: The Delany Sisters' First Hundred Years* (New York: Dell, 1993), 108.

38. Fannie Poole, interview.

39. Shaw, *What a Woman Ought to Be and to Do*, 24; Fannie Poole, interview.

40. Shaw, *What a Woman Ought to Be and to Do,* 25.

41. Ibid., 25–26.

42. Elizabeth and William spelled their last name differently. She spelled the name as Drewry, and he spelled it with an extra "e," Drewery.

43. US Census Bureau, *Thirteenth Census of the United States Taken in the Year 1910: Abstract of the Census with Supplement for West Virginia* (Washington, DC: Government Printing Office, 1913), sheet 7A, Enumeration District 86.

44. Memphis T. Garrison, "The Negro of McDowell," *West Virginia Review,* 17, no. 7 (April 1940): 186.

45. Fannie Poole, interview.

46. *West Virginia Marriage License Records for McDowell County,* 1904, vol. 8, p. 151, West Virginia Cultural Center Archives, Charleston.

47. Elizabeth Drewry to Lucile L. Drewry, n.d., ESDC-ERCA.

48. Deborah Gray White, *Too Heavy a Load,* 88.

49. Mildred Bateman, interview, April 11, 2003.

50. Vincent Harding, Robin Kelley, and Earl Lewis, "We Changed the World, 1945–1870," in *To Make Our World Anew: A History of African Americans,* ed. Robin D. G. Kelley and Earl Lewis (New York: Oxford University Press, 2000), 445–46, 447.

51. Patricia A. Schechter, *Ida B. Wells-Barnett and American Reform, 1880–1930* (Chapel Hill: University of North Carolina Press, 2001), 1.

52. Arrienne Beasley, *Lynching in West Virginia,* The Carter G. Woodson Project, Marshall University, Huntington, WV, http://www.marshall.edu/carterwoodson /adrienne_beasley.asp.

53. Gaines, *Uplifting the Race,* 234.

54. Ibid.

55. Trotter, *Coal, Class, and Color,* 217–18.

56. Women were granted suffrage prior to 1920 in some western states and territories, including Wyoming, Utah, Colorado, California, Illinois, Arizona, Oregon, and Montana. On the East Coast, women were granted suffrage in New York in 1917.

57. Trotter, *Coal, Class, and Color,* 228.

58. Rosalyn Terborg-Penn, "Discontented Black Feminists: Prelude and Postscript to the Passage of the Nineteenth Amendment," in *Women and Power in American History: A Reader, From 1870,* vol. 2 (Englewood Cliffs, NJ: Prentice Hall, 1991), 138.

59. Ronald L. Lewis, *Black Coal Miners in America: Race, Class and Community Conflict 1780–1980* (Lexington: University Press of Kentucky, 1987), 152–53; C. Stuart McGehee, "Politics and Education in the 'Free State': Elizabeth Simpson Drewry, Pioneer African American Politician" (paper presented at the Sixth Annual West Virginia Black History Conference, Marshall University, Huntington, WV, September 24, 1993), 10.

60. Memphis Tennessee Garrison, interview, tape 4, side 1, transcript 1:3, Marshall University Oral History of Appalachia Special Collections, James E. Morrow Library, Huntington, WV.

61. Ibid.

62. Bickley and Ewen, *Memphis Tennessee Garrison,* 141.

63. "Highest Post Held by Negro: Dr. Bateman Is Appointed Mental Health Director," *Charleston Gazette,* December 18, 1962.

64. Dr. Mildred Mitchell Bateman, interview by author, February 20, 2003; Melinda Hamilton, "Dr. Mildred Mitchell Bateman," *Herald-Advertiser,* April 25, 1971.

65. "Biographies of Prominent African Americans in West Virginia," *West Virginia Archives and History,* http://www.wvculture.org/history/drewry.html; "Woman Candidate for Legislature," *Welch Daily News,* May 4, 1948.

66. Robert Kelvin Holliday, "The Contribution of the Negroes to Politics: A Portrait of Fayette County" (Oak Hill, WV: Fayette Tribune, 1960), 219. This essay was found in the West Virginia Cultural Center Archives file under the general heading "File 1 African Americans."

67. Joe Myers, "Retired School Teacher Tabbed by Caperton for Delegate Slot," *Montgomery Herald,* December 19, 1990.

68. Hawks and Staton, "On the Eve of Transition," 101.

69. Ibid., 101–3.

70. Stephanie J. Shaw, "The Creation of the National Association of Colored Women," in Hine, King, and Reed, "*We Specialize in the Wholly Impossible,*" 487.

71. Thomas E. Posey, *The Negro Citizen of West Virginia* (Institute, WV: Press of West Virginia State College), 59; Trotter, *Coal, Class, and Color,* 2.

72. Jo Boggess Phillips, "Women Pioneers of the West Virginia Legislature," 2.

73. Ibid.

74. Mamie L. McMechen, "And Still Another Club," *The Woman's Era, Organ of the National Federation of Afro-American Women* 3, no. 4 (November 1896).

75. Jo Boggess Phillips, "The Women Pioneers of the West Virginia Legislature," 2.

76. Cynthia Newman-Morton, *Afro-American Women of the South,* 3–5.

77. Bickley and Ewen, *Memphis Tennessee Garrison,* 130–31.

78. Ibid., 130, 207–8.

79. Lillian Scott, "Lady from McDowell Does a Man's Job," *Chicago Defender,* February 24, 1951.

80. Elizabeth Drewry to Lucile Drewry, November 29, 1936, Elizabeth Simpson Drewry Collection, ERCA.

81. Scott, "Lady from McDowell Does a Man's Job."

82. House Resolution no. 18, "Resolution Urging President Bush to Support Civil Rights Initiatives to Help Minorities and Women," *Acts of the Legislature of West Virginia, Regular Session, 1991* (Beckley, WV: BJW Printers, 1991), 1675.

83. Hamilton, "Dr. Mildred Bateman."

84. Susan Williams, "Making a Difference: Dr. Mildred Bateman Broke Barriers of Prejudice and Ignorance to Help the Mentally Ill," *Charleston Gazette,* March 21, 1998.

85. Hamilton, "Dr. Mildred Bateman."

86. House Resolution no. 18, xviii.

87. Susan Williams, "Making a Difference."

88. Katrina Bell McDonald, "Black Activist Mothering: A Historical Intersection of Race, Gender, and Class," *Gender and Society* 11, no. 6 (December 1997): 1–2.

89. Paula Giddings, *When and Where I Enter: The Impact of Black Women on Race and Sex in America* (New York: Bantam Books, 1984), 81.

90. McDonald, "Black Activist Mothering," 4.

91. Lucile Meadows, "The African-American Woman, A Foundation Builder," 1994, 1. Found among Meadows's personal papers, this document contains a long list of African American women who have made history in the United States and West Virginia. It also includes the name of Elizabeth Drewry and was prepared for and presented to her granddaughter, Jeri Monique Austin. Lucile Smallwood Meadows Papers, in possession of her daughter, Mrs. Louanne Austin.

CHAPTER FOURTEEN

Ethel New v. Atlantic Greyhound

Fighting for Social Justice in Appalachia

JAN VOOGD

On the night of June 11, 1944, Ethel New, a black woman from Lynch, Kentucky, purchased a ticket to take a Greyhound bus from Blackstone to Appalachia, towns in Virginia about 350 miles apart. The crowded bus had passengers standing in the aisle, so, despite being three months pregnant, New stood up for the first 80 miles, from Blackstone to Lynchburg, Virginia. In Lynchburg, many passengers disembarked, and New found a seat. The bus driver took notice of her choice, however, and citing a rule requiring black passengers to sit behind the white passengers, he asked her to move back. She did, but not far enough, and when the driver told her to move further back, she refused. The driver called the police, who were unable to persuade her to change seats, at which point they forcibly removed her from the bus. Once she had arrived home in Kentucky, having suffered bruises and injuries as a result of her ejection from the bus, Ethel New consulted her physician. On June 18, 1944, she had a miscarriage. Her physician testified that in his opinion there was a causal relationship between the injuries she had suffered and her subsequent miscarriage.[1]

In June of 1945, Ethel New sued to recover $10,000 in damages for her treatment at the hands of the Atlantic Greyhound Corporation.[2] As such, Ethel New's case stands as one of the earliest examples of the nascent civil rights movement's challenges to segregation in transportation, as well as a groundbreaking example of an African American Appalachian woman's fight to obtain social justice using the conventional legal system. Yet New's efforts have been obscured by time, although her struggle was remarkably similar to that of Irene Morgan, whose successful suing of the state of Virginia in the landmark case *Morgan v. Virginia* served as the catalyst for the desegregation movement.[3] Considering Ethel New's story in light of the culture of Appalachia, the state of race relations at that critical wartime and postwar moment, and the subsequent civil rights movement, this essay will explore the meaning of Ethel New's courageous struggle for social justice in Appalachia. Breaking out of widely held and long-standing myths about Appalachia and its people, along with facing down narrow views of the proper behavior for black women in the 1940s, Ethel New forged a path many civil rights activists have since followed.

THE STATE OF RACE RELATIONS IN APPALACHIA IN THE 1940S

Traditionally, according to Memphis Tennessee Garrison, "Appalachian" has suggested an agriculturally based, rural people who create quilts, crafts, and country music.[4] Samuel R. Cook insists that Appalachia "is quite simply an enigma. While the vast and diverse natural resources of the region offer the potential for local economic prosperity, much of the region is characterized by widespread poverty."[5] The enduring stereotype of Appalachia is that of an isolated and homogenous society,[6] and a typical Appalachian is "from a suspicious people, people who watch you make your way up the road, across the bridge, along the path. People who give you a long slow look before they invite you on the porch. People who are hospitable once you're in, but don't entertain many who aren't their relatives; and they weren't always too sure what to make of a relative . . . who lived in town."[7] In his novels, William Demby describes a "cultural and social claustrophobia [along with] a peculiar tangle of race and expectation, and the informal and formal rules that limit the ability of individuals to sort out that conundrum."[8]

The word "Appalachian" has been used by many journalists and scholars too specifically to refer only to the Scotch-Irish settlers. In a recent example, Peter Boyer, writing in the *New Yorker*, calls their descendants "a proud, ornery lot, deeply patriotic and always ready for a fight." He continues, saying the "southwestern region, rising from the Roanoke Valley up to the Appalachian Plateau, is a place of small farms, coal mines, and chronic economic hard times. It was settled in the 18th century by Scots-Irish Calvinists who fled Anglican-dominated Ulster and, eventually, came to that portion of Virginia which the planter aristocracy didn't want."[9] Tellingly, although in his essay Boyer is writing about Barack Obama's strategy in the presidential campaign and the relevancy of race, from the article it is not readily apparent that there are any Appalachians who are black. This oversight is not unusual.

Nell Irvin Painter suggests that black Appalachians have been an invisible people, as "southern blacks outside the plantation economy who were able to forge their own destinies and pay their own way." Black Appalachian women, in addition to invisibility, as women have been oppressed by gender constructs, as well as being, as William Turner puts it, "a racial minority within a cultural minority."[10] Far from being invisible, black people do live in Appalachia, but in so many ways resist the stereotype of the Appalachian. As Memphis Tennessee Garrison, a social activist and one of the few black Appalachian women from the twentieth century to have had an account of her life thoroughly documented, described the situation thusly, "We didn't live up in the woods. You couldn't get Negroes up in those mountains. They lived down in the coal camps . . . we Negroes didn't move to the mountains. You won't find any Negro up in the mountain living on nothing. You find him down where the action is."[11]

Cook points out that during World War II, "Virginia miscegenation laws would be elaborated with a fervor previously unmatched," because of whites' fear of, and confusion about how to deal with, "mixed race" people. The existence of Native Americans and people who did not fit into established categories created ethical questions about the long-standing racial policies in the state. In order to avoid examining the ethics of the policies, whites simply became more and more vehement in observing those policies, minimizing, discounting, and ignoring the racial variety in their midst.[12]

The 1924 Racial Integrity Law was actively promoted and enforced through the 1940s, agitated and advocated by Walter A. Plecker, Virginia's first director of vital statistics. He worked hard to make the Indian presence in Virginia disappear, attempting to ensure that any people of mixed race or Indian descent were classified as "black," or "Negro." He worked aggressively and creatively to revise old records, committing "documentary genocide," to change the past. For example, in 1943 he sent a list to all county clerks and registrars containing surnames that were from then on to be classed "Negro," many of which were, in at least one county, prominent Indian names.[13] By instituting a policy in which the names were dissociated from the identities of actual individuals, Plecker faced less resistance from people who otherwise did not identify as "black" or "Negro."

Forces did exist exerting a counterinfluence on white racism. Labor union activism, for example, had succeeded by the 1930s to the extent that black workers no longer automatically worked for less pay or accepted the least appealing or most dangerous jobs.[14] While segregation persisted, the concept of equality had been introduced. Mining employed many of the residents of the Appalachian region, and many of the miners were African American. The primary labor union, United Mine Workers of America, had always had a race-blind attitude in its membership policies, in part to disallow for any race-baited strikebreaking; hence, less racial tension simmered there than in other unions.[15]

Appalachian miners were at the heart of the union movement, and about a third of these miners were black. Black coal miners worked hard and had strong expectations for improving their lot. They placed a high priority on education and sent their children to school and college.[16] It was a struggle for selfhood in postwar American society, according to literary critic James Hall, the construction of race and masculinity being central to the struggle.

For Ethel New, it had to be a struggle for selfhood that was about race, but also as much or more about volition, agency, and power apart from gender. It was not "masculinity," but rather self-determination, humanity, adulthood. As a lone black woman challenging institutionalized segregation in the heart of Appalachia, New was also challenging regional mores, cultural expectations, and gender constrictions. Of note is that the African Americans challenging as individuals the bus segregation in the 1940s were women (see *Morgan v. Virginia*, *Day v. Atlantic Greyhound*, and *Whiteside v. Southern Bus Lines)*, or a minister (see *Simmons v. Atlantic Greyhound*), all representing versions of what in American society would be viewed as a compromised masculinity.

SPECIFICS OF ETHEL NEW AND HER CASE

Kentucky, Ethel New's home state, had, even at that time, a long history of black activism for social justice. The NAACP had been active in Kentucky since the first branch was founded in Louisville in 1914. An especially active branch in Frankfort was established during World War I, and this group "aggressively pushed for enforcement of the law" regarding mob violence. Also very active was the Kentucky Commission on Interracial Cooperation (CIC), formed in 1920, and an adjacent group, the Kentucky branch of the Association of Southern Women for the Prevention of Lynching (ASWPL).[17]

Ethel New was from Lynch, Kentucky, near Cumberland. Lynch in the 1940s was still a coal camp, built in 1917 by U. S. Coal and Coke Company, a subsidiary of U. S. Steel, and not incorporated as a town until the 1950s. The world's largest coal camp at the time, it comprised 19,000 acres near the Virginia border, at the southeastern tip of Harlan County. Information on Ethel New herself is slim, but records suggest New was the wife of miner George Tucker, although it is not clear why she did not use her married name in the suit. She may have used her maiden name in order to protect her privacy and deflect the judgment of her neighbors. While the diverse population of the town may have offered her an expanded world view, as the more than four thousand employees of the company represented thirty-eight nationalities, the fact remained that Lynch was a company town, with a company police force and paternalistic control of social services, political processes, economics, and culture. Living under the company's narrowing perspective may have radicalized her. An even more likely radicalizing force was the coal company policy for routing union activism and intimidating organizers with violent tactics. These policies and their enforcement led the county to be known as "Bloody Harlan." The struggle of the United Mine Workers there in the 1930s drew the concern of the nation to the county, along with a US Senate subcommittee investigation into potential civil liberties violations.

This town of Lynch being the home of Ethel New, there in the heart of Bloody Harlan County, might suggest she was part of a social justice movement. Just what was she doing in Virginia? Was her social activism against segregation premeditated? Or was it spontaneous, incidental to her other purposes, and she, traveling alone, simply lost patience with the practice of segregated travel? The answers may never be known. The organized protests against segregation, sponsored by the Congress of Racial Equality (CORE), were to come years later, with the Journey for Reconciliation in April of 1947 and the Freedom Riders in May of 1961.

Ethel New's journey started in Blackstone, a village known in the early 1800s as "the village of Blacks and Whites," for the rivalry between two innkeepers, Mr. Schwartz (German for "black") and Mr. White. Blackstone is located in the Southside region of Virginia, eighty miles east of New's fateful stop in Lynchburg. At the time of New's trip, Blackstone was just becoming accustomed to Fort Pickett, an Army base established in 1941 for the purpose of training units from all branches of the military to serve in World War II.[18]

Whether, or how much of, Ethel New's experiences in the originating location influenced her journey, and the decisions she made during it, is indiscernible. Blackstone being a military town may have added a chaotic atmosphere. Depending on what troops were stationed there, New may have had friends or supporters as she embarked. Her purpose in Blackstone may have affected her situation, her state of mind, and her resolve, as well. Something motivated her to challenge the suspicion, the judgment, the constricted nature of Appalachian society and strike out for the cause of civil liberty.

The destination on her ticket was a town called Appalachia, Virginia. She had in mind to go all the way home to Kentucky, eventually, but for some reason bought the ticket only as far as this town. New's home in Lynch was just ten miles further on, across the state line into Kentucky. The bus line may have only gone as far as Appalachia. If she had bought a ticket all the way through to Lynch, her trip would have been "interstate" and her court case would have paralleled the influential *Morgan v. Virginia* case that transpired at the same time. The town of Appalachia is surrounded in the immediate area by several coal-camp communities. If New was a union operative, in addition to being a miner's wife, she may have had business with the miners in this town.

Ethel New v. Atlantic Greyhound 407

Silas House, in his novel *Clay's Quilt*, evokes the pull of home for people from this part of the country. "Alma fell asleep just outside of Asheville. Clay turned the radio down and sang to himself as the landscape began to look more and more like home. When they crossed into Virginia and he was sure the mountains he saw rising in the distance were those of home, he shook her gently and she started, rising up on her seat as if she thought they were in a wreck. 'Look up yonder,' he said. 'That's Kentucky.'"[19] The members of the Eastern Kentucky Social Club, an organization of African American miners from the area of Lynch, voice a rousing affinity for the land, and their ongoing reunions for those who have moved elsewhere are a testament to their love for the mountains.[20] Before she got to Appalachia, though, New had to get through a stop in Lynchburg.

When Ethel New first sued Atlantic Greyhound, the jury found in favor of the bus company. Ethel New appealed, but the appeals court affirmed the judgment, convinced by the evidence that under the circumstances "no more force was used than was necessary." The court went on to explain that "minor disadvantages in travel did not necessarily indicate discrimination."[21] Was what happened to Ethel New on the night of June 11, 1944, really just a "minor disadvantage"? That New faced down the segregationist policies that night, in light of the societal pressures against her, and knowing that doing so would delay her from her homecoming, with most of her journey left to go, suggests that a "minor disadvantage" it was not.

The bus stopped at the Lynchburg terminal to discharge and take on passengers. The town of Lynchburg began as a tobacco-based economy, but by the turn of the twentieth century it was "a small, tightly knit manufacturing city." Its citizens valued education and the arts and founded three colleges: Randolph-Macon Woman's College (1893), Sweet Briar College (1901), and Lynchburg College (1903). Lynchburg's factories ran constantly during World War II, and the airport was used to train pilots.[22] It was into this vibrant hubbub of culture, prosperity, and wartime bustle that Ethel New's social activist spirit leaped.

Someone called the bus driver's attention to Ethel New, sitting on the front seat of the bus. The driver asked her to move behind the white passengers, telling her there was "a rule under which colored passengers were required to sit behind the white passengers." While the driver went into the terminal to check in, New did move, taking the last aisle seat, the seat next to the long seat running across the rearmost wall of the bus. When the driver returned from checking in, he assessed New's position and dissatisfied with it, asked her to move further back. He wanted her to sit on the five-passenger rearmost seat with three other black passengers, freeing her seat for two white passengers standing in the aisle. The driver reiterated the rule of the company that required "colored passengers" to be seated behind white passengers. He claimed a Virginia statute to the same effect and threatened to call the police if she did not change her seat. Ethel New refused to change seats, and said she had no intention of moving.[23]

In the trial, Atlantic Greyhound argued that sitting on the long, rearmost seat was no sacrifice, its "quality and convenience" being "equal to those of the seat she occupied." The company admitted that the back of the long seat was not adjustable, a feature of the other seats, but argued that the long seat had the same springs and covering. The long, rearmost seat's windows were not adjustable either, but, the company argued, there was a ventilator above it for the removal of hot air and odors, something the seats with windows did not have.[24] Still, in a mode of transportation in which heat, fumes, odors, and motion sickness were rampant, and the physics of motion guarantee a less pleasant ride the further back one sits, the company's arguments for equal quality and convenience ring shallow. Ethel New's preference for the seat she had claimed for herself is no surprise, especially given that she had been standing for the previous eighty miles. Her resolve in the face of such adversity, however, with so many arguments stacking against her by such powerful entities, remains impressive.

The driver called the police. Lieutenant W. N. Smith and Officer Bagby of the Lynchburg city police responded. In the course of about thirty minutes to an hour, Smith twice attempted to convince New to move to the rear seat and make the seat next to the rear available for the two standing passengers. Witness accounts suggest that Smith, politely and patiently, explained to her both the law and the company rules. New maintained her refusal to move and later stated that Smith, assisted by the driver, roughly pulled her off the bus. Smith and others

Ethel New v. Atlantic Greyhound 409

testified, however, that it was Officer Bagby alone who took her by the arm and led her off the bus, and that Bagby had used no more force than was "necessary under the circumstances of her passive resistance." New testified that she told the bus driver and officers that she was sick, but the police officers, the bus driver, and several passenger witnesses contradicted her.[25]

A jury in law and equity court in Richmond, Virginia, denied New's initial petition for damages. Justice Willis D. Miller took under advisement the plaintiff counsel's motion to set aside the jury's verdict.[26] At first, only the *Washington Post* described the case in terms of race. A few months after the first trial in June, when Judge Miller confirmed the previous jury decision in favor of Atlantic Greyhound, the *Post* referred to the matter as a" racial segregation case" and reported that New's "Negro attorneys" would appeal the decision.[27] Subsequent articles followed the *Post*'s lead, referring to the events in the context of race policies. A headline in the *Atlanta Daily World* used the phrase "Jim Crow Case" in describing New's motion to the Virginia Supreme Court of Appeals and also compared her case to the United States Supreme Court having reversed a Virginia decision the year before in the *Morgan v. Virginia* case, declaring passengers in buses that cross state lines cannot legally be segregated. Ethel New's intention to travel onward from Virginia to Kentucky was deemed irrelevant by the court because her ticket was from one point to another within Virginia.[28]

The confusion and inconvenience of passengers traveling from one state to another amid segregation policies that varied among states led the Supreme Court to act in the case of *Morgan v. Virginia*. This case involved a Virginia statute requiring motor carriers to "separate white and colored passengers and required that all passengers should observe and obey the directions of the agent of the carrier in respect to such separation." The Virginia statute made a criminal offense the "failure of either the carrier or of a passenger in the performance of the respective duties imposed on them." This statue was invoked when a black passenger, Irene Morgan, traveling home to Baltimore, Maryland, from Virginia, refused to move to the long, rearmost seat to make room for a white couple, as requested by the driver. She was arrested, tried, and convicted. The Virginia appeals court affirmed the decision, but the US Supreme Court reversed it. The Supreme Court ruled the statute invalid "as constituting a burden upon interstate commerce," because of the situation, recognizing that as people traveled through various states with differing policies, seat changes could be disturbing. If national travel was to be promoted and protected, uniform rules and policies would be necessary.[29]

On August 15, 1946, to clarify the *Morgan v. Virginia* decision for employees and customers, George S. Engle, executive vice-president and general manager of Atlantic Greyhound, issued to all of the company's drivers a letter containing instructions for the seating of passengers. Initially emphasizing passenger safety and comfort, the letter falls back on the traditional justification used to defend racial segregation, saying, "This company is under a duty to operate its coaches in such manner as will promote the comfort, security and safety of all of its passengers, and will preserve the public peace and good order on its coaches." Claiming the right to determine and change passengers' seats, the company asserted the necessity for this power in order to ameliorate situations involving "intoxicated persons whose conduct becomes objectionable to others, the illness of passengers, particularly children, while enroute, differences in the attire or cleanliness of passengers." The heretofore reasonable letter then makes the segregationist leap of logic to observe the "established usage, custom and tradition induced by the general sentiment of the community that passengers of different races be not seated in adjoining seats or in the same part of a public conveyance," specifically that "colored passengers be seated from the rear forward, and white passengers from the front toward the rear."[30]

The segregationists asserted that "the seating of white and colored passengers indiscriminately would increase the occasions for arguments, altercations and disturbances among passengers leading to annoyance, discomfort and possible danger to passengers of both races." Segregationists were determined to believe that when "racial prejudices and antagonisms do exist . . . they are the source of many unhappy episodes of violence between members of the white and colored races," and "the separate seating of white and colored passengers" would simply "lessen the occasions for such conflicts."[31]

In his letter to employees, Engles argues that relegating black passengers to the rear of the bus offered "seats which are substantially equal, in comfort and convenience to other available seats in the coach." In enforcing this policy, the letter suggests that all courtesy was to be observed, and no force used. Drivers should call the police in cases of recalcitrance or dispute.[32] If the seats at the front and rear of the bus were in fact substantially equal, a question begs, however, as to how whites would have dealt with a policy in reverse, wherein they were seated from the rear forward. It is telling that such was not the case. Ethel New filed her suit a year before Engle issued his letter, which was two years after the incident in Lynchburg.

In January 1947, noting that the case bore on the applicability of the Jim Crow law in intrastate bus service, the *Washington Post* reported that the Virginia Supreme Court of Appeals granted a writ of error to Ethel New.[33] This step allowed the appeals trial to take place the following September, but New lost this trial as well. Despite New's testimony that she suffered bruises and injuries during her forcible removal from the bus, despite having a miscarriage once being home in Kentucky, and despite her physician stating his opinion that a causal relationship existed between New's injuries and her subsequent miscarriage, the Virginia Supreme Appeals Court ruled in favor of Atlantic Greyhound, affirming the decision of Richmond's Law and Equity Court.[34]

STATE OF ACTIVISM AFTER *NEW V. ATLANTIC GREYHOUND* AND *MORGAN V. VIRGINIA*

Eleven states had laws in place that required segregated bus travel: Alabama, Arkansas, Florida, Georgia, Louisiana, Mississippi, North Carolina, Oklahoma, South Carolina, Texas, and Virginia. Kentucky, Maryland, and Tennessee had only de facto bus segregation, but they did have laws in place requiring segregated railroad facilities.[35] During the next few years, several other cases against Greyhound and other bus companies followed on Ethel New's failed legal action, including *Simmons v. Atlantic Greyhound* in 1947, *Day v. Atlantic Greyhound* in 1948, and *Whiteside v. Southern Bus Lines* in 1949. The details of these cases involving individual resistance to segregation policies offer a view of the impact of New's efforts, an impact that relies on an accretive effect and illustrates the incremental drops of resistance wearing away at the stone of segregation.

Reverend Simmons of Roanoke, Virginia, in October 1946, planning to attend the annual Synod of his church convening in Salisbury, North Carolina, purchased a round-trip ticket from Roanoke, Virginia, to Salisbury, by way of Winston-Salem, North Carolina. On the bus, waiting in the station, were only about three other passengers. Reverend Simmons took a seat in the forward part of the bus, about four seats back from the front. When the driver noticed where Simmons had seated himself, he asked him to move to the rear of the bus. Simmons asked if there was any law requiring him to change his seat. The driver replied that his instructions were to "seat colored persons in the rear of the bus," and Simmons would have to move . Simmons alleged that the driver spoke loudly, and in a rude and threatening manner, but witnesses said the driver was "courteous and spoke in a normal conversational tone."[36]

Reverend Simmons left the bus and in the office of the bus terminal asked for the manager. J. W. Saunders, Roanoke area supervisor, appeared. Simmons reported the incident on the bus and stated that since he was an interstate passenger, the action of the bus driver was wrong, according to the recent US Supreme Court decision. Saunders disputed this and defended the driver's actions as abiding of company policy. Simmons left the terminal, although the bus was still waiting for its scheduled departure time. In his suit, Reverend Simmons charged that because of the offending bus driver, he was forced to travel to Salisbury by train. This was an uncomfortable trip, requiring extra expense, and in taking the train Simmons incurred a delay that caused him to miss a committee meeting. The court recognized that Simmons, "had he chosen to submit to the rule as to the seating of passengers, could have made his trip on the bus and avoided any of these consequences of traveling by train." The court also recognized that what Simmons hoped to achieve through the legal action was "to establish a right to be free of any compulsion in regard to his choice of a seat on defendant's bus where that compulsion is based solely on the plaintiff's race."[37]

In the context of these challenges to segregation, the case of *Day v. Atlantic Greyhound* destroys any previous argument made by segregationists, yet the court found in favor of them. Day, a sixty-seven-year-old black woman, refused to move her seat or to leave the bus.

The driver summoned police, who forcibly ejected her from the bus, arrested her, and confined her on the charge of disorderly conduct.[38]

Day purchased a roundtrip bus ticket from Syracuse, New York, to Florida, stopping over at Richmond, Virginia, for three weeks over the Christmas holidays. On January 22, 1946, Day boarded an Atlantic Greyhound bus at Richmond to go to Winter Haven, Florida. The first person aboard the bus, she took the second seat from the front on the side opposite the driver. A white woman sat next to her on this seat, without objection, all afternoon as far as the stop for supper at South Hill, Virginia. Day stayed on the bus while all the passengers and the driver left it. When the driver came back in, although she was alone in the bus, he ordered her to move to the last seat. Day refused to move because she believed "the Supreme Court in the Morgan case had declared the segregation of the races in public vehicles a violation of the constitutional rights of colored persons." Not only that, but she had been sitting next to a white passenger during the two-and-a-half-hour ride from Richmond to South Hill. When the police officers attempted to eject Day from the bus, the sixty-seven-year-old resisted and clung to her seat. Out of the bus, they tried to get her into a police car, but she resisted that as well. The officers had to walk her some distance to the jail, where they charged her with disorderly conduct and locked her up. Three hours later, Day paid twenty dollars in lieu of bail and left Virginia shortly after on another bus.[39]

Despite Morgan, this US appeals court ruled against Day, stating that when "the plaintiff was requested to move, the bus was empty except for herself, and the shift could have been made without substantial inconvenience either to the other passengers or to herself."[40]

As a young lawyer in the midst of arguing cases against residential segregation and segregation in education, Thurgood Marshall served on Whiteside's counseling team in *Whiteside v. Southern Bus Lines.* Whiteside purchased a ticket in St. Louis, Missouri, for transportation to Paducah, Kentucky, via Cairo, Illinois. From Cairo to the Kentucky state line she sat in the front part of the bus to no complaints, but in Wickliffe, Kentucky, the driver told her to move to another seat in the rear of the bus. Whiteside refused, and the driver summoned a Wickliffe police officer. Together they ejected her from the bus,

414 JAN VOOGD

injuring her and causing the loss of personal property. Whiteside sued for damages.[41]

The district judge dismissed the suit and an appeal followed, on the grounds that the bus line's segregation rule was "neither reasonable nor necessary for the safety, comfort, and convenience of its passengers." As in other cases, the bus company argued that "the separate seating of white and colored passengers was both reasonable and necessary [and] that upon a number of occasions there had been trouble upon its buses when the rule was not observed."[42]

The US circuit court considered *Hall v. DeCuir* and *Morgan v. Virginia* in its deliberations. Yet the court found that although Kentucky had no racial segregation statute, the company was buttressed by "long-settled usage and custom in Kentucky, crystallized into its unwritten law." Still, the US circuit court did not allow the district court to dismiss the case and sent it back for trial.[43]

SCHOLARSHIP ON THE civil rights movement, and the fight against segregation specifically, often mention aspects of the three cases *Simmons, Day,* and *Whiteside,* though they vary in method, mode, technicalities, and outcome. Why has Ethel New's case been ignored? The striking similarities between the New case and the Morgan case raise some puzzling questions. Both New and Morgan were asked by their drivers to sit in the rearmost seat to make room for a white couple, New in June of 1944, Morgan in July. Both refused. Both were forcibly removed. Both sued. The differences in the cases are telling. New was injured, Morgan was not. New was Appalachian, a coal miner's wife. Morgan was from urban Baltimore. New sued the bus company, Morgan sued the state. The key difference—that New's trip was intrastate and Morgan's was interstate—proved definitive. New lost her case. Morgan won hers, and the case became precedent, catalyzing components of the subsequent civil rights activism, including the Journey for Reconciliation and the Freedom Rides. Ethel New, her courage and her struggle, rested in obscurity.

While certain specifics regarding her life and motivation cannot be verified and further research is warranted, if she was the Ethel New who married miner George Tucker, they moved to Muncie, Indiana, in 1952, where they lived until George Tucker's death in 2003. According

Ethel New v. Atlantic Greyhound 415

to various genealogical database sources, Ethel New Tucker is in her nineties and still living in Muncie with her daughter.[44] Still, the simple uncontested facts of the case remain significant. In 1944 a black Appalachian woman named Ethel New challenged the segregation laws of Virginia, in action and in court. Doing so, she became a part of a nascent civil rights movement and counters much of the received wisdom about Appalachia by representing an example of the breadth and diversity of those who are the women of the Mountain South.

NOTES

1. Ethel New v. Atlantic Greyhound Corporation and W. N. Smith, Record no. 3224, 186 Va. 726, 43 S.E.2d 872, 1947 Va. LEXIS 193, September 3, 1947.

2. "Asks $10,000 for Ejection From Bus," *Pittsburgh Courier*, June 9, 1945. Same article ran as "Ejected From Bus, Sues for $10,000," in *Atlanta Daily World*, June 10, 1945.

3. Day v. Atlantic Greyhound Corporation. No. 5803, 171 F.2d 59, 1948 US App. LEXIS 3392, December 7, 1948.

4. Ancella R. Bickley and Lynda Ann Ewen, eds., *Memphis Tennessee Garrison: The Remarkable Story of a Black Appalachian Woman* (Athens: Ohio University Press, 2001), 213.

5. Samuel R. Cook, *Monacans and Miners: Native American and Coal Mining Communities in Appalachia* (Lincoln: University of Nebraska Press, 2000), 2–3.

6. Bickley and Ewen, *Memphis Tennessee Garrison*, xxv.

7. Meredith Sue Willis, *In the Mountains of America* (San Francisco: Mercury House, 1994), 6.

8. James C. Hall, "Afterword" to *Beetlecreek*, by William Demby (Jackson: University of Mississippi Press, 1998 (orig. 1950)), 226–27.

9. Peter Boyer, "The Appalachian Problem," *New Yorker*, October 6, 2008, 36–41.

10. William H. Turner and Edward J. Cabbell, eds., *Blacks in Appalachia* (Lexington: University Press of Kentucky, 1985), xi, xix.

11. Bickley and Ewen, *Memphis Tennessee Garrison*, 93–94.

12. Cook, *Monacans*, 84.

13. Ibid., 108–10.

14. Turner and Cabbell, *Blacks in Appalachia*, 79.

15. Ibid., 163.

16. Bickley and Ewen, *Memphis Tennessee Garrison*, xxvi.

17. George C. Wright, *Racial Violence in Kentucky, 1865–1940: Lynchings, Mob Rule, and "Legal Lynchings"* (Baton Rouge: Louisiana State University Press, 1990, 200–6.

18. Blackstone Chamber of Commerce, Blackstone, VA.

19. Silas House, *Clay's Quilt* (Chapel Hill: Algonquin Books, 2001), 285–86.

20. Thomas E. Wagner and Phillip J. Obermiller, *African American Miners and Migrants: The Eastern Kentucky Social Club* (Chicago: University of Illinois Press, 2004).

21. New v. Atlantic Greyhound.

22. Ibid.

23. Ibid.

24. Ibid.

25. Ibid.

26. "Dismiss Bus Jim-Crow Suit," *Pittsburgh Courier*, June 29, 1946.

27. "Court Upholds Segregation on Va. Buses," *Washington Post*, October 9, 1946.

28. "Virginia Bus Jim Crow Case Further Appealed," *Atlanta Daily World*, October 13, 1946.

29. Simmons v. Atlantic Greyhound Corporation, Civil Action no. 315, 75 F. Supp. 166, 1947 US Dist. LEXIS 1849, December 30, 1947. Whiteside v. Southern Bus Lines, Inc., no. 10799, 177 F.2d 949, 1949 US App. LEXIS 3857, November 23, 1949.

30. Simmons v. Atlantic Greyhound.

31. Ibid.

32. Ibid.

33. "Va. Supreme Court Grants Error Writ in Jim Crow Case," *Washington Post*, January 10, 1947.

34. New v. Atlantic Greyhound; "Kentucky Woman Loses Bus Case," *Pittsburgh Courier*, September 13, 1947.

35. Pauli Murray, ed., *State's Laws on Race and Color (Studies in the History of the South)* (n.p.: Woman's Division of Christian Service, 1951; Athens: University of Georgia Press, 1997).

36. Simmons v. Atlantic Greyhound.

37. Ibid.

38. Day v. Atlantic Greyhound.

39. Ibid.

40. Ibid.

41. Whiteside v. Southern Bus Lines.

42. Ibid.

43. Ibid.

44. Rootsweb, MyFamily.com, Ancestry.com; Eric James, *Stray Leaves*, www .ericjames.org; "George Tucker obituary," *Muncie Starpress*, November 18, 2003.

CHAPTER FIFTEEN

"Remembering the Past, Working for the Future"

West Virginia Women Fight for Environmental Heritage and Economic Justice in the Age of Mountaintop Removal Coal Mining

JOYCE M. BARRY

"We want to save our communities, we want clean communities, we want sustainable communities, and we want jobs."

>—Patty Seebok, member of the Coal River Mountain Watch

"We're trying to preserve something, and save this creation. . . . We're trying to push the state forward, you know, and to stop the destruction and diversify the economy."

>—Judy Bonds, codirector of the Coal River Mountain Watch

In the late 1990s, local and national newspapers began reporting the practice of mountaintop-removal coal mining (MTR) in West Virginia and the concomitant public outcry over this socially and environmentally devastating form of coal extraction. As awareness of MTR grew, citizens became polarized, with many protecting the coal industry for the jobs provided and also because of its long presence in the region. Other citizens were appalled by this indefensible industrial practice, which alters the Appalachian mountain range, dislocates residents, and compromises the area's rich biodiversity. These tensions were manifested early in 1999, during an annual march commemorating the historic labor battle of Blair Mountain in Logan County. During this public remembrance, Blair Mountain became a newly and differently contested site, with proponents of MTR pelting those opposed with eggs while shouting, "This is coal country" and "Lizard lovers go home."[1]

Today Blair Mountain is no longer a site where labor struggles are recognized, or where tensions over MTR are expressed; this historical space is targeted to become the latest West Virginia mountain to be destroyed by mountaintop-removal coal mining. Recognized by the National Trust for Historical Preservation as one of the eleven most endangered historic sites in the country, Blair Mountain is noted as the place where the largest labor insurrection in United States history occurred in 1921, as 7,500 coal miners seeking a union faced a 2,500-man oppositional force organized by the Logan County sheriff, Don Chafin.[2] This battle, an integral part of West Virginia's culture and history, ended with the intervention of 2,000 National Guard troops.[3] Today, instead of protecting this historic site, West Virginia politicians are currently standing by as coal companies seek to obliterate Blair Mountain with a powerful mixture of amyl nitrate and dynamite—an explosive, everyday reality for the people and environment of West Virginia in the age of mountaintop-removal coal mining.[4]

The most active grassroots movement in West Virginia today is the collective resistance to the effects of MTR on small communities in the state, and women constitute the majority of membership in most anti-MTR organizations. This essay examines the activism of West Virginia women in this age of mountaintop removal coal mining and argues that while historically women's activism in West Virginia has been linked to male resistance and to reforming work in the coal industry, MTR activism charts a separate path that seeks to dislodge King Coal from its privileged position in West Virginia's economy. Current women's activism operates outside this industry and the interest of male labor, leveling broad critiques that seek to eliminate coal's very presence in West Virginia, ending the social, economic, and environmental destruction by this billion dollar industry. Today's activists, while cognizant of the coal jobs currently created in an area with limited economic opportunities, possess a long view that sees alternative energy as a way to diversify the state's economy, end the coal oligarchy in the state, and save the natural landscape and communities of West Virginia.

Current research suggests that women make up the majority of environmental justice activists in both the developed and developing world.[5] Environmental justice is community-based responses to social and environmental problems. Defining the environment as where humans live, work, and play, environmental scholars and activists, unlike mainstream environmental practitioners, link social justice with environmental concerns.[6] Environmental justice scholar Rachel Stein suggests that because environmental ills "strike *home* for vulnerable communities," women are frequently the first to respond to social and environmental crises.[7] Some academicians argue that the noticeable presence of women in environmental justice activism also reflects women's position in the natural and social world. For example, ecofeminist scholars Heather Eaton and Lois Ann Lorentzen note that environmental problems disproportionately impact women in most parts of the world:

> The increased burdens women face result not only from environmental deterioration; the sexual division of labor found in most societies considers family sustenance to be women's work, and women, as primary caregivers, generally bear primary responsibility for the food and the health of family members. Providing fuel, food, and water for families becomes increasingly difficult with environmental degradation. To make matters worse, economic resources—ownership of land or commercial businesses—remain inaccessible to most women.[8]

While ecofeminist scholars have noted the social arrangements that relegate women to the private, reproductive sphere and precipitate their environmental justice activism, existing environmental justice scholarship has not adequately accounted for the overwhelming participation of women in these campaigns. Environmental justice scholarship effectively highlights the connections between class, race and the natural world, but additional research emphasizing the importance of gender to the environment and to environmental justice activism is needed. This essay seeks to contribute to existing environmental justice scholarship by focusing strictly on women's MTR activism in Appalachia.

My focus also departs from existing literature on MTR in Appalachia. Recently, several books were published on the impact of mountaintop-removal coal mining, including three journalistic accounts and one scholarly study of MTR in West Virginia. Erik Reece's *Lost Mountain: A Year in the Vanishing Wilderness* (2006) follows the life of one mountain in Kentucky, providing a social and natural history account of MTR in this area; Penny Loeb's *Moving Mountains: How One Woman and Her Community Won Justice From Big Coal* (2007) focuses on West Virginia resident Patricia Bragg and the major litigation in the story of MTR, *Bragg v. Robertson,* where local residents sued the West Virginia Army Corp of Engineers for illegally issuing mining permits; and *Coal River* by Michael Shnayerson, which examines the political-economic forces behind MTR and those fighting it in Boone County, West Virginia. These journalistic texts help raise public awareness about MTR, spotlight those involved in ending it, and contribute to the existing literature on MTR in Appalachia. The only scholarly study, Shirley Stewart Burns's *Bringing Down the Mountains: The Impact of Mountaintop Removal on Southern West Virginia Communities,* examines the social, political, and economic forces that promote MTR in West Virginia, providing a thorough history of the events important to the emergence of MTR as a prominent means of coal extraction.[9] While these texts mention the prominent women involved in anti-MTR activism—among them Judy Bonds, Patty Seebok, Vivian Stockman, Freda Williams, Pauline Canterbury, Mary Miller, Janice Nease, and Maria Gunnoe—none highlight the gendered component of this activism. Mountaintop-removal coal mining, arguably, is one of the most serious social and environmental crimes of our time, and women are leading the fight against it. If we accept Eaton and Lorentzen's position that women suffer disproportionately from compromised environments, a gendered analysis of MTR is crucial.[10] West Virginia women's committed efforts against MTR deserve recognition to ensure that their involvement is not tossed into the proverbial dustbin of history but is instead central in anti-MTR accounts.

"Remembering the Past, Working for the Future" 421

CONTEXTUALIZING WEST VIRGINIA WOMEN'S ACTIVISM

History teaches us that oppressive social conditions frequently elicit contravening responses by vulnerable populations. Exploitation consistently generates collective resistance to oppressive forces, and West Virginia coalfield labor history is a prime example of this phenomena. It should be noted that not all exploited people in West Virginia have participated in grassroots resistance efforts. In Appalachia, and other regions, residents have often collaborated with outside forces against their own material interests. However, the historical precedent of vigorous collective action in Appalachia is well established. Considering the Appalachian case, Thomas Plaut wrote three decades ago that "Appalachian history is full of rebellions and rebels: of men and women who demand ... that their existence be recognized. From mine wars to roving pickets, Mother Jones to Widow Combs, Black Lung and Brown Lung movements, Appalachians have fought domination."[11] In addition, this history reveals that West Virginia women long have engaged in grassroots activism against the coal industry to change and improve their communities. For the sake of brevity, I will only cite two examples of such activism, even though there are numerous instances one could examine.

In the early days of coal (late nineteenth to mid-twentieth centuries) women fought to unionize the coalfields in order to ensure better job conditions and equitable wages for male coal-mining relatives. For similar reasons, women participated in coal-mining strikes and other organized labor activities. In the 1980s women continued to form and join grassroots labor organizations, including groups that supported striking coal miners. During the Pittston coal strike, many Appalachian wives, mothers, daughters, and widows of coal miners formed the Family Auxiliary, a group with strong, but contested, ties to the United Mine Workers Union.[12] These women, as Virginia Seitz notes, initially viewed themselves in relation to male workers at the beginning of the strike but over time broadened their activist perspective, envisioning themselves as not just working for their immediate class interests but for a larger constituency of working-class people.[13]

From the 1960s through the 1980s women still engaged in labor activism, but they also fought to limit the practice of string mining—a process that used fewer miners for coal extraction, thus limiting the economic opportunities in the region.[14] They resisted strip-mining activities because the transition to this form of coal extraction resulted in the loss of jobs for many miners, but they also fought to save the lush Appalachian environment from further despoliation. Mary Beth Bingham, an Appalachian scholar and activist, notes the contributions of women anti–strip mining activists in Knott County, Kentucky, in the 1970s, asserting, "There is some value in the kind of direct confrontation we took. We helped publicize the issue of strip mining and may have served as an inspiration to other people in various struggles. Our action was a conscientizing experience for many of us, and important part of our political education."[15] These examples illustrate the extent of women's grassroots responses and support the historical point that rural Appalachian women have rarely accepted coal industry abuses— they consistently exert collective agency in personally empowering, and politically transformative, ways.

The Appalachian studies scholar Karaleah Reichart says that the very cultural identity of the coalfields of southern West Virginia has been formed by the coal industry *and* by organized protest. She argues that the "varied actions of women in labor activism and industrial conflict have played an important role in the development of the coal industry across the Appalachian region."[16] Women have not been employed by the coal industry in great numbers, yet they have been equally active with men in grassroots activism. Reichart says that women in this region historically have been involved in nonviolent resistance, "including participation in picket line demonstrations, boycotts of company stores, businesses, and local government offices, and organizing and implementing food distribution systems during strikes."[17] Women's activism long has crossed the traditional boundaries of the domestic sphere, as they fight to protect the class interests of their families and communities in the face of the Goliath coal industry. In West Virginia these activities, what Virginia Seitz has termed "proxy activism," were ultimately to improve the socioeconomic conditions of families in state communities.[18] Women activists working in anti–mountaintop removal campaigns today are linked most obviously to the anti–strip mining activism of the 1960s and 1970s. The connections between anti–strip mining activism of the 1960s and 1970s, and current anti-MTR activism

"Remembering the Past, Working for the Future" 423

are conveyed succinctly by perhaps the most famous anti-MTR activist, Judy Bonds, who calls MTR "strip-mining on steroids."[19] Not only is MTR more massive on scale than older forms of strip mining, but its threats to both the human and nonhuman environment are also far more grave than previous strip-mining operations.

Compared to past grassroots activism in Appalachia, current women activists are not explicitly fighting to save coal jobs, or to work for reforms within this industry. They serve as watchdogs against big coal abuses, while fighting for green economic alternatives that will preserve their communities and environmental heritage. There are several groups within the Appalachian region fighting the devastating forces of mountaintop removal, with the Coal River Mountain Watch (CRMW) and the Ohio Valley Environmental Coalition (OVEC) being two of the most prominent. OVEC is a grassroots regional state organization formed in 1987 to fight toxic waste issues, but since the late 1990s it has focused most of its efforts on MTR. The CRMW is a locally based community organization, situated in Whitesville, West Virginia, formed in 1998 by residents directly impacted by MTR. These groups engage in political lobbying, direct action, and public education campaigns. Recent actions include Mountain Justice Summer, designed to raise awareness about MTR in West Virginia, Kentucky, Virginia, Tennessee and North Carolina; the Pennies for Promise campaign, a fund-raising effort to build a new school for children of Marsh Fork, dangerously located next to a massive coal-processing silo; and the Coal River Mountain Wind Project, a renewable energy plan that could create two hundred jobs in Boone County, West Virginia.[20]

In the coalfields of West Virginia, white working-class women's current anti-MTR activism is informed by the sexual division of labor that associated women with the private sphere of home and family and men with the public arena of industrial work. Coalfield women, acting out of a need to save their homes, communities, cultural heritage, and the lush Appalachian environment from the ravages of the coal industry, are influenced by entrenched gender ideologies shaped and solidified by coal in the region. Arguably, these women are defying separate-spheres conventions by exerting collective agency that can be personally empowering. Separate-spheres ideology, and its manifestation into the real lives of people, existed prior to coal's entrance in Appalachia, and some scholars have argued that these upper-class gender conventions were never attainable for poor and working-class Native American, African American and white women in the region.[21] However, gender ideologies and cultural notions of the best and most natural spaces for men and women became uniquely solidified when this industry began producing coal in Appalachia in the late nineteenth century.[22] While coal did not create separate-spheres ideology, when operations began in parts of Appalachia, cultural values and gender and family arrangements changed to better serve this profitable industry. Increased gender segregation came to fundamentally shape and inform local culture.[23] Many West Virginia men entered the public, albeit dirty and dangerous, work of coal mining, gaining their cultural identity as hard-working patriarchs who risked their lives for the socioeconomic survival of their families. While men worked in exploited, unsafe working conditions, for very little pay, they enjoyed autonomy, cultural privilege, and power at home, a sanctuary away from their public life as industrial workers. Conversely, many West Virginia women further retreated into the private sphere of home, gaining their cultural identities as wives and mothers. While some West Virginia women also worked for wages, particularly those from the working class, many public means of good employment were denied to coalfield women, and both their class and gender positions became increasingly compromised, as they grew more dependent upon their husbands. Unlike men, they received no sanctuary away from their work as wives and mothers of working-class coal miners. Sally Ward Maggard suggests these coalfield gender ideologies helped establish family patterns and systematize the coal industry in West Virginia, where coal towns had numerous "disciplined miners" and women who "provided the unpaid domestic work to support the miner labor force and increase profits for coal owners and stockholders," who, invariably, were located outside the state.[24] While similar gendered cultural arrangements are evidenced in other places, and at specific historical moments, the composition of these social patterns, and their cultural value is, of course, contextually bound. The coal industry has changed considerably over the years, but these well-established ideologies about men,

"Remembering the Past, Working for the Future" 425

women, and work continue to inform the culture of West Virginia's coalfields. The gender ideology that seeks to consign women to the private sphere, caring for children and husbands, is the same ideology that has propelled some anti-MTR activists out of the home and into coalfield communities, mining sites, the state legislature, stockholder meetings, and any number of public spaces to educate the public about what is currently destroying Appalachian communities. As such, current anti-MTR activists are simultaneously embracing traditional gender ideologies and protecting their families and communities, while also defying these prescriptions by their very public activism against mountaintop removal coal mining. Divisive gendered notions, and lack of opportunity, as well as concern for their homes, communities, and the Appalachian landscape that surround them, inform anti-MTR activism and ultimately serve as powerful tools for women to justify their resistance. Celene Krauss has argued that ideologies of motherhood, in particular, have led to politicization of some environmental justice activists. She notes:

> Ideologies of motherhood, traditionally relegated to the private sphere, became political resources that these women used to initiate and justify their resistance and increasing politicization. Rejecting the separation of public and private arenas that renders invisible and insignificant the world of women's work, they developed a public, more politicized ideology of motherhood that became a resource to fight gender and class oppression.[25]

Krauss suggests that women working in environmental justice campaigns do not necessarily reject traditional ideologies of women and motherhood but, rather, reinterpret and redirect them into a source of social and political power.[26] Many of the anti-MTR activists, as stated above, are mothers who can be viewed as reinterpreting the traditional coalfield gender ideologies and redirecting them into political action. Of course, there are some anti-MTR activists who are not mothers or wives. Nevertheless, connections among women, traditional gender ideologies, and political activism are frequently linked and are cited by many women activists when explaining the large presence of women in the movement. For example, Judy Bonds says:

> It's a protection issue . . . a woman just feels that she has to protect her children, and her grandchildren and her homeplace. And that's why there is so many women involved in this because we have that instinct inside of us and that stubborn streak and the convictions to protect . . . through the traditional people I've studied, the women has been the ones that managed things, that protected things, that basically did what they needed to do to protect their children. The mother hen syndrome.[27]

While Bonds's comments may strike some feminists as reducing women to their supposed maternal capacities, her activism ultimately challenges traditional notions of women and their place in the public, political arena. Bonds depicts anti-MTR activists as determined, driven women whose activism is virtually an automatic reaction to the assaults on their homes and communities. Her use of the mother hen metaphor is particularly interesting, as she likens her female counterparts to fierce protectors of both the human and nonhuman environment. While West Virginia women such as Nease, Seebok, Stockman, Bonds, Gunoe, Lorelei Scarbro, and others strive to save communities, mountains and their environmental heritage, they are simultaneously involved in fighting for economic justice by promoting the use of renewable resources and green energy projects in the mountain state.

Most members of OVEC and CRMW are working-class white women—many of them wives, mothers, and grandmothers whose homes and communities have been directly impacted by MTR operations. Some have no prior political experience; however, others have participated in regional reform efforts, such as labor activities associated with the United Mine Workers Union. Some anti-MTR activists did not participate in past labor activists but joined these organizations because of environmental concerns. Anti-MTR activism also has a vigorous youth base, with many college students from the larger Appalachian region, both women and men, active in the fight to end MTR.[28] Regardless of the various backgrounds of the grassroots women activists, all are involved, to protect their communities, promote alternative energy sources, diversify the economy, and preserve West Virginia's rich cultural heritage, which is inextricably tied to the mountainous geography.

"Remembering the Past, Working for the Future" 427

WEST VIRGINIA'S ENVIRONMENTAL HERITAGE: COAL OR MOUNTAINS?

In May 2007 I traveled west on Route 3 in West Virginia from my mother's house in Eccles to the offices of the CRMW in Whitesville. In the small town of Surveyor, I passed a billboard with black background and white lettering with this directive: "Stop Destroying My Mountains," signed "God." Anti-MTR activists, intent on raising awareness about the large-scale decimation of Appalachia's lush mountains and biologically diverse environment, sponsored the billboard. The next day, when traveling the same route, I was disturbed by the sign's overnight alternation. Someone had scaled the billboard, and using white spray paint, had crossed out the original message, changing the signer from "God" to "Tree Huggers," an obvious message to environmental activists. The vandalism of this public sign speaks to the ways in which coal-industry sympathizers denigrate grassroots activists as environmental extremists who seek to destroy West Virginia's economy and cultural ties to coal. The alteration of this billboard also reveals the divisiveness created by MTR. On the one hand, West Virginia has a strong contingent of grassroots activists who fight to save the mountains and small communities located near these sites and to promote new economic enterprises, such as alternative energy projects. On the other hand are the pro-industry forces—coal employees and state political leaders—that continue to serve the interests of big coal at the expense of state citizens.

The defining marker of the Appalachian region is, of course, the expansive Appalachian mountain chain. Mountain residents express personal ties to the surrounding landscape, and many have great difficulty leaving the area for other environments. Mountains are inextricably tied to the history, culture, and environment of the region. This cultural, environmental phenomenon has existed in the region for over one hundred years. For example, in 1905 Emma Bell Miles explained:

> Only a superficial observer could fail to understand that the mountain people really love their wilderness—love it for its beauty and freedom. . . . Nothing less than the charm of their stern motherland could hold them here. . . . Occasionally a whole starved-out family will emigrate westward, and, having settled, will spend years in simply waiting for a chance to sell out and move back again.[29]

This sentiment is still expressed today by those living in the region. In addition to a sense of longing and ownership of the natural landscape, many people in Appalachia, particularly in West Virginia, express the sense of being comforted and protected by the enveloping mountains in which they live. For example, West Virginia poet Maggie Anderson says:

> I know, of course, that the mountains can narrow our horizons,
> lower our ceilings, and hold us in, both literally and metaphorically.
> But I must also admit that these hills comfort me. Perhaps because
> of their great age (the range of mountains that makes up the
> Appalachian region from Georgia to Maine is two hundred million
> years old), the hills provide a sense of history, and, therefore,
> of implicit continuance. The fact of their long past suggests the
> possibility of a long future.[30]

Anderson wrote this in the mid 1990s—a decade that saw the rise and expansion of mountaintop-removal coal mining in West Virginia. While Anderson is optimistic in her belief that a long history ensures a long future, many grassroots activists in West Virginia worry that if mountaintop-removal mining does not end, people in Appalachia will lose the source of their comfort and devotion, the sublime mountainous landscape. Many residents view mountains as God-given and created, revealing the strong influence of religion in coalfield culture. Whether or not one considers mountains divinely created and gifted, environmental activists in West Virginia are keenly aware of how the mountainous landscape is part of their environmental heritage. Patty Seebok, long-time member of the Coal River Mountain Watch, expresses the views of many in West Virginia and Appalachia concerning the historic and cultural significance of the mountains:

> Mountains *are* Appalachia. We *are* the Appalachian Mountains. We
> are the mountaineers, we are the pioneers . . . My ancestors trace
> back on one side, on my dad's side, of the family to the 1700s. They
> settled this area when nobody else wanted it. It was too rugged, too
> rough. It had no roads, no railroads, no nothing. You know our
> people were pioneers who came in and carved this out and now all
> the sudden they [coal operators and abetting politicians]want it?
> Excuse me?[31]

Seebok's comments call into question the real ownership of this natural landscape and reveals, by invoking the history of settlement, the danger of losing this environmental space to current political-industrial forces. The land, like that of most white Americans with European roots, that Seebok currently protects was originally occupied by numerous Native American tribes, who were forced off the land to make way for white settlers, African slaves, and free blacks.[32] Nevertheless, Seebok's familiar ties to the Appalachian mountains is an important incentive for her work in protecting this landscape.

Janice Nease, one of the charter members of CRMW and lifelong West Virginia resident, claims mountains are also important to her family history:

> They [mountains] gave us our sense of time, and place and identity. And we would go there. If you were happy you were in the mountains to celebrate . . . it made you understand your connection to the universe and to the creator. And we went there when we were very sad for solace. The mountain would, you know, replenish you.[33]

With Appalachian mountains falling prey to MTR, activists increasingly and consistently highlight the cultural link to their environmental inheritance. They remind people that mountains—not the coal industry—define the region. Asserting their connection with land, culture, and history in the destructive age of mountaintop-removal coal mining, CRMW member Lorelei Scarbro says simply: "we don't live where they mine coal. They mine coal where we live."[34] Scarbro's comments expose what defines West Virginia culture for many environmental activists in the region and privileges long-standing Appalachian communities over coal extraction.

While many residents and anti-MTR activists see West Virginia culture as forever tied to mountains, business interests claim that West Virginia culture long has been shaped by the coal industry, which ultimately owns the Mountain State. A conscious effort on the part of business and state politicians stresses the industrial connections between coal and West Virginia. For example, over the past few years coal officials have changed the language from the well-known and arguably more descriptive designation "mountaintop-removal mining" to "mountaintop mining," omitting the word "removal," in an attempt to soften the connotations of this destructive process in the public mind.[35] This shift, from mountains to coal, was dramatically apparent in 2006 when the state's welcome sign was changed by the Joe Manchin administration from the long-standing welcome slogan "Welcome to Wild, Wonderful West Virginia," stressing its connections to the mountainous geography, to "Welcome to West Virginia: Open for Business," with coal, of course, being the primary business in operation.[36] Indeed, for many residents of West Virginia the coal industry defines the culture. One can read sentiments such as "West Virginia *is* coal country" on billboards and bumper stickers throughout the state.

In addition, the pro-industry group Friends of Coal (FOC) distributes yard signs and bumper stickers to citizen supporters, as part of its well-funded propaganda campaign. In the 2006 West Virginia Coal Association's publication, *Coal Facts,* Friends of Coal asserts the connection between West Virginia and this industry, by claiming, "It is likely that no state and industry are as closely identified with one another as West Virginia and coal.[37] FOC says the state is "full of people who understand and appreciate the value and the importance of the coal industry to the Mountain State and its people . . . These people have always been around. But they have never before been organized into a cohesive force capable of demonstrating just how many West Virginians are directly and indirectly involved with the coal industry."[38] Certain industries do influence the culture of particular areas, and to a large extent this is the case in West Virginia, but one must note the impact of that influence and question the efficacy of such arrangements, particularly in regions ruled by extractive businesses. The coal industry, despite the jobs created, has not been a positive influence in West Virginia. One must certainly question why and how this profitable business works in the second most impoverished state in the country. One must also question why and how Big Coal can readily build roads and create massive mining operations but contribute very little to West Virginia's infrastructure in non-coal-mining economic development, education, and health care and other social programs that contribute to the well-being of the citizens of the state. Instead, this industry has shifted its tax burden to state citizens, polluted the natural environment, jeopardized the quality of life, and dislocated small communities throughout the state.[39] Today King Coal has both the human and nonhuman environment literally on the run, fearing for their survival in this age of mountaintop-removal coal mining. Vivian Stockman, OVEC activist, eloquently describes the frightening realities of current life in the coalfields:

> Already mountaintop removal has claimed nearly 400,000 acres of forested mountains. Entire communities, built long ago in the hollows the companies now desire for valley fills, have been bought out. For other communities, mountaintop removal grinds ever closer, and worried about the blasting damages become routine, and even bigger problems claim attention. Every time it rains, folks who live close to this greed-crazed form of mining get scared. Really scared.[40]

ECONOMIC JUSTICE THROUGH RENEWABLE NATURAL RESOURCES AND GREEN ENERGY IN WEST VIRGINIA

The logo for the Coal River Mountain Watch is a large blue eye, whose center is a green mountain chain topped by a bright sun. Accompanying this logo is the slogan "Remembering the Past, Working for the Future."[41] The first part of this motto is a historical awareness of the social, political, and environmental exploitation of the state as well as the legacy of grassroots activism in West Virginia. The second half of the catchphrase reveals its commitment to making transformative changes that will benefit the human and nonhuman environment. The group describes their mission as "to stop the destruction of our communities and environment by mountaintop-removal mining, to improve the quality of life in our area and to help rebuild sustainable communities."[42] Similar sentiments are expressed by OVEC, whose broader mission is to "organize and maintain a diverse grassroots organization dedicated to the improvement and preservation of the environment through education, grassroots organizing and coalition building, leadership, development and media outreach."[43] Its logo is a large tree that sits on top of the group's acronym, OVEC, which is in green. Anti-MTR activism of groups such as the CRMW and OVEC in West Virginia has two primary goals: to stop the destructive influence of coal, including its adverse impact on the natural environment, and to promote the development of renewable natural resources, that, in turn, will improve local economies by creating sustainable industries and communities.

While interviewing many women anti-MTR activists over the years, and reading interviews with them in local and national media, it has become clear that these activists, unlike past grassroots resistance, do not focus their energies on saving coal jobs or fighting for reforms within this industry. They lodge critiques of coal primarily as environmental justice activists who are part of a larger national and international movement that seeks to raise awareness about global warming and the impact of fossil fuels on the global environment. While these women possess an international perspective, they are solidly situated in their local and regional communities, making the crucial connections between the global and the local. They engage in what the noted global scholar Vandana Shiva has labeled "Earth Democracy," an ancient perspective that promotes peaceful, just, and sustainable communities.[44] Shiva claims that "Earth democracy connects the particular to the universal, the diverse to the common, and the local to the global," and "evolves from the consciousness that while we are rooted locally we are also connected to the world as a whole. And, in fact, to the entire universe."[45] CRMW codirector Judy Bonds conforms to this worldview, as she considers herself an environmental activist as a way of "paying rent for living on this planet . . . if you're not an activist, you're not paying your rent for living on this planet. You're just, you're just, a parasite."[46] Bonds, like many environmental justice activists, adopts an unequivocal position in her perspective about anti-MTR activism by boldly exclaiming, "There's no neutral. You gotta be either/or. And if you're neutral, you are a parasite."[47] Bonds's comments dramatize the linkages between past and current Appalachian activism and are reminiscent of Florence Reece's famous call-to-arms labor anthem, "Which Side Are You On?" and its strong condemnation of political moderates or those unwilling to take a stand. In addition to her unambiguous stance on MTR, Bonds reveals her knowledge of the larger picture and the importance of making local and global critiques:

> You know, I could go on about West Virginia and mountaintop removal but I can see the big picture. And the big picture is

"Remembering the Past, Working for the Future" 433

renewable energy. The big picture is America's reliance upon fossil fuels. . . . I can see what it's doing to the earth. I mean here in West Virginia, you know, the mining and the extraction of coal is filthy. It's nasty. But, the problem is, on the other end, the burning of it is poisoning our unborn children . . . there's no such thing as cheap energy and here's your proof."[48]

Bonds became active in the anti-MTR movement in 1999, when her community of Marfork, in Boone County, West Virginia, was destroyed by MTR operations and many residents were forced to relocate when living conditions became unbearable.[49] She won the prestigious Goldman Environmental Prize in 2003, one of six people in the world who annually receive the award.[50]

Organizer for the Ohio Valley Environmental Coalition and the 2009 winner of the Goldman Prize, Maria Gunoe joined anti-MTR campaigns in 2001 when her home was impacted by a massive flood, which many residents blamed on MTR's alteration of the natural landscape. Gunoe supports Bonds's critique of fossil fuels, and her claim that "there's no such thing as cheap energy," by revealing the health risks linked to the toxic environments many people in West Virginia occupy as a result of the national and, indeed, global use of coal:

> People around here are swiggin' down contaminated water all day long, every day. The health effects are sometimes long-term. It's usually pancreatic cancer of some kind of liver disease, or kidney stones, gallstones—digestive tract problems. And then, too, people's breathing. The blasting is killin' people—just smothering them to death through breathin' all of the dust. The computers and electronics and stuff in my house stay completely packed up with black coal dirt and rock dust together. Why do they expect us to just take it in the name of jobs?[51]

Gunoe's comments also reveal many activists' unwavering commitment to fight coalfield injustices and to save local communities. She affirms the historical reality that vulnerable populations frequently resist their own oppression. They fight to change social and economic conditions of their immediate environment for both present and future generations. Through their critiques of coal extraction, women such as Bonds and Gunoe promote what Vandana Shiva terms "living economies," which are "people-centered, decentralized, sustainable, and livelihood-generating." They are based on "co-ownership and coproduction, on sharing and participation. Living economies are not mere concepts: they exist and continue to emerge in our times. Living economies are being shaped by ordinary people in their everyday lives."[52] For Shiva, living economies unite the human and nonhuman environment. Women in West Virginia promote living economies through sustainable development of the area's renewable natural resources and the promotion of green energy projects.

Recently, activists have begun to promote green alternatives to coal, including the economic development of natural resources, such as medicinal plants, ginseng, and black cohosh.[53] Many activists view the cultivation of these renewable natural resources as another alternative to the economic reliance on coal, the state's most noted and finite natural resource. Ginseng, a medicinal plant used for centuries in Asia and North America, grows in all fifty-five counties of West Virginia, and is a state-regulated activity, whereby residents are able to dig their own ginseng from September 1 to November 30 every year.[54] "Ginsening," known by locals as "sangin," has a long history in the Appalachian region. In some West Virginia communities such as Coal River, digging ginseng is a fundamental part of local culture and "represents an intimate, harmonious relationship between the people and the environment as much as an economic activity."[55] This medicinal herb is used to improve physical vitality and to treat a wide range of afflictions, including digestive problems and hypertension, and it is certainly profitable, as it sells for $300 a pound.[56] According to the West Virginia department of forestry, in 2002, 6,400 pounds of ginseng was extracted in West Virginia, worth $2 million dollars.[57] CRMW activist Patty Seebok maintains that MTR is threatening these indigenous plants and hopes their efforts can curtail the threat and provide economic alternatives to the extraction of coal:

> There's other things growing here ... medicinal plants, the ginseng, black cohosh, yellow root, all the things that are being destroyed ... that's another thing we're trying to revive that might come under sustainable communities. That, I mean, as much as the price of ginseng and cohosh and stuff is up, why can't we stop destroying it, and have businesses out of that?[58]

"Remembering the Past, Working for the Future" 435

Black Cohosh, another renewable resource promoted by local activists, has been used for centuries by healers and doctors to treat fever, arthritis, and women's health issues, including menstrual and menopausal symptoms and reproductive diseases.[59] Black cohosh is found in rich hardwood forests east of the Mississippi, including West Virginia. At most health stores today it sells for roughly seventeen dollars for sixty capsules.[60] There are many such roots and herbs growing naturally in the mountainous landscape of West Virginia. The production of these renewable natural resources, when combined with other environmental assets, can provide viable economic alternatives to the destructive force of MTR.

Some activists also promote the use of West Virginia's expansive forests, and the valuable timber that is currently being destroyed by MTR. The first step in the MTR process is to clear trees and other vegetation from the permitted site. Instead of using the trees from MTR sites productively, coal companies burn them in their haste to extract the coal and get it to international markets. Many activists want this timber used productively, instead of the wasteful and destructive ways in which the coal industry currently handles West Virginia's trees. Patty Seebok says, "Why can't we have furniture stores with all the wood that's being razed? A lot of this weed doesn't even leave here, and it's on a mountaintop-removal site but they don't want to wait. They slash it and burn it."[61] While the extraction of timber can be environmentally problematic, this renewable resource can be managed in sustainable and economically just ways, such as those advocated by theorists like Shiva, and her emphasis on the cooperative, "living economy."[62]

In addition to the promotion and development of natural resources such as timber, ginseng, and black cohosh, anti-MTR activists also promote the use of green energy, most notably wind energy. Currently, Massey Energy Corporation intends to mine roughly ten miles of Coal River Mountain in Boone County for nonrenewable coal extraction. A coalition of forces, including Coal River Mountain Watch; Appalachian Voices, a regional organization in Boone, North Carolina; and WindLogics, a national wind development modeling firm, proposed the Coal River Mountain Wind Project as a source of alternative energy in the southern region of the state.[63] Area resident Lorelei Scarbro, an activists committed to this project, says, "Our concern today is our homes, our environment and the sustainability of the environment. The house I live in and raised my children in, which my husband built, and he is buried in the family cemetery next door, would be in danger from this mine. The wind farm would preserve the mountain."[64] Predictably, coal forces contest the proposal because they realize the threat that green energy development poses for enterprises reliant on the extraction and sale of non-renewable fossil fuels. Patty Seebok counters King Coal's opposition to the wind project by saying "they like to tell everyone that you can't produce electricity without coal, but at the same time they say, well, the windmills are not going to make enough wind to see a difference. Well, if it's not, why are they fighting it?[65] The Coal River Mountain Wind Farm is, indeed, a viable economic alternative. This cooperative study on wind energy production contains data on the economic benefits of this alternative. During construction of the wind farm, $20 million a year would be generated in local spending, creating over two hundred construction jobs. In addition, after construction, $2 million a year in direct spending would be generated, and forty to fifty permanent operation and maintenance jobs could be created. The local tax base would also benefit, as the project would provide $400,000 annually in state tax revenue, and $3 milion in county tax revenue. Developers of this project claim it has the potential to provide the city of Beckley and all of Raleigh County with electricity generated by clean wind energy.[66]

State activists, in addition to their public education and direct action campaigns, are posing tangible solutions to the current crisis in West Virginia and other parts of Appalachia. They foster systemic changes that can save their communities from extinction and protect West Virginia's lush, mountainous environment. Most of the activists are ordinary citizens impacted by the excesses of greedy, multinational coal companies who do not care for human welfare or the fate of the natural world. Their local, community-based activism also makes important connections to the global world. In doing so they promote the use of renewable natural resources to facilitate the end of King Coal's reign over the people and environment of West Virginia.

ANTI-MTR ACTIVISTS are keenly aware that the survival of their local communities, and the beautiful Appalachian Mountains, are at

"Remembering the Past, Working for the Future" 437

stake in their reform efforts. Current women activists represent links in a long chain of organized protest in West Virginia. In addition, West Virginia women are influenced by the dictates of separate-spheres gender ideology, but their activism also represents a direct challenge to the status quo as they transfer energies outward into Appalachia's public sphere of anti-MTR environmental justice activism. They represent a formidable presence against the destructive forces of coal in West Virginia, and the gendered nature of this activism should not go unattended by environmental justice or Appalachian studies scholars. These women are, indeed, remembering the past by acknowledging traditional agrarian practices, such as root digging, as infinite, sustainable forms of resource extraction. They remind us that mountains, the rich biodiversity, and the human communities that lie within them are what defines West Virginia, and not, contrary to prevailing opinion, coal or the coal industry. These women also continue to work for the future, developing renewable natural resources and promoting green energy that will not only benefit their local communities but set a precedent for other areas compromised by nonrenewable, fossil fuel extraction.

NOTES

1. Ken Ward Jr., "Miners Marcher's Ideal Collide," *Charleston Gazette,* September 1, 1999, http://www.wvgazette.com/news/News1999085144.

2. Rudy Abramson and Jean Haskell, *The Encyclopedia of Appalachia* (Knoxville: University of Tennessee Press, 2006), 362.

3. Ibid.

4. I Love Mountains, "Mountain Monday: The Legacy of Labor: Blair Mountain, West Virginia," http://www.ilovemountains.org/news/432, accessed December 15, 2008.

5. The high proportion of women environmental justice activists has been noted in numerous sources. See, for example, Joyce M. Barry, "A Small Group of Thoughtful, Committed Citizens: Women's Activism, Environmental Justice, and the Coal River Mountain Watch," *Environmental Justice* 1, no. 1 (2008): 25–35; Rachel Stein, "Introduction," in *New Perspectives on Environmental Justice: Gender, Sexuality, and Activism,* ed. Rachel Stein (New Brunswick, NJ: Rutgers University Press, 2004), 1–17; Lois Ann Lorentzen, "Indigenous Feet: Ecofeminism, Globalization and the Case for the Chiapas," in *Ecofeminism and Globalization: Exploring Culture, Context, and Religion,* ed. Heather Eaton and Lois Lorentzen (Lanham, MD: Rowan and Littlefield, 2003), 57–71; Karen J. Warren, *EcoFeminist Philosophy* (Lanham, MD: Rowan and Littlefield, 2000); Robert Bullard, "Environmental Justice in the 21st Century," in *The Quest of Environmental Justice,* ed. Robert Bullard

(San Francisco: Sierra Club Books, 2005), 19–43; Robert Bullard and Damu Smith, "Women Warriors of Color on the Front Line," in Bullard, *Quest of Environmental Justice*, 62–85; John G Betting and Diane-Michele Prindeville, "The Role of Indigenous Women Organizing in The Communities," in *Environmental Injustices, Political Struggles: Race, Class and the Environment*, ed. David Camacho (Durham: Duke University Press, 1998), 141–65; Mary Mellor, *Feminism and Ecology* (New York: New York University Press, 1997); Giovanna Di Chiro, "Environmental Justice: Reflections on History, Gender and Expertise," in *The Struggle for Ecological Democracy: Environmental Justice Movements in the U.S.*, ed. Daniel Faber (New York: Guilford Press, 1998), 104–36.

6. A number of sources define environmental justice and describe how it differs from mainstream environmentalism. See, for example, Robert Bullard, *Dumping in Dixie: Race, Class, and Environmental Quality* (Boulder: Westview Press, 2000); Bunyan Bryant, "Issues and Potential Policies and Solutions for Environmental Justice: An Overview," in *Environmental Justice: Issues, Policies and Solutions*, ed. Bunyan Bryant (Ann Arbor: University of Michigan Press, 1995), 1–8; Luke Cole and Sheila Foster, *From the Ground Up: Environmental Racism and the Rise of the Environmental Justice Movement* (New York: New York University Press, 2001); Daniel Faber, "Introduction," in Faber, *Struggle for Ecological Democracy*, 1–27; Ronald Sandler and Phaedra C. Pezzullo, *Environmental Justice and Environmentalism: The Social Justice Challenge to the Environmental Movement* (Cambridge, MA: MIT Press, 2007); David Naguib Pellow and Robert Brulle, *Power, Justice, and the Environment: A Critical Appraisal of the Environmental Justice Movement* (Cambridge, MA: MIT Press, 2005).

7. Rachel Stein, "Introduction," in Stein, *New Perspectives on Environmental Justice*, 2.

8. Heather Eaton and Lois Lorentzen, "Introduction," in *Ecofeminism and Globalization: Exploring Culture, Context, and Religion*, ed. Heather Eaton and Lois Lorentzen (Lanham, MD: Rowan and Littlefield Press, 2003), 2.

9. Erik Reece, *Lost Mountain: A Year in the Vanishing Wilderness* (New York: Penguin, 2006); Penny Loeb, *Moving Mountains: How One Woman and Her Community Won Justice from Big Coal* (Lexington: University of Kentucky Press, 2007); Michael Shnayerson, *Coal River* (New York: Farrar, Straus and Giroux, 2007); Shirley Stewart Burns, *Bringing Down the Mountains: The Impact of Mountaintop Removal on Southern West Virginia Communities* (Morgantown: West Virginia University Press, 2007).

10. Eaton and Lorentzen, "Introduction," 2.

11. Thomas Plaut, "Extending the Internal Periphery Model: The Impact of Culture and Consequent Strategy," in *Colonialism in Modern America: The Appalachian Case*, ed. Helen Matthews Lewis, Linda Johnson, and Donald Askins (Boone: Appalachian Consortium Press, 1978), 358.

12. Virginia Rinaldo Seitz, *Women, Development, and Communities for Empowerment in Appalachia* (Albany: State University of New York Press, 1995), 161.

13. Ibid., 182.

14. Stephen L. Fisher, "Introduction," in *Fighting Back in Appalachia: Traditions of Resistance and Change*, ed. Stephen L. Fisher (Philadelphia: Temple University Press, 1993), 6.

"Remembering the Past, Working for the Future" 439

15. Mary Beth Bingham, "Stopping the Bulldozers: What Difference Did It Make," in Fisher, *Fighting Back in Appalachia*, 29.

16. Karaleah Reichart, "Narrating Conflict: Women and Coal in Southern West Virginia," *Journal of Appalachian Studies* 7, no. 1 (2001): 6.

17. Ibid., 7.

18. Virginia Seitz, "Class, Gender, and Resistance in the Appalachian Coalfields," in *Community Activism and Feminist Politics: Organizing Across Race, Class, and Gender*, ed. Nancy Naples (New York: Routledge, 1998), 218.

19. Judy Bonds, interview by Joyce M. Barry, Whitesville, WV, June 14, 2006.

20. Ohio Valley Environmental Coalition, http://www.ovec.org; The Coal River Mountain Watch, http://www.crmw.org, both accessed December 15, 2008.

21. Wilma A. Dunaway, *Women, Work, and Family in the Antebellum Mountain South* (New York: Cambridge University Press, 2008).

22. Scholars have recently debunked the long-standing myth that Appalachian people lived an idyllic, purely agrarian, nonpatriarchal existence before the coal industry was developed in the region. This scholarship argues that most Appalachians participated in mixed economies, combining subsistence agriculture with waged labor. See, for example, Wilma Dunaway, *The First American Frontier: Transition to Capitalism in Southern Appalachia 1700–1860* (Chapel Hill: University of North Carolina Press, 1996); and John Alexander Williams, *Appalachia: A History* (Chapel Hill: University of North Carolina Press, 2001).

23. Sally Ward Maggard, "From Farm to Coal Camp to Back Office and McDonald's: Living in the Midst of Appalachia's latest transformation." *Journal of Appalachian Studies* 6, no. 1 (1994): 16–17.

24. Ibid.

25. Celene Krauss, "Challenging Power: Toxic Waste Protests and the Politicization of White, Working Class Women," in Naples, *Community Activism and Feminist Politics*, 148.

26. Ibid., 149.

27. Judy Bonds, interview.

28. Mountain Justice Summer, http://www.mountainjusticesummer.org, accessed December 15, 2008.

29. Emma Belle Miles, *The Spirit of the Mountains* (Knoxville: University of Tennessee Press, 1975), 18–19.

30. Maggie Anderson, "The Mountains Dark and Close Around Me," in *BloodRoot: Reflections on Place by Appalachian Women Writers*, ed. Joyce Dyer (Lexington: University of Kentucky Press), 33.

31. Patty Seebok, interview by Joyce M. Barry, Whitesville, WV, June 21, 2006.

32. Wilma Dunaway, *The First American Frontier: Transition to Capitalism in Southern Appalachia 1700–1860* (Chapel Hill: University of North Carolina Press, 1996).

33. Janice Nease, interview by Joyce M. Barry, Whitesville, WV, June 21, 2006.

34. Deborah Feyerick, "The Battle Over Coal River Mountain," October 7, 2008, http://www.cnn.com/2008/US/10/07/coal.river.

35. "Glossary of Terms," in *Coal Facts 2006* (Charleston, WV: West Virginia Coal Association), 2.

36. Fred Pace, "Open for Business," *Register-Herald*, March 16, 2006, http://www.register-herald.com/business/local_story_077192446.html?keyword=topstory.

37. "The Friends of Coal," in *Coal Facts 2006*, 2.

38 Ibid.

39. Shirley Stewart Burns, *Bringing Down the Mountains: The Impact of Mountaintop Removal on Southern West Virginia Communities* (Morgantown: West Virginia University Press, 2007), 62.

40. Ken Ward Jr., "Woman Makes Environmental Movement Move," in *Charleston Gazette*, March 9, 2005, http:www.ohvec.org/links/news/archive/2005/fair_use/03_09.html, accessed December 15, 2008.

41. *The Coal River Mountain Watch*, http://www.crmw. net/.

42. Ibid.

43. *The Ohio Valley Environmental Coalition*, http://www.ohvec.org/.

44. Vandana Shiva, *Earth Democracy* (Cambridge, MA: South End Press, 2005), 1.

45. Ibid., 1, 5.

46. Judy Bonds, interview.

47. Ibid.

48. Ibid.

49. Ibid.

50. Joyce M. Barry, "A Small Group of Thoughtful, Committed Citizens": Women's Activism, Environmental Justice, and the Coal River Mountain Watch," *Environmental Justice* 1, no. 1 (March 2008): 28–35.

51. Maria Gunoe, "My Life is on the Line," http://www.stopmountaintopremoval.org/ marias-story.html, accessed December 15, 2008.

52. Shiva, *Earth Democracy*, 63.

53. Judy Bonds and Vivian Stockman, interview by Joyce M. Barry, Clinton, NY, November 13, 2008.

54. West Virginia Department of Forestry, http://www.wvforestry.com/ginseng.cfm?Menucall=ginseng, accessed December 15, 2008.

55. Anthony Cavender, *Folk Medicine in Southern Appalachia.* (Chapel Hill: University of North Carolina Press, 2003), 63.

56. Emily Grafton, "The History, The Mystery of Ginseng," *West Virginia Wildlife Magazine*, http://www.wvdnr.gov/wildlife/magazine/archive/02Summer/TheHistory_the_Mystery_of_ Ginseng.html, accessed December 15, 2008.

57. West Virginia Department of Forestry, http://www.wvforestry.com/ginseng.cfm?Menucall=ginseng, accessed December 15, 2008.

58. Patty Seebok, interview.

59. Cavender, *Folk Medicine in Southern Appalachia*, 128.

60. *The Vitamin Shoppe*, http:www.vitaminshoppe.com/store/em/browse/sku_detail.Jsp?id=SO-1954&st=cs&source, accessed December 15, 2008.

61. Patty Seebok, interview.

62. Shiva, *Earth Democracy*, 13.

63. "Wind or Mountaintop Removal?: Study Shows West Virginia Mountain Could be Permanent Power Source for 150,00 Homes," *Earth Times* http://www.Earthtimes.org/articles/show.wind-or-mountaintop-removal-study,510055, accessed December 15, 2008.

64. Ibid.

65. Patty Seebok, interview.

66. "Wind or Mountaintop Removal?"

The Petition of Margaret Lee

Margaret Lee was an African American woman who in 1795 appealed to the Superior Court of Law of Washington District, in the Territory South of the River Ohio (popularly called the Southwest Territory), for the freedom of herself and her two children. The lands of the Southwest Territory were those western lands formerly controlled by North Carolina but ceded to the federal government. The Southwest Territory lands in 1796 became the state of Tennessee; as of 1795, however, the territory fell under the rule of the Ordinance of 1790. The ordinance—unlike the Ordinance of 1787 that created the Northwest Territory and which the 1790 ordinance resembled in every other respect—not only allowed slavery but also forbade emancipation.

At the time of her appeal, Lee lived with her two children in Sullivan County, Washington District. Slavery coexisted with the pioneer settlements of the county; moreover, the buying and selling of slaves was common in the county. Two major roads in the area, Island Road and Blountville Highway, served as trade thoroughfares for material goods and human beings. Slaves easily could be transported west to auction in Knoxville, Tennessee, and north to auction either in Abingdon or nearby Bristol, Virginia. The slave population of Sullivan County was not that high—as of 1787, for instance, tax lists reveal that there were 223 black polls (slaves between the ages of 11 and 60), contrasted to 782 white polls (white adult property-holding males); and as of 1812, there were 384 black polls and 2,042 white polls. Nonetheless, slave labor in pioneering activities (such as clearing land), agriculture, and domestic work was invaluable to the economy of the county.

DOC 1

To the Honorable the Judges of the Superior Court of Law for the District of Washington.

Your unfortunate petitioner Margaret Lee on behalf of herself, and her tender little Infants Maria & Abraham, humbly begs leave to represent to your honors—

443

That she is the immediate offspring of Lucinda and Thomas Lee free Citizens of the Town of Boston in the State of Massachusetts.

That her Parents although of a black hue had the happiness to be born free [scratched out (citizens)] people, and as such, enjoyed all the benefits of freedom, in the above mentioned state.

That your petitioner sometime in the year 1774 (as she believes) and a little after sun setting, happening to be on the Town Wharf, was suddenly seized by a certain Samuel Latin, bound with Cords, and hurried on Board of a vessel, which sd [said] Latin commanded.

That your petitioner was immediately lodged in the Hold of the vessel, where she bewared her [. . .] situation [. . .] and unseen by any humans Eye:—After undergoing for some time this melancholy confinement, her fetters were unloosened, and the Light of [scratched out (Heaven)] the sun, once more she experienced,
But new Sorrows now filled her Breasts—the Land which she had been accustomed to dwell in was now vanished from her sight
—And every Gale wafted her further and further from her affectionate Parents, Relations, friends and Country.—Every (scratched out [rev]) revolving day now hightened her sorrows, till at length her Destiny was fixed, Villainy triumphed, and her misery became complete:—the vessel having escaped the Dangers of the sea, your petitioner was landed in the state of Maryland, and there doomed to servitude. The cruel Latin then treated your petitioner as a Slave, and Labour, oppression & their attendant grief, hovered around her; But recollecting the invaluable Blessing of which she had been so unjustly deprived, she communicated her situation, to some benevolent Men with a view of obtaining relief; but Latin fearful least [lest?] truth might appear from Investigation, sold her to a certain George Johnson, who sold her not long afterwards to a Mr Francis Hawkins, who sold her to a Mr Butcher Bozlin of Frederick County in the state of Maryland, and by this past mentioned Gentleman, she was sold & delivered to a certain Samuel Gammon of Sullivan County, in the south western Territory, in whose possession she now is, in the capacity of a humble Slave.

Thus your Honors must discover, that your Petitioner, for the period of twenty years, has suffered a life of servitude, in a Country, where she had inherited from her Parents Liberty.

Your petitioner's situation, need only be recollected, to convince your Honors, that she is unable to defray the expences of a Law Suit—

—She therefore humbly solicits the interposition of this Honorable Court, in favour of herself and her two little Infants;—And if it should seem meet to your Honors, that the most gracious writ of Liberty, of a Habeas Corpus cum causa, may immediately [. . .], directed to Samuel Gammon of Sullivan County, commanding him to offer before your honor, [hole worn in document; illegible] with the Bodies of Margaret Lee & her two children Maria & Abraham, together, with the cause of their Detention; or that your Honors may take such steps, as will give to your petitioner an opportunity of shewing that freedom was her Birthright. And your petitioner will [. . .]

18th of September 1795   Margaret Lee in behalf of herself and her two children Maria & Abraham

DOC 2

Territory of the United States Washington District
South of Ohio—   Superior Court
of L

To Samuel Gambell Manter in the County of Sullivan, in the Territory South of Ohio

We Command you, that you have before us at Jonesborough on the third Tuesday of March next, under safe, and secure conduct the bodies of Margret Lee, and her Two Children Maria and Abraham who are said to be detained by you as Slaves, together with the day, and cause of their being taken, and so detained,—and further that you do and Reserve all and Singular those things, which the Superior Court of Law, for the District of Washington, Shall then and there Consider of, and Direct in the behalf, and have you then and there this W[. . .]t, Witness James [P]iken Clerk of our said Court at office this third Tuesday of September A D 1795, and in xx year of our Independence

(Signed

To Sam ᵉ Gambell
1795
To
Sam ᵉ Gambell

Read by Me to Samuel Gamble
(. . .) Shelby

Source: Washington County Court Records, Box 3—Superior Court, Folder 117, Archives of Appalachia, East Tennessee State University.

The Fight for Suffrage

Women's suffrage, hotly debated throughout the American South, was a controversial issue in the Mountain South as well. Unlike Northern women whose quest for the vote began in Seneca Falls in 1848, most suffragists in the South, including the mountain areas, did not establish suffrage clubs until the 1890s, and their growth remained slow until after the turn of the century. The majority of suffrage and antisuffrage leaders in the South were middle- and upper-class women, well educated, and often involved with other reform movements such as child welfare, public health, education, and protection of women. Arguments for or against suffrage were often regional in nature and class based. Urban women who had access to more activist groups, suffrage speakers, and institutions of higher education and, therefore, more access to progressive ideas were more likely to favor suffrage than were rural women. Women from areas whose economic interests, political sympathies, and cultural identity bound them to the established southern ideals of social order and gender roles often rejected progressive reforms, including women's suffrage.

The issues of states' rights and race not only divided suffragists from antisuffragists but also split the suffrage movement in the South. While states' rights suffragists supported women's right to vote, they did not want a federal constitutional amendment. Since most southern states had enacted legislation to disfranchise black men, they firmly believed that the right to decide state voting requirements belonged to the individual states. Antisuffragists warned that white dominance would be in jeopardy if black women were given the vote; suffragists argued that white women voters would outnumber black women voters.

Suffrage studies that focus on individual states make it difficult to assess the support, or lack of support, for suffrage in the Mountain South. West Virginia is the only state that lies entirely within the Appalachian region, and there are detailed studies of the suffrage movement in the state. Regional patterns on suffrage within the state paralleled patterns found in the South as a whole. West Virginia counties in commercial and industrial centers bordering the northern and western states of Pennsylvania and Ohio had the largest support for suffrage, while most of the isolated, rural south-central counties opposed it. And despite high hopes for suffrage in West Virginia following the state legislature's passage of a woman suffrage referendum in 1915, the referendum failed overwhelmingly when the electorate voted in November 1916. Still, bordering the west and the north, Kentucky, Tennessee, and West Virginia demonstrated support for suffrage earlier than the rest of the Mountain South. Kentucky allowed women to vote in school elections as early as 1838, and Tennessee granted women the right to vote in presidential elections in 1919.[1]

In June 1919, a federal suffrage amendment was sent to the states for ratification. Alabama legislators viewed the amendment as an infringement on their authority by the federal government and rejected it. Kentucky and West Virginia ratified the amendment in January and March 1920. After a nine-day special session in August 1920, Tennessee became the thirty-sixth state, and final state needed, to ratify the Nineteenth Amendment. It was decades before other southern states with mountain counties ratified the Nineteenth Amendment. Virginia ratified the amendment in 1952; Alabama, 1953; South Carolina, 1969; Georgia, 1970; North Carolina, 1971; and Mississippi, the last state to ratify the amendment, 1984.

THE TASK WHICH TENNESSEE SUFFRAGISTS HAVE SET FOR THEMSELVES

SOME LOCAL FACTS—(GROWTH OF SUFFRAGE IN GENERAL)

BY CARRIE C. CALLAWAY

Like New York suffragists, the Tennessee suffragists have set a task [for] themselves. For the New York women it is "Suffrage in 1913," which date (owing to the fact that in that state an amendment to the constitution has to pass two successive legislatures before it becomes a law) is the earliest at which the question can reach the voters. At that time Woman's suffrage is sure to pass in New York state for all New York political parties have indorsed the submission of a woman's suffrage amendment to their platforms. The task that Tennessee suffragists have set for themselves is to make Tennessee the first equal suffrage state in the south and it seems to me that the Tennessee woman's task is going to be the hardest to accomplish. And why? There are several reasons.

The Fight for Suffrage 447

In New York state equal suffrage has practically arrived. The question there has been agitated for forty-four years, from the time of Susan B. Anthony and Elizabeth Cady Stanton, who worked for the political emancipation of women in 1868, and the sentiment for woman's suffrage in that state is now too strong and too universal to be longer disregarded. But in Tennessee we have not this mass of sentiment in sympathy with the cause. It is comparatively of late years that the matter has been generally discussed in the press and in polite society. It is only within the past half dozen years that equal suffrage has been regarded other than a joke in this section. Far be it from me, a native of the "cracker state" to disparage the south's fair name, but it is a fact that the group of states known as "The South" are the most conservative in the country, and are the last to give up their traditions and customs; to them changes come slowly in all departments of life and especially are they slow to see that the granting of political independence to women will not detract from their charm and womanliness but rather add to it dignity and self-respect. For those reasons—which might be enlarged upon indefinitely—the Tennessee suffragists have set for themselves no easy task. If they accomplish their goal, they cannot sit idly by and dream of the beauties of a society where man and woman stand shoulder to shoulder in solving the larger social and political problems of the home, city and state. They must work; they must create favorable sentiment; they must agitate—not in a militant manner, but in the way the women of the south know how to work; in the way they worked in pioneer days, in Revolutionary days; in the days of '61–'63, and in the days of the reconstruction period. The woman of the south, now struggling for her political independence, is this same woman working out her destiny now, as then. And they must work together. Every woman in the state, who is interested in the cause, should, connect herself, in some way, with the movement and do her part. If the women of Tennessee WILL work together they will succeed in making the Volunteer state the first in the southland to grant the franchise to its women for week by week the gates swing more widely open and more southern women pass through them.

Some State Facts. As the result of interest manifest in Tennessee in woman's suffrage within the past two years, this state has been put, by national leaders, in the list of those most likely to immediately follow in the footsteps of the nine equal suffrage states already in existence. Dr. Anna Shaw, president of the national organization, says that Michigan, South Dakota, Maine, Missouri, Montana and Tennessee are the states most apt to grant equal suffrage in 1913 and 1914. Kentucky and Virginia rank next to Tennessee in the south, in interest in the cause.

The organization of the Tennessee Equal Suffrage association was effected about 1885, but at that time it was very weak and little was known or cared about equal suffrage in the stale. In fact the cause practically died after the organization of this association and was not renascent until about two years ago.

It was not until the fall of 1910 that any vital interest was manifest in Tennessee in the cause. It is true that be-tween 1885 and 1910 there were periods when the movement seemed to take on new life but these periods were brief and were followed by periods of indifference. But since 1910 the growth of the movement has been prodigious and there are now equal suffrage leagues in Memphis, Nashville, Knoxville, Chattanooga, Morristown, Jackson—with leading women in other smaller towns interested.

The state league, of which Miss Sarah Barnwell Elliott, of Sewanee, is president, now numbers its membership into the thousands. There seems to have been a concerted awakening throughout the state, and there is no doubt about the permanency and potency of this awakening. With sentiment growing, as it is in this state, for equal suffrage, it is no wonder that Tennessee has been placed in the list of "probable" equal suffrage states for 1913–14. At the convention of the Tennessee Equal Suffrage association, held in Nashville January 6 and 7, the delegates adopted as their slogan, "Make Tennessee the first southern equal suffrage state," and the women of this state, with the courage of their convictions behind them, will soon be in a position to demand their enfranchise-ment . . .

Source: Carrie C. Callaway, "The Task Which Tennessee Suffragists Have Set for Themselves. Some Local Facts—Growth of Suffrage in General," *Knoxville Journal & Tribune,* January 19, 1913, in Lizzie Crozier French Scrapbook, p. 30 b, Calvin M. McClung Historical Collection, Knoxville Public Library, Knoxville, Tennessee. Accessed January 30, 2013, at http://cmdc.knoxlib.org/cdm/singleitem/collection/p265301coll8/id/448/rec/13.

Bolivar, W. Va.,
Feb. 27, 1918

Dear Sir,—

I am in receipt of your very kind letter of the 26th inst., and desire to extend the thanks of the W.C.T.U., as well as my own appreciation, for prompt reply and the assurance of your conscientious consideration of the woman's cause.

With reference to the question you ask, as to how you shall regard the vote of 1916, in our state, on the matter, permit [me] to say that I cannot see why W.Va.'s vote in 1916, on a state constitutional amendment, should be viewed in the light of "instructions" to govern your vote in a federal constitutional amendment, in 1918.

The Fight for Suffrage 449

Since it will rest with the Legislature of W.Va. to voice the sentiments of a majority of our people—whose views have undergone a radical change since 1916—it seems to me that you might conscientiously vote—in the U. S. Senate—for a *submission of the question* to the state—Legislature (which is the usual method employed I think, to ratify or reject an amendment to the Federal Constitution) without jeopardizing your sincerity and fair-mindedness [sic] as a representative of a state which is almost sure to reverse its vote on Equal Suffrage should the question be considered by referendum vote again.

The hostile sentiment displayed in our state, in 1916, was due largely to ignorance of the real merits of the question, and the suspicious attitude assumed by most men toward anything new and implied in regulating affairs of home, state, and nation.

Then, too, we had not sufficient time in which to conduct an educational campaign to a successful finish. However, the change in sentiment is very marked throughout the state. Our only real opponents are the vicious, the predatory and the incurably "moss-backed."

Now, we know you are either favorable to open-minded, and we feel sure you will do what is just and right by the mother-half of the state and nation. In this era of wonderful progress, we object very naturally—to the status assigned us by a government which does not hesitate—to call upon its voteless women for patriotic support in service not limited to home economics—service in which we must face supreme sacrifice, many of us.

We are giving that service to our country—to our "Uncle Sam," whose blind eye and deaf ear are invariably turned to the female side of his house, and who develops amazing "skills" of inconsistent stubbornness whenever his "nieces" endeavor to argue him into a better frame of mind, and would strengthen and purify his body politic.

In every way possible to us we are helping to win the war for World Freedom. I myself, have given my only child—the son of a widow for service in France, and I am proud of the fact that he was the first to volunteer from his hometown. Yet we mothers do not enjoy the full rights and privileges which a democracy should bestow upon its own citizens (from whom the government expects, and deserves, loyal support) before it seeks to democratize the world.

We give our sons and our services to help make the world safe for Democracy. Will Democracy give us the vote to help make the world safe for our sons? We ask nothing for our services. Surely, what we ask of the Government is very small in comparison to the sacrifices *we* are called upon to make.

Men do not enjoy the right of franchise because they are moral, intelligent or sound in judgment, but because they are *men.* Therefore, because we are *women*—the other necessary half of Humanity—we want the voting privilege on equal terms with men—as a matter of simple justice.

As a nation, we have allowed half of the countries of Europe to forge ahead of us—the world's greatest democracy—in granting tardy justice to women. Are we going to lag behind with only brutalized Germany left to agree with us that woman's place is wherever men choose to place her? Is it not true that the German vote in the United States is always against extending the franchise to women, and in favor of woman's greatest foe—the Liquor Traffic?

I cannot think that our Government will line up alongside of the German Kaiser in its attitude toward women.

With my best wishes for your health and happiness as well as for your future success, and thanking you personally and in the name of our W. C. T. U., for whatever support you may give us in our bloodless battle against Injustice,

I am,

Respectfully,

Blanche A. Wheatley, Cor. Sec'y
W. C. T. U.,

Bolivar, W. Va.

Source: Letter from Blanche A. Wheatley to Howard Sutherland, Howard Sutherland Papers, Feb. 27, 1918, Box 10, Correspondence, FF2, WVRHC.

NOTE

1. See Anne Wallace Effland's entry "Suffrage" in *Encyclopedia of Appalachia,* ed. Rudy Abramson and Jean Haskell (Knoxville: University of Tennessee Press, 2006), 1618; and Anne Wallace Effland, "'Exciting Battle and Dramatic Finish': The West Virginia Woman Suffrage Movement," *West Virginia History* 46 (1985–86): 137–58 and "'Exciting Battle and Dramatic Finish': West Virginia's Ratification of the Nineteenth Amendment,"ß *West Virginia History* 48 (1989): 61–92. For Tennessee's pivotal role in the passage of the Nineteenth Amendment, see Marjorie Spruill Wheeler, ed., *Votes for Women! The Woman Suffrage Movement in Tennessee, the South, and the Nation* (Knoxville: University of Tennessee Press, 1995).

Abortion in the Mountain South

The debate over abortion and reproductive control in the United States has been, and continues to be, shaped by religious and moral beliefs and layered with the politics of gender and class. Before 1973, abortion was a states' rights issue and in most states abortion was illegal. In *Roe v. Wade*, decided January 22, 1973, the United States Supreme Court ruled that women have the right to an abortion under the Fourteenth Amendment to the Constitution.[1] However, challenges to *Roe v. Wade* and the growing power of the pro-life movement have placed increasing restrictions on legal abortions. The Hyde Amendment (1976), a legislative provision attached to the annual federal appropriation bill for Medicaid, prohibits the use of federal Medicaid funds for abortions; and *Planned Parenthood v. Casey* (1992) upheld the right of states to impose waiting periods and parental notifications in their requirements for legal abortion.[2]

Now, as in the past, poor and rural women are less likely to have access to contraceptive services and abortions; and in Appalachia, contradictions exist between, on the one hand, the traditional religious world view and conservative morals of the region, and, on the other, the economic necessity for birth control. In the nineteenth and early twentieth centuries, Appalachian women sought aid from female family members and midwives for birth control and childbirth. Many of these "Granny" women and midwives relied on plant-based concoctions made from buck vine or partridge berry, pennyroyal, cotton roots, ginger, or May apples to initiate premature labor or recommended the drinking of quinine or turpentine to induce abortions. The case *State of North Carolina v. Elizabeth Shaft* featured below illustrates not only the common reliance on midwives for reproductive control but also the attempts of state officials and the medical profession to curb the "dangerous practices" of midwives. Elizabeth Shaft, a sixty-three-year-old midwife from Asheville, North Carolina, was convicted of providing capsules containing aloe to seventeen-year-old

Annie Kraft and was sentenced to three years in jail and a $1,000 fine. The conviction was upheld.

However, doctors also engaged in dangerous "remedies" and illegal practices to control reproduction and, sometimes, to make a profit. Women who could not obtain legal and safe abortions often resorted to "back-alley" or self-induced abortions. In an interview with Deborah Baker for *Mountain Life and Work,* Ethel Brewster recalled that as the wife of a coal miner, a "kid" herself with two small children and most likely pregnant again, she asked the company doctor for something so she wouldn't be pregnant all the time. He told her to take "a big dose of turpentine." A dose consisted of ten or twelve drops, but without specific instructions, she drank a cupful, making her terribly ill.[3] In a dying declaration, Bessie Kouns accused Dr. H. C. Dorroh of Ashland, Kentucky, of performing an abortion using an instrument he dropped on the floor, then picked up and inserted into her uterus. Dorroh maintained that Kouns suffered from gonorrhea, and that the peritonitic condition of her abdomen stemmed from the use of a lead pencil she used to self-abort.[4] After his conviction for criminal abortion, Dorroh appealed his case to the Supreme Court of Kentucky, where his conviction was overturned. In one of the worst cases, Dr. Thomas J. Hicks of McCaysville, Georgia, charged $100 to fix the "problem" of young women from Georgia and East Tennessee. Between 1951 and 1965, Hicks provided everyday health care to local farmers and townspeople in the front of the clinic, while he performed illegal abortions in the back rooms. During that time, he also sold more than two hundred babies born to mountain women for $1,000 each on the black market.[5]

As the second document from the West Virginia Abortion Reform Committee reveals, despite the U.S. Supreme Court decision *Roe v. Wade,* women continued to be forced out of the region to seek abortions. West Virginia was one of eleven states where public hospitals offered no abortion services a year after *Roe v. Wade.* As a result, women in the Mountain State utilized four nonhospital clinics offering abortion services in Cincinnati, Ohio.[6] Traditional value systems along with states' rights issues increased restrictions on abortions and, as always in poor and rural areas, "those with money can obtain abortions; those without, suffer."

Abortion in the Mountain South 453

State v. Elizabeth Shaft.
[No Number in the Original]
(Filed 20 May, 1914.)

1. Criminal Law—Abortion—Trials—Evidence—Harmless Error—Interpretation of Statutes.

   Upon trial of a defendant for unlawfully, etc., administering a certain "noxious drug" to a pregnant woman with the intent to produce a miscarriage, against the provisions of Revisal, secs. 3618 and 1619, testimony as to sexual intercourse is immaterial, and its admission harmless error.

2. Criminal Law—Abortion—Expert Evidence—Effect of Drug——Trials—Evidence—Interpretation of Statutes.

   Where the defendant is being tried for an intent to produce an abortion upon a pregnant woman, contrary to Revisal, secs. 3618 and 3619, and there is evidence that a capsule given contained a certain drug, it is competent for experts to testify as to the effect of such in producing a miscarriage.

3. Criminal Law—Accomplice—Trials—Evidence—Abortion—Interpretation of Statutes.

   While the judge should caution the jury as to the weight to be given the testimony of an accomplice to the crime upon which the defendant is being tried, a conviction may be had upon the unsupported testimony of the accomplice; but it is held that the victim of the defendant in the latter's effort to produce a miscarriage upon her, contrary to Revisal, secs. 3618 and 3619, is not an accomplice in the crime, in a legal sense, whether she consented thereto or not.

4. Criminal Law—Abortion—Intent—Interpretation of Statutes.

   It is the intent with which a noxious drug is administered, and the purpose to produce an abortion, that is made indictable under our statutes, Revisal, secs. 3618 and 3619; and it is not necessary for the State to show that administering the drug named would have had the desired effect.

5. Criminal Law—Judgments—Cruel and Unusual Punishments—Constitutional Law.

   The defendant was indicted, tried, and convicted of administering to a pregnant woman a noxious drug for the purpose of producing an abortion, contrary to Revisal, secs. 3618 and 3619. Held, a sentence to the State Prison for three years and the payment of $ 1,000 as a fine is not objectionable as cruel and unusual punishment.

Appeal by defendant from Carter, J., at November Term, 1913 of Buncombe.

This is an indictment for a violation of sections 3618 and 3619, Revisal.

Attorney-General Bickett and Assistant Attorney-General Calvert for the State.

R. S. McCall and Mark W. Brown for defendant.

Brown, J. The first and second assignments of error relate to the admission of testimony tending to prove sexual intercourse upon the part of the girl, Annie Kraft. This testimony was wholly immaterial, and certainly harmless as to the defendant.

There was no dispute as to the pregnancy of the girl, and the only question to be determined was whether or not the defendant had administered to her medicine for the purpose of procuring an abortion.

Exceptions 3, 4, 5, and 6 relate to the competency of certain witnesses to testify as experts, and to their qualifications as such. A previous witness had testified that the capsule offered in evidence, and some of which had been administered to the girl, contained aloes, and these witnesses as experts were permitted to testify as to the effect of this drug upon pregnancy, when administered in large doses.

We see no objection to the competency of this evidence.

Exceptions 7, 9, and 11 were taken to the sufficiency of the evidence to go to the jury, and seem to rest upon two grounds:

First. It seems to be contended by the defendant that a conviction cannot be had in such cases on the uncorroborated testimony of the woman, as she is said to be an accomplice in the alleged offense.

Assuming that the girl, Kraft, was an accomplice, the testimony of an accomplice is competent in this State, and a person may be convicted upon the unsupported testimony of an accomplice, though the jury should be cautious in so doing. While Annie Kraft may be, in one sense, an accomplice of the defendant, it is only in a moral and not in a legal sense.

In a note to 12 A. and E. Annotated Cases, p. 1009, there is a full discussion of the cases showing that the victim of an abortion or attempted abortion, whether or not she consents thereto, is not in law an accomplice in the

Abortion in the Mountain South 455

commission of the offense nor within the meaning of the statute providing that there shall be no conviction of a person upon the uncorroborated testimony of an accomplice.

Second. A further contention of the defendant under these exceptions seems to be that the testimony does not show that the defendant advised and procured the prosecuting witness to take or did not administer to her a noxious drug.

There is abundant evidence that the defendant, at the solicitation of Annie Kraft, gave her the capsules containing aloes for the purpose of producing a miscarriage. While there is evidence that the drug furnished her would produce such an effect when administered in very large doses, yet it is not necessary that the State should prove that aloes are a noxious drug and capable of producing the intended effect.

The language of the statutes of the different States describing this offense varies, but they nearly all provide that whoever, with the intent to produce a miscarriage of any pregnant woman, unlawfully administers, or causes to be given to her, any drug of noxious substance whatever, with such intent, shall be guilty of the offense.

Under this statute it has been generally held that the offense may be committed by administering any substance with intent to produce an abortion, whether such substance be noxious or not, and whether it be capable of producing the intended effect or not.

There is a full discussion of this subject in the notes to Abrams v. Foshee, 66 Am. Dec., p. 82, where all of the authorities are collated.

The defendant excepts to the judgment of the court on the ground that it imposes a cruel and an unusual punishment, and relies upon the case of S. v. Lee, ante, 250. That case is no authority in support of the defendant's contention. The statute in this case limits the punishment to not less than one year nor more than ten years, and a fine in the discretion of the court. The sentence in this case is within the limitation prescribed by law.

Upon a review of the whole record, we find No error.

Source: State v. Elizabeth Shaft, *North Carolina Reports: Cases Argued and Determined in the Supreme Court of North Carolina*, Vol. 166 (Raleigh, NC: E. M. Uzzell & Co., 1914), 407.

West Virginia Abortion Reform Committee

Almost two years have passed since the U.S. Supreme Court decision of January 22, 1973, made abortion legal anywhere in the United States.

Unfortunately, the situation within West Virginia has remained relatively unchanged. Since that time, informal studies have shown that several thousands of West Virginia women each year have been forced to go out-of-state for abortions. Further study shows numbers of women going to the emergency rooms of hospitals because of septic abortions, that is, uterine infections caused by the introduction of a foreign object by themselves or someone else. The number is high even yet, and the reporting of these figures is often disguised. One large hospital in the Charleston area has at least three or four "septic" abortions reported a month.

Many people feel that septic abortions are a thing of the past, but in West Virginia, at least where there is no law in line with the Supreme Court Decision and where many women can't get the money to go out of state for a safe abortion done by a licensed physician, septic abortions continue to be a real threat to life and health. It's much the same as it has always been in West Virginia . . . those with money can obtain abortions; those without, suffer.

The West Virginia Abortion Reform Committee (WVARC) was established in November, 1974, under the sponsorship of the Charleston Women's Center and works in close cooperation with national organizations and local chapters of such groups as the American Civil Liberties Union, National Organization for Women, National Association of Social Workers, National Abortion Rights Action League, major church denominations, clergy, social agencies and individuals concerned with defense of the U.S. Constitution and the right to individual choice.

WVARC members have been involved in court cases challenging the old state law, which in late February was struck down in Kanawha County Circuit Court in the ACLU case. A March Federal Court hearing will likely see the law clearly struck down for all of West Virginia. Another Federal suit seeks to force a Charleston hospital to allow doctors at that hospital to perform abortions.

During the 1975 regular Legislative session, letters from WVARC people equaled the number of letters from opponents to legal abortion. Before, letters have run 8 to 1 from the opposition. Unfortunately, the legislators once again refused to bring the state law in line with the U.S. Supreme Court decision. The governor, despite the state court's ruling, said he would veto such a measure anyway.

Source: National Organization of Women (NOW) Papers, Box 1, "Abortion," West Virginia and Regional History Collection, West Virginia University, Morgantown, West Virginia.

NOTES

1. Jane Roe, et al. v. Henry Wade, District Attorney of Dallas County, 410 US 113 (1973).

2. Planned Parenthood of Southeastern Pennsylvania v. Casey, 505 US 833 (1992).

3. Deborah Baker, "Interview with Madeline James & Ethel Brewster," *Mountain Life and Work* 50, no. 6 (June 1974): 3–7.

4. Dorroh v. Commonwealth, Court of Appeals of Kentucky 236 Ky. 68; 32 S.W.2d 550; 1930 Ky. November 14, 1930, Decided.

5. Rick Bragg, "Town Secret Is Uncovered in Birth Quest," *New York Times*, August 23, 1997; Larry Copeland, "The 'Hicks Babies' Ga. Doctor's Dark Secrets Haunt Towns," *Philadelphia Inquirer*, June 8, 1997; Stephanie Saul, "Adoptee Finds Baby 'Black Market,' Not Her Roots, in Long-Closed Clinic," *Los Angeles Times*, July 6, 1997.

6. Ellen J. Stahl, "Legal Abortion in Cincinnati and Appalachian Women," *A Magazine of Appalachian Women* 5 (July–August 1978): 7–14.

Helen Louise Gibson Compton
Founder and Proprietor of The Shamrock

CAROL BURCH-BROWN

In 1964 "Miss Helen" Compton, daughter of a coal miner from McDowell County, opened what she claimed was the first gay bar in West Virginia. The Shamrock was on the main street of Bluefield, Mercer County, West Virginia, in the heart of coal country. From 1964 until Miss Helen's death in 2001 the bar was an underground haven for Appalachian queers from the Virginias to Kentucky and North Carolina. Helen and her friends kept The Shamrock running for thirty-seven years despite regional homophobia and squabbles among the bar's patrons. Helen was pragmatic. She kept a baseball bat stashed behind the bar. She threatened to reveal embarrassing secrets about local public officials. She cozied up to the police. Some say she kept a gun in her back pocket.

The bar operated for many years as a restaurant during the day, serving rail workers and the local, downtown Bluefield community. During the day it was a base of operation for a loyal clientele and for discrete heterosexual assignations. In the evening it was transformed into a gay bar, with local drag shows, which included annual "Miss Shamrock and Mr. Shamrock" pageants and regional competitions. The bar was temporarily closed when Miss Helen was hospitalized in the late '90s and had a leg amputated from a previous injury and lingering infection. However, her good friends reopened the bar under their own ownership and for the last couple of years of her life Miss Helen ruled the scene from her special table.

HELEN GROWING UP

Carol: So, when you were growing up nobody talked about homosexuality.

Helen: Oh, no.

Carol: How'd you find out about it?

Helen: I went home one time and told my Daddy, I said—well I did—'I seen two guys kissing.'

Carol: Where'd you see that?

Helen: In the coalfields where I was raised. And I told Daddy, I said, 'Daddy, guess what I seen a while ago.' He said, 'What?' I said 'There was two guys down there a'kissing.' He said, 'Who?' I said, 'That Smith boy and that Wren boy.' He said, 'Yeah. Yeah. You just stay away from them people.' He said, 'There'll be a cross burnt in their yard, later on.' Which sure enough it was.

Carol: How old were you when that happened?

Helen: I was about 10, 12 years old.

STARTING THE BAR

Helen: Why I started it [The Shamrock] was because of four guys that couldn't get in a gosh-durn bar. It was back in nineteen and sixty-three. They rung the buzzer [to a 'private' club] and they came to the door and they said, 'No, y'all can't come in here.' And I looked at them—I was behind them. And I thought well, they look nice and well dressed and everything, what's wrong with them? You know, they didn't look like rough necks. And so I went on in and I asked the guy when I got in, I said, 'What was wrong with those four guys there, that you wouldn't let them in? Has there been any trouble or something?' And he said, 'No. They're queers.' And I thought, oh gosh, [they] wouldn't let them in here! And I been coming here for a long time, you know, didn't know that they felt that way. And so I didn't stay but for just a few minutes and went back out. And the guys were still standing on the sidewalk. And I asked them, I said, 'Why wouldn't they let y'all in a while ago?' And they said, 'Because we're gay. We should-a had a woman with us and then they would have let us in.' See, back then if a man wanted to get in a bar he had to have a woman with him. If a woman wanted to get in a bar, she had to have a man with her.

We stood and talked I guess for about thirty, forty minutes. And I said, 'I tell you what I'm gonna do.' I said, 'I'm gonna get a bar on the main street in Bluefield and open it up to the gay people.' And the next day I called the guy about the bar that I'm in now—[it] was a little hot dog [place], urban renewal had come through and tore his place down. I talked to him, asked him how much he'd take for it, and he said, 'Ten thousand dollars.' And I said, 'Okay.' Well, I kept a Clabber Girl Baking Can hid [with money in it]. I said, 'I'll go dig it up and I'll lay the cash money on your desk.' And that's what I done.

It was just exactly like I said I was gonna do it, that's what I done. I paid ten thousand dollars cash for the place the day I bought it. And I said, 'Within a year I'm gonna have my ten thousand dollars back.' And I had it back in six months.

RESTAURANT BY DAY, GAY BAR AT NIGHT

Helen: Well, daytime was mostly straights. Of course some of the gays come in to eat lunch or eat breakfast or something. But mostly it was straights of the day and of the evening, why, I got where I'd tell them—the older guys and their wives, you know, in there drinking beer and just sitting, [to] have a place to go and listen to the jukebox and everything. Back then people was really into stuff like that. They're not anymore, but they was back then. I'd tell them of an evening, I'd wait till about six o'clock, and I'd say, 'Boy I tell you, these young people's gonna come in here in a minute and that music's gonna get so loud, and I can't stand this loud damn music.' They'd say, 'Miss Helen, I can't either. I think we'd better go.' And they'd get up and leave. And then the gay people'd start coming in. Then I'd be there all night with them. Most of the time we'd leave out of there when the sun be coming up. Lot of the older ones that was coming there back then can tell that sun, about ever weekend, that's when we'd be walking up that street, singing, drunk.

DRAG SHOWS

Carol: What about the drag shows? When did they start?

Helen: In nineteen-and-seventy-two. I'd sit and talk to them of a night, you know. I was talking to a bunch of them and they was talking about dressing—stealing their mother's dresses and their sister's dresses and dressing up. And then having to sneak them back in. And I said, 'Well, y'all like to do that?' 'Lord God, yes, Miss Helen! You don't know how good we like to do that!' I said, 'I tell you what I'll do. Y'all come in here next Saturday. We'll have a show and you do it.'

And I hung a sheet from that wall right there to the kitchen wall and let them come out from behind the sheet to perform. And the jukebox

Helen Louise Gibson Compton 461

was sitting right here. And I would have K&K Music to put the records that they wanted on the jukebox that day. And I'd put a quarter in it, because it was a nickel a punch then. I'd put a quarter in it and punch off whatever record was to be played.

And they'd go to that little old place right on the corner there, [in] the Weinberg building—[it] got tore down. Miss East run kind of like a flea market or something, where you bought second hand stuff. They'd go down there and buy their little old dresses and pocket books and their hats and their shoes. Some of them couldn't find a pair of shoes to fit them and they'd wear bedroom shoes. Flip-flops and such.

HELEN ON DRAG QUEENS

Helen: I like to call them 'Girls.' My Girls. I do not like to hear 'drag queen.' They are a Lady on that stage. Nothing but a Lady. In my book they are a Lady on that stage. They are not a drag queen. I sit here on Saturday nights when they're having the show and they'll say 'What drag queen is that?' and I'll think, God, I don't like to hear that. And I'll look around and I'll say 'I don't know.' And I don't. But if they were to ask me 'What Lady is that?' Then I would tell them 'That's Cortney,' or whoever that is. I do not like to hear drag queen. It's the same thing to me as queer, lezzy, all of that. I don't like to hear none of it. They're Human. You're you. I'm I. And he's he.

We're women. We can't make nothing else out of it. Although we like an opposite—I mean we like the same sex. He is a man. He can't make nothing else out of it. Although he likes men. [Helen falls apart laughing.] He's not a 'drag queen.' He's a Lady when he's out there. They've went to a lot of hell to be a Lady. You understand what I'm saying? They've went through a hell of a lot, when nobody knows, to be a Lady. Not a drag queen. I'm *sorry*, but that's the way I feel.

CUCUMBERS

Helen: Well, the first Mr. Shamrock show was to be the girls, you know, for Mr. Shamrock and the guys for Miss Shamrock. So the first one was just a bunch of girls and they was gonna do 'The Village People,' was what they was gonna do. The manager down at Deskin's—Deskin's was there on Raleigh Street then. Mr. Duff was his name. He came in every evening and got him a quart of beer to take home with him and he'd get a quart and drink it while he was there. And that evening he come in, he said, 'Miss Helen, can I ask you a question?' And I said, 'Yes sir, what is it?' It was on a Saturday evening, they was gonna do the show that night, they was all in the back. And he seen them back there. And he said, 'Uh, that bunch of girls back there, they was down at the store today and they was getting cucumbers and laying them down here and measuring them. [Helen demonstrates against her pants leg.] Could you tell me why they was doing that?' I said, 'God, I don't know why.' They all had them a cucumber. And duct tape. Had their cucumbers taped to their leg with duct tape.

HELEN ON KEEPING PEOPLE IN THE BAR SAFE

Helen: If somebody'll go in Macdonald's, or some place like that, and shoot up a bunch of people, what do you think they would do to a gay bar? Well, why do you think I'm sitting in that window watching every move that everybody makes on the outside there? And every move that they make on the inside? That's the reason—a lot of people will come up there and talk to me and they'll say, 'It seems like you're irritated or something, Miss Helen.' I say, 'Hey, I'm not irritated or nothing like that. My mind is out there.' There'd been a car went real slow by. And I'm a'waiting. If I don't see that car, see, I'm watching the headlights coming across the hill. If that car don't come on down, you'll see me get up and walk out to see why they stopped out there. Because they'll do it [harass people in the bar]. So, that's the reason I'm sitting there. To protect the ones that's in there.

You don't know when somebody's going to decide to come in here and start shooting up and carrying on. You never know that, you see? So that's the reason I watch everybody that comes in there [pointing to the door of the bar]. And if somebody strange comes in there, some man—strange—or a woman, and they just don't look right to me when they come in, you'll see me watching every move they make. I have mirrors—over here—that I can watch them over there. I have mirrors—over there—that I can watch them over here. I can be standing there and I can watch everything that's inside the place. And I could stand up front then and watch everything because I've got it marked—how the car lights comes across the hill when anybody comes up the road. From the time they leave that corner I can see them.

Helen Louise Gibson Compton 463

POLICE AND AUTHORITIES

Helen: See, when they found out that I was having a gay bar, well the city, I had to buck them, the state and the county.

Carol: How did they find out?

Helen: Oh, the people coming there all the time. They had patrolmen back then that would come and check your doors of a night, see if they were locked, you know, walking the beat. They don't have that now, but they did back then. So, the patrolmen would be walking the beat, you see, and you'd see them see all that was going on there, because that whole front was glass then. Even the doors was glass. Everything was glass. Couldn't have curtains—only halfway up, at the windows . . .

Carol: What about your encounters with the police?

Helen: Well, I told them I would not allow them [the bar patrons] to hang out front and holler at people and carry on, like some places does.

Carol: You had a liquor license?

Helen: No. A beer license. I've never had a liquor license. And I've sold it for upwards of thirty years, but I've never had a license. [I told the police] I'd not allow them to stand out front and carry on. Which I don't. People will tell you that. It irritates me when they say, 'I'm going out here and get a little air,' and they'll stand out there and flip around and holler at people, you know, cars that goes by. And I'll tell them right quick, 'Now, you done got enough air. Get back inside or go to your car. I'll not allow that.' And I'd not allow them to harass nobody around. I didn't want no harassment.

But, if the police wanted to come in on it [shut down the bar], I think that I could call around enough, all over the United States, and other places too, and they might be fifty or sixty thousand gay people marching in the street, if they wanted to buck me. I told the City Hall, State Hall, and County Hall. So, I've never been harassed. A lot of nights they'll call me and tell me they have one of my 'Sweets,' what must they book him on? See, you can't ask for any more than that. Like I tell them: show them respect. Therefore, demand respect from them.

HELEN ON RACE RELATIONS

Helen: For years if a white woman was with a black guy they got strung up, you see. I mean, it's about the same thing. They're getting a little used to it, but

464 WOMEN AND ACTIVISM IN THE MOUNTAIN SOUTH: DOCUMENTS

they're still not used to them being together. And having kids together. They're still not used to that. Well, it's the same way with the gays.

The gay people is kind of like the black people. You ever notice it? They dress about alike. They like about the same things. They like to party, they like to do this, that, and the other. Gay people won't come out until ten, eleven, and twelve o'clock of a night. Well you won't see a black person out until ten, eleven, twelve o'clock of a night.

AIDS

Helen: When they first started talking about it, it scared the hell out of me, because I used to—well, I 'run up and down the road' all the time—didn't matter to me. But you don't see me doing it now, I can tell, you and it's not age either. I tell you, I put on rubber gloves to pick up beer cans. It scared the f—k out of me, the way they talked about it, you know. And nobody in the bar at that time, that we knew of, had it. But they had heard about it, you see. And there's been several of them that has died with it.

GAY LIFE IS THE HARDEST LIFE

Helen: I believe there's a little gay in everybody. . . . [but] gay life is one of the loneliest lives you can live. I don't care—you got a lover? That lover cannot fulfill that lonely spot that's in your body. I bet you have one. Everybody does that leads a gay life. I don't know what it is, but it's one of the loneliest lives you can live. We can't do what other people does. We've never been able to. We never will be able to.

Carol: Is that why you've had the bar all these years?

Helen: That's why I done it. I tell them, strange people comes in, I say, 'Hey, get over and there and talk to them because, make them feel at home, this is a family bar.' That's what it's supposed to be, a family bar. You come in there you're not supposed to be harassed, you're not supposed to have no trouble, you come in there to enjoy yourself and let your hair down a little. Let your feelings out. Relax. That's what you come in there for and that's what it's for. And that's what it's going to be like as long as I live—I don't know how much longer that'll be.

Source: Helen Louise Gibson Compton (January 4, 1924–Died April 18, 2001), interviews with Carol Burch-Brown, Bluefield, West Virginia, 1997–2001. Interview tapes, transcripts and photographs are located in the Smithsonian Museum of American History's Archive Center, Washington, DC.

At the Intersection of Cancer Survivorship, Gender, Family, and Place in Southern Central Appalachia
A Case Study

KELLY A. DORGAN, KATHRYN L. DUVALL, AND SADIE P. HUTSON

In March 2007, three women met in the coffee shop of a local bookstore in South Central Appalachia. Two of us were researchers, one from communication and one from nursing; neither of us was a cancer survivor, but the disease had touched both of our lives in intimate and heartbreaking ways. The third woman was an amazing, passionate woman, a longtime breast cancer survivor and local advocate for survivors. For several hours, we talked about so much, including the experiences of women rooted to and living in southern Appalachian mountain communities and the experiences of survivors surviving in a place with high rates of cancer mortality and morbidity.[1] All three of us had been involved in various cancer-related research projects for several years, so we knew the gaping hole in the literature: How do women in this region actually *survive* cancer survivorship?

Over the coming months we worked, we planned, and we pondered how to tackle this question. A graduate student joined our project team, devoting many hours to the study, a devotion lasting years after she completed her MA program. Starting in September 2008, after receiving grant funding[2] and approval by the Institutional Review Board, the project team collected illness narratives from twenty-nine female cancer survivors from Northeast Tennessee and Southwest Virginia. First, we invited participants to a day-long story circle (n=26) where they literally sat in a circle and provided their testimonials. Sometimes they were guided by a trained moderator, but most of the time participants' stories were organic, free-flowing. Enlisting the help of the Tennessee Cancer Control Coalition, we were able to provide participants with a $25.00 gift card to a local grocery store that also sold gas, thereby offsetting participants' transportation costs.

Second, following the story circles, Kathryn Duvall, one of the team members, conducted in-home interviews that permitted us to include stories from women who could not attend the story circle event for a variety of reasons (such as chemotherapy, work, and/or financial issues). Here we provide excerpts from one interview of a dual-cancer survivor (breast and ovarian), allowing student-researchers to examine emerging themes and ethical considerations, as well as the intersection of cancer survivorship, gender, family, and place, Southern Central Appalachia in this case.[3]

EXCERPTED INTERVIEW DATA

[Duvall Researcher Note: Upon arrival in the interviewee's home, it was obvious privacy could not be ensured. The two-bedroom house was small; at least six people lived there. Family members and home health workers came and went during the interview. The interviewee chose to involve her family because she believed a cancer diagnosis affected all members of the family. Several family members smoked throughout the interview.]

EXCERPT 1

Interviewee: That one right there has helped me more than anything, my husband. My daughter-in-law who's walking to the kitchen. She helped me a lot [....] she's got two small children. So there was a lot of times she was able to take me to the doctors, sat right there with me, you know. If they had to admit me on more than one occasion, she'd sit with me, she'd call my husband, "Hey you need to get over here," you know. He always went too, my husband. He always went to chemo with me, you know. If I got sick he was always there to help me. [...] I did not get home health care till well, well after my breast surgery. I'd already been through the ovarian and everything. He's drained tubes when I had tubes coming out, he's drained them. He's patched me up. He's kept the dressings clean and dry. So I could not, I could not, not have made it [...] without my family. I couldn't have done it. I really couldn't have because he's been my mainstay through all of it. And like

Cancer Survivorship 467

I said my daughter-in-law as far as taking me to appointments and that sort of thing. And the morale, my sons weren't quite as involved. They're—I was a single parent for years and years, so all I had was them and all they had was me. So they didn't deal with it quite as well. You know, as maybe girls would have, but although they weren't there for the appointments and that sort of thing they were there to cheer me up, you know. Or, I'd start to do something and then one of them would jump in and do it. And you know just little things like that they would do.

Duvall: Have you found any challenges in your family while you've gone through your cancer experience?

Interviewee: Well I think so, don't you [husband]? I think maybe the biggest challenge is trying to keep the family together. Because it's like I said I mean between the both of us we've got a large family so of course this, this is the nucleus of the family. Holiday dinners are here. You know, family functions are here. All of that is here. But for the last year and a half that has been really super hard to do. Because at that time the bulk of it fell on him [husband] and here he is trying to take care of me. And I'm frustrated because it is really challenging to try to keep the family together when you're not together yourself. So that's been my biggest, biggest challenge is keeping the family together through all this [. . .].

EXCERPT 2

[Duvall Researcher Note: In this part of the interview, the Interviewee describes her gynecologic oncologist and how she, the oncologist, "saved" her life "with the ovarian cancer," the interviewee's first cancer diagnosis; however, the Interviewee explains, when concerns over possible breast cancer arose, the gynecologic oncologist had to refer her to another oncologist]

Interviewee: So she [the gynecologic oncologist] tried to get me with a good breast cancer doctor, but she wouldn't take my insurance. So at this time—Oh I probably shouldn't say this—No I'm going to say it anyway. At this time [the state Medicaid program] was threatening to drop me because the ovarian cancer was not enough to keep me on [the state Medicaid program]. Well, needless to say, I'm a writer. I mean I believe in using the people that I vote for. So honey I sent a letter to the Governor, I sent a letter to the Congressman, and I sent a letter to

468 WOMEN AND ACTIVISM IN THE MOUNTAIN SOUTH: DOCUMENTS

the President of the United States. When I go, I go big. So I explained, and they were like 2- and 3-page letters. But I mean I had names, dates, you know, all my facts were in a row. I had everything that I needed. So what had happened was the Governor [name omitted] actually got a hold of somebody in the [state Medicaid program] bureau, and I don't know what he done—He [the Governor] kept my [state Medicaid program]. I know I was so tickled. So she [the gynecologic oncologist] got me in to the health department because she said if I go that route, and it is cancer they can get me in quicker to see a doc, and I didn't know that. I didn't know that. So [. . .] I had my mammogram. They went ahead and done a mammogram. Then they done a spot mammogram. So I got the results from that, and they said it's definitely a lump so we're going to do a biopsy. Okay well that's not a problem. So I went out there. You know I'm still doing this by myself because I'm thinking we're—I'm still being checked for ovarian cancer so my mind is like, it can't be breast. So they done the biopsy and thank the Lord. I can't remember, you [husband] must have got off early because we were having, we went out [. . .] got us some chicken. And we were going to go to a park and just chill. And we got our chicken and got to the car, and [the doctor] called me and told me the biopsy showed it was cancer and it was malignant. And we were like, okay, what do we do? [. . .] And if was just like a regular appointment then she'd [daughter-in-law] take me other than that he [husband] would take me. And immediately of course shortly after they took my breast, they wanted to start chemo [. . .].

[Duvall Researcher Note: The interviewee's husband and daughter-in-law are both in the room where the interview is being conducted. Conversation begins between Interviewee, daughter-in-law, and husband about lack of resources available to ovarian cancer survivors versus breast cancer survivors. The husband mentions how the interviewee was sent home after her ovarian cancer surgery with drain tubes sticking out of her].

Interviewee: And see he had to change them [drain tubes] before he went to work. He'd have to come home from work and change them. I mean and that's something if the Lord will let me live and provide for me financially to do this. I want to change that. I'm here to tell every man in this country that ovarian cancer kills. It is a silent killer. It will sneak

Cancer Survivorship 469

up on you and you will be gone before you ever know what happens. And this mess of it's just ovarian cancer we don't really know that much about it. No, that's unacceptable. That is totally unacceptable. And I have found out a lot around here. She's [daughter-in-law] right you know. I got no assistance whatsoever. Honey, somebody from the Cancer Society come to see me the day I left after I had my breast removed. I got gas cards to go down for my chemo. You know I got, we got help with some of our bills because of course I couldn't work. And he [husband] was the only income we had. And like I said for chemo he had to take off from work because sometimes I got sick, you know. So it was a whole different ball game. I still talk to certain people, and I keep telling them I'm going to do something about this ovarian cancer. Because all they talk about is breast cancer, breast cancer which is totally important too, but you've got something going on there. You don't have anything going on for ovarian cancer. Those women need just as much help, if not more, than the women that have breast cancer. Cause there's already help out there for them. But not people that have ovarian. So that is something that [the state capitol] will probably hear about from me. Because I do think it's a very important thing.

NOTES

1. Joel A. Halverson, *An Analysis of Disparities in Health Status and Access to Health Care in the Appalachian Region* (Washington, DC: Appalachian Regional Commission, 2004), 42.

2. Kelly A. Dorgan and Sadie P. Hutson, Survivors' Revival: Appalachian Women Testifying on Surviving Cancer. Grant funded by East Tennessee State University Research & Development Committee, #RD0105, Johnson City, TN, 2008.

3. See details of research procedures in Dorgan and Hutson, Survivors' Revival.

Mother Jones. *West Virginia and Regional History Center, WVU Libraries.*

Temperance Election of March 11, 1907, Vera Smith singing. *Jas. E. Thompson, photographer. From the Abby Crawford Milton Collection, Calvin M. McClung Historical Collection, Knox County Public Library, Knoxville.*

Women working at suffrage headquarters, Birmingham, Alabama, 1913. *Alabama Department of Archives and History, Montgomery.*

The women's suffrage booth, State Fair, Birmingham, Alabama, 1914. *Alabama Department of Archives and History, Montgomery.*

Picket at Loveman's Department Store, Birmingham, Alabama, 1963. *Birmingham, Alabama, Public Library Archives.*

Women on vigil in support of striking coal miners in the Pittston mines, Southwest Virginia. Camp Solidarity, near Castlewood, Virginia, July 1989. *Archives of Appalachia, East Tennessee State University, Johnson City.*

Helen Compton, late 1990s. *Photo courtesy of Carol Burch-Brown, photographer.*

Part 3: Women and Activism in the Mountain South

Questions for Discussion

1. How have women of the Mountain South used the concept of motherhood to advocate social, economic, and political reforms?

2. Discuss women's health care and the role of women providing health care in the Mountain South. Who has provided health care and how has it changed over time? What are the biggest obstacles to quality health care in the region today? Have women been marginalized in regard to receiving health care? And if so, why?

3. Discuss discrimination in the Mountain South. What forms has it taken? How has it changed over time? What explains the variations from place to place?

4. What social, economic, and political factors have shaped women of the Mountain South's arguments for or against issues such as suffrage, abortion, and mountaintop removal?

5. What role has geographic location or place played in those arguments? Are women in certain areas of Appalachia more inclined to speak out against injustice that those who live in other areas?

6. In the quote at the beginning of part 3, sociologist Helen Lewis maintains that "love can be a real revolutionary." How has love served as an impetus for social, economic, and political activism in the Mountain South? How often has anger been the incentive for activism? Which one has been the stronger incentive and why?

EPILOGUE

Reflections on the Concept of Place in the Study of Women in the Mountain South

A Roundtable Discussion with the Authors

The essays and documents in this book show that the Mountain South, or "southern Appalachia," is diverse and that no one generalization holds true for the entire region at any point in time. It is a land of many "places," with a diversity of people from many places. It embraces many cultures. It is mountains and ridges and valleys. It is urban and it is rural. It is ever changing. Whether as America's first frontier or one of the centers of American industrialization, each stage of its history has witnessed a transition of people and resources.

In the following roundtable discussion, the authors of this volume reflect on their concepts of place and its relevance to the study of women in the Mountain South.

Marie Tedesco: Central to studies of any region, be it New England, Appalachia, or the West, is the idea that the region is special in some way. Perhaps it is the geography or climate of the region or the inhabitants of the region that make it special. The region takes on an identity of its own that popular writers and scholars alter over the years. Any region is a social construction, one given characteristics and boundaries by humans. A place, named as such, is also a social construction, given identity by those who gaze upon it and then write about it or depict it in image. Appalachia is a social construction, as both Henry Shapiro and Allen Batteau have written; the boundaries of that social construction have changed from the nineteenth century

(Mountain South, the mountainous areas of that other social construction, "the South") to the twenty-first century (the region's boundaries now have been reified by the Appalachian Regional Commission map).

Until recently, say twenty or twenty-five years ago, the region called Appalachia—one invented by white local color writers of fiction (e.g., Mary Murfree), educators who sought funds for deprived sections of the region (e.g., William. G. Frost), or professionals who cared for the region but viewed it mainly as "victim" (e.g., Harry Caudill)—was one inhabited by whites. Sure, the Cherokee lived in the region before whites barged in, so to speak, but they receded to the background after the 1838–39 Trail of Tears forced most of them to remove to Indian Territory. But neither the Cherokee nor the enslaved and free blacks and their descendants, nor the "not quite white" ethnic and religious groups (e.g., Italians, Poles, Jews) were integral to the region. The region was white, and many writers and scholars wrote of "the Appalachian" (white male) or "the Appalachian man" (white male, again) or "the Appalachian woman" (white woman). Usually, these Appalachians were residents of mountainous areas: no one called "Appalachian" lived in cities or towns. A "typical" (or maybe revered) Appalachian lived in a rural area, usually on a farm. Only the incursion of outsider-dominated extractive industries that destroyed farmland forced the Appalachian to leave his land and to take work in a coal mine. Such simplifications, while exaggerated here to an extent, have resulted in the essentializing of the women and men of the region known as Southern Appalachia. From the seventeenth century on, the region has been home to persons of varying colors and heritages. While for convenience's sake, scholars and lay writers speak of "New Englanders" or "Appalachians" as a way to locate persons, so doing should not point to the essentializing of a region's inhabitants. New England is no more inhabited entirely by Yankees (that is, by white persons of northern European descent, Protestant in religious belief), any more than Appalachia is inhabited entirely by mountaineers of northern European stock. To essentialize the inhabitants of any region is to ignore the variety of persons who live in said region and to simplify the complexity of life for different types of persons.

What does it mean, then, to study a region and its inhabitants? Critical regionalism (CR) studies the region as it links to the nation and to other regions. CR rejects the idea that any region is, or can be, isolated from the larger nation or a larger region. While any region or locale may display unique cultural attributes, these attributes did not develop in a vacuum; rather, they developed as a consequence of inhabitants—be they Cherokee, Anglos, or blacks—borrowing from one another and forging new patterns of behavior. Women in Appalachia lived diverse lives in the many locales of the region and learned from and borrowed from one another, as demonstrated by Cherokee, white, and black women who lived in Cherokee lands in the years before the removal. The history of Appalachia reveals that many women of different races, ethnicities, sexual preferences, and socioeconomic classes have lived in the region. As it usually does, the study of the past reveals complexity, not simplicity.

Karen W. Tice: Some general comments I would make about place are that it is not inherently prescriptive but can also be a source of political possibility and solidarity making. Here I am thinking of the work of Barbara Ellen Smith and others—for example, Ann Kingsolver and Dwight Billings—and not just about binaries of insider/outsider and borders. A focus on place can help to direct analytical attention to historicity and specificity of particular and distinctive locales. When I think of Appalachia, I think of place in the plural sense, since I see Appalachia as a multifaceted region of many "places."

Penny Messinger: Ever since the 1978 publication of Henry Shapiro's book, *Appalachia on Our Mind*, scholars who study Appalachia have wrestled with the dilemma of studying a region that, according to Shapiro, most people understood primarily as an idea—a social construction of novelists, home missionaries, educators, and others. This creates a certain discomfort, for how does one study a place that exists as an idea? How much was the *idea* of Appalachia grounded in the reality of the people who live there? And most important of all—if Appalachia is an idea, a social construction, does it really exist at all? I think that some of the discomfort with the idea of Appalachia as a socially constructed place is related to the thought that, somehow, a place

Epilogue: Reflections on the Concept of Place 477

that is socially constructed is one that is not "real." Yet we live comfortably within many social constructions, including race and gender, and accept them as real. As social constructions, race and gender change over time and are defined differently in many places; they are social creations but they have also shaped people's lives and behaviors in important ways because people accept them as real. One way through the social construction-essentialism dilemma for Appalachianists is via the idea of "social location," a virtual place that lies at the intersection of racial, class, gendered, and other social identities. For me, social location is grounded in a sense of place and in their connection to the land. This shapes a standpoint grounded in identity. I believe that this identity-grounded social location is shared by many people who come from Appalachia, as well as by scholars who study it.

Louis C. Martin: "Appalachia" is a social construction as surely as are all other regions, but place has exerted a powerful influence over history as perceptions of place have motivated individuals and as distinctive cultures have formed in geographical locations that in turn have shaped identities. Moreover, the differences between certain rural and urban values and attitudes led to divergent beliefs and behaviors within the United States in the nineteenth and twentieth centuries. Finally, place played an important role in the political economy of those centuries as capital relocated in an effort to escape powerful working-class organizations and to tap into new sources of labor, especially low-wage female labor.

These factors all played roles in the history of women steelworkers in West Virginia. Steel magnates relocated factories, especially sheet metal plants, to Northern Appalachia and the Ohio Valley, in the 1890s and early 1900s in order to have access to cheap fuels and both experienced and inexperienced steelworkers. They often believed that rural places were places free of discord where land was cheap and plentiful. Working-class families that came to the small mill towns and countryside around them brought a diversity of attitudes and values. For example, they viewed women's work differently in the various factory towns, and their views changed over the decades. In some families, it was acceptable, if not expected, that married women would work for wages to increase the family's standard of living. Others strove to achieve a single-income household where the mother's household labor would improve their standard of living and the children would stay in school longer. While no homogeneous Appalachian working-class culture existed, rural-industrial workers commonly valued local control and a "make do" attitude that helped them survive hard times and achieve higher goals in good times.

Messinger: For the female mountain workers who are the subject of my essay, place was both a geographical location and a social concept. They understood Appalachia to have an actual physical location, but they also understood it as a social construction, and, in fact, they actively participated in shaping the social understanding of the region. The mountain workers of the early twentieth century inherited and built upon the understanding of Appalachia that had been shaped by local color writers and home missionaries; indeed, the Conference of Southern Mountain Workers (CSMW) was founded by John C. Campbell, who began his career as a missionary but ended it as a social scientist. Campbell's understanding of region—marked by diversity and grounded in sociological theory—serves as Henry Shapiro's ending point in *Appalachia on Our Mind*. (Actually, it is important to give credit to Olive Dame Campbell—John's wife—for this understanding of region, since she wrote *The Southern Highlander and His Homeland*, which Shapiro discusses in his book.) The CSMW reflected the continuing involvement of mission workers and other reformers for many decades after its establishment in 1913, and the group was instrumental in creating our current understanding of the Appalachian region: where it was, who lived there, what it was like, what needed to be preserved, and what needed to change. In other words, the CSMW was instrumental in defining and shaping the *idea* of Appalachia as it was understood during much of the twentieth century. Mountain workers promoted that social construction and institutionalized their vision of region for insiders and outsiders alike. Not only did they publish the first magazine devoted to the region (*Mountain Life & Work*), they established

Epilogue: Reflections on the Concept of Place 479

the field of "mountain work," the precursor to Appalachian studies; worked to professionalize the field; and claimed the right to interpret the region to the outside world. In the time frame of my essay (1920s–1950s), this vision of region was strongly shaped by gender. Like female reformers elsewhere, in Appalachia the mountain workers emphasized education, health care, cultural work, a cooperative vision, and the use of maternalist arguments. They did so while also seeking to preserve Appalachia's regional distinctiveness.

Evelyn Ashley Sorrell: There is a proliferation of scholarly work on reform in the Appalachian region, but it cannot be ignored that the same was occurring among immigrants in the North and poor whites and blacks in the South. The history of public health movements is a particularly telling example of how stereotypes of ignorance extended beyond Appalachia and were shaped by race and class. In this sense, public health reform in the Mountain South is a part of a larger historical narrative about the role of gender, class, and race in the venereal disease panic of the twentieth century, but there is a marked difference in how medical officials and social reformers addressed issues of sexuality and disease in Appalachia. The belief that the "place" of Appalachia was culturally, socially, and regionally isolated gave rise to the policy of taking children from their homes to larger urban areas where they were often secluded from contact with their mothers.

Cultural and social constructions of ignorant, neglectful, and sexually irresponsible Appalachian mothers shaped Linda Neville's venereal disease treatment and prevention work among children of women afflicted with the same diseases. She not only used these constructs to justify her work, she also became involved in the creation of an Appalachian maternal stereotype at odds with not just the cult of domesticity but also the the cult of science surrounding domesticity. The historical example of Neville's intervention in the region demonstrates the power stereotypes have in impacting the lives of those targeted by a discourse of difference that extended beyond the Appalachian region. The perceived isolation of Appalachian residents shaped how reform was approached in the area, which speaks to how "place," or at least social constructions surrounding a "place," influenced methods of public health reform. However, historians must be careful not to examine Appalachia in cultural and social isolation from the rest of the nation, or even the world. The motives and ideologies of the social reformers and public health officials working in the region were representative of the larger movement. Thus, Neville's work with Appalachian mothers is a significant and illustrative part of the twentieth-century public health movement against venereal disease that must be understood and incorporated into the narrative of the history of public health that, with the exception of scholarly works related to race and public health, has widely focused on the urban North.

Barbara J. Howe: "Place" is extremely important for my essay. As noted, all history happens in a place. Even great thinkers lived somewhere and that, presumably, influenced their thoughts. Wheeling is a particularly important place in Appalachia. One might argue that it isn't even really Appalachian. At the time period for this study, it was the largest urban enclave between Pittsburgh and Cincinnati along the Ohio River or even elsewhere in what we now call Appalachia. That may be hard for people to appreciate now. The fact that it was on major transportation routes meant it had a transient population that drew in women who sometimes got trapped into prostitution, as well as men looking for prostitutes. That has happened throughout Wheeling's history. When I make presentations about prostitution in Wheeling in that city now, I always get stories about recent prostitution. Cities are always magnets for people looking for work, and that was the case for Wheeling in the mid-nineteenth century. It had the nearby natural resources to develop heavy industry. The transportation networks brought immigrants to work in those industries, meaning the population was far more diverse than elsewhere in Appalachia at the time, and the fact that there were these immigrants and so little agriculture and an orientation that was far more northern than southern (it is, of course, north of the Mason-Dixon Line), meant very little slavery and very few African Americans. The fact that it is even in West Virginia is an accident of history in some ways, as it was predetermined by the western boundary of

Epilogue: Reflections on the Concept of Place 481

Pennsylvania. Would we call it Appalachia or pay much attention to it if it were in Pennsylvania? Probably not. We'd focus on Pittsburgh instead. Wheeling residents are always clear that they live in a valley, not near mountains. They are *not* mountain people. The river determines their lives, not mountains. Because Wheeling was on major transportation routes, especially the railroad, Civil War troops moved through the area on their way to war. Certainly there was prostitution before and after the war, but it increased during the war because of the soldiers. That was common—it happened in Parkersburg, too, but maybe more so in Wheeling because it was a larger city. Even more local, the fact that the soldiers were camped on Wheeling Island meant that prostitutes went there and could be "sheltered" there with soldiers and be even more "hidden" than in the city itself or even in the wards where most of the documented prostitution took place (who knows what happened in private homes more out of sight, although, given the fact that many of the houses were row houses and that it was a crowded city, I'm not sure how much was really hidden). And even within the city, prostitutes were held in jails or camped along the river. Mapping these spaces gives pretty graphic evidence of the world the prostitutes knew. I don't know how you could understand these women's lives without knowing how/where they moved within the city.

Katharine Lane Antolini. In my larger work on Anna Jarvis and her Mother's Day movement, I do not portray her as a woman fighting to protect the integrity of an Appalachian holiday. Moreover, my research has revealed four other figures besides the Jarvis women who had either crowned themselves, or have been championed by others, as the true founder of Mother's Day. Of that group only Mary Towles Sasseen resided in Appalachia; Sasseen was a schoolteacher from Henderson, Kentucky, who promoted an April celebration of Mother's Day in 1893. The rest represented different regions: Julia Ward Howe in New England (1873) and Juliet Blakely Calhoun (1877) and Frank Hering (1904) in the Midwest—Michigan and Indiana respectively. But it was Anna Jarvis who took the idea of a maternal memorial first suggested by her mother and made it a national and international holiday.

That Jarvis led her movement from her home in Philadelphia has further distanced the holiday's connection to West Virginia. (Even Ann Reeves Jarvis is buried in Philadelphia). There is no evidence proving that Jarvis ever celebrated a single Mother's Day in Grafton either, preferring instead simply to send carnations to Andrews Methodist Episcopal Church as she spoke at more prestigious services across the country. Nonetheless, West Virginians take great pride in claiming Anna Jarvis and her Mother's Day as our own. This, of course, begs the question of exactly why? Why the need to anchor the origins of a national holiday to the hills of West Virginia? In my opinion, I think it comes from a desire to show the cultural relevance of Appalachia, beyond its association with folk art, coal mines, and family feuds. It is important to stress how a woman born and raised in West Virginia went on to establish one of this country's most endearing holidays. Just as Jarvis herself refused to relinquish her ownership of Mother's Day once it became a national holiday, we, too, refuse to relinquish our claim on her.

Lois Lucas: The concept of place for African American women in Appalachia represents the same that it does for African American women in any other region of the United States. The concept carries with it the idea of carving out a contribution niche. To do so recognizes that Appalachian African American women have made contributions not only in West Virginia but in the larger American society as well. Recognizing their contributions goes beyond acknowledging their location. It denotes that they indeed have a place in the historical record.

Jan Voogd: Every historical event results from a confluence of factors, with location providing a context. "Place" is how we try to understand the effect of that context. Our understanding is dynamic, being endlessly complicated and clarified, and this is why the meaning of words like *Appalachia* continue to be debated. One way to complicate and clarify our understanding of the power of location is by bringing stories to light that change what we thought we knew. I write at this moment surrounded by mountains, but in these California mountains, instead of "ridges" and "valleys," the people say "mesas" and "canyons." Could Ethel New's social justice activism have played out in this

Epilogue: Reflections on the Concept of Place 483

mountain region the way it did in Appalachia? Maybe it could have, but it didn't. There was opportunity enough for some kind of activism, but just as the vocabulary is different here, injustice has manifested in different ways and other factors brought to bear. Place is crucial for understanding the unique forces of location, but it serves best when allowed to encompass many facets over time, broadly considering both sides of any binary we may construct or dispute. Appalachia is distinct, and it is just like everywhere else, for there are at least as many Appalachias as there are people who live in the region. *Place* constantly evolves, while *location* endures.

Carletta A. Bush: Many Appalachian people are known for their deep sense of place. We have a deep affection for the region's steep, densely forested mountains and hollers, wide, green valleys, and numerous rivers, creeks, and runs. We, like many others, treasure family ties that extend to the days of exploration, and celebrate our history, culture, and traditions. Because of this, the preservation and protection of family and community is of utmost importance today as it was in the earliest days of settlement. As it did during those earliest days on the Appalachian frontier, when settlements were scattered and isolated by the region's harsh terrain and weather, times of crisis still frequently call for individuals to take drastic action and for communities to pull together. When civil rights legislation opened the door to employment in the coal mines for women in the 1970s, women who had never previously considered working underground eagerly offered their employment applications to human resources personnel.

With its lack of economic diversification and overdependence upon the coal industry, the economy of the coal-dominated areas of Appalachian had been in a downward spiral since the postwar period when the 1973 oil embargo turned a long-drawn-out "bust" in the coal industry into a "boom." Experienced miners and aspiring miners, from eighteen to fifty years of age, eagerly applied for mining jobs. Many of these aspiring miners knew that mining jobs meant a way out of poverty that did not require moving out of the mountains, as many of their friends and families had been forced to do when the coal industry mechanized during the 1950s, causing employment to plummet. However, it was not just men who needed the wages and benefits that mining jobs offered. Women, especially single mothers with children, knew that working underground offered their families a way out of poverty and a way to remain in their communities. Thus, while the oil embargo was a crisis for the American economy, it created an opportunity in the Appalachian coalfields. Women seized this golden opportunity with fear and trepidation. Tradition and cultural mores had kept women out of the mines except during the days of family-owned and -operated truck mines and wartime emergencies. Furthermore, the demand for employment far exceeded the number of opportunities available. As a result, those presently employed in the mines and members of their families and communities had little qualms voicing their disapproval toward women, especially women of color, who dared to go to work underground.

Are Appalachians unique in terms of their deep attachment to the land, its communities, and its culture? Was its communities' negative reaction to women entering the mines unlike those in other rural communities across the nation whose women obtained work in the mines and other nontraditional fields of work? I strongly believe that the answer to both of these questions is no. I have studied the experiences of women of various racial and ethnic groups across the United States throughout the twentieth century. Women living in urban and rural areas all encountered a great deal of resistance when they sought employment in male-dominated industries. For those living in rural areas, the resistance was greater. While Appalachia is a region that exhibits a typically strong lack of economic diversification, rural areas across the nation are rarely diversified in terms of economic opportunities. As a result, good paying jobs with benefits are in strong demand and highly prized. Until civil rights legislation passed during the 1960s and 1970s, most rural women worked as teachers and nurses (for the highly educated minority), retail clerks, waitresses, cooks, housekeepers, and child-care workers. Like their Appalachian sisters, these women hoped to remain in their homes and communities. And like their Appalachian sisters, they also faced

Epilogue: Reflections on the Concept of Place 485

resistance when applying and obtaining employment in areas such as mining and the construction trades. Obtaining the American dream sometimes came with a price.

John C. Inscoe: For the three films I analyzed, along with the fictional source material they're based on, place is certainly integral. Each film focuses on outsiders moving into the southern mountains, and their interactions with the highlanders they come to serve. All three female protagonists are exposed to a distinctive culture that we're meant to recognize as Appalachian, and by filming on location in the mountains of North Georgia, East Tennessee, and western North Carolina, respectively, all three filmmakers establish a pronounced and authentic sense of place, and they embed their characters and their culture firmly within that setting, which they render in unabashedly idyllic and scenic terms. As such, these films reflect one of the great paradoxes of the region and a recurring theme in its history and literature: that so glorious a natural environment could, and long did, breed such miserable and unfulfilled lives—at least as those lives were perceived by outsiders—yet also provide such healing and restorative powers to others, as it does in subtle ways for at least two of three women portrayed here.

Joyce M. Barry: In my research on women and anti-MTR activism, I see the coalfields of central Appalachia as a contested place—historically and culturally. MTR is a polarizing issue in Appalachia, with many arguing that coal mining is a part of our cultural and economic heritage—a heritage that should be recognized and supported, even if it means lopping off mountain tops. Others see the mountainous landscape as our cultural heritage, which should be recognized and supported, and many see mountaintop removal as destroying that heritage. West Virginia is still considered "the Mountain State," and yet mountains are being destroyed by the coal industry, which does have the support of many people. So the coalfields of central Appalachia are a very contested place in my mind.

Tice: In terms of my piece on embodiment, the template of beauty pageantry has been stretched across the globe with many different local inflections and articulations. There are multiple agendas for beauty pageantry, including consolidating notions of citizenship, nation, and belonging/exclusion; claiming modernization or upholding traditions; normalization and idealization of gender, class, race, ethnic, religious, and cultural relations; tourism; promoting corporatization, branding, and marketing of commodities, bodies, and places. Beauty pageantry is international in scope and not unique to Appalachia.

I would argue, however, that Appalachian pageants are variant and distinctive, since they are embedded in local agendas, rationales, sponsorship, and contexts, so one finds differences and similarities across the region itself. I would argue too that there are overlaps and differences among Appalachian pageants themselves. For example, there have been numerous pageants throughout the region that celebrate coal, and I would argue that such coal pageants have both overlapping and distinctive components rooted in time, place, and context. To me, the approach should not be to flatten and erase these differences and overlaps but rather to allow the complexities of place—just as folks do with gender, race, ethnicity, and so on—to come to light by showing that even within the Appalachian region ("place"), one could find wide variations in beauty pageantry, so a fluid definition of place is important.

Barry: In today's globalized world, conceptions of the place of Appalachia must be broadly conceived, because there are many national and transnational links between the culture, environment, and economy of Appalachia. As such, Appalachian scholars, artists, activists, and others should conceive of Appalachia as a local region with broader, national and international implications. For example, the extraction of the fossil fuel, coal, is occurring through the process of MTR because of increasing national and international demand for coal. While the production of coal is causing major changes in central Appalachia, the burning of it in massive coal-fired power plants throughout the world is accelerating climate change. West Virginia coal travels to twenty-three states and thirteen countries, so it is important to make these broader links and contextualize the place of Appalachia nationally and internationally.

Epilogue: Reflections on the Concept of Place 487

H. Adam Ackley: For those like myself who identify as urban Appalachian migrants, Appalachia is neither ethnically, racially, or economically homogenous, nor is it exclusively linked to the geographic southeastern mountains of the United States. For example, my own family's roots are in the Pennsylvania coal camps of the northern Appalachian mountains and the Ohio border with West Virginia in the central Appalachian foothills.

Appalachian identity for urban migrants such as myself thus derives more from a particular multidimensional understanding of extended family, one that is deeply rooted in, but not entirely limited by, an Appalachian regional sense of place. People from particular counties in the Appalachian mountains tend consistently to migrate to the same neighborhoods in particular cities, so that outsiders (local neighbors) perceive the migrants to be a distinct cultural group ("hillbillies"). The migrants themselves, however, tend not to define themselves as Appalachian because it is socioeconomically stigmatizing but remain loyal to their local communities of origin, usually a particular county or mountain. Urban neighbors in areas where many Appalachian migrants have settled incorrectly perceive this group as homogenous. Often viewed as maladjusted, problematic, and unassimilated to the dominant culture, these stereotypes are reinforced by the "shuttle migration" behavior common to Midwestern urban migrants who could and did return to mountains of origin for frequent visits with seasonal and family changes. Scholars like William Philliber and Phillip Obermiller have thus argued that Appalachian cultural identity, especially for urban migrants from the region and the first few generations of their descendants, is thus embedded, rather than visible. Shuttle migration, romanticized images of mountain home and kin in film, literature and popular song, all express this longing for a sense of place, so deeply felt that literary critic Ron Willoughby calls it "primal" for Appalachian people.

Deborah L. Blackwell: Living as I have outside of Appalachia for the last sixteen years (fifteen of those on the Texas-Mexico border), the notion of "place" in relationship to my research has evolved since I started my research journey. Because the majority of my scholarship focuses on the late nineteenth and early twentieth centuries and the reformers and benevolence workers that arrived in the southern mountains during that period, I tend to think of Appalachia in terms of an invented place where the anxieties of modern life either found a solution (through the values of the "contemporary ancestors") or a foil (in tales of evil backwardness). Both stereotypes, of course, served the needs of the newcomers more than the natives, and they said little about the actual conditions of the place itself or the people who called it home. That said, the fact that events unfolded in a particular place and at a particular time matters. The isolation of the mountains combined with industrial expansion fostered the impoverishment that the Progressive Era benevolence workers so vigorously sought to address. In order to do so, however, they transmitted ideas about this place called Appalachia and helped to create something that was as much a mythology as a literal place. I must say, though, that I tend to see a bit less uniqueness in some aspects of the Appalachian place than I once did; similar forces are at work here in South Texas. Personally, I retain my emotional sense of "coming home" whenever I am near my mountains again; that sense of place has never really left me, and I doubt that it will. From a research standpoint, though, I am as interested in those ideas and mythologies of place as I am the literal place itself.

Connie Park Rice: As a historian, it is important to study the social, economic, and political realities that have shaped, and continue to shape, people and places throughout Appalachia. It is also important to understand that individual, local, and regional identities have often been shaped by our *concepts* of place, rather than our realities of place. It is interesting to look at the symbols we created in order to recognize and maintain those concepts of place, because they also become part of our identity. For example, contributors to this volume made several thought-provoking comments about West Virginia's symbols. Asra Q. Nomani stated, "I definitely feel that the mountaineer spirit and the notion of mountaineers as always free resonates for me, as a woman challenged by rules about what I can be or do in this world. I get much of my sense of social justice from having grown up in West Virginia." As a West Virginian,

Epilogue: Reflections on the Concept of Place 489

I know the state motto, "Montani Semper Liberi," resonates in the heart of all mountaineers, past and present. What we don't know is the actual impact this simple motto has had on the people who embrace it. In his Native American blog, Isaac Emrick discusses West Virginia's iconic symbol, the mountaineer. Emrick writes that "the Mountaineer remains the model of American rugged individualism, the banner-man of modernity's taming of the wilderness," but asks, "What about his negative side?" Indeed, the rugged individualism of the mountaineer that symbolizes Appalachia, led to the displacement of Native Americans throughout the region. By embracing such symbols, do we automatically exclude important contributions to our past? More importantly, do we reconstruct the past to fit our vision of ourselves? Clearly, the identity of people and places throughout the region is based on both real and constructed "places," and when we choose to create and identify with the symbols associated with those places, place becomes an important element of who we are. Obviously, the realities of place are complex.

In a discussion about place, historian Ronald L. Lewis noted that academic disciplines use the concept of place differently. Literary people use it as a vehicle for creating stories and characters without allowing details to get in the way of a good story. For them place becomes the larger world impinging on people, a force bigger than the individual, who has no power over it—or something a hero struggles against and wins. It also provides an analytic for them to peel away layers, revealing deeper and deeper meanings. Historians, in an attempt to reconstruct the past, cannot substitute place for analysis. A factual analysis of rural life, poverty, power relations, and so forth provides a framework for understanding not only what happened but also why people, places, or events are alike or apart. Place, however, is important because local variances are important in shaping historical events, and, like politics, all history is local.

Too often the term *Appalachia,* imbued with socially constructed meanings, is used as a place name to cover a lot of things that people take as a given. For almost four decades, scholars have discredited the myths and stereotypes of the socially constructed place we call Appalachia that have evolved over the last century and more. In the process, we have learned about the "other" Appalachia . . . the *real* one; one full of diversity and complexity, and nothing illustrates this more than the lives and experiences of the women of the Mountain South.

Contributors

H. ADAM ACKLEY is a university professor of gender studies in religion, writer, certified yoga instructor, and consultant based in the greater Los Angeles area who received his PhD in philosophy from Claremont Graduate University in 1997 and has spent almost two decades teaching philosophy, history, and spirituality as a full-time college professor. He is the author of *Women, Music and Faith in Central Appalachia* and a Huffington Post Religion blog. He also serves as an ordained minister in the Church of the Brethren, Pacific Southwest District.

KATHARINE LANE ANTOLINI has an MA in sociology from Rutgers, the State University of New Jersey, and an MA and PhD in History from West Virginia University. She has published articles on the topics of women in the American Civil War and the history of American holidays. Her recent work includes a book on the history of Mother's Day, entitled *Memorializing Mother's Day: Anna Jarvis and the Struggle for the Control of Mother's Day*. She is currently an assistant professor at West Virginia Wesleyan College, offering courses in both American history and gender studies. She is also a trustee of the International Mother's Day Shrine in Grafton, West Virginia, an organization dedicated to preserving the site of the first Mother's Day service and the holiday's history.

JOYCE M. BARRY, Visiting Assistant Professor of Women's Studies at Hamilton College in Clinton, New York, holds a PhD in American Culture Studies from Bowling Green State University. Barry's research interests involve the connections between gender and environmentalism, with particular interest in women's environmental justice activism against mountaintop removal coal mining in the Appalachian region. Barry, a 2006 recipient of a National Endowment of the Humanities fellowship, has published in *Women's Studies Quarterly*, *Environmental Ethics*, the *National Women's Studies Association Journal*, and *Environmental Justice*. Barry is also the author of *Standing Our Ground: Women, Environmental Justice, and the Fight to End Mountaintop Removal*.

DEBORAH L. BLACKWELL is Associate Professor of History and Director of the University Honors Program at Texas A&M International University. She received her PhD at the University of Kentucky, where her dissertation considered the gender dimensions of Progressive Era benevolence efforts in southern Appalachia. Her publications include "The Maternalist Politics of Road Construction at Pine Mountain Settlement School, 1900–1935," in *Appalachian Journal: A Regional Studies Review* 37, nos. 3 and 4 (Spring/Summer 2010). She teaches US southern, women's, and Gilded Age/Progressive Era history, as well as historical methods and Honors courses.

CAROL BURCH-BROWN is Professor of Visual Arts and Director of the Master of Fine Arts Program in Creative Technologies in the School of Visual Arts at Virginia Tech. Her intermedia exhibitions and performances investigate issues in life sciences, gender, and natural history. She is photographer and coauthor of *Trailers* and the recipient of an NEA Artists' Fellowship. She received her MFA from the University of Chicago.

CARLETTA A. BUSH is a senior lecturer in the History Department at West Virginia University, where she designs and teaches online courses. Her master's thesis, "Women Coal Miners: Another Chapter in Central Appalachia's Struggle against Hegemony, 1973–1998," focused on the experiences of women coal miners. Her dissertation, "Faith, Power, and Conflict: Miner Preachers and the United Mine Workers of America in the Harlan County Mine Wars, 1931–1939," examines the work of preacher-organizers in the coalfields of Harlan County, Kentucky.

KELLY A. DORGAN is an associate professor and research coordinator in the Department of Communication at East Tennessee State University. She has an MA in communication from the University of Kentucky and a PhD in speech communication from the University of Georgia. She specializes in the intersection of gender, health and illness, and culture. She has published peer-reviewed articles in several journals, including *Academic Medicine, Women & Health, Oncology Nursing Forum, Women's Studies in Communication,* and the *California Journal of Health Promotion.*

494 CONTRIBUTORS

WILMA A. DUNAWAY is a professor of sociology in the Government and International Affairs Program School of Public and International Affairs at Virginia Polytechnic Institute and State University, Blacksburg, Virginia. She has published numerous books and articles on Appalachia, including *The First American Frontier: Transition to Capitalism in Southern Appalachia, 1700–1860; The African American Family in Slavery and Emancipation; Slavery in the American Mountain South; Women, Work, and Family in the Antebellum Mountain South;* and most recently, *Southern Laboring Women: Race, Class, and Gender Conflict in Antebellum Appalachia.*

KATHRYN L. DUVALL is tutor coordinator for the federally funded TRiO program for Student Support Services at East Tennessee State University. She has a BA in public relations and an MA in health communication from East Tennessee State University. Kathryn's research interests include cancer communication, women survivorship, and Appalachia. She has published articles in *Journal of Appalachian Studies, Women & Health,* and *Preventing Chronic Disease.*

BARBARA J. HOWE taught women's history, women's studies, and public history at West Virginia University. Some of her articles and presentations have focused on aspects of women's work in mid-nineteenth-century Wheeling, including articles in the *Journal of Appalachian Studies, West Virginia History, U.S. Catholic Historian,* and *Appalachian Journal.* She has also published on this topic in *Feminism and Hospitality: Gender in the Host/Guest Relationship,* edited by Maurice Hamington; *Beyond Hill and Hollow: Original Readings in Appalachian Women' Studies,* edited by Elizabeth S. D. Engelhardt; and *Neither Lady, nor Slave: Working Women of the Old South,* edited by Susanna Delfino and Michele Gillespie. She was chair of the National Council on Public History, president of the National Women's Studies Association, and on the Governing Council of the American Association for State and Local History, and she is on the board of directors of the National Collaborative for Women's History Sites.

SADIE P. HUTSON is an associate professor in the College of Nursing and coordinator of the Nursing Honors Program at the University of

Tennessee, Knoxville. She obtained her BSN in nursing from the University of Wisconsin-Madison; an MSN (Women's Health Nurse Practitioner) from the University of Pennsylvania; and a PhD in nursing science from the University of Pennsylvania. She has expertise in women's health, psychosocial oncology, and end of life care among HIV/AIDS patients in Appalachia. Hutson was the recipient of the Regional Cooperative for Professional Nurses Week RN Clinical Excellence Award in 2013. She has recent publications in *Annals of Behavioral Medicine, Health Expectations,* and *Journal of Appalachian Studies.*

JOHN C. INSCOE, the Albert B. Saye Professor of History and University Professor at the University of Georgia. is the author of *Mountain Masters: Slavery and the Sectional Crisis in Western North Carolina; Race, War, and Remembrance in the Appalachian South; Writing the South through the Self: Explorations in Southern Autobiography;* and coauthor, with Gordon McKinney, of *The Heart of Confederate Appalachia: The Civil War in Western North Carolina.* For the past fifteen years he has edited the on-line New Georgia Encyclopedia. His current book project is tentatively titled "Appalachia on Film: History, Hollywood, and the Highland South."

MARIA ALEJANDRA LOPEZ is a native of Argentina and holds a BS and MS from the University of Buenos Aires in clinical psychology. She obtained her PhD in educational psychology and education from the University of Tennessee, Knoxville. Lopez worked extensively with the Hispanic population in the United States as a therapist and educator in the fields of psychology and social work and with at-risk students in the East Tennessee area. She currently practices in Irving, Texas.

LOIS LUCAS earned a PhD in American history from the University of Kentucky and is currently a professor of history at West Virginia State University in Institute, West Virginia, where she teaches courses in American, African American, world, and women'shistory. Her research interests include the contributions of women and African Americans in the early twentieth century. In addition to other sources, she is published in the *African American National Biography Enclyclopedia.*

LOUIS C. MARTIN is chair of the History, Political Science, and International Studies Department at Chatham University in Pittsburgh, Pennsylvania. His research interests include labor and Appalachian history and twentieth-century political economy. He has done extensive research on the pottery and steel industries of West Virginia, and his forthcoming book examines rural-industrial workers in northern West Virginia. He teaches twentieth-century US history, American environmental history, working-class history, and oral history.

PENNY MESSINGER is a native West Virginian who earned a PhD in history from The Ohio State University in 1998 with a dissertation about the Conference of Southern Mountain Workers. She is currently an associate professor of history at Daemen College in Amherst, New York, where she teaches courses in American history, women's history, and women's studies. Her current research interests include gender and reform in Appalachia during the Progressive Era, missionary movements in the Appalachian South, and Northern Appalachia. She is also conducting research for a biography of Boris Reinstein and Anna Mogilova Reinstein, radical political activists in both Russia and the United States from the 1880s through the 1940s.

ASRA Q. NOMANI is a former reporter for the *Wall Street Journal* and the author of *Standing Alone: An American Woman's Struggle for the Soul of Islam* and *Tantrika: Traveling the Road of Divine Love*, a journey into the corners of her identity as a Muslim born in India and raised in America. She teaches journalism at Georgetown University's School of Continuing Studies and is a cofounder of Muslims for Peace.

CONNIE PARK RICE earned a PhD in history, with an emphasis on Appalachian regional history, from West Virginia University. A lecturer in the History Department at West Virginia University and the assistant editor of *West Virginia History: A Journal of Regional Studies*, she has published numerous essays on black West Virginians and women in Appalachia. She is currently revising a manuscript titled "'Don't Flinch nor Yield an Inch': The Life and Legacy of Civil Rights Pioneer J. R. Clifford," on West Virginia's first practicing African American editor

CONTRIBUTORS 497

and lawyer, and working on a new project titled "West Virginia Women in the Civil War Era: A Documentary History."

EVELYN ASHLEY SORRELL is a PhD candidate and teaching assistant at the University of Kentucky. She is currently working on her dissertation, which analyzes how social reformers and government officials in the United States used the public health movement against venereal disease in the twentieth century to justify the policing of poor and working-class female sexuality and motherhood.

MARIE TEDESCO has a PhD in American history, earned in 1978 from Georgia State University, Atlanta. Director of the Master of Arts in Liberal Studies program at East Tennessee State University in Johnson City, she teaches interdisciplinary core courses in that program and the history of women in Appalachia for the Department of History at ETSU. Research interests focus on work, gender, and race in Appalachia.

KAREN W. TICE is chair of the Department of Gender and Women's Studies and a professor of Gender and Women's Studies and Educational Policy Studies at the University of Kentucky, where she teaches courses on gender and education, feminist theory, activism, and popular culture. Her publications include *Tales of Wayward Girls and Immoral Women: Case Records and the Professionalization of Social Work* and *Queens of Academe: Beauty Pageantry, Student Bodies, and Campus Life*. She has also published on reality TV makeover shows, gender, social reform and activism, beauty, race, and religion, and popular culture. She is currently doing research on the micro-politics of feminism, class, and region.

JAN VOOGD is author of *Race Riots and Resistance: The Red Summer of 1919* and *Maynard, Massachusetts: A House in the Village*. Formerly a librarian at Harvard University for ten years, she received a Bryant Fellowship from Harvard and a Mudge Teacher Fellowship from the Boston Athenaeum.

Index

Page references in italics denote illustrations.

Abbott, Mather Almon, 360
abortion, 15–17, 452–57
Ackley, H. Adam, 15, 488, 493
activism: MTR, 422–32
Adair, James, 23, 30
Adams, Johnnie, 361
Addams, Jane, 82, 220
African American(s): discrimination in
    transportation and, 402–3, 406–12;
    education for, 373–74; inequality and, 395–
    96, 402, 412–15; middle-class, 377–79, 394;
    middle-class values and, 380–84; National
    Association for the Advancement of
    Colored People (NAACP), 373–74; politics,
    372–73. *See also* African American women
African American women, 13, 128–30, 244–45,
    254–55, 257–58, 275, 285, 372, 380–84,
    386–387, 394–96, 483; activism and, 385, 395,
    412–15; beauty pageants and, 128–30, 134–36;
    discrimination against in beauty pageants,
    134–36; free, as manufacturing workers, 188–
    89; prostitutes, 212–13; slaves, 77–78, 176, 178,
    179, 184–85; slaves, as farm laborers, 176–79;
    slaves, as transportation workers, 189
Alice Lloyd College, 239
All That Is Native and Fine (Whisnant), 84
Amalgamated Association of Iron, Steel, and Tin
    Workers, 280, 282
Amax Coal Company, 260
American Sheet Steel Company, 274
Anderson, Rufus, 4
Anglin, Mary K., 8, 9, 171
anti-Semitism, 127–28
Antolini, Katharine Lane, 11, 482
Appalachia: definition of, 218; discovery of, 66,
    81, 95–116; diversity of, 2; idea of, 477, 479;
    social construction of, 2. *See also* Central
    Appalachia; Mountain South
Appalachia, VA, *xii*, 402–7
Appalachian Oral History Project, 174
Appalachian Regional Commission, 5, 476
Appalachian Studies Association, 5
Appalachian Voices, 436
Appalachia on Our Mind (Shapiro), 75, 477, 479
Arch Coal, 255
Archer, Elizabeth, 209
Archie, Elizabeth, 206
Archie, Sarah, 206
Ar'n't I a Woman? (White), 77–78
Asheville, NC, *xii*, 101, 232, 452–56

Association of Women in Industry (AWI),
    256–57
Atlantic Greyhound Corporation, 402
Attakullakulla, 29
Ault, Hewetson, 212
Austin, Jeri Monique, 91, 401

Bailey, "Mad" Anne, 3
Baldwin Felts Detective Agency, 297–301
Banks, Alan, 7
Banner Elk, NC, *xii*, 118, 147–52
Bannerman, Arthur M., 233
"Barbara Allen" (ballad), 108–9, 111
Barber-Scotia College, 376
Barney, Sandra Lee, 7–9, 356
Barnhart, Jacqueline Baker, 195
Barnum, P. T., 125
Barrabino, Dr. E. A., 205–6
Barron, Gov. Wallace "Wally," 376
Barry, Joyce M., 9, 16, 486, 493
Bartram, William, 23
Bateman, Mildred Mitchell, 376
Batinkoff, Randall, 104
Batteau, Allen W., 2, 75, 79
beauty: hegemonic ideals of, 119, 125–26, 128–130;
    racialized femininity, 125, 129, 134–36
beauty pageants and festivals, 12, 117–36; African
    American women and, 128–30, 134–36; as
    celebrations of regional heritage, 120–23,
    131; as commercialized promotions of place,
    117, 120–22, 131; display of female body and,
    125–27, 133; Native American women and,
    128–29; opposition to display of female body
    and, 126–27; as promoting coal, 120–23;
    as promoting commodities, 120–24, 130;
    segregation and, 129; socioeconomic class
    and, 125, 129–30, 132–33
Beaver, Patricia D., 7, 9, 329, 335
Bedlar, Margaret Baunan, 200
Bell County, KY, *xii*, 131–36, 330, 339, 342
benevolent workers, 5, 10–11, 95, 107, 112–14
Berea College, 81, 130, 223–24, 228–29
Berkeley, William, 79
Berry, Martha, 112
Bethania, NC, 141–43
Billings, Dwight, 7, 477
Birmingham, AL, *xii*, 256, 471, 472
Biskind, Peter, 337
Bituminous Coal Queens of Pennsylvania
    (film), 122

Blackwell, Deborah L., 9, 11, 488–89
Blair Mountain, 297, 419
Bledsoe, KY, *xii*
Bluefield, WV, *xii*, 459–65
Bluefield Colored Institute (Bluefield State University), 374
Bolivar, WV, *xii*, 449–50
Bonds, Julia "Judy," 345, 418, 421, 424, 426, 433
Bontemps, Arna, 378
Boop, Betty (in *Musical Mountaineers* cartoon), 74, 90–91
Bostona, No. 2, 208
Boudinot, Elias, 35
Bradley, William Aspinwall, 85–88
Brady, Caroline, 199, 205
Bragg, Patricia, 345, 421
Breckinridge, Mary, 8, 355
Brookside Mine, 338
Brophy, John, 331
Brown, Carol Burch, 459
Brown, Gizella Dull, 276, 287
Brown, Patricia, 257–59, 262
Buckhannon, WV, 210
Bufwack, Mary, 328–29
Burns, Shirley Stewart, 421
Bush, Carletta A., 13–14, 484
Butler, Elizabeth Beardsley, 274, 279
Butler, Marguerite, 227–29
Butler, Viney (in *Songcatcher*), 109–10

Caldwell, Atty. Gen. Aquilla B., 203
Campbell, John C., 107–8, 222–23, 225, 227, 229, 231, 479
Campbell, Olive Dame, 96, 107–8, 219, 223, 227–29, 231, 333, 479
Capehart, Harry, 385–86
Caperton, Gaston, 375, 389, 393
Capp, Al. *Li'l Abner*, 119
Catatoga, NC, *xii*, 26
Central Appalachia, 17, 23, 254, 327–28, 330, 332, 335, 343, 466–67, 486–88
Chafin, Don, 419
Chambless, Mrs. C. O., 364
Charleston Woman's Improvement League, 391
Cherokee: identity, 10–11, 25–27, 33–34, 38; identity and race, 33–34, 38; marriage and marriage laws, 27–31; Moravian missionaries to Cherokee, 25, 30, 35; patriarchy, 36–37; patrilineal descent, 36–37; people, 4, 7, 10–11, 23, 476–77; removal, 36–37; women, work of, 175–76, 180, 184–85; women in home-based textile production, 180, 190; women in putting-out system, 184. *See also* Cherokee Nation; Cherokee society
Cherokee Hosiery Mill, *320*
Cherokee Nation: citizenship, 34–37; citizenship and 1827 Constitution, 34–35; East, 36–39; West, 37–38
Cherokee National Council, 31, 34–39
Cherokee Phoenix, 180

Cherokee society: black women in, 25, 36–37; clan in, 27–28; free blacks in, 34–37, 38; matrilineal kinship, 26–27, 34, 38; polygyny, 30–31; roles of men in traditional society, 28, 32–33; roles of women in traditional society, 25, 28, 32–33; sexual mores, 29–30, 36; slavery in, 33–34, 36–37; white women in, 25–26, 35
child care, 65–66, 330, 389, 485
child rearing, 55, 158–66, 381
Children's Free Hospital, 362, 366
Chilhowee, 26
Chota, TN, 26
Christian media, 103, 106
Christy. *See* Huddleston, Christy
Christy: book (Marshall), 96, 102; film, 96, 101; TV series, 101
Christy: Return to Cutter Gap (TV miniseries), 103–4
Circuit Rider's Wife, The (Harris), 96–98
civil rights legislation, 16, 157, 244–48, 264–66, 386, 393, 415, 484–85
Clampett, Elly May (in *The Beverly Hillbillies*), 119
Clarksburg, WV, 272, 274, 282
Clayton (in *A Mountain Europa*), 80–81
clubwoman, clubwomen, 16, 351, 381, 384, 390
coal companies, 249–50, 252, 253, 255, 260
Coal Employment Project (CEP), 5, 248–49, 262, 315, 322
coalfields, 5, 13, 16, 244, 246, 249, 298, 316, 332, 374, 422–26, 432, 460, 485–86, 494
coal mine, 121, 128, 151, 248, 256, 263, 316, 337, 344
coal miner, 5, 80, 119, 120, 121, 245, 246, 250, 255, 257, 259, 260, 263–64, 276, 297, 317, 327, 328, 331, 334, 338–42, 419, 422, 425, 459, 494
Coal Miner's Daughter, A (film), 119
Coal Mining Women's Support Team News, 315–19
Coal River Mountain Watch (CRMW), 345, 418, 424, 429, 432, 436
Coal River Mountain Wind Project, 424, 436
Collins, Patricia Hill, 381
Colored Republican Club, 387
Colored Women's Republican Club, 387
Compton, Helen Louise Gibson, 16, 459–65, 473
Conference of Southern Mountain Workers (CSMW), 13, 217, 217–19, 222–33, 479, 497; education programs, 221–24, 226, 231, 233; female leadership in, 222–24, 226, 231–32; female mission of, 222–26; gendered hierarchies in, 226
Congress of Industrial Organizations (CIO), 283
Congress of Racial Equality (CORE), 407
Conroy, Jack, 378
Consolidation Coal (Consol), 249–50
Cope, Dorie, 184
Cowen Railroad Festival, 124
Cowles, Anna B., 362
Cox, Henry, 144–46
Cox, Peggy, 144–46

Crescent Mill, 203
critical regionalism (CR), 477
Cronemeyer, W. C., 273
cross-cultural interaction, 96, 106–7, 109
cross-dressing, 118
Crozer, Upland, and Page Coal and Coke
  Companies
cultural brokers, women as, 107–12, 114
Cumberland, KY, 252, 406
curtsy: in pageants, 134–36
Cutter Gap (in *Christy*), 102–4

Daisy Mae (in *Li'l Abner*), 7, 119
Dalmanutha, Aunt, 83–84
Daly, Tyne, 104, 106
Dawson, Kipp, 254
Day, Coroner Elijah, 201
Debo, Angie, 24
Del Rio, TN, 101, 103
Dingman, Helen H., 224, 227–29, 233
divorce, causes of, 144–46
domestic abuse. *See* violence against women
Dorgan, Kelly A., 466, 494
Drewry, Elizabeth Simpson, 372, 373–74, 383;
  health care reform and, 375; McDowell
  County politics and, 374
Duke, Daisy (in *The Dukes of Hazzard*), 119
Dukes, Joyce, 317–18
Dunaway, Wilma A., 7, 13, 173, 495
Duvall, Kathryn L., 466–67, 495
Dykeman, Wilma, 1

Easter (in *A Mountain Europa*), 80–81
East Tennessee, 12, 26, 158, 181, 248, 306, 315, 453,
  466, 486
East Tennessee Research Corporation, 248, 315
Ebenezer Mission School, 102, 104
economic justice, 432–37
Edens, Bessie, 306–11
education: African Americans and, 373–74, 380;
  college programs, 81, 130, 131, 135, 223–24,
  228–29, 239, 276, 376, 380, 408; schools, 81,
  82, 84, 85, 87, 101, 102, 106, 108, 111, 112, 114,
  147, 227, 231, 228, 229, 231, 240, 306–11, 321,
  351, 379; social class mobility and, 373–74;
  women and, 147–52, 306–11
Elbert County, GA, 97
Elberton, GA, *xii*, 97
Elizabethton, TN, *xii*, 6, 89–90, 306–11; women
  rayon plant strikers in, 89–90
Elkhorn, WV, 374, 378
Empire Laundry, *320*
Engelhardt, Elizabeth, 8, 9, 77
*English Folk Songs from the Southern
  Appalachians* (Sharp and Campbell), 109
environment, 418–21, 423–24, 426, 428, 487, 493
environmental justice, 422–32
Estrada, Pat, *322*
Etowah County, AL, *321*
Everidge, "Uncle" Solomon, 88

farm laborers: African American women (slave
  and free), 78, 176–79, 184; Cherokee women,
  175–76; white women, 177–79
Farr, Sidney Saylor, 4, 6
feminine values, traditional, 126, 133–34
feminism, 113–14
festivals and pageants: Georgia, 124; Kentucky,
  123; West Virginia, 120–22, 125
fictional depictions of white mountain women,
  95–114. *See also* film depictions of white
  mountain women
film depictions of white mountain women,
  95–116
Finley, Mrs. John, 66
Fisher, Steven L., 9
Flora McDonald College, 102
Fogelson, Raymond D., 29
Fokker Aircraft, *321*
folk traditions, 344
Follansbee, WV, 272
Follansbee Brothers Company, 274
Foreman, Carolyn Thomas, 24
Fort Hinckley, WV, 205
Fort Nichols, WV, 200, 204–7, 213
Fort Pickett, 407
Fort Wayne Women's Bureau of Industry, 260
fotched-on women, 6
Fox, John Jr., 80; *A Mountain Europa*, 80–81
Frank, Susan, 206
Friends of Coal (FOC), 431
Frontier Nursing Service, 8, 355, 357
Frost, William Goodell, 2, 81, 476
Furman, Lucy, 81–84, 86, 329

Gadsden, AL, *xii*, *321*
Gaines, Kevin, 379
Gambold, Anna Rosina, 35
Garland, Mary Magdalene, 15, 327, 338–44. *See
  also* Jackson, Molly
Garrison, Memphis Tennessee, 372, 373–92,
  403–4; Christmas Seals and, 374; civil rights,
  373; education and, 374; NAACP and, 374
Garrison, William Melville, 373
Gatlinburg, TN, *xii*, 229, 233
Gearhart, Donna, 263
gendered analysis, 75–76
gender roles, 78. *See also* Cherokee
Giddens, Earl (in *Songcatcher*), 110
Giddings, Paula, 394
Gist, Joetta Ann, 251
Glendon Baptist Church, 339
Glenn, John M., 225
Glick, Larry, 128
globalization, 9, 118, 433–34, 437, 487
Goans, Melanie Beals, 8
Gold (Gould), Mrs. Margaret C., 202
Golden Brown Chemical Company, 129
Golden Brown National Beauty Contest, 129
Golden Rule Foundation, 61–64, 66, 67
Goodell, Florence, 227–32

Goodrich, Frances L., 228
Good Samaritan Hospital, 358
Gorn, Elliot, 327, 331–32, 334, 337, 341
Grafton, WV, *xii*, 45, 48, 51–52, 55, 208, 483, 493
Greenbrier County, WV, *xii*, 144–46, 385
green energy, 432–37
Greenwald, Maggie: *Songcatcher*, 107–8, 109, 110–11
Griggs, Charlene, 259
Gunning, Sarah Ogan, 327, 328, 339, 340–44
Gunnoe, Maria, 345, 421

Hafey, Bishop William, 126
Hall, Betty Jean, 248, 249, 262, 315–16, 322
Hall, Caney, 178
Hamlin, Kimberly, 126
Hampton, TN, *xii* 14, 306–11
Hampton Institute, 380
handicraft, hand-crafted, 179, 226, 229
hand-weaving, 180, 182, 184–85, 229
Harkins, Anthony, 76, 78, 80
Harlan County, KY, *xii*, 229, 245–46, 252, 255, 328–29, 335, 337, 338, 345, 406
Harlan County, U.S.A. (film), 338
Harney, Will Wallace, 2
Harris, Corra, 96–97, 101, 112; *The Circuit Rider's Wife*, 96, 97–98
Harris, Emmylou, 111
Harris, Lundy, 97
Hart County, GA, 97
Hayward, Susan, 98–99, 100
Hazard, KY, 123, 316, 364
health care, 5, 8, 16–17, 222, 224, 226, 233, 271, 312, 338, 355, 375, 392, 431, 453, 467
Heaton, Margaret, 275, 277
Heaton, Patricia, 122
Henderson, Alice (in *Christy: Return to Cutter Gap*), 104
Henderson, Herbert, 392
Hening, William, 196–97
Highlander Folk School, 240
hillbilly, 75, 89
Hillbilly (Harkins), 78
Hindman, KY, *xii*, 81–85
Hindman Settlement School, 81–82, 85, 87, 229, 231, 351
Hines, Ramona "Boots," 276–77, 279, 287–89
Hollens, Mary, 295–96
Home Mission Movement, 147–52
Howe, Barbara J., 9, 13, 481, 495
Huddleston, Christy (in *Christy*), 102–7, 112
Hugens (Huggins), Nancy, 206
Huntington, WV, *xii*, 128, 271, 376; as beauty pageant capital of Appalachia, 128
Hurwitz, Erica, 329
Hutchins, Francis, 228, 233
Hutson, Sadie P., 466, 495–96

I'd Climb the Highest Mountain (film), 96, 98, 105–6, 112–13

informal section trading, 185–87; African American women (free and slave) and, 185–87; Cherokee and, 186; white women and, 185–87
Inscoe, John C., 11, 486, 496
International Council of Women of the Darker Races, 387
International Harvester, 252
International Iron Molders' Union (IIMU)
Islam, 153–57; marginalization of women in, 153–57; Wahhabi teachings, 156
Island Creek Coal, 249, 253
Ivanhoe, VA, Jubilee Festival, 118

Jacksboro, TN, *xii*, 248, 249, 315, 316,
Jackson, Molly (Mary Magdalene Garland), 15, 327, 338–44
James, Johnnie, 261
Jarvis, Anna, 11, 45–50, 54–60, 62–64, 67, 482–83
Jarvis, Ann Reeves, 11, 45, 46–59, 67, 483
John C. Campbell Folk School, 227, 229, 231
Johnson C. Smith University, 276
Johnston, Brittany Lea, 134
Jones, Carol Davis, 322
Jones, Maggie, 210
Jones, Mary Harris "Mother," 15, 327, 331, 334, 335, 341, 344, 422, 471
Journey for Reconciliation, 407, 415

Kahn, Kathy, 329, 337
Kana'ti, 33
Kendall, Norman, 50
Kentucky Commission on Human Rights, 250, 260–61; sex discrimination and, 250; sexual harassment and, 260–61
Kentucky Commission on Interracial Cooperation (CIC), 406
Kentucky Mountain Laurel Festival, 130–36; as promoting regional heritage, 130–31; and racial discrimination practices, 134–36
Kentucky State Medical Association, midwives and, 356
Kester, Howard, 232
Kimple, Nancy, 208
King Coal Association, 121, 122
Kingsolver, Ann, 477
kin work, 13
Knell, Merion, 277
Knott County, KY, 423
Kopple, Barbara, 338
Kostur, Anne, 257
Kresch, Mary, 65

Ladies' Home Journal, 46, 125
Lakin State Hospital, 376, 379, 384
Landon, Michael, 128
land ownership by white Appalachian women, 177
Latina/Hispanic women, 4, 12, 135, 158–66, 496
Lavenda, Robert, 117

Lederer, John, 79
Ledford, Katherine, 78–79
Lee, Margaret, 443–45
Lees-McRae College (Institute), 147–48
lesbianisn, 110, 113
LeSueur, Meridel, 331, 334
Lewis, Helen M., 5, 325
Lewis, Ronald L., 490
Lexington, KY, *xii*
LGBTQ, 459–65
Li'l Abner (Capp), 7, 119
Lippincott's Magazine, 2
local color writers, 2, 4–5, 10, 75, 79–84, 89, 476, 479
Locklear, Erica Abrams, 9
Loeb, Penny, 421
Logan County, WV, 419
Lomax, Alan, 333
Lomax, John, 333
Long, William, 202
Longe, Alexander, 23, 27
Lopez, Maria Alejandra, 159, 496
Loudon, TN, *xii, 320*
Louis-Philippe, 28, 30
Louisville Free Children's Hospital, 366
Loveman's Department Store, *472*
Lucas, Lois, 16, 483, 496
Lucy Laney School for Nurses, 379
Lynch, KY, *xii*, 245–46, 251–52, 402, 406–8
Lynchburg, VA, 402, 407–9, 412
Lynchburg College, 408
lynching, 145, 385, 406

Maggard, Sally Ward, 6, 425
Maid of Cotton festival, 123–24
Maloney, Michael E., 10
Manse, David, 108
Markham, R. H., 285–86
marriage, 144–45; hardships of, 144–45
Marshall, Catherine, 96, 102
Marshall, Thurgood, 414–15
Marshall, Veronica, 318–19
Marshall University Medical School, 376
Marsh Fork, WV, 424
Martin, Kellie, 103, 105
Martin, Louis C., 14, 478, 497
Martinsburg, WV, 271
Martins Ferry, OH, 274
Marx Toy Company, 273, 282
Massey Energy Corporation, 436
maternal authority, 15, 327, 329–36, 344, 480
maternal façade, 49, 480
maternalist politics, 334–37
maternalist rhetoric, 84–85
maternalist state, 221
Maternity Center Association (MCA), 60–66
McBain, Anna D., 4
McBride, Neil, 248, 315
McCan (McCann), Mary Ann, 199, 201, 203, 213
McCormick, Helen, *169*

McCormick, Hilda, *169*
McCreary County, KY, 365–66
McDannell, Colleen, 334
McDonald, Katrina, 394
McDonald, Mary, 199
McDowell County Colored Republican
    Organization (MCCRO), 386
McKenzie, Marian, 208
McKinley Tariff: importance to steel industry, 271
McKinney, Becca, 363–64
McKinney, Goldie May, 363–64
McKinney, Madgie, 363–64
McTeer, Janet, 109
Meadows, Lucile Smallwood, 372–73, 396, 375–77,
    382, 384, 388–89, 393–96
Meeks, Mary, 361–62
Meeks, Pauline, 361–62
Messinger, Penny, 9, 13, 477, 497
Midway Coal Mining, 250
midwives, 356; regulation of, 356–57, 452–57
Mildred Mitchell Bateman Hospital, 376
Miles, Emma Bell, 21, 428
Miles, Tiya, 27, 30
Miller, Alderman, 206, 212
Miller, Angeline "Sally," 282
Miller, Mary, 421
Miller, Rita, 261–62
Miller, Justice Willis D., 410
Mine Safety and Health Administration, 263
mission school workers, 101–6, 108–11, 112–14
moonlight teachers, *321*
Moravian faith, 35, 141
Moravian *Lebenslauf*, 141–43
Moravians, 35, 141–43
Morgan, Irene, 403, 410
Morgan, Lucy, 229
Morgan Gap, TN, *xii*, 102
Morgantown, WV, *xii*, 153–57
Morgan v. Virginia, 403–11
mother: negative images of white Appalachian,
    361–64
motherhood, 47–48, 54–58; ideology of, 58;
    scientific, 60, 63, 65, 66, 352; sentimental
    model, 49, 63, 66
Mother's Day, 45–49, 55–56, 58–63, 66–67; legacy
    of, 59
Mother's Day Flag Resolution, 61
Mother's Day International Association, 46, 49,
    58, 59, 62
Mother's Day Movement, 46, 57, 61–62, 66
Mother's Day Proclamation, 47, 62
Mothers' Day, 55–56, 58–60, 66–67
Mothers' Day Work Clubs, 50–54, 63–64
Mothers' Friendship Day, 54
Mountain Europa, A (Fox), 80, 86
Mountain Fund, 352, 354, 357, 358
Mountain Justice Summer, 424
Mountain South (region), *xii*, 1–3, 147, 475–91
mountaintop removal (MTR), 418–38, 486–87;
    grassroots movement for, 419, 422–24

INDEX 503

Ms. Foundation for Women, 249
Murphy, Maggie, 365–66
music, Appalachian, 75, 107–11, 333, 344, 345;
   folk traditions, 333, 338, 342–45; mountain
   ballads, 96, 107–9; protest songs, 328, 332,
   344–46, 338–40, 345
Musical Mountaineers (cartoon), 74, 90–91
Muslim women, 4, 12, 153–57, 497
Myerson, Bess, 127–28; as victim of anti-
   Semitism, 127–28

Naoma, WV, *xii*
National Association of Colored Women
   (NACW), 130, 390
National Committee for the Defense of Political
   Prisoners, 339
National Industrial Recovery Act (NIRA), 282
National Labor Relations Act, 283, 312
National Labor Relations Board (NLRB), 283–84,
   312
National Miners Union, 336
Negro Artists Series, 374
Neville, Linda, 15, 350, 480
New, Ethel, 402–16
New Echota, GA, *xii*, 26
Nomani, Asra, 153, 497
North Georgia, 26, 35, 96–98, 114, 141, 486

Obermiller, Phillip, 10, 488
Ogresovich, Theresa, 281, 285, 287
Ohio Valley Environmental Coalition (OVEC),
   424, 427, 432
Olmstead, Frederick Law, 79
Opportunity Schools, 228
O'Toole, Col. Edward, 391–92
out-migration, 227, 244
Owens, Virginia "Jennie," 364, 365
Owens-Illinois Glass Company, 271

Paint Creek, WV, *xii*, 297–99
Paint Creek Collieries Company, 297–305
Painter, Nell Irvin, 404
Pardo, Juan, 33
Parton, Dolly, 119–20; bifurcated image of, 120
Peabody Coal, 249, 252
Peer, Ralph, 333
Pendleton County, WV, *xii*
Penlaric, Elna (in *Songcatcher*), 109–10
Penlaric, Lily (in *Songcatcher*), 108–9, 111–12, 114
Pennsylvania Bituminous Coal Festival, 120–21
Perdue, Theda, 7, 29, 38
Perkins, Francis, 62–63
Peters, "Zonk" (in *Musical Mountaineers*
   cartoon), 74
Pettit, Katherine, 81, 85, 87, 112, 352
Pickering, Mimi, 339, 341
Pikeville, KY, *xii*, 361; hospital strike, 14, 312–14
Pine Mountain Settlement School, 84, 87, 227, 231
Pineville, KY, *xii*, 130–36
Pittsburgh Coal (Gulf Oil), 249–50

Pittston Coal Corporation, 249–50; coal strike,
   316, 345, 422, *473*
place: cultural relevance of, 483; identity, 475–77,
   488–89; plurality and, 277; political economy
   and, 478–79; public health and, 466–70,
   480–81; reality of, 477; social conditions of,
   477–79; symbols of, 489–90; urban v. rural
   and, 481–82
Plaut, Thomas, 422
Plecker, Walter A., 404
Pocahontas County, WV, *168*
Porter, William Wesley, 205
Presbyterian Mission Board, 229
Progressive reform, 218, 221, 225, 229–30, 233; in
   Appalachia, 218–34; maternalist state, 221;
   and New Deal, 221, 229–30; and social work,
   225, 233; women as integral part of, 218–19,
   222–24
Progressives in Appalachia, 219–20
prostitutes, 195–213; crimes committed by, 200–
   203; why attracted to Wheeling, 210–11
prostitution in Wheeling, WV, 195–13, 210–11;
   African American houses of, 212–13; causes
   of, 213; city council ordinance against, 204;
   legal codes against in antebellum Virginia,
   196–97; legal codes against in Wheeling,
   WV, 197–98; police attitudes toward, 209;
   prosecution of, 205–7
protoindustrialization, 179, 182–84. *See also*
   textile production: putting-out system
public health, 50, 65, 212, 219, 225, 227, 480–81;
   cancer and, 17, 434, 466–70; venereal disease
   and, 15, 350–67, 480
Pudup, Mary Beth, 271

racial discrimination, 244–45, 247, 252–53, 254,
   261, 265, 266, 270, 275, 276, 303, 311, 341,
   395–96, 402–16
Rahel, 141–43
Ralsovich, Deborah, 318
Randolph-Macon Women's College, 408
Reece, Florence, 15, 327–28, 337–38, 433
religion, 3–4, 17, 23, 35, 56, 97, 106, 147, 151, 154,
   334, 417, 429
Rice, Connie Park, 489–90, 497
Ridge, John, 35
Roan, James O., 131
Robertson, Alderman William, 200, 204
Rockefeller, Jay, 375, 393
Romalis, Shelley, 334
romanticism: Appalachia and, 6, 76, 81, 114, 488
Rome, GA, *xii*, 320
Rooks, Noliwe, 129
Roosevelt, Eleanor, 62, 66, 284
rural life, fictional depictions, 96–101

Sabraton, WV, 272, 274
Sampson, Gov. Flem D., 131
Sasseen, Mary Towles, 482
Satter, Beryl, 379–80

504 INDEX

Saunders, J. W., 413
Save Our Cumberland Mountains (SOCM), 248, 315
Schneider, Martin, 23
Scott, Lillian, 392
Seals, Sarah, 167
Sebok, Patty, 418, 421, 429, 435, 436, 437
Seitz, Virginia, 422–23
Selu (Corn Mother), 33
separate-sphere ideology, 13, 23, 173–78, 190, 334–37, 359, 424–27
Sevier, Catherine S., 3
sex typing of jobs, 14, 270, 286, 289
sexual discrimination, 5, 14, 156, 249–53, 254–62, 284, 287–89, 315, 349–51
sexuality, 4, 9, 15, 16, 29, 118–19, 134, 354, 380, 459–65, 480
Shaft, Elizabeth, 452–56
Shamrock, the, 17, 459–65
Shapiro, Henry, 75, 475, 477, 479
sharecropping, 177
Sharp, Cecil, 109, 111
Shiva, Vandana, 433, 435
Shnayerson, Michael, 421
Sight to the Blind (Furman), 83–84
Simpson, Grant, 378, 381, 374
Skocpol, Theda, 221
Slaughter, Lenore, 126, 128
slavery, 141–42, 176, 189. *See also* slaves *under individual headings*
Smith, Barbara Ellen, 7, 9, 76, 477
Smith, Capt. John, 78
Smith, Vera, 471
Smith, Lieut. W. N., 409
Smith, Walter, 131
Smoky Mountains (TN), 96, 103
social justice, 373–75, 403, 406, 412–15, 420, 483, 489
Songcatcher (film), 107–11, 113
Sorrell, Evelyn Ashley, 15, 480, 498
Southern Highlander and His Homeland, The (Campbell), 479
Southern Highlands Handicraft Guild, 228, 232
"Southern Mountaineer in Fact and Fiction, The" (Williams), 114
Springplace, GA, *xii*, 35, 141
Stack, Carole, 13
steelworkers, 14, 270–71, 277–79, 288, 478
Steffey, Jean, 316–17
stereotypes: of African American women, 77, 79, 379, 382; of white Appalachians, 82, 87, 109–10; of white mountain children, 82–83; of white mountain granny, 77; of white mountain men, 74–75; of white mountain women, 4–5, 74–78, 82–89, 119, 147–52
Steubenville, OH, 274, 281–82
Stockman, Vivian, 421, 432
Stone, May, 112, 229, 352
Stucky, Dr. J. A., 352, 365
suffrage, 15, 16, 78, 126, 377, 385–86, 389–91, 446–57

Tazewell County, VA, 186
teachers, women, 6, 19, 83, 89, 108–9, 220–21, 224, 226, 231, 278, 333, 375, 378, 380, 485
Tedesco, Marie, 33, 475–76, 498
television depictions of mountain women, 102–3
tenant farming, 177
textile production: factory, 306–11; home-based, 179–84; putting-out system, 183–84
Thompson, Mary (in *The Circuit Rider's Wife*), 97, 105, 112, 114
Tice, Karen W., 7, 12, 66, 82–83, 329, 477, 486–87, 498
tourism, 117–18, 128, 131, 136, 189, 487
Townsend, TN, 103
trachoma, 351–53, 361, 364
Tufts, Edgar, 147–52
Turkeytown, AL, *xii*, 26
Turner, William, 404
Turtle Town, NC, *xii*, 26

United Mine Workers of America (UMWA): women and, 247, 258, 266, 312, 327, 331, 336, 345
U. S. Steel, 245–46, 251, 253, 373–74, 391–92, 406

venereal disease, 15, 353–68, 480
violence against women, 87, 198, 201–3, 209, 297–301, 304, 316, 336, 345
Virginia Justice, The (Hening), 196–97
Voogd, Jan, 16, 483, 498

Wachovia, NC, *xii*, 141
Waters, Maggie, 14, 297–305
Weirton, WV, *xii*, 272, 277–78, 282, 283
Weirton Steel, 274–77, 279–83, 285, 287
Weirton Steel Employees Bulletin, 277
Welsh, Maude, 169
West Virginia Association of Fairs and Festivals, 124
West Virginia International Pageant, 122
West Virginia Legislature: black women and, 373, 388
West Virginia Oil and Gas, 124
Wheeling, WV, *xii*, 183, 195, 197–98, 199, 204, 208, 210
Wheeling Intelligencer (WV), 196, 197, 199, 204, 206, 207, 211, 212, 213, 272, 278, 281, 282, 495
Wheeling Island, 199, 207, 482
Whisnant, David, 84, 95
White, Deborah Gray, 77, 78
Whitesville, WV, 424, 428
Wickliffe, KY, 414
Williams, Cratis: "The Southern Mountaineer in Fact and Fiction," 114
Williamson, J. W., 75–76, 89
Wind Logics, 436
women and trade unions, 247, 258, 266, 271, 284, 312, 327, 331, 336, 345
Women's Christian Temperance Union, 351, 450–51

women's clubs, 51, 64, 130, 221, 377, 387, 388, 390, 391

work: as part of everyday life for white mountain women, 148–49; conditions for women, 14, 297–305, 315–19, 184–85, 274, 276–77, 282, 284–85, 295–96, 306–9, 312–14; household, 174, 176, 179; household production, 174–75; married women and, 14, 63, 255, 265, 275–76, 278, 309–11, 478–79. *See also* Cherokee: women, work of; Cherokee: women in home-based textile production; farm laborers: white women

Yokum, Daisy Mae (in *Li'l Abner*), 7, 119

Zande, Ethel DeLong, 84, 87, 90, 329
Zane, Elizabeth, 3
Zinaich, Katherine, 283